FOR MERCY'S SAKE

A Preparation for Jesus' Return

By: Carol Ameche

Scottsdale, AZ Published, 2006

LOVE + MASS MEMMENTOS, CAROL
Fr Peter MARY Rookey, OSM

ISBN-10: 1-58776-846-1

Manufactured in the United States of America

1 2 3 4 5 6 7 8 9 10 NetPub 0 9 8 7 6

For additional copies:

Carol Ameche
7814 E. Northland Dr.
Scottsdale, AZ 85251

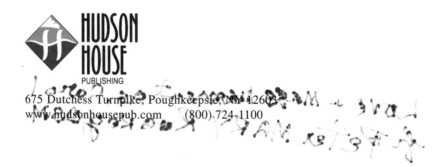

675 Dutchess Turnpike, Poughkeepsie, NY 12603
www.hudsonhousepub.com (800) 724-1100

Dedication

This book is dedicated to the Perfect Will of God, Our Heavenly Father, Who has allegedly Spoken and guided me through years of preparation of This Book.

Acknowledgement

I wish to publicly thank and praise the support and technical Help of Gary Schaefer, a Webmaster par excellence; Our children: Kevin, Don III, Kathleen, Susan and Michael, whose technical support and loving patience were my salvation for my husband, Don for his patience and Understanding and support throughout years of my answer to an alleged special call.

According to the decree of the Congregation for the Propagation of the Faith, A.A.S., 58, 1186, approved by Pope Paul VI on October 14, 1966, it is permitted to publish, without a Nihil Obstat and Imprimatur, works relating to revelations, prophecies or miracles.

It is hereby stated that the messages contained in this book must be understood not as words spoken directly by our Lord and our Blessed Mother, but received in the form of interior locutions by Carol Ameche. In accordance with the regulations of the Second Vatican Council, the publisher and author state that we do not wish to precede the judgment of the Church in this matter, to which we humbly submit.

TABLE OF CONTENTS

Introduction

FOR MERCY'S SAKE!

Carol Ameche

Throughout all of 1998 travel filled my life nearly every weekend which answered invitations to speak to prayer groups all over the country. The Lord had been speaking to my heart with new warnings to share with all those who were listening to Heavenly messages. The substance of these locutions contained directives to the people of the world that would save them from the results of nuclear attacks and the radiation fallout that could burn and disfigure all those who experienced these events. I dreaded sharing the details of these warnings with the groups of people who gathered. The reaction was always the same when upturned faces of those who listened intently heard the words of Jesus or Mary telling their beloved people the absolute probability of nuclear war by the end of 1998. All the color drained out of those faces, as I repeated words from Heaven, and many of them were lost to the present moment after that. Eyes were not focused as they had been. Attention was not as keen, nor was there awareness of any words spoken after the words *nuclear war* were announced. I dreaded each encounter and prayed so hard to God and Our Blessed Mother to give me the strength to continue to fly to new destinations week after week. Jesus gave me so many assurances of this necessity, and of course, there was present a desire to help save as many as possible from terrible annihilation, and remain faithful to the obedience to these requests. Prayer was mentioned repeatedly as our primary response, as well as having supplies ready to take along on a hasty retreat from danger. Angels would be sent by Heaven to lead us to refuges where we would be protected from nuclear destruction. The return to our homes would occur when the signal was received that all would be safe after God, the Father, miraculously cleared the air of radiation. Many people cancelled plans to travel to relatives for the Holidays. It was a grim and tense time, even though we had been promised protection by special gifts of the Father. Events in the world at the time also supported the extreme possibility of nuclear war, as we watched Kosovo become the focal point of renewed hostilities among the Serbs and former Yugoslavia in what was termed *ETHNIC CLEANSING.*

In the beginning of July, 1998, Jesus began to give to my heart words to be shared with the world regarding the necessity of preparing for, but also praying to prevent the possibility of nuclear hostilities amongst nations capable of such aggression. Our Lady even said that during the summer then-President Clinton was in China meeting with other leaders of super powers, deciding who would receive the first nuclear strike in these plans, to which all had agreed, for world domination by those who will attempt to conquer the entire world!

FOR MERCY'S SAKE!

Jesus' words on 7/30/98 included these:

Your prayers are always working to impact the lives of others for good; are always being heard by the Father and moving Him to give more mercy to the world. But you must ALL PRAY MIGHTILY to stop these threats of nuclear war. Great destruction is a heartbeat away! Please, dear, dear ones whom I love with all My Sacred and Merciful Heart, take the energy you are using for fear and doubt and arguments, and kneel in peace and humility, begging the Father to remove this nuclear threat while at the same time gathering supplies for the great possibility of leaving your homes to escape nuclear fallout. If enough of you cry out continually to your God and Father, He may then be moved to interfere with plans of the evil one to annihilate different parts of the entire earth.

Evidently enough people took those words to heart and action, although there were many who railed against Jesus and His words when there was no nuclear attack. Until midnight on December 31, I was in nervous Adoration in union with people everywhere in the world who had also seen these messages and prepared for the worst. The terrible realization that so many people had expected and prepared for the annihilation of possibly two thirds of the world, and were praying and waiting as I was, made me physically ill. The seriousness of all the words shared those many months and the weight of this task sat heavily on my body and spirit. NOTHING HAPPENED! There were many who accepted a new level of understanding of the power of prayer and praised God. But many lashed out in rejection of any further reception of words of warning from a loving and merciful God on this subject anyway. No one wants to feel "taken", and I guess some very frightened people did. The important point about accepting God's plan and Will for our lives is that sometimes we will be frightened and see destruction; but in accepting His Will, we must accept it just the way He presents it to us and on His timetable. Not until January Third did the Lord speak again, as you will read in the succeeding chapter. He said, "the world is waiting for a word from Heaven about the recent expected events." And, God help me, I said, "Well?" In receiving locutions, (an inner voice in my head and heart), there is also an experience of the emotions of the person speaking that is felt in my whole body and spirit. Jesus was very serious. He continued:

"There are no words except the mercy of My Father. He always desires to act in response to your response to His warnings and requests. You asked for mitigation, and you received it! You were obedient to all We asked of you, and you are now seeing the power of your prayer, even over mighty events."

At Medjugorje, in the 1980's, Our Lady had explained that prayer could stop wars, prevent natural disasters and effect great change in the world. She has repeated this many times everywhere in the world. Most of us who attempted to pray and change as Mary requested, still did not understand this prayer power she had defined. The Father had just shown us in a mighty way (in this *NOTHING HAPPENED*) the mighty power to mitigate and delay, and in some instances defeat the plans of Satan. As you read the words in this book, you will see how the

FOR MERCY'S SAKE!

Father repeatedly calls us to be prepared for anything, to live a 'long time or a short time' and to trust in His promises of protection as His Remnant people, His instruments of mercy and healing and explanation of His plans to ultimately remove evil from the world before the Second Coming of His Son. When you read these Heavenly words, you will weep for your God, weep for the world and weep for yourselves. You will bask in the beauty of Our God's loving explanations and elegant prose. You will find repeated themes (which Heaven readily admits!) for our good and to stimulate our poor attention! Above all, "we are loved!"

To focus on the event we all await, we turn for a moment to what we have come to know and understand as the Father's Warning or the Illumination of our minds to the state of our souls, as God sees them. Nothing has filled the minds and hopes of those who pray like the arrival of this enormous gift of the Father to the world, which needs to see honestly and truly the truth about themselves in order to accept the opportunity to "get right" with God, to repent and renew their own lives in God's mercy and forgiveness. The world's greatest theologians, the finest minds and intellects can explain mysteries of God, offer answers and pose new challenges about God; but only God Himself can reveal our sins to us. Only the One, Who know us and is closer to us than we are to ourselves, has the perfect knowledge of our innermost being, the reality of our hearts, our thoughts, our lack of charity and good will. It is in the silence of listening and truly desiring a deeper revelation of the truth about ourselves that we will encounter God, the Father, the Physician, the Spirit of Truth Who only desires to save us from the father of lies.

Freedom from the world is absolutely necessary for all who desire to remain in the capacity of remnant people, chosen ones of God, instruments of His Will for His lost ones whom He WILL send to us after the Warning. Jesus says to us: I need the prayers of all who will spend entire days in deep union with Me and with My Mother for the lukewarm, for the worst sinners, to pray in reparation for their sins! The one who stays on the Path reaches the goal most quickly, without unnecessary delays. Time spent away from the world and in silence is necessary to heal us quickly, to free us to serve the Father's people now and in the future, and do His Will COMLETELY. It allows us to be emptied of noise and distractions that we might be filled with peace and grace, trust and wisdom, with Jesus Himself. This is surrender to transformation and learning to live in the Divine Will. It is not that we need purifying for our own honor and glory, but that we might be readied to be united to Him Who is Purity itself! We are invited to dwell in the Perfect Will of the Father, His perfect love for us and His desire to save and bring into Paradise as many as possible.

Carol Ameche, 2006.

All the messages in this book are discerned carefully and prayerfully by Fr. Elmer Torborg of Holdingford, MN and Mesa, AZ.

FOR MERCY'S SAKE!

This has been a huge endeavor. I apologize to Queenship Publishing that the first copies I gave to them were not acceptable because of the disorganization and need for much greater editing. Still God's Will is done. I apologize that some of the many changes I've had to make are not always uniform. The computer quite often said: 'Enough!' Carol

Jesus said: "Thank you for remaining faithful, for it is a long wait! All of Heaven sends you new ability to wait; for My Father's plan is perfect, and it molds you and causes you to be what you have not been, to become who you are not and what you are not in this plan filled with wisdom and gentleness. A wise and loving Father molds His children gently, slowly, mercifully, tenderly. You are becoming tenderness, My children!"

FOR MERCY'S SAKE

"BLESSED IS THE MAN WHO DOES NOT LOSE FAITH IN ME" (Matthew 11:6)

MESSEGES FROM 1999

1/4 "Daughter, it is I, your Lord Jesus Christ, King and Spouse to your soul.

THERE IS NO EXPLANATION, SAVE THE MERCY OF THE FATHER OF US ALL! When you pray for mitigation of war and nuclear destruction, and for mercy on the world, you should realize that this is the reaction and response the Father waits for! He must have your prayers, your sacrifices, your sincere love and fasting. When you comply with HIS requests, He is then able to choose to comply with YOUR requests! My Father loves His people and is deeply moved when you, His faithful ones, pray in love and concern for the salvation of the world, for true peace and mercy to be given. I have told you before, dear ones of My Heart, these events cannot be removed completely, but are and can continue to be, lessened in severity and incidence. He is showing you the MIGHTY RESULTS OF YOUR PRAYERS in order to convince and encourage you to persist in your prayerful pleadings to Him. The gifts of obedience and trust and humility, so sorely needed by Our children, are being released in greater numbers now, since the numbers of prayers and time of adoration also increases. It is so necessary that all of you, who read and believe, listen to My voice within your hearts. I wish to tell you directly of My great love for you, and gratitude for your surrender to the plans and perfect Will of My Father. You must simply continue in prayer and adoration, as you are, until the Angel appears to lead you to safety. Be at peace in your minds and hearts, dear ones. Be filled with the knowledge of the special graces you have received that will allow you to be all you are called to be. The plan of My Father includes many different directions for all who remain to teach and heal, to fight and win the battle over the evil in the hearts of so many. Be assured that you are loved far beyond your comprehension and understanding. Your fidelity will be outdone by the faithfulness of the Triune God and all in Heaven. Know that I love you with an everlasting tenderness and supreme joy! Be encouraged by this love, which is your refuge along with the Heart of Our dearest Mother, Mary. Come to Me again in the Sacrament of Reconciliation. Surrender ALL of yourself, My people. Give EVERYTHING and EVERYONE in your life back to Me through the Heart of Our Mother. **I will return them to you at the appointed time, according to My Father's Will.** Again I say to you, be at peace and DO NOT BE AFRAID. I am Jesus, Who stands before the Throne of My Father, pleading graces and healing for each one of you."

FOR MERCY'S SAKE!

1/8, Jesus said: "Dearest one, please write My words of love to you. Do you TRULY believe I would lead you astray with false promises and words that would confuse and lead Our people to certain destruction? I am your Jesus, your Lord and Savior, your Spouse and your King. The types of messages you receive are very necessary to bring Our people to a place of preparedness. If these words were to prove false, then there is no truth. But there IS truth because I Am Truth, and I AM! You must listen to Me now, in everything I tell you. You have remained calm in the face of much ridicule and rejection, and I commend your trust and surrender. Once again, daughter, every word that has been given to you WILL BE FULFILLED. You will continue to have powerful words with which to convince Our people of the need to remain prepared and strong in their belief in Our words of warning to them. Please convince them with your sincere ways and strong words to go out and defend themselves against all those who would laugh and walk away from them.

'It is you, My faithful ones, who will remain by My side, whom I will need to serve all My lost ones who come to you, **who will fight in the great battle against all of Hell itself when I will defeat Satan and his followers, and lead you into the era of peace and purity, of truth and honesty.** No more will you be sad and subjected to Satan's attacks. No more will you wander in loneliness and pain, suffering cold and hunger. My people, you are the ones the Father has given to Me. I am your Jesus Who died to save you, to open the gates of Heaven. I am your Jesus Who will come again so very soon to avenge the innocents killed by inhuman tactics. I am your Jesus Who will lead My faithful into the land flowing with the peace and purity of Eden. Won't you please TRUST Me a small while longer, My beloved ones? Please tell Our people in the coming weeks that the messages of all My faithful messengers do not contradict each other, as you shall see in the near future as you begin to live out each one."

1/19, "Dearest one, it is I, your Mother who comes with new words of warning for the world. Tonight, my child, there will be a series of secret tests in an important place in the world known to the One-World people, who escalate plans once more, now that other plans are in place and occurring on schedule. Thank you for praying first to my Spouse, daughter. I am Mary, the Mother of all people in the world, even those who reject me. My Heart overflows with sorrowful love for all, who are not aware of grave dangers surrounding them. In this new year of attack and counterattack, so many are being killed, as one would practice with a new toy! The concern for human life is no greater than that, my little soldier. This sort of casual killing leaves all of Our beloved breathless with horror. In Heaven there is great weeping over senseless killing of innocent villagers who want no part in these wars for control over small pieces of territory by men who have no regard for anyone. THE CALL WILL NEVER BE OTHER THAN A RENEWED PLEA FOR PRAYER FOR THE FATE OF THE WORLD. So many of Our faithful ones say, *I suppose I should be praying more*, and I tell you NO ONE is praying as they could, or as much as they SHOULD. Much of the grief in my own Heart is caused by this knowledge and the realization of how much more COULD be mitigated, how many events COULD be lessened in severity, how many more COULD receive the graces of conversion if all of our loved ones truly gave every spare minute of their time to praying for these intentions.

You will weep in great sorrow, My people, when you truly realize all you could have done, all the time you wasted, all the warnings and pleadings from Heaven that you ignored or reacted to in a casual way. If you knew that members of your own families were suffering from bitter cold and hunger, being forced from their homes, wandering about, lost, without the knowledge and grace of Jesus; you would be working feverishly to send them aid, to ease their plight, to fill them with the Peace of Jesus and the joy of knowing My Son and Myself. And yet, dearest ones, THESE ARE YOUR BROTHERS AND SISTERS. You are ALL members of the SAME family! PLEASE, children everywhere, BELIEVE this and respond IMMEDIATELY to the needs of so many who suffer terribly during these times! New destructive weather patterns continue to bring disaster to different areas of the world. What are you doing to help those who have lost nearly all their possessions? Are you praying that they will respond to the graces also present in these terrible events, and turn to God at last for His help and mercy? Will you allow people of all ages, especially the precious unborn babies who are helpless victims of greed and the callous indifference of those who should be loving and nurturing and protecting them, to be systematically robbed of life? Nothing, my dearest one, NOTHING is as important, and certainly never more important, than the salvation of souls.

You all have stories of loved ones, or people you know, who suddenly had an amazing conversion experience that surprised everyone, or a miracle cure and healing that occurred in a sick one's life. THIS IS ONLY THE RESULT OF PRAYER, MY PEOPLE! When you pray sincerely and steadily for someone, this is obeying the Father's Will for you; and if mitigation or healing is what is best for that event or that person, He is delighted to grant your requests. But you must persist, and ask for the healing of your own hearts and souls at the same time

'HAVE MERCY ON THE WORLD, FATHER, HAVE MERCY ON ME; FORGIVE THE WORLD, FATHER, FORGIVE ME; HEAL US, LORD, LEST WE PERISH.'

Please, dear ones, who listen and love Us, REALIZE THAT YOU WERE CREATED FOR THIS TIME. God, the Father, knows your hearts and the love and compassion HE PUT THERE and sees growing daily. He also knows all that you are capable of doing on behalf of the world. And He sends His Love and encouragement to you through words from Jesus and myself, these many years. We have used every word of warning and begging and caution to you. You DO have all the understanding you need, but you are resisting the degree of service to which you are being called, and saying again the very words of Satan: '***I will not serve* to the degree you, Jesus, and you, Our Mother, are requesting. I will not give up my own pleasures and my own important pastimes in order to pray**

for hours at a time. I will not be made uncomfortable by Your irritating reminders of suffering people I don't even know....' And I tell you, you DO know them, My dearest, little ones. They are your family. They are YOU.

What judgments and critical observations will you rush to share after you have witnessed your own souls and the results of critical behavior? You think my words harsh, children? These are words of love, sent to you by a loving Mother who wishes to wake you from your self-induced sleep, the busyness of your important lifestyles, events that fill your thoughts and plans. **The Father has a plan too, My dear ones! He plans to bring as many of His people to Heaven, as He is allowed by each of you. You hold your own fate in your busy hands and hearts. You hold the opportunity for salvation for as many as you will accept now, here, today, for the rest of your lives! This is a major part of the Father's plan for your own salvation, people of My Heart**. Please say softly to yourselves many times in these coming days and weeks:

FOREVER AND EVER AND EVER AND EVER, I WILL BE IN HEAVEN OR HELL!

The decision is yours, beloved of my Heart. We in Heaven are waiting for all of you with open arms filled with love. Reread these words, dearest ones. Allow them to sink deep into your subconscious. Let these words give impetus and new direction to all your thoughts and actions. I love all of you, my dearest children, beyond your earthly ability to understand. This night you are given the strength of perseverance and renewed prayer effort. As you read my words, please believe that these graces will enable you to do whatever is needed, all that is requested by Heaven for the good and salvation of the world. Say, *YES*, dearest ones, PLEASE say *YES*!"

1/26, Jesus said: "Dear child, please write these words: You are all about to be victims of war. (A great example of the amount of delay we have experienced, but which is still in our future…cta.) The greatest battle with Evil the world has ever known. **The thought and remembrance of My Victory will need to be a constant source of strength for My people.** I am your Jesus, daughter, Who will lead all of Our faithful ones into this battle after My Return. Think of it! You will see Me on the clouds, surrounded by the Angels, and My Mother will be there, too! What an incident to experience! What a gift! What a miracle! What an event to take in, to internalize, to live for, to anticipate now, to participate in, to record and enjoy, to rejoice and give thanks for! Think of the graces, the gifts, the purification and mercy that will accompany My Return. I Am Grace! I Am Purity. I Am Gift. I Am Mercy, My dear one. You, who will remain faithful, and remain according to the Father's Will for you, will witness the greatest event and gift from the Father since I returned to Heaven. And I remind you of My Mother's words, '...You were created for this; you and all of the Faithful Remnant who will behold My Second Coming to the Earth.'

My people, please let your hearts be at peace about everything. Please wait in a prepared and prayerful way. Please trust all Our words to you from

Heaven, and continue to practice charity and mercy with all your brothers and sisters We send to you every day and, most especially, your own dear loved ones who are closest to you. Charity can only come from a merciful heart and a mind that sees the need of so many in the world and responds to that need in every way possible. Each of you is so blessed with the goods of this world. But if you are not, I have told you to TRUST that you will be cared for by those who are able to share from their store of food and clothing. This is the law of Justice and Charity, My loved ones of the Earth: when you are given more, you MUST share it and invest yourself in the needy. My people, you will be repaid in a thousand ways, in ten thousand ways by My Father and yours. He will never be outdone, and most of all in pouring out and increasing the love and gifts you already have!

I need for you to be faithful and diligent. You need to see your preparedness as a living out of the stories of the Gospel when the virgins wisely kept plenty of oil on hand, and stayed awake watching for the Master's return. There are so many beloved ones who work in secret, praying and suffering for all of you in the world who must persevere through unimaginable trials and horrors. Is this not a way I would speak to you, My people? How else train for war than to know to a certain extent the difficulties you must face, the strength of the Enemy, his tactics and battle plans? This is not some exercise in fear sent by the Evil One! This is a HEAVENLY warning, meant to give you the proper ammunition for each onslaught of the Anti-Christ and his followers. You will not succeed in eluding him unless you TRUST in My promises to you. You will not succeed in remaining here (on Earth) unless the Father wills it for you, but that does not mean you are doomed! Think of Heaven with a joyful heart, because that is where every one of you is going at one time or another! This is My greatest wish for you, My people. I hope it is yours!!"

1/28, "Daughter, please take these words for Our people: 'My beloved and faithful ones of the Earth. I, your Jesus, send words of love and gratitude to each of you. Your prayers and sacrifices are continuing to release mercy from the hands of the Father of us all. Do not be anxious for the appearance of the Anti-Christ, but continue to guard yourselves against the lure of the world. The plans of Satan go forward and result in continued hateful crimes against Our poor defenseless ones. Do you not wonder what will be the end of such atrocities? These will continue, I tell you, as long as Satan remains free to fill the hearts and minds of men with greed and lust. Do you think it unfair, little ones, that only a FEW of you are spending all your time now in prayers and silence? **Please do not consider conversation with God and His holy Mother, or a daily visit before My Blessed Sacrament a chore! Please continue with your prayers and novenas to Our Holy Spirit for the gift of openness and understanding of the great graces and gifts of preparedness, and courage and strength you are receiving.** In this time of quiet, before the storms of the Evil One rage across the country, be filled with greater certainty than ever that your God WILL protect you. What more do you need, when you have the promise of the Triune God that you are, indeed, His Faithful Remnant who will remain (according to the Father's

Will) to serve all those We send to you? What more can I tell you, other than these words of encouragement and peace that I will continue to give your hearts? You are becoming stronger, more flexible, more docile and obedient, more pliable in the hands of your God. You will soon enough be emptied of all your possessions (and perhaps many of your loved ones), and will know the time has arrived to take your faith and trust into hiding from all that threatens you.

It is a great privilege you have been given. You are ALLOWED to suffer in union with Me for the winning of souls. I remind you again of all the miracles you will see performed on your behalf, and by your own intercession. The Father knows what is necessary in each life to bring you to a more perfect readiness to serve. Continue to pray and serve My Mother. Continue to TRUST and be at peace about the perfect timing of My Father. Continue to believe, I beg you, that you ARE loved by Me and My dearest, holy Mother. Be at peace and persevere, My faithful ones."

2/1, Adoration St. Augustine Church, Des Moines, Iowa

Jesus said: "My dear child, I am your Jesus Who comes by the Will and grace of My Father. Please stop now and pray to Our Spirit for complete openness to My words, for a complete union with all of My desires for you. Daughter, PRAY. Dearest child, your patience is in constant need of purification because there will be much waiting in My Father's Plan. You must teach others this part of surrender, and docile waiting in peace and obedience. There is so much to occur before I return, and Our people must be purified of their impatience, their busyness, and their own way of doing things. Because the world has gone so far beyond the original plan and Covenant with My Father**, you must now all be purified to a much simpler way of life and state of soul**. This will be necessary for everyone entering Heaven or remaining to begin life in the New Era. All of you only THINK you know what this simplicity is, this purity of mind, and heart, and spirit. In all of your observations. You are filtering through the world-view of *right and wrong*, of *simple*, of *obedience* the requests of My Mother and Myself. She has spoken to you of the *Kingdom of Self* where most of you worship at the *Altar of Pleasure and Self-gratification.* You know NOTHING of deprivation, of self-denial, of a way of life that includes not only a great deal of prayer, but service to our poor ones and charity to the needy. It is possible to do all this without leaving your homes, yes; but My Father wishes all of you to serve each other, to touch hearts and spirits DIRECTLY, whenever that is possible. If you are to be ready to serve the needs of hundreds of thousands of lost ones after the Warning, do you not agree that SOME practice would be in order?

Do you think one who dances with a ballet troupe is able to perform without hours and years of practice daily? What is your level of dedication to this call, My beloved people? The position of *prima dancer* is open in most cities! Would you care to try out for this? Are you prepared to lead the rest? Are you familiar with every step delivered with the greatest ease and grace? Do you appreciate what it takes to make something very difficult appear quite easy, a joy?

FOR MERCY'S SAKE!

This is the task ahead of you, My remnant flock, My leaders of those who will come to be nurtured by your performance, who will be moved to wish to join your troupe, to learn your routines! I have chosen you for these tasks because I have given you the ability to serve in this manner! But first, you must get up and come forward. Listen to the words of instruction. Hear the music of Heaven's praise. Learn the words that teach you each step, take you in the right direction at the proper time. Become so familiar with the music and words that you can respond without having to stop and think, without missing a step, perhaps even falling down! The angels are chanting this lovely refrain at every moment:

'Come back. Come back, dear loved ones. Come back and praise the Father. Obey the Son. Enjoy the Spirit. Reflect the Mother and shine with the Light!'

Learn to be docile, and sway in the wind of the Spirit. Be able to move in whatever direction you are led for the moment.

'Bow and curtsey, pirouette. Leave the world for our duet!

Take My hand and pas de deux. Take My Heart and hide within.

Let Me lift you up on high. See the shores of Heaven nigh!

Throw all caution to the wind. That's it, dear ones, let's begin!'

Can you feel the rhythm of My love, My dearly loved ones? Let go of all your baggage of preconceived notions and criteria, of ritual and form. Be FREE, My partners, and allow Me to lead you up the stairs ahead, to fly on wings of hope, to land ever so gently at the top where My Father awaits us. He it is Who has chosen you to perform, to work at all the intricate steps of His DANCE INTO ETERNITY! There are springs and fountains everywhere along the Way with which to refresh yourselves before the next step. But always, you will be climbing and swaying and twirling as you hold My Hand and we rise higher and higher toward the top! It IS simple **if only you stay with Me and follow My lead, imitate My steps.** There, see in the wings a cloud of angels ready to help you get up when you trip or fall. Count on their assistance, dear ones. They are unencumbered by the weight of the world. They are eager to help you learn, and move on at the right moment. The music swells at times, ushering in a time of praise and thanks, allowing you time to rest and renew, when the music slows almost to a quiet halt! Let our hearts beat together to the rhythms of My Father's Will. Become familiar with the stops and starts, the ebb and flow. Be ready to watch and listen with attention, when different dancers take the spotlight and deliver their own practiced segment of the whole. This composition is composed of many 'solo numbers,' many times of individual performance that add strength and meaning to the rest of the dance.

So much beauty awaits you in this waltz of service, this thrilling ensemble of faithful ones who have cared enough to practice each new step, to do whatever it takes to be in shape for this spiritual blending of human and divine. Be filled with understanding now, dearest of My Heart, of the great opportunities which await you, as you come forward into the Light and the glow of My Father's love for you. Be the ones who are able to perform whenever you are called upon. This audience will eagerly await all you have to share with them from your own store of talents, the results of your hard work and training. The Orchestra is warming up, My people. The curtain is about to rise. Are you ready for this great drama to unfold, to dance right into My arms?'

Daughter: Stay with Me forever! I am your Jesus Who speaks, Who is here in the union of the Trinity. My Father sends greetings of love and appreciation. My Spirit fills you with new resolve and fire. Now praise the Father with Me, with all of Heaven, for His gracious Goodness and Mercy."

2/6, "Dearest daughter, yes it is I, your Mother of Sorrows.

'Dear people of the world. Rejoice! **It is the *time of your life,* this preparation for My Jesus' return** to Earth. It is the fulfillment of all the reasons you were born at this time, brought to this moment in history through all the experiences of your life. This is your training from the earliest days, your environment whether easy or a painful struggle, your learning at each new level of progress, especially the mistakes you have made and, oh yes, continue to make, my loved ones! Please pay more attention to the roots of your behavior: your pride and selfishness, your self-gratification and, I am sad to say, arrogance on many occasions. Ask again, dear faithful, struggling ones, to see these sins and behavior patterns. When you discover more, rejoice again! Then beg the Father for the grace to overcome these faults, for the strength to reject old habits and critical attitudes. Let go, once and for all, of all that hinders the great progress the Father desires for you at this time. Please reread Our words to you since the beginning of this new year. How do you think you have changed? How have you grown? Where have you changed, or have you slipped farther back on the path to my Jesus? Have delays (Mercy) caused you to gain new insight and conviction, or have they provided you with a license to relax, to pray less, to lose your sharp edge of preparedness and concern for souls, ESPECIALLY your OWN? I know that SO MANY of you are lonely and hurt by the ridicule and rejection of others. YOUR DOCILE ACCEPTANCE OF THIS PART OF YOUR JOURNEY HAS DONE SO MUCH TO RELEASE GRACES FOR THE ENTIRE WORLD. Read Our words many times please, and the words of My Jesus in holy Scripture. Be an able warrior and a gentle protector. Let your spirit soar with love for the Triune God, and lift you up to a place of greater protection from all the taunts and criticism hurled at you by uncaring people whom Satan has in his grip.

Remember to offer these hurts for those who are filled with hatred and jeering over the words of Heaven, who are made uncomfortable by your increased prayer and visits to the Most Blessed Sacrament where my Son waits for you in an agony of anticipation and longing. Have mercy on Him, My people. Spend every spare moment you can find in adoration of the Trinity, no matter WHERE you are. Your loved ones, who are here with Us, are praying in constant supplication for your continuing conversion, and in union with your prayers for continued mercy on the world. There are so many events yet to occur to challenge your faith and cause your struggles to increase. I am praying for increased patience and peace in the hearts of all of you who listen and respond to Our words.

My plea to you is the same: Pray and TRUST. Love and have mercy. Do not ask or anticipate or have expectations. Put yourselves in the boat with my Jesus and call to Him in your fear and need. He will calm the storms within and without. He will protect you from the elements that would capsize your vessel! Fear will do no good, My children. What is needed is TRUST. Allow your God and mine to do everything for you and with you. Remain in the protection of My Heart and Mantle. Prepare for all that is even now unfolding in the world. DO NOT WAIVER IN YOUR COMMITMENT TO MY SON AND TO ME. ALLOW NO ONE TO MAKE YOU TURN AWAY FOR THE SAKE OF KEEPING A SORT OF PEACE IN YOUR FAMILY, IF THAT IS YOUR CHALLENGE. ALLOW NO ONE TO TALK YOU INTO CHOOSING THE MARK OF THE BEAST FOR CONVENIENCE' SAKE. DO NOT CHOOSE THE EASY WAY, MY SOLDIERS AND FRIENDS. CHOOSE JESUS' WAY AND RUN QUICKLY INTO THE WILL OF THE FATHER, WHO WAITS FOR YOU WITH GREAT ANTICIPATION. AGAIN, MY LOVED ONES, I SAY.... REJOICE!"

2/8, 1:30 a.m. "My beloved people, continue to come to Me daily in My Blessed Sacrament. Know that you are receiving increased strength for the preparedness of your hearts for My return. I am your Jesus of Mercy, of Love and of the greatest devotion to you. Be in peace, knowing that you are My Chosen Remnant who will remain faithful, many of whom will see Me coming on the clouds with My Angels to defeat the Anti-Christ, to defeat Satan and all his cohorts and followers. You will fight with Me, My dear ones. You are *precious* to Me, and I bless you now with new joy and new hope for the Victory already won, that will usher in the New Era of Peace and Purity. You are brave and faithful children of My Heart, and I will bring all of you to Me according to the Will of Our Father. Persevere, My dear ones, and know how much you are loved."

2/10, "Dearest one, I am your Jesus. Be at peace. There are so many sad events for all to encounter. Once the Antichrist makes himself known to the world, the plan of My Father will be so much closer to completion for the Earth and all the people on it. A humble display of obedience before the world will do much to convince many hardened hearts of the authenticity of Our words. This is the only way to win souls. I, Myself, will save many from drowning in the sea of their own pride and arrogance! When a person allows her/himself to be used as an instrument in the hands of God, great miracles can occur that very few will ever even know about. **Conversion only occurs in the life of one who has honestly accepted the truth about themselves, who has seen their error and then comes to My Father in sorrow for sinful behavior.** But first, something must happen in that life to arrest its behavior, stop this one in his or her tracks, as you say: *Bring them up short!* You are allowing yourself to be ridiculed and rejected by many, who see themselves as faithful warriors for a Heavenly cause. How can one come to know Heaven's desires, when that one never takes time for silent LISTENING? How can you hear the softest whisper of My voice, My Mother's, the Father and Our Spirit, unless you take the time for quiet listening and reflection? No, My child, this cannot occur, and so you must explain to all ***how necessary is this time spent with Me, away from the world each day.*** This is the only way to prepare the soil of your being to receive the water of grace and the seeds of My Father's Will. Tell Our people **how necessary it is to make the repeated decision that whatever the Father needs for the salvation of souls, you are there to relinquish all of who you are in service to His desires for you.**

A knife does not suddenly decide to become a fork! An arm cannot be exchanged for a leg. A brain can only function in a way that is compatible to its construction, its God-given abilities and the way it is put together. Each of you is 'put together' just a little differently according to the Father's particular plan. You cannot possibly know all the ingredients your Creator has used for your own personal makeup. So how can you know what is the best way to serve God and His people, unless you reflect and meditate on your life, on God's Word in Scripture and all the teachings passed down through the generations?

WHO ARE YOU in the Light of My Love, the searching, probing ways of the Spirit, the (sometimes not so gentle) molding and remolding of the Father, the urgent and concerned call of My Mother, the great needs of your brothers and sisters and tiny innocent victims of abortion, the madness of world leaders today, especially in your own country? My people, time will run out on you if you do not stop! Unless you realize your sinful ways NOW, you are in the greatest danger of being lost forever in Eternity. **The Antichrist will have his eyes and ears *everywhere. He will make opportunities to follow him so easy, so much the only intelligent choice to make*. And the greater number of people in the world will choose to follow him!**

WHO ARE YOU in the light of the absolute possibility or probability of leaving your homes and most of your possessions and perhaps even loved ones? What will your choice be, My people? What will you do when the Angel of the Lord appears to you with the command to depart hastily to follow him to a place of safety from nuclear fallout? (Followed in most cases by a return to our homes after the Father has miraculously cleared the air of radiation… see messages from 1998 in “BANDS OF LOVE”, QUEENSHIP PUBLISHING…. CTA.) Have you developed (by accepting the grace and strength that has been offered) a distance from all that would possess you, from all who are an occasion of sin, from places and people that are detrimental, even deadly, to your spiritual life? Have you learned to look at yourself honestly, without your usual excuses? Are you seeing clearly now through the rays of Divine Mercy and the humble Heart of Mary? There is so much to be accomplished and so little time left! DO NOT continue on your path of present behavior, controlled by your schemes to convert at the very last minute! Your hourglass may be empty! Perhaps it is broken!!!

I love you, My dearest people. I do not wish to lose you to the wiles and lies of Satan. Ask Me for the gift of new eyes, new ears, a new heart. If you do not allow My Father to make of you a new creation, you are ALREADY dead!! My words are meant to convey the strongest urgency for your return in sorrow and contrition to the Covenant of the Father, to His Laws, to the Spirit of God, to My love, to the mercy of the Triune God. STOP whatever you are doing, even serving His plan of salvation; and LISTEN, RECEIVE and ACT upon all the Father wishes to give you anew. The most critical time of a soldier's preparation is immediately before entering the battle. Come NOW, this INSTANT back to Me, all of you created (in the beginning) in the Image of your God. Do not put this off another SECOND. DO NOT map out a new schedule that would include your reconciliation with Me ... when time PERMITS! SURRENDER and come back IMMEDIATELY ... TODAY. Find out who you really are and all the possibilities available to you. Do NOT continue to commit spiritual suicide. Do NOT listen to the Father of Lies. Listen to ME. I Am Truth. I will NEVER deceive or betray you. I will NEVER leave you. I will ALWAYS love you, if you will ALLOW Me into your heart and mind and soul: TODAY, My dear, dear people."

2/12, At Adoration Blessed Mother said: "Child, please write. I am your Mother of Divine Mercy. I come at the request of God, Our Heavenly and Merciful Father. Daughter, this day is a black one, indeed, in the history of your country. Who can be surprised that a man of great cunning (President Clinton and the Monica scandal) and ability to lie in the face of all that is just and true, should be allowed to go free by the Father of Lies and his followers? Yes, Our people must pray for each other and for this country. This leader of your country leads all, who will allow him, into the darkest times in all of history. He has publicly received pardon for criminal activity EVERYONE KNOWS HE COMMITTED! THE FOLLOWERS OF SATAN HAVE WON ANOTHER VICTORY IN THIS COUNTRY THAT IS NO LONGER THE ***LAND OF THE FREE***. The brave ones who are left are quietly praying and preparing to survive the terrible oppression of the Antichrist. Know that your country will not see honor or valor or the blessings of Almighty God until after the return of My Son, and the defeat of Satan and his hordes. Those of you, who are faithful to the promises of God, the words from Heaven and the service required to your needy brothers and sisters will be brought together many times in heart and spirit to pray for Mercy on the world. This now signals the rest of the One World Order to escalate plans for the Third World War to begin. You, as a nation, have been given every chance to vote, to choose, to demand the preservation of **the freedom your ancestors died for. They weep in Heaven for the terrible state of affairs and loss of just principles within your government.** Be aware that YOU HAVE CHOSEN TO ACCEPT THIS BEHAVIOR, this OBVIOUS deception, this FLAGRANT disregard for truth from one whom you have chosen to lead you, to make laws that rob you of freedom and destroy the lives of innocents. THIS PUBLIC REJECTION OF GOD AND HIS LAWS WILL BECOME EVEN MORE OPEN NOW: ACTIVITY THAT ALL WILL SEE AND BE HELPLESS TO STOP. Redouble your prayers for mercy NOW. Do not neglect the duty of soldiers of mine to fight to protect the gifts freely given by the Father of ALL people. These gifts are grace and strength and the opportunity to come back to God, to be nourished by my Son, to be sanctified by my Spouse, the Holy Spirit of God. More than ever, faithful ones, ***it is my desire that you quit the world, that you leave behind all frivolous and empty behavior***. This destruction of justice, this mockery of truth is much more serious than it even appears. The ramifications (of this refusal to acknowledge wrongdoing on the part of your elected officials) reach far into your homes and families. **You have invited martial law, confiscation of personal property and goods into your very existence.** This man of dishonor and lies will never stop deceiving you, will become a stronger tool of the Antichrist and will not lift a finger to save your country or any of you from the great and imminent threat of WAR.

HEAVEN WEEPS THIS NIGHT AT THE WANTON BEHAVIOR OF THE LEADERS OF THIS GREAT LAND, THIS LAND THAT WAS SO BLESSED, SO GIFTED BY THE FATHER. For now you have said *yes*, once again to those who will destroy freedom, destroy the peace and security that has always been yours.

PRAY AMERICA, IN REMORSE AND SORROW FOR YOUR SINS OF OMISSION, YOUR LAZY ATTITUDE TOWARD ANY RESPONSIBILITY TO THE HEALTH AND PROSPERITY AND DECENCY OF THIS COUNTRY. Do not think that these leaders do not know about me, all of the messages being received worldwide, all of the warnings about the secret plans to give away this country and the world to the domination of the Antichrist, to the 'power' they believe they will have from him. What sad and foolish men they are! What poor examples for the younger ones who look for heroes, for honesty and all the qualities meant to be found in REAL leaders! The darkness has increased this day, my poor loved ones of the Earth. This acceptance of flagrant violations of truth will now give even freer reign, more possibilities to lie and cheat and betray and steal and get AWAY with it! Everyone in the world can look around at the dreadful state of affairs and say, '*through my fault, through my fault, through my most grievous fault.*' Daughter, My heart is so heavy with sorrow tonight. You can feel this, and are sobered by a new awareness of the dangerous results of this day's *legal* activity. Please ask everyone to bring all these national sins to me, that I may take your petitions for mercy to the Father and plead (along) with you. When you follow My Jesus, you agree to accept the sins of the world, just as He did; and beg the mercy of the Father on the millions of selfish, thoughtless people who truly do not know what they have done, or the awful results of their indifference. Do whatever you can to promote a greater response from Our people whose eyes are still blinded by the busyness and frantic activity that seems so important and necessary. My children of the world, and especially this country, please unite. Come together in the Immaculate and Sorrowful Heart and the Glorious and Sacred Heart of Jesus. Remain there united to Us and to each other in a renewed effort to fight Satan and all his followers, and to beg the Father's mercy on the world."

FOR MERCY'S SAKE!

2/16, Jesus said: "You see now that it isn't necessary for you to know what is occurring in the world, as long as you are praying in unity with My Mother for her intentions and in union with Me for the perfect Will of the Father to be fulfilled at every second by yourself and all Our faithful ones. Now, please take these words: 'Dear people of the world who listen and act upon all the words you are receiving from Heaven, I am Jesus Who worships and obeys God, My Father; Who is united with Him and Our Spirit, Three in One, in the perfect unity of this Trinity that We Are. I bring you new strength for the waiting, for the persevering, for your increased ability to remain in the state of grace for answering every request of My Mother with all your heart and all your mind and all of who you are. Satan is attacking all of you in a more powerful and more constant way now. Have you noticed?

If you are preparing each day with prayer and repeated acts of praise and thanksgiving, then you can be sure that your struggles have increased! Your weaknesses are causing you greater discomfort, greater challenge, more difficulty than ever before. Yes, beloved ones, this is to increase your resistance to temptations to ***Take a brief holiday*, or *time off for good behavior*!** The times seem quiet in the world, but each one who has eyes to see and ears to hear realizes that this quiet is meant to lull you into a sense of ease, of complacency. In order to destroy your sharp edge of alertness, Satan and his demons are working constantly to distract you, to fool you with days that reflect a peace that does not really exist. Before every battle there is a calm atmosphere, but one that is charged with emotion and expectations. This is what you are feeling, dearest beloved; and no one is exempt who has made the commitment. Each of Our messengers, more than the rest, struggles these days with personal weakness and sinful inclinations. **The more you do by way of service to My Mother, to the Trinity, to the people of the earth, the more Satan wars against you with temptations to loneliness, doubt, fear, and critical judgments.**

You must all be more patient with each other, My people. If you make an extra attempt to understand another's behavior, you will be able to treat one another in a kinder way, with less irritability and impatience. Please listen more closely to each other and realize the tremendous strain you all feel from the increased waiting and wondering. You are all being greatly purified by the obedience you practice. You are being made to glisten in the fires of each trial, each struggle in order to be melted, made more pliable and reformed by My Father. You become a sharper, more efficient weapon and instrument the Father will use in His plan for the salvation of all His people. Do not be put off by the weakness you observe in each other, most especially in Our special messengers! <u>Do not be moved to turn away from this Plan for your own salvation because of the deeds of another. Focus on My Face, little ones, on My beauty, on My perfection.</u> Allow these to draw you more deeply into My Sacred Heart that burns with love for you and a longing to hold you near forever.

I send My compassion to you this night. I have told you before what it was like for Me ... waiting for the final word from My Father before beginning the march to Golgotha. WE ARE MORE AND MORE UNITED THAN EVER, MY PEOPLE, AS YOU SHARE MORE AND MORE OF MY PASSION. HEAVEN HAS THE GREATEST NEED OF ALL OF YOU, THE GREATEST DESIRE TO HELP YOU, THE GREATEST DESIRE TO SEE YOU SUCCEED IN ALL YOUR ENDEAVORS TO BECOME ALL YOU ARE CALLED TO BE!

I ask you to receive these gifts and use them with JOY, My own dearest ones. Come to Me in My Blessed Sacrament. Rejoice when you discover a weakness, a bad habit, a tendency toward sin in the company of certain people or particular places! Run joyfully to My Sacrament of Reconciliation to be cleansed, to be renewed, to be freer to climb more quickly over your failings and all that would burden you and hold you back on the Path to the Kingdom. Feel My own excitement and joy for you as I see you accepting graces and making the right choices. **Do not be disconsolate at the need for constant visits to confess sins! Most of you are beyond much of the repeated, habitual sins now, and are able to give more attention to asking Our Spirit to show you hidden sins and weaknesses.** You should have more time to reflect on daily occurrence, verbal exchanges with others, working with others or in greater solitude. Reflections on daily behavior are so necessary because of the very small amount of time that is left before destructive events in the world and the Warning of My Father. PAY VERY CLOSE ATTENTION TO EVERY WORD, EVERY ACTION OF MINE, AS I WAS LED THROUGH THE WILL OF MY FATHER TO THE ULTIMATE SACRIFICE ON CALVARY. DIE WITH ME TO THE WORLD, MY DEAR FAITHFUL ONES, THAT YOU MAY RISE TO BE THE HOLY AND PURIFIED ONES WHO GREET ME AT MY RETURN. I have great faith and trust in you, My people. Please have the greatest faith and trust in Me. YOU ARE MINE!"

2/21, "Dear one of My Heart, I am your Jesus Who invites all to partake of My Beauty, My Strength, My Peace.

NOTHING is real without My presence in it!

NOTHING will last without the Will and support of My Father.

NOTHING can live and grow properly without the life and love and vitality of Our Spirit; and

NOTHING can approach the throne of God without the humility and obedience of My Mother.

The Virgin Mary said: "Daughter, let us begin: The world slumbers in a vague uneasiness, aware something is 'wrong,' but not really grasping the portents on its horizon. Everywhere, intrigue is the framework for the dealings of one country with another. **More than anything, lies and hatred are the food of international repasts.** Everyone knows that all the decisions have been made and agreed to by leaders of the major powers. Each country plays its role in the events that ultimately set up the reign of the Antichrist (and the fulfillment of Scripture for these End Times) that will allow the One World Order to take over the

ENTIRE world! Each smaller nation will be a puppet in the hands of those who have the first and last say.

Your own country will be devastated by the plans of your leaders to allow foreign governments to take control and further subdue any retaliation on the part of loyal Americans. This is NOT about patriotism. This is about TREASON at the highest level of CRIMINAL activity. The One-World people are CRIMINALS, first and foremost, without consciences or an understanding of right and wrong. **There is a stage of development in the criminal mind when all prior understanding or rejection of evil, immorality or injustice DIES!** Plans and preparations are made on the basis of greed and lust for power.

Nothing can stand in the way of these plans, except God Himself. Only the love of Jesus in the hearts of the few Faithful Remnant (in union with HEAVEN'S PLANS) will ultimately defeat the might that Satan has been allowed (by the Father) in order to accomplish the ultimate renewal of the world after My Jesus, your Savior and your King, returns to the Earth. You will be more convinced of this truth as you see and experience the growth of evil in the world and the *apparent* success of the Antichrist and his followers. **According to the minds of terrorists, no one must be allowed to rest in peace again until they have conquered and subdued the *enemy*, which is the ENTIRE WORLD! The criminal element in every part of the world will become more powerful and apparent, as major powers legislate any and every change that suits their needs.**

Please have all of your Sacramentals and your souls in order! Plan to depart for safety with pure hearts and a mind filled with humility and obedience. Trust in these words, dear ones of My Immaculate Heart. You will NEVER be without direction or words of warning regarding impending events. These words are meant to encourage you to believe in Our promises of protection, and to keep you vigilant and alert. You will not need to figure out anything on your own. Just be aware and praying every moment you can, and know that your future is assured as a child of God and heir of His Kingdom. Daughter, these words are meant to assure Our people of the Earth that they will never be abandoned or left wondering what to do.

The Father's plans include EACH ONE who remains faithful and perseveres on this journey into Heaven or into the New Era on Earth! There are so many events of a mighty nature to occur before My Jesus' return. It is most important that you continue to pray for patience for yourselves and all of those who pray. Only those good intentions that are supported with action will bring you into an eternal bliss and joy in Heaven. Please do not become lethargic in your responses to my requests. I am coming to you with the greatest love and gratitude for your love, but with a motherly concern about your ability to endure the **long periods of waiting included in the Father's desires for His people.** ABSORB ALL THE LOVE I BRING TO YOU, MY CHILDREN. It will protect you from the attacks of the evil intentions of the Antichrist and his followers. Stay close to me now, dearest ones. Come in peace and trust and faith in all the words of Heaven.

THE VICTORY IS WON. SUCCESS IS YOURS; BUT IS ACCOMPLISHED ONLY BY ALLOWING US TO LEAD YOU, TO DIRECT YOU, TO COMFORT AND STRENGTHEN YOU AT EVERY STEP, EVERY TURN. Be filled with anticipation for all that is about to take the people of the Earth through the most momentous times in history. Praise and thank the Father for choosing you to live at this time and be an integral part of His plan of salvation for all His people. PERSEVERE, MY LOVED ONES, WITHIN THE TWO HEARTS! **You must stay so very close in order to survive all that will attempt to interfere and destroy your mission and your soul.** I know that your trust is great, and you do not fear whatever lies ahead."

2/28, Jesus said: "Child, please take these words now for Our people: Dear ones of the suffering Heart of Jesus, I listen and watch and walk by your side. I dwell in your hearts and fill you with My Light, My Power and My Mercy. ***I call you to be the center of healing and reconciliation wherever you go.*** People will see this and be drawn to you by a special gift of My Father. You will notice that you are able to speak (to those who come) with words that are filled with My Spirit, that flow from My Heart through yours as a soothing balm to the wounds of all these dear lost ones. Do not be alarmed, or allow your own progress to be stayed by your loved ones who refuse to accept My words and those of My Mother! You know in your hearts, (by a special grace you have accepted) what is true and holy, what will occur in the nearest future, and all you are called to become during these serious events.

DO NOT WAIVER IN YOUR RESOLVE, MY FAITHFUL ONES. BE AWARE THAT YOU ARE SURROUNDED BY MANY ANGELS WHO DO BATTLE AT EVERY MOMENT AGAINST DEMONS ALSO PRESENT, WHO FIGHT TO WIN YOU AWAY FROM ME, FROM TRUTH. No one will escape the experience of grief and loss! No one will be saved from persecution of one kind or another. Please remember that your prayers, your fidelity, your service, are the means of sanctification for loved ones, in spite of choices they make in the immediate future. The salvation of your own soul, the gift of My Love and friendship are worth ANYTHING you are required to suffer. Some of you will even give your lives on account of My Name. Be filled with joy at this possibility, My people. Accept all the crosses you will meet, and carry them with joy, knowing that each event, each struggle brings the world that much closer to My return. Be filled with peace and be encouraged in spite of many delays and seeming abandonment by Heaven! **I am living proof that the Father keeps His word and all His promises at the proper time, at the appointed hour.** Read your Scripture daily, My people. Reread all I have taught through My Apostles, all I have promised for the New Era about to be realized upon the Earth. SURRENDER YOURSELVES AND ALL YOUR POSSESSIONS AND TALENTS TO MY FATHER. OFFER TO HIM ALL OF WHO YOU ARE, ONCE AGAIN. Do not be discouraged. You are sending a mighty cry for peace and mercy to the Father, Who is then responding with Peace and Mercy for the world. Avail yourselves of the opportunities to receive graces for yourselves and your loved ones as often as possible. You are held in My arms as you read these words. Can you feel the beating of My Heart next to yours? It is real, children. I love you and send this love and delight into your heart with each beat of My Own. Persevere!"

3/4, Jesus said: "My child, please write. Daughter, **the need for patience will be satisfied when the fruits become apparent in the future.** Some day you will know all the graces and benefits won for your loved ones. The ability to transform a person into the fighting weapon of My Father's desire is only that of My Father's power, His Wisdom and great Love for His people. When you say *YES* to the call of God and Our Mother, you agree to allow Us to make <u>any changes in you in the best possible way.</u> You are allowing and cooperating in this action in your life in a new and more beneficial way and degree. For the most part, Our people of the world are NOT remaining faithful to the amount of prayer requested by My Mother. <u>That is why it will be only a few who remain to greet Me upon My return.</u> All of you will need every help and prayer possible from the faithful who will be taken in large numbers to Heaven! Please remind Our people that EVERY WORD We have given to you to share with them will be fulfilled. When the word of God goes forth, it is ACCOMPLISHED! No, perhaps not 'immediately', or without a certain amount of delay, but it IS fulfilled because it is living and Life-giving.

If all of you would offer each other and each other's sins and weaknesses to the Triune God, in union with My suffering and beg mercy for each other, you will see a new and greater healing given to all. <u>Bring your brothers and sisters of the world into My Presence whenever you come to adore. And then pray in reparation for these sins and these sinners you have brought along and offered. Please consecrate sinners to Me DAILY, My dearest faithful children. Carry the world in your heart!</u> Accept the responsibility of being your brother's keeper.

Be the sin offering for the WORLD with Me, in union with My sufferings, children of My Sacred Heart. <u>Be the ones who carry this cross-that-is-the-world and all the evil in it.</u> Bring this cross to Me. Ask My Mother and all her Angels, all of the Saints, and your loved ones in Heaven to help you lift the cross of the World. Lift it high in supplication and reparation to My Father and beg mercy and healing, conversion and transformation for them, for the WHOLE WORLD. Prepare to kneel with Me in the Garden, to give your blood if necessary, as you look at your own sins and see also the sins of the world lived out in terror and the bloodshed of innocent people. DO NOT WAIT, MY PEOPLE, TO BRING THE WORLD TO ME. Much prayer is needed to fill the time that is left before My Return. Get rest and peace for your increased strength and perseverance. Especially hold up My suffering Church that moves inevitably toward its crucifixion. HOLD MY SHEPHERD IN ROME WITHIN YOUR HEARTS TO PROTECT AND COMFORT HIM THERE. Hold each other in reverence, and cherish and appreciate the gift that you are to one another.

Our Spirit is working to bring all of you to a deeper knowledge and understanding of your own pride and selfishness. Please allow Him every opportunity that you may bring them to Reconciliation. There are so many gifts that are waiting for those who persevere to the end. There is so much peace and healing for you now, when you visit Me in My Blessed Sacrament, when you take time after receiving Me in the Eucharist, when you absorb My Goodness and My Beauty. I beg you to come in silence and adore! Praise Me, little ones, thank Me for the mercy of My Father, for the gifts of our Spirit, for the great gift of My Mother and her virtues. Realize and accept the fact that you are NOTHING, My people, without your God, Who makes all things possible, Who will make all things new.

Yes, daughter, I am your Jesus Who brings all the love and help and renewal that you need. I wait for you, daughters and sons of My great longing. Come children, COME! I long to love you and to bless you and caress you. Give Me the chance. Give Me the *OKAY* to save you and your loved ones, and the whole world. Do not become sad, but rest. Be renewed and filled with energy and joy, My faithful ones. I increase your strength and grant new patience and TRUST! Good night and sleep in My arms."

3/9, "Dear one, you may begin to write. I am Jesus, your Lord. Daughter, the state of readiness for war is present in enough countries now, and only awaits several hostile moves on the part of another. This is planned, as We have said all along, for the inevitable World War that will develop out of these initial conflicts. The United States will make no effort to hide its aggressiveness. The results will be a taking of sides, according to plans. You will see weaker nations destroyed very quickly, as well as renewed weather aberrations. The world is about to explode on many fronts and will soon be the scene of so much bloodshed in many countries at the same time. This will be unlike any other conflict that has ever existed. It is not necessary that anyone has knowledge of these events, as this would only increase the fear already present in the hearts of so many. And I tell you, My faithful ones, THERE IS NOTHING TO FEAR, nothing to dread, nothing to anticipate, for all will occur for each of you exactly according to My Father's Plan for you. Those of you who believe, and wait in trust, are so very prepared for whatever occurs. Remember that you have a God of Mercy! Think of that, every time you are tempted to panic. Count on each other for strengthened encouragement. Remember to expect miracles to bring you through every trying event. When you have the gift of My Peace in your heart, nothing can disturb you, or make you turn away from Us. My Mother and I pour out Our gratitude to you in the form of increased graces of strength and patience. When you are in Heaven one day, you will see the results of your fidelity and prayer, and be filled with joy and amazement. It is important that you are very flexible and ready to leave at any hour, any moment. **If there are those loved ones, who refuse to accompany the angel who comes to lead the way, I bid you: have courage! Heaven needs you to come away to safety in order to serve those We send to you. Always believe that this is your primary goal and responsibility in the coming days.**

FOR MERCY'S SAKE!

Because the Father has a perfect Will and has made perfect plans for everyone, you need not worry about each other, if some of those you love choose not to respond to this call. Again, this will require the greatest trust on your part, who work so hard to protect your families. Remain faithful yourself and know that the promises We have made (to save your loved ones for Eternity) are a gift to all who pray and serve until I return, **no matter what your past life has been like!** The Father's Mercy is beyond your understanding, so please do NOT impose your own criteria on Him in regard to your family or yourselves. Be assured that MERCY IS FOR EVERYONE WHO WILL ACCEPT IT. This great gift has been won for you by My Passion and Death and Rising again. All of the gifts and graces you need are here for you. Come to Me. Come back to My Father. Come by the help of Our Spirit and His holy spouse, Our beloved Mother. Spread word of My Goodness, My precious friends. Spread the light of My love which burns in your hearts. Love each other with My love and be there to greet Me upon My Return. This will be the answer to every struggle, every dilemma, every attack by the Evil One and his followers.

YOU WILL CRY AND SING AND CHEER, MY DEAR ONES, AT THE GLORIOUS SIGHT OF ME! BE FILLED WITH EAGERNESS FOR THIS DAY. PRAY IN ANTICIPATION OF THIS DAY. WAIT FOR ME, MY PEOPLE. I, your Jesus, Second Person of the Trinity, Son of the Living God, call out to you: obey each directive that will be sent to protect you and bring you ultimately into the New Era where you will live in love and purity to help build My Church anew. Persevere, My very much-loved ones. I LOVE YOU!"

3/14, "My child, I am your Jesus. Let us begin: 'My dear ones of the Sacred and Immaculate Hearts, be convinced in your minds and hearts now, once and forever, of the truth of the words I now give to you. You must care not about the attitudes of the world, especially those closest to you, who have a greater ability to fill you with pain and sorrow, hurt and humiliation. **Ask every day for new ability to suffer ridicule and rejection.** The God of all sees into the hearts of all. Let Him find abandonment to His Will and mercy for others in yours! Let Him see your sincere motives to please Him; to give praise and honor, love and thanksgiving for all He allows to occur from now on, for all of His gifts, for holy companions, for the love that grows and the desire to obey that blossom in your hearts. Let Him see these promises lived out in the service that will be required to all who come to you for help. These most important aspects (of the rest of your time here on Earth) will bring you the salvation desired first and foremost by your Creator and Lord. You will be able to let go of the world completely now, if even only in your heart. But this is where your surrender must happen. **This heart of yours must be swept clean now, emptied of people and the props you use to identify how 'well' you are doing, how much you love Me and your extended family members. Seek no equality with anyone**. Be emptied now and accept the life of a slave, no, a friend, for I call you all friends who keep My Father's Commandments.

FOR MERCY'S SAKE!

Become mercy, become obedience. Become the patient, loving instrument you find in Me! Do not limit My gifts by your obstinacies and disbelief. Become victims of Love, along with Me, for the salvation of the world. This understanding and action on your part has NEVER been more important. TRUST in Me **and persevere through all the trials that now increase in your lives**. These are the jewels in your heavenly crowns, the coins with which you purchase salvation for all of your families and loved ones. Tell the world to get behind you! Leave behind all who are not of Me. Continue to carry them on the cross of isolation from all the allurements of Satan in preparation of yourselves, and death to sin in your hearts and the whole world. **Give up doubt and critical attitudes, rejection of Our words and all the plans of My Father for your own salvation. Give up. Give in to the Father's agenda for your life, His gifts and graces, His choices for your time spent in greater union with Me and our loving Mother.** Reread these words, My special, faithful ones. I am your Jesus Who knows you intimately, every hidden desire, every area of resistance to Our requests. When you are standing in the Light of Christ, there is no place to hide, no dark corner in which to make devious plans. This Light which now envelops you will never be overcome by the darkness of Satan. Remain in the light, children of My longing, while time and light remain! Stay forever in My Heart. Continue to become one with Me."

3/25, Jesus said: "Dear little one, welcome into My Presence. The pure of heart WILL see God, and will be brought into the Kingdom immediately. Warn My dear ones that many will need to receive My Sacrament of Reconciliation in order to be healed again of all that continues to hold them bound. This, along with prayer for Mercy on the world, is the only important consideration for you at this time. **Also, there must be more visits to Me in front of My Blessed Sacrament if you wish to continue to serve all the poor and needy who will begin to appear on the scene.** I am your Jesus, Who joins with you to honor My Mother on this special feast. I love you with all of Who I Am."

3/26, Jesus said: "Loss of property is always a result of war-like aggression; and believe Me, My dearest children, YOU ARE ALREADY AT WAR! The Holy Spirit will always help those who have spent all of themselves in order to feed the hungry, clothe the naked, and give a drink to all who are thirsting for the Living God. My people, you are loved mightily by your God. You are appreciated by all of Heaven. Remember that prayer is NOT enough. **You must change and pour yourself out to heal the wounds of your brothers and sisters. This will be your way of life until My Return**. This response to the needy ones (who are sent by Our Spirit) will bring you quickly to perfection will heal all selfishness and critical tendencies embraced by so many who think they are serving to the best of their ability. I tell you, the widow's mite is your example, your reminder of the need to give (from your own want), all of who you are freely, generously, lovingly. You will no longer be lonely or bored, I ASSURE you!

Grab the brass ring attached to more gifts from My Father. **Fish in the bottomless pool of His grace and mercy.** Be assured that you, too, will become fishers of men, once you have let go of your 'perceived' ownership and control over the possessions My Father has granted to you. Admit to yourselves, once again, that all is a gift of God that you have been given in order to share and distribute among the poor. The lost ones of the world are many. Will you stand in the way of their salvation, too? Will you hoard these gifts, thinking to keep them for yourselves? I tell you, **they will be taken away from you, if you do not share with EVERYONE you meet, and multiply them as you feed the five thousand, and more! Learn the joy of sharing.** Discover your hearts filling with the happiness of reciprocal love and appreciation. LET GO OF YOURSELVES AND ALL YOU 'OWN' before all is removed by the brutality of the Anti-Christ and his followers. Empty yourselves now, children, in charity to the needy, or suffer the consequences of a failure to respond to the requests of Heaven. **You will wish you had answered the call of My Mother when you see the condition of your souls, when you see the greed and power of the Anti-Christ conquer nearly the entire world**!

Tomorrow and today, choose to belong to the victorious Army led by Our beloved Mother. You were created for this great mission. Please say 'yes' to the call of your God to become the best possible Warrior in the fight against evil. Come now and sit before Me, begging the ability to give away all you have received. These will quickly be replaced by greater gifts from My Father. I am waiting, dear ones. Please hurry!"

3/29, "Dear child of My Heart, I am Jesus, Who loves you dearly. **Learn to meditate upon what's important in your life, so that you can let go of what is not!** The only way to be ready for all that is about to occur, My beloved faithful one, is to be EMPTIED OF ALL THAT IS OF THE WORLD, AND FILLED WITH MYSELF AND OUR DEAR MOTHER, ALL THAT IS OF THE KINGDOM. Dear, dear people of My Heart, **I wish to save you from the *residue of the past, a way of seeing and thinking and behaving that was far from My Father's Will for you*.** Be assured that each struggle and sorrow that comes your way is meant to prepare you for your ultimate place at My side forever in Eternity. You are so dearly loved, My faithful ones. Be assured of victory. Be assured of Our continued love and protection, be assured of a special place in Heaven with all who remain faithful. Be healed once more of all the effects of the world and previous behavior. Be sure of My Presence with you at all times and the absolute truth of all you receive through My special messengers. Be filled with the healing power of My Love. I am your Jesus, Who comes by the grace of My Father, as a special gift of direction and support for all of you who struggle to remain faithful. Be filled with Me in the unity of prayer and obedience, of suffering and love. Be blessed, My dear, loved ones."

4/3, Jesus said: "Daughter, please write. As I lay in the tomb these many hours, daughter, I contemplated the works of all those who would serve Me in the future. These days were very present to Me, and I saw all those who are serving now in the different capacities of messenger, healer, evangelizer and teacher. Please continue to pray (with all who are in Heaven) that the Father will begin to act in a greater way to bring about the Illumination of the minds of all Our people in the world to the state of their souls. I will be pouring Myself out in union with you requesting His Mercy to hasten the day of My Return. Do not sit in fear and trepidation. Be full of JOY as you again receive My Sacrament of Reconciliation.

Be filled with the excitement of one who waits for the One Who will come back to dry every tear, to comfort those who hunger and thirst and mourn, who wait with great longing the arrival of their Dearest Friend and Savior. Welcome to the Day of My Resurrection, when I defeated the power of death, when I overcame the darkness of the tomb and rose into the light of promise, of fulfillment, of the accomplishment of your salvation! Spend this time of My Feast in praise and thanksgiving to My Father for His Mercy and generosity to all the people who would ever live on the Earth. **The Mercy of My Father is the ONLY answer to the amount of evil present in the world.**

Only YOU can decide your future, My people. Only YOU can accept or reject all the new gifts and freedom We wish to give you. The entire world is in peril from the attacks of terrorists and those of the One World Order who would conquer all people. The future is more and more yours to choose, to protect, to surrender yourself in service for. Do not ever be discouraged for a minute. Remember everything IS possible for God, Who desires only peace, and His great love for you. Remain My Faithful Remnant who are led every step of the way. Be filled with Peace, once again, people of My longing."

4/4, "Daughter, please write. I am Mary, the Mother of the Savior, Jesus Christ. I come to you tonight with news for the world. Please pray again to my Spouse for His gift of openness, and I will accompany you. I am pleased also, child, at the gift of speaking to you at this time. The words I give now, daughter, are sent from the Father. Please believe them with all of your heart. Let us begin:

'As you look back in history, My dear ones of the world, and as you reflect on your own lives, you see how God has sent His messengers and prophets to warn His people of impending disasters and chastisements. All throughout the history of mankind, there were VERY FEW who listened. We in Heaven, **Who see all time as one,** have sent every word of warning. Assurances of Our love, and promise of protection are sent in order to prepare you of the Earth once again for the Father's mighty action **to cleanse the world and return it to a state of beauty and peace, purity and obedience to His Laws**. The response this time has been NO BETTER than ever in the past; and so the **Father has determined to act swiftly now to allow the plans for war, present in the hearts of many in the world, to escalate to a full-world involvement. I am telling you this in order to alert you to the very great danger hovering over the Earth.** Weapons of a new and more destructive nature are already in the hands of major powers who wait for the right moment to unleash them on unsuspecting nations and even on each other!' Daughter, please pray at this point with me, once again. Thank you, daughter. We continue: 'The great petition in My Immaculate and very Sorrowful Heart is that all who read and believe in these words to you will not be cast into despair, and cease your prayerful assault on Heaven for Mercy on the world. The events of the coming weeks and months and years demand the greatest fidelity to prayer and TRUST in Our promise to protect you. We wish to join all of you in begging the Father for a period of time in which events move swiftly to **the completion of the Age and return of Jesus, the Beloved Son.** Once again, My dearest ones of the Earth, reach out with all of your strength to the Father and Creator of all, for Mercy on the MANY who will be entering Eternity from now on. The Father will allow the annihilation of so many at this time (this includes the rather long period of time contained in the "Day of the Lord ... cta.) in order to fulfill Scripture and renew the Earth and its people. Do not be frightened for yourselves, My dearest children, and do not EVER despair. <u>You will be made so much stronger, as you survive each event, each playing out of the evil plans</u> of those who listen to the destructive suggestions of Satan and use his power to accomplish his plan of destruction of the Earth**. The ones who plot to take over the world do not realize Satan's plans to destroy his Earthly FOLLOWERS, as well, once his objectives are met.**

Even though it may appear to you that your prayers have failed or not been heard, this is NOT so, beloved ones. Your prayers and praise and adoration are needed more than ever, now that initial steps have been taken in the plans of the Antichrist and his followers. I know, my darling faithful ones, how difficult it is to receive these words. We only attempt to prepare you for the fact that these terrible plans of the evil one are about to begin on a level of destruction NEVER seen by any human before! PLEASE, MY CHILDREN, DO NOT BE FRIGHTENED. Do not reject these words, thinking, 'Heaven would not send such words of warning.' Do not be anxious about this messenger or the others that bring news of terrible war on your horizon. Your future will be filled with great turmoil and upheaval. **The only way to survive these last days is to depend totally on your Triune God, your dear, loving Mother who loves you with her tender heart, and all the Angels with Michael, the Warrior, and all the Saints who pray for all of you constantly**.

Each prayer for Mercy for the world will result in the Father acting sooner now to rid the Earth of all evil, all sin, all the residue of sinful aggression and hatred. You do not wish to live for long under the oppression planned for the people of the Earth by the puppets of Satan. You do not wish to wait for another MOMENT to pass by without the increased action of our Triune God to allow the Angels of these End Times to begin to pour out each plague and difficult circumstance that will fill your days until Jesus returns. Because no one is praying enough, because not enough of Our people are listening, it is necessary to MOVE UP these plans of Our Father, so that time will again be shortened, as will the reign of the Anti-Christ then be shortened. You are weary of waiting now, my loved ones. <u>Think of being granted the reprieve of months and years of living under the DREADFUL conditions planned by this son of Satan.</u>

Because you have not known war in this country, because the world does not know this degree of evil, many will be HORRIFIED at the perversity and treachery about to occur. Many will think that all is lost, and that is when you must encourage each other to persevere, to hang on just a little bit longer before the victorious return of Jesus to drive Satan and all who follow him into Hell. Do NOT pass quickly over these words, dearest ones. Read them and allow them to become the impetus for greater obedience to the call for increased prayer and service. You have nothing to fear, or things to plan, since Heaven will be with you, sharing its strength and the power of Jesus. There is NO REASON TO PANIC, children. LISTEN to your Mother who bids you, ***Be at peace***! Listen to My Spouse speak to your hearts, and fill you with renewed vigor now and a renewed trust in Our protection. THE WARNING OF THE FATHER WILL BE EXPERIENCED AT ANY MOMENT BY THE GREAT MERCY AND LOVE OF GOD. (Remember, *any moment* simply means sooner than soon and is nothing like our time!.. cta.)

You have built up a great edifice for yourselves through obedient response to My call. Do not allow this to be destroyed. The evil one is a cunning and subtle destroyer, who wishes nothing good for anyone. Do not be surprised from now on at ANYTHING that happens. Just remember that it is ultimately for the good of all, even though you cannot see it (at the time). There will be more words in the coming days to warn you of evil plans about to occur. Just TRUST, and follow the directions you receive. Praise and thank your Father, dear ones, for His tender mercy and care for you. Thank you for listening to all these words. Kindly pray for weary messengers, who spend long hours each day in this service to all who read and believe. Children of the world, I love you! Be on guard, dear little soldiers of My special army of faithful ones, the Remnant of My Heart!"

4/14, "Dear loved one, I, your Jesus of Love and Mercy, speak with joy to your heart. 'BELOVED ONES OF MY FAITHFUL REMNANT, HEAR MY WORDS: A good soldier continues the discipline and behavior necessary to maintain a high level of fitness and the ability to enter combat at any moment. Since the Enemy (Satan) is relentless in his attacks on each of you, it is obvious that you are already in a continuous battle mode. Your state of preparedness is accompanied by the prayers and loving support of your loved ones in Heaven and all the Angels and Saints. Be convinced that the **reign of the Antichrist has been shortened by your prayers and pleadings**. More mitigation and mercy will always be possible, and that is why you must remain faithful and prayerful and trusting, no matter WHAT you see and experience. No matter what, you MUST endure! Be assured of the Victory of My Father over evil and sin. Remind each other of the promises you have been given. Continue to expect protection and grace throughout the entire time before My Return.

I am your Jesus of Mercy, and I tell you, you will see in Heaven each result of your efforts, as you now begin another year of mercy with cleansed hearts and souls, free of the residue of past sins. Begin this very minute as a NEW creation, washed clean and ready to fight the ongoing battle against the evil one who lies in wait, plotting your fall, your destruction, as well as that of the entire world. He is more than ever filled with hatred towards those who remain faithful, wrapped in the Mantle of Mary, our Mother, and the Mercy of God! You will win every battle, My people, when you remain clothed in this heavenly armor and protection. Persevere and remain faithful to your family of the world, who suffer cold and hunger, disease and displacement from the growing aggression of Satan and his followers. **The many who will continue to enter Eternity will immediately begin praying for the conversion of their loved ones and for all of you who are praying now for all of them! THIS IS THE LAW OF RECIPROCAL GRACE, My dear ones."**

4/19, "I, your Jesus of Mercy and Love, tell you the people of the world are slumbering from frantic running here and there to satisfy their perceived need for entertainment! Please pray for those about to be shocked in the near future by the illumination of their minds to the state of their soul, (***Yes, and here we are in 2006 still waiting. No wonder so much patience and mercy is needed!***) as the Triune God sees them: clearly, honestly and without the interference of human foibles and reprehensible self indulgence! Yes, daughter, there will be immense shock for many, and all of Our faithful ones can cushion this event with your prayers for them. It is true that some will even be taken into Eternity through this experience. This will be an act of mercy by My Father for those who would not fare well under the coming events. YOU HAVE A GOD OF MERCY, MY PEOPLE, Who has given you every opportunity to see, to hear, and to believe. What good would it do to send you into Hell when I only wish to SAVE My people and bring everyone into Heaven? Remember how much I wish to save you FROM YOURSELVES in My great love for you. Remember that I died for you, that I suffer now all of your rejection and ridicule of My words. Remember to thank My Father for all of His gifts, and He will give you more! **Remember that Mercy continues to forgive, long after forgiveness makes any sense!** Remember that I only wish to heal and forgive you, and bring you into My Kingdom forever.

Please do not be afraid. Oh yes, you will see frightening things! You will continue to be tempted and deluded and distracted by the evil one, but <u>I WILL FORGIVE YOU EVERYTHING YOU BRING TO ME IN REMORSE AND REPENTENCE. This is so important for you to believe, to live by and to hope for.</u> If all of you were deceptive parents, it would be easy to understand your doubts and fear of Me. But so many of you had loving parents, and bring that same love and concern to your children. People, **I weep tonight over the earth, as I did over Jerusalem**. I weep for those who will not listen, and choose to remain in a life of sin. I especially weep for those who destroy life, the most precious gift of My Father. I weep for those who allow pride and personal criteria to get in the way of the Light that would, first of all, heal their blindness. I weep for the little ones who are abused and left to wander in fear and confusion. And I weep for you, My people, who refuse to see, refuse to hear, refuse to accept My love and mercy, who must now experience My Father's justice. I tell you again, I AM A GOD WHO SAVES, WHO CALLS HIS PEOPLE TO PEACE, TO PURITY OF HEART AND MIND. BE ONE WITH ME, DEAREST OF MY HEART. Receive Me again this very moment into your hearts and lives. Give up everything that does not honor My Father and build His Kingdom. Give up distractions of every kinds. Give up your fear of Me and every doubt about My words to you. Live in peace and the tranquility that comes from trust in all of Our promises to you. Put Me first in your lives, and all else will be accomplished according to the Will of My Father for the good and salvation of your souls! You are loved mightily by your Lord and God. Please accept this Love and be saved."

4/22, "Dear children, your Jesus is here with you. Offer to Me all of who you are, and I will bless and cleanse you. The focus on My Face, the visits before Me, the lifting up of your hearts is the way to maintain the strength to persevere in this prayer mode without giving in to fatigue, or worse yet, anxiety. **Those who believe in My Mercy will have every opportunity to be saved by it! Each of you must ACCEPT it,** however, and live according to My Father's desires and demands.

YOUR BEHAVIOR CANNOT REFLECT THE WORLD AND ME AT THE SAME TIME!

The prayers of My Mother pull at your heart constantly, as she constantly pulls at you to come closer to Me, to Our Two Hearts. Hidden in Our Hearts, you are safe from the Evil One, safe from the demands of your own ego, your own 'self' which clamors for gratification."

4/30, "Daughter, I am Jesus Who speaks to you from the Cross. Know that this (in Washington State) will be a place of community in the New Era where the Will of the Father will be lived as perfectly as possible on the Earth. There will be many miracles and conversions here. Many of Our heartbroken ones will find renewal and reconciliation. The Mercy of the Father will flow through the Immaculate Heart of Mary and heal the sick and the broken who come seeking the light and mercy of God. Graces and miracles will be given here. The trumpet is sounding again. Let us rush in where no one has gone before. Let us shine the Light of Christ into the dark corners of hearts gathered in trust and hope."

5/5, Jesus said: "Child, please write. Pray now to Our Spirit, once again, for the grace to receive this message.

*AFTER TOMORROW, YOUR COUNTRY WILL BE THE VICTIM OF A SURPRISE ATTACK AGAIN IN YOUR HISTORY. But this time the results will impact all in this land directly. Be alert and expectant that the promised Angel (who will lead all to safety from nuclear fallout at the proper time .c.a.) will arrive for all who believe in Me. The power of My arm will protect all who follow in obedience to a place of refuge from nuclear fallout. Everywhere there will be great need and great sorrow. Please ask Our faithful ones to keep up constant prayer and attempts at reconciliation. Your souls cannot be too well scrubbed, and you will need every ounce of grace you can attain.

The more time you spend with Me, the more you will become like Me, become Me! Put on your armor daily and march to the sound of My voice and that of My Mother calling you to the battle, to victory over evil in your life and in the world. YOU ARE NEEDED BY YOUR GOD AND BY HIS SUFFERING CHILDREN ALL OVER THE WORLD. Be renewed in joy. Be filled with Me! I am your Jesus Who ministers to your every need and fills you with peace. The Spirit pours out His strength and healing to those who pray and believe."

*Webster's Dictionary tells us: tomorrow means on or during the day after today 2. at some time in the indefinite future!

5/9, "Child, please write. I am Jesus, your Lord and Spouse, Who comes with special words: **The more Satan is listened to and his plans obeyed, the stronger he becomes.** What is all the killing and destruction except a living out of Satan's hate-filled suggestions and lies? We in Heaven weep over the necessity that the Earth must endure such scourging, that Our people must endure so much suffering and privation, such hardship and sorrow.

WE WILL DEFEAT ALL THAT IS AND OF EVIL IN THE WORLD AND I WILL SEND SATAN AND ALL HIS FOLLOWERS INTO THE DEEPEST LEVEL OF HELL TO BE CHAINED THERE. These are words that you must believe and count on to be fulfilled, that you must spend the rest of your time before My coming back to save you from the Antichrist, remaining in faithful endurance, being the weapons of prayer and service to all those We send to you. There is NOTHING to fear, and nothing to give you doubt or worry. Your role has been defined; your path laid out. It is only for you to be obedient and surrender all of who you are to the Father's Will for each one. Be filled now with the anticipation of seeing Me in Heaven or at My *Grand Return!"*

5/13, Jesus said: "Child, you may write. A greater perfection is rèquired of all My people who would be instruments of the Father's Will. **Change is most of all simply a greater uniting of your heart with Mine, your will with the Father's, your behavior with that of Our dear holy Mother.** Every place in the world longs for peace, but the power of Satan is strong now, and overcomes with plans for war and destruction. Be encouraged to be more disciplined in your fasting and penance. You must all become soldiers of strong inner conviction to serve in the manner required by Heaven. That is, at once and forever, **you must give up things that gratify your senses and comfort your 'self'!**

ALLOW ME TO COMFORT YOU WITH MY PRESENCE, MY SWEETNESS, MY BEAUTY. Become a major weapon against doubt and fear. Explain to Our people why they can believe in Our words, so that they can be changed into soldiers who are willing to follow orders and serve Our people until My Return. Be prepared to answer their questions and still the minds filled with confusion.

FOR MERCY'S SAKE!

The world watches as political figures all over the world play games and vie for attention. The irresponsible actions of leaders are due in most part, to goading by well-placed strategists behind the scenes. Pray that people all over the world, who are able to comply, are storing food and water for serious events that will destroy MANY natural resources. My Heart is breaking over the sad state of the hardened hearts everywhere. The walls of pride and arrogance built around the rich and powerful and especially those who are not rich, but powerful in their own opinions, will come crumbling down. But not until My Father's Will and Power is unleashed in their lives. Oh, My dear, sad people, be obedient and humble before My Father and His Commandments. Return to Him TODAY. Do not require the more powerful events and experiences at His disposal to send you, to be used as a last resort to get your attention, topple your defenses, cause you to stop, look, and listen to **the *Father's Voice speaking through tragic events.***

Once the war plans spread to every part of the globe, it will no longer be so easy to return to His loving, waiting arms. You are not living out the intelligence and worldly gifts you have worked so hard to acquire. You have corrupted the talents given you by your Father and Creator. Do not wait to discover this at the time of My Father's Gift of the Merciful Warning to you! Do not allow yourself the shock and grief this sudden discovery may cause. COME NOW, TODAY, TO ME IN MY SACRAMENTS. BRING YOUR OLD LIFE AND YOUR OLD SELF, YOUR TIRED HEART AND MIND, YOUR BURNED-OUT BRAIN AND SPIRIT, AND ALLOW ME TO TAKE THEM FROM YOU AT MY ALTAR! Let us go together to My Father after you have shared your life of sin and waste. Be emptied of all your harmful thoughts and actions, and the people and places that would take you away from Me again. Unburden yourself and be cleansed and renewed by My grace, given by the hand of My Mother who waits to be accepted by you, also. Fill the emptiness of your lives with the sweetness and joy of My gift of peace, and the comfort and tenderness of My Mother. You don't know what you're missing! Taste and see MY Goodness, My beloved people of the Earth. Your choices now have EVERLASTING results. I want them to bring you to Me, to My Father, to Our Spirit, into Our Kingdom of Eternal Joy. It is the Will and desire of your God that you do this and that you allow the Virgin Mother of God, Mary, into your hearts and lives! WELCOME her. WALK with her. LEARN from her. Be at peace in her Immaculate Heart; be protected in her Mantle of Love.

5/16, Jesus said: "All My Mother and I tell you IS of the Father. It is He Who decides when to act on these words, and Who has included many delays in response to the pleas of all who pray. He is so pleased with all His faithful ones who have become stronger now in obedience and love. The Father desires all of Our dear ones to know that He acts in ways that will PROTECT ALL from as much suffering and oppression as possible. More of your loved ones will be converted by the Warning of My Father! Your increased prayers have allowed greater gifts to be released for your dearest relatives and friends! The Goodness of the Father has continued to find ways to shower new graces upon the world, relieve the suffering of many, and shorten again the reign of the Antichrist and his followers!

If all will continue this new level of prayer, you will affect the greatest amount of mitigation and mercy to be given AT THE SAME TIME Satan is allowed to begin conquering the world through the followers of Hell! Be absolutely assured of the need for ALL OF YOU TO REMAIN RESPONSIBLE FOR THE GRACES TO BE ACCEPTED (by others) THAT WILL ALLOW SO MANY MORE TO CHOOSE FOR MY FATHER AND HIS KINGDOM AS THEY ENTER ETERNITY. If this seems to be an increased burden, please **remember that this will be the way you will live out your time until My Return! PRAYER AND SERVICE ARE THE HALLMARK OF MY FOLLOWERS, MY BELOVED ONES. Without this 'Way' you, too, would succumb to the wiles of Satan. Your salvation HAS BEEN WON for you, but your salvation must be ARRIVED AT through hard work and sacrifice on your part. Whatever you must endure will be worth the Glory and Peace and Joy of the Kingdom!"**

5/18, "My lamb, it is I, your Mother, who speaks. Daughter, please be at peace. The world is on the edge of a major turn in this warlike behavior of its leaders. The Antichrist waits for the right moment to allow increased involvement by more countries, and will allow a major conflict to erupt in several places at once. Give praise and thanks to the Father, dear ones at every moment in spite of developments. I am Mary, your Immaculate Queen and Mother."

5/20, Jesus said: "Child of My Eucharistic Heart, please take these words of warning for My people: If I came to your door, and you invited Me to come in, would you not prepare a feast for Me and invite all your neighbors? I have invited all your loved ones in Heaven to join us, all your special Saints and Angels who love you so much and pray for you constantly. What can be more important than coming to Me daily and partaking of My Body and Blood, all of Who I Am? What keeps you from tasting My Goodness, the sweetness of Myself as Eucharist? Is there truly something that overwhelms your ability to spend time with Me, even if you CANNOT leave your home? Is there a love in your hearts, My dear ones, that is greater than your love for Me? There **should not be**, My beloved ones.

There MUST NOT BE another that takes My place in your life and love. I am the One Who gave you EVERYTHING you have. I AM your Creator. Without Me, you would not be alive, or continue to live. I have given you rules by which to live out your journey back to your Triune God, and all the means and graces with which to accomplish this. Your journey is moving toward its end, its goal, for I AM RETURNING TO THE EARTH. Everyone on the Earth will see Me soon, either in Heaven or on the Earth when I come to defeat the Antichrist and his followers; when I defeat Satan and all his demons, and send every one of them to Hell! You may choose Hell, if you wish, My dear ones of the world. You are ALL creatures of the One God Whom you either deny and reject, or accept and choose to follow because you have a free will. If you choose to return to Me now in deed and action, in heart and in love, you will be assured of your salvation. You will know truth and see truth, and have the greatest opportunity to choose to accept truth. I AM TRUTH. ACCEPT ME. COME BACK TO ME. Stop worrying about your own kingdom of self, of comfort, of wealth, of prestige, of power, of gratification. Give me that small kingdom that is yours (allowed by My Father) and We will give you Our Kingdom which is mighty, which is heavenly, that is FOREVER!

THERE IS NO CONTEST, MY DEAR ONES. I WIN!

The power of God is greater than Satan and all his empty promises that are illusions that will vanish in a breath of My Father's Will, like Satan will upon My Return. I AM THE VICTORIOUS ONE, children of My longing. I wish for you to live forever! But you must come to Me NOW. DO NOT AWAIT THE APPROVAL OF ANOTHER! If you have been touched by My Spirit already; if you know, or even suspect the Truth of God and His need of you, your need of Him, come to Me TODAY and surrender to My Heart, My love. Pray for the heart of the *other,* who tries to interfere with your life and your freedom. People *die* for other's freedom, My dearest ones. Won't you LIVE for yours? Receive a baptism into My Body and come totally into My Church, My Sacraments, all of Who I AM. Oh, My dear ones, it is not too late to do this; **but soon it will be so much more difficult, nearly impossible! The graces given now will begin to be diminished shortly, as darkness grows in the world, as Evil is given more power, more of a place in the many lives given to its worship.** I call to you in anguish, My people, for time is gone that sees your world as you have always known it. Satan WILL have his day, and many will be in that number, in his company for eternity. Be the strong one you were CREATED to be. **WITHOUT YOU, not as many will be saved, not as many will have the opportunity to come back to their Father,** Whom so many don't even know, and learn of His Love and unfathomable mercy and forgiveness, and accept Him as their own Lord and Savior, as their Sanctifier.

CAN YOU HEAR ME? **Do not wait to be 'intellectually convinced.' Allow your HEART to be transformed, your LIVES to be transfigured by My Love.** When you allow Me to be your God, that simply means love and peace, forgiveness and mercy. It means every answer to your needs and struggles, all the freedom and truth you have always searched for has at last become part of your life now and throughout Eternity. It means that you are moved along quickly on the *Way*, the *Path,* in the *Light* of becoming all you have received; and sharing them, being a SOURCE of love and mercy and peace and forgiveness for all those We will send to you. It means you will be united with all the members of the Communion of Saints. Oh, My people, I love you with ALL My Heart and Godly Power and Might, and with My Divine Mercy. I wish only to give you ALL of Who I Am, to use that power and might, that Supreme and Infinite Love, to nurture yourselves and your brothers and sisters, who are the world. Reread these words often, My dearest ones. Share them with everyone, especially those whom pride or hurt, bitterness and anger hold bound. Free yourselves first and then free them, if they will choose to accept life without harmful thoughts and feelings, healed of the results of the sins of others and themselves. Reread and realize, dear ones, the seriousness and URGENCY in My Heart, in My Voice, the greatest concern for YOUR heart, YOUR future. I am Jesus, Who pours Myself out this day before the throne of My Father, with Our Spirit of Love, on YOUR behalf! [weeping] There is no more time, daughter. I weep for those who will die without the forgiveness of My Father, without the peace and love that is rightfully theirs, the salvation I suffered and died to procure for every person ever created. Continue here (in adoration) daughter, and plead that many more will heed this tearful, loving plea from My Sacred and Suffering Heart."

5/24, Jesus said: "Child of My love, please write. The world will tremble in many ways. It will shudder at the ferocity of the elements, and as it beholds the ferocity of the evil with which man deals with man, others who are poor and weak, helpless and pawns of power displays between nations. Your own country continues to be aggressive, in the name of honor, to destroy unprotected ones, people who are dependent on the kindness of others. You will see even greater atrocities visited upon the helpless victims of war. The world will gasp in horror at actions of government that are then explained away with empty and callous words. More and more, the decency and honor that once marked your own country will be noticeable to all by its ABSENCE from the attacks of nations united,

A brother carries his sick or wounded brother. A sister ministers in joy and delight to her ailing and sorrowful sister.

Reach OUT, My beloved, faithful ones, with your wealth of money, of goods, of love and time! Give of yourself more now please in honor and joyful service. Pray more for each other and the conversion of family and dear friends. Welcome this new opportunity for sanctity. Run to My Presence in silence and joy."

5/27, Jesus said: "In the world, much is illusion. You have been chosen for reality, MY reality! There will be increasing attacks by hostile young ones, who are filled with bitterness and resentment, for the sake of excitement and revenge. This abuse of elderly by gangs of thugs will escalate; will highlight the lack of respect in the minds and hearts of many of the young today. (This could be reflected in what we are reading about now in 2006 in Florida ...cta.)

MAKE WATER A PRIORITY, MY PEOPLE, and do without some frivolous beverage and even harmful excesses in order to purchase more. Organize your bedding and clothing, My dear ones. Keep only what you will need for VERY COLD WEATHER in the event of the aftermath of a nuclear attack on your country. Pack in boxes to store all you DON'T NEED for living in the type of environment that will be of your everyday life after the Warning and until My Return. You will never be able to transport much, so be generous in your plans to give away either now to the poor or to those who will come in such desolation.

Pray to the Spirit of Truth, of Light, of Action. Let the power of His breath blow you into action, clear your mind, re-prioritize your lives. If you have plenty, but refuse to believe in the need to gather for the needs of all, YOU WILL NOT FARE AS WELL OR RECEIVE THE AMOUNT OF MERCY RESERVED FOR THOSE WHO COME IN TRUE POVERTY AND NEED! Give of your stores, My powerful soldiers, you who have been so gifted by My Father and the legacy of your own family! **Prepare to give back what you have received, and trust that you will lose the surplus anyway!** It is written in My Word and in the Heart of My Father's Will. Find the true meaning of being alive, when you empty yourselves of self and 'ownership.' **See the handwriting of My Love on your hearts!**

LEARN TO HAVE BY HAVING NOT.

LEARN TO RECEIVE BY GIVING.

LEARN THAT MY ALL IS THE *ALL* YOU WILL EVER NEED.

5/30, Jesus said: "Dear child, know that I love you. Evil has the power to intimidate, to frighten, to coerce, to bully, to force Our poor helpless ones into submission.

The only surrender you are to consider is the resignation of your will to all the plans and requests of Heaven. My Father looks out for your best interests, and will decide the time of your service on Earth and the time of your departure to Heaven. This can be agreed to by each of you and cooperated with now, as you wait peacefully and prayerfully for His perfect Will to be accomplished. Only My Father knows what is best for you. What could be more fatherly than a total sharing of His plans to save you either here, or by taking you to Heaven? What more can He do, after all Our words of explanation to increase your understanding, to give you directives that will allow for your safety? Is this not the action of a loving and protective Parent? Yes, My people, it IS! Begin to give more praise to the Father now for all that will be allowed in order to fulfill all of Scripture until the time of My Return. Praise Him for His mercy and forgiveness that have nothing to do with your worthiness, but everything to do with His Love and desire to save as many as will accept Him for all eternity. Praise Him, dear ones, for His loyalty in spite of your infidelity, and the opportunity to return to Him before it is too late, and the Anti-Christ and Satan turn this world into total darkness. Praise Him for the Light of Christ, and accept It into your hearts for all to see in the darkness. Praise Him for choosing you to be alive at the most important time of this particular century in union with My Mother's appearances and words of warning at Fatima. Praise and thank Him for showing you Truth in the Great Warning. Praise and thank, love and adore Him, your Creator and Lord, Who calls you into His Eternal, Loving Embrace." (When we hear words like this, we see Heaven in the words "there is no time in the Kingdom, only an eternal NOW! ..cta.)

6/9, Jesus said: " Begin today a new consecration of all that is, and who and what you will become as, moment by moment, you are created anew to love and serve all those We send to you. There is no peace in the heart of Satan, My people! There is not one peaceful desire in the hearts of those who follow him. There is only hatred and destruction planned by the forces of Hell who would bring this and every country to ruin. There is nothing to do now, but pray and trust the Triune God, My dear faithful ones. You now must begin to live out the time of the **Antichrist who has been created for this moment in history, who has chosen to be the Puppet of Satan, the *man of iniquity*, the one who will personify evil and darkness. In the future, you will be astounded at his brazen claims and displays of power; all of which Satan will effect within him. Let no one sway you with emotions and begging! DO NOT listen to them, as they would not listen to you who tried to bring them to Truth!**

Mary, the Mother of all people on the earth and above the earth, has called out these many years to you. She, who is My Mother and who has suffered every wound, every pain and rejection and humiliation in union with Me, has wept tears of sorrow and anguish over the refusal of so many to accept her words, her warnings, her love, her promises of guidance and grace. Those, who see themselves as possessing an intellect above any known to God or man, have decided what Heaven would say or do, or how We must act in Our dealings with mankind! They have proclaimed Our words to Our messengers as false according to lofty guidelines created by their own ego. How sad and stunned they will be when the Father presents them with absolute Truth and the absolute reality of their own sinfulness and wretched souls. Pray more, My Faithful Remnant, for those whom reality will shock with an unrelenting look at their greatest enemy... themselves!

Oh My dear ones, how I love you and will welcome you back instantly into My Heart and Mercy, My Grace and Forgiveness; even though you have continued to reject all of Our attempts to purify you now; and prepare you for this gift of mercy of the Father's Warning, and ultimately for My return to defeat Satan and all his followers: the worst and most evil on earth who is the Antichrist.

After the Warning, people of the earth, hurry back to your God for reconciliation and forgiveness and peace. No longer listen to the world, but be assured of the opportunity to be forgiven when you bring your sorrow and remorse for the life you have wasted, thus far, building your own kingdoms. Your Creator and Father in Heaven waits eagerly to embrace you and fill you with gifts of grace, and a renewed soul and spirit, life and love.

Spend the last ounce of yourself, until I return, warning Our poor lost ones of the evil intentions of this Antichrist who will appear with false claims and hidden plans to take away as many lives and freedoms as possible. The leaders of your country have made a pact with each other, based on the lies of the evil one, for power and immortality. **Trust no one save those marked with My Cross on their foreheads.** The days race toward the time of total world conflagration. The plans of the Antichrist and his One World proponents are changing the shape and destiny of the earth even now. Remain in My arms, in My Father's Will, in the power of Our Spirit, in the Heart of Our Mother, and never leave Us again. **Never even glance back at the world and** all the ***lies that feed the Satanic illusions*** **created by the king of the world who would destroy your soul the minute you come towards him.**

'Beloved ones, the plans of My Father will overcome the plans of Satan and his One-World puppets. I WILL DEFEAT THEM all upon My Return. This victory IS assured, is already won, for those who remain in the Sacred Encampment of My Mother's holy army of faithful ones. ***Pay no attention to anyone who offers promises of grandeur without MY Cross.*** YOU KNOW ME, MY PRECIOUS LAMBS. I AM YOUR SHEPHERD, AND I CALL ALL OF YOU TO COME INTO THE SHEEPFOLD OF MY HEART, WHERE I WILL CARRY YOU FOR ETERNITY! Repent and believe in Me, people of the earth. The King of Heaven and Earth is about to return in glory to defeat the powers of Hell. You are loved, My people. Come back to Me. Accept this Love!"

6/18, "I am Jesus, Son of God, Son of Mary, and Lord and Savior of the world! Let us begin the message for the world.

'My loved ones of the world, rejoice. A new period of peace, and a renewed and cleansed earth, will be the setting in which you will live out My Father's plan for yourselves after My Return to defeat Satan, the Antichrist, all the demons and the earthly followers. Stop and look and listen to yourselves, My dear ones. What do you hear? What do you see? **Are you scrutinizing your own behavior as thoroughly as you sift the actions of others?** Please allow the Holy Spirit to take care of those who might be working for the evil one by causing confusion among the faithful. PRAY FOR EVERYONE, for your own protection, for the Truth to win out in the battle of good and evil, for the help of Our Spirit, and for proper discernment before every message you read. Listen to the small voice of the Spirit of God leading you in safety and in Love. Thank you, My people, for your strong love and defense against anyone who appears to be leading you down an alternate path"

6/28, At Adoration, Blessed Mother said: "Fires are about to break out in the parched areas that will bring record devastation to this country. The ability of your government to control weather has brought emergency conditions to a new level of experience. **The followers of the Antichrist do not stop their work meant to conquer the world, and make slaves of survivors. They do not allow words of government, of media reports, to lull them into acceptance of a false peace. Satan does not give himself a vacation from his plans to defeat your prayers and prayerful behavior! He works, with his demons, harder than ever to attempt to convince you that your increased prayers are not needed."**

7/9, Jesus said: "Without your obedient response at this present moment, My dear ones, how do you expect to be able to be obedient to a call from Heaven in the future when Our requests will call for a difficult and immediate response on your part? A soldier is NOT prepared who sits back and says**:** ***oh, I'll be there when it's time, when things get really tough, when my life is threatened by unfolding events!*** No, My dearest ones, everything you do in this world requires practice. A method of behavior is not just imagined, does not occur as a result of vague mental plans.

In the heat of battle or any crisis, only a trained and seasoned response, one that occurs as a result of repeated practice, is the one that wins the day! You must be prepared to MOVE IMMEDIATELY WHEN HEAVEN CALLS UPON YOU FOR HELP DURING SERIOUS EVENTS THAT ARE LIFE THREATENING AND DANGEROUS. You are seeing pre-drought conditions developing everywhere that will certainly lead to times of famine and increased hardship even in your own land of plenty.

I am your Jesus of Mercy, Who requests your mercy for your brothers and sisters everywhere. Prepare to serve them in a greater way in the future by serving them NOW with your prayers that will save them for that future and a life without the terrible suffering of radiation burns and disfigurement. I call you all to begin to serve now in a more direct and more committed way, the entire world that is in the greatest danger of annihilation! YOU ARE ALREADY AT WAR, AMERICA. **What will you do who have the weapons at hand to combat Satan's plans to take as many lives as possible in the very near future? Band together in prayer and love, My beloved warriors.** Defend all who will accept your valiant attempts to save them. Those who fought and died once for your freedom are gathered, once again, with all the warrior Angels, who daily battle fiercely the demons, who would destroy your souls. Join these brave ones in prayer and adoration and obedience to the call of Heaven in order to defeat those who have every plan in place to destroy most of the world and its inhabitants. THE VICTORY IS ALREADY WON, MY BRAVE ONES, BUT MUST BE FOUGHT NOW!"

7/12/99, Our Lady said: 'In the coming days, little children, you will begin to see the signs in the sky I have mentioned for so long. These will be mysterious to all, even your scientists. These are meant to focus the attention of the world for the time when words of warning will be delivered to this country and then to the world. The Father will take care of every detail of this most important of all the missions of Our messengers. Nor is this the first time so much was required of Our people whom the Father's Will has saved, has led, has carried. The Israelites wandered forty years in the desert under the harshest conditions before Yahweh's promises were fulfilled with a land flowing with milk and honey. You will not follow Heaven's directions for nearly as long a time or in conditions nearly as harsh; but **you must be willing to accept events given by the Father's hand in His Way and according to His desires for you. This trust, this obedience is cleansing you, my precious children**. It is emptying you of your self-will, your stubbornness, your self-gratification. You are being turned into strong and faithful soldiers who follow their Supreme Commander wherever He would lead them. Believe also that this level of training is necessary if you are to survive and persevere through all the events of the future. **You will be the strong ones on whom all will depend, to whom all will look for help and guidance, in whom all will seek peace, from whom all will expect answers and understanding, by whom all will request healing!** Do you really believe in all of Our words and promises, dearest of My heart? Do you wish to follow the call of your Mother, so that you may lead when others call to you? Do you wish to remain and serve God's people and help them return to their Creator? Do you care about the salvation of the world? Do you desire you own salvation and a life of splendor and sublime happiness for all Eternity? If your answer is *YES*, my lambs, then you are invited **to be prepared to leave your homes at any *moment* and flee from a nuclear attack (still, this is in the Plan!) on this country resulting in never-before-seen and experienced levels of destruction here and in the world.** You know what to do, My children. Act swiftly, all the while giving praise and thanksgiving to the Father for words of warning, designed to save as many people in the world as possible."

7/22, "My dear and faithful people, your Lord and God calls out to you. I am your Jesus, My dear ones, Second Person of the Trinity and Son of God. I send My blessings and new healing upon all of you this night for your continuing trust and endurance. COME TO ME and discover, once again, the peace I Alone can give, the mercy and forgiveness of My Father, and the strength and healing power of Our Spirit. Believe that WE ALWAYS LOVE YOU. Believe in Truth, no matter what you see or hear or experience that is designed to lead you astray. Come before Me again, My children, and sit in silence. Allow Me to teach you, to touch you with My tenderness, to transform you with My love for you. It WILL happen. You must be at peace before you can hear Me speak to your heart. I MUST speak My words of love for you. I MUST have your soul to bring to My Father. I must heal you and cleanse you, together with My Father and Our Spirit, that you may remain close to Us and Our Mother, protected from the dangers of the world that are presented as pleasing and good! DO NOT CONTINUE TO ARGUE, My dear ones. COME TO ME. Give Me TIME with you: time (for you) to be emptied of all the noise and hurry and arguments that fill you to overflowing. I am your Jesus, your God, your King, your Savior. FOLLOW ME, My dear ones! **Go to My Mother, once again, and take her hand. Ask her to bring you to Me, to help you empty yourselves, to sit in silence and absorb all of Who I Am. I will calm the perturbations that assail you to the point of distraction and division. Let nothing divide you, My OWN DEAR ONES! In unity you are strong, and My Body is made stronger and able to withstand every attempt by Satan to divide and conquer your hearts and minds and souls!**

Do NOT rush to judge another, My sweet ones. The Spirit of God is the One Who will heal and restore and rebuild. Pray for each other, dear people of

My Great Love. Call down the Spirit of Truth, the Fire of Love upon the world, especially on those who attempt to serve their God and His people. Send all your remorse and prayers for reconciliation for all, for each other, for sins committed in the heat of exchange, amidst heightened emotions and thoughtless words! **It is so necessary that a united front be presented against every attack of Satan.** Be strong in your understanding of Truth, My dear people. Be humble and gentle in presenting and defending it! Do not leave Me, My Own, lest you perish!"

7/28, In Grand Haven The Lord said, "Dear people of God, who live in this most beautiful region of this country, (Michigan), praise Him for His many gifts to you. Thank Him for bringing you here to live out your days and the Father's Plan of Salvation for His people. Ask Me now for a listening heart, and pray in the days ahead that I will nurture the seeds sewn in your hearts, that these words will burst into full bloom very quickly. Time is truly short, My beloved ones, before the Father allows events of catastrophic proportions to devastate certain areas. By this you will know that the words of warning from Heaven are true. There will be no coincidences found in these specific acts of the Father, which begin a greater time of calling out to you for your attention and response. These words are meant to SAVE YOU FROM DESTRUCTION. THEY ARE WORDS OF LOVE GIVEN BY THE SPIRIT OF LOVE! Do not be fearful and disbelieving. YOU KNOW ME AND LOVE ME! YOU HAVE SEEN MY POWER, and now I ask you to accept the new power, new strength, new joy that I wish to give you. Stay in much prayer and quiet throughout these days. Allow Me to build up your conviction and trust. You will need all of these gifts in the days to come. YOUR GOD NEEDS YOU, DEAR, DEAR PEOPLE. DO NOT BELIEVE YOU HAVE ALL YOU NEED FROM GOD ALREADY! That will never be true, children. **You will always learn and grow into more knowledge and union with the Triune God forever and ever.** Allow your God to lead you NOW, My people. Allow Him to teach you, and bring you to understanding and knowledge and wisdom. This will be so necessary if you are to serve the Father's plan. This is His Will for YOUR salvation. I am the Spirit of the Love of the Father and Jesus. I bid you be at peace and renewed. Believe in these words of Mine with all your heart!"

<u>A new prayer was given by Our Lady on June 10, 1999 in Tulsa Okla.</u>

"We praise you, Father, and beg Your Mercy on a sinful world. Without Your Kindness and Mercy, the world will not survive. Have pity on us, Father, and forgive us we pray. Amen."

8/11, Jesus said: "Child, please take My words of love and encouragement. Our words will always contain the promise of protection and forgiveness and love and mercy to those who come seeking these gifts. Nothing can stand in the way of My Father's Mercy for those who are sincerely repentant. Fear not the words of bullies that threaten and frighten My lambs. "A bruised reed I will not break" (Isaiah 42: 3), My faithful remnant. Come close to Me now and never leave Me again, even for a moment! <u>The danger is too great now to chance</u>

an encounter with the world without My Presence to sustain you. I LOVE YOU, MY BELOVED PEOPLE, AND WISH TO SAVE YOU FROM HARM; but you must come to My arms and remain locked in My embrace, no matter what anyone else thinks or does or says! IT IS YOU I LOVE AND YOU I WISH TO SAVE! Be the one who comes now with your heart in your hands, offering it to Me along with ALL of who you are. Come immediately and confess your sins. Come now and spend the rest of time and beyond as close to Me as you will allow Me to bring you. IT IS SAFETY, I OFFER YOU, MY PEOPLE. IT IS SALVATION I WISH TO GIVE TO YOU. Do not waste another minute arguing and wondering and refuting these words of warning I give you. If you truly care about your place in Eternity, surrender to all We are requesting of you, everything that is required of one who fights in My Mother's Army of faithful ones!

I call to you for not much longer, My people, for soon it will be too late, and devastating tribulations will rock the serenity of this land wherever you are! Please, **prepare for the time of nuclear destruction that is most certainly in your future. (It was obviously not the very near future, but unfortunately is still a present danger, more than ever. .cta.) Prepare and gather the belongings and supplies you will need to sustain you for a short period of time away from your homes, in a place of protection from radiation fallout.** Do you doubt My words, children? Do you doubt this messenger? Can you afford the luxury of avoiding words that warn of the effects of radiation and your own demise? Do you no longer recognize loving words given to save you from terrible suffering, My own loved ones? Does not a loving Father always call out to His children with words designed to save them from harm? Follow Our instructions, people of God. Listen to Our pleas. I am your Jesus of Love and Mercy, and I am begging you once again to open your minds and hearts to believe in the advent of terrible danger lurking around tomorrow's corner! HEAR ME, MY PEOPLE, AND LIVE!"

8/12, Jesus said: **"Be assured of being healed, My loved ones. Do not be afraid now or at any time in the future. Learn to know the Triune God and the great love and peace that awaits you, that is yours for the taking, once you are reconciled to your Creator, your Savior, your Sanctifier.** Thank you for your love for My Mother, for you are also loving Me, as I desire to be loved. If you will only stay close to her at every moment, you will be further purified and readied to come instantly into Heaven or to greet Me when I come again to drive Satan and his followers into Hell and rid the world of evil. Have mercy on yourselves. Have mercy on Me!

"Remain faithful, My dearest ones, as the events in the world continue to spread darkness everywhere. Be the light of My Son that will lead all who come to you back to the loving embrace of Our Father and Creator. Be a sign of the mercy of the One Who is Mercy Itself. Be purified today and become united more deeply with Him Who Is Peace and Purity! Look forward to the fulfillment of every promise given to you by Heaven. Bask in Our love and the favor that falls upon you now. Listen to these words, My children everywhere, and praise and thank the

Father of us all, Who has called you into service to His lost ones of the world, and Who gifts you in new and powerful ways. Love and serve and cherish each other, My faithful companions. Know that you are loved by your Mother and are gifted by Me today with many more Angels of protection to help you to persevere in joy and hope throughout these difficult days that loom on your horizon (that's for everyone who reads and prays and believes). Stay focused on the promises and directives of Heaven, and live in trust until the day we are together in the bliss of the Heavenly Kingdom."

8/17, Jesus said: "Dearest child, please write these words. The days are few, My dear one, before many more devastating events around the world take the lives of many of Our people. Know that EVEN THESE ARE BEING ENHANCED BY THE ABILITY OF GOVERNMENTS TO ALTER OR INCREASE THE DEGREE OF DESTRUCTION OCCURRING! This is difficult to believe, My daughter, and you can only wait to be more convinced as you see the increase in severity of all the weather and natural events from now on. Please tell Our faithful ones to pray more for all those going into Eternity as a result of these destructive events. Daughter, be prepared with your supplies in a more orderly and organized fashion now, please. Obtain more water immediately, and then finish the tasks of organization this week, daughter. **I am Jesus, your Open Door into the Trinity!"**

8/18, "My dearest child, please write. I am your Mother of Sorrows. Carol, **tonight there is another meeting of major powers who are agreeing to the dates, once again, to begin hostilities in several places. The earthquake victims hold the attention of most of the world, while evil men plot the demise of so many more almost immediately."**

8/22, "My child, I your Mother of Sorrows, come with great sadness at the devastation taking so many lives of Our dear ones in many places. Believe, daughter, that it is according to plans of the 'One-Worlders' to cause as much death and destruction as possible. Child, I would speak directly to Our many faithful in the world, so please pray to My Spouse, once again, for His gifts of strength and openness to a long and difficult message. Let us begin.

'To Our precious faithful ones everywhere, I, your Mother of Sorrows, send greetings, blessings and love. Your fidelity warms the chill of the sight of destruction that fills My Heart with horror and grief. When there is such a huge loss of life, as in the present earthquake in Turkey, there is a hush in all of Heaven at the might of events the Father will allow at the hands of evil. **Know that this, and many subsequent acts of violence, is indeed the result of the enhancement of the workings of technology now existing in your world.** We have repeatedly warned all of you of terrible hatred for God, Our Father's creation and creatures; that you would see many people brought and sent into Eternity from now on. Please, My darling children who love My Son and Myself, who listen to Our words: pray for mercy on all these unsuspecting victims of earthquakes whose strength and ability to destroy are part of Satan's plan to destroy God's people and the world. You see the results of such a force. You see how unprepared one is for the suddenness of a mighty quake that even splits open the earth, that simply washes people away and crushes them under tons of concrete. These ARE your family, My people of the world. These are brothers and sisters who need you now to pray for them constantly, to beg for the release of graces that will assist them in their eternal salvation. **They are close to you now, these brothers and sisters, and will hear your prayers and concern for them. They will respond, as graces are poured out on them by the power of your prayerful pleading to the Father. These would be enabled to go to Heaven and begin praying for the conversion of their immediate families!**

The people in this part of your world are, for the most part, not acquainted with the Father, or My Son, or Their Spirit. They have other gods or do not pray or worship at all. **Please accept them as a new responsibility for which you will spend added time on their behalf, asking the Father to pour out His mercy on them.** This work of salvation for so many has just begun! This is just the first group (of these end-time events) that is coming into Eternity and in need of so much conversion, healing and the grace that will allow them to choose for God and His Kingdom. **There will be so many more, as the plans of the Antichrist strengthen, before My Son returns to defeat him and all his followers. You are witnessing a 'first strike' of brutal natural disasters. The 'success' of this attack will give more surety to those who control these events, and move them on to more and greater devastation.** I do NOT wish to frighten you. Once again, I warn you to be on guard, as Satan continues his plan through his puppet leaders of nations and enemies of Our Church. Once again I bring words from the Father, Who weeps at the destruction of His world and innocent people. Of course, you are all at risk before the power of evil. Are not the innocent, unborn of the world at risk? Are not their lives in danger and sacrificed to the gods of pleasure? Does all of this not show you how indifferent are so many today to the great gift of life given by Life Itself? Share My sorrow now, children of My Immaculate Heart, just as you have often shared my joys. Be aware. Wake up to the very real danger everywhere from the attacks of Satan. Have your hearts and souls cleansed by the great Sacrament of Forgiveness when you bring your sins in remorse to the priest, to My Son present there in Reconciliation; after confessing them, receiving the forgiveness of the Father and the graces not to sin seriously again!

COME NOW, My people of the world. Bathe yourselves in the healing waters of this grace and live in the comfort of the Father's arms, knowing your salvation is secure as long as you remain in the state of grace and minister to those we send you! Do not be afraid, children of My love. Do not let anything or anyone keep you from this great Sacrament of Mercy and the salvation My Son, Jesus, died for! Do not deny yourselves, any longer, the great gifts waiting for you, the peace only My Jesus can give, once you are forgiven and unburdened of your sinful lives. **Once confessed and forgiven, My children of the world, your sins no longer exist. They are no more!** Please come now to the foot of the Cross (beautiful image for the Confessional here) and beg forgiveness from the King and Savior of all mankind. He waits for your honest admission of guilt and sincere desire to repent and sin no more. I will help you, if only you ask for it. All of your faithful family of God is already praying for your conversion. Accept the strength and graces being poured out as a result of their love and pleading for your salvation... forever in Eternity in Heaven! No longer listen to Satan, My beloved children. Accept the reality of the One, True God Who reigns in Heaven and calls out now while time remains, ***Come back to Me, My people everywhere. I love you and want to save you from an eternity in Hell and eternal suffering.***

My dearest ones, who pray, I am with you at every moment. Please be aware and be comforted by this fact. Let the Communion of Saints resound with a mighty call for mercy for all of God's people, so that as many, many, many as possible can come to Heaven and begin to pray immediately for their own dear ones still on the earth. They will be overcome with gratitude and joy when they realize the great mercy they have received through the Father's love and all of your prayers for their intention! Be at peace about yourselves, My faithful ones. Be assured of a high and special place in Heaven as part of your heavenly reward. I love you, My precious ones. **Be fierce in your attack on the Father for His mercy!'**

Daughter, thank you for taking this message and getting it out immediately. Your own strength and fidelity are especially aiding those who hear you speak. The Holy Spirit works to open the hearts of many more to bring you into their areas where you can joyfully share Our words of preparation and directive, Our love and promises of protection. Stay focused on the face of My Son. I am your Mother of all people in the world. Along with these words, I send graces of healing and new trust to many this night. Be filled, once again, with Jesus, My Beloved Son."

8/25, "Dear one, please write. I, your Jesus, **WILL BE RETURNING TO EARTH IN A WAY THAT YOU WILL SEE ME, BUT I WILL REMAIN SACRAMENTALLY! THE TRIUMPH OF THE TWO HEARTS WILL OCCUR AFTER THE SECOND PENTECOST when so many everywhere will come back to the Father. There is need for more water for each of you and your families**. There must be extra water for cleansing yourselves and clothing and utensils. There must be a greater focus than ever, from now on, on the requests of Heaven. Yes, many of you will be remaining in your own homes as a refuge for others. Your families will unite under one roof, and those who have not believed you in the past will know of the truth of all you share of the words of Heaven.

If you make no move to show your faith, how can you work out your salvation according to My Father's Will for you? My beloved followers, what will it take to convince you, to move you, to capture your hearts once and for all. Each time one of Our messengers is ridiculed and insulted by someone, that person offers this hurt for the conversion and healing of the one causing the pain, the distress and sadness in that life! You are loved and served mightily by Our warrior servants. Instead of attacking, pray for their strength and endurance. Satan will cause this judgmentalism and criticism to continue until the end of his worldly reign! You are all about to change so much, and will be able to love and serve each other better and more easily. You indeed are in need of this transformation, especially those of you who have all the answers, and think all is well and good because of your keen minds and ability to judge another. Prepare for great surprises, some of My faithful ones, who are in reality faithful to your own agenda and **perception** of your relationship with Me. Continue to beg for mercy on yourselves and the whole world. Every one of you still needs a great deal of purifying of the worldly 'self' and your secret sins and attitudes. Come to Me now in My Sacrament of Reconciliation. Ask Our Spirit to guide you to honesty and trust in the Trinity.

America, you will also see great damage in the future.

Those of you who have made plans to keep up your frivolous and sinful lifestyle until 'the very last minute' before My Father's wrath erupts in your midst, I tell you: THE VERY LAST MINUTE IS HERE! The time of your personal suffering is upon you, with many people in this country removed from the earth. Listen to Me, dear ones. Act upon these words. Make a sacrifice of your own plans, your own desires, and spend all the time remaining in this era in prayer and remorse and repentance. Those of you who laugh at your spouses and parents because of their new gifts of love and service to God and His Mother, beware that **you will suffer intense sorrow and remorse when you see the state of your own soul.** Repent and return now, My little spoiled children. Pray to Our Spirit to open your minds and hearts NOW to accept these words of love and warning given to save your lives eternally! I promise you this, people of the world, you WILL BE SORRY FOR YOUR STUBBORN AND WILLFUL ACTIONS AGAINST YOUR GOD AND YOUR FAMILIES. Know that Our faithful followers will remain faithful ... if only in order to effect your salvation through even greater trials and persecution by the evil one, even to die for My Name in order to win your freedom from sin's oppression. THERE IS NO GREATER LOVE, MY PEOPLE, THAN TO LAY DOWN YOUR LIVES FOR ME AND FOR THE LEAST OF YOUR BRETHREN. Be a well-balanced, powerful source of My Father's mercy to the people in your life and to the One God Who IS Life! Continue to extract yourselves from the world and all its distractions!

You are truly loved, one and all. And so We continue to call to you for prayer for the suffering victims of hate and greed; the lives that count for nothing, but a means to money, less responsibility and more of the opportunities to live in the glare of false excitement and gratification. These are NOT HARSH WORDS, dear ones. They are a REFLECTION OF YOUR REALITY, PEOPLE OF THE WORLD... even many of Our faithful ones! I remind you, once more: your life as soldiers in Heaven's Army cannot reflect both My Father and the world! I am Jesus, Who is *present now* at your *creation*, and again at *your departure* from this world. This world of false glitter will be gone so very soon. Hear these words, My dearest people. They are meant to save you. You must accept them NOW!"

8/30, Jesus said: "Dearest child, please write. I am your Jesus, Who accompanies you at each moment of your life. Your suffering has been only a struggle with self, My precious one. Wait until you must struggle with the cold and discomfort of hiding from the Antichrist(!) This WILL come to pass, child. Cling to Me, daughter. Cling to Truth, to the Way, to My Light. Show these to Our people who are lost and filled with grief and profound remorse. Hold them and caress the wounds of their hearts and souls with the soothing and comforting words of Our love. Constantly reassure them of the ease with which they will be received INTO the mercy of My Father, BY His mercy and THROUGH His mercy. BELIEVE that you will indeed have every grace and gift required to serve and support these dear ones in their journey back to the Trinity, the Holy and Blessed Mother, and an eternity of bliss and joy. Who could refuse this offer, My beloved faithful ones? Know that there WILL BE SOME WHO REFUSE THIS OFFER OF MERCY, and many who will accept it and come back to Me, only to fall away again in fear of the Antichrist and his wicked plans to destroy all those who follow Me!"

9/6, Jesus said: "My return will greatly strengthen all who choose to accept Me. THE NEW ERA OF PEACE AND PURITY WILL EXIST on the Earth for a **LONG period of time**. My Eucharistic Presence will be so strong among and during your lives then, until the last days of that Era and the release of Satan from Hell. But first, **My world will shake from explosions and eventually will fall out of its present orbit. It will go crashing through space from the blows of a mighty comet! As you know, (Isaiah 13:13) I WILL ACT to return the earth to its proper place.** I am so pleased to see your instant acceptance of this truth. All of Heaven is praying for you."

9/8, "Dear child, please write. I am your Mother of Sorrow and Joy. Please continue to pursue your understanding of the ways in which Satan lies and fools Our people, and **attempts to get all of you to worship your own will and opinions!** These are such true understandings, child. I will help you sort out this knowledge that you might put it on paper and use as a teaching for all. The Holy Spirit shines on you and fills you with new insight. Praise and thank the Father for these new gifts. Daughter, be not afraid to stand your ground for what is right and true and just. Do not allow any other event or person or behavior to interfere with your membership in the Communion of Saints. Yes, you do see that life in the next months and years, but especially in the Era of Peace and Purity, will be much like life in Heaven for those who serve their brothers and sisters who come to them according to the Father's Plan for each one." (The need for surrender now is so great because of the difficulty we will have in our humanity, a TOTAL giving [DYING TO OURSELVES] of ourselves and our time and energy when these people come into our homes and live with us, and we need the practice! C.A.)

FOR MERCY'S SAKE!

"Many events will occur very quickly now. Our people need to understand all you have come to know. It is the Father's Will that you share His words to you with His people. Do not hesitate, little soldier, for fear of the attack of words on each teaching and explanation you give from now on. Great clarity is needed in order to combat the confusion and chaos that is rampant in the world now. When you see so many misled and divided by phenomena that lends importance to already exaggerated egos, you understand why We weep so often and even tears of blood. The heart of the world is filled with evil. But the Light of My Son will always shine above and through the darkness of evil deeds and plans. It is the Light that also shines in the hearts of Our faithful remnant, and the Light that the darkness of evil will NOT overcome. (John 1:5)

Daughter, I am nearly overcome by the rejection of so many, since this human heart still resides in my human, though glorified, body! And the love you lead others to bring to Me, is a soothing ointment poured over My breaking heart! There is no joy now that is not tinged with the sadness of seeing Our children reject and deny their God, those who use their free will as a means to choose whatever pleasure delights them most at the moment. The difficult choices you and all Our faithful children are making, are the kinds of penance and self denial that build giants of hope, of trust, of strength and most of all, loving and generous hearts toward the Triune God and Myself! Stay with these decisions, the narrow path you know you are being called to please, child of My Heart. Discover the strength and peace this sort of choice will immediately place within your mind and heart and limbs."

9/9, "Child, be at peace! I, your Jesus, am here. When you let go of everyone, little one of My Heart, you also let go of anxiety and wondering and mind games! *YOU MUST LOVE ME, DAUGHTER, MORE THAN YOU LOVE YOURSELF!* Yes, it is as simple (and difficult) as that. How will you put the enormous needs of all these people first, if you cannot put Me first in your agenda, in your heart? I say again, child, be at peace."

9/17, In Tucson Jesus said: "Child of My Heart, hello! You are loved. THERE IS DEVASTATION ABOUT TO POUNCE ON THE WORLD. AN EVENT OF SERIOUS AND SEVERE MAGNITUDE WILL ROCK THIS COUNTRY EVER SO SOON. Be one with Me in the Father's plan. To all Our dear ones who wait: 'Come one. Come all to the banquet table of your Lord!'"

9/22, At Adoration, Jesus said: "Dearest little warrior, please pray to Our Spirit for openness and healing. Now, child, let us begin. When My people are submerged in self glory, self pity, self abuse or self absorption, there is no room for another. Least of all, is there room for My Spirit even to enter into this closed fortress of SELF. Picture a castle, surrounded by a moat filled with savage crocodiles, waiting to tear apart anyone who would dare to attempt to cross this barrier. Picture cold and forbidding walls with few tiny openings for light or air. 'See' the inside of this edifice: cold and dark and evil smelling. This is what so many of Our people in the world are like today. Nothing can penetrate these defenses. Nothing about this fortified city welcomes a traveler or visitor. Nothing of warmth or welcome graces its facade or invites one to come in.

The Triune God waits outside the battlements of many such cities, knocking, begging, calling out to be allowed entrance. Only silence greets Our plea. Only indifference meets the needs of anyone passing by, especially the need of God, Himself for a response, an invitation, a welcome, a gesture of hospitality, an offer of rest and refreshment, a shelter from the storm outside! The interior darkness of this edifice is such that it seeps through every crack and crevice, every porous area of stone upon stone. Not long is the time anyone can spend in the presence of such negative rejection! Not long is the ability of darkness to encourage life to remain, to be maintained, nourished, protected. And so, One moves on to other castles, other mansions, other houses, other shelters. As a building becomes more simple in design, more doors are already open behind welcome mats adorned with flowers in cheery colors. There are many windows in these smaller and simpler designs allowing abundant light to enter, often open to the warmth of a soothing breeze. Gentle music, even singing, is heard wafting above the sounds of daily industry and reflecting the joy within. One is instantly drawn to this temple of peace, and encouraged to seek comfort and nourishment by its cheery countenance. These are My Remnant who are filled with the peace and joy of My Presence; the knowledge of My Love and Friendship; the trust in My promises, My help and consolation; the acceptance of My burden and yoke, who carry My Cross and theirs. The Triune God, Our holy Mother and yours, Our people in great need of Life and the essentials of life, hurry to these cottages of caring concern, those lit by the spark of Life that shines from deep within and the individual offers of refuge and safety. These houses are built of sturdy materials that have withstood the test of time. All are care worn, but burnished and polished by storm and heat, violent acts of Nature, predators and every challenge imaginable, threats of fire and floods and wind and the devastating effects of age. Ailing areas have been rebuilt: torn down, replaced with stronger stuff, renewed with many and varying coats of protective finish. One feels at home here, and filled with the knowledge of a ready niche already carved out and waiting for each visitor, no matter how poor or how lofty. It is possible, as each of Our dear ones knows, to be simple and unobtrusive, yet mighty; humble in appearance, yet strong in construction; able to sway with the changes of time and season, yet built on a firm foundation. **What sort of structure are you, My beloved people?** I am your Jesus of Love and Mercy. I am a Master Builder Who wishes to come into your house to rebuild and shore up, replace or renew, rearrange and realign, refurbish and restructure. I cannot enter a highly fortified and well-defended castle! I INVITE YOU TO CONSIDER A MAJOR MOVE AT THIS TIME. THERE ARE MANY SIMPLE COTTAGES WAITING TO BE OCCUPIED. THEY ARE FILLED WITH GRACE AND CHARM, AND AN ENCHANTING CHARACTER ABOUNDS THROUGHOUT. If you will allow Me, I will arrange for a trial visit at no expense to you! There are so many benefits to this new lifestyle and transformed neighborhood! I can be found at any time on any day! I await your interest and encourage your call!"

FOR MERCY'S SAKE!

10/2, At Adoration, "My child, I am your Jesus. I desire to speak to My people. Please pray again to Our Spirit for strength and openness to these words. Let us begin. 'Today, My children of the world, you have celebrated the Feast of Guardian Angels, given to you by the loving mercy of My Father. He knew how much help you would need in this life on your journey back to Him. He knew of the many dangers in the world and the strength and cunning of Satan. He knew you would need an Angel to guard you and bring you through many dangerous times and struggles. The love of My Father for His children is a love that is all-powerful and never ending. The love of all of us in Heaven is a constant flowering that helps to sweeten your lives and beautify whatever path you choose. Today's society is greatly in need of protection, greatly in need of guidance and companionship. The mode of living at present is one that isolates Our people and makes them feel lonely and unloved! The repeated rejections and humiliations leave so many of you without hope, or even an understanding and knowledge of Your God. You have closed yourself off from sharing your warmth with anyone, leaving yourselves further isolated and seemingly abandoned. You are NEVER ALONE, My people. I tell you this over and over, yet you continue to live with your gaze focused upon yourselves first and most strongly. You resist anyone who reaches out in friendship or (most of all) in need. You have turned away from the Triune God, and are bitter and unloving. You have no mercy or compassion in your hearts, beloved ones. Yet, I tell you, you always have your own Angels with you, ready to help you at every moment. You are always loved by Our Father in Heaven. You are in My Presence and My Mother's as much as you desire to be. Choose to accept, My dearest people, the gifts being offered that will allow you to come even closer to Us, to live in greater peace and unity. They will give the intended meaning and value to your lives, bring you safely through every event of the future according to the Father's Will for you!

The reason you were created, My people, is that you might receive all the love of the Triune God more and more each day as you live the Commandments, the Beatitudes, all the directives and directions you would receive from Our Spirit. How can you not understand the need to rid the world of evil? Why do you turn away from Me as Present in My Blessed Sacrament, from the opportunity to receive All of Who I Am daily in My Eucharist? Why do you continue to live a life of sin when you know and feel the results of sinful behavior, knowing your God sees every deed, hears every word, knows even your deepest thoughts and longings? The God Who created the Universe and every creature in it, is calling out to you to surrender to His love, His desire to heal you and bring you into His arms forever. You must first spend some time daily in silence in order to hear My voice!

I am returning to the Earth in a way more powerful than you have ever known or imagined. You will experience My Presence and Power and Love in deeper and stronger ways than ever, since I first walked the earth. I will live in your hearts and reign in the world as your Eucharistic Lord! All evil will have been removed from the world. Satan and his followers will be

chained in the deepest levels of Hell, and you will live in a renewed world with My people, ***renewed and changed totally into Eucharistic people. You will converse with your God in a most beautified environment on the earth, if you are meant to do so in the Will of the Father. You will have no trouble living in peace and purity and friendship and love, all centered around My Eucharistic Presence.*** **I have invited you for so very long to spend some of each day with Me, before Me, absorbing My sweetness and love for you, being filled with My strength and My obedience to the Father. IF YOU DO NOT ANSWER THIS REQUEST, MY DEAREST ONES, YOU WILL NEVER BE ABLE TO LIVE IN THE NEW ERA ON THE EARTH WHEN ALL OF THESE CONDITIONS WILL EXIST. YOU CANNOT BE OVERNIGHT ONE WHO HAS BECOME FAMILIAR WITH SILENCE AND LISTENING FOR MY VOICE! You must learn to desire My Presence, love to be with Me, long to be healed as you sit before Me and pour out your hearts and needs and love for the Trinity. When you do this, a friendship, a bond, a knowledge based on complete conviction in My words develops in your heart. In no other way will this intimate relationship be given to you, nurtured, deepened, become the center of your existence, and result in your own healing and perseverance through all My Father desires for you. You will be TOTALLY TRANSFORMED, PUT ON CHRIST, AND BECOME WHATEVER THE FATHER NEEDS YOU TO BE. THERE IS NOTHING TO BE AFRAID OF, MY BELOVED PEOPLE.**

Since the beginning of your life on earth, you have lived in the protection of your Angels, and now even more (Angels) have been given to each one of Our faithful remnant. The plan of My Father is based on His deep desire to SAVE AS MANY PEOPLE AS POSSIBLE. There is ALWAYS ANOTHER CHANCE when you return to My Body and confess your sins; accept the Commandments of My Father as the pattern for your life; become as a little child; allow the Father of all to take care of you, and surrender to His Will for your life. YOU MUST DO THESE THINGS NOW, BELOVED OF MY HEART. DO NOT THINK IT IS ENOUGH *to say prayers and fast and do penance, go to daily Mass and Eucharist, IF YOU ARE STILL LIVING IN THE WORLD IN ANY WAY!* ***For many of you, major changes have been necessary, I know, resulting in new tensions, new distancing, even total removal of friends and family or spouses from your lives. Fear of these developments keeps many of you from taking the final step of conversion. Return NOW, all you who hear and remain paralyzed by fear. Trust Me to heal relationships or to bring you into a better life of grace and rebirth here on the earth, or in Heaven where you will be totally united to Love Itself forever."***

10/9, Jesus said: "My daughter, I invite you to write, without distraction, words for Our people. Serious words are being shared at this time (see Marytalk for messages from 'Timothy in Africa') that speak of an earthquake which threatens the western coast of this country. Pray now to Our Spirit, please, My dear child, for openness and truth. NO, DAUGHTER, THIS INFORMATION IS

NOT TRUE. THE EVIL ONE HAS SET UP THIS CHILD OF OURS TO BELIEVE ALL THE MESSAGES HE RECEIVES; BUT THIS ONE IS FALSE. PLEASE, MY PEOPLE, DO NOT PANIC. DO NOT BELIEVE IN THESE WORDS THAT GIVE YOU ONLY DAYS TO PREPARE, ONLY A SMALL WHILE TO EVACUATE, ONLY A FEW DAYS IN WHICH TO OFFER YOUR PRAYERS FOR MITIGATION.

CONTINUE TO PRAY FOR MITIGATION OF *CERTAIN DESTRUCTION* FOR THE STATE OF CALIFORNIA. **Know that enough prayers have been said to cause the Father to have** ALREADY LESSENED THE DEGREE OF DESTRUCTION PLANNED FOR THE ENTIRE LENGTH OF THIS STATE! You must continue to beg for more to be given by way of lessening of destruction. Pray for the mitigation of all that is planned, yes, at the HANDS OF THE ONE WORLD ORDER, WHO ARE ABLE TO START EARTHQUAKES AT ANY TIME NOW AND ESCALATE THE NUMBER OF MINUTES ONE IS EXPERIENCED, AND THE DAMAGE THAT IS CAUSED. **I tell you this, My people, so you will increase your prayers for protection from the total devastation desired by the Antichrist.**

Different areas of this state, as you know, are centers for pornography and the filming of ever deepening levels of lewd conduct, blasphemous talk and vulgar words, an increasingly casual acceptance of illicit sex and every type of lifestyle that challenges the natural and moral law. You know that these industries are centers of evil meant to produce films that offer every sort of evil conduct under the guise of the accepted "conduct of the '90s", including witchcraft and satanic worship. When evil is glorified and made to seem acceptable entertainment, the Father must allow the plans of other evil ones (one world people) to interfere through devastating events to cause the destruction of these 'Capital Cities of Evil'. This must be allowed to occur as part of the Father's plan to rid the world of all evil, and replace it with peace and beauty and love of God and neighbor. All licentiousness will be removed from the earth and the hearts and lives of Our people who remain (on the earth) into the New Era after My return.

A Eucharistic Reign cannot co-exist with evil. Peace and purity cannot conquer hearts and minds and desires filled with the attitudes that now prevail, the chaos and filth of those who espouse evil. The beauty planned by My Father for all of you will capture your eyes and minds and hearts, and fill them with love and happiness and appreciation for all of His gifts. When you see large-scale destruction, it will be terrifying (momentarily) until you quickly remember the evil that is a way of life in many places in your country. The innocent ones who are taken into eternity will come quickly to Heaven to pray for their loved ones who remain, and an end to the level of evil that exists elsewhere in the world. My people, you are fooling yourselves when you deny this evil, or that the lifestyles glorified in present day movies and pornographic films **are *not that bad*!** Believe the words of Heaven, My dear ones. Believe Me when I tell you this is a large part of Satan's tools and weapons with which he plans to bring as many as possible (especially the youth) into Hell forever and ever and ever!

Innocence and decency have nearly disappeared from the film industry, people of My Sacred Heart. Can you continue to watch stories filled with suggestive talk and immoral behavior, that is presented as attractive and desirable, and then come before Me in My Blessed Sacrament and adore? Of course not! You have already chosen your gods of lust and gratification. YOU DON'T WANT ME, MY PEOPLE. You prove that with every action that shouts louder than any words or beliefs you claim to uphold. THE TIME FOR TOTAL HONESTY IS NOW, MY DEAR, DEAR LITTLE ONES, AND MUST BE USED AS A BASIS FOR EVERY DECISION, EVERY CHOICE YOU MAKE. There is no time to slip in one more movie, or video, or Television program where the worst scenarios and talk are presented every day and night to poison the minds and hearts of those given by the Father into your care and love and responsibility. These programs, these movies, these *popular* songs get worse, (a lot worse) every day, My people. Pay attention to your children and their activities. Replace the toxic material your children are ingesting with healthy, life-giving, heart nurturing games and family prayer and outdoor activity. Visit institutions of learning about history, that develop an appreciation for your country and the values it once accepted and supported. TIME IS VERY, VERY SHORT, MY PEOPLE. There are many in your world today who have definite plans for the destruction of a great portion of the earth and MANY of the people on it! Listen and believe and prepare for all you have heard by way of warning and suggestion from Heaven these many years. Act now, beloved ones. IT IS NEARLY TOO LATE.

I love you, My people. I desire to rid your world of all evil and to save you from unbelievable plans of the Antichrist to dominate the world. I tell you the Father will allow whatever is necessary to rid His people of their evil pastimes and inclinations (the residue of sin) and the annihilation planned for them by Satan and his demons. Reread these words. Hear the serious tone and grim determination that accompany them. Realize how serious are the threats to your salvation from all the present evil in the world, and to (your) increased enslavement and the ultimate damnation planned for the very near future. Come back to your senses. Come back from the insanity and disease that identifies and gradually destroys those who allow themselves to be misled and deceived by the father of lies. DO NOT SPEND ONE MORE MINUTE OUTSIDE OF MY GRACE AND THE PROTECTION YOU ARE PROMISED WITHIN MY MERCIFUL AND FORGIVING HEART. Let nothing stop your return to My Father. ALL I HAVE IS YOURS, BELOVED. Return to peace and the prosperity of a life filled with grace and mercy and the providence of your Lord and God. Hurry, My dearest ones. Storm clouds gather. LOOK MORE DEEPLY INTO MY EYES, MY FACE, INTO YOUR OWN HEARTS! Please, My sweet, vulnerable ones, come today and listen, repent, reconcile. I will give you every grace and strength and help to come now and be renewed and reborn."

11/9, "Daughter, I your Jesus, Bridegroom of your soul, have returned to comfort you and visit this night. I wish you could see the glee that results as each heart is touched (of people who come to listen to His words in personal messages.) Another reason to bring many into Eternity is to save them from losing heart over all they would witness at the hands of the Antichrist and his followers. Impress upon Our people, little one, ***that coming to Heaven is a far better role to play than living through the evil plans of evil men! Yes, dearest one, this will be a long time of trial by your own estimation. Time will seem to have stopped, when in reality, the tribulations and chastisements WILL NOT BE AS LONG AS ORIGINALLY ALLOWED FOR!"***

11/12, Jesus said: "ONLY THE MULTIPLICATION OF THE FEW PRAYERS (SAID BY OUR FAITHFUL REMNANT), BY THE PRAYERS OF ALL OF US IN HEAVEN WILL BE ACCEPTED BY MY FATHER! Remind My faithful ones of the Loaves and the Fishes, daughter, that FED THE 5,000 AFTER THEY WERE BLESSED BY MYSELF. My agony is at the greatest, the highest level at this time, even beyond the Night of My Agony in the Garden of Olives. That night I contemplated and awaited only My own death; but now there is an unbelievable number of lives in jeopardy from instruments of death and destruction. Do not be frightened, My people. BE MOVED TO PRAY, TO PLEAD WITH YOUR FATHER AND CREATOR TO ACT TO SAVE HIS PEOPLE FROM SATAN'S PLANS.

Encourage each other. Reach out to each other, My precious children of the world. Stop protecting yourselves from your unnecessary but overwhelming fear. Open your hearts to My words. Believe in them and act. Act on behalf of your world family who are held in the clutches of the evil one and his lies and empty illusions. Be strong now, My soldiers of Mary's Army. When I say 'there is nothing to fear,' I do not mean there is nothing of danger to expect in the future, or nothing to be done by way of added prayer and fasting at this time! I mean: if you are trusting in My power, if you are busy praying and gathering necessary foodstuffs and the proper supplies for daily living in the case of ANY EVENT, you will not have the time or the inclination to be fearful or unbelieving in the words of Heaven, given to many in the world now as a gift of love and mercy by My Father. ***Do not let a hostile attitude overtake your hearts, My beloved ones. Root out, cast out in My Name, all these negative spirits that continue to goad and drive you away from the true Spirit of God and all He wishes to effect in your lives and hearts. It is up to you, I tell you once again, children of the Two Hearts. Be humble in your words and actions. Be not critical and righteous. Your judgmental attitudes could be the 'death of you' yet, My loved ones."***

11/16, Jesus said: "Child of My Heart, be at peace and sleep well until you come to receive Me in My Eucharist. You are correct in your perception, daughter, that all the information We have given to you is and will be most acceptable to those who are balanced in their understanding of My return. Only time and study and fulfillment will convince those who think they have all the answers! (Just then I was aware of the house beginning to sway and shake! I realized it was a real earthquake and just sat in the kitchen and watched the floor move, heard the house creak and the wind chimes outside begin to clang until the moving of the house and floor stopped! I was amazed, since this was a first in my own experience!) All got very quiet again and Jesus said: **"Child, this sign, given by My Father, points to the imminence of a very large quake that will more than shake your homes in this area!** You are prepared here and will not see destruction to this house! Aren't you grateful that protection is promised you, daughter? Do not be fearful for a moment! Remember what you always tell Our people: ***Heaven has everything planned and a plan for everyone!***

Let us return now to Our recent theme. The plans of My Father are evident in so many places in this world. Those who reject and ridicule the events of weather as signs of My Father's displeasure will learn quickly and be humbled by Him! The bitter words all of you must experience are necessary as (you become) an instrument of healing for the hard hearts and heads that make noise reflecting the emptiness inside them! A brief, silent 'thank you' to My Father, along with the words: 'Be healed in the Name of Jesus,' is all the response necessary from anyone. Be happy for the opportunity to join your humiliation to Mine as a further means of unity with all of Who I Am. Please know, beloved faithful ones, that YOU WILL PERSEVERE and REMAIN FAITHFUL, IF YOU DESIRE THAT! It is always your personal choice that will determine your future, no matter how often you feel the temptation to weaken and walk away. Simply cast out that temptation, again in My Name, and continue about your industry or prayer of the moment.

Expect to be tempted, fiercely at times, throughout the time until I return; but also, BE CERTAIN THAT YOU HAVE THE STRENGTH AND GRACE TO RESIST ANY ATTACK BY THE EVIL ONE! Deal with each event in the power of My Name. Do not be confounded or confused, but continue on in confidence and trust. As you do this more and more often, your confidence will grow and overcome any tendency toward doubt or fear of the power and strength of Satan and his demons. You will see them overcome by My Power that has been given to you for these serious and sometimes perilous events and occurrences. You WILL be able to do these things to protect yourselves and others! They will be weakened by a lifetime of sin and ease, as many of you once were. They will also gain confidence in Our words and promises, as they see and hear the power of Heaven coming through all Our remnant holy ones. You WILL be holy ones, My precious people, more every day. Please look forward to these times of grace and extraordinary gift. Pray mightily for each other, people of God, and that as many as possible will accept the graces and opportunities to change and come to the Father as His beloved children and heirs of Heaven. It is your choice, My people. Will you accept it?"

11/26, Jesus said: "Child, time moves along so quickly! I tell you, My dearest one: THE REMORSE WILL BE NEARLY OVERWHELMING FOR THOSE WHO RIDICULED AND REJECTED THE OPPORTUNITY TO PRAY AND OBTAIN THE FATHER'S MERCY TO DEFEAT PLANS FOR NUCLEAR DESTRUCTION IN THE WORLD. DO NOT GIVE UP HOPE, DAUGHTER. DO NOT STOP PLEADING WITH OUR PEOPLE TO CONTINUE PLEADING WITH MY FATHER TO INTERFERE WITH AND

DEFEAT THE PLANS OF THE SONS OF EVIL TO ANNIHILATE SO MANY AND DESTROY SO MUCH OF THE EARTH. Believe in every word I have given you, My people: your ability to stop completely these plans if enough of you pray and fast and plead for mercy. I tell you, My little lambs, it is NOT now for you to DO, but just to BE! Prepare your hearts to receive your Infant Savior by first pouring out all traces of the world from your minds and hearts. Sit in silent adoration before Me and believe that you are being healed of MANY things that are the residue of harmful behavior in the past!

Believe that you need this emptying, this pouring out, this death to your worldly self, that you might be reborn in My Image. Your heart must be formed into an empty and shining Manger in which My Mother will lay the Infant Christ, born again for you who are born again for Me! Oh My dear ones, this is real! This can be. There are many of you who say, 'Oh no, I don't wish to spend Eternity in Hell'. Yet you are not willing to fight for your salvation and freedom from the slavery to sin, which places you in the greatest danger of giving your souls over to Satan and certain damnation! My people, who have worked so hard all your lives that your children might have 'more' than you did at their age, listen to the sane reasoning of My plea.

There will be nothing left of the world, as you think it is, to pass on to your children! There will be no freedom, no opportunities to succeed, as you see them through your worldly eyes. There will be nothing for them to inherit, as all will be destroyed or in the hands of the Antichrist. ***You are close to the most devastating destruction ever planned by any group of people in history for the rest of the world. Their plans for world domination are formulated by Satan himself; and therefore, (they) do not seek life and growth and improvements for the earth, only death and terrible living conditions in which a small remainder of conquered humanity will exist, serving every need and whim of their conquerors. My beloved of My Heart, I present this bleak picture of a future without peace or freedom or the grace of My Presence,*** in order to shake you from your slumber, a slumber caused by your lazy indifference. This indifference is a cover, a mask for your sneering disbelief that a loving, merciful God would not make up (or allow the evil one to fool you with) words such as these. You believe such events, such conditions are untrue and could never exist on the earth as it is today. People of the earth, open your eyes, open your ears, open your hearts to the words of your God Who created all and everyone, Who sees all, Who knows the plans of evil men who listen to Satan, the great destroyer, and his lies and totally empty promises. He has nothing and no power of his own! He has only that which My Father allows, and even that he is losing rapidly, that Scripture and My Father's Will may be fulfilled!

Be a part of the most important time in history since My first coming to the earth: My appearance and revelation as the long awaited Messiah, true God and True Man, Son of God and Second Person of the Trinity, Savior and King, My proclamation of the Kingdom of God, My Passion, Death and Resurrection! Do you wish to miss the excitement, the grace and gift, the healing and wonder of this period of time preceding My return to fight Satan and his followers, to renew this world reduced by evil to an ugliness and slavery to sin and self worship? YOU HAVE BEEN IN PAIN AND BONDAGE FOR SO LONG, MY POOR LOST ONES, YOU NO LONGER RECOGNIZE THE HOPELESSNESS OF YOUR CONDITION!

Awake, My sleeping revelers! Respond to the final calls of your God to cease your dreadful sin, your wretched behavior, your murderous scheming. Repent of this lifestyle which is more rightly called death style! COME BACK TO ME, PEOPLE OF THE WORLD, THIS VERY MOMENT, AND BE FREED OF CORRUPTION AND THE ADDICTION TO HATRED AND A CULTURE OF DEATH. CHOOSE LIFE, MY BELOVED. CHOOSE FREEDOM. CHOOSE ME! I AM JESUS WHO LOVED YOU BY GIVING MY LIFE TO RANSOM YOU FROM THIS CAPTIVITY! Because of My love for you, you are freed from Death, given the opportunity to spend Eternity with My Father and with Me, with Our Spirit in everlasting bliss forever and ever and ever. How can you turn away and disbelieve My plea? How can you reject the truth of what you see and hear and live every day you spend in the world of Satan and his cruelty and murder and abuse?

Ponder these words, My people. There will not be many more given, by the Father's Will. This time of grace is about to be replaced by tribulations and suffering that are unknown in the history of mankind. You have rejected the warnings of Heaven, and are about to see them begin. The man of perdition is at your 'doorstep', about to walk into your lives. Prepare, My faithful ones, for all you have heard revealed these many years. Reread Our words to faithful messengers. Be on guard and vigilant. The enemy is at the gate, but your God will be your sword and your shield. Put on Christ, My faithful ones, and prepare to face the Day!"

Blessed Mother then said: "Child, please write these words. I am your Mother, Mary, bringing words from God, Our Father, and My own words to follow. Pray again, little one, to the Holy Spirit, My Spouse, that you will be open to everything you need to know and hear. I will pray with you, daughter. Be at peace now, child. Let us begin. (Words of God, the Father, given by the Virgin Mary)

'Our people are hardened in heart and therefore not responding as they should to this call for increased prayer. When this country is shredded by nuclear attack, when another government takes over your present leadership, when all that has been prophesied about the Antichrist begins to occur, then will My people believe in all We have revealed to them these many years. What hard and ungrateful hearts My people possess. What sneering attitudes My Own creation maintains when they hear Heaven's words or see new gifts being given. Know well that all the bitterness in the hearts of those who consider themselves followers of Jesus, My Beloved Son and Mary, His Holy Mother, is known by the Triune God. Search your hearts now. Ask for the help of Our Spirit, His Wisdom and Knowledge. I, your Father and Creator Whose words are given this night by My Beloved Daughter, Mary Immaculate, tell you that many of Our faithful ones do not know their hearts and the evil that still resides there. This is not said in judgment, My people, but in love and concern for Truth and your healing through acceptance of Truth. You puff up your own importance by judging and rejecting signs and gifts I wish to give for the benefit of all.

Do not interfere with My gifts, dear children, by rejecting them! Do not be fearful, you who are already frightened by your own imagination. It will become darker in the days ahead, and I need all of My Remnant people to be in UNITY, filled with the Light of My Son, able to give good example to those who come to you for help, whom you will need to bring back to Me. My heart is grieved at the stubbornness of all who turn away from God and make gods out of men!! Once again I, your Father and Creator, ask you to search your hearts. Find out what still resides there to cause any division between your heart and My Divine Will! I wish to continue to pour out My Mercy upon the world; and only those who seek it in humility, who continue to accept My desires for each of you, will receive the abundance I wish to give to you. Fall on your knees and beg for My mercy and forgiveness. Surrender to My plans for each one. Allow Our Spirit to lead you freely into the Truth, more deeply united to Truth, more trusting and dwelling in Truth.

Children of the world, rejoice in My Son Jesus and His words of promise to you. Rejoice in your Beloved Mother Mary and the graces she waits to dispense through the power of Our Spirit. My blessing of paternal love and favor pours out upon all who listen and believe in all the words given this night. I give you all the mercy and trust and forgiveness that you ask for, My people! I give to each one increased faith and hope, *if you truly desire these gifts.* ***My people, do not turn away from the gifts I have for all by turning away from gifts I give to the few.*** And remember, you are forgiven as you forgive others! It is time now to let go of all sin, all critical words and attitudes, all association with worldly pursuits outside of legitimate means of employment. You cannot be cleansed of the world while you are still following any of its ways. Read the words of Scripture every day. Receive My Son in His Eucharist. Adore Him and beg for the healing of your hearts. Praise and thank your God, for all is a gift of My generosity and love for you. My Son and I stand at the Banquet Table ready to seat you and begin to serve you. When will you wish to join us there, My people? When will you accept My Love?' "Daughter, I your Lord and God, Father and Creator, bring My gratitude and delight to your heart this night. I give you these words as a special gift to you and Mary, the Immaculate Queen."

12/12, Blessed Mother said: "IT IS A TERRIBLE TIME OF WAITING, I KNOW! OUR FAITHFUL REMNANT IS AT A BREAKING POINT AND NEEDS ASSISTANCE TO WAIT PATIENTLY A LITTLE MOMENT LONGER! I do wish to give them encouragement this night. Let us pray together to My Spouse, the Holy Spirit of God.

FOR MERCY'S SAKE!

'As you gaze upon the Infant in the Manger remember, My beloved ones, His future was understood by myself and by Joseph from all we had made part of our hearts with the words of Holy Scripture. We wept for joy that such a Gift was entrusted to us, but also at being in the Presence of our God Who lay before us as a tiny, humble Babe. It was difficult to take my eyes from Him, so filled with wonder and joy was I. As Joseph continued to make that little cave more comfortable and protected from the cold, I knelt before My Son and adored. His tiny body was perfect, and I trembled as I held Him to Me to keep My Jesus warm, Who had also created me! There was no need for words, as the night was filled with Angel's songs. My own heart was overwhelmed with awe at the beauty of this Child of mine Who was God's Own Son! When you gaze at Him, My dearest faithful ones, look through My eyes and see Him Whom you also carry within you, Who is born again and again in your hearts. Prepare your hearts to receive the Infant, to cuddle and keep Him warm with all of your love residing there. Clothe Him with hymns of welcome. Wrap Him in layers of joy. Tell Him stories about His people waiting to greet their Messiah. Tell Him how much you love His Mother, and watch Him smile and gurgle with glee!

Nurture this Infant King with promises of faithfulness and service to all of His needs. Rock Him gently, My precious ones, and sing to Him a lullaby. Feed His Presence in the manger of your heart, My dear ones. Keep Him there, made comfortable by your love. You can do this, My dearest and most loving children! Feel the coldness of the night. Hear the voices of Angels singing Hosannas. Kneel with Me, and pray and adore Our Savior and Our Lord. Come, My children, prepare your hearts. Scrub them clean in the sacramental waters of grace. Allow the mercy of the Father to remove every stain of sin. Can you not feel the newness of this resting place for His Son? Ponder the magnitude of this Gift to the world in every age, at every moment. Spend your days preparing for His coming as a helpless baby. Adorn your hearts with the prayers of longing, songs of praise and litanies of thanksgiving. See the flowers of these offerings fill your hearts with a sweet perfume that reaches out to all who approach. My precious children, allow Me to help you prepare, as I did while waiting for the blessed time of that first Christmas morn. Together, Joseph and I will lead, as you follow along on that road to Bethlehem in silence and wonder...Be filled with awe and a joyful expectation for all to be fulfilled as the prophets have foretold. Wait with Me, My children. Be filled completely by the Gift of My Son!'"

12/20, At Adoration, Jesus said: "Hello My dearest one. I am your Jesus of Mercy, little one. You see and feel the hardness of hearts everywhere, and these are Our faithful ones! The number of people believing and acting on Our words will be smaller yet, even with the advent of earthquakes and so much destruction. I ask you to pray now to Our Spirit for the grace to take My words to the world, and to remain in prayer tonight before you send it. These are perilous times, My beloved, and you must be totally consecrated and united with Me and My Father's Will for you and for the world. Child, let us begin.

FOR MERCY'S SAKE!

'My beloved ones of the world, I bring you peace and strength and blessings for this week of preparation for the Feast of My Birth. It is with sadness that I share the fact that very few in the world are focused in any way on the meaning of Christmas. Most are consumed with shopping and plans for meals and gifts and parties. Each year the feast of My Birth is understood less and less by My young ones who are not properly taught the true reasons for the solemn celebration of the Christmas season. In fact, with your newer laws banning religious symbols in secular places, no one is reminded of Me at all as they shop and prepare. Your President (Clinton) gives weak and sad explanations for his legislation and words about public displays of a religious nature. I wonder if he has really looked at a penny lately, if he is familiar with the words of your Constitution, if he hears any of the words used in the Sunday church services he attends for all to see.

There is so much hypocrisy in your nation now, My people, that you have become blinded to the truth and numb to the words of ridiculous disparity, (inequality: Webster) lack of even rational thought. You have become deadened by words pronounced with such authority by your leaders and the media. You no longer discern the truth, My poor lost lambs, nor are you able to recognize falsehood anymore. Your God calls out only a moment longer to call you back to reason, to truth, to sanity. This is truly a world gone mad from too much gratification, too much of whatever is the perceived need of the moment: whatever you desire, too much noise and frivolity. You have heard these words before, My dear ones, but they are more easily discarded during this time of holiday and rich foods and revelry. My people of My Sacred Heart, I call out to you to STOP, to LISTEN in quiet, to ALLOW Me to share Myself with you at this special time of grace in your Church Year. (and every year from now on… cta.)

The need to pray more for mercy and mitigation of expected events means that you will not have time for parties and distractions, My dear, dear children. Return to the simplicity of your own childhood. Anticipate My Birth with the Holy Mother and Joseph. Hear the Angelic voices and the Shepherd's words of wonder and awe. You must fast and prepare spiritually for this Day which is now a greater reminder of all I lived and how I died for you; that I will be coming again soon to destroy every ounce of evil in your midst and from every one on the earth. Wait for the time of My Second Coming, My precious people, by reliving the Sacred Night of My First Coming into the world! It is My desire that you do this, dearest ones, that you refrain from noisy feasting, and celebrate instead the silence and awe of the ones who greeted Me on that first Christmas Night. Join Me in the simplicity and poverty with which I entered the world. Listen for My voice and My cries, My Angels promising peace to men of good will. I have always offered you peace. Never have you needed this gift more. Never have you needed Me more, My dear little warriors. Again I say, gaze on My Tiny Infant Body wrapped in the love and preparations of My Mother and earthly father. Remember that I will return to the earth to bring peace once again, the peace that has all but disappeared from the entire world.

FOR MERCY'S SAKE!

Watch and pray, My loved ones, that the graces of this time when Love was born into the world are so greatly needed by each of you for the days that follow. Do this for Me, those of My faithful friends who profess to love Me. Do this for yourselves, My needy ones. Overcome all of your fears and trembling with the mighty power of this Infant King Who comes again soon in battle array to do battle with the hatred and destructive plans of Satan. Be filled with hope of new life and love in the world, as you see the Tiny Baby, Who is your God and Protector. Come daily to Me, My people, and pray and listen. Nothing is more important for you now. No one is more important or necessary for you than I Who Am your Savior and King. Praise My Father, children, for these words of encouragement and love from your God. Listen to all the words of Heaven again, and to those who come to share them with you. Be not distracted or doubtful because My words do not agree with your plans for the future. GIVE Me YOUR WILL totally, My faithful ones, and ACCEPT MINE totally. I bless you with new strength this day, all who read and believe and act upon My words. Be filled with gratitude to My Father Who loves you with so many words of love and warning. Be filled with My peace again, My beloved, as you read what I have come to tell you today. Reach out to those in real need. Give shelter to the poor in your prayers and hearts and gifts. Pour yourselves out. Do as I have done for you. Rejoice, My beloved ones. I AM COMING AGAIN AND I AM NEAR! I love you, My people. I am waiting for the gift of your hearts that I may place them in the Manger right now, beloved ones. Do not wait. Time is gone. Time has fled on the wings of My Father' s Will and plans for you. When you read these words, dear faithful ones, come then directly to see Me, to visit before My Sacrament to prepare your hearts for My Birth, for My return to the earth so very soon. (It is more important in light of these urgent words, to remember that 'very soon' are words given in Heaven's time and not ours... cta.) My beloved lambs, rejoice!"

At Adoration, 12-25, 6 p.m. Jesus said: "My dearest little one, give praise to the Father of all that I am here to be with you in these closing days of this century. How great is the goodness of My Father, child, Who gifts His people with Love. My Birth signified the beginning of an Era of fulfillment of words through many of the Prophets who lived before My advent into the humanity of God's Creation. **My Birth was the single most important event in all of History and remains so today. My Death and Resurrection are hailed as the second most important event as they opened, once again, the opportunity of mankind to return to their Creator in Heaven whose gates had been closed to this return by the sin of your first parents.** Each year My Church celebrates these Events as the major Feasts of its history in joy and thanksgiving. Today has been such a Feast of remembrance and reenactment of My appearance as the God/Man, the King and Messiah, the Savior and Redeemer. Many such celebrations have been held since My Birth, each year seeing the world grow colder and more disinterested in the Sacred Character of these Events that resulted from the incredible Mercy of God, Our Father. Now all who live are being prepared by prophecy and signs and wonders for My Return to the earth. I AM STILL THE LIGHT THE DARKNESS WILL NOT OVERCOME. (John1: 5)

FOR MERCY'S SAKE!

My coming back to the world to fight the power of Satan (which will reach its zenith by that time) will mark the Day of the Lord and the third most important Sacred Event in the history of mankind. All who live shall see the saving power of God. As I ascended to Heaven, you will see Me descending on the clouds with My Angels. (Matthew 24:30) As My Apostles gathered to watch Me depart for Heaven (Luke 24:50-51) at My Ascension, so many of My faithful will gather to greet Me when I come again. Yes, caught up into the air with joy will you be at the sight of Me. (1Thess 4:17) to greet Me and to join Me in the battle that will result in the defeat of Satan and his followers and his demons, and the removal of all evil from the earth and from every person on it. What cause for rejoicing, My daughter. What reason to prepare yourselves to be present for this Great Event, according to My Father's Will for each one.

Do you not feel My excitement as you read My words? Can you not imagine the grace and favor and love of My Father that has created you to be alive at this time: the culmination of so much struggle and bloodshed throughout the intervening time, the continuing battles between Good and evil, the fulfillment of Scripture that is about to occur right through the events involved in and around My Second Coming into the world? Please, My faithful ones, allow the magnitude of these gifts to fill you with awe and amazement. Allow the time of expectation (that filled the known world before My Birth) to be an example of serious preparation for all your expectations for My Return, based on the early prophets and words given by Heaven today to those chosen to be messengers for these End Times. Can you truly believe in all My prophet's words of warning, shared by your God for the world, and not be moved to act upon the loving directives of Heaven? Must you also weary your God? (Isaiah 7:13)

As parents, most of you know the frustration and helplessness that result in your hearts, as errant children refuse to listen to words designed to protect them. You know the heartache of seeing your children adopt lifestyles that are sure to lead them into danger and certain disaster. I tell you, it is the same for your God and Holy Mother. We weep from the pain of the rejection and ridicule that greet all Our words given in love, and designed to save Our children from the certain disaster and destruction contained in the choices for evil and gratification of the world. Those who refuse to listen and refuse to see and acknowledge the presence of this evil in the ways of the world, will be doomed forever by it unless they accept the grace and opportunity given by the Gift of My Father's Warning! Those who continue to accept the deception and empty promises of Satan will lose these graces ultimately and belong to those followers of the Antichrist who will also be defeated (with him) by Me, and driven into Hell. These will be like the fallen Angels who followed Lucifer into Hell that first time My Father was rejected by satanic pride. This time the world will be completely renewed, and MANY will live in the beauty as was present in the Garden of Eden. Although the blemish of Original Sin will still exist on the souls of all who enter there, **evil will not be allowed to tempt Our purified and renewed ones who will live in peace and purity in My Eucharistic Reign as a Eucharistic People.** Oh My children, ponder these words and rejoice! Return to these words often and to the pictures they paint.

Long to see the earth covered with the beauty always intended for it by My Father. Allow yourselves the gift of believing in this possibility because I have said it will be so!! Lift your hearts and minds in praise and gratitude to My Father that the fierce oppression and suffering that always accompanies the evil one and his ways will be totally removed from the earth and the lives of Our faithful remnant. You are already redeemed, beloved of My Heart. Now return to My Father and live according to His Commandments and the Beatitudes. Accept His mercy, win your salvation and live eternally in the bliss of Paradise. Yes, yes, yes, My children, these words are truth. They are filled with wisdom and light, for they are My words and I Am Truth. I Am Wisdom. I Am Light and Life. By the Power of My Holy Name, My people, believe in these words and be saved! RETURN TO ME, MY LOVED ONES, IN OBEDIENCE TO MY FATHER, FOR I RETURN TO YOU IN OBEDIENCE TO MY FATHER! PRAY, MY PEOPLE. SAY IT: 'COME, LORD JESUS!'"

12/30, At Desk, 1 a.m. Jesus said: "Daughter, together let us pray to My Father and Our Spirit, Who also have words for you and for the world. Let us continue, little one. Safety in the streets will not really exist again until I return! Daughter, I, your Jesus, bring these words to you from My Father (and yours).

'I ask you to believe that I am your Father and Creator speaking to your heart because of My immense love for all My people. Hear now words of importance for the future of the world.

I am Lord and God and Creator of all My dear people. Another only has the power I allow that one to have. And I will not allow My world and My people to be completely destroyed. However, My dear children, you will see My anger released in the fury of Nature, the plans of Satan, and the fulfillment of Scripture until the time My Son, Jesus, returns to defeat the evil one and all his demons and earthly followers. I, your God and Father, tell you these things again in order to convince you of My Omnipotence, My Power, My Wrath at the terrible carnage of My innocents; but also My Love that will last forever unless you continue to reject Me at the last possible opportunity. You alone can choose for yourself.

How foolish you appear (enemies of the church and freedom) with all your plans and war games! How inadequate you are, as you will discover at the last moment before your personal and collective defeat. And My dearest people who love Me, I will continue to allow most of you to be protected and renewed and empowered for the good of all those lost ones who survive approaching events and come to you for help in finding their way back to Me. I will continue to gift you, My faithful remnant, with whatever you will need to guarantee your success in this most important mission of your lives. Continue to be faithful to your increased prayer now and never do less for My lost souls who are your own gateway to salvation! As you read My words, children of hope and joy, I shower you with My great love and admiration for your perseverance, your endurance in the face of the fatiguing challenge of waiting for Me to act in such a way that will allow many more of your loved ones and Mine to see the truth in all the words of prophecy shared by Heaven these many years. My people, lift your faces and hearts to Me, your Creator. I am everywhere, dear little ones. Feel My love and Presence all around you. You are immersed in Me, My beloved faithful ones who seek only to obey and serve and glorify Me! Thank you, My own. You will be so happy and grateful that you believed and listen to Me and served Me! I shower you with blessings as you read, My children.'

My Spirit speaks to the world now:

'People of the world, I am the Spirit of God Who speaks in order to calm your concerns and strengthen your faith and trust in these loving words of the Father and Creator of all. I tell you, as you read these words, I am healing all God's faithful ones of many, many aches and pains and ailments, large and small! Yes, some of you have agreed to suffer for the conversion and salvation of souls, but the greater number will know an increase of strength and courage, and the ability to pray longer and without as much distraction. You have done well struggling to answer the call of Heaven to pray and prepare, to change and trust. I will be pouring Myself out upon all who are open to receive these new gifts and healing decreed by God, the Father. These are to encourage you to remain faithful in spite of severe hardships. They are also the result of the Father's gratitude for all you do for Him and His people even now. Call on Me constantly also, people of God. Ask for My assistance, My gift of openness to help you receive lovingly and joyfully the many who will come in terrible need and desperation. Be filled now with My Gifts, with new conviction, with new delight about your future in Heaven or in the New Era on a beautified earth. Rejoice that you are chosen, strong and prepared soldiers in the Army of the Holy Mother, My Spouse, the Virgin Mary!'

FOR MERCY'S SAKE

"The Lord, your God, has chosen you from all the nations on the face of the earth to be a people peculiarly His own. It was because the Lord loved you and because of His fidelity to the oath He had sworn to your father, that He brought you out with His strong hand from the place of slavery and ransomed you.... Understand then that the Lord, your God, is God indeed, the faithful God who keeps His merciful covenant to the thousandth generation toward those who love Him and keep His commandments." (Deuteronomy 7)

Messages, Year 2000

II

½, "My dearest faithful one, rejoice! I am your Jesus of Mercy and Love. I repeat, child, all We have told you WILL occur at the proper time. 'Do not waste precious time, My precious ones, in a world that is running at breakneck speed into the jaws of the evil one who waits to snap up Our unsuspecting, unprepared and uncaring children dancing non-stop to the world's tune! I need you to be the victims of Love for these End Times. You are held tightly against My Sacred Heart beating with love and gratitude for all who love and serve Me. I tell you, it **is only in trials and disappointments of delays that you reach the final place of preparedness and obedience to My Father's Will.** Do you believe His Will contains what is best for you? Do you? DO YOU? You are being strengthened and purified and cleansed of your agenda, your desires, your will each time you patiently await and accept every period of waiting, every turn the Plan of My Father takes. Be at peace and be filled with My Presence and increased Love. ALL WILL BE ACCOMPLISHED."

1/6, At Home, 11 p.m. "Dearest little one, I am your Jesus, come to give you peace. Daughter, Our people are more than dejected, more than bored or impatient with waiting. They are angry at delays My Father continues to decree, and they lash out at all of you who bring Our words to the world. They lash out in anger at some of you because you are 'available'. You are a 'source' of these words, a vehicle for their being shared with all of them after you have received them. I told you many months ago that this would happen, and so it is. Of course, I am showering graces and strength upon My faithful messengers. You will continue to receive and must endure the scathing attacks and words of ridicule from those who see themselves as self-appointed leaders of Our people. It is not enough that these revile all of you, My faithful, but they cite their own reasons for this supposed discernment. Remember, My dear ones, it is Myself and My words they are rejecting... not yourselves. My faithful and concerned people, please stop wasting time on this frivolous exchange of ego-centered judgments. How long will you dwell in the Kingdom of Pride? It is not My Kingdom, I assure you! When will you surrender to Me, and embrace silence and humility and a firm trust in your God? Stay close to My words, My little ones. They are wisdom and light.

You will not be the first ones who have reacted angrily at My Father's methods of purification of His people. The Israelites got fed up waiting for Moses to return to them, and built a golden calf to worship!! Imagine how far from understanding what Moses was telling them repeatedly, when they would turn all their finery into a golden calf and worship it! This is what you are doing, My people! You are sick of waiting and wandering in uncertainty already. You are lashing out at anyone who brings you words regarding the future; and you are worshipping your own intellect, your fine way with words of explanation, your own opinion! Come to Reconciliation, My truly faithful ones. Stop being misled by those who speak as someone with authentic authority. Put not your faith in man, My beloved ones. Put your faith in Me. Only I can lead you safely around and away from the dangerous pits dug by Satan and his followers. Only I, in union with the Trinity, know every plan. Will you leave Me, too, My people? For you know the words of Peter are true, and I DO HAVE THE WORDS OF ETERNAL LIFE! (John 6: 68) My people, it is to bring these weaknesses (within so many) to your attention that We allow situations that will show you, once and for all, that the power lies with My Father; that NO ONE is more powerful or clever or discerning or like unto God than Our Heavenly Father Who IS the Creator of the Universe and all people and creatures and things in it! I repeat, My irritable ones, do not get rid of the supplies and water you just gathered. YOU WILL NEED THEM. It is My Father's Will that you, too, wander in the desert of uncertainty, as did the Israelites of old, who followed Me for forty years not being sure of anything. They grumbled constantly and rebelled often, also! Be careful! You may not reach the Promised Land of the New Era either. It is only by trusting the leader that anyone can be brought safely to a destination. In wartime, it is only the leaders who know all the plans at first, the destination and the means to arriving there. THIS IS WAR, MY PEOPLE. I and My Father and Our Spirit are your Supreme Commander. We know the goal. We see the whole picture. We have the means and the power to help you arrive. Otherwise, you will not make it! We also know the best way to train you, Our beloved warriors! Be filled with peace, My dearest ones. There is nothing to fear. The Israelites, the Chosen People of God, were victorious and well cared for along the way; and you will be, as well. You cannot see all We can see, My dear ones. You do not know all that We know! You must trust your Triune God, My little lost and helpless and frightened ones. It is the only way to the Kingdom. I am the only Road, the only Way with My Father and Our Spirit. Please, allow My Dearest Holy Mother to bring you to Me, once again. Recognize another new beginning for yourselves. Realize that any time you surrender more, you are brought to a deeper level of unity with Me but also, you begin to live on a higher plane of service and intimacy with your God and Precious Mother Mary. Invite all of Heaven to pray with you constantly. You are loved beyond telling, beloved ones. You are held in My Heart at this moment of your reading or hearing these words. Keep Me in your hearts, and I will keep you in Mine! Persevere."

1/25 & 26, Jesus said: "Dear one, I have told you your mission includes visits to Our faithful ones until I return. This renewal and encouragement will be so necessary **as all of you are hidden from the Antichrist's followers in a special place and miraculous way during long months and years of waiting (!)** Do not be overwhelmed by these words, little one, but continue to focus on the present moment, one day at a time. More gifts are being given to all Our chosen messengers now as a sign to the faithful who wait, that We are with you and see into every heart, read and hear every thought and word you speak. Our people grumble when their expectations are not met, and they turn away from prayer in disgust and jump into the world once more. My Heart is grieved by the callous attitudes of the many who think of themselves as My followers, yet abandon Me the moment things do not occur according to their plans. It is the world you must abandon. It is Me you must trust and embrace and follow through any trial and disappointment."

1/26 At Adoration, continuation of 1/25. Jesus said: "My people, you DO understand many new dynamics of prayer and grace as you accept the Wisdom poured out by Our Spirit, if you are asking the Holy Spirit for the gifts of openness and trust in Our promises. My dearest children of the Two Hearts, please persevere in this routine of prayer and especially ask Our Beloved and Blessed Faustina to pray with you during this important time of cleansing and deep reflection on all the events that opened the Gates of Heaven and redeemed mankind. Praise and thank My Father for all who DO accept His Divine Mercy, and all who serve and promote Mercy in a quiet and humble way. You will not believe how strong you have become through your prayers and devotion to Me, to My Father's Mercy, to My Mother, to so many of Our Saints and Angels. My Sacred Heart fills with rejoicing at your increasing levels of holiness and prayer. Yes, there are MANY times you could do better, but you HAVE RESPONDED to offered graces and allowed yourselves to be inspired and uplifted by the Holy Spirit. This new level of response and joy will not leave you, My precious ones, in spite of some times of fatigue and influence of the vessels of clay our bodies!) which house your spirits. Remain within My Light. Remain in the joy that comes when you finally begin to realize how much you are loved and cherished and appreciated by your God. All your loved ones send prayers and love from Heaven. My Mother's Mantle holds all of her faithful ones close to Her Immaculate Heart. Remain focused on Me, My people. You ARE Mine. You DO belong to Me. I love you completely and with All of Who I Am."

2/4, "My dearest, precious, faithful ones: I am Jesus, the Son of God, Son of Man, Second Person of the Trinity, your Redeemer and King. You are lifted higher each time you become a new creation by your ongoing surrender to His Perfect Will, your ever-more purified 'YES' to that Will, to that growth into new unity with Our Holy Mother (and yours), with your Triune God. You are already transformed beyond your ability to understand by your fidelity to the requests given to the world by My Mother and Myself. I see what you cannot see, My people, and that is the process by which you are being transformed in all the many ways that allow you to become more and more Jesus, less and less the person of the world you used to be. Some of you will reach your heavenly goal more quickly than others, where you will dwell in peace and eternal bliss, praying for your loved ones still on earth, or working out the punishment due to your sins and attaining your heavenly reward after this level of purification. Some will remain on the earth to serve your brothers and sisters who come in desperate need after the gift of the Illumination of your minds is received by the entire world. **You will live and serve according to My Father's Will for you until I return, all the while being purified and sanctified yourselves as you lead all these lost ones back to the Father, away from the Antichrist and the slavery and death he has planned for the earth's inhabitants.** Along the way, at the proper time, Our faithful will come into Paradise, while those chosen to work out their salvation on the earth will remain until My return to fight the ultimate battle of Armageddon. You will assist Me in this battle and remain on a renewed earth, cleansed and purified for a new Era of Peace and Purity.

This plan of My Father is necessary to cleanse the earth and its people that an Era would be given to His faithful remnant in which they will live as perfectly as possible on the earth, in the Divine Will of Our Father and Creator. Dwell on these words. Dwell on the promises of protection you are offered that will bring you safely through each event and the evil designs of Satan's puppets in the world under the leadership of the Antichrist. My faithful children, THERE IS NOTHING TO FEAR! THERE IS NO POWER LIKE THAT OF YOUR GOD. THERE IS NO POWER THAT CAN PREVENT THE MIRACLES YOUR GOD WILL PERFORM IN ORDER TO ENABLE THIS PROTECTION AND ALL THE HELP YOU WILL NEED. There is no love like Love that will heal and renew and strengthen you to withstand the hardships of future events. YOU MUST DWELL IN HOPE. You are invited to remember that all will be gifted and graced and transformed along the way, so as to accomplish every task and request and difficulty you encounter.

YOU ARE THE DELIGHT OF THE HEAVENLY FATHER. YOU ARE THE APPLE OF HIS EYE. YOU ARE THE FLOWER GROWING DAILY MORE BEAUTIFUL WITHIN HIS GARDEN! BELIEVE, MY CHILDREN, IN ALL THE WORDS I HAVE EVER GIVEN TO THE WORLD; AND CONSTANTLY, I BEG OF YOU, RENEW THEM IN YOUR HEARTS. REFRESH YOURSELVES THROUGH TIME SPENT IN MY BLESSED COMPANY, MY PRESENCE IN MY BLESSED SACRAMENT, AS MUCH AS POSSIBLE EACH DAY. Oh My dearest ones of My Sacred Heart, I speak directly to you. My holy ones, My followers who are becoming My obedient and humble lambs sacrificing yourselves (in union with Me) to My Father and His every desire, rejoice! Now all Our words take on new and deeper meaning. Now the Word sent to you from My Father is truly accomplishing its good, which is the Will of My Father and yours. You are being formed into fighting weapons that My Father is using to defeat the plans of the evil one, to free His people from the burden of sin, the bondage of Satan's lies, the traps set to ensnare the innocent and unsuspecting children, many of whom never even reach the world!

Listen to your Jesus of Mercy Who calls out with a breaking, suffering Heart: My people everywhere are starving and freezing, abused and abandoned, subjected to unspeakable horrors. Bring all of these to Me before My Blessed Sacrament, and consecrate them to Me. Share all you are and all you have with them NOW, MY dearest ones, who cry out to know God's Will for you. THIS IS HIS WILL FOR YOU, MY BELOVED ONES. BEGIN TO LIVE MORE AND MORE FOR OTHERS AND NO LONGER ONLY FOR YOURSELVES. Serve Me in My poor, lost, helpless and terrified ones everywhere in the world. This is your salvation. This is the Father's Plan for all! Read My words many times, My people."

2-16, Jesus said: "Each day sees a further development of the plans that will result in the crucifixion of My Church and the greater sufferings of Our faithful ones. Please tell Our people of the dangers that lurk everywhere, that the evil one waits daily for an opportunity to distract all of you with events or people that seem, at first, to be part of My Father's plan, but disintegrate quickly into just distraction and a further diluting of your prayers and your focus on My Face! My dear ones, people are suffering and dying daily everywhere in the world. You cannot continue to insulate yourselves with your money and possessions and education, to live your lives as privileged and above the struggles of this part of your journey back to My Father and yours.

Realize, My dearest people, the power of celebrating and remembering and renewing the events of My life as a means of an ongoing nurturing, an example to follow for your own lives. Without these reminders, this call to deny yourselves available opportunities for any and every type of food and entertainment, you would lose Me completely. These choices on your part strengthen and build up discipline like nothing else can accomplish. You are not hurting yourself when you fast, My dearest children! (Please keep in mind that prudence and balance must be brought to fasting by people who are seriously ill or on special diets and need certain medicines that cannot be taken on empty stomachs, etc. Jesus is talking to our maturity here. C.A.) You are aiding your spiritual growth enormously, as well as allowing your body a much- needed rest from frantic activity and an overload to your senses! LESS IS BETTER, MY PEOPLE, and allows you time to live, to be more fully alive; to be healthier, more at peace, more able to enjoy the simple beauty of everyday life. Discipline is sadly lacking in today's world. I GIVE THE GIFT OF DESIRE TO FAST AND RETREAT FROM THE WORLD DURING THESE FORTY DAYS OF PREPARATION, MY DEAR ONES. And blessed are you who have the company of your spouse and family to live in this way of your family and spouse.

Blessed are you who pray, children.

Blessed are you who fast. You will be prepared for the blessed, meager existence of the future by living it now!

Blessed are you who hear the words of Heaven and live them. You are very close to the Kingdom of My Father on earth as it is in Heaven!

Blessed are you, My beloved ones, for loving My Mother, for your devotion to her.

Blessed are you who love your Triune God in the Father and the Son and the Holy Spirit.

Blessed are you who try to love, to pray, to change, to become all We are calling you to be.

Blessed are you when you are humble enough to admit that you have sinned AGAIN that same weak sin of lust or greed or aggressive behavior; or laziness or covetousness or dishonesty or gossip or idol worship; or murder of another's reputation or good name.

Blessed are you, My beloved ones, who return for Reconciliation and seek forgiveness from your God, and promise to accept My graces to go and sin no more!

I am waiting to forgive you, to heal you, to renew you, to strengthen you, to guide and protect you. I send these words to you with every ounce of My love and pleading for your return in trust to My Father, Who waits to make of you a new creation; born in love and tenderness, and the longing of your God to save you and bring you one day to Paradise and Eternal Bliss forever! You are not aware of this, My faithful ones, but you ALSO have need of rebirth in My Purity, My love for you, My Self! Just get to know Me, My dearest little ones. Just love Me, My people of the world. All else will be taken care of by Me and the intercession of Our dearest, holy Mother Mary.

BEGIN A NOVENA TO THE HOLY SPIRIT ONCE AGAIN. ASK TO HAVE YOUR WEAK WILLS SHORED UP! REQUEST A CHANGE IN ATTITUDE FROM COMPLACENCY TO BEING SET ON FIRE WITH THE SPIRIT OF SURRENDER TO THESE REQUESTS, AND THE JOY TO LIVE THEM IN PEACE AND GENTLENESS. Stop whatever you are doing, and feel My love in these words to you. Be changed by them. Be renewed by them. Be blessed by them! I am your loving, suffering Savior. Accept My gift of peace now!"

2/28, At Adoration Jesus said: "My dear people of My Sacred Heart, I speak as One Who continues to offer from My Divinity information about all that is about to break upon the world; and with **directives for you to follow in order to be saved from the plans of the One World Government agenda,** bloated by greed for power and amassed wealth. Think of a Giant Toad, My dear ones, who is blown up with itself tenfold! This is the present condition of the people of power in the world, grossly enlarged by their own egos and the flattering lies of others. Satan has convinced them of the success of their coming endeavors and the might of his arm! They will continue to believe they are invincible throughout the victories allowed the Antichrist and his followers, all Satan's puppets. They are allowed these perceived successes by My Father that all of Scripture might be fulfilled. I mention this, once again, because you have not been taught to evaluate world events in the light of the fulfilling of Biblical prophecies. The Word of God is living. The Word was made Flesh. I Am that Word Who Will accomplish everything I was sent to do. All has been accomplished and **you are the generation, the people who are chosen to see and live the accomplishment of every word recorded there (in Scripture) until My Return.**

You will see the victory, (already won), being fought, being realized, as Satan is actually defeated and chained in Hell with his demons; as the Antichrist and his accomplice, the Antipope and all their followers, are thrown into Hell following the annihilation of much of the earth and its inhabitants. But you do not listen because it seems too impossible, because you too accept the lies and distractions of the world. AND I TELL YOU: I AM YOUR LORD AND YOUR GOD. THERE IS NO OTHER! There is no argument or modern, watered down philosophy or heretical theology that can EVER change that fact. I was born into the world, a Son of God, as son of Mary, who has always been Immaculate, a Virgin, the one whom Scripture foretold. When the skies open and rain floods the earth, no one can get together with like-minded people and convince you that it is not raining! The obvious truth cannot be denied, cannot be changed or rationalized away. I AM TRUTH, MY PEOPLE. I AM THE WORD OF GOD AND SO, MY WORD IS TRUTH. Fall on your knees, My dear, dear people. Repent of your rejection of My words and those who share them with you. Cast out (in My Name) the critical judgments with which you cast My words, My Presence, out of your midst! Oh My beloved ones, would a loving, caring God not continue to offer you the opportunity to repent and return, to give you the means to walk away from chaos and into the Arms of Peace?

You are not going to survive your immediate future without Me! You will not reach Heaven without Me and all the help and protection I continue to offer you in the Name of your Triune God. You will not survive a world that is ruled completely by Satan through the Antichrist. I weep, My poor lost ones of the world, for you are far from the salvation I died to obtain for you. You are lost for all eternity unless enough graces are released (by the prayers of My Remnant Flock) that will enable you to choose to accept the mercy and forgiveness I wish to give you at the time of My Warning (Illumination) that will convince you I exist and have the power to save you. Love is the only answer, people of the world. Reject hatred and eternal death, My dear ones whom I loved unto My Own Death. Choose Life. Choose Me, for I AM Life. I AM ALL YOU NEED. Through My faithful chosen ones, I will bring you back to My Father. I have always promised this, and have fulfilled this promise for all who have and will allow Me into their hearts and lives. **Your stubbornness and hardened hearts are without equal in all of history**.

No, My little ones, I am not speaking to someone else. I am looking directly at, I am speaking directly to YOU! Let the souls of your brothers and sisters everywhere on the earth be your reason to respond with all your heart and soul and mind and strength to the need for constant prayer for peace and conversion, mercy and mitigation, for the glory of God Our Father, and for your own forgiveness and salvation. I only want to love and heal you, My dear ones, to protect you from certain devastation, to share My strength and power with you until I return to drive evil from the earth and return it to the Beauty-of the-Garden waiting to be accomplished. Choose Me. Spend time with Me, all day wherever you are, whatever you are doing. You say you desire love, My people. ACCEPT ME. I AM LOVE! When I return, daughter of My Heart, will I find anyone waiting faithfully in joy and hope? Only prayer, united to My suffering and the suffering of all who will accept it in joy, will determine the answer!"

3/13, At Adoration Jesus said: "Child of My Heart, I am Jesus, hidden before you in My Blessed Sacrament, filled with joy by your presence before Me: 'My dearest people, I, your Jesus, come to you to say: Rejoice, for the graces of increased love in your hearts for prayer and adoration. My beloved faithful ones, some among you are receiving new gifts that will allow you to suffer for the salvation of souls, the reparation of sins, and to give new honor and glory to My Father. You are slowly, but most assuredly, becoming the mighty warriors you were created to be. The backbone of steel, the gentleness of My Mother, new gifts of Our Spirit, new joy and hope, new love for each other, new desire to spend more and more time with Me in prayer and adoration fill your hearts and spirits, healed and renewed to a new level of surrender and service by special gifts of healing from My Father. How close you have become to the Kingdom of God on earth as you were always meant to live it. How beautiful have your souls become: gleaming with the purity and new innocence, the strength and healing of the beauty and luminous glow of sanctifying grace and reconciliation with your God and each other. You have become seekers, and you have found truth. Welcome, My children. Rejoice, for the Kingdom of God is at hand. The mission I began two thousand years ago with My birth into your world continues to unfold and brings now a renewal of the lives and souls of many by the new outpouring of the Spirit of God in a time to equal, even surpass, the first Pentecost! Who would not rejoice at the joy and gifts of conversion and salvation promised to the greatest number of people in this world ever given in one brief period of time? All, who serve, as you each will serve, will receive this outpouring of Spirit, as well. BELIEVE IT, My people! Eagerly await and prepare for this time, this Second Pentecost (the Warning or Illumination …cta.) that will enable millions to return to their God, or meet and embrace (accept) Him for the first time. Can you feel the gratitude and love and excitement in My Heart for all to be accomplished? It was like this for Me as I contemplated and then approached My Crucifixion and Death on the Cross, all the while dreading the events necessary to obtain your Redemption and fulfill My Father's Will. Reread and contemplate these words, friends and companions in My Passion and Death and Resurrection. Allow them to penetrate to the deepest levels of your being by the special gifts of the Holy Spirit. Be renewed and cleansed again in My blood, My loving Wounds. Rejoice! YOU WERE LOST, BUT NOW ARE FOUND!'"

3/14, At Home: "Child of the Immaculate and Sorrowful Heart, I am Mary, Mother of all people. Child, give praise and thanks with me that we are able to visit once again. Let us call upon the Holy Spirit, my dear Spouse, for gifts of openness and attention to my words meant to encourage and comfort Our faithful people everywhere in the world:

'My dear ones of the world, I Mary, the Mother of God and your Mother, call out to you in love and gratitude for your fidelity and devotion to My Beloved Son and to me. See the intensity of the pain in their eyes, the swollen bellies of starving children, the victims of terrible floods, epidemics of virulent diseases in areas of ongoing poverty and extreme neglect. No one in the world should be living in these horrible conditions. These conditions will continue to worsen until entire nations die of disease so rampant, nothing can be done to save them. These conditions have existed for hundreds of years because of the greed and terrible evil in the hearts of leaders of too many powerful countries of the world. Only unimagined evil and hatred for others, different and less fortunate, could allow such an inhuman environment to exist. Only the lack of heart and soul, produced by Satan himself in his followers, could allow the entire world to degenerate to this level of cruelty and absence of any concern for God's people, the ones He created to simply love and be loved by Him.

HEAR THE CRY OF THE POOR, MY PEOPLE. Hear children weep, and infants sob and cry themselves to sleep in the exhaustion that results from chronic hunger. My children, these are your brothers and sisters who belong to the same world family as you do; who are loved by Our God in the same way you are; who were created to live in peace and harmony on the earth as you were. They are helpless to stop the invasion of greed that first creeps silently and then roars destructively across their land, destroying everything in its path. Allow your eyes and hearts to be opened by these tragedies existing in many places, most of which you know far too little about, by the designs of these same governments who will present these situations and ongoing disasters and killings as a reason for uniting the world under one government for the 'good and safety' of the world! Allow yourselves to be touched in the deepest part of your soul, your entire being, so much so, that you will act at once in defense and heartfelt outrage by sending mighty prayers and aid to these helpless victims of Satan's plans to destroy as many in the world as possible. I speak stern words to you in order to present a picture of the reality in which you live, My dearly loved ones. There is no rational excuse for the money that pours into sports arenas, sporting events and on and on for the gratification of the privileged in the world of which there are so many.

You are called to love the Lord, your God, with your whole heart, your whole soul, your whole mind and your whole strength, and your neighbor as yourself! (Matt. 22: 37-39) Hear the echo of My Jesus' words in your liturgy readings this first week of Lent.... 'As often as you did it to the least of your brethren, (feed the hungry, clothe the naked, etc.) you did it unto Me.' (Matt 25:40) Could anything be clearer, my people? Will you be taken joyfully into Heaven one day, or sent away with the words, 'Depart from Me, you accursed, into eternal fire' (Matt.25: 41) on your day of judgment? If you are generous with your time and self and wealth, you will find an honest comfort in My words, for you are found faithful and rich in good works. If you are selfish and mindless and unconcerned about the poverty so prevalent in the world and do nothing to help others, then these words, I pray, will be a challenge to your comfort and the proper encouragement to move you out of your complacency to become your brother's keeper, to do what you can to overcome the evil plans of Satan and soon to be experienced Antichrist. You will begin sincere and loving prayer now for the defeat of existing plans for world war, and the continued injustices and inequities between the rich and powerful and the weak and impoverished people, all created equal by God.

Oh my beloved ones, the darkness of evil descends and deepens. You reject these words as 'doom and gloom', my dear ones? Indeed they are meant to paint an honest picture of actual conditions in most of the rest of the world, and concrete plans of evil men and women everywhere. It is the evil one's doom and gloom of which I speak! I plead with you, beloved of my Heart, use this time of Lent to pray and fast and do penance to a greater degree than you ever thought possible, if you have the good health and strength to do so. When Jesus invites you to be united to Him through prayer and self discipline and generosity, He means for you to give as He gave, to live as He lived, to minister to His people, to share out of your abundance, to pray to the Father in order not to lose any of those He has sent to you at home and in the entire world. Feel my love for you, children. Feel my concern and sorrow for all who suffer so terribly on the earth. Feel the urgency I hope to convey at the shortness of time, the length of eternity and the need of so many RIGHT NOW! I hold you in my Heart, precious children, and I call out with a mother's heart and concern. Pour yourselves out for others, little dear ones, as My Son has poured Himself out for you! I am Mary, your loving and grateful Mother."

4/7, Jesus said: "Please people of this holy and very blessed area of your country, pray especially for patience for all Our faithful ones everywhere. At a time when waiting is becoming more difficult and fidelity a sheer act of will and trust, each of you needs (more than ever in your lives) a renewed strength and ability to await in joy and hope the Father's Will. WHEN ONE EVENT IS DELAYED, MY CHILDREN, ALL EVENTS ARE DELAYED AT THE SAME TIME. If you spend time in reflection on the Mercy of My Father in your own life, you will clearly see the benefits of receiving more time before events of a destructive nature begin. Know that you are responding very well and being turned into mighty warriors in the Father's plan to remove every vestige of evil from the world and ALL His children. Say often to yourselves, My sweet ones:

'I am a child of God, Who has created me in His Image to become more like Jesus Christ every day through the help and intercession of Mary, the Immaculate Mother.'

Continue to consecrate the world daily, especially the worst sinners. More than ever is the call from Heaven to be summed up simply: Pray, Trust, Surrender, Adore, Fast and Do Penance in preparation for the time when the Spirit of God pours Himself out to all who will accept His power and healing of conversion and reconciliation. Abandon your own will, your own plans for the future, and receive totally the Will of My Father for all your time and energy, becoming the perfect instrument of His Mercy and service to all the lost souls He will send to you. (Recently this thought has come to me through reading and listening to these messages: All this delay is not about our waiting for God, it's about His waiting for us to 'get it', to comply with His desires for us and the world. Perhaps I am the last one to discover this?)

"Remember, when you trust completely, it matters not when a promised event occurs or even when it doesn't. Continue to believe in the power and love of God. Continue to see each delay, each word... new or old... as the best for yourselves and for the whole world. Focus on Me, dearest ones of My Heart, not on frivolous activity that would distract or dilute your concentration on prayer and the sincere Consecration you make to My Mother and to Me. CHOOSE LIFE, CHILDREN. CHOOSE JOY. CHOOSE ME!! I love you so deeply, My Sacred Heart burns with longing and delight to accomplish your Baptism by Fire that you might become spotless lambs before the Throne of My Father. BE FILLED WITH HOPE. BE FILLED WITH PEACE. YOU ARE MINE! I am your sweet Jesus Who died for love of you."

4/23, Jesus said: "**New nations and new peoples will grow into a land blessed by the cleansing hand of God, and learn to praise and thank Him in the beauty of the new era of peace and purity**. There is so much suffering and loneliness ahead for Our people. They will need strength and love and encouragement again and again, as **years of hiding stretch into a long period of time filled with tedium and hardship. This will be the time of ultimate purification that will render Our faithful remnant cleansed and ready to be led into a renewed earth, as the renewed and Eucharistic people on it, in My Eucharistic Reign.** I have told you long ago that before you can lead, you must be strengthened and purified even more than those you will lead into My New Era of Peace and Purity. You have strength that allows you to understand the action of My Father's Will for you. This gives you the needed ability to surrender immediately and bounce back stronger and more convicted than ever of His Mercy and Love. This response on your part is only made possible by a special gift from the Father Who is filled with great love and gratitude for your instant acquiescence to each event He desires that brings you most quickly to a place of greater obedience. As more events in your life occur, you will see even more clearly why all this suffering is necessary at this time. Do, please My little one, be at peace now. All WILL come to be, daughter. You must believe more than ever now. I am Jesus Who has died and risen to save you from death."

5-2, Jesus said: "Please tell Our beloved ones who gather to pray, for **this waiting and wondering is but a shadow compared to the time in hiding that you will spend avoiding the Antichrist under the protective Mantle of My dearest Mother!** You are all so blessed in the world today, living at exciting times of struggle and pain; but also partaking of the many graces showered from Heaven, as Our specially chosen servants are honored by Heaven and Earth!

(Many of the Lord's servants of bygone years are being elevated to Sainthood by John Paul II …cta.) Your beloved Holy Father and leader of millions of souls, responds to the Holy Spirit to bring many of Our outstanding examples of an extraordinary degree of love and obedience to a place of honor in the hearts and minds and annals of the Church. A good soldier is faithful to a regimented lifestyle expected by the 'Commander of the camp!' **A true test of trust and faith is the ongoing observance of repeated drills and exercises, in spite of fatigue or less than obvious results! Hear My words, My warriors. Build up your gifts and defensive maneuvers by repetitious prayers and pleading, all the while becoming the expert fighting machines needed to ultimately defeat the evil in the world and in all its people."**

5/3, "My beloved children, I am your Mother of Sorrows and of Joy. What a glorious Feast in Heaven: Mercy Sunday, celebrated all over the world in greater numbers than ever with such joy, such hope, such rejoicing in all of your hearts; such rejoicing in Heaven! How beautiful was this day for Our beloved Faustina. How radiant she was; how filled with joy and smiles that never ended, that were never finished until the celebration is done! Always, my children, with a great celebration of this kind, there is an Octave of ongoing celebration, and I remind you of this Octave, for you are still celebrating this new Saint, this precious one of Ours, who is such a precious one of yours, I know. Rejoice and thank Our Father for the great gifts you are being given, for the opportunity to share the joy of Heaven and all the gifts that are being given at this time. Absorb the joy, children, the happiness that reigns in Heaven this night; for soon, for what seems like a long while, you will not know joy. You will not feel happiness, and you will need to think back upon these days, upon this time; and remember and rejoice, once again, that you have been given so many gifts. I am so very close to you now. I hide you in my Immaculate Heart, and I purify you with special gifts this night to celebrate this great victory in Heaven for Our Faustina and for all of you, servants and lovers of Divine Mercy. Thank you, children, for all you do, for the many ways you serve and love. You know I love you, children everywhere. Think of it every moment of every day, for I am with you, loving you and protecting you."

5-5-00, Jesus said: "My beloved people of the world, I am your God and Father, calling out to you with words of the greatest love for each of you. My faithful ones, you are about to enter a time of tribulation, unlike any the world has ever seen. Part of this suffering will be the absence of apparitions of the Most Holy and Blessed Virgin, Mother of God, and all public messages of words from Heaven given to chosen messengers these many years. There will be some places continuing to receive these gifts, while others remain centers of prayer, but seeing an end of messages. This is My Will for you now; but also a sign to you that My Plan escalates and moves forward. You are ready to endure the hardships that must develop, as I begin to cleanse the world of evil that you, too, must experience: tremendous changes brought about by the plans of Satan to destroy

My children and all of My Creation (that will also fulfill Scripture). You are strong and willing, My people, yet few in numbers and fewer in the future, as belief in the Name of Jesus, your Messiah and King, brings with it greater dangers to life itself. You will see martyrs. Some of you will be martyrs; but all will (at least) leave your possessions behind and flee into protected refuges until the return of My Son in Whom always, I Am well pleased! My gratitude to you and for you is only surpassed by My love for you and eagerness to share whatever power and gift you will need to continue to live out My Will for you and all My lost ones I will send to you. You will become more excited and more believing as you finally see these promises fulfilled. I speak to you as faithful members of My Perfect Will, who will be filled with joy and amazement as you see and are allowed to mediate many miracles of healing and conversion.

The Apostles and Martyrs (of the era following My Son's Ascension to Heaven) pray for all of you at every moment. You will believe and trust and shout for joy in the midst of struggle and pain and the fight against evil and despair. I ask you to **pray for each other's perseverance from this moment on. Pray for the response of as many as possible to the very great showering of the gifts of Our Spirit on the world. Pray in reparation for the sins of so many to whom I wish to give My Mercy. Beg mercy for the world, My own. Beg for an unflagging trust and conviction for each other in spite of long years of waiting that will contain many victories for the Antichrist and sorely try your patience. Continue to fight against your weaknesses and vulnerabilities, My beloved victims of love.** I am honored by all of you who accept My grace, My love, My need of you, My plan for your salvation. I bless each of you in the Name of the Triune God: your Strength, your Goal, your Protection. Believe these words from your God and Father of Mercy and Love."

5/24, "My dear ones, welcome again to this night of prayer. I am your Jesus of Mercy Who comes this night to bring you good news. I also bring you perseverance. Along the way, I will gift you to allow you and help you to persevere. From now on I ask you to **begin your prayers with praise**. Already some of you do this; but for the most part, praise is not something all of Our children do enough of and you, My children, you are praying more in reparation of sin. You cannot imagine how many souls will need to be prayed for in this way, for mercy will be given to very many and **you must make reparation for their sins**. You must continue to pray for each other and support each other, for there will come a day when these events are suddenly upon you!"

5/31, These are all also for the entire world, who read and pray: "My dearest ones, I am your most Holy Spirit, the Spirit of God, the Spirit of love and joy and peace; the Spirit who dwells within you in power and strength. I come on this very special night to tell you how happy I am with you, how pleased, how grateful, how overjoyed I am as the Spirit of love in your lives. As soldiers in the army of My beloved spouse, the Holy Virgin, you will see many battles. You will know that you are energized by Me, by My power. I am sent this night to encourage you to remain convicted in all you have come to believe, in all you have come to understand. This night I give you new wisdom, new knowledge, new understanding. It is not as though you are suddenly filled with new knowledge or bursts of understanding this very night; but as events begin to unfold now, you will understand them in a deeper way, that you might live them in a greater peace and trust for all of the words that you have been given.

Your future, My children, fills with amazing events; with miracles, new healing and conversions, in numbers you can only strive to imagine. Believe My words! Remember, you will be able to handle every event, every difficulty, every struggle and even every attack of the evil one, for I am with you always and you are filled with My light, with My love and strength. Part of the new knowledge you are given this night will take you through any event**, knowing that you will overcome with the power of God**. As the Word of God that is sent to the earth fulfills what it is sent to do, so your prayers that are sent now to Heaven fulfill all that you request. Believe in the mighty power of your prayers. Expect miracles, My faithful and obedient ones. Accept My love now and My presence within you. Even though you hear these words, you have no idea of the great gifts you are being given and how much you are loved."

6/14, "I am your Jesus of Mercy, here to share My words. My children, you will suffer much! You will be ridiculed more and rejected more. It will become more difficult to persevere, and the evil one will incite many to think that you cannot trust these messages or this messenger. The evil one will incite many to attack you at every turn, to try to undermine your commitment, your conviction, your consecration. There will be sickness and fatigue that you will battle. Although it will be minor, it will wear you down, My children. Be on guard for this. Be on guard for the attacks of Satan through many of those who are close to you now. I say this, children, not to frighten you, but to give you an understanding and a preparation for the days ahead. This will be true of prayer groups everywhere, for Satan is raging at your successful prayer, your successful commitment to My Mother.

My dear ones, it is the Father's Will that you receive many new gifts this night, for these attacks will begin shortly. You will find more ridicule, more who scoff at your faithfulness and the many hours of prayer you are giving to Me, to My Father, to Our Spirit, to Our Mother. You will begin to realize more how much I suffered for you, what it was like for Me when I did go into the desert to be with My Father. There were times when I could hardly make it to My destination, so weak and sorrowful was I. Angels would come to minister to Me, and My Father would speak loving and encouraging words and fill Me with new strength and the ability to continue, for there was such hatred in the hearts of so many. There is hatred today that you have not yet seen. I tell you there will be Angels who minister to you along the way! Believe this for all of Our faithful ones everywhere. The time is coming soon when you would be unable to continue another step without this kind of Heavenly intervention and help and strength. All of Heaven prays with the knowledge of what is ahead for you. Their love pours out upon you: all the Angels, all the Saints, most especially My Apostles (My first followers and disciples,) all of the holy women and holy men just like yourselves. You are turning into faithful ones, just like they! Truly, you are becoming centers for mercy yourself! Truly, you are becoming like My Mother's Mantle that will be a refuge for so many, a place of hiding and healing for so many! There are no words for My gratitude and My love for you. I weep with joy over you. How precious you are indeed in My eyes. Be at peace, My little ones everywhere, about everything and anyone and anything. Continue to persevere at this level of strength and prayer and faith and trust. You are mighty warriors, and I love you. Amen."

6/16, "My dearest child, I, your Jesus, wish to continue our visit. My words for the world will be those of My Father, given for the instruction of all. Pray again to Our Spirit with Me and with dear Mary, My Mother. Here now, My dear one, are words from My Father for all to hear:

'My dearest daughter of My Will, I am your God and Father, your Creator, the One Who sustains your life at every moment with My Love and Mercy. Events in the world that will result in an ultimate reshaping of the earth and its people could NOT BEGIN until each of you (I count on) had reached the appropriate place of change and renewal in My Son, Jesus, and in My Will. This HAS COME TO PASS to the desired and necessary degree in all those specially chosen to lead and teach and encourage all those who will listen after the minds of Our people everywhere are illuminated to the exact state of their souls, as seen by their Triune God. The plans of all who are involved in following Satan in the End Times before the return of My Son (to complete the fulfillment of all of Scripture until His defeat of the Antichrist and his followers, Satan and his demons and the beginning of the New Era of peace and purity,) begin to take shape in your media reports and in plans to make public international changes. The events about to erupt on the earth will result in an enormous amount of destruction, and My people will be moved quickly to repent and return to Me. Another reason for increased prayer now is the nearness of these events. (Please remember that, in all of these words, there is the new direction for us first, which takes a long time to adjust to, along with all of the personal suffering we must experience and learn how to 'handle'... and so a lot more time goes by in waiting... cta.) A new direction begins for all of you who are faithful to Me and the call of Mary, the Immaculate Queen. If you are truly praying, My beloved people, you are no longer plagued with doubts about My Plan to save My people who accept My help and grace and mercy. Thank you again a "million times", dearest ones, for being faithful and trusting. Your hearts are melting in the Heat of My Love and delight for you. 'Tomorrow' yet another visit such as this will continue."

6/21, "My dearest, dearest children, I am your Mother of Sorrows and Joy. I am your companion at every moment of every day. I am your Mother who loves you, not just with a motherly love. I love each of you as my dearest sister, my dearest brother, my dearest companion in the world. By that I mean that you are never alone in this very difficult world. I am with you, remember, bringing you solace and comfort; and the very fact of my presence with you, my children, is giving you joy without an awareness of your own. Look at every occurrence, every little annoyance, every little irritability that life brings every day as nothing compared to the great gift of Our Presence with you. Realize, my dear ones, that this is a gift beyond the ordinary gifts of Jesus' Presence in your heart, of my presence in your heart ... that WE ARE ACTUALLY WITH YOU. You just cannot see Us, children. We ARE there! This MUST lead you to begin living more completely in an atmosphere of mercy and joy, an environment of peace, an environment of recollection. I am telling you this night that it is possible to do your chores, to clean your homes, to cook your meals, to wash your clothes, to shop for all the staples you need, and still be very recollected in Our Presence! Yes, my dear ones, this will take more work on your part. It will take energy and concentration and focus, but it can happen for you because the Father has decreed this gift for you out of His wonderful love, His great mercy, His appreciation for each of you everywhere who pray and listen to Our words.

I accompanied my little Jesus everywhere He went, as He was growing stronger and wiser and learning and traveling about. I was always at His side for protection, but also to answer His questions, to give Him proper explanations and understandings given to me by my Beloved Spouse, the Holy Spirit. I WISH TO DO THIS FOR YOU, MY LITTLE ONES! Ask me questions, children; not just on your knees in Church, or by your bed at night ... ANYTIME! You ARE my little ones, just as my Jesus was and is my Little One. I love you in the same way and wish to teach you and guide you in the same way. It will give me such joy, my children. It will give me an opportunity to be closer to you, that we might be more united and become as one, and I will help you love Jesus more, as I do! Rejoice, for as you hear this good news, you realize a great gift is being given to you and it is only for you to accept it! I long to see you healed completely, and strengthened and filled with the knowledge and wisdom of the Holy Spirit. My children, let us help each other. Let us give each other joy! My Beloved Son sends His peace to you this night. Send each aggravation to the foot of the Cross. **Cast out every irritability in the Name of My Beloved Jesus.** Stay close to me. I am close to you. There is so much we will do together!"

6/22, "My dearest child, I am your God and Father, speaking these words as Jesus delivers them: 'Each of you is more united to the Communion of Saints! What a lovely phrase to describe the wonderful synergy of grace and prayer directed towards the salvation of as many souls as possible, as a glorious fulfillment of My Will for all who dwell upon the earth. No one can even imagine how much help and mercy are given by their God, and think most of what they do is a matter of their own initiation, instead of realizing that everything (each of you has) is a direct gift from Me! I need to be praised by a grateful people! Your praise and gratitude adds nothing to My stature. **It is YOU who benefit from this call to you from Heaven; you whose being is enhanced, transformed, made to grow in all the gifts of the Spirit and virtues of My Son.** It is you, the people of

God, who grow in the fulfillment of all you are created to be, as a child of God and heir to Heaven. My people, if you would only believe all the words given in the Commandments and Beatitudes and My promises of unimagined love and mercy and protection from evil. There would be immediate change in the entire world, and no longer would the danger of the Antichrist and his followers threaten your future! There has always been punishment for sin. The understanding was given immediately upon the sin of Adam and Eve that life on earth would now be filled with struggle to survive and many painful experiences. To sin (seriously) is to choose eternal death, My people. To be obedient children of My Desire and Will is to choose life and healing and wholeness NOW, and everlasting life and happiness in the bliss of Paradise, the Kingdom of Heaven.

Again and again, you are given the gift of forgiveness when you seek it, when you resolve not to sin again in ways that bring instant death to your souls, when you turn to Me and surrender to My Perfect Will for you, and remain in My grace and mercy forever. Millions of people throughout the ages have accepted My gifts of freedom and forgiveness, and are living in the joy of unity with Me in Heaven for all Eternity. Some wait still to be finally cleansed and brought into Paradise. Others, far too many, My beloved ones who read or hear and listen to My words, never repent, never learn to accept My Love and promises of mercy, and choose eternal death in a place of horrible suffering FOREVER.

Ponder My words, people of the earth, and return to Me today. I am offering you true freedom, true peace, true happiness forever with Me, your Creator and God, the Almighty and All Powerful One Who waits to share all My love and power with you forever, My beloved children, FOREVER! Listen with your hearts, with your intellect that allows you to recognize truth; to know that the God Who created every living being, the Universe and all it contains, is speaking with a Heart and Words filled with a loving desire to save you from harm, from pain and the heartbreak the world (this kingdom of Satan) will always give; to save you from death and give you the strength NOW to accept the means NOW. Receive the gift of salvation made possible for you by My Own Beloved Son Who suffered and died a Passion and Death in agony to obtain for you the gift of Redemption, the possibility of attaining your salvation in spite of your own unworthiness. Call upon Our Spirit TODAY, My people. Ask for a firm desire to return to Me and remain faithful for the rest of your lives. Ask, My precious ones, and a change of heart WILL BE GIVEN TO YOU, a firm commitment to My promise to be your God, that you might be My people. COME BACK TO ME, DEAREST PEOPLE. **That's all there is to it!**

Seek Me, My precious children. You WILL FIND ME and receive the strength to remain with Me forever! I am your Loving Father. Do not let a life of sin keep you away from Me. Do not accept from Satan any more lies or life threatening suggestions. No matter how evil your former, or even present behavior, return to Me; ask My forgiveness; expect My Mercy to be given. Anticipate an eternity of joy and peace to result from these choices. Expect miracles, My dearest children of My Own Creation. Reread these words. Share them with everyone. Please, act quickly. Do not delay. Believe that I love you. I wish to shower you with healing, with peace, with a renewed heart and soul and mind and **even body**. I wait in joyful hope for each day you spend with Me, My loved ones, living more deeply in My Divine and Perfect Will."

6/26, "Dearest child, please write. The words, I, your Jesus, speak now are from My Father. Peace is only found in Me, little one. The real battle has yet to begin! Here now are words from My Father to continue His visit with words for the world.

'My dear child, begin to come into My Will for you, once again. There are so many new things to reveal this day. I am your God and Father, little dear one. Nothing and no one can compare to Me. 'My people everywhere: I am come, once again, to plead with you for a return to Me, your God and Creator, not in the spirit of the law only, but especially in the Spirit of Love. DESIRE to be with Me in prayer, one with My Will for you and the entire world. I tell you, nothing of the world is important! Nothing else, save union with Jesus and with Me and Our Holy Spirit will ready your heart and soul for the struggles ahead. When you are emptied of worldly pastimes and pursuits, you are free to serve My desires for you and the needs of others. YOU MUST PRACTICE, MY DEAR, DEAR FAITHFUL ONES ... LOVING! You must realize that this sort of love and service and mercy to your brothers and sisters is NOT FOUND in your human nature (your worldly self) in a very great degree because of Original Sin (the inclination to sin, and gratification of self) without being united to the power and strength and goodness of your Triune God. This takes time. Allow yourselves to be emptied, to be filled in an ongoing, ever increasing way. It is NOT YOUR virtue or gifts that enable your progress in your return journey towards Me and My Kingdom. Only the gifts and grace I give to you: the goodness, the changed heart, the reconciliation you need to desire Me, to desire to do My Will to become a child of Mary and follower of Jesus.

To be a child, a follower, a holy one of God entails an acceptance of the initial graces of your Baptism and a living out of My Commandments in joy and love; to go beyond this basic way of life and accept every request of My Will for you personally, as recognized in each event of your life as meekly but joyfully as possible, always saying 'yes' and accepting MORE! This is the way of the Father for an obedient child. Your ARE learning to walk, My faithful ones. Now I am calling you to RUN, that I may soon teach you to FLY! Believe these words, My highly blessed and favored ones. You have a future filled with awesome gifts, miracles and healing. I need your 'YES'. I need your surrender. I need your joyful acceptance of preparation NOW, that you might fly later! Reread and ponder My words. I am your loving and merciful God. I offer you My power, My gifts, My strength. You MUST return to Me totally, dears ones. WILL YOU ACCEPT?"

6/28, Jesus said: "My daughter, it is My Father's desire to speak briefly once more, so I ask you to pray again to Our Spirit.

'My people of the world, I am your Merciful God and Father, children. Are not all people moved to speak tender, loving words to their children? Because of My great and merciful love for each of you, I deem it necessary to speak Myself now to give you a last warning before serious developments within the governing structures of all countries. I wish to give you a last direct call (as the end of this age draws near) with My loving guidance and reminders and promises. My dearest faithful ones, I have such wonderful plans for you, for the entire earth and for all who accept My Will and Commandments in their lives. You cannot possibly know that which you are saying NO to, or that which you contemplate saying YES to!

On the one hand, there is no power of your imagination that could embrace the miracles and healing and joy-filled times ahead; or the beauty of a renewed earth without evil and temptations, and full of peace and tenderness and joy. On the other hand, there is not one particle of your being that could imagine the terrible suffering planned by the Antichrist and the destruction of the earth that would return it to the darkness and chaos of a pre-human state. My dearest ones, you cannot wait to be convinced by the intellectual criteria you set down for My messengers, or the fulfillment of My words. Delays in events are also designed to bring out the worst characteristics hidden within you, My people, that you might better see and recognize your pride and arrogance, and bring them to Reconciliation.

How will mapping out all the events with answers (you think you have) save you from suffering or a difficult future? Only I, your God and Creator, can defeat the plans of Satan that will begin so shortly to unfold before the world. It is good to have the ability to gather information from many sources, but please, do not continue to batter and reject those who continue to share the words of Heaven despite the increasingly difficult and harsh treatment they receive from so many. **None of you has any clear understanding of the heartache and pain caused by those who think theirs is the only mission or ministry or blessed call on this earth. All who have been vocal in helping to form the beliefs of others by condemnation and ridicule and criticism must bring that to Reconciliation quickly.** This activity, this judgmentalism must end, for it is causing your hearts to close and harden again, to become callous and cold and very arrogant. I see and hear you, people of My longing. I tell you, if you are not seeking the help of Our Sprit to know your hidden sins, to 'see' your own behavior, to hear your attitudes, you have no place in My Kingdom, for you are already deeply and firmly planted in your own kingdom! There are tears in this plea from a loving Father Who desires to transform you into a more perfect Image of Jesus, My Beloved Son. Do not be caught sleeping when the Bridegroom arrives! These are not harsh words, My people. They are loving words from One Who loves you and wishes to save you from your greatest enemy, your SELF."

7/2, Jesus said: "My dear child, please let us continue the words of My Father: 'My dearest faithful ones who read and listen to all the words of Heaven in these critical times in your history: BEWARE OF STRANGERS BEARING

GIFTS! BE ON GUARD AGAINST SMOOTH SOUNDING WORDS OF FLATTERY. DEFEND AGAINST WHATEVER WOULD DISTRACT YOU FROM YOUR NEW LEVEL OF SERVICE TO THE WORLD THROUGH PRAYER AND DEED. Protect your hearts, My beloved, against those who would divide them with plans for your time, for your energy, your love. Satan, the great enemy of mankind, is using every subtle means to ensnare you, trap you once again, entangle you in webs that catch you and hold you fast. These hot days of summer are a temptation to take life and responsibilities and commitments a little (and often a lot) less seriously; to treat the loving words of warning I have sent for many years now as a matter of work from which you also need a vacation! I remind you and reiterate, evil takes no vacation; but is always looking for new ways to entice you, to lead you in a direction that seems good at first, but quickly disintegrates into a trap that has the power to hold you fast, to dilute your first love, your commitment to the holy Mother and your Triune God. Remain calm, My dear ones, but do not be lulled to sleep or stupefied by the false peace that seems to exist in the world.

Remember the quiet that descends just before the storm erupts! See the sun and warmth as the symbols of the loving embrace and peace of your Creator God that is all the while renewing your strength and increasing the heat of your passionate love for Me that MUST accompany the degree of service to which you are called. Oh, My dearest people, how much you are loved and appreciated and cherished and needed for the days of upheaval ahead for the world. Enjoy these present days in the constant Presence of My sustaining love, of Jesus' embrace, of life wrapped in the protection of Mary's Mantle and filled with the gifts of the Holy Spirit. THIS IS THE KINGDOM WITHOUT END, My beloved ones.

Do not be distracted, or leave your prayers and fasting and penances; your daily Mass and Eucharist; your frequent reflection and Reconciliation at home, while you hurry off for a 'break', a time away from your newly found relationship with My Beloved Son, your Heavenly Mother, the Spirit of Love and Joy, My Plan and Will for you! Make time for prayer amidst the summer activity, and realize that all is gift from Me, your Father and Creator. Praise and thanksgiving is as necessary a part of your daily routine as breathing, as food and water are to your growth. I love you, My adorable children. Believe it. Count on it. Trust it. Thrive on it. Be with Me forever and ever: NOW, LATER, HERE, THERE, every moment in the freedom and joy of children dancing under the loving gaze of their Father Whom they adore!"

7/12, **Beginning of *External Locutions to group via Carol unless otherwise noted**

"My dear ones, I, your Jesus of Mercy, come this night with My arms overflowing with mercy; with My Heart pouring out mercy and forgiveness, nourishment and peace upon each of you and your families. There is much talk of a comet. Mention of a comet has been made to many of My messengers in the world. AND, MY DEAR ONES, THERE IS A COMET! Again, when a possible danger is mentioned, the possibility of diverting this danger is always offered, and your prayers are the vehicles of the Will of My Father. Your prayers determine which path this comet will take, for it is headed this way, My little ones. It has been sighted by astronomers, scientists, those who's knowledge and education allow them to discover, to track, to explain. I tell you this tonight because many, many prayers are needed; and you are My warriors. You are mighty in deed and strength.

You cannot believe how few remain faithful. It was written, and it is thus. You have no idea how much you will do for My Father by way of service and ministry. Believe that you are strong, for it is this strength My people will need most, even Our faithful ones. It is most natural to be frightened and I remind you, THERE IS NOTHING TO FEAR. For whatever occurs, I have promised you safety and protection. Do not forget this. I have said you will see many miracles. The time for miracles begins: necessary miracles, life changing, world-changing miracles. I need you, My dear ones. I need you with Me every moment in your hearts and minds and spirits: with all your might, all your strength, all your desire. You have a world full of brothers and sisters. My Presence is enough! Come with Me, My little ones, stay close to My Heart. Stay wrapped in My arms. Pray for each other more. I love you. We will be victorious in spite of every obstacle, every event. Be at peace, My children. DO NOT BE AFRAID, BUT REJOICE!"

*A spoken message through Carol, as opposed to a written one received internally by Carol and written down. All the following messages will be spoken ones at her prayer gathering unless noted otherwise.

7/19, "My Children, I am the Holy Spirit of God. You will be leaders of Our people. You will be a sign of hope, each one of you and everyone who comes to pray in this place. Many of Our people everywhere are faithful ones and will, of course, be leaders as well. This leadership will be a quiet leading. Lead by example, lead with love, lead with service, lead in patience, lead in forgiveness and mercy. How you shine with the Light of Jesus! How Heaven rejoices over each of you, and sings hosannas to the Father in your name. And, yes, your names are chanted before His Throne. Believe this! Believe that you have persevered well, that you have overcome yourselves in so many ways, that you are gifted far beyond your knowledge or your understanding. Be happy for each other, My dear ones. Be happy for each other's gifts. Let joy, peace and gratitude fill you and remain with you. Let nothing disturb this within you now. Practice this equanimity. These are the things that strengthen you, that give you a backbone of steel, that prepare you for war. Again remember you have become mighty warriors, and praise the Father. Be a person of gratitude. I fill you with the fire of love, the fire to serve and to care for the needs of others, to forget about yourselves and your own needs or discomforts, your own desires. Oh My dear ones, how healed you will be once you are serving to this degree, at this level. Rejoice! Give thanks, give praise, be a source of joy. Everyone who meets you knows of My Presence within you; knows that your spirit is guided by Me. Thank the Father for bringing you to this level of holiness; and look forward to service and new joy, new compassion and new healing. I love you, My dear ones. I am the Spirit of Love. Be filled now with all of Who I am!"

7/26, "Dearest Children, it is I, your loving Mother, who has come to speak this night to your spirit, your heart, your mind and to your strength. Oh my beloved ones, how could I stay away? What love you have in your hearts for me, for my Son, for Our mighty Father and Creator and for my Beloved Spouse, the most Holy Spirit. What vessels of mercy you have become. Believe it when I tell you that St. Faustina is here with me, sending you blessings and kisses. She is so grateful for your devotion to her and to the Divine Mercy of God. Each of you is a special vessel of mercy united with St. Faustina by a special gift of the Father this night. All will be very well, my little ones. Never, for an instant, be afraid; never, ever, my dear ones. You are wrapped so tightly in my mantle and protected so totally in my Immaculate Heart. I love you. Great mercy is being poured out upon you now. Accept it, children. Steep yourselves in mercy. Amen."

8/3, Our Loving Father said: "My dearest one, please write My words given for your protection and comfort. I am your Lord and your God, speaking by means of a special gift for you and all My faithful people. The summer days hurry to a close of the season when young ones will return to school. The carefree routine of sunshine and sand, games and camps, days filled with play and exercises leave them with renewed vigor, renewed anticipation of yet another year full of challenges and choices and decisions. More and more you will see freedoms removed as the Antichrist displays his power through new laws and restrictions and requirements. All of you will know and recognize immediately what has occurred. As changes are enacted, freedom of travel and movement will be surrounded **by certain restrictions which render you unable to comply with new circumstances that require special passes or cards. Finally, the implantation of a chip will be required in each person in the world who desires to continue life in the world.** My faithful ones, you have been repeatedly warned of the need to prepare for a time of danger and great change in your lives. THAT TIME IS HERE.

If you have allowed delays to turn you away; if the absence of fulfillment of your own expectations has caused you to become more critical of those who deliver the words of your Triune God and Holy Mother; if you have not remained faithful to the requests of Heaven, but have turned away in disgust and joined the hardened hearts of the world once again, you are NOT PREPARED OR STRENGTHENED to the degree that will bring you through this time of struggle and grief. You will not have the grace needed to walk away from the offers of an easier way to get along, to be part of the great progress offered by government leaders. You look for a message without struggle, without pain, without difficulty or discomfort on your part. How could this be, when My Own Son lived a life of poverty and struggle and hard work and rejection? Life on this earth with all its comforts and gold and possessions is not the way of My Beloved Jesus Whom you profess to follow. Those who are truly following Him are experiencing inner turmoil, challenges of every kind, increase of temptations and the lure of the enticements of the world.

If you have not developed a loving relationship with your God and Mary, the Immaculate One; if fear has been your motive for prayer and you have not allowed this fear to be replaced by increased trust; if you have not accepted the cleansing fire of Our Spirit, the love of Jesus and the graces and virtues of dear Mary, you are not in the frame of mind and spirit to love Us to the point of total surrender to My Will for you, My plan for the salvation of the entire world, of the obedience required of a soldier in the Army of Mary Immaculate.

Unless a total consecration is made daily to the Two Hearts and a dedication and devotion to live all the requests of Heaven given by the holy Virgin, you cannot survive all that is about to occur in the world by order of the New World Order governments everywhere. I watch your behavior, hear your words and see your disdain with a great sadness. I see the annihilation of brother by brother that has reached the millions, and the coldness of hearts dedicated to ruling the world without their God and Creator. Man has always been impudent and proud, but never to this degree of hatred of decent values that escalates minute by minute. You, who think you are prepared for anything, will be horrified at the evil that is about to erupt and flow like molten lava destroying everything in its path. My people, get over your judgmental and critical attacks based on suppositions and false data. Allow Me to continue to be the Lord and Master and Life Giver Who sustains your very existence.

Think, My beloved ones. Stop, look, listen to the mayhem that grows and roars in every corner of the earth. Pay attention to all the signs that are being given, prophecies being fulfilled, lives being discarded and weather anomalies wreaking havoc and fire in your own country. I speak with sorrow to you who have had every opportunity to be prepared for what arrives. When you say: we've heard that one before, and laugh off new warnings, a new call for conversion in your hearts; it is yourself you are destroying, not My faithful messengers who seek only to be obedient to the request to deliver the words of Heaven. Do not turn away now, My spoiled children. Do not give up on your God and His plans; but remember those who follow My Son will suffer as He did as **a servant of the needs of others**, pouring yourselves out as He did and does for you. Believe that My words are designed to protect you, to stop you from destructive behavior, to share My gifts and power with you in a time unlike any other in your history. People of the earth have become more and more rebellious throughout the ages.

The amount of evil in the entire world defies My Will for your good at every turn; demands My response to purify you quickly and in a way that is best for each of you. Your very rejection of delays, meant to strengthen and cleanse you, is a sign of the times, a sign of the great need you have of ongoing conversion and rescue from the strong clutches of Satan. Nothing is impossible or unknown to Me, and I tell you, each development or what you see as lack of development, has been **designed to expose the anger, the haughty attitudes, the lack of humility and obedient nature present in most of My people.**

Listen to Truth, My beloved ones. Remain faithful to a routine of prayer and reflection, quiet time before My gift of Beloved and Obedient and Hidden Jesus Present in the Blessed Sacrament of your Altar. There is no other way to reach Heaven, but to live in the constant Presence of Jesus and Mary and the many Angels I have given to the truly faithful ones who hear these words and live My plan for your salvation. Scripture once again, I remind you, must be fulfilled; and this requires the power of Satan in your world to reach the present level. Sin is the result of so many giving in to self-gratification in a life of greed and lust for power and possessions.

You must look into your hearts, My dear people, and see with the help of the Holy Spirit and through the eyes Mary, the coldness that creeps into every corner, as you allow doubt and fear and ridicule to rebuild walls of defense against the warmth and healing power of My Son's love for you. Of course, it is difficult to persevere! It is only possible for your God to persevere in love for you when you turn away, when your behavior creates an atmosphere (in which) only the love of God could continue to give mercy; to continue to offer another chance to be forgiven; to be cleansed and be transformed into the likeness of Jesus, My Beloved Son. I offer you Life on My terms, My dear ones! Will you continue to reject My Perfect Will for you personally and collectively? My terms are filled with offers of love, healing, peace and protection and the promise of an Eternity in Paradise. Won't you accept My terms and discover the peace and joy and trust that will allow you to rise above the earthly struggle to live and serve in the protection of My arms, of My Kingdom now? Pray to My Spirit that you can accept these words, My beloved ones, everywhere. Do not listen to the disdain of the evil one. Listen to Truth, and live! I bless you, My beloved ones. Accept My gifts, My words, My love."

8/9, "Dearest children, I am your Holy and Immaculate Mother, and I praise the Father for allowing me to be with you again this night to speak. I come to share my love and to tell you how much the gratitude of all in Heaven is raised to the Father, for you are each a little miracle, my dear ones! When you answered my call, you were not quite as prayerful as you are now. You were not quite as docile. Your hearts were not listening then as they are now. I mention these things, my children, to encourage you, to help you to remember and notice how much you have changed. There will be many changes. Change is a word that people reject. It is a word that tends to frighten many. It is about control, my children. There has been enough evil. There has been enough destruction. The Father has just begun to display His anger and His rejection of the murder in the hearts of so many of His people, His children. Oh my dear ones, stay close to me. Stay close to each other. How well you have learned to handle adversity, humiliation, obstacles that you overcome with ease now. Truly, you are model soldiers. Rejoice, my children, rejoice in peace. Praise and thank the Father for all of this."

FOR MERCY'S SAKE!

9/16, Jesus said: "My dearest children, My dear ones, you know in your own hearts, you still need much healing! And so My Mercy pours forth upon you. Rejoice, once again, My little ones, for you are being highly blest this night. How happy you have made Me in honoring My Mother with so much love for her great feast; for the remembrance of her wonderful, glorious Assumption into Heaven. Recall with Me once again, My children, how all of Heaven filled with shouts of joy. The Angels sang like never before and joy rang through the heavens, more than ever could be imagined, My children. There was gratitude in the hearts of everyone present for the final return of My beloved Mother and yours. Picture this, My dear ones: My Mother, so beautifully gowned and crowned; so radiant with joy and gratitude to the Father; so filled with love; so humble and shy before the great love, the hosannas of all in Heaven. I tell you it was the brightest day ever seen in Heaven. I wish you to share this knowledge, this lovely mental and spiritual picture, and to keep it closely guarded in your heart forever. One day you will see us face to face. And before that, many times, you will catch glimpses of My Mother when it is necessary for your strength, for your perseverance, for your continuing joy. But until you come to Heaven, you will never see the radiance that exists, the beauty of My Mother glorified. Long for this day, My children. Let it be a goal: a motive for prayer, for fidelity, for perseverance. Allow it to give you strength. Allow it to be your joy. My Mother is My joy! The Will of My Father is Our joy; and it must be yours, My dear ones.

How I wish you could hear Me saying every day, every moment, as I do: My dear little ones, be brave, be strong, be loving, be merciful, for I love you; and I cannot wait for the day when I hold you in My arms ... forever! My children, be healed by these words. Be encouraged by them and by My love. Believe in My words, My little ones. You are precious, more precious than diamonds. I fill you again with My Peace and new joy. Return this joy to Me through the heart of My Mother and, together, we will take your joy to My Father in Heaven. Remember My love every moment. Amen, My children, amen."

Note: Some people have asked if these words are only for the prayer group. I believe that all messages are for everyone. When a message seems to be specifically for one group, it is still to be shared, since we belong to the One Body, and every message always contains words of encouragement, and some 'how to' phrases, and the wonderful loving appreciation for all God's children who are faithful. Everyone can learn and benefit from any words from Heaven. They are not exclusive with love and patience and mercy. These messages are never shared in order to boast, but to just plain share the joy of a Heavenly Presence, and as a motive to pray more and live in the ways that are suggested... cta.

8/23 "My dear ones, I am your Jesus of Mercy, come this night. My children, thank you for coming to pray, this most important of all your gifts of your entire mission, of all the requests of Heaven. I hear you, children, say at times, I've done enough for today. My dear ones, I understand your fatigue, believe Me, most certainly I do, but there is never enough prayer. Reading scripture, My children, is prayer. Reading My messages, all the messages of Heaven, is prayer. Sitting in quiet reflection, My little, dear ones, is prayer. Remember now it is not for you to do but just to be. Be with Me, My children. I am with you. Be aware of My Presence at every moment. This will help you more than you can imagine, of course. My dear ones, I am like and AM a lover, who wants every good thing for His beloved. You will be leaders in ways you cannot imagine yet. There is a certain mystery when I mention all of the things you are not aware of yet. This is as it should be, My children. A lover keeps loving secrets about the gifts he has planned for the future, and so it is with My Father and Myself and Our Spirit. Let gratitude overwhelm you, that you are loved so much by your God and your holy Mother. Gifts and graces are being given to you and all of Our faithful ones more than ever in history for this great number of people. Surely, one suspects something is up! Is this not true, My little ones?

My Mother has told you in the past that followers of Mine work long hours, work hard and have little sleep. This sounds very difficult, but I have promised you the help you need. And I have promised that this will unite you to Me, to My Heart, to My life more than ever. Always you are called to more; but gently, tenderly, and with God's great patience. My dear ones, remember I want the best for you, for I love you. You are like My little proteges, little saints in the making, little hearts in the blossoming, little warriors in training. How I love you. My Mother sends her love. We bless you now in the Name of My Father and in My Name, and the Name of the most Holy Spirit. Amen."

9/9, "My dear child, please write these words given by the Will of Our Father in Heaven, and by My own desire to share them and all My encouragement with you. I am Mary, your Immaculate Mother, Queen of all in Heaven, Hope of the Afflicted, Refuge of Sinners. Tell Our people, little one, that the times require a greater commitment to all the requests for prayer and a willingness to allow the Father to effect greater changes within them that will result in an increased love for God, for me, your holy Mother, and for all the lost souls who will come to them. Remind those, who have remained faithful and open to the Father's Will for them and for the world, that they HAVE RECEIVED INCREASED GIFTS AND STRENGTH in recent weeks that have brought them to a place of total readiness for all that now unfolds. They will notice a calm acceptance of these words, as opposed to the frantic response of many times in the past. It is necessary to be at this place of acquiescence to God's Will for those who will serve in mighty ways, performing mighty deeds for those in near collapse from remorse and grief. A businesslike response (those who can quickly overcome emotions and get right to work ministering to others, I believe this means, C.A.) to each event is only possible in those who believe Our promises of protection and Heavenly aid; who trust in the power and strength and love of all of Us Who comprise your Heavenly Family and loved ones, the Angels and Saints and all who pray for each of you every moment of your time, your day.

The Day of the Lord is the Gift of the Father's love for all His people ever created until now and in the future. It is His mercy in response to the weakness of all mankind that will save the earth from certain extinction and renew it, once again, for future generations. Remember how blessed and graced and gifted are all those who will accept His desires for the salvation of every person in the world. Praise and thank the Father for all those who do not praise and thank Him, who will soon be shown the absolute truth of the fact of God's existence and supremacy, as Creator of all that has ever and will ever exist. How beautiful and peaceful and loving will the world be, once it is renewed with every living creature into the glory of Eden; the happiness of life in the Kingdom of God on earth as it is in Heaven; led not into temptation, delivered from all evil! The peace and love you are feeling, daughter of My Immaculate Heart, is but a shadow of the same feelings that will be enjoyed in the New Era of Peace and Purity. The Father's Will is Perfect at all times for all people, in every event of your lives. This, my little warrior, is what awaits Our people, what inspires and strengthens all to persevere, to pray and fight with the last ounce of time and breath you have; to wait in joyful hope for the return to the earth of Jesus, My Son, your Savior and King. Oh children, rejoice with me. Invite all to rejoice and be renewed in commitment to me and to God's Will for the earth and all its people. Be joyful, little ones."

9/13, "My dear children: I am your Mother, little ones, gathering you into my mantle this night, as a mother hen gathers her chicks at the end of a long day. She takes them under her wings, my children, to protect them from the wolf, from any predator that lurks, ready to cause harm, ready to cause death, ready to disrupt the quiet and the order of the little house. Oh my dear ones, there are predators; there are wolves who lurk. I tell you this night a matter of great importance, my children, that all of you who are faithful to me must let go now of all your irritations. Bring to my Son all of those people, all of those things, who distract you, who irritate you, who cause you inner turmoil. I have told you, my little ones, in the past with great love, let no one and nothing disrupt your peace. If you are doing this now, my children, it is because you are giving in to something within yourselves that must be purified. Only peace can reign, my little ones. Only a focus on my Son is the answer to every turmoil. There will be so much turmoil, my dear little ones, that you must allow me to save you from, to protect your from, to guide you.

I shoo you into my mantle, as that mother hen shoos her baby chicks, for you are my little ones. You are my precious little ones. I have promised and my Son has promised to protect you from harm. But you, my children, must allow this. You must bring all of your distractions to the Sacrament, that you might be purified even more, again and again, my dear ones. Old habits are difficult to relinquish. They have a hold of you, my children, but you are holding on to them, also! I ask you to think about this in the coming days. Ask my Spouse, the dear, dear Holy Spirit of God, to show you once again what you cling to, to comfort yourself, to serve yourself, to give yourself a feeling of being unloved, of being rejected. It is now time, my children, when you must drop everything but the weapons you have received from heaven: my rosary, adoration and silence before my beloved Son, unity with the peace you must accept. It is up to you, my little ones. Each one of you has an area that you cling to: areas of unforgiveness, areas of resentment, areas that need the light of my Son to shine upon to bring you to the Light, His Light, my children. These are more gifts to you to prepare you, to render you the finest of fighting weapons, that we might fight together in this great battle that looms ahead. Oh my children, allow me to protect you. Allow me to strengthen you with my gentleness, with the openness to all who will come to you by opening to all who are here now. If you cannot be open to those you pray with everyday, how can you be open to strangers who will be very, very difficult? You will see, my children, what a struggle this will be. You will need all the grace, all of the cleansing, all of the purification that will render you this supreme instrument of the Father's Mercy.

There are no words to convey my feelings for you, my gratitude for you, my joy. You fill my heart, my dear ones. How precious you are to me. Come closer yet. Allow your heavenly Mother to prepare you in these last times, these last days, the final and finishing touches on your soul and your heart and your spirit, my children. Be free, my little ones. Be joyful in spite of sadness, in spite of hurt and humiliation. Be free of this, my children, and be filled with joy. You will see how joy will transform you that you might transform others from sorrow to joy. I love you, my little ones. I'm right here with you always. Call to me. I wish to help you. You need my help, all of you, everywhere! I love you."

9/20, "My dearest children: I am your Jesus of Mercy. I am your sweet Jesus. I come to you once again asking that you believe in My Presence, that you believe in My words, that you believe Me when I tell you I am standing in your midst this very moment. I walk among you. I touch your hearts. I take your hearts and I hold them next to My Own. See this in your minds, My children. See this in your hearts, in your spirits. See Me standing before you. See My eyes looking at you, gazing at you with love. So much love I have for you. I praise and thank My Father, too, that I might be here with you, spend this time now: healing you, strengthening you, bringing you closer to Me. Thank you for coming together to praise My Father, to invite My Mother who stands here with Me. Believe this, children. She is gazing at you with her incredible love for each of you. Feel her presence. You have no idea how close We are to you at all times. You have no idea of the love We are pouring out at this very moment again to heal you, to strengthen you. Pay no attention to anyone who scorns you, who laughs at you, who rejects the love you have for Us. It was so for Me, My dear ones, and so it will be for you! Rejoice, My children, for We are more closely united in this humiliation, in the pain of the scorn, in the heartbreak of rejection.

My children, you hear Us speak so often of My Mother's Army. I tell you, My faithful ones, YOU ARE GENERALS! You are attaining the highest rank. Expect surprises in the near future, My children. Expect gifts, for you have suffered and accepted joyfully so much pain, so much loneliness, so much misunderstanding, so much scandal. It is scandal, My children, when people say things about My faithful ones that are untrue. My Heart weeps to see you suffer, but I know the joy in your hearts, for you have learned to unite this suffering with Mine. Oh My children, some day you will know how many you have saved; how many you have allowed to receive the grace to come to Me. Rejoice now, My children, for all of Heaven is rejoicing for you. Know that I wait every moment of the day until you arrive before Me in My Blessed Sacrament. How happy I am when you come and kneel before Me, and I see that smile on your face and your own delight and your joy to be with Me! I speak words of love this night, My children, for My Heart overflows with love. You are My dearest ones. Again, I thank you for allowing My Mother and I to take respite in your hearts. How cold it is in the world, in the hearts of so many of Our people. Thank you again for your love. Feel My love for you. Believe every word, every promise, every gift. I fill you now with My peace, with new strength. Yes, children, strength to experience new degrees of persecution, of ridicule, of rejection! You do this for ME, My little ones, as I have done it for you. Greater love has no man, than he lay down his life for his loved ones. WE ARE ONE, MY CHILDREN. I love you. Amen."

9/23, Jesus said: "My dearest little one, I am your Jesus Who loves you. THERE IS NO OTHER WAY TO PERFECTION THAN TO STAY FIXED IN THE FATHER'S WILL BY ACCEPTING EACH EVENT WITH JOY, WITHOUT MURMUR OR QUESTION.

Corruption and self-gratification boils out of the pit of Satan's plans for the earth and its people. Do not be concerned about those who have turned away in disgust. With the revelation of the truth of each individual soul's condition before God, MANY, MANY will accept the error of their ways. Your prayers for mercy on the world ARE BEING ANSWERED, MY FAITHFUL ONES, and once again, the many are being saved by the faithful few! No matter how events unfold, your future in Heaven for Eternity is assured, as you remain close to My Mother and yours and allow her to lead you ever closer to the Triune God. THERE CANNOT BE NEW WORDS, MY CHILDREN, BECAUSE THERE IS NO OTHER WAY!

As the Heavenly messages are fewer in number and less frequent in reception by Our faithful messengers, you will mourn your own foolish criteria and grumbling these many years, making impossible demands on these dear ones who have sacrificed their lives in order to serve your needs and the requests of My Father. More and more, you are about to recognize your own pride and puffed-up egos that have given life and energy to all your criticisms and judgments. HURRY, My poor misguided ones, to My Sacrament of Reconciliation with true remorse and rejection of your own behavior and sinful words and ways. I am reaching out to you with mercy, and a Godly desire to forgive your sins and cleanse your actions and purify your souls NOW. STOP, LOOK AND LISTEN AGAIN, My people. The reflection in the waters of grace is you! HURRY, CHILDREN. Run to Me through the Heart of My Mother. Be ready to walk through the Gate, My precious ones. I AM THAT GATE. Heaven cannot help you, little pools of large resistance, if you do not allow it! I go before you and smooth the way. I am Jesus Who loves you."

FOR MERCY'S SAKE!

9/27, "Dearest ones, I am your Mother. The world is filled with confusion. This is only the first volley from the enemy that has its weapons trained upon each one of My faithful children. How my heart weeps. What a shame, my children, for all the loss you will see, all of the destruction, families turning upon each other, **friends turning in friends.** You will not believe, many times, what you will be seeing. Believe these words now, children. The idea of betrayal is not a new one. It was also experienced, most dreadfully and deeply, by My Son. Our Father's plan also always allows the worst to come out in people who are turned against The Son. And so you will see this. More and more there will be division and hatred coming to the surface within governments, within communities, within churches, within families. This is not news to you, but of course, I mention these things in order to ask you to pray more for these intentions, for those who will be rejected by many of those nearest to them. This will be the ultimate betrayal for this generation of Our beloved ones. You have not known this kind of pain, this sorrow, this hatred. You will understand more the hatred of Satan for the Father when you see this upon the earth.

Oh, my children, the tragedies ahead, the broken hearts, the broken spirits! You need not wonder why I take such delight in you, why I am so grateful for the love in your hearts for me and for my Son. What peace you bring to my heart, torn by the hatred I see everywhere, even now. My dear ones, stay close to me. Stay close to each other, as you are. Pray for each other for strength, for perseverance. The words (messages) that you have become so familiar with now, learn to appreciate and learn to pray for. Again I mention how far you have come in the Father's plan for all of His people. Be encouraged, my children, by the encouragement of all of Heaven. Be filled with the joy of Heaven at your honesty, your sincerity, your increasing purity every day. Give thanks to the Father, my dear ones, for you would be nothing without His mercy. I would be nothing without His mercy given to me so very long ago; but given again now in these times, allowing me to be with you like this, to visit with you, to love you, to guard you and to guide you, to teach you: all the things I love to do! How I love to see you blossom and become more beautiful each day. Be at peace, my dear, dear ones. I love you. Always, I love you!"

10/4, 3:50 a.m. Jesus said: "My dearest child, you may write My words that are of the utmost importance. Please pray with Me now that your heart and mind are renewed to a new and higher and keener level of development as the Father desires for you now. Then I have much to tell you, little faithful one. Let us continue: Today and for the next days, all the world is poised on the brink of a new day. Hundreds of thousands of people are praying in union with dear John Paul II, Our chosen and beloved Pope and Shepherd of the flock My Father has given to Me. It is this union and the obedience of so many that will ensure that none of these (the Flock) will be lost. None of the plans for such total destruction (that Satan believes will be accomplished) will in fact be successful to the degree expected by all of his followers or by the Antichrist and his political schemers.

When you see the amount of destruction that will still occur, I tell you people of the world, you will quake with a new realization of what might have been! You will be brought to a new level of praise and gratitude to My Father for allowing your prayers to have such power, and effect such change in the future. I am still returning to fight and win the victory in the battle against all the forces of evil. I will still drive out all of the evil in the world and in the hearts of mankind; Satan and his puppets and demons into the deepest fires of Hell to remain chained there for another long period of time. I will lead you into the New Era of Peace and Purity that will be My Eucharistic Reign, and all who remain will be My Eucharistic people. I tell you too, that all I have revealed to this little one and many of Our messengers throughout the world will be fulfilled! However, there has been a great altering of the degree and duration of the remainder of this time of purification and tribulation for the earth. Please remember, My dearest people, that all of Scripture must be fulfilled before My return to defeat Satan and rid the world of evil. **Please recall how very different is the timetable of My Father and the time experienced by all the inhabitants of Earth. DO NOT BECOME DISCOURAGED, My precious ones**. Do not have particular expectations, or think you have all the answers to the many questions regarding the complete unfolding of My Father's Plan: (Please read these often and pray to the Spirit to recognize the information given in what seems to be an outline of all that is to come in the plan of the Father for the earth…cta.)

A time of evangelization,
A time of drought,
A time of great blessing and outpouring of Our Spirit,
A time of dying,
A time of rising,
A time of upheaval,
A time of action,
A time of seeming victory for the powers of Hell.
A time of hiddenness,
A time of protection,
A time of fasting,
A time of celebration,
A time of waiting,
A time of fulfillment,
A time of defeat,
A time of victory,
A time of renewal,
A time of peace.

Recall that there are many people in the world, and My Father's Plan includes the salvation of all of them who turn back to the Father and learn to be His obedient and loving child. Recall, too, that there is much to occur about which you still know nothing, and add this rather lengthy category to your list of events about to begin. My Mother's triumph is so near, My dearest ones. Focus on her triumph, her victory over Satan and over his power to drag her dear children into the flaming abyss. I tell you, dear precious ones of My Heart, you MUST REJOICE, YOU MUST BE PEOPLE OF JOY AND HOPE AND TRUST. Who could have the power to overcome the might of God? NO ONE, I tell you, in spite of how the world will appear for a relatively short period of time. There is nothing to fear; but there is no way to avoid the justice of the Father and Creator of life. Reparation must be made for the grievous sins against nature, against the innocent, against the Creator and all His children, His creatures, His creation.

I tell you: to wait in joyful hope is the greatest gift you can give to yourself, to your God, to the entire world. Remember, praise and gratitude enable more gifts to be given; trust enables more and more mercy to be poured out upon the whole world and the many suffering, needy ones everywhere. If you could see them; if you could hear the cries of anguish and despair, you would wonder anew how such conditions can prevail. Evil, I tell you, greed, lust, avarice; self propulsion to the top of the hill, the head of the line to be the one who has more and more and more of this world's glitter and glamour and empty thrills.

I tell you, you are already the recipient of every gift you require, every strength to overcome yourselves: the jealousies, the position-consciousness of the multilevel class system that exists in your hearts and daily behavior! Remember Lazarus and the rich man in the Gospel story, My dear children. IF YOUR OWN SPIRITS HAVE BECOME HUMBLE AND DOCILE AND GENEROUS AND HONEST AND CHILDLIKE, YOU HAVE NO FEARS OF PUNISHMENT OR CHASTISEMENTS! Have you done; do you daily seek to accomplish all the requests of Heaven to render yourself cleansed and becoming a new creation for the Father's Kingdom on earth as it is in Heaven? You are already loved with a love that is Divine!

I AM THE BODY TO WHICH YOU BELONG. I AM THE HEAD. YOU ARE ITS MEMBERS. I AM THE VINE. YOU ARE THE BRANCHES. WE BELONG TO EACH OTHER, MY BELOVED ONES. YOU AND I ARE ONE WHEN YOU ARE LIVING THE REQUESTS AND DIRECTIVES OF HEAVEN, WHEN YOU KEEP MY COMMANDMENTS, WHEN YOU REACH OUT TO THOSE IN NEED, WHEN YOU ACCEPT MY MERCY, WHEN YOU TRUST IN MY PROMISES, WHEN YOU SURRENDER TO MY PLAN FOR YOUR LIFE! Come, My people. Run to My arms. Live in My Heart in My unimaginable love for you this very minute. COME TO ME NOW! It has never been so important to act on My words immediately, to trust Me completely. There will be signs, My children. Will you be one who sees them?"

10/4, "My dearest children, how good it is to be with you again. Make no mistake, each person who comes to you, wherever you are, has been sent by Our Holy Spirit. I am Jesus. I am the Bridegroom of your souls. My Dear Ones, I am your One and only, and each of you is My one and only! I love you. Each of you is a new creation. Imagine, My dear ones, how much you have learned, how many insights. Oh yes, through struggle and through mistakes, even through stubbornness. Yet each time you learned a lesson it has been of great value to your soul, a great aid in altering your behavior and in helping you to become a more perfect instrument of My Father's Will. There is so much unrest in the world among all of Our faithful ones, as well as those who plot and scheme to begin wars everywhere; to support the slaughter of the innocents; to take away from Our people, Our children everywhere in the world all of their possessions, all of their freedom, all of their peace and security. Praise and thank My Father, for each of you has a grasp on reality, on the truth. You do not spend your days arguing or imagining what things might be like. You have learned patience, and to surrender your questions and your impatience to Me. How blessed you are. I will always tell you that, My children, to help you remember to thank My Father for all of His blessings, for choosing you, for perfecting you along this way of tears and struggle; and yet from each new struggle you emerge shining brightly, more purified, more docile, more humble, more joyful. There will be many to comfort. There will be many questions to answer, children. Be ready for this. Look back. Reread, reflect, meditate and be in silence more.

More and more the chaos builds in the world and in the hearts of evil men and in the plans of Satan. You have learned to see yourselves more honestly than most; and this will always bring a greater humility, more gratitude for gifts and graces in spite of yourselves. Yes, you are weak, little ones, but you are strong in My love. You are strong in mercy. You are strong in your love and your commitment. You are strong soldiers and warriors ready for **a long, long time of unfolding events** that along the way will be supported by miracles, gifts of the Spirit. Listen for My voice, My dear ones, for all day long I am saying to you, I love you. All day long I tell you: you are Mine. Be filled with new joy, new hope, new peace. You are precious and you belong to Me, My dear ones."

10/12, "My little dear one, I am your Jesus, come to renew your spirit and strength. The EVENTS in the MIDDLE EAST SPEAK LOUDLY TO ALL MY WORDS ABOUT WAR IN THIS AREA OF THE WORLD. HOW OBVIOUS ARE SATAN'S PLANS TO DESTROY MY HOLY PLACES OF MY BIRTH, LIFE, DEATH AND RESURRECTION. (And here in 2006, we see this pattern repeated…cta.) What better way to quickly call for a public announcement of countries' taking sides, causing further division in the world and bringing the danger of further destruction to a boiling point. There is no need to play at peace, spending the time AGREED UPON TO LULL THE WORLD FURTHER INTO SLUMBER, RIGHT BEFORE THE CATS POUNCE UPON EACH OTHER IN ORDER TO OBTAIN OWNERSHIP OF THE CHOICEST MORSELS! AGAIN, I REMIND ALL OF YOU WHO LISTEN TO THE WORDS OF HEAVEN AND BELIEVE, THESE ACTIONS AND COUNTERACTIONS ARE BY AGREEMENT OF ALL INVOLVED. The timetable is Satan's, but it is also ALLOWED BY MY FATHER WHO waits for the entire world to see the extent of greed for land and power. There is a very great possibility of mutual destruction of the sacred ground where I, your Lord and God of all people, walked peaceably. It is throughout this very land being desecrated by those who care nothing about truth, but follow the lies and suggestions of the evil one through the prompting of crafty men skulking in the background, spreading further hatred and corruption.

If you are praying in union with Our beloved John Paul II, My Father will act to save the Shrines built to honor the time when your Jesus, the Son of God, became Man and lived and died to open the Gates of Heaven to all mankind. These who are against each other are putting an end finally to the deceit of peaceful words and the hypocrisy of talk of honor and shared trust. No one but My Father will be the One Who has decided to allow men of destruction to make war, and destroy each other and themselves. Pray, My faithful ones, that My Father will allow signs that will strike terror in the hearts of terrorists, that He will act with mercy once more and reach out in an overwhelming way to capture those who seek to capture each other's possessions in order to show them that their God is One. He is Omnipotent. He is All-powerful, clothed in majesty and peace. When My Father acts to stop the sacrilegious killing and mindless destruction, all will know it is He, bringing justice to a people steeped in pagan beliefs and practices. If Yahweh were truly worshiped and adored, there could be no murderous plans for large-scale slaughter, as now exist in the hearts of the WHITED SEPULCHRES of your day!

What you see unfolding upon the pages of history is AGREED TO BY ALL INVOLVED WHICH INCLUDE THE LEADERS OF ALL THE MAJOR WORLD POWERS. PRAY, CHILDREN. PRAY BEFORE YOU THINK OR SPEAK OR ACT! PURIFY YOUR PRAYERS WITH PURIFIED BEHAVIOR AND SACRIFICES MADE BY GENEROUS HEARTS WILLING TO SHARE WHAT LITTLE YOU WILL HAVE. DO NOT FEAR. I AM ALWAYS WITH YOU, SEEKING TO HELP YOU TO RESPOND TO WORDS DESIGNED TO TURN YOU AWAY FROM THE WORLD TOWARD THE OPEN, WELCOMING, MERCIFUL FORGIVENESS AND WARMTH OF MY FATHER AND YOURS."

10/27, "Daughter, I your Lord Jesus, am here with you, bringing words of love and comfort. There is no one who suffers in the same way; but each one is patterned by My Father to turn His chosen ones into specific instruments, to fulfill particular roles, and effect unique healing and conversions for Our poor lost ones who will wander in terrible fear and desolation. The time right now is absolutely critical, as the evil one will soon (again, please bring your understanding of Heaven's 'soon' to bear here...cta.) gain nearly total control and power in your own country and in many throughout the world. This will signal a time for other countries to begin aggressive moves and a power take-over in their own land. The leaders of all the large countries in the world are about to reveal the intentions agreed to by all, and introduce oppressive measures and maneuvers to gain greater control of property and personal possessions.

Those who love Me are about to face ever greater challenges which lead them to increased hardships. I ask you, My beloved people, to PRAY FOR AN INCREASE IN THE PERSONAL DISCIPLINE THAT YOU WILL REQUIRE TO REMAIN FAITHFUL AND JOYFUL IN SPITE OF MORE REJECTION

AND RIDICULE FROM LOVED ONES AND PEOPLE WHO HAVE UNTIL NOW BEEN YOUR FRIENDS.

Satan is being allowed to sift your hearts that you might know exactly, once and for all, where you stand in your love for your Triune God and Holy Mother. Yes, there will be times of more or less weakness and conviction in My promises to protect you from harm according to My Father's Will for you; but now will be a time of renewed commitment and promise of obedience to all of Heaven's direction. You will find many things in your lives changing from ways you have always lived them, and even in the names and faces of many with whom you have always shared them! Just please believe My words. Do not fear or be caught up in imaging events that may not happen! I only urge you at this time to plead with My Father for a greater discipline that will be needed from now on in order to persevere through sometimes painful decisions on your part and those of others. Your world is changing rapidly now, still hidden to some degree, but about to erupt in startling events that are initiated by the very ones who are the CHANGLINGS, the traitors, the GREEDY ONES WHO WILL EXCHANGE YOUR FREEDOM FOR THEIR POWER.

Reread Our words given these many years to faithful messengers who have stood the test of time and trial, temptations and threats against their safety and the little serenity left in their lives. I TELL YOU, SUFFERING OF SOME KIND IS THE WAY OF LIFE FOR THOSE WHO CONTINUE TO FOLLOW ME, TO ANSWER THE DIRECTIVES OF HEAVEN WITH ALL OF WHO YOU ARE, TO REMAIN FAITHFUL in spite of hardships and enormous changes in your life, as you now live it. I speak directly this night. I ask all, who listen and believe, to MAKE ANOTHER NOVENA TO OUR HOLY SPIRIT TO ASK FOR HIS DISCERNMENT, an increase of His gifts, a listening heart, a new level of patience and holiness and sanctity; an iron will that accepts whatever the Father's perfect Will desires for you and of you. The battle between good and evil, Heaven and Hell, the Kingdom of God and the kingdom of Satan is escalating! These measures are meant to strengthen and prepare you for the ultimate victory over evil and the total renewal of the earth and all God's people. I speak again to alert you, dearest ones of My Heart, to prepare you for greater struggles over very difficult choices to bring you to the place of absolute readiness needed for all of you, who will serve and minister far beyond your present gifts and abilities all those sent by My Father in His plan to give salvation to the entire world.

Be at peace, beloved faithful ones. Just pray in union with all Our faithful ones who respond to these requests, who are effecting unimagined mercy for the world and its inhabitants. Do not delay, My people. You will certainly perish at the whim of the evil one, who waits to fill you with laziness, a lack of interest, a sneering response to all the words of Heaven to Our faithful messengers everywhere. I speak from knowledge of all of Satan's plans, as carried out by his followers in the New World Order and led by the Antichrist. DO NOT BE DISBELIEVING, I BEG YOU, MY PRECIOUS CHILDREN, BUT BELIEVE! THE TRUTH WILL SET YOU FREE; AND I REMIND YOU, ONCE AGAIN, I

AM TRUTH. Do not fear. My strength is with you. Be healed more. Be filled with the fire and energy and Presence of Our Spirit!"

10/25, "Dearest ones, I am the Holy Spirit of God. I greet you this night joyfully, children. Thank you for gathering in the Name of Jesus to honor My beloved spouse, the Immaculate one, Mary, your Mother. I come to ask you several things, My children. First, it is necessary to be conscious of dear Mary's presence with you at every moment now. Events in the world speak to developing difficulties, warlike aggression, suffering; and you will need the strength of her presence. You will need to hold her hand. You will need to be purified, calmed, sanctified, blessed as only she can do; as only the influence she can be for your needs in the coming days. The future of the world, My children, hangs in balance. So many more could be praying; so many, many more are not. Heaven calls out to all who listen everywhere in the world to pray, to beg for mercy, to beg that the Father will stay the hand of those who would destroy shrines, holy places, sacred places (Palestine, Jerusalem), little ones, places you have longed to see yourselves. These are places that give honor to the life of Jesus, that remind you of all He suffered for you, of all His love. You recreate these days in your own lives, My dear ones, and as you are living faithfully, you too are shrines of Jesus' life and death, as you suffer for Him and die to yourself and your selfishness, and live for the Father, His Will, which was all that Jesus ever wanted, ever desired, ever lived. Think of this and praise the Father, little ones who are tall in love, in service, great in the eyes of God and all of Heaven. How you are loved and supported by the prayers of all in Heaven. How close they are to each of you everywhere who pray.

Dear Children of God, rejoice once again. The Father desires to share more of His power with you, to give more power to your prayers to enable Him (with your prayers) to defend sacred places, to defend life in all of its forms, as you do pray, as you do desire as your Father desires. My dear ones, as you pray, unite these prayers to (those of) everyone else in the world. A mighty united prayer must go up to the Father. There is so little unity in the world today. Show Him in this way there is unity in your hearts: unity of purpose, unity of hope, unity of desire, unity of your work, your prayerful work, your work at prayer. My dearest ones, I also tell you to be on guard more than ever, for the evil one roars, and he is like a lion who is very hungry. Do not be afraid of My words. By now you know these are loving words of warning. When you were little and you crossed a busy street, someone always said, 'Be careful. Watch for cars.' It is the same today, My dear ones. Heaven knows what could happen to you. Heaven desires to protect you. Allow us to do that. Help us in that way too, My dear ones, and recall how closely you are living the Father's Will now; how closely you are living to all of those in Heaven. Realize that this is part of your new way of life, the new creation you are becoming, and rejoice!

My dear ones, all will be well as you listen to all of Our words and directives, and are obedient to them. This is all it takes, children, dear, beloved ones of the Heart of God. I pour out upon you now all of My gifts: strengthening you, giving you more courage, all of the ability to surrender and to suffer (if that is necessary) freely, gladly, joyfully for the whole world, for souls. Enjoy new wisdom this night, dear ones everywhere, new understanding in the days ahead, increased knowledge, fortitude; all the things you need to become a stronger, more loyal soldier, fighter, warrior. Be at peace, dear, dear people of the world. **Let your prayers fight for peace**. You are loved."

11/8, "My dearest ones: I am you Mother. You have noticed that messages from me are fewer throughout the world. You are only to look for signs, children, to read them. You are not so much to desire signs, as the pagans do, but to discern them, to recognize them and to give thanks for them. My little ones, you have grown close to me in ways you cannot understand. Know that they (these ways) give great honor and glory and delight to Our Father in Heaven. Know that all you do and struggle to do and desire to do for My Son and for me fills Heaven with joy. But also, they are gifts from the Father through His Spirit. This night I come to tell you children, that no matter what happens in the world, in your own country, in your own city, in parishes and homes, all will be well for you; that I will be with you; nothing new perhaps, but always a reminder. I give thanks constantly for this gift, children. It would be well if you thanked the Father for the gift of my words, of my presence with you, of my prayers for you, my pleading for you; the gift of my heart and my great love, my compassion and understanding of all you do, all you go through.

My children all over the world struggle. They struggle because the evil one is stronger. He is called a fiend, children, for this he is. These plans of Our Father include every safety for you, for your loved ones; every safety for those you pray for, for those who are close to you. Realize that these will change quickly now as the leadership of your country changes. Either of these leaders has plans to take the world, but especially this country, into particular directions. And the world will follow. You must not let up on your prayers. You must not let up on fasting, on reflection of all my words and the words of my Son. It is so important that you have words of Scripture, words from Heaven during your present day woven into the fabric of each day, each chore and each task; for they are all based upon Scripture, the life of my Son, my life, the life of those who followed my Son. Recall that there **is no time in Heaven, that all time is one.** Reflect on this, that you might not feel so separated from Jesus and His life, from myself and the time we lived on the earth during Jesus' first coming and His life, His examples, His teachings. **All of that, all that you live now, is NOW in Eternity! If you can grasp that, just a little, my children, you will be able to have more patience.** You will be able to wait calmly, without distractions, without discouragement, without the lack of discipline that causes distractions, that causes one to run in many directions to stay busy; to avoid the silence, to avoid the nothing that is happening, as you see it. Can you not feel how close the world is, and you yourselves are, to the escalation of events in the world, to another time of danger, of building tensions and challenges; of the need for prayer in hopes of going beyond present tensions, present possibilities of warlike aggression? Imagine. Each one of you is so important in the whole picture, the whole defense against Satan and his might. Appreciate, my children, the power you are being given against the might of Satan and his plans. **Long ago, you would have been living in the reign of the Antichrist, had it not been for your prayers and mine.** We are so closely united, children.

The more you pray, the more you give your hearts to me in your lovely consecration prayers; in the lovely flowering in your hearts of all that your consecration means; the lovely blossoming of your spirits, the coloring of YOU as new creation set within the Will of Our Father. You cannot appreciate this now, but believe it, just as you believe so many things through faith, through gift that Heaven is telling you: my words, the words of my Son, Our Father and Their Spirit. Do not for one moment become distracted. The holidays have a way of gripping the focus, the attention of all people. This must not be. In the past we have led you closer and closer to the focus that must exist in your hearts, even during times of distraction like holidays with parties, with projects and different events. You will see an escalation now, as I said earlier, of the plans of new government**, new leaders who are actually and truly no different than what you have lived in the past! Accept that the plans of Satan will become more obvious, more public, more experienced and felt by all of you. And over all of this, my little ones, you must have joy**: your own joy given by my Spouse, the Holy Spirit of God; the joy of the Father and the Son and the Spirit; the joy only grace could allow in this time of preparation.

As you wait in expectation, not even knowing the results of all of your prayer for this time of election of leaders that will mean so much to your country and your lives, we must be joyful together. As I contemplated the death of my Son, His passion and suffering first, I was able to have joy because of my Jesus' Presence, His beauty, His sweetness, His love for me. The same is possible for you, and for the very same reasons. Think about my words to you this night. They are meant to bring you into deep thought and reflection, into a quiet place in your mind and in your heart, your spirit; where you will discover new strength, new ability to wait patiently, new awareness of my presence, new joy. Always, we shall seek and find new joy. I love you, my dear ones. How I miss the times when we do not visit like this. Know that they will continue as long as the Father allows this. Pray for each other. Love each other. Appreciate each other, for each of you is such an important part of the whole of the community here; of all that unfolds for your future. The future is now, my children. Be at peace. FEEL MY L0VE. KNOW MY LOVE. BELIEVE MY LOVE. LIVE IN THE PRESENCE OF MY LOVE."

11/11, "My dearest little one, I am your God and Father. Yes, little daughter, you are seeing a first fulfillment of My Son's words to you long ago about splitting this country in two, (Country waiting for results of election of Bush or Gore) Whether or not this will also occur physically to the earth depends, of course, on prayer for your land, taken over now by pagan practices and plans of Satan. There can never be a time when Our people could reflect upon these facts too often! Each of you must keep before your mind and understanding the fact that SATAN WILL SEEM TO RULE THE WORLD COMPLETELY FROM NOW ON. The number praying and fasting (of so many of the faithful listening to Our Spirit) has added to this time of delay in order that more prayers may be said to ask Me to touch the heart of the new President and remove all vestiges of evil plans for the unborn, and preservation of life at every age. **Pray, My beloved people, that enough will pray!** My dearest children of the earth, this is just one of many choices and decisions you begin to make that will determine the future of your country and then the world. You are seeing the greedy characters of participants in this almost deadlock. You will see laws discarded by the powerful, and powerful takeovers precipitated by the hidden machinations of the One World Government people who will then follow the Antichrist (one day) into Hell.

Pause, My dearest ones, and reflect upon the fact that you are chosen to live at this time of world changing events. Even though you possess a great deal of knowledge about your future and the different possibilities with or without prayer, there are still bits of information that have not and will not be revealed. This, too, will purify each of you who think you have the future all figured out! You know, deep in your hearts, that this is the mindset of many. You know that you are still paying enough attention to every word that comes from your Triune God, the holy Mother and even Saints and some Angels allowed to speak to some at this crucial time in the history of your world. Do not wait to be convinced of these words of warning. **Begin this moment to clean your household, your heart and spirit of people and things and expectations.** Allow Me to empty you of all pastimes that waste the valuable hours and moments still remaining now. I will continue to pour out My mercy upon you by the desire of My Will for you and through My Beloved Son, Jesus. You should be able to prepare for the sacred celebrations that are upon you, and still have time to pray and visit Me in the Blessed Sacrament, where the Father and the Spirit wait for you in union with the Son. These priorities must be made and lived out! **The future of peace or war depends on how all My faithful ones respond to My requests!"**

11/15, "My dearest children: I am your Jesus. My little vessels of mercy, you are becoming more and more the Father's desire. I will never stop telling you this, for you will need all of the encouragement Heaven can send to you. You will be in constant need of new strength, of renewed hope and of renewed perseverance. Faith is a gift you have received long ago, that you have nurtured and protected within yourselves. This was one of the first gifts each of you learned (about) after My Mother began appearing here in your parish. (St. Maria Goretti, Scottsdale.) This faith has never left you and it never will, for your hearts are loving and open and desirous of service. This night I ask you to consecrate yourselves again to the Perfect Will of Our Father. Often it will not look like the Perfect Will in action. What is occurring will not seem what might be best, what you might hope for, what you might desire yourselves. These are the times when you will need your faith and Our strength, your commitment, your consecration of every fiber of your being, every gift that you are given, that you might consecrate them to My Father. Every day I remind you: sometimes it will be to **consecrate every moment in order for you to continue to be brave, to be patient, to surrender and ALLOW ME to lead you.** YOU cannot do this. You cannot lead each other into this kind of battle, this level of evil, these plans to destroy you, destroy the world.

Oh My children, surrender to MY leadership, to MY wisdom, to the hope found in MY Heart. Never tire of hearing Me say, 'there is nothing to fear'; for you will be tempted mightily to be fearful, to give up hope, to think that all is lost. Truly, My dear ones, to a certain degree (as this election farce continues), it will seem for a while that all is lost. The government that will take over will quickly implement tools of Satan: relaxed attitudes against life and the importance, the sacredness of life. You are ready for this in your hearts, but when you see this actually unfold, you will be horrified and greatly saddened; and you will find the time to pray more than ever against this terrible slaughter, against the plans of the evil one. You are surrounded by danger as you are surrounded by Angels, by the strength of My Father, protection in His promises. Do not forget His promises. As the election dilemma continues, people will turn away from prayer. People will be distracted completely or become discouraged or bored, just as Satan desires you. Do not play into his hands. Do not give in to his suggestions that all is lost, that your prayers are worth naught, that your God is beginning to abandon you. All of these thoughts he will put into the hearts of each of you, especially My faithful ones, for he desires NOT your success, your fidelity, your perseverance. My little ones, pray more for each other. Ask for strength and discipline and patience for each other that these might be given in response to your request.

The waiting is more difficult than ever, I know; and you are more faithful than ever, and stronger than ever and able to withstand whatever happens next in the plan of My Father, or allowed in the plan of Satan. If you are staying close to My Mother and holding her hand and appreciating her, you are not impatient, you are not anxious or curious. You are healed to the degree My Father needs you to be, but if you are anxious and focused on events, then you will not be living My Father's Will for you. Think about these things. It will make every day easier, for My burden is light and My yoke is easy. Never ever will you be abandoned. Never ever will you be without the presence of My Mother and Myself. How you will need Me then, and My Mother. My children, your prayers enable gifts like this to be given and these wonderful visits we are having because of My Father's mercy and His gifts to you, His delight in you. My dearest ones, again I say, 'you are precious in My eyes.' Be at peace. Be at peace. Be at peace. Amen, My little ones. I love you. I love you. I love you."

11/17, "Daughter of My Will, I am your Father, come once again with words for you and for My people that point to the time after My Warning to the world that will give each a view of their souls through the eyes of Truth, through the eyes of the Triune God. Oh My dearest people of My loving Will, how your fidelity and prayer are touching the hearts of My suffering ones everywhere. You are MY hope, MY delight, MY joy! Believe that you shall see the good things of the Lord in this place of the living. Believe that miracles will abound, that every promise given to you by your Triune God and Mary, the Immaculate one, will be fulfilled. Continue to praise and thank Me, for **My gifts to you will continue to be given and grow in strength and power as you have need of them. Be absolutely at peace about every event allowed by My Perfect Will for you!** My Precious and Beloved Son holds you in His Heart and supplies you with every need.

Your country is in deadly peril. All of your time must be given to prayer now, for the situation in the world grows more serious at each moment. I am your God, My little ones. I have proclaimed these promises to you AND ALL WHO LISTEN. You will never be overcome; you will never weaken; you will always be My instruments of peace and salvation as you wait obediently for the return of Jesus, your Savior and King. Continue, as you do now, to fight the evil one and his demons, **who will wreak havoc in order to fulfill Scripture**, BUT WILL BE DEFEATED AND CHAINED IN HELL IN IGNOMINY. For who is like unto God? I tell you, **I have created you in love for these times, and you will be victorious with the might of My Arm.** I wait in union with Jesus and Our Spirit in the magnificent, humble, glorious Gift of the Eucharist, My gift to you for all ages. You are My holy ones! You are mighty in your Lord!"

11/25, 3 a.m. At Desk, "Dearest daughter, I am your Immaculate Mary, Mother of God and your own Heavenly Mother. All of Heaven prays for the patience and surrender of the faithful remnant, who long for the gift of Enlightenment to convince so many of the truth of Our words of warning these many years and the actual state of each soul as seen by God through the gift of this Illumination. All of Heaven waits and prays in the same anticipation of millions of souls returning to a life centered on their Creator and Savior and Sanctifier. But remember also, dearest people of the world, (all of you, my precious children), **many events of great upheaval and destructive forces of nature will be loosed upon the earth first, and the Father's Mercy delays this suffering as long as possible.** Yes, many of the lukewarm souls have turned away in the impatience over many delays, but the hearts of Our faithful ones are stronger than ever! All of Heaven prays for your perseverance, dear ones, and cheers the increase in numbers of prayers: the prayers of the heart that have grown within all of you. There are still newly informed fledglings who flock to hear Our words through messages and messengers everywhere. Never lose hope. Come to me with your sorrows and hurt feelings. The rejection and distancing by others will ONLY INCREASE AS IT BECOMES MORE AND MORE DANGEROUS TO PROFESS BELIEF IN MY SON, HIS FATHER AND THEIR SPIRIT. It is the wisdom and mercy of Our Heavenly Father that enables and allows the perfect timing and experience of each event. Remember, dear people, His Will is perfect; what is absolutely the best for each person will occur. You are loved and longed for, my precious children, and the events that ultimately remove all evil from the world and all of its people, will escalate quickly once they begin to fulfill the plans of Satan for a one world government and religion**. It will be neither**

government nor religion that will exist, but a succession of wars and oppression, as evil reaches its greatest power allowed by the Father to fulfill His plans and all of Scripture up to the return of my Jesus. That is why you must be joyful, my dear ones. You are promised help and protection at every turn, at each new development according to the Will of Our God.

Jesus is returning to the world, and this is the first reason to rejoice! MANY souls will receive the gift of salvation and spend eternity in the Kingdom of Heaven. The world WILL BE RENEWED and beautiful, and the era of peace and purity will begin: the Eucharistic reign of My Beloved Son Who will remain with His Eucharistic people more powerfully than ever before in history. Yes, My dearest ones, REJOICE. There is nothing to fear! These events will occur that will contain suffering in direct proportion to the number of people praying, and their constancy. Heed Jesus' words to pray that more will pray! All My words this night repeat warnings and teachings given these many years. Our beloved Slavko (well loved Medjugorje priest who died recently) has entered Paradise triumphantly. His hard work on your behalf and a life given to giving praise and honor to the Father brings him immediately to His Throne to continue sending more prayers and support to all the earth, and especially those of you who have suffered to follow and accept my words and appearances in his beloved land. (Medjugorje) Pray to him, children. He waits to assist you more now! The love each of you has for me is the soothing balm to the wounds in my own Heart and the Sacred Heart of My Son.

Reread Our words to you, and bolster your faith and courage. Read them now while you still have time and peace in your world. This condition will change drastically, and you need a renewal of commitment to me and the Triune God most of all, that you are willing to accept whatever is necessary for your own purification and that of the world. NOTHING ELSE IS IMPORTANT BUT THAT YOU SURRENDER COMPLETELY NOW TO GOD'S LOVE FOR YOU. It is a love that will overcome all evil and the evil deeds of destruction planned by my adversary. Oh my dearest beloved ones, time is so very short now. I love you with all the love in my aching and Immaculate Heart. Be at peace, loved ones. Pray."

12/06, 11:25 A.M.

(While some of this is addressed to pilgrims on ship, much is for the world. C.A.) Jesus said: "Child, please write. I am your Jesus, Beloved of your soul. Thank you for coming here, daughter. I have many words for Our people. Let us pray together again to Our Spirit for the gifts of openness and surrender. Let us continue now....

'People of My Heart, I speak only what the Father tells Me to speak for the preparation and purification of your minds and hearts and souls. Your bodies, My dearest ones, will be renewed to the degree desired by My Father and yours, that you might do whatever is needed for Our suffering, lost ones. You will suffer at different times in varying degrees. It is suffering which unites you to Me, breaks and remolds you constantly, that you might emerge from this fire of Love and cleansing a burnished sword, a glowing and mighty weapon in the hand of God! **It is only by living out your promises to My Mother and to Me that you will be able to experience the promises of My Father!** You are feeling an increased level of My peace, given as a gift of love to you. Do not abandon this level of peace, but remain focused in generous prayer and adoration to Me, living now in a gentle atmosphere of mercy and patience. Let your holiday gift giving be (especially) gifts of prayer and time spent in silence, sending peace and love to the suffering little ones everywhere in the world. Your prayers are given renewed and increased power this day. **Send out your love and compassion and concern for all who will wander in confusion and loss and fear.** Begin to comfort them now, to pray for the gifts of the Holy Spirit for them, that they may open to the action of Our mercy, Our forgiveness, Our longing for them to return and be healed and forgiven again and again. My beloved ones, you have no idea how much GOOD your prayers are obtaining for your own countries and for the world. My Father pours out His gifts of power and might that you might help to lift the burdens of addiction and suffering and self-hatred from the shoulders of the entire world. It is not a game I play with you... leading you to the brink of powerful and destructive events, only to delay these events; but an opportunity to allow the Father to hold back His wrath another second, another minute, and to make you that much holier, better prepared, more totally changed and transformed YOURSELVES in order to do His Will for the whole world. Praise My Father and yours. Thank Him for allowing you to share in His power and gifts when you respond with all of who you are to the needs of His lost souls everywhere. I cannot repeat these words too often or too strongly. Please believe that your loving prayers are effecting miracles in hearts and souls that have been hardened by lives filled by the world: the Kingdom of Satan. Are there still behaviors in you that are of the world? Do you NOT follow up with generous and humble surrender all your words, your actions, dressed up for the entire world to see, but meant to impress greedy eyes, and only seeking approval of others?

My dear ones, WRITE A SPIRITUAL SCHEDULE FOR THESE BUSY HOLIDAYS! Stick to it as best you can. Do not be discouraged by interruptions; yet, do not allow any person or event to distract you from a focus on My Face, or allow yourselves to have a divided heart. Give Me all of yourselves. My lost ones need you. You need them to lead you closer to Me! How I love you, precious ones. My Mother with all her Angels is here with Me now, bringing new strength and grace for the growth of stillness, and a deeper union with Us and with each other. Receive the blessing of your Triune God, children."

12/13, "My dearest little ones: I bring greetings once again from all in Heaven. I am your Jesus. The Father counts on you so very much and you are fulfilling His desires so very much. There are going to be events of destruction very soon. I know you have heard these words before, but pray as though it were the first time**. Each time something like this is mentioned you are much closer to these events.** How very much closer all of you come to events you have been warned about all of these years. More prayer is needed, My children. You can do this! You can remain in more silence, spending more time with Me. It is your future I discuss. It is the future of the world I speak of; it is My Father's Will I present. Many gifts will be given for this great season, this celebration of My birth that you prepare for. Your hearts will be the Manger in which My Mother will lay My tiny form. This will gift you beyond anything you have known, My people. My people everywhere who hear these words: focus on these words, on this possibility, for you have grown to this level of receiving very, very precious gifts. It is My Father you must once again give your gratitude and praise. You are special to My Heart, to the Father's Heart, to the Spirit. Expect miracles, My children. Expect to live more closely now with the Communion of Saints, within the Body of Christ of Mine, of which I am the Head.

There is so much evil, My people. Heaven weeps, as this part of the Father's plan develops, as He allows Satan's plans to develop, to grow and to gain power. It must be, My little ones. How We pray for you; for all of your hearts that still experience ridicule and hurts: people turning away, fewer than ever who have patience and understanding to wait while, all the while, everyone should be praising and thanking My Father for every delay. Stay close to Me. Stay close to My Mother, that she might give you this gift, this Presence of the newborn King, as you have never experienced it before. Look forward to every gift that is mentioned, every promise and every event; for as each one occurs, we move on to the day of My return, to the day of the defeat of evil. Oh My dear ones, how I long for that day. Long for that time with Me. Pray the Father will hasten this day. Look not for new answers or new messages. Look to Me, to My Face, to My love, My perfection and My beauty. Think not of your own weaknesses or your inabilities. Count on Me, My children. You have Me. I will NEVER let you go. My love for you is complete. Your love for Me is growing and growing. Is it not wonderful, My little ones, to feel My love, to love Me, to have your heart cleansed and renewed and softened: made gentle and tender, just like My Mother's?

From now on, My children, we dig in! We prepare more for certain battle. Satan's plan has been defeated in your election, but not forever, or by much; and he will be allowed to go forward, and every word I have told you all these years will be fulfilled. Live in the joy and the certainty of My love and My promises, your certain victory. I love each of you beyond words. Listen closely, for you will hear the voices of many Angels singing hosannas and praises for each of you. Be filled with My peace. Be filled with love, and rejoice once again. Amen, My dear ones, everywhere in the world."

12/21, AT ADORATION "I AM YOUR JESUS: I AM YOUR SAVIOR AND KING, JESUS, THE SON OF GOD, YOUR INFANT KING WHOM YOU PREPARE TO GREET AT THIS TIME OF CELEBRATION OF MY BIRTH. MY WORDS ARE SENT TO SOOTHE AND COMFORT, TO CALL OUT AND CARESS YOUR WEARY WAYS, YOUR LABORED PREPARATIONS FOR THIS SACRED TIME OF THE HOLIEST NIGHT OF YOUR CHURCH YEAR. THE INCREASE OF SECULAR ACTIVITIES ADDS GREATLY TO YOUR FATIGUE AND FURTHER LOSS OF SLEEP. AND SO I CALL OUT

WITH LOVE AND CONCERN FOR YOUR WELL-BEING AND PEACE. I SAY AGAIN, COME TO ME, MY MUCH LOVED CHILDREN. COME TO ME AND BE RENEWED. BE REVITALIZED; BE ABLE TO REDIRECT YOUR ENERGY TO YOUR TIME SPENT IN QUIET BEFORE ME: LOVING ME, LISTENING FOR MY VOICE AND WORDS OF LOVE AND DELIGHT FOR YOU, AND YOUR LOVE FOR ME. PLEASE, APPRECIATE THE FACT THAT MY WORDS OF INVITATION AND OFFER OF PEACE AND HEALING CONTINUE TO BE GIVEN BY THE GRACIOUS WILL OF THE FATHER OF US ALL. THIS FRANTIC PACE OF LIVING IS ONLY A SHADOW OF THE LACK OF PEACE AND LOSS OF REST THAT WILL FILL YOUR BEINGS WHEN THE DEVASTATION BEGINS, ESCALATES AND RESULTS IN NEW TRIBULATIONS. THE WORLD AND ESPECIALLY THIS COUNTRY IS REELING BENEATH BLOWS (REPEATED AND PROLONGED) OF STRONG WINDS, SUBZERO TEMPERATURES AND HEAVY AMOUNTS OF SNOW AND ICE THAT SNARL TRAFFIC ON THE GROUND AND IN THE AIR, CAUSING SEVERE DELAYS AND INCREASED HEARTACHES. I OFFER THESE WORDS AS REFLECTION ON THE FACT THAT MY RECENT WORDS ARE BEING FULFILLED POWERFULLY AND CONTINUALLY. YOU "MUST" OBTAIN A FURTHER MEANS OF HEATING YOUR HOMES OR MANY WILL PERISH. THE COMBINATIONS OF WIND AND COLD ARE NEARLY IMPOSSIBLE TO OVERCOME WITHOUT ADDED HEAT SOURCES, BETTER INSULATION (JESUS ESPECIALLY MENTIONED FOR WINDOWS RECENTLY. C.A.), AND VERY WARM CLOTHING. PREPARE TO SEE AND HEAR OF MANY FREEZING TO DEATH, AS WINTER CONTINUES TO SEND FIERCE STORMS THAT SLOW OR DENY OPPORTUNITIES OF RESCUE OF THE POOR ON THE STREET OR WITHOUT MEANS OF HEAT OR ADEQUATE SHELTER. PREPARE YOURSELVES AND YOUR HOUSES, I TELL YOU. BE READY TO OFFER SHELTER TO MANY WITHOUT THE PROPER DEFENSE AGAINST STORMS DESIGNED BY HIDDEN PLANS TO TAKE MANY (WHO WANDER HUNGRY, NEEDY AND FREEZING) OFF THE STREETS AND OFF THE LISTS OF THOSE WHO SHOULD HAVE THE PROTECTION OF GOVERNMENT AGENCIES. NOTICE HOW MANY TIMES YOU HEAR THE WORDS UNPRECEDENTED, UNEXPLAINED, BEYOND EXPLANATION, MYSTERIOUS FORCES (AND THE LIKE) TO BE USED BY THOSE WHO REPORT WEATHER CRISES WORLDWIDE. BELIEVE THAT ALL WILL HAVE THE OPPORTUNITY TO LEARN ABOUT MY FATHER'S KINGDOM AND DECIDE FOR GOD THEN. BY THE GREAT MERCY OF OUR LOVING AND FORGIVING FATHER, HE DESIRES TO SAVE AS MANY OF HIS CHILDREN AS POSSIBLE. PRAY FOR ALL THOSE WHO WILL BEGIN NOW TO SUCCUMB TO THE BITTER COLD OR VOLCANIC ACTIVITY OR WHATEVER OTHER MIGHTY ERUPTIONS OF NATURE ASSAIL THE PLANET AT THIS TIME. BELIEVE MY WORDS, BELOVED OF MY HEART. THEY COME TO YOU TO SAVE YOU FROM

SUFFERING; TO PREPARE YOU WITH NEW UNDERSTANDING AND WISDOM THAT YOU MIGHT BE READY TO REACH OUT TO THOSE YOU MIGHT SAVE FROM UNBELIEVABLE COLD AND SUFFERING, HUNGER AND THE GREATEST ANGUISH. (This has yet to occur in this country to the degree mentioned here, but have been lived out to a greater degree by those in Europe; and we are told all that He has prophesied WILL BE fulfilled before His return.) DO NOT BE FRIGHTENED, MY DEAR ONES. BE GALVANIZED INTO ACTION IMMEDIATELY FOR THE PROBABILITY OF THE VERY EVENTS I AM DESCRIBING TO YOU. BE MOVED OUT OF YOUR PRESENT PLACES OF COMFORT AND DISBELIEF INTO AN ORGANIZED TEAM OF LIFE-SAVING, CONCERNED CITIZENS AND MEMBERS OF THE BODY OF CHRIST. MY PEOPLE, HEAR ME! SAVE YOURSELVES FROM SINS OF OMISSION AND GREAT REMORSE OVER A PITIFUL RESPONSE OR NO RESPONSE TO MY PLEA, MY WARNINGS. I LOVE ALL OF MY CHILDREN EQUALLY. YOU ARE ALL MINE, AND I WISH YOU TO BE PREPARED TO ANSWER THE CALL FOR HELP THAT WILL EXIST. BE AT PEACE, MY PEOPLE, BUT BE ALERT AND READY TO SERVE, TO HELP, TO SAVE."

12/27, "My little ones: It is I, your loving Mother: a Mother who prays and watches and protects you. Never will you imagine, my children, the joy that filled our hearts at our first sight of my Jesus, a tiny, tiny babe. A precious, adorable, beautiful Baby, my dear ones, my beautiful Baby: Son of God, Savior for the world, King and Messiah. I wonder, my dear ones, if I am still completely over the amazement, the gratitude at seeing the only Son of God, our Father, born into this world to fulfill all of the prophet's words concerning my Son. No, I suppose not; for each time I meditate, those joyful times come to me. Each time I am in prayer, I am united once again with all of Jesus; all He lived, all He experienced, and all I experienced with Him, because of Him, through Him and by Him.

Your prayers have been powerful, my children. They have been heartfelt and filled with hope for the promise that all of Heaven gives to her faithful ones: all of you who listen, who love, who welcomed Jesus, my Baby, into your hearts once again. Oh my children, the world is much colder at this time than it ever was in that outdoor manger: a stable, a lean-to in your words, a cave inhabited by animals, farm creatures, creatures of sustenance, gathered to see the One who sustains all in their midst. Think of this, my little ones. Think of my joy. Ask me, again and again, and I will share that joy with you, that deep, grateful joy, that deep gratitude. I fill you with the graces of the Season. I pour out upon you the mercy the Father sends this night. I tell you, at this special time, there will be a special healing in some area of your life. This gift is from the Father, this gift of His gratitude, His Christmas gift to you: a new gift, one that is needed most especially and uniquely by each of you who are so special and unique. Come to me to pray more. Come together more often, my dear ones, and pray. I have told you, my Son has told you, my Spouse, the Holy Spirit and God Our Father have told you, and I remind you again: this is a special group to the Heart of God and to my heart. Special gifts, special graces, special miracles will be given to you and through you, my dear ones. Make gratitude a focus of your prayer for the New Year. Thank Him for bringing you together, for bringing you to this place: this blest parish, this blest core group of faithful ones; of hearts softened and made more beautiful by love, by your love for me and for your God and for all of Our people in the world, especially the lost ones, and those terribly cold and hardened hearts in so many of Our people. Hold tightly to my love for you and my overwhelming joy with you. Be at peace, my children. Again I say, come everyday to be with my Son. He waits for you; and I am there, waiting with Him in a special, adoring way. Amen."

12/29, 3 a.m. "Oh daughter, it is truly I, your Jesus. Happy are those who have answered the call for increased surrender, a deeper commitment to the Father's Plan of Salvation, a renewed consecration of yourselves and all of your prayers and obedience to the requests of Heaven. These facts are also celebrated by all of Heaven, and great joy rings out to Our people of good will! A new understanding (of the serious days ahead) and preparations made for the probability of extremely cold weather and the poorest of poor (who have no home) given shelter in their great need, develops in the hearts of those who listen and believe and are acting on My pleas to be ready for any emergency in the days and weeks ahead of you. Gratitude and increased gifts are the response of the Father and Creator of all. It is imperative that the faithful receive immediate words of encouragement that they will persevere until the frigid weather is tempered, once more, by the change of Season and arrival of the temperate days of Spring.

People of the world, make another list this very week of things you need for keeping out wind and cold, and maintaining a livable environment. Take steps to seal windows and doors with products and cover cracks with material impervious to winds and stinging cold. The colder areas of this country will be even more susceptible to the subzero weather that will last long into Spring time. You can see how this will weaken those already exposed to inadequate shelter. You will also see scandalous misuse of the funds being reportedly set aside by your government for the shelters promised to those pitifully poor living on the streets, or in very poorly built housing. Remember, it is My Father's mercy at work allowing the suffering people on Earth to be brought into Eternity, to come as quickly as possible into the glory of the Heavenly Kingdom. Continue to pray for mercy for all people everywhere, that they will allow My Father and theirs to grant them all the mercy He wishes to pour out. They are indeed fortunate and blessed who are brought quickly and soon out of this earthly struggle into the greater opportunity to choose Heaven and their Triune God for all Eternity. Praise the Father Who acts to make the gift of salvation possible, available to all who will listen and repent. Oh My beloved people everywhere, you are My faithful ones whom I love as the apple of My eye! How My Heart thrills at the facts that surround you now: many Angels, more strength of perseverance, a greater understanding of your role in the coming events. Be at total peace. I am your Savior and King, little dear ones. Rejoice!"

FOR MERCY'S SAKE

"Work with anxious concern to achieve your salvation. It is God Who, in His good Will toward you, begets in you any measure of desire or achievement. In everything you do, act without grumbling or arguing; prove yourselves innocent and straightforward, children of God without reproach." (Philippians 2:12b-15a)

III

Year 2001

1/4, At Adoration Jesus said: "Dearest child, please take My words of love and instruction. 'My faithful people who brave each day, each struggle, each setback from your own weakness, but continue to persevere and grow stronger, it is I, your Lord Jesus, speaking words of wisdom that, like My Apostles, only those who have persevered to this point will understand and believe and learn from. I ask each of you, as you read or hear these words, to stop now and pray with Me asking Our Holy Spirit to grant even newer and increased protection and openness to the spirit of My words. The need for serious response on your parts is imperative. Do not succumb to the temptation to disbelieve and dismiss for any reason every word, every directive, every request, every promise I give to you now. My precious ones, this messenger has not seen, nor learned the content of, words I have just shared with others. Remember this, please My loved ones, and believe I am speaking as if for the first time this warning of particular events.

First I wish to thank you again for your response to words designed to alert you of a prolonged and extremely cold season of Winter throughout the world. I also bring gratitude and blessings and renewed mercy from My Father and yours for your focus on prayer of direct preparation for the celebration of My Birth. All of Heaven prays for you and with you when you struggle to answer a request for particular prayer and behavior before a Feast or before the possibility of dire events occurring. Behold, little precious ones, you have not only mitigated and delayed and defeated Satan's plans on many occasions, but are responding more wholeheartedly, more powerfully when new requests are given. This certainly has been part of My Father's desires for your own conversion and cleansing, your own growth in love and trust.

My Mother and I also cheer your efforts. You have filled Our Hearts with certain joy and delight over the new level of grace and gift given to you when you obey and love and work ardently for the Kingdom of God on the earth as it is in Heaven. Let us pray together once again, My people, for new eyes to see, new ears to hear, a new heart filled with new understanding for each of you. In the past, I have told you that each of you was chosen to live at this time and, before you were born, given particular gifts in order to **serve the people My Father would send to you after certain events of destruction and the Great Gift of**

His Warning to you, that the opportunity to be Our faithful remnant during these End Times was offered to all, but few accepted and even fewer will persevere in the face of possible martyrdom at the hands of the Antichrist. Nothing is impossible to the Triune God, but it is and always was and will be His Will to act in response and according to the will and response or lack of it in His people in each Age. Now this Law of Love and Mercy and Justice must begin to respond and act upon the evils of this Age, and the lack of enough response in enough of His people.

I tell you, there will be many more wildfires, **airplane disasters**, weather anomalies, disasters of unbidden storms never seen at this time of year. There will be entire areas in different parts of the world that will be totally removed from the earth by one or more of these hostile conditions. When I speak of tribulation, My precious ones, I do not simply mean a very cold winter or fierce storms of the kind you have yet to see, or even that your ancestors and relatives used to talk about, but the kind that destroy enormous numbers of people and large portions of the earth. I know most of you are terrified by these words and I ask you not to fear! I tell you, new strength and trust pour out upon you as you read these words of warning. Reread all of Our words and hear and see how often I have spoken of the real possibility of this type of destruction. Remember too that, although many wait in prayerful hope for the coming of the Illumination of all to the state of their souls as your God sees them, you are to remember that great destruction will usher in this Warning from My Father and many, many people will be taken into Eternity by an act of His mercy, as He also allows the plans of Satan to escalate to this degree, that His Own plans might begin (in this Age) to bring salvation to all who will accept it. You know in your hearts that a nuclear war is being prepared by the followers of Satan through the Antichrist. And make no mistake, My people, **the threat of a nuclear attack has been agreed to by all the superpowers even to the agreement of which nation receives a first strike!**

Listen not to those who say, 'God wouldn't talk in this way or try to frighten us with threats of war.' It is not My Father Who plans wars, but it is He Who warns you to be on guard and ready at all times for the great possibility. Believe that your prayers for mercy in the past held back My Father's hand that was ready to fall and allow a nuclear exchange: It WAS DELAYED AND DEFEATED (at that time) by His merciful response to your prayers. Isn't that what you count on your God to do: hear your pleas, answer your prayers, fulfill your needs, protect you when you pray to Him for help of any sort? My dear ones, do NOT BE CAUGHT OFF GUARD BY YOUR ARROGANCE and mighty egos. Read the story of each Age and each prophet sent by God to warn His people to repent and return. Do you not agree, My doubters, that Moses was an instrument of Yahweh who repeatedly asked the Pharaoh in the Name of the God of Israel to let His people go?

Stop your own critical airs and clever, harsh words and sorry judgmentalism against My messengers who have agreed to suffer for your resistance and rejection of My words and of Me. This will be one of the last times such strong words are used by Heaven to shake you from your complacent and lofty slumber and disinterest. Do not listen to the voices of the evil one and those who scoff at these renewed warnings for large scale disasters and cold that freezes and kills. When you were little, My precious ones, perhaps you were never harmed in any way. But loving parents still reminded you every day of the things, the behavior or places to avoid. Most of you learned to swim, but were never once in danger of drowning. You were sent to school and brought to Church and learned about how much you are loved, if that was the Father's Will for you. You had warm clothing and heated houses, most of you, and were protected as much as possible from any kind of harm although never actually did you experience danger or harm. But you knew what to do when a fire bell went off loudly in school, and you learned what was necessary to grow and develop your talents in order to take care of yourselves and others. All of these instructions were and are gifts of My Father's great love for you.

Now the possibility and threat of the annihilation of this planet is greater than ever in history, and My Father sends more people for more years (than ever before in history) to speak the words given them by Heaven with promises of protection against the most overwhelming power ever allowed to Satan and His remember followers. Remember this too, My beloved: THE GATES OF HELL SHALL NEVER PREVAIL AGAINST MY CHURCH. **It will nearly become extinct except in the hearts who love her, in the hearts where My Mother and I have triumphed. Do not be concerned about the past or trials or seemingly unfulfilled prophecy given also to purify Our faithful ones.**

GO FORWARD, MY DEAR ONES, ALWAYS FORWARD WITH MY MOTHER AND I AT YOUR SIDES, SURROUNDED BY MICHAEL AND HIS WARRIOR ANGELS AND THE MANY ANGELS YOU HAVE ALL BEEN GIVEN.

Begin to pray for peace in your own hearts, once again, as well as the hearts of all. Follow all My directives now, little ones. Come to Me every day for one hour (or fix a place of quiet in your homes...cta) and be in silence and listen and believe I am finishing the work of final preparation at that time with the healing and quiet strength and calm you must have to be the gift of mercy My Father has created you to be. DO NOT BE SAD OR FRIGHTENED, MY DEAR, DEAR LITTLE WARRIORS. REJOICE! The plan of My Father moves forward, and we go with it arm in arm, step by step, prayer by prayer. I love you, My own. You ARE Mine. You belong to Me."

New Locution: "Dearest children, welcome, welcome, welcome! (Many visitors have come from other states). How happy you make My Heart this night. I am your Jesus, your Lord and your God, your Jesus of Mercy. In the future it will be so important to remember that you will NEVER, EVER, EVER FOR A MOMENT BE ALONE; that My Mother and I and so many, many of her Angels accompany you, stand at your side, My children, give you strength and courage you know nothing about; but remember that it is there, and **it will always be**

there, to whatever degree you need, with whatever gift you need. Rejoice, My children, you are highly favored; you are beloved of My Father and you find great favor in His plans.

I come filled with gratitude. You ARE Mine. I have placed each of you in My Heart, deeply within My Heart, for I protect you, of which you are too often not aware. **When you are being protected, you are being comforted, you are given solace and encouragement.** Encourage each other, My dear ones. Comfort each other. Respect and cherish each other. No one knows the secret sorrows of each one, and so I encourage you to be aware, that each one be a delight to each other as you are a delight to Me. Pray for each other more, pray together more, laugh more, be joyful. I pour out joy upon you this night. I pour out My love. Remember, there is nothing to fear. I will remind you of that until the day I return! You will fight at My side, as you have been, but more now, from now on, and until you see Me coming on the clouds with My Angels.

What surprises and astonishment await you, as you discover gifts you are not aware of, abilities you didn't have before! How you will rejoice then. You fill Me with joy. **I count on you! Count on Me, My dear ones**. Whatever happens, whatever you see or hear, do not be afraid. Fear is not of your God, fear is a distraction and leads to doubts. REJOICE! Whatever you suffer, suffer in My Name and praise the Father and thank Him; for suffering is gift. **Suffering with joy will save the world, My dear ones.** Remember this! Invite all of Heaven to pray with you always, and you never know what gifts My Father has in store! Expect miracles. Expect great healings: many, many hearts converted. Come every day. I wait for you. We shall visit and you WILL HEAR MY VOICE, I promise you. Continue to pray and sing and praise My Father. Amen, My little ones."

At Adoration, "My dearest little soldier, be at peace for I, your Lord and your God, come today with words of wisdom and understanding for you and for all My people. They will be brief, but filled with love and gratitude to those who persevere in the law of love lived in Our Spirit, allowing your hearts to be further transformed and cleansed by My Will. Do not become anxious, My dear people, by what you perceive as 'waiting for events to begin', but focus on the events of cold and fire and continued oppression all over the world...and PRAY! Recognize the lack of new words from Heaven as an event in itself, and an escalation of My plan to cleanse your souls and behavior by requesting more time in quiet surrender, allowing Me to heal you anew and form you by the desires of My Perfect Will that turns you into a more obedient and more perfect instrument of mercy and love and compassion.

The people you will minister to and comfort, after My Great Gift of Merciful Warning to all, will **need you to be trained and tempered and transformed by your own gifts of new wisdom, knowledge and understanding,** given to you during this time, but also learned through experience of the struggle and hardship involved in your own personal loss of control of 'your world', as you know it; living in the world, but not of it; living now in a world of My choice, dying more to your choices of self-gratification and empty pleasures; living a life of self-sacrifice instead of self service and selfishness; living in a world filled with the peace of My Son instead of the world of chaos and noise and busyness and games. All of this change took time; but also has slowly and deeply prepared you to be who and what the poor lost and frightened and needy ones will need you to be in order to be the effective means of their comfort and renewal and conversion, more open yourselves to the Spirit of God and His gifts to them through each of you. Continue to pray for patience, My beloved ones. I am gifting you with perseverance and new patience (as you read), a deeper understanding of these times and My desires for you. TRUST YOUR TRIUNE GOD, MY PRECIOUS ONES. TAKE ALL I OFFER YOU, AND REJOICE! To praise and thank your Creator and Lord, to be filled with joy and love for your God and all His creatures is the quickest way to My Perfection ... all through the Heart of the Immaculate One, Mary the Mother of all people, the Queen of all hearts who have accepted her. Unite (YOURSELVES TO) each day with its waiting, its hardships and painful events, (but also its joys), to My Will for you and for the world; and **do not waste precious time analyzing, searching for reasons to satisfy your own egos, your own sense of justice (as you perceive it), for the justification of your own pride, your own puffed up egos.**

Oh My dear, dear ones, ego and pride are present in all people. Subdue these enemies to your peace of mind and heart by surrendering to the requests and directives of Heaven given by My Beloved Son and the Immaculate Mary to messengers in every part of the world. Ask Our Spirit to make you aware of egotistical behavior especially that contained in criticism and judgmentalism of others. It is time that is critical, My people. You will, believe Me 'Who has created you in love, Who sustains you in My love', **you will survive the nature of this critical period in history only by abandoning your own critical nature!** Be emptied of your sinfulness TODAY. Begin again in a new spirit of peace and patience, and trust that your God WILL remove every injustice, WILL expose to the light all the deeds of evil held now in darkness, WILL remove evil from the world and the hearts of those living on the earth at the proper time and in the right way. Trust Me, My beloved! Believe in My words this day and all that have been given through My Son, by His followers and gathered in Scripture, as well as today in loving words of warning and promise. Without you and your prayers, I continue to choose to be hampered, to be guided and enabled by your own choices, your own pleas for mercy.

I, your Father God, love each of you personally, deeply, in the greatest hope for your eternal future. Please, beloved children of My Creation, accept My love and forgiveness and mercy this moment. Love Me. Have mercy on Me. Forgive Me for My very necessary and perfect timetable for your lives, for the salvation of the world. My Son beckons to you with words of friendship, an offer of friendship and peace with all that is of My Kingdom here and in Heaven. Pray, My most beloved children of the earth, for those who continue to resist. I am your Father, your Lord and God, the One Who loves you!"

FOR MERCY'S SAKE!

At the end of the message given by the Father in the morning, He said, "Be assured of words of love this night and special gifts given to all who gather: "My dearest children, I tell you, I am your Lord and your God. I am your Father and come to you as Father, and invite you to come to Me as Abba. I invite you to come to Me, My dear little ones, without fear; to come to Me and just be. BE with your Daddy, My little ones! For it is true I am your Father, your Creator God. **I ask you to come without expectation, without need, without an agenda, to be in My Presence that I might fill you also with the peace of Jesus, My Beloved Son, in Whom I always am well pleased.** I tell you, more and more you are also ones in whom I am well pleased! I tell you this again to encourage you, to strengthen you, to help you to persevere, to promise you once again the might of My Arm, the protection that has been promised you all of these years.

How pleased and grateful I am for each of you; for the beauty of your soul; for your commitment again and again, more deeply each time, more committed each time to My Will for you, My desires for you: accepting whatever comes as My Will, as what is best for the moment.... not just for yourselves, but for those around you; learning through you to open up, to blossom, to knock down their walls of defense, of fear, of mistrust. I remind you again, I am your Heavenly Father, My dear ones. I AM LOVE. How could I wish to harm you? How could I desire anything other than good, to share Myself with you, to lift you higher, to place you upon My lap that I might caress you and soothe you, to comfort you, to cleanse you, as a Father Who places His child upon His lap after the child has come in from 'playing in the world'; Who then cleans off his face, perhaps with the corner of his garment; Who cuddles with this dear child He cherishes; Who looks at His child with shining eyes filled with delight, nearly overcome by His own love for this child? IT IS THUS I LOVE YOU, My children. Believe it! Believe every word you hear. It is so important, so necessary for your eternal future, for the present moment, for your life, My beloved ones: life now and life eternally in My Presence. Thank you again for learning to love Me, for accepting My mercy, My forgiveness, My plans for you. Know that everything about you delights Me! Remain so very close to Me. Be aware that you are held in My arms of love at every moment; that My love sustains you; that you were created in My love, by My love and for My love. Dear ones, **all will be well, never forget that**. Do not fear, My little ones. Stay within the protection of My arms, the shelter of My love. Reread My words many times. They will sustain you through times of difficulty. I love you."

(An exceptionally good look at our future.. C.)

"My dearest children: I am your Mother, here with many, many, many of my Angels this night. If you listen closely, you can hear them singing and praising God for you; singing hosannas to the King of kings, the Lord of lords, to the Creator of all; chanting your names, my children, (each of you before the throne of the Father), praising Him and thanking Him for all the beauty in your hearts, for allowing me to come and visit, to be with you in this special way, to tell you once again of my gratitude for you. My dear ones, you have no idea of the good your prayers are effecting. You have no idea of the souls that are being touched with new conversion: receiving new understanding, new wisdom every day, new strength to persevere, new openness to believe in all of Our words. Rejoice with me, as I rejoice over you for the great gifts waiting to be showered upon you at the proper time, at the time they are needed. Time will see this vast array of people who come to you, who stand before you in terror, so helpless, filled with grief over enormous loss; and you will say to yourselves, 'how will I ever help all of these people?' And I tell you, IT SHALL BE DONE, not just by your ministering to them then, but most of all, because of your FIDELITY NOW, BECAUSE OF THE PRAYERS YOU SAY FOR THEM NOW; because of the love in your hearts for people you have never seen, for your trust in all the words of Heaven these many years: the trust that remains in spite of the fact that you know there will be more waiting!

My children, there will be times of action and then again times of waiting and then again new events. This pattern will strengthen you even more, and will show you (even more) **the necessity of total surrender to the Father's Will**. For you see how totally He is in control and how much of Satan's plan He will allow in order to cleanse the earth and all the people on it. Already you are seeing history as it has never been. Praise the Father for your new leader. Pray for him every moment with all of your strength. He is a precious child of the Father and a great gift to this pagan country. Pray that he will be protected. He, too, is surrounded by Angels. Pray that the evil one is not victorious in his plan to destroy the good present in this man, for he is the greatest gift this country has seen in many a leader. My children, whatever the future brings, remember all the gifts I bring you this night: too many to enumerate, but you will feel them. You will find it easier to pray. You will find it easier to do whatever-it-is you are called to do, to become that instrument the Father calls you to be, desires you to be.

The Father has loved you into being. He maintains your very existence in His love, and He loves you into NEW BEING CONSTANTLY. You will live in this love forever! Think of it, my dear ones, growing constantly in His love, into the Heart of my Son, into unity with Him, (with your Triune God), and with me, my dear ones. I bring new conviction for each of you this night in all my words and promises. I bring you new awareness of my presence with you and my strength within you. I love you, my dear ones. You are still my little ones! You will always be my little ones, but you are growing into strong soldiers who will fight and help my Son to win the great battle, every battle ultimately against the evil one. My dear ones, rejoice that you have Me by this great gift of Our Father, as I rejoice that I have you."

Wednesday night: "My dearest ones, I am your Jesus of Mercy, Who comes this night. Welcome, My little ones, welcome. How happy you make Me, as you gather, seeking My Mother's prayers for yourselves, for your loved ones, for all the world; coming here together as My Father's children, as sinners admitting your sinfulness, your littleness, your weakness, and asking My Mother to pray for you as sinners. My Father is filled with gratitude when you come in humility asking blessings, asking new strength, new ability to overcome yourselves: this selfishness that resides in every person, the self-centeredness that continues to be an enemy of your own humility, the noise of the world that blocks out the voice of Our Spirit, the noise within your own hearts from living in the world for so long; but also, I rejoice over your CHANGING. YOU ARE BECOMING STRONG. Believe in strength you don't even feel yet! Believe in gifts you don't even see yet. Believe in all of My promises. How far faith in My words will carry you. **How much stronger you have yet to become**. How much delight and joy you have yet to feel, to see, to become. Is it not a great gift, My dear ones, to BECOME JOY, TO BECOME MERCY, TO BECOME THE COMFORT, THE GENTLENESS THAT WILL BE NEEDED BY SO VERY, VERY MANY? Thank you for remaining faithful, for it is a long wait. All of Heaven sends you new ability to wait; for My Father's plan is perfect, and it molds you and causes you to be what you have not been, to become who you are not and what you are not in this plan filled with wisdom and gentleness. A wise and loving Father molds His children gently, slowly, mercifully, tenderly. YOU ARE BECOMING TENDERNESS, MY CHILDREN!

Imagine right now being in the midst of an earthquake, as so many of Our little ones in the world have just experienced. Pray in reparation for their sins, for many did not know My Father, did not know Me. Yet, My Father will have mercy on them; and you, My very special ones, will pray in reparation for their sins, for their lives apart from Me, that they might accept the mercy My Father offers them now. The many, many He has brought into eternity will discover the Kingdom of My Father. Pray that they choose to accept it, for this is your mission. This is the greatest gift My Father can give you on earth; and all of Heaven prays that you will accept this merciful gift, this mission (a mission of love) of pouring yourself out for them as I pour My self out for you. I love you so much: totally, completely beyond, beyond anything you could imagine. Stay close to Me, My dear ones, every moment. We have much to do together! Amen. Be at peace."

2/8, At Adoration Jesus said: "My daughter, please know of My gratitude this day. There is no time for anything now, save a focus on every request: a living out of your consecrations, your vows of humility, purity and obedience, patience and fidelity. Human nature is weaker and more selfish and frivolous today than ever in history. This is no new statement! The understanding of the decadence in the lives of the greater percentage of people would be too much for anyone (on earth) to bear. The weeping in Heaven by My Mother is reflected in many signs given now in weeping statues, in the blood that flows from icons and pictures and likenesses of her; but these, though miraculous events to remind all of you, are merely a shadow of the great sorrow that exists within her Sorrowful Heart and Mine. The suffering of Our little ones is beyond belief by the human hearts of those who love and cherish their children and little helpless ones throughout the world. There are so many ways to help the children.

FOR MERCY'S SAKE!

I CALL UPON YOU TODAY, PEOPLE OF THE WORLD, TO RENEW YOUR ASSISTANCE, TO MAKE THE FOCUS OF YOUR PRAYERS THE DELIVERANCE FROM EVIL AND THE CLUTCHES OF SATAN, ALL OUR PRECIOUS, ABUSED, ABANDONED, SUFFERING CHILDREN EVERYWHERE: THE SQUALOR AND POVERTY, THE HATRED THAT CREATES AN ENVIRONMENT OF ANGER AND REJECTION OF THESE DEAR ONES WHO LIVE IN FEAR OF EVERY KIND OF ABUSE, THE LIVES SPENT ON THE STREETS OF A WORLD OWNED BY THE FOLLOWERS OF SATAN, THE LURE OF EVIL THROUGH DRUGS THAT SEEM TO ALTER THE MISERY, THE POOR EXISTENCE, THE LACK OF ANY KIND OF LOVE, AND LEAD THEM TO GANG-STYLE LIVES IN THEIR SEARCH FOR MEANING AND ACCEPTANCE. These few words of explanation, these grim pictures of the reality of life in the world now, are just a small and pale reflection of the results of Satan's successful plans to destroy the Father's creatures and creation.

I APPEAL TO YOUR HEARTS TODAY, MY PEOPLE. I CALL OUT TO YOUR SENSE OF OUTRAGE AT THESE INDIGNITIES, THESE TERRIBLE, SINFUL CONDITIONS: THE LIFESTYLES OF SO MANY THAT ALLOW THESE CONDITIONS TO EXIST, THAT FOSTER THE MANIPULATION OF INNOCENT CHILDREN WHO ARE SUBJECT TO THE INHUMANITY OF SO MANY, WHO ARE IN SO MANY CASES MURDERED BEFORE THEY TAKE A BREATH OR SEE LIGHT OUTSIDE THEIR MOTHER'S WOMB. THE WEAK AND HELPLESS HAVE ALWAYS BEEN THE VICTIMS OF MEN AND WOMEN WHO HAVE BECOME FOLLOWERS (VICTIMS THEMSELVES) OF SATAN AND HIS TOTALLY HATE-FILLED DEMONS. SHARE YOURSELVES. SHARE YOUR PRAYERS, YOUR TIME, YOUR GIFTS, YOUR LOVE, YOUR ENERGY, YOUR COMPASSION AND CONCERN FOR THE CHILDREN OF THE WORLD WHO HAVE NEVER KNOWN LOVE, WHO HAVE NEVER KNOWN 'LOVE'. THERE ARE SO MANY. THERE IS SO MUCH CORRUPTION OF ALL THAT WAS MEANT TO BE GOOD AND HEALTHY AND HOLY. THE POWER OF EVIL SHOUTS IN TRIUMPH FROM THE LIVES OF THOSE DEVASTATED BY ALL THE SINFUL ACTIONS OF THE DEPRAVED FOLLOWERS OF THE PRINCE OF LIES, THE KINGDOM OF SATAN, THE KING OF THE WORLD. GREED AND AVARICE, PRIDE AND ARROGANCE.... FIGHT THEM IN THE WORLD, IN YOURSELVES, AND BECOME MY PURIFIED WARRIORS, SOLDIERS OF LOVE AND MERCY. HAVE MERCY, MY PEOPLE; HAVE MERCY ON THE CHILDREN. I COME THIS DAY CRYING OUT ON BEHALF OF ALL THE VICTIMS OF HATRED; I, YOUR LORD AND KING, THE CHRIST CHILD OF YOUR HEARTS."

2/14, "Dearest ones, I am the Holy Spirit of God, the Spirit of Love. I wish to speak this night, for it is a celebration of love this day: a day to remember each other, friends, relatives, loved ones, spouses; to remember each other and your love for each other in a special way. Know that all of Heaven sends their love this night to you, their Valentines! Valentine is a Saint here with Us in Heaven. The many little cards and gifts that you exchange are a reflection of the love he had in his heart for the Triune God, for My holy spouse, dear Mary, for the poor and the wretched who lived in his day. I come to remind you of the poor and the wretched of your day. You have accepted My gifts over the years. You have been renewed in My gifts, strengthened. You have responded to the call of Mary, My spouse, bringing you words from Heaven, requests for prayer; challenging you to grow, to allow your heart to fill with concern for the poor and the wretched: the murdered innocents, the abused, those who cast off life as trivial, those who cast out loved ones from their hearts and their homes, and those who are cast off, who have never known love. Imagine, My dear people, what this must be like: you who are gifted and loved, who have cherished each other and been cherished in your families, in your growing up, in your learning to love as you have been loved. Yes, many families today do not know love, and this is why I come with more of My gifts. You know that where evil increases, grace abounds and, as Satan becomes more powerful in these times, I am more present with grace, with gift, with renewal, with fire! Children of the Triune God, how blessed you are, how fortunate ...beyond your imagination. I tell you this night, (this night of gathering of the faithful waiting for the Father's Will in your lives and in the world, waiting for Jesus), is like the Apostles gathered in the Upper Room with the Holy Mother, My spouse; and thus I tell you, I pour out the fire of Myself, the fire of My Love, the fire of My gifts upon each of you this night as you have never known them. (and these gifts are renewed and new for each one who reads everywhere … cta,) Gifts you already have are renewed and increased this night. Know that above all, you are given love as I pour Myself out upon you. You are given the ability to love more and to accept love more. Let your hearts be glad. You are being made holy by the Will of the Father. Rejoice!"

2/19, 2:15 a.m. "Dearest child of My Immaculate Heart: greetings dear one. I am your Mother in Heaven, bringing new gifts of patience and perseverance. You are correct in your perception of the increased attacks by the enemy of all that is good. It has been, and will continue to be, a difficult wait as the Father's plan unfolds so slowly upon the Earth. The time spent in prayer is strengthening Our faithful ones like nothing else could do. This final cleansing before battle is a branding (of hearts), an emptying of the world and its empty glitter. How few have remained willing to allow this degree of painful scouring, this scourging of old habits, old ways of being and doing, old behavior that included time spent frivolously and vainly; this further stripping of worldly garments that prepares your souls to wear the purple gown of fasting and penance, not only requested by Heaven, but eagerly donned and worn with humility and gratitude and joy for this great Season of Lent about to begin.

I call all My children (who listen and respond) to live these weeks detached from everything that is not building the edifice of faith and trust, hope and obedience, love and surrender within your hearts and will. This edifice is being built upon the Rock, the Foundation that is My Son, His Word, all the words given these many years by faithful messengers and accepted as the **building blocks of your house of virtue and grace**. The gifts of the Father of all have enabled every new addition.... added slowly and lovingly through His great love and mercy, His Perfect Will. Believe and marvel at the designs of Our God and Creator Who allows this new creation, this Mansion of Hope to be built according to His Will and desires for each one, that you might be guided and protected within this new structure of His Perfection! These rooms are illuminated by the Light of My Beloved Son. The pattern and design of this holy architecture is textured by layers of grace: the simple, yet beautiful designs of His plan for each of you and for all. Every room is designed to draw you ever closer to the throne room that springs forth at the center of this mighty building of God's plan, where He dwells in peace and harmony, tending to the upkeep and further development of the entire, perfect dwelling. Lent is a specific time in the Master Plan of the Divine Builder, a time for the inhabitants of His Will to spend discovering new gifts placed within each room contained in every heart that longs to find Jesus at the center of its existence, together with the Father and Holy Spirit, My Beloved Spouse. I am there in silence, worshipping, interceding, ever obtaining new graces to adorn and add to the strength and beauty of each room of your own heart-mansion. Come, My dear ones, come into the palace of your heart. Come and be in silence in union with my own (silence), discovering new vistas, new gradients of color, new arrangements of the Father's Will within each area of this growing edifice of mercy and love. You will find all the new treasures of your own choosing, many NEW POSSIBILITIES of choice, each one placed there by the desire of the Father, each patterned after the Life of Jesus and leading to His ultimate Sacrifice for you. Here are possibilities to add new furnishings (that glow with the fire of the Spirit) to your Mansion, that will attract and urge you to place them in just the right spot everywhere. Light shining from beyond will lead you on and on through each room, selecting and decorating with the particular beauty of each gift. These gifts, my children, will far outshine the beauty of former items that once filled your hearts. You may decide to spend more time in some rooms than others, moving out former items of attraction, that newer and more appropriate ones might blend with the new simplicity and austere beauty of the Architect's arrangements! I urge you to set aside a time each day in which to wander and ponder each room, contemplating the possibilities for improved arrangements of fewer, but more appropriate furnishings. I will gladly be present to assist you, if you invite me to come along with suggestions I have already discovered before you! You see, I know the Heart of My Son and His perfect obedience to the Will of the Father, as He emptied Himself to allow the furnishing of His Sacred Heart Mansion to be accomplished by that Divine and Perfect Will. My own heart has also been furnished: first with the words of Scripture, and then all the events and words of My Jesus that I stored up as my only treasures there. Many are the sorrows and memories of My Son's sufferings and my own in sacred union with His that adorn the rooms of this Immaculate and Sorrowful Heart. Many are the joyful memories of Jesus' birth and growing up obediently in the simple home provided by dear Joseph. Many are the memories of the incredible events of our lives spent in perfect trust in God's Will and the protection that led us through hardships and peace, ever further into the Will that allowed the perfect formation of the Perfect Victim of Love.

Call on me to assist you, my children. Call upon the Saints who spent much of their lives exploring developments in their hearts, always choosing new opportunities to decorate this growing edifice of holiness with treasures patterned after the Heart of Jesus and my own. Give this journey into your heart as much time and reflection as possible, my beloved ones. It is time, once again, for Spring Cleaning! Continue this journey of discovery of new treasures waiting to be claimed. These are opportunities you cannot afford to resist... and they are life giving and soul satisfying and free for the asking!! The Triune God beckons. Please, dearest little ones, let me help you. My dear Carol, these difficult and powerful words of imagery are meant to open the eyes and ears of hearts cluttered with shabby and worn furnishings filling hearts that have shopped only in the markets of the world. These hearts will shine with new treasures chosen with a deeper understanding of their value... eternal value, child. I am your Immaculate Mary, Queen of your heart, Queen of the world of faithful ones who have answered my call. All will be well for each of you, daughter. I stand at the door of your hearts ready to guide you through each room. I love you, little ones. You are mine, also!"

2/21, "My dear ones: I am your Mother. Praise Our Father with me, my children. THANK HIM FOR ALLOWING ME TO BE WITH YOU, for I tell you, THESE GIFTS WILL NOT CONTINUE FOR MUCH LONGER. THERE WILL BE RARE OCCASIONS, SPECIAL OCCASIONS, WHEN THIS GIFT WILL BE GIVEN, BUT NOT AS OFTEN, NOT AS INTENSELY AS YOU HAVE KNOWN THEM. So it is with special gratitude and great love in my heart for each of you that I come this night. My dear ones, what can I say to reach the deepest level of your understanding, of your hearts, of your souls? I wish to tell you and I wish to beg you to remember and to believe that I am always with you; that I love you beyond words, beyond anything you can imagine, beyond any love in this world, even beyond your needs, my children! Believe me, your needs are many, (a gentle smile here... cta.). I take all of your needs in my hands this night, your desires, your hopes, your dreams, all of your petitions. I hold them against my Immaculate Heart and I purify them for you, and I take them to the throne of our Father. Believe this. Believe that you are ever protected in my Mantle. The Father has many plans for all the gifts you have been given. This is not news, but I remind you this night and I beg you to remember every loving word I have given to you: the written word and my spoken word. I tell you this night that events are about to escalate again. You can see them everywhere. You are reading about them. You are praying about them. You are listening with your hearts and praying with your hearts with all of your might. I see your resolve, your commitment to me and your love for me. What joy you give me. How close we are, my dear ones, how much you are mine. How I love you. How precious, my little ones, you have become. The littler and more childlike you become, the more mighty you will be in the Father's plan. Remember these words. There will be nothing you are unable to do, for you will have my protection and many, many more Angels now.

Satan and his demons fill the air, fill hearts bent on destruction, fill plans for the demise of the world. You must be serious and joyful. You must be hopeful children, as I am hopeful, for your prayers and love have shown me hope. I know, because it is written, that my Jesus will overcome and defeat Satan and his demons and rid the world of evil. But you have added to my hope for a glorious victory: A VICTORY FOR YOU, MY DEAR ONES, WHICH HAS BEEN MY HOPE. Your hearts become more and more like the Immaculate Heart I have been given. You shine with my love, with the power of my Jesus. You are ready, my dear ones, for anything and everything. But most of all you are ready to carry the banner of joy. This is your banner.

YOU ARE JOY. Most certainly, my children, YOU ARE MY JOY! How close you are to the Kingdom of Heaven. How closely you are living the Father's Will. Think of how far you have come in a twinkling! Think of the Father's great love for you, His many, many gifts. Rejoice with me for each other, for gift, for grace, for miracle in your lives. YOU ARE MIRACLE, MY DEAR ONES! Know that I am with you, and be aware of my presence. This will help. DO NOT BE AFRAID. THERE IS NOTHING TO FEAR, although fearful events are on the horizon. You have heard these words before, and they have been delayed. And now it is difficult to believe in the imminence of these events. Children, do not fool yourselves. Do not let your guard down for one moment. The evil one, more and more, attempts to distract you, to place obstacles in your path. Be aware of this. Be on guard. You have me, my Angels and the Might of the Arm of God. You have become my little, holy ones. Imagine! Stay very close to me, as I will lead you more and more deeply into the **Heart of My Son, your ultimate protection.** I am with you, my children, always loving you, caring for you, praying for you, lending my maternal strength. Be of great peace. Let us spend this Lenten Season together, side by side, (and during every one that follows until Jesus returns) as we adore EVERY DAY, my children. Live in my great love for you. Remind each other. Remind yourselves of my great love and that all is well, that all will be well, FOREVER! I love you. Amen."

3/2 At Adoration: "Daughter, be at peace! I am Jesus, Son of God, Savior and King. Be refreshed now, little messenger of My words to all. I have words for Our faithful ones this time of days that are one day, the Day of the Lord. Only in My peace, in My grace, in My Heart do you know and understand these words. Only as one who is obedient to My request for more prayer, more time spent in silence with Me can you realize the seriousness of obeying every desire of My Father, of desiring to appease His Wrath, of the importance of the fulfillment of His Plan for the salvation of the whole world. As you read and hear of devastations, yet see the continued protection against great loss of life, (except in those places where My Father's Will calls many to Him that they might choose His Kingdom, come quickly to Heaven and pray for their families and countries), you realize that His mercy is still poured out vigorously where there are faithful ones to pray for His mercy. To understand My Father's plan; to recognize His Perfect Will, especially in areas that need a vigorous shaking to wake them up to the shame of their conduct, their 'wild behavior'; this in itself is a source of peace. This is wisdom and understanding and other new levels of gift from Our Holy Spirit. This time of watching and **waiting for all is a necessary time of testing of all your own promises, all you profess to offer to do, to become.**

My beloved children of the world, I your Jesus, am speaking. To sit in My Presence in the Tabernacle, to bask in the peace only I can give you, to join others in times of special prayer and Lenten observations is the path to joy! To gather with the faithful in My Name is to live out one of the primary duties as My followers. To persevere in the repetitious actions of daily prayer and practices is the pathway to life and holiness. This will strengthen you like nothing else in your commitment to Me, (to your Triune God) and dearest Mary, your holy Mother. Do you notice the world and its noise and empty demands fading into oblivion, My precious ones? Do you notice the peace and harmony of an existence without the noise of television and movies and other worldly distractions? Please take time to look around and appreciate nature, even though this might contain cold and rain and snow and difficult conditions. Let your senses be healed by the effects of My Father's Will. Recognize the escalation of His plan and the fulfilling of events prophesied by Heaven. Be filled with gratitude as you see possibilities of miracle through new eyes of faith, where once you saw only hatred and loss.

The understanding of each day as a blossoming of My Father's Will for you and for the world brings new comfort, new trust in your place at this level of His desires for you. The Saints had this wisdom, this knowledge that all is working for the good of those who love the Lord. Nothing else can bring this peace and joy to your hearts in the midst of daily trials and struggle. Then as these difficulties increase, so will your level of understanding and the strength of your consecration to all the Father allows, your total surrender to His providence, His wisdom. To be at true peace amidst true chaos is impossible without special gifts and preparation by Our Father in Heaven. To receive these gifts, one must be open and anxious to receive them! **To be faithful to this 'routine' is the practice that makes perfect!** Persevere, My loved ones. Stay little and humble in your devotions, your increased acts of charity, even to sending packages of compassion and love and prayers for healing conversion to those who suffer abuse and poverty and the cruelty of destructive habits or the devastation of nature. Increased power is given your prayers at this time, and I send you increased joy and gifts of Our Spirit to carry you to new heights of love and service. You are overcoming yourselves! You are becoming mighty in word and deed and humility. You are being transformed by My Father each time you accept docilely whatever each day brings: the little ways, the humble ways, the secret ways you allow others to ridicule and reject, cover you with harsh words and jeering attitudes at your new way of life in Me, your increased meekness and patient compassion. This is the new level of unity with My life and suffering that the world cannot accept, cannot see, cannot understand. Be filled with new conviction and comfort. You are living in the Kingdom of My Father's Will ... about to come into a renewed earth cleansed of evil and ugliness. All of My promises to you WILL BE FULFILLED, My dearest, My own faithful ones. Be filled with peace and assurance of victory. The best is yet to come. The victory is yours, is Mine!"

3/7, "My little ones, I am your Jesus of Mercy. My Father's plan escalates, and you will see new events in the world **and closer yet, to home**. Within this country, this very week, you have seen more tragedies: children killing children, threatening, carrying weapons, reflecting the degree of evil in the world now; allowed by My Father to cry out to you the seriousness of the times, of all My words of warning and preparation for each of you. I have died for you, My children. I cannot do more except that I rose from the dead for you. I have offered you freedom again and again and again: freedom from addictions, from harmful behavior, from habits that are less than My Father requires of you and desires of you. I need all of who you are.

I NEED YOUR HEARTS COMPLETELY, not divided; not yet still, partially even, in the world, but totally now, your total focus on My Face, your total surrender. **Give Me all your free time**. You have more than you realize. I ask you tonight to stay away from the telephone as often as possible. (When you read or even reread, take this request as now, tonight! Cta.) This can be an instrument of comfort, I know, and help to others, and you have used it to reach out for comfort; but I ask you now to realize in these times it has become more and more a distraction, an interruption in the quiet I call you to, in the silence, in the very meditation that you are able to keep. Even, children, you might consider turning off your phone during the day, if this is possible! Only in silence will you hear My voice, will you be more aware of My Presence with My dear, dear, dear Mother and so many Angels. Feel and hear the seriousness of this request! I plead with you this night to be very, very generous about these words, these requests, these reminders of the seriousness of the times; but also that you might live recollected in this Presence in joy. It is joy that will win the day, EVERY day! It is joy alone that overcomes fear and doubt, anxieties... both concerns you needn't have at all, My dear ones. You are Me, My dear ones, and this time of Lenten preparation is an opportunity to become more united with Me; yes, with My sufferings, with the deprivations I had every day as part of My entire life, I ask you to share for this brief period of time. You will hear otherwise, but I tell you, **it is still most important to deprive yourself. This will strengthen you, your discipline, your resolve, your commitment to Me, to My Father's Will, to My dear Mother's requests to you.** Children, I ask you for nothing but love. Could you deny love to Love? I am Love. I am your Light, your Peace, your Mercy. I am All in all. Believe all My words, but most especially when I say to you, 'I love you', know that nothing else is more true. My little ones, 'I love you!'"

3-14, "My dear ones, I am your Jesus. I come again this night through this special gift to each of you from My Father: a gift to all who hear, who listen, who pray, who respond to all the requests of Heaven, especially those given through My dear, dear Mother who is with Me now and has been praying along with you, walking among you, blessing you, pouring out her love and her gratitude upon each of you. My children, you have MY gratitude! You know this, but the human heart needs to hear again and again of the gratitude, the appreciation, the love of their Lord and their God. I am your Lord and your God. I am your Savior. This is the time of preparation for the time in My life when I suffered and died to redeem, when I rose and opened the gates of Heaven to all. No one can appreciate how great a gift this has been; but as you pray, more and more your understanding grows: your appreciation, your ability to praise and thank My Father for sending Me to you at a crucial time in history. HE IS ABOUT TO SEND ME TO YOU AGAIN AT THIS CRITICAL TIME IN HISTORY. Over and over again I have told you there is nothing to fear. Over and over My Mother and I invite you to pray for suffering souls, suffering bodies, minds and hearts and spirits everywhere.

This very week will see new events of Nature, My children. Begin to pray now for those who experience them, for those who see new hardship, new struggle, new loss; who will be living in groups as refugees because of the destruction around them. Pray that their hearts will be touched and opened by these events; that they will begin to be open to My Holy Spirit, the Spirit of Love. It is a time of struggle for all. You can believe this, as you struggle in your own lives, as one thing or another seems to go wrong, or that you are not feeling as well as you might. The strength you expect just isn't there! My Father calls you to quiet and if you do not voluntarily choose this, My children, My Father will make it possible for His faithful ones to comply with these requests! These are such important requests now for the final preparation of your hearts, the final healing of hearts: hearts dedicated and consecrated to My Mother, to My Father's plan. It will take many, many prayers and hours of silence to enable the gift of salvation for the entire world, My dear ones!

How easily you are distracted, and yet, My Father understands this. He has given you many gifts, and you are using them well and wisely and fully; but My dear ones, **you must make time each day for quiet:** quiet listening, that I might pour the gift of quiet strength into you now as a preparation for later when the many (people) you have heard about for so long will descend upon you. It will be as a cloud of locusts (the people...cta), My children. The numbers will be great. The noise and confusion from the chaos will be great, and you must be strong. You cannot just decide that you are going to do these things, as I have mentioned in the past. Everything takes practice**. Only practice will make My dear, dear ones perfect!** I love you so much. I wish for you to succeed, that you might be filled with the joy waiting for you in the service of Our lost people. There is no way you can see now or understand now what it will be like then, so I simply continue to repeat the requests of Heaven asking that you follow all of My directives meant to protect you, to build you up, to open you to all the gifts you will be offered when you need them. My own dear ones, these beautiful days, spend time, (part of your prayer time), walking among the gifts of Nature from

My Father; walking in the sunshine, even in the snow, if it is wherever you are; but walk, My children, and appreciate My Father's gifts. Allow that time to slow you down, to fill you with peace.

You are loved so mightily by all of Heaven. My Father is gifting you in special ways this night. You will know these gifts when you discover them. You will think of this night and your new gift and say, 'Praise you, Father. Thank you, Father. You knew how much I needed this. You know my vulnerability, my weaknesses. You know my unfaithful nature. Thank you, Father, for this gift. Thank you for Your gracious goodness to me, Father, for Your mercy, for your providence.' My children, as you pray, as you walk, as you work, be aware of My Presence. As you practice this, there will be times of greater Presence when suddenly you will realize strongly that I am standing right there where you are; and this will be another gift, and you will smile, remembering My words, feeling a rush of gratitude that you are so blessed. Listen, My children, in silence. Listen for the prayers that accompany yours. Listen for the voices of Angels in the silence. Listen for My voice. Again I remind you, children, I am whispering in your ear constantly: 'I love you. You are Mine. You belong to Me."

3/21, "My dear ones, I am your Jesus, come again this evening to be one with you in this gift of unity of prayer; one with My Mother, with Our Father's Will, one in Our Spirit. My Father gifts you with greater unity this night because He loves you, because, My dear ones, you ARE lovable! I remind you of these two reasons for My Father's love, for you must remember that He has loved you first, that you are created in love and that you are sustained in love and you are called to love. Love covers all: every action, every word, every thought, every urging of the Holy Spirit, the Spirit of Love. I ask you more than ever from this day forward, to be aware of the Spirit of love, to speak gently to everyone, everyone, especially those closest to you. I ask you for an honest appraisal this week of your loving behavior. Look at yourselves, My children. Are you gracious? Are you patient? Are you appreciative of those around you? Are you grateful for all that is done for you by others; again, especially by those closest to you? Are you thoughtful of the needs of everyone? Are you compassionate, My dear ones? **Compassion comprises all of the other gifts, for it requires patience and all the virtues, and understanding and wisdom, to be compassionate.** You are called to compassion in a greater way. Yes, as a preparation for those who come. As you know, **everything We have spoken of, everything We call you to do, to become, is a preparation for those dear ones who will come to you so helpless and needy, so very nearly at death's door themselves**. Your heart will be moved to pity. Always the sight of one in need moves the heart, but it is the continuation that makes up compassion. That is the stuff of patience!

Think again and again, My dear ones, how patient My Father has been with each of you and His faithful ones all over the world. Throughout all of history My Father relented again and again of just punishment to His people and held back His hand wherever He could, as often as He could, as He is doing now, this day. It cannot last forever. It cannot continue, for as your hearts continue to soften, there are too many hearts that continue to harden: too many who turn back to the world, (the world of frivolous, mindless, empty activity) too many who return to gratification, too many who have turned away from the Father. This season of Lent, My children, you can do more. There is more fasting. There is more prayer. There is more obedience to the call of My Mother and to the call to spend time with Me in silence. Please, My children, reread the words I am giving you (this night) many times. I AM CALLING YOU TO PERFECTION, MY DEAR ONES. You have the gifts and the grace and the strength to do all of these and more, for it is in joy I call you to joy of response, to joy in action and surrender. In total surrender, My children, there can be nothing but joy, for you are doing My Father's Will. What could be more blessed, more freeing? Little holy ones, you are Mine, beloved of My Father, precious children of My Mother, instruments of the Spirit of Love. Be filled with My peace this night, My children, for all is very, very well for you. I am hiding you now from the world. I am hiding you in My Sacred Heart, My Sacred Wounds, My great, great love. I am with you. Feel My Presence. Know My Presence. Rejoice in My Presence!"

3/28, "My dear ones, I am your Jesus, here with you by the great gift of My Father, by a new outpouring of Our Spirit, by a new level of mercy from the bountiful store of mercy that is My Father. You fill My Heart with joy. I tell you again, your hearts are a respite for My Mother and Myself from the rejection in the hearts of so many, from the coldness there in the hearts My Father has created, My Father sustains with His power and His love. My dear ones, you only need to look around in this very city, in your country, most especially in the world, and you understand the need for mercy, for humble servants of My Father's Will. **Humility, My children, is rarely what My people think it is.**

It is not to be last. It is not to be the tiniest voice.

Sometimes it will be necessary to be the voice that leads.

You have mercy on people when you help them by leading them, by showing them the way, by making them feel comfortable, by your graciousness, your hospitality, your welcoming and your sincerity. A humble servant of My Father is a handmaid of the Lord; patterns his or her life after the life of My Mother; begs to have her generous heart, her ability to sustain the unkindness of neighbors, people everywhere. How cruel people were to My Mother. How kindly she always responded to any word thrown at her, to any challenge, to any bitterness, ridicule, all on account of Me. I wept at the suffering My Mother endured for My sake, and yet I knew it had to be, just as she knew My suffering had to be. My dear ones, you can be little as you are leading. You can be humble explaining a mystery, answering a question, leading prayer, leading song, expressing your love for your God and your holy Mother, rejoicing in Us, being unafraid to suffer. A humble one merely acknowledges the source of all gift. A humble one reminds everyone: 'to God belongs the glory! Praise you, Father, for your great gifts and goodness and patience with me.' A humble one serves the needs of others without grumbling, is the first to come forward to look to the comfort of others, who puts the needs of self behind and thinks only of the needs of another. It is one thing to do this occasionally, but you will be called upon in the future to sustain this activity, to make this a way of life. Although I will be giving you all the gifts you will need, you will know fatigue, you will know exhaustion at times, My children.

You must practice humility, become humility and be emptied first that you might be filled with the honest understanding of your own weaknesses, your own vulnerability and yes, My children, your own sinfulness; not to dwell in these, not to become maudlin or beyond sorrow, but what is normal for sin. For this, too, is pride; but to focus on My face, to focus on My beauty, My children, to realize that you are being beautified in Me and in My Mother; truly, as each of your hearts becomes more honest, more sincere, more grateful for the gifts of others, becomes more beautified, more radiant, shining with the light of purity. When you gather, My children, there is a light of community light, not only around you, but from within. Others see this, My children, who accept this: to live according to this great community spirit and light. The light of My Presence that shines from within each one (and collectively) can bring you to a great humility and gratitude, My dear ones, to more surrender, more peace. This gift of My peace is to be the environment in which you live out the rest of your days. Without My gift, without a humble and grateful heart, you will not survive the chaos. You will become an example, a leader, yes, that My Father will need you to be: not in any way you can imagine now, My children; but you trust My words after all these years, and I speak tonight to give you reflective thoughts, to bring you to a new place of understanding, a new peace of humility, surrender. Only surrender, My children, brings you face to face with truth. I AM TRUTH, My children. EMBRACE ME! I love you so much. Amen."

4/7, "I am your Lord and God, Three in One, present and united in the great Sacrament of the Altar with Jesus, the Word. Trust My words: The world hurtles towards further destruction, as confrontation and ego surges on every front. The plans of Satan are obvious in snares and plots meant to lure countries into a World War of terrible proportions and consequences. My people who have remained faithful are praying like never before in history and responding to My Will for them in a powerful and trusting manner. I tell you, nothing can prevent many victories by the Antichrist before the return of Jesus, My Beloved Son, but the ultimate victory is His.

MERCY WILL ALWAYS REMAIN ALIVE IN THE HEARTS AND LIVES OF PRAYER AND SERVICE OF THOSE WHO CONTINUE TO SURRENDER TO THE NEEDS OF HELPLESS BROTHERS AND SISTERS WHO RETURN TO ME AND RECEIVE THIS MERCY AS THE GIFTS OF FORGIVENESS AND LOVE AND SALVATION. EACH OF YOU WILL BE THE SOURCE AND ONLY EVIDENCE OF MY MERCY IN THE COMING DAYS. EACH OF YOU WILL BE MY INSTRUMENTS OF HEALING AND RENEWAL IN HEARTS AND LIVES NEARLY DESTROYED BY THE DEATH CULTURE OF YOUR DAY: THE PRESENT VICTORIES OF

SATAN'S PLAN TO DESTROY ALL OF CREATION AND EVERY PERSON, EACH A PRODUCT OF MY CREATIVE LOVE. MY PLAN TO GIVE SALVATION TO MY PEOPLE WILL NEVER BE COMPLETELY DEFEATED, OR EVEN OVERCOME BY THE POWER OF EVIL. NEVER FORGET THIS, MY DEAREST PEOPLE. WHATEVER IS THE NATURE AND UNFOLDING OF MY PLAN, WHATEVER SEEMS TO BE THE END - MANY TIMES - WILL IN REALITY BE ANOTHER BEGINNING OF A NEW LEVEL OF MY PLAN, A NEW DEVELOPMENT AND DIRECTION OF WHATEVER MUST OCCUR TO ULTIMATELY FULFILL SCRIPTURE, FULFILL AND COMPLETE MY WILL UNTIL THE MOMENT WHEN MY JESUS RETURNS VICTORIOUS AND REMOVES ALL EVIL FROM THE EARTH.

I hold in reserve for you every grace and gift necessary for your own perseverance and victory. Believe every promise, every word given these many years and live, My beloved holy ones. I call on you, once again, to become mercy for the world, to become the face of Jesus in the face of danger and destruction, despair and disillusionment. With each new event, remind yourselves, 'sin and sickness, evil and darkness are about to be removed from every life, every soul, every action of every faithful one!' Be strengthened by hope, by joy, by an outpouring of love and mercy from your own hearts that will transform all whom you meet. Be humble as befits a child of God. My daughter, thank you for taking My words meant to encourage the faithful who wait in peace and hope. The suffering seems nearly unbearable at times, but is forming the endurance necessary for battle. **Tell My people to go slowly and carefully, gently and gratefully each moment of each day.** The Spirit of God is upon each of you. Amen and Amen. Be at peace, child. All is well. I am your God and Father."

4/10, Jesus said: "I must remind you again to praise and thank My Father, for He will allow you to perform amazing feats of healing to enable conversion, to enable the return of many, many, many of Our lost ones. I repeat this often to you, for I wish you to remember it as a focus of your prayer, as an impetus, as a motive. Finally, to remain faithful for your own sake and for the lives and the salvation, My children, of all those you will touch, whom you will bring to My Father; for whom you would provide (along with My own redemptive action) salvation for all eternity. I ask you this week for as much quiet throughout the day as possible. This is more possible than you think, My children. Come away with Me on My walk through the days before My suffering, before the questioning, the ridicule, the terrible torturous beatings. Allow Me to look into your eyes, to touch your heart with My loving glance, to transform you as I hold you closely to My Sacred and Suffering Heart. I wish to transform you, My children, into pure joy: a joyful instrument of whatever is needed at the moment, by whoever stands before you; whoever it is, even one who may be close to you now.

As you put on My face, as you put on the face of mercy, people will see and be drawn to you even more, not by what you do or even by what you say, but by the beauty of My presence: the strength, the power to draw others, not to yourselves, but to Me. That will be My power working within you, pouring forth as My blood (would pour out...cta) to cleanse others by your forgiveness, by your patient listening, by your gentle compassion. My Father's plan could never succeed without you and faithful ones just like yourselves. Focus on nothing else but My love for you and whatever arrangements you make to be with Me, to walk in My footsteps. Walk not before Me or behind Me but with Me, My children, next to Me. Help me, My children, help Me carry this cross as I am helping you carry yours. I die for love of you, My children. All of the Angels will sustain you through this week in a new way, in a special way; and you will know their presence, a gift from My Father: like the Angels He sent to sustain Me as I knelt in the Garden, as I carried My cross and fell three times. Only with the help of the Angels was I able to rise and continue. Count on this help, these Angels, these gifts: new gifts from My Father. Amen."

4/11, "My beloved children, I am your God and your Father. I come this night to be with you because of My great love for you and because of the seriousness of these times, because it is Holy Week, the most sacred time in your liturgy, in your year, in history. Thank you for gathering once again. I remind you what great honor you give to Me and to all of Heaven. My children, this night I simply gather you in My arms to tell you that you are My faithful ones, to welcome new souls who are here, new faces upturned with love and prayer, answering all of My requests, responding obediently and joyfully. I gather you to comfort you and sustain you, for you are My beloved and precious ones. It is you and people like you all over the world, (My children, My chosen remnant) who will bring My mercy into the world, who will help many, who will co-redeem, who will bring salvation to so very many. Remember these words, for it will not appear to be so, as you view the events of the future. And yet, you will be actively involved with many who return to Me. Remember that this will be multiplied many times all over the world; that your prayers will be given added strength by Jesus, My beloved Son, and dear Mary, the Immaculate one, and by all the people in Heaven: all who have ever lived and are there now in the happiness, the bliss, the joy of Heaven. Keep this in mind, My dear ones, for it will be a source of strength. It will give you new hope when new hope is needed, and new reason to continue; for there will be times when you will feel that your prayers are useless, for you have been told **there will many victories by the evil one, by the Antichrist in the beginning of his campaign.** But all of these things must occur to fulfill Scripture and are part of My Will. My little ones, you are chosen to participate in events, in healings, in conversions, in greater numbers than anyone who has ever lived. Believe this and rejoice. Although I am your God and Creator, mere human words are not enough to explain My love and My gratitude for each of you. You have filled all of Heaven, not only with joy, but hope. Allow yourselves to be filled with hope now and cling to that hope, My children. It will be a valid hope. And, again, it too will sustain you and build on itself and spread like a stone that enters a pond, whose ripples reach the shore and come back again to touch it.

My children, My Son begins His sorrowful march to the Cross now, but He began with a great victory: the victory of the Eucharist, the victory of remaining with you throughout all of the time since that first Last Supper, that first sharing of His Body, His Blood. Focus on Eucharist. Focus on being Eucharist as well as mercy. Focus on the transformation of yourselves this very week. In these days ahead, focus on the great love of My Son as He suffered and died for you. Allow this to penetrate, as never before, your understanding, your gratitude; for it is these that will transform you, that will open you more to the power of Our Holy Spirit, the Spirit of healing, the Spirit of love, the Spirit of sacrifice, the Spirit of surrender which I pour out upon you again this night in My great, great love for you. I wish only to gift you, My children, to make you joyful and grateful that you are My child, that you belong to your Triune God. When My Jesus returns, you will have been united with your God, more than anyone, through all the service, the outpouring of love you will be giving to Our people. What great gifts await you, My children, what great love. I bless you tonight, My dear ones, and I thank you again in My Name, in the Name of My Son, Jesus, and in the Name of Our most Holy Spirit. Praise Me, My children; thank Me for choosing you, for all your gifts. It is fitting that I, your God and Father, would be praised. You were created for this, My dear ones. I love you. You are everything to Me and to My plan for the world."

4-24, At Adoration, Jesus said: "My Carol, please write. Again I tell you, new levels of healing are being experienced by those with whom you share My words. Your Heavenly relatives and friends are helping sustain you through long hours of speaking and prayer. Here now are words for the world meant to bring a new level of appreciation for the mercy of My Father.

'My dearest people of My Merciful Heart, thank you for your increased devotion to My Divine Mercy throughout the world in spite of so little response from those within My Church, who should be shepherds of Mercy, leading you closer to understanding, and the opportunity to gather and offer one mighty voice of praise to Me for the revelations to dear Faustina and opportunities to bring increased mercy upon the world. Without your love for My Divine Mercy, and humble pleading for the world, those who were gifted in new and special ways could never be touched by this free gift from My Father that has brought added peace to the hearts of Our faithful ones, and merciful protection and conversion to many who will be added now to the numbers of Our faithful ones. All of Heaven rang with joy from the love in your hearts and your level of gratitude for the mercy in your own lives and the world in general. My Father's plan goes forward once again to add to your strength and discipline for the coming days. People of the world, rejoice, for you are still receiving prophecies of events about to erupt everywhere. I tell you especially today of plans of the New World Order members to launch all-out war in the areas where conflict has already occurred. Why do you suppose there are renewed challenges in Bosnia, the Far East and Africa? To increase tensions and dilute your protection from the military at home, these renewed hostilities will 'require' (His emphasis...cta) added numbers of forces to be sent out to protect the mentioned territories. I have told you many times that My Father will allow the plans of Satan to escalate now, and this will include many smaller wars that will set up the divisions between major world powers and result in taking sides. These had been delayed as elections and holidays and other distractions allowed a greater concentration of military aggression to seem to suddenly break out in many areas. You will see this renewed now because of the subtle movement of troops and money among the world's super structures.

For those of you who watch and wait and believe in all Our words to you, you see now the obvious plans to control your world markets and remove money from those, who thought they were increasing their personal holdings, who watch as all their new money derived from manipulated and inflated stock prices and holdings purchased with new mortgages, lose personal wealth and homes; savings, (educational and retirement funds) disappear. My words may seem harsh, My people, and I remind you that ONLY MY GIFT OF PEACE WILL PROVIDE YOU WITH TRUE WEALTH AND GIVE MEANING TO THE STRUGGLES THAT NOW UNFOLD!

Because an escalation in My Father's plan includes the greater presence of evil influence in the world, the next events must be ones of renewed war and destruction, the ultimate plans of Satan to conquer the world. The Antichrist is hidden for now, but his own powerful followers are very much in position to initiate warlike activity fomented behind the scenes, as I have already explained to you. As you see these words fulfilled one after another in many places of renewed combat, be assured of the TRUTH OF ALL MY WORDS. Fear is never the object of words of Heavenly warning, but a calling out to obtain renewed trust and prayer from all of you, Our faithful ones. These events begin immediately (this, it seems, is such a different type of word to us who wait … cta.) in order to convince you to persevere in your response to Me and to Our dearest Mother, the Immaculate one. Remember, you are living in critical times, and all the actions in this battle between Good and evil will be of the nature of critical threat to the safety of the entire world, another reason We promise so often the protection of Heaven from so much destruction according to My Father's Will for each of you. Praise His Perfect desires for your lives, My beloved ones. You are loved mightily and completely. I am your Jesus Who has suffered and died to open to you the opportunity of redemption and salvation. Choose Life, once again, My children. Choose Me."

4/25, "My little ones, I am your Jesus of Mercy, come to thank you, to bless you, to pour out new mercy upon you for your deep devotion, for your sincere love for My Feast of Divine Mercy and for My Merciful Heart, for the Novena prayers that you poured out upon the world in all of My requests to you through dear, dear Faustina, Our little Saint of mercy. Do you realize how well prepared you are, how truly you are soldiers of mercy, how this great army of mercy will swell in size and numbers, how Heaven sings hosannas? What great feasts are now together in the calendar of your Church, My Church: first, My glorious Resurrection and then, holding up for the world the rays of My Divine Mercy pouring forth from My Sacred, Suffering and Eucharistic Heart. It is a more important time in your history than you can realize, My children; but it is, believe Me, My mercy that enables you to cooperate with Our requests, to bear the requests of My mercy, to bear the changes within you and around you that must occur, that Mercy might become the atmosphere in which you live.

Imagine the people who will come to you, who will come out of a lifestyle of the world of sin and many times, of evil, into a climate of mercy. They will be uncomfortable, as you can well imagine; and part of your merciful mission will be making them comfortable, explaining that mercy is for everyone, that without mercy, Our people are lost. As obedient as you have become, as much as you pray for the world to embrace My Mercy, to return to My Father and be saved; as many promises as My Father gives that many, many will receive His Mercy, still you could not possibly do any of these things without the outpouring of Our Holy Spirit Who prepares your hearts, Who opens your heart just as the sword opened Mine, My children. The sword opened My heart, and blood and water signifying grace and mercy poured out into your hearts that have now been opened by the sword of Our Spirit: My Father's desires. His plans are always perfect, always beautiful and always full of symbols that catch your imagination, that stay with you and grow in beauty, as your understanding increases. This is all part of My Father's care for you, His providence, His incredible love that you might be tendered at every step of your journey (through Mercy) back to My Father.

My Children, these are important and exciting and grace filled days, and you do well to continue to beg for My mercy. These very days are a preparation for the enemies of Mercy to begin wars once again, as I have just told you. These wars will contain much senseless killing; but remember, the people who enter eternity are being given an opportunity through My Father's Mercy to choose His Kingdom, to pay their dept to His merciful justice, assisted by your prayers at every turn, at every development in My Father's plan. These developments will unfold more quickly at this point, at this time in His plan. As more occurs on the world front, you will see this as a personal call to increase your surrender: the surrender of your time and your energy to more prayer and reflection and quiet. Much quiet is needed within all of you, and I mean every one of you! I only mention this again because silence will secure for you so much of the strength you need, the healing, the blessings; and I wish to see you receive all of these, as much as possible in My great love for you. I have spoken many words tonight that need your reflection. Praise My Father that He moves forward toward My ultimate return through all the fulfilling of Scripture, all the events that must occur before you see Me coming on the clouds to defeat the evil one. Rejoice, My children. You are so highly favored, so deeply loved. Cling to Me. I am with you forever, but most strongly in these days. Do not be afraid. I love you. Thank you for loving Me. Thank you, My children, more than you will ever know. Rejoice!"

5/2, "My dear ones, I am your Mother, come once again to be with you by a special gift of Our Father. There are so many people to pray for. There is so much evil escalating in the world. DO NOT FEEL PUT UPON WHEN YOU ARE

ASKED TO PRAY MORE, MY DEAR ONES. If your heart truly understands your state of emergency in the world because of the escalating plans of Satan, then you will happily, gladly give every spare minute to this call. And yet I remind you, that you never give more than you are given; that you cannot outdo your God in generosity. Already, so many times, you have experienced this showering of the Holy Spirit shortly after you have given of yourselves in a greater way. All have agreed to wait more patiently or have discovered new sorrow in your hearts and brought some new discovery of behavior to My Jesus in the Sacrament of Reconciliation; and then the Father will shower the gifts of the Spirit, some consolation upon you. How many times have you said to yourself, 'whatever is necessary, My Lord and My God, for the world's conversion, I will do'? This is the pouring out of mercy you can have on your God and on me, your loving Mother. How much I love you. How I have been with you every moment in all your prayers, in all of your hours of adoration. I was there, my children, in deep prayer with you and for you and for the world.

This great Feast of the Ascension of My Son can correspond in your minds and in your hearts to the times when Jesus does not seem as close, when maybe He will hide Himself in order to draw you, once again, closer. Think about that, my children. Think about the different ways my Son interacts with you: always calling you more deeply into the Father's Will and His plan, but closer to Himself certainly, always closer; like the bride seeking her spouse who is present one moment and seems to be gone the next, who wanders through the town asking people, 'have you seen my beloved?' (Song of Songs) The Angels and the Saints know how important it was when my Jesus returned to His Father. The gates of Heaven had been opened. The Father's Will had been fulfilled for the world. But that was not the end, and it is not only at the time of this Feast that these moments, this time is relived and celebrated by you and by all of Heaven. This great dynamic occurs again and again in your minds and your hearts, in your lives, bringing you new conversion, new understanding, lifting your minds and your hearts to Heaven where my Son dwells now at the right hand of His Father.

Oh my children, there is so much to be revealed to you at the right time! I am eager for this to happen to increase your understanding and appreciation and gratitude to the Father, for so much more is given and done for you than you ever realize. That is why We simply ask you to praise and thank the Father for all of His gifts. As you prepare for my Son's return to Heaven at His Ascension, you are also beginning to prepare for the great gift of Pentecost. PREPARE WELL, MY CHILDREN, FOR THESE FEASTS. IT IS NOT ONLY IMPORTANT FOR THE WORLD, BUT FOR YOUR OWN FUTURE AND THE FUTURE OF SO MANY OF OUR LOST ONES. I love you, my precious children. My dear, dear little darlings you are! I praise and thank the Father every moment for giving me YOU, for your fidelity, your devotion to me. Thank you, my children, for loving me, for loving My Jesus, for pleasing me so much in this way. Be filled with my love. I pour out sweetness upon you this night and an increased love for My Son, an increased joy at prayer, joy at giving and joy at receiving. Amen, my little ones. We shall prepare together once again. Amen"

FOR MERCY'S SAKE!

5/6, "My dear ones, thank you for gathering this day. I am Jesus, the Son of Mary the Immaculate One, the Virgin; Son of God, Son of Man. I come with thanksgiving to you once again from all of Heaven. My Father is blessing you this day for making this special effort to be here to pray in this way to honor His precious daughter, His prophet to you for this age, for this time, for this Day of the Lord. My dear ones, how blessed you are. Always I remind you of this, for always you are blessed more, and placed more deeply within My heart and within My Father's plan for you and for the world. What faithful ones you are; what love courses through your veins, a driving force for all you do: for your obedience, for your delight in each possibility to praise your Triune God, to give Us thanksgiving and gratitude. Only the gift of My Father could allow this new delight, always this new urgency and understanding for the need of more prayer.

Wisdom shows itself in your faithfulness and in your eagerness to do whatever is requested of you, and to show special honor to this glorious Mother and Queen in her special month dedicated to her under all of her titles; but most of all, Queen of your hearts: Queen of every heart ever created, even Queen of those fallen angels for whom she weeps, Queen and Mother of the whole world. I tell you, because of your fidelity, you will know more of her love in a very obvious way from now on. You will know a deeper bonding between your heart and hers, a bridge between your heart and hers that will be beautified as the months and years go by, encrusted with jewels, I tell you, ever covered with flowers of the most beautiful fragrance. This beauty will spill over into your hearts to beautify them in a new way, to bring a gentleness and a beauty not given to many. This too will become apparent to others and yourselves, and secretly and constantly you will rejoice and praise and thank My Father. You are loved. Never tire of hearing that. Never tire of desiring to hear that. Never cease giving praise and thanks for the love that pours out on you every moment of every day.

There will be new persecutions within your own families soon. As the Summer unwinds, unfolds in a seemingly gentle, easy going way, (and so it shall be in some areas of your lives) you will know secret sorrows, My children, for the Mother of Sorrows also visits you this day to share herself completely. As the long days of Summer approach, once more I remind you as I have in the past, do not be distracted by the plans of others. Although you might accompany them, I ask you for greater energy in staying recollected with My presence and the presence of My Mother. This need not interfere with plans or vacations. On the contrary, it will only enrich all of your activities.

My heart is heavy this day, as well as rejoicing over your love, heavy because of the plans coming to fruition now in certain parts of the world. I have been speaking of these plans in the last few weeks, and now the world waits for a sign from one leader to go forward to begin a time of challenge, of new conquests, of increased loss of life, of a further unfolding of Satan's plan. This plan, My children, unfolds more quickly now, for it is time that the words I give you are fulfilled. It is time to show you, in a greater way, how necessary are your prayers; how necessary is your faithfulness; how necessary YOU ARE, My dear, dear ones, to the success, to the victory of all of Our faithful ones and as many of Our lost children as possible. Let compassion rule your hearts for the rest of your lives, as you reach out continually in prayer and service. **Prayer is service, My children, service is prayer.** All of these, on many different levels, allow Me to raise you to a new level this day. Let your prayers be even more efficacious, more powerful, more far reaching: deep into the hearts of Our people everywhere. Rejoice, My dear ones, the Kingdom lives!"

5-13, "My dear children, I am your Mother. I have hastened this day to be with you, my dear ones, because of the great honor, the glory, the praise you are giving me, the devotion in your hearts, your beautiful prayers this day, your lovely song which grows out of the love in your hearts. My dear little ones, I speak to everyone this day, those who could not be here, everyone who has ever come to pray with this group; but also to the entire world who listens, who prays, who practices obedience to my directives, the directives of my Son. My children, I shower you with grace this day, beyond anything you have ever received. I fill you with virtue this day beyond any you have yet received. I fill you with new ability to persevere, my children; for you are beginning to realize that it is a long, long journey through the perfect Will of Our Father. The wait is much longer than you desire, my children, I know; and when you surrender your own will to the Father's perfection, YOU are perfected! You are given new patience, new purification, a new joy at waiting, a new joy at surrender, a new joy at being the instrument of the Father's Will. To become an instrument, you must be formed and reformed and formed again to be understanding and compassionate to all of those who will be (aware of) experiencing the Father's perfect Will for them and for the world, perhaps for the first time in their entire lives. Imagine this, my dear ones! You know the struggle against your own nature, your own will that surges to the top every chance it gets, that is still alive and well and kicking, often having tantrums, even like a child!

There is much within each of you that reflects the child you were, that reflects the **need for purification of that child who still wants his or her own way, who still rebels at the waiting, who still resists the gifts that are necessary for that child to grow, to mature, to become a soldier who will lead, a soldier who will perceive and focus on the needs of others rather than personal needs.** I know that you know this; and I repeat it because the gifts being given this day are specifically for that little child, for all the needs within each of you to mature, to become more than you imagine you can be. The Father sees who you are becoming! The Father knows who you will become; and therefore, has every confidence in each of you, for He knows too from whence you have come. It is a miracle in all of you, my children, that you are at this place in your lives, in your hearts, in your minds; that you come (to prayer) eagerly and not resisting. Not for show, not because you think it is expected of you; but because you desire to be here, wherever you are, to pray or whatever kind of prayer you are offering: be it adoration or group prayer, or simply hidden but never alone, united with all of Heaven and never alone: never, ever, ever alone, my dear ones. Always, always in the actual presence of my Jesus and me, my special Angels that you have been given to protect you now, to increase the prayer around you, the joy poured out each day by these Angels. I tell you, these Angels love you, yearn for your acknowledgment, your invitations to them for prayer and your invitations to them to actively join in each task.

Invite them, children, to help you fix dinner! Invite them to help you do the laundry! Whatever it is, whatever seeks your attention, your time and energy, invite Us, my children, and in this way you WILL find more joy. You WILL discover you are not alone, that you are surrounded by all of us who love you, to whom you are precious; who cherish you, who appreciate you. My dear ones, allow this to be a shield against the ingratitude and the harsh words of others, the hurts they would throw at you, the torments, the real sadness that you feel from this behavior. Allow us to do everything possible to shield you now from behavior, from attitudes, from words We do not wish for you to experience one moment longer; while at the same time, uniting all of these hurts to the suffering of my Jesus. Take joy where it can be found to keep up your strength, to bolster you, encourage you and strengthen you; for you cannot only know the sadness and negative attitudes of others. You must allow a balance. Allow the love of those (who love you) to heal you each day, each moment.

I COME TO SAY, I LOVE YOU, MY CHILDREN. MY CHILDREN YOU ARE. MY CHILDREN YOU WILL REMAIN. MY CHILDREN WHO'S MOTHER I AM! Be filled with peace this day, my dear ones. Bask in my love, in the love of your children. Be filled now with my spirit, with my joy, with more of the love in my heart for you and for the world. Amen, my dear ones. Amen. I love you!"

5-21, Jesus said: "My beloved ones, I wish to speak to all of you as one. Again you must believe that I am your Jesus, your merciful and sorrowing, but joyful Lord. Is it not a great gift to be here together, My children? I have brought you here. These martyrs (Isaac Jogues, John de Brebeouf, Kateri Tekakwitha and others honored here, C.A.) join Me today, greeting and praying for you, to ask with Me that you PRAY FOR ALL OF THOSE WHO WILL ONE DAY BE MARTYRED IN MY NAME; THAT THEY WILL HAVE THE STRENGTH, THE PERSEVERANCE, THE GRACE TO ACCEPT THE GIFT OF MARTYRDOM, FOR THERE IS NO GREATER GIFT YOU CAN GIVE TO YOUR GOD THAN TO LAY DOWN YOUR LIFE TOTALLY IN DEFENSE AND ACCEPTANCE OF MY NAME. I ASK YOU TO INCLUDE THIS PETITION AT YOUR PRAYER GROUPS FOR THE PEOPLE OF THESE DAYS. THEY ARE NOT USED TO SUFFERING. THEY ARE NOT USED TO COMPLETELY GIVING UP EVEN THEIR POSSESSIONS, WHICH WILL OCCUR FOR ALL OF YOU. THEY DO NOT KNOW THE SPIRIT OF SACRIFICE THAT WILL BE REQUIRED OF ALL OF YOU SOME DAY. It is another reason to pray for each other, another reason to come together, to learn to know each other and love each other, to desire to pray for gifts of protection and strength. All of these gifts will be given, but each one must be open and believe, trust that My words are true. My promises will be fulfilled, each one of them.

How I love you. How grateful is all of Heaven this day, every day for you. To see you in this special place (Shrine of the North American Martyrs in Canada.) is a cause for joy, and I know you feel the presence of Our Spirit. Many gifts are given to you now, many new graces, much strength, for you will work harder than most. You have generous hearts. You have the mind and the heart-set that will be needed to lead Our people, even Our faithful ones. There are few, My children, who have a true understanding of all that will be required, of the difficulties you will encounter, the hard work, the fatigue, the difficulty encountered in each person who comes to you. You have never seen anything or could imagine anything such as this will be! My dear ones, do not be concerned. Be prepared! Be prepared through prayer and more surrender, more time with Me, before Me in My Tabernacle, before Me in My Holy Sacrament of the Altar. How blessed you are, how favored by My Father. My Mother sends her love and gratitude that you are in this place, the place of the first martyrs on this continent. How grateful she is for your prayers and your devotion, your love. It is the love from her heart that courses through your own, (and everyone who loves her…cta.) which raises your hearts and your minds and your spirits to your Triune God. Rejoice, rejoice that you are loved and gifted beyond your knowledge.

Your constancy in prayer is a marvel to all in Heaven, the depth of your commitment, your joy in prayer. Again, you have no idea how many you touch every day. They simply see you because your love itself, your sincerity shines, shines through your eyes and on your faces and around you! Believe this. This is seen and felt by the people who are meant to see and feel. Do not be concerned about My words or give them another thought. Just accept the reality of these gifts. I love you. You are so close to Me, to the Kingdom of My Father. SATAN WILL SEEM TO HAVE ALL THE VICTORIES NOW FOR A LONG TIME. DO NOT BE CONCERNED ABOUT THIS. THIS MUST BE. THIS MUST FULFILL SCRIPTURE. THIS MUST FULFILL MY FATHER'S WILL. Continue to be faithful. Continue to love Me and My Mother. Only in that way will you survive all that is to come. Be encouraged. Be at peace. Know that you are following and are totally grounded in My Father's Will, and deep, deep within the heart of My Mother and My own Heart and the gifts of My Spirit. Never forget for an instant that I am with you with My Mother and her Angels. Call on your Angels, My children. Develop that relationship, that gift. You will need them in the future. Call on them now! Be filled with peace and joy. Amen."

5/27 Continued. "Dear one, rejoice, for I am your Lord and your God, here to take you into My Heart, into the secrets of My love for you and all who are faithful. Is it not peaceful to be here, away from the noise and confusions of the world and all its demands? Believe these words this day of feast, this time of celebration and gratitude for My return to My Father in Heaven. So great was My Father's joy, so powerful was Our mutual joy and love at the fulfillment of all My Father had required of Me, that words could never convey the enormity of this event and Our uniting upon My return as God AND Man. All of Heaven exploded in a symphony of joy and loud song. Heavenly music rang throughout the completion of My Sacrifice, the ultimate price to be paid to purchase the redemption of every person ever created throughout all of time/Creation. As I was already God and King, present with My Father at Creation, I returned to what I knew, to Who I AM and had remained; but this time, I brought with Me Human Nature and all of you, as well! AS YOU WERE PRESENT TO ME HANGING ON THE CROSS, SO ALSO YOU WERE PRESENT TO ME IN MY RETURN TO MY FATHER IN GLORY! The awesome mystery of these truths can be better appreciated and understood as you reread My words. **What takes place in time is lived out step by step, one event following another. What takes place in Eternity is the fully accomplished and completed victory for all at once, at the same time in a NOW environment of completion. The Will of My Father allows a veil to remain before the eyes of your understanding in order to feed the feeble faith and understanding slowly and perfectly according to His Merciful Will. Some day you will stand in the fulfillment of Paradise to see and understand everything you have ever heard and believe in, and will marvel further at this perfection.** The actual fulfillment for each of Our faithful ones occurs long before their new awareness of this action by Our Spirit. This is what brings each one along the path of My Father's Will and allows the victory to occur for each faithful one. Continue to rejoice over the favors given to so many of those who struggle to follow Me."

5/30, "My dear ones, I am the Holy Spirit of God, come this night to prepare you for the great feast, the great celebration of My first outpouring upon the earth, upon the Apostles who were gathered just as you gather this night in prayer, in trepidation, in fear and trembling of different things (as some of you are and as each of you has been at different times in your life). I come this night to pour out new graces and gifts, to pour out My power upon you, dear faithful ones, to cleanse and purify and refresh your spirits. I use these words, most especially refreshment for each of you, My dear ones, for you are weary; you are filled with the tasks, the challenges, the harsh words, the lack of understanding, **the difficulties that will ALWAYS ACCOMPANY YOUR JOURNEY, as you follow Jesus and you attempt each day to live God's Will in your life.** So many times, little ones, you hear the words, 'I give you new gifts this night,' and always you have received gifts; but I am here to tell you, the gifts I bring you tonight are unlike any you have received in the past, (this happens again as you read these words… cta.) and I ask you to believe this, to meditate upon this. I bring also with Me the gift of openness to these new gifts. **With every gift, there is a responsibility**. With every task and new direction, you are called upon to learn more, to let go more, to surrender more, to BE more and to be LESS, My little ones! You have learned these things, and because of this and because of the fidelity in the hearts of each of you and all of Our faithful ones all over the world, there will be an outpouring on this great feast such as you have not seen in your own lifetime. (This seems not to have happened yet.. '06, at least not to our conscious perception!) Perhaps you will not recognize this at first. Perhaps you will! In either case, My dear ones, you will ultimately feel the power of new gifts, the result of new Wisdom and Understanding, the Peace that comes with new Fortitude, new Courage, the Hope that blossoms within your hearts as Trust grows again for every new gift and from all of these things. **I give you the trust you will need to withstand each event of the future**, everything you will see, many of which, My dear faithful people, will be shocking or frightening at first. Believe that you will overcome each emotion, each reaction you experience along the way. I mention these, dear little ones, that you might know everything that is being arranged for every possibility.

Every experience will be accompanied by all the strength, by all the grace and gifts and help you could possibly need, although you will still experience initially human reactions. Once again, it is requested that you do not allow these words to alarm you, to frighten you; but that you see them as more love, more mercy, more preparation, more protection for the future. The future, My children, will not always be a distant future, as it seems right now. As time passes, the future becomes more immediate. You can see this in situations developing all over the world. As Jesus has reminded you in the past, Satan takes no vacations. You are reminded, once again, not to be distracted, and you are requested to remain focused and faithful and joyful in your prayer, in your commitment, in your love. You are My children, too! Child of the Holy Spirit, Child of the Spirit of God, Child of the Spirit of Holiness and all of My gifts. All is well for you, My dear ones. How blessed, how gifted, how graced you are. what joy you bring to Me, as well, and delight that we work together, that we work with our spirits united, that we work reaching out, spreading joy and mercy and hope. You are loved, My dear ones, you are loved! You are blessed every moment. You are precious and cherished by your God and by My beloved spouse, the Immaculate One. Rejoice, people of the Spirit of God. Amen."

6/2, 12:15 a.m., "Happy Birthday, My dearest one. I am your Jesus Who loves you as no other could. I am the One Who will care for you forever with the might of My arm. You have only to remain obedient and humble in the face of My Father's Will, trusting in all you hear from Us and are allowed to experience. Events have exploded in the world today. These are signs to the 'One Worlders' to begin rash behavior in their countries, to escalate Satan's plans to leave several countries without leaders and vulnerable to neighboring territories. Believe the seriousness of these developments, little one. They have set the world stage for new and unbelievable events from now on. The world will seem to have gone mad, and hysteria will reign on several fronts. Your own President will be challenged again by the Chinese whose power is far greater than even the U.S. realizes. These will all seem like random events, but soon a pattern will emerge that will be chilling for all wise enough to observe. The earth will rumble with the devastation recently described, and you will know that My Warning is at hand. It is so important for you, little teacher and messenger, to continue to reach out with words of deep truth and explanations to all who will listen. My Father is about to give you more words about His mercy this very week that will reach new levels of Our people's consciousness. This will further prepare all to accept each new word of warning in the future.

Please Pay Attention to this (C.) "For many months this warning phase will continue with new teachings and explanations of My Father's mercy and unequaled love and forgiveness. Then all will begin with sudden and acute destruction that will set up the period of time that includes the Warning, the caring for huge numbers of people and the brief Golden Age of Our Spirit resulting from unimagined conversions and return to My Father. Continue to hold fast to this pattern of development in your own understanding. Your own fidelity has brought you to a place of deep trust by My Father, that His plans for you might be fulfilled. Simply remain focused and in deep listening for all My Father will be telling you. You are surrounded by all who love you, little one, and the prayers and love of all of Us in Heaven. I am your Jesus, your Life."

6/5, 2001 At Adoration, "Little one of My Will, please take these words meant to teach you and the world important 'heart data': information that will solidify the commitment and understanding of all who wish to remain faithful to My call for ongoing change and sanctification. Daughter, I am your God and Father. Pray again now for openness from Our Spirit, and for the grace to concentrate and become one with My Word and My words. You must concentrate on writing and finishing one last book upon your return, daughter. **It will be a powerful vehicle of teaching and change for the entire world. I am increasing your ability to express and to explain those things you have come to understand, as well as the strength to undertake this final compilation of words and prophecies from Heaven. (This is the book you are finally reading in His perfect time, and my fatigue!)** The world must come to appreciate more deeply, more completely the degree of mercy I am about to pour out upon the world in this **gift of My Warning; but also, it must be 'moved' to a greater surrender to My need for the total sacrifice of each faithful one as a vehicle, an instrument of this mercy. A gift is received more eagerly when it is wrapped in a package that is both interesting and brightly colored! By this, of course, I mean each of you who understands My call to you these many years, who has survived the delays and disappointments, the embarrassment before family and friends caused by My merciful Will for you, the mitigation and lessening of destruction allowed in answer to your prayers; the trust you have developed as you have allowed My Will to replace your expectations of instant fulfillment that would have made you seem so powerful or special or wise in the eyes of the world! You have truly learned many painful lessons, My people, that have led you away from taking ownership of promised events or even being the 'cause' of delays, or gifts given or postponed. You have**

come to realize and accept the need for all of this cleansing and renewal; to smile and nod in agreement with each development in your life and in the world that has emptied you of self, of the ways of the world, and filled you with new wisdom and new peace. My plan goes far beyond what you perceive still! The change that will be required within each of you to render you 'fit,' and able to serve all who come to you, has not yet been seen or experienced by any of you, My dearest faithful ones. These are not words of disapproval or condemnation, but once again a matter of preparation for more gifts of understanding and conversion in your immediate future.

Becoming an instrument of My Perfect Will begins with an acceptance of whatever it takes in your own life, your mind, your heart to render you that newly molded, reshaped, reformed person who will allow Me to pick up and lay down again your new self, wrapped and packaged in shining trust and all the colors of obedience and joy! As you live the next weeks and months, My dearest ones, do not please be overcome by great changes that will occur. Remember these words and be strengthened by them and by My promises to sustain you through each event. A resilient nature, a docile acquiescence to all that is required to bring each of you to a new readiness to comply, to serve, **is only acquired through a living out, an acceptance of the events as My perfect and merciful and loving Will for your life. When you are pliable in the hands of the One Who molds, Who turns the wheel of events, you will not break; but allow a smooth and rapid transition and transformation from one creation to another, all the while gaining new luster and color and form! This is truth, My lovely ones. This will be an ongoing process that ultimately brings each of you to a place of fulfillment in My plans for each one. Trust the Divine Scheme, the Potter Who continues to add new designs and increased methods of employment in the wonderful economy of Heavenly plans to reach the greatest number of people possible in a short period of time.**

I ask you, more than anything, to trust My love and providence for you and your loved ones throughout these life-changing events; to accept My words of explanation that I am strengthening you, preparing you to become a warrior, a lover of My broken people, the Samaritan to each wounded one you encounter, the absolute instrument of My healing and mercy, My love and forgiveness, a source of all these facets of Myself and the gifts most needed by the lost souls of so many, especially those who continue to reject Me and My words to the world. You have read enough words repeated to many faithful messengers that have convinced you of the gravity of the times and expected events, but you need to realize to a greater degree the amount of change still necessary for each of you to ready you for the battles ahead. When you begin to see and experience the continued cleansing of your minds and hearts and spirits, you will understand even more **the need for delays that allow you to come to a place of new creation in My Will. Remember, My precious and cherished ones, all is for your own good and to bring you most quickly into My Perfection: that place**

of unity with your Triune God that only My mercy can give you. Begin to praise more and thank Me for what is, what has been and all that will be, My beloved ones. Breathe deeply of Our Spirit so recently poured out upon the world in such a great and total way. Remember, too, **you already have every gift, every grace necessary to enable you to do whatever is required of you in the furnace of My cleansing fires of love! Be filled with peace, My dear, dear ones. I love you.** Be joyful and trusting in the Hearts of the Sacred and Immaculate Ones. Daughter, continue to be in silence and peace. Believe My words and love for you. I am your Father Who loves you and will continue to gift you with My need of you."

6/13, "My dearest little ones, I am your Jesus, with you tonight once again by a special gift from My Father. I see in your hearts, My children, a deep desire to honor Me this month of My Sacred Heart, and I thank you. I can only encourage you more to be faithful to this devotion and to those who begin the Novena this day of the Sacred Heart. I offer you special blessings, conversions for your own hearts and the hearts of your loved ones. This day also, children, sees many events in the world: events of destruction, events of importance where world leaders are meeting at various places. Pray for these, My children, that they will be guided by the Holy Spirit; for you are already aware of the plans of the evil one, the plans to disrupt peace even more in the world, the plans to inspire one country to take over another country. You see countries at this moment without leadership. This, too, is by design as I have told you. My dear ones, each day the situation becomes more serious and more in need of prayer, special Novenas, special times of silence by all of you; silence in which you can be with Me, united more closely to Me. My dear ones, what could be more important, what could be a greater gift to you, what could be a greater sign of My Father's love for you? This unity will just grow and grow and bring you to that place in My Father's plan where you need to be: a place of service, but a place of joyful surrender. Yes, I know you have heard these words before, but each day they become more important. Each day they need to be a focus of your prayers, of your own words personally.

Surrender, My children, is a word that means so much more than it seems at first, that means something different in the lives of each one of you. Oh, the overall dynamic of surrender is "letting go," yes, is dying to your will, to your selfishness, but it goes so much deeper than that. Mercy, My children, ask for My mercy for yourselves. Ask for mercy that you might surrender more. You have come so far. I tell you again, you are an example to prayer groups everywhere, to faithful ones everywhere and you cause all of Heaven to sing for joy. They are praying with you so seriously, My dear ones, this special month of My Sacred Heart, for they know the power which pours out from My Heart upon the world, upon each one of you, the love, the cleansing, the gifts.

There will always be gifts, My children, yes, because you need them; but more than that, because you are loved....loved so mightily. Never before in history has there been a time like this, a degree of giftedness such as this. You are all greatly fortified by the gifts of the Spirit now. Since this great Feast most recently, you were brought deeply within the Trinity of God. By that I mean a closeness to Us as one: as Father, Son and Spirit and as Trinity. My Children, I mention these things to remind you that you are blessed beyond the understanding of anyone, so we can simply rejoice together, you and I, and I can bring you more deeply into My Sacred Heart. As you pray these special prayers, these litanies and novenas during this month of My Sacred Heart, My Heart is your heart. Your heart is hidden deeply within Mine forever, forever, My dear ones, forever. I love you.

I am so grateful to you for all of your prayers and your struggle; for those who come closer to Me now, perhaps for the first time; for those who are turning to My words uttered in this place but reflected all over the world. My dear ones, I welcome you here this night. (4 or 5 new people...cta) I thank you for opening up to Our Holy Spirit Who inspires all good, all prayer, all good intentions. Persevere, My dear ones, all of you. Again, I remind you of the distractions of summer. Take Me with you everywhere. I am already standing at your side! Be aware of My Presence. Be aware that I am loving you and protecting you and blessing you every moment. Be at peace about My words. Believe them. Reread all My words to you now in these days of summer, My children everywhere. They are more important to you than you realize. I love you, My dear ones. Thank you for loving Me. Amen, amen. Rejoice."

6/6, "I, your Mother, am here with you now, praising the Father with you, thanking Him also for the gifts He has given to you, for your new place in His plan. Most especially, my dear children, I praise and I thank Him for the love in your hearts, the love which has grown, as you have accepted my love and share it now with everyone and so very well with each other. Your patience....what a joy to behold; your generosity and tenderness with each other and all you meet; your patience with those who try you, who hurt you, who refuse to give an inch. Is this not true, my dear, dear ones? Again I say, 'how precious you are to all of us in Heaven!' I remind you, my little ones, this very month is the month dedicated to my Jesus and His Sacred Heart. I ask you to make this a special dedication in your own lives; a special focus for all of your adoration and love, your praise and your thanks to the Father who gifted each of us with Jesus to begin with. My dear ones, ponder the beauty and the love of my Son. Ponder once again His suffering for you. This becomes more apparent in your lives as you suffer more for Him, for the whole world, for souls, my children, **always for souls**. Would it be possible that you might find more time to spend with Him, adoring Him, being in His presence in the Tabernacle or in His Sacrament of the Altar, exposed for all to share, to love, to adore: would it be possible, my dear ones? Only you can answer that. Ask yourselves this question this very special month of this very special year. You know, my children, that time has gone by, a much longer period of time than anyone of us had expected, even myself! And so you know that time has brought the world to a place that is closer to events for which you have prepared for many, many, many years.

How you have grown; how you have become instruments; how you have become the people of God, the chosen ones of God, the people on whom God counts to fulfill His plan for the world. What a task, my dear ones, what gifts you are given by the Father's need: His need for you, for courageous and generous hearts, for loving, surrendering, loving hearts. Loving hearts, my children! What loving hearts I see which beat in each of you. I am overwhelmed this night, as I see your love for me; overcome with joy, with gratitude, with humility at your response to my call these many years, your fidelity. Never will it be that I could mention this too often, for it becomes more difficult, a greater struggle, not easier with the passage of time. Because you have grown, you are stronger and carry greater burdens. I salute you, gathered here and my faithful ones throughout the world. I salute your tenacity, and it is courage required to persevere in the face of more hostility, more words that hurt and cut and wound so deeply.

I thank you for the sacrifices, for your surrender in allowing whatever the Father wills in your own lives. You are my obedient and precious little ones, and I see in your hearts that you have joy over being my little ones. Is it not better, my dear ones, to be hidden and little and dependent upon the Father? I knew you would discover this, my children, as I did. Let us begin each day together with a new yes, a new fiat, a new surrender to all the Father has in store for each of us and for the world**. Evil will be overcome, my children, never forget this!** The Father will defeat evil, the evil one, the evil ones who follow him and all the plans ever made to spread evil in the world and in the hearts of men. Rejoice in this! Become more focused now, for during this month, this special month of the Sacred Heart of my beloved, more strength is given you at my request because of my love for you, because I know you will do whatever I ask you because of the love in your hearts. Feel my love for you, my little ones everywhere. Never ever turn away from me, my dear, dear children. Be joyful in me as I am joyful in you, because of you, with you, through you. Is it not wonderful to be so united, my dear ones, in joy? I am your Mother. I LOVE YOU!"

6/19, At Adoration, "Child of My Will, please take My words. They are meant to further instruct My faithful ones in requests that have already and always been given to those who would come to Me through the Heart of My Beloved Son. Jesus is the Lamb, the Obedient One, the Son Who shows to all My Face, My Mercy, My Will. If no other gods have filled your hearts, My people, you are living as My child, made in the My Image and likeness. If you are still listening to the call of the world, the lure of its enticements or even just its distractions, you are not the follower of My Jesus and all His words and teachings you think you are! It is (beyond) time to look at your lifestyle, your heart and your motives for each action, be it prayer or service to the poor, or a turning back to the empty excitement promised by the empty games of Satan. My beloved ones, his call and snares, his lies and deceptions are so subtle! Yes, I your God and Creator, am calling you to become as perfect as possible in this life; as saintly in your thoughts, words and actions as possible through an on-going surrender to My Will. I call you to a total focus on prayer and change.

I call you to time spent daily before Me in union with My Son, Jesus, and Our Spirit Present in the Sacrament of the Altar, waiting in the Tabernacle in the form of Sacred Host: Jesus Hostia, the Bread of Heaven, the Precious Eucharistic Host. I am your God and Father Who calls out in these times of preparation of your souls for the greatest devastation known to mankind. When you hear of an outbreak of some disease, you immediately take every precaution to avoid contracting, or even being in the vicinity of, this dreadful danger to life: your own and especially your loved one's. How is it that Heavenly warnings of the advent of worldwide exposure to dreadful, life threatening warfare, unheard-of diseases and deadly chemical weapons do not move you to then accept the precautions and directives of Heaven, sent through many faithful messengers that (even your hardened hearts must realize) receive no personal gain from their role as those who carry Our warnings to every corner of the world?

Have you heard people say (who have had a powerful conversion experience, even perhaps a near death experience and have in a special, personal way come to know My Jesus; maybe even have seen Heaven? Do you recall at this moment that all who receive special gifts from Our Spirit will say, "It's all about love"? What is all about love, My dearest ones? Why do so many people who have been powerfully enlightened by an experience of near death or new life always say the same thing? Why do those whose life is altered by a sudden change of direction, a life-changing event, recover with a new understanding of the importance of love as the principal and guiding dynamic: the only thing that defines life, that makes sense in a world of chaos and people bent on destruction? Spend time on these questions, dearest children of My creative love. Again I tell you, you were created in Love, are sustained and called by Love, invited to become Love!

Love IS the Mercy you receive. Until you accept mercy, you cannot give it to others. Until you accept Love, you cannot give Love to others. Your greatest task as My children is to live in My love, to continually accept it, to give it away to others by emptying yourselves in Love through mercy and service to all those I send to you; and even those you will never meet, but with whom you are one when you are one with your Triune God and the holy Mother. This is not too much to expect of you, if you are truly motivated by Love and desirous of spending Eternity united to Love and in Love. Yes, this requires a radical change in your thinking, speaking and behavior: everything about you.

This is more than possible, My dear little ones. JUST ACCEPT MY WILL FOR YOUR LIVES IN SURRENDER TO ALL MY DIRECTIVES, MY DESIRES FOR YOU. **Mercy, My beloved children, is the atmosphere, the climate in which love thrives and blossoms into a fullness of the potential I have set in the very building blocks of your soul!** Find out for yourselves now, quickly, immediately, My people, that you too are love when you begin to live love as the guiding principle of a renewed self in the excitement of discovery, when you allow love to burst forth from the depths of your being as it is nurtured by the waters of Sanctifying grace and all the gifts of the Spirit of God.

Reread My words, people. Reflect upon your own lives in the light of Love and becoming Love, not only a possibility, but a fulfillment of all you have received from Me, all the potential for the greatness found in silence and simplicity and service! I love you, My own dear ones. I desire your desire to become instruments of My love and mercy. When I tell you that every faithful one has not yet seen the changes necessary to become this instrument (6-5-01) in My hands (and, yes, defended and protected by the might of My arm. It is a portent of serious times in the future requiring a serious response on your part now, an acceptance of a new level of understanding of all I tell you to perfect you, to prepare you, to cleanse you completely, to change you into a vehicle of My Will for all those I will send to you shortly.

Do you desire to be part of the great gift of the Second Pentecost; to be present at the outpouring of Our Spirit as never before seen or known by the world; to be a sharer, a partner with your God and holy Mother in My plan to give the gift of salvation to the entire world? Ask yourselves all these questions, My beloved people. Your future in Eternity will be determined by the choices you make now to accept My mercy, My gifts and graces, My protection and strength that will carry you into the very Day of Jesus' return to the earth to defeat Satan and renew the face of the earth. His Eucharistic Reign will be triumphant!"

6/20, "Children, I am your Mother, the Mother of all people, the Mother of everyone in the world: everyone who has ever lived and who will live. Please know that I had a great hand in bringing you here, my dear, dear ones. How happy I am to see you. I bring greetings from all of Heaven. Believe this, for it is a special gift this night from the Father and greetings most especially from your own dear loved ones here. Know that they are praying for you and with you every moment of everyday. They have had a great hand in bringing you here also and they have had much to do with many graces being released for you; graces that had been saved for you since before you were born! This is again by a special gift of Our Father Who is always giving you gifts, and always hoping you will receive them and that you will use them, share them; allow them to help you grow; allow them to overflow onto others, most especially gentleness, tenderness, patience, a sincere attitude toward others, a listening heart. All of these things Our people have needed, and you as well. These are given again tonight, as well as more gifts, the everyday gifts, the gifts that help you get along: to be gracious and welcoming; to be pleasant to be around; to be merciful; to be helpful, all of the things you like others to do for you. These are the everyday gifts. It does not mean they are plain or ordinary by any means, for every gift from our Father is special as you, my dear ones, are special......so special to my heart. What joy you bring to Heaven. This room, full of faces uplifted, hearts uplifted; joy pouring into your hearts and reflecting from your faces. Peace, my children, in this place, peace radiating from your being. It is so true, how I love you! How Heaven rejoices for you that you have answered an invitation, either mine or someone else's; but I too have been part of that invitation, how ever you received it; for I have waited for your response, your arrival at this place, in this group where you have been called by my Spouse, the most Holy Spirit of God.

My dear ones, you have a life, each of you, that will be full beyond your understanding. Even now, all of you still have much to learn. The Father calls out to you, reminding you that there is more change required in the lives and the hearts of everyone who is faithful, everyone in the world; but most especially those who have responded, who have been praying, who have allowed the gifts of Our Spirit to change them, to strengthen them. There are many, many more events and trials ahead of you, my children; but you will experience these joyfully, I tell you, for you will be aware of my presence with many, many Angels, and your own Angels greatly increased now. As the weeks and months go by, you have developed more wisdom. You are seeing the need for the Father's plan in just the way it happens in your life and in the world. My dear ones, you fill me with joy.

Accept my joy this night which I pour out upon you now: a deep abiding joy that will remind you constantly that you are my own dear little ones; that I am your own precious, loving, cherishing, caring, prayerful, watchful, interceding Mother. You are precious gifts to me from the Father. We are about to begin a great adventure for which you are nearly prepared. It will be an adventure unlike anything you have ever heard or read about. As events begin in the world, I ask you to begin to jot down these events: changes that you notice, even the weather that is occurring all over the world now so strangely, so out of Season in many places. Just a few words each day, my children that you might have words to look back on, words to chart the Father's plan, the events planned since time began! Above all things this night, believe that I love you, that I am closer to you than you are to yourself! Thank you for loving me. Amen."

6-24, "My beloved ones, I am your Father God. Be aware of My Presence with you now, united to My Son and to Our Spirit: The Triune God. Thank you, My dear ones, for honoring My Son and His Mother, My dearest daughter, on this day. There has been great feasting in Heaven, shouts of joy, praise and thanksgiving for these special feasts, but also a feasting and a thanksgiving for each of you here and My faithful ones all over the world. We come closer to times of fulfillment in spite of delays in the past. Believe My words. Believe that the plans of the evil one have escalated greatly; for each plan so far has seen success, has seen a passive acceptance by the people in the world, has seen greater oppression manifest itself in many parts of the earth. I mention these things to remind you of the need to remain faithful, to remind you of all you will be called upon to do in the future; but to ask you now to remain more faithful to prayer than you could ever imagine before. I give you grace this day. I call out to you, My people everywhere, to ask you to receive new strength, new ability to focus, to concentrate, to be one with the prayers being said continuously in Heaven to Me, to praise and thank Me, your God and Creator, to ask of Me increased mercy; for **it is only mercy that saves you**, that allows you to come to Me in the first place, as I wait with open arms, eagerly welcoming you into My embrace, into My perfect plan for your salvation and that of the whole world.

My people, realize how you are being gifted mightily. Realize that all the struggle and trouble and loneliness, all of the unhappiness, all of your plans that seem to be confounded, that bog down, are merely trials to strengthen you and to bring you to that place of understanding that only My Will is important now. More than ever before in history, My dear ones, is My Will your all, and My Jesus your ALL; for He lived My Will with every breath, every motion, every thought, every desire, and you have been promised and already given all of the help from My Angels, as He was given. Come away with Me, My children, in the next days and weeks. Find time for retreat. Retreat in silence; not just for one hour or even one day, My dear ones, but several days; a true retreat to prepare yourselves even further. The heat you endure, My children, is a sign to you of the truth of all the words spoken by Heaven, all of the warnings; but more than that, all of My promises to you that you might believe in the truth of every single word given to you over these years, that everything will be fulfilled as it has been announced. My dear ones, be aware of the gift and the privilege you are given to serve Me, to serve Our children, Our lost ones. When you were in school, you prepared for testing; you prepared to be examined in order to pass to the next grade, the next level of education. I tell you that this is what this retreat will be; for I wish to lift you much higher in My plan in sanctity and holiness, in ability to serve, to be My instruments, to be a source of mercy and holiness for all you meet. Let this make you humble, as it is meant to do; not proud, not taking ownership, but being humble and grateful in silence. Away, My dear ones, away from the noise, away from distractions and the emptiness of the world. I love you. I AM LOVE. I have created you to be love for the world. You will never know how much you are loved, but (you) know more today, children, understand more how much you are loved. All of Heaven sends their love. Joy to you, My dear ones. Thank you for loving Me."

6/27, "My dear ones, I come again this night, your God and your Father. I come to remind you of the **need for balance**, for trust, for a remembrance of all the promises given to you. Future frightening events will be something that each of you will experience wrapped in the Mantle of the Immaculate One, held securely in the heart of My Son; held fast in the protection and the might of My Will for you; held in the power of Our Spirit; held in love, My dear ones, a nurturing, Fatherly, saving, redeeming love. I wish to thank those who gathered today and encourage the rest of you to gather tomorrow or the next day or both, (days of retreat). You wonder why I, your God, would speak of these few hours; and yet you cannot see the Angels and Saints who accompany you each time you gather, each time you pray, each time you respond in obedience to My requests, My desires. Your prayers, your efforts are multiplied beyond your imagining by all of these who join you, who pray for you, who call down new graces and strength by the merits of their own lives, their own obedience, their own responses in their lifetime; who know the struggle to follow My Jesus, to relinquish your own will in order to follow Mine, to surrender completely to all you are called to do, to be, to become. As much more as you are realizing the seriousness of these times and the things to come, you can never completely imagine the future; and it is well, it is mercy, it is protection that keeps you from this total awareness. Do not be concerned for one moment. Concern will not save you! Worry never changed anything, did it, My dear ones?

Remember all you have learned. Remember the increase of wisdom and understanding and knowledge you have been given many times. Remember the protection, the promise; remember My need of you and for you, and rejoice, for you will live to see incredible events. Your names are written in the Book of Life. They shine, My children, believe it! Even your names reflect the goodness, the light that now lives in your hearts and your spirits. You have no idea the degree of blessedness and holiness and sacredness you are becoming, you are given, you will be for others. Oh My children, rejoice! Praise and thank Me. Think about these things. Think about My gifts and My love and My mercy to you. **Do not think about things to frighten yourself. There is nothing save prayer and obedience that you can do about them; and yet, this is everything and has already accomplished so much.** What mighty little ones you will be! Live in My gratitude. Run to Me everyday upon your awakening. Tell Me: **'Thank you, Father. Thank you for this day, this time, these opportunities to learn more about You; to come closer to You in unity and love and purpose and fulfillment of all You have given to me, all You have created me to be.'** I love you so far beyond any words, but it is always this way. Feel My love for you. Hear My love for you in My voice. The intensity will save you, will free you finally of the world. Allow Me to love you into perfection, My children. You ARE My holy ones! Amen."

7/1, "Dear children of My Precious Blood, I welcome you here again, come as My faithful obedient ones. I am your Jesus. I speak to you and to My dear ones everywhere. I pour out My blood upon the whole world this day in answer to your prayers. Are you noticing how the Father is still protecting so many of His children in areas where destruction occurs? He is yet allowing destruction to occur away from heavily populated areas. He is yet showing His mercy to the world, giving each one an added opportunity to benefit from graces given through your own prayers. **Believe that your prayers are touching every person in the world**, whether they know Me or not; whether they believe in the Triune God or even know Him or not, your prayers are given added strength and power again this day. Please realize and appreciate the degree of sacredness of your lives and your prayers; the degree of unity being given to you with the Trinity, most especially through My Sacred Heart, through My Precious Blood, through all of My suffering, My Passion and Death and Resurrection. The Cup of My blood IS the blood of the new and everlasting covenant. A symbol of that covenant is the Cup. And I tell you, you too, as you are filled with Me, are a symbol of that Cup which must be poured out, which must be emptied more and more of self, of self-giving, with joy. It is no good to grumble! It is defeating to grumble, to complain about prayer, to appear at this place or that place with resentment in your heart, or even worse, with fear in your hearts. It is joy I call you to, My dear, dear ones. **How else could I have shed every drop of My blood except for joy in My Father's Will; joy at being the Lamb, the Sacrifice Who opened the gates of Heaven; joy at being your Savior, your Redeemer; joy at being the bridge between yourselves and My Father.** Think about these things, as you spend more time in quiet, in silence before Me. Joy is flooding your soul, your heart, your mind from the peace that is given during these times.

Joy brings patience, docility and acceptance of the time it takes for My Father's Will to be fulfilled. Without joy you will not survive, for joy brings with it all of these gifts I have just mentioned, and it is these gifts which will carry you through every event. **As chaos and fear surrounds you, only the gift of My peace, that is the result of joy, will keep your feet on the ground; will keep your heart grounded in Me,** in trust of all these promises, for it will be a super human effort. There is no imagining the degree of destruction you will see, or the life style the Antichrist has in mind for you as he lives out the desires of Satan. Only in joy and complete trust that you will be protected, saved, live to serve, to pray, to be the instrument of My Father's Will. Ask Our Spirit for a deeper understanding of My Father's Will; not what it is for you, so much, but the fact that it is everything for you, it is everything in your life; and **everything in your life is the Father's Will allowed for a larger, deeper, more important reason than you can see at first; than you could ever see on the surface. Deeper, Children, dig deeper into the treasures found in My Father's Will. The Blood that I pour out upon you today seeps deeply into this ground. Dig more deeply each day with the help of Our Spirit. These are important and deep words this day, so I ask you to plumb them.** Take time that will not be interrupted or distracted by other events, by worrisome thoughts, by schedules that are always leading you away from Me. Do these things, and you will see and understand more, and I will reveal even more to you.

You are doing well, and My words today speak to increased gifts because you ARE doing well; because the Father's mercy and love is always pouring out upon you; because you are loved so mightily by all of Heaven; because you are precious to all of us. I love you. I am so grateful for you. <u>It is your fidelity that I saw from the Cross as I shed My Blood to the very last drop.</u> I ask you to shed your very last drop of energy, of commitment, of focus and of joy for My sake, for the glory of My Father through the power of Our Spirit, for the conversion and the salvation of the whole world, My children, the whole world."

7/8, "My dear ones, I am your Jesus. Welcome, once again, My dear faithful ones. All of Heaven lights with JOY for you! It is difficult to reconcile salvation and peace and purity in your minds with the state of affairs in the world today. As you pray and reflect, you are also discovering new things about yourselves that need to be reconciled, as it is meant to be. I tell you, My dear ones, no matter what you see or discover or experience, bring all of them with joy; for each discovery, each time you pray for anyone or anything, for yourselves in gratitude and praise or in remorse, more mercy pours out upon the world. **When one is prayed for, all are prayed for!** For in spite of the disparities, the divisions, the distances between people, you are all children of God in the world. Let nothing cause a wall, a separation between yourselves and anyone. More and more it becomes necessary to recognize and to practice the oneness, the unity to which you are called with the entire world. There is no difference, My children, to the Father**. It is the perception of the world that requires healing, purifying, a proper perspective, a oneness with the Will of My Father and yours.** These words may sound repetitive and yet they are mentioned and brought to you with more seriousness than ever; with more reason than ever to put the entire world, it's needs, it's conversion, it's salvation at the very top of your list; the very forefront of your understanding, of your petitions, of your desires for mercy, especially those who are perceived as 'enemies', who are instruments of the evil one in carrying out all of his destructive plans. Oh, My children, do not be fearful as you see weather escalate, as you hear stories of horrors, of things that have been kept hidden in the past, but have occurred recently. You will realize more of what I say to you this day, the terrible conditions in the world. I tell you truly, you cannot imagine them; and because of this, you tend to forget**. Do not forget, lest My Father forget you**.

Acknowledge your family, your world family. **Who else will pray for them?** Who else will bring them to My Father and obtain mercy for them? **This is your mission:** caring for, ministering to, comforting. Healing all of Our lost ones began with the first call to prayer that you received in these times and has only escalated since then. Realize this call as the greatest gift you have ever received. Realize this as your lifeline, **the Golden Rope that ties you to your own salvation**. Oh, My dear ones, rejoice! Allow My Blood to cover you now, once again. I pour it upon the world this day and I take your prayers to My Father. I take you to My Father, My children, and in return I shower you with love. We are one, My precious little ones, we are one! Think often about the fact that you are Mine. I love you. Amen for now, My dear ones. Remember the world. Amen."

July 11, At ADORATION: ST. BENEDICT, PRAY FOR US! Jesus said: "Dearest child, be at peace now. Do not succumb to dismay or despair over the evil intentions in the hearts of your enemies and Mine. The world will never be the same in a very short while. Destructive events are about to erupt, as Our people need immediate signs of the truth of the warnings of Heaven. (Only three months until September! C.) The arrogant attitude of those who judge with the weak discernment of pride will be brought to a place of humility. Wait on the action of Our Spirit to reveal error and danger that might be present in the words of Heaven corrupted by the hearts of false messengers. This is not meant to frighten Our people, but to **increase their patience** and trust in directives and warnings meant to protect them; meant to assure them of the safety in trusting Our

Spirit to allow error to become obvious to all without the pious words of self-appointed guides to the minds and hearts of faithful sheep who know and follow their Shepherd and His words. Words of attack cannot hide the underlying fear present in the haughty observations of some.

Stay close to My Mother and Myself, your Eucharistic Lord, and **be assured of protection and guidance and proper discernment from the Spirit of God, My dear people. Do not waste time exchanging words puffed up by a false sense of the worth and superiority of your own opinions.** I beg all of you who judge and criticize, spend this time before Me humbly begging forgiveness and mercy for yourselves and for the world. It is I, your Jesus, Savior Who speaks these words from the depths of My Heart full of love and concern for your future. Hear Me, My beloved ones. Look into your own soul for the enemy of peace, the peace I am trying and hoping to give you, the light that darkness will not overcome. Come to Me, My people, for ALL of your needs and concerns. I AM TRUTH! You are reminded again this day. Live in the Presence of Truth. I LOVE YOU! I long for the healing of your hearts; and to empty them of fear, of the world completely at last. A soldier trusts his or her Supreme Commander. Trust Me and My power, My love. Remember how much you are loved. **Remember!"**

July 11, "My dearest ones, I am your Lord and your God, your Father, your Creator. I come again with words of love, with many blessings, with many gifts this night and an increase of those you already have been given, especially those that have been with you throughout your lifetime, gifts that you have honed and polished; that you have made part of what you do and who you are; that you have learned to praise and thank Me for; that you have consecrated to Me; that you have surrendered to Me to use according to My plans for the world, for their salvation and My plans for you and for your salvation. Again I remind you how far you have come as you climb the mountain of My Will, My little ones and all of you all over the world, My faithful and weak but strong in desire to please, to be obedient; broken but becoming whole in My Will, integrated in My Will, healed in My Will. I thank you once again for patience that you have gathered, that you have practiced in spite of the impatience which picks at the corner of your mind, which threatens the peace of My Son; but each time, you overcome the temptation to give in, to walk away, to give up. Thank you again and again for trusting your God, for having patience with your God Whose only desire is your own sanctity, your salvation, our unity one day in My Kingdom in Heaven. It almost seems like a dream, does it not: all you have been told to expect, all the gifts and miracles that you will see? But it is not a dream. It WILL come to fruition and fulfillment. Live in deep belief in the fact that your God loves you. This is beyond your comprehension, I know. Try repeating it, My dear ones, often. This will help: **'My God loves me. I love you, My God.'**

My children, when events begin, you will not be shaken, you will not be frightened or caught by surprise because of the long time and the depth of your training, your preparation; and, like soldiers, you are prepared for battle, strong in the areas of combat, filled with trust in your Leader. These are the things that give foundation to your trust, to your obedience, to your ability to wait upon My Will and My desires for you. Know that the gifts I give you this night are decorations for valor; for duties above and beyond the call; for learning to become a fighting unit that takes care of each other, that prays for each other, that loves each other! All of Heaven joins Me in this gratitude. Words fall short, My dear ones. I tell you again: We are grateful and you are loved!"

7/16, At Adoration: "My dear child, I your Jesus, call out to you. Please give thanks and honor and praise to the Father of all, Who gifts you anew from His store of mercy.

YES, THE WORLD AND THIS COUNTRY TEETERS ON THE BRINK OF MIGHTY EVENTS. IN LIGHT OF INCREASED PRAYER AND FAITHFULNESS, EVENTS HAVE ESCALATED THAT WILL SET UP THE TIME OF THE WARNING. OF COURSE, DESTRUCTIVE EVENTS WILL OCCUR FIRST, AND CONTINUE TO GROW IN INTENSITY ALL OVER THE WORLD. SATAN GOADS LEADERS OF NATIONS WHO VIE FOR THE SAME LAND AND POSSESSIONS. HEARTS ARE HARDENED AGAINST PEACE OR THE SUCCESS OF NEGOTIATIONS. THE ONE WORLD ORDER MEETS IN SECRET, WHILE MEETING FOR REASONS GIVEN THE WORLD THAT WOULD SEEM TO HAVE YOUR INTERESTS AT HEART. THERE IS INDEED INCREASED GLOBAL WARMING AHEAD; BUT IT WILL BE AIDED GREATLY BY FIRES AND WARS AND PLANS OF THOSE WHO PLOT IN SECRET TO TAKE OVER THE ENTIRE WORLD.

IF YOU ARE PRAYING MORE AND LIVING A SIMPLER EXISTENCE, UNITED IN HEART AND SPIRIT AND EXAMPLE WITH OUR BELOVED POOR, (YOUR SISTERS AND BROTHERS WHO LIVE IN POVERTY AND PERSECUTION,) YOU NOW POSSESS A GREATER UNDERSTANDING OF THE WORKINGS AND DESIRES OF MY FATHER'S WILL. YOU HAVE OVERCOME IMPATIENCE AND SUSPICION AND CRITICISM, AND ARE ABLE TO WAIT IN JOY AND TRUST AND SURRENDER FOR THE TIME IT TAKES MY FATHER TO ACT UPON THESE PLANS FOR THE CLEANSING OF THE WORLD AND FULFILLMENT OF ALL OF SCRIPTURE BEFORE I RETURN. IT MATTERS NOT TO YOU WHEN CERTAIN EVENTS OCCUR, AS YOU FOCUS ON MY FACE, MY DIRECTIVES, MY WORDS, TIME SPENT EACH DAY IN MY COMPANY ENJOYING THE SWEETNESS AND MIGHT OF ALL OF WHO I AM. THANK YOU FOR YOUR SURRENDER TO EACH DAY'S EVENTS IN YOUR LIVES, AND YOUR PRAISE AND SINCERE GRATITUDE FOR MY FATHER'S WILL FOR YOU. ENJOY THE PEACE I GIVE YOU FOREVER! REJOICE IN MY LOVE AND THE GRACE GIVEN THAT ENABLES YOU TO ACCEPT AN ABANDONMENT OF YOUR OWN WILL AND AGENDA.

THIS DAY OF OUR MOTHER'S FEAST OF MT. CARMEL, RECEIVE RENEWED STRENGTH AND FAITH IN THE PROTECTION IN THE SCAPULAR, (GIVEN BY HER,) THE BADGE OF TRUST IN HER GIFTS AND HER LOVE. HEAVEN RINGS WITH JOY FOR ALL OF YOU ENROLLED IN THIS POWERFUL DEVOTION AND HUMBLE ADORNMENT OF THIS SACRED SIGN OF YOUR LOVE AND OBEDIENCE. YOU ARE TRULY HER CHILDREN IN SPIRIT AND IN TRUTH; HER FAITHFUL ARMY OF FOLLOWERS AND WARRIORS POISED TO FIGHT THE EVIL ONE WHENEVER AND WHEREVER THE NEED. BE FIRM IN YOUR BELIEF IN THESE WORDS, MY PRECIOUS ONES. BE THRICE BLESSED BY THE SPECIAL GRACES OF THIS SPECIAL FEAST FOR THIS SPECIAL AND GLORIOUS, IMMACULATE ONE. BE FILLED WITH JOY THIS DAY. YOU ARE UNITED TO THE JOY AND HAPPINESS OF ALL IN HEAVEN. I AM YOUR JESUS, SON OF MARY, SON OF GOD WHO BLESSES AND LOVES YOU THIS DAY. REJOICE!"

7/18, "My dear ones, I am the Spirit of God, your Holy Spirit. Each time you gather, you receive new gifts; but this is a special night for a renewal once again of your commitment to your Triune God, to the Holy Mother, My beloved Spouse, a recommitment to prayer, to adoration, to surrender, to all the Father calls you to be, and to joy, My children. I increase your fidelity and strength this night, as things escalate in the world (that could lead to war), that lead even now to more bloodshed, more unrest setting up the plans and the example for many, many more to challenge the authority of your beloved Pope John Paul. It is a time of challenge between countries, between neighbors, within families. You will need new strength, a firm purpose of conviction in all you believe, a firm promise within your own heart to remain faithful in spite of every hardship. Certainly in the hearts of all those gathered here is a clear understanding of events to come, of the hardships, of the temptations that will come to give in to the temptations to give in to the temptation to accept an easier path, an easier way! None of it will be easy, My dear, dear people; and yet all of it, every event, every moment, will be accompanied by enormous grace, enormous help: the strength of your God, the power of your God, the gifts given you again and again and again over time; and at the moment they are renewed, the moment of greatest need. Remember all of this, FOR YOU WILL BE AFRAID, YOU WILL BE MOVED TO DOUBT AT TIMES. YOU WILL WISH TO TURN AND RUN! Pray to the Apostles, those first followers. THEY KNOW! They will help you and bring compassion to your situation.

You are surrounded by Angels. Remember that. Call upon them. It was requested of you to begin to write, to keep track of events in the world, and your own life experiences: your own salvation story. Have you begun, My dear ones; and if not, will you begin??? You cannot see the need for this now; but there will be one, and you will have what you need. Every word that comes from Heaven IS IMPORTANT. Every word is important to reread, to understand, to delve into the meaning always present, deeper than what you perceive at first. Call upon Me. Ask My help, My discernment, My gifts of deeper understanding. There is more to see, My dear ones everywhere in the world. There is more to understand; and from this will come more nurturing, more strength and even MORE understanding. Your God is revealing, not only events of the future, not only calling you with directives for your safety, for your protection; your God is revealing Himself more! Learn more, My dear ones!

You are loved mightily. You are gifted far beyond your ability to grasp. Grasp these things now, that you might come to a final place of preparation and strength and courage and hope and perseverance and trust! **So many people will be depending upon you, so VERY MANY, My dear ones.** Cheers resound through Heaven because of you, for you, about you. Be even more grateful. Be even quieter and in more silence, alone with your God and the Immaculate One, My Spouse. Come, people. Come. Experience that love, experience the joy of Heaven for you! That is all this night, but I have given you much to do, if you will reflect upon My words."

7/22, "Dear ones, I am your Lord and your God. I come this night and see in your hearts that I am welcome, and I thank you. I am your God and Father, your Lord. I gaze upon this group with all of Heaven who hear with Me your prayers for conversion of the world that truly blossoms, for the continuation and the spread and acceptance of My mercy. My children, I know the outcome of your prayers! I know who will accept mercy and who will not, but in My justice and in My mercy, I must allow each one to choose within his or her own lifetime. Praise and thank Me for the freedom of will I have given to each of you in the whole world. I come this night to thank you again, but also to encourage you, to tell you why My plans are escalated now because of your prayers. You have questioned this in your hearts, hoping always to delay and yet, even you know this cannot be. Events must move along. Satan is allowed to plan and to execute those plans. I must work and act and react, as well. I am God Who sees all and knows all, even the innermost secret plans and thoughts, especially those motivated by Satan, who is My enemy, who is your enemy and against whom we battle together; whom you battle even now with your prayers. Most strongly you battle with your prayers. Events are taking place in secret, at every moment now around the world. It will never be secret to Heaven, to Me or to you, when I choose to reveal things to you that are for your good, or for your safety, to give you a new reason to pray. My children, it is why I can tell you that all will be well. It is why I can offer you protection as I have done so many, many times.

Continue to bring Me your praise and your thanksgiving again in the coming days, for always new gifts are being given, as they are tonight. **Never, My children, do I speak without it being a gift in itself**! My very words to you are a gift to you. I ask you to listen with all of your hearts to everything I am telling you. **I have chosen you since before you were born to serve in special ways at this special time in history.** What a gift this is. As events begin to be even more serious and more apparent, more obvious in the world and in your own lives, you will come to a deeper understanding and appreciation and gratitude. Learn from all the words of My Jesus. Learn from all the words We have given you from Heaven, My dear ones. Learn by the delays and through them. Look at the mercy and the patience I have had with you, and realize My great love for you, My great desire to save you; and that even more, we are one! Continue to come to Me, united to Jesus in the Blessed Sacrament of the Altar with Our Holy Spirit, with your prayers, with your love. I give special thanks this night to those who have brought new ones, who evangelize, who reach out and attempt to bring more to hear the words of Heaven so important, so serious for these times. You are becoming giants of prayer! Amen to you, My dear ones. I give you My gratitude."

7/29, "My people, I am your Jesus. Welcome to all of you again. I am happy to be here with you for this celebration of My Precious Blood which I once again pour out upon you. I am cleansing you again this day of the little sins that cling. Repeated sins, even though they are small, My children, must go. I call you, as I have told you in the past, to the perfection of My Father; and I have told you this is possible with My grace and My strength. I call you out of your resistance, My dear ones everywhere in the world: to Me, to My Mother, to Our call for as much prayer as you can possibly say each day**, to more prayer than you have ever said in your lives!** The situation in the world worsens. Misleading words come from false prophets. Satan works overtime to trip you up, to trap you, most of all to distract you. My dear, dear ones, you know how I love you and why I wish to save you, why I wish to elevate you in holiness and sanctity, why I wish to strengthen you that you might take every advantage of all the gifts you are given and become all you are called to be and more, to accepting every person in the world. The summer is hot in this area, especially. Do not allow weather or vacation plans or company or tasks to dilute your prayer. My dear ones, whenever you come together**, pray first, then celebrate**; for prayer is a celebration of your brothers and sisters throughout the world. It is recognition that you are all one family. It is a saying 'yes' to accepting every person in the world as your brother, as your sister, into your family and into your heart. My dear ones, ponder these words. You will see. It is always a matter of acceptance, of openness. So, I pour out the gift of openness upon you this day, that you might accept and bring into your hearts and your lives the whole world and their needs, their coldness of heart in so many places; even the sins of the world….. that you take them on as I did, that you suffer for them, not as I did on the Cross, but carrying your own crosses without grumbling, carrying them with joy!

How many times have I spoken to you, My dear children, of joy? It will always be so! Joy will gladden your own hearts in the midst of any chaos, any hardship, any loss, and gladden the hearts of others because only joy comes from My Father, the deep joy I call you to have and to share and to be for each other. Praise My Father, children, once again for allowing this time of visitation, this time of hearing My words; for the opportunity to reread them, to meditate, to change, to grow, to become. My Mother, who is with Me, showers you with kisses and wraps you again in Her Mantle. There is coolness under her Mantle, My children; a relief from the heat, from the pressing tasks of the day, from all your struggles! Recall every minute that We are with you with many Angels, that you are never alone, that I am in your very hearts. Be blessed and healed according to My Father's Will, My little ones. Hear Me say to you every moment, 'I LOVE YOU!'"

8/1, "I am your Jesus, come once again to be with you, and I welcome you once again. How much I love you, and there are no words (that are) adequate, no words to 'contain' My love. So again and again, I come to tell you to hope that the love I am pouring out upon you now will heal you more, will change you, will open your hearts to new gifts from My Father, will open your hearts and your minds to each other, who are also gifts from My Father. Believe Me when I tell you how close you are to My Heart. Deep within My Heart I place you all once again this night for protection, for comfort; that I might lavish you with mercy, with all the healing you need to become strong, to become gentle, to be come mighty, to be able to die, My dear ones, to the world that you might live in My Father's Kingdom now in your hearts and in Mine, in Me. You are not only gifted far beyond your understanding, but far beyond so many, many, many people who have ever lived in history. Yes, the responsibilities are greater, also. All that you are being called upon to become; all that you will do, the acts you will perform, the services, the ministering: they are greater, too, than at any time in history for a group as large as yourselves, all over the world, faithful ones. You must be excited, filled with encouragement, eagerness for each event to begin, that I might return soon. That all of the evil in the world and in people's hearts will spend itself at last, and My Father will rid the earth of evil. You cannot imagine the beauty that will exist upon the earth and in your hearts and on your faces. Again I say, rejoice!

Unrest grows. There is a great danger of increased conflict. You know where these things are occurring. You read about them and hear about them, and I see in your hearts that you pray about them. **My Mother and I pray with each of you every time you pray.** We love you so much. We need you. My Father showers you this night, My children, with a mercy as bright and glowing as any light you can imagine. Mercy will shine upon your faces with the new joy that comes, as you see more and more of Our words fulfilled, as you see more and more people healed and returning to My Father. What joy lies in your future. How joyous I am for you, beloved of My Father. I love you. Thank you for loving Me. Your love is growing. Persevere, My dear ones!"

8/5, "My dear ones, I am you Mother. I come filled with happiness and joy, with delight and blessings. How wonderful to celebrate this day with you and my faithful ones all over the world who have noted the day of my birth. All of Heaven celebrates with you. I have prayed with you, today, as I had gathered in that upper room with the Apostles the day My beloved Spouse, the Holy Spirit, poured Himself out upon us gathered. My companions, the Apostles, had been gathered in fear. I wish you could have seen the change that took place in them once the fire of the Holy Spirit nestled in their hearts; and once it nestled there, it then became like a tornado filling them. Fire, indeed it was, excitement glorifying God and praising Him, praising the Father for Jesus, their beloved Master and teacher and friend and Lord. It was as if an explosion had occurred, which indeed it had: an explosion of grace and gifts. Mighty wonder filled all of us, once the experience had ended: not just wonder, but an impetus to go out. The Apostles could not contain themselves. They rushed to share this great gift, this fulfillment of my Son's words to them with everyone gathered. People had begun to gather as they heard the noise like a mighty wind that filled the house where we were. It was, of course, the plan of the Father that they should gather; that the next miracle should occur instantly, as all gathered could hear the Apostles speaking in his native tongue. And you should have seen the looks on their faces! It was marvelous to behold and in my heart, I praised the Father and the Son and My Spouse, the beloved Spirit of God.

My dear ones, contemplate this as a further gift for my birthday. Remember the words I am giving you today. You will be like this in the days ahead. You will know a greater fire, a greater impetus to go out, to reach out, to speak out and to pour out yourselves and your love, your service, your comfort, your welcoming, your hospitality, your loving compassion. O, my dear, dear ones, how blessed you are. You will look at each other on occasions, incredulous at what you have just witnessed: miracles, mighty healings, amazing grace! Reflect with me on these times, as I look at your own future as a mighty portent of things to come. Rejoice, my children, as I rejoice for you this day; as I give praise and honor with you to God, Our Father, Who has gifted each of us far beyond your understanding. As grace increases, my children, so will your understanding and your wisdom and your knowledge and your ability to do whatever is needed at the moment. Prepare yourselves for this time, my dear ones. Begin now by once and for all turning away from the world, letting go of all the residue of the past once again, all the ways of being and speaking and thinking and acting that you have been and done in the past. Think of yourselves as a new creation. That is not proud, my children. It is something for which to rejoice, a reason to give praise to Our Father, and thanksgiving. Find all the gratitude in your hearts, in your spirits, in your minds and your souls. Offer it up to the Father for His great gifts to you in the past and again this day, and all of those that will come to you in the future. I love you, my dear ones. We go forward together marching in this vast army of my faithful ones. You are my precious ones."

8/9, in Iowa Jesus said: "Child, please write My words. Events in the world worsen and move toward a major and formalized confrontation. The very fact that China has adapted their 'superior' attitudes poses a threat and challenge to your President. Each event that is of a world shaking nature will then take time to reverberate throughout the world and My Church. Here is another reason there is seeming delay and long periods of waiting before the next event. The Masonic interference and presence in My Church must not become a matter of public knowledge too soon in the One World Plans! A domino effect will be present in the breakup and break down of all the moral and physical structures (you will see begin to collapse) in the coming weeks and months. As wars develop, social structures are weakened by the separation within families and the weakening that occurs from terrorist attacks and spreading fear. This pattern will continue to appear in different parts of the world and result in the 'need for' the reaction and taking sides by the entire world that I have already mentioned. You can see this developing, daughter, in announcements of renewed 'friendly relationships' moving countries toward an allied condition and state of internal and external affairs.

I am maintaining a general application of My words until the very time of overt aggression on the part of major powers that will lead to obvious divisions and a fracture of the false unity pretended by so many at this time! The games being played and the lives of those, who are pawns, are a disgrace to the intelligence and integrity of all who watch and pray and fight from a position of blessed strength in My Mother's Army of faithful ones! Do not leave her side for a moment, My children. You are formed into the fighting unit that will assist My victorious defeat of Satan and all the "SECRET" PLANS that begin to unfold, and set the stage for world war and annihilation of epic proportions, as foretold in My revelations to My beloved John 2000 years ago!

Be aware, My beloved warriors, of the serious words I speak about oh-so-serious developments everywhere in the world now, that bring you to the first of many confrontations, wars, destructive events in Nature and an ongoing unfolding of all you understand to be the Father's Plan and My ultimate return. My dear ones, prepare for My Mother's Feast and pray mightily at the same time for your Pope John Paul II, Our beloved, chosen leader and lamb. DO NOT FEAR, PRAY! I love you. I am with you. My Mother is pouring out grace and strength upon all (who pray) by the Will of Our Father. Consecrate yourselves to her once again. Be in constant preparation for this great Feast of, not only her Assumption into Heaven, but the fulfillment of her life on earth that serves as the source of enlightenment and hope for the fulfillment of your life on earth and entrance into Heaven to live eternally in the bliss of unity with all of Us there.

As members of the Body of Christ, you groan in the pain of waiting for your own delivery from the sufferings of living out My Passion and Death in your own lives with an eye to the future glory of Heaven. All you await is about to begin to move the world, and especially My Church, into the final stages of your death to the world of Satan and rebirth into the Light of Christ, either in Heaven or in the New and Renewed Era of Beauty in Peace and Purity on the Earth in My Eucharistic Reign. Rejoice, My people, as My Father continues to wrest you from the clutches of Satan and deliver you into the freedom of His Divine and Merciful Will."

8/22, At Adoration, Jesus said: "My dear one, yes, write My words of direction for My people on this great feast of My Mother and yours. The Queenship of Mary is a feast and fact to ponder, children of her Immaculate Heart.

FOR MERCY'S SAKE!

To be a child of a Queen means special gifts are reserved for her royal offspring; that is, those who are members, who are one in the Body of Christ. It means a certain level of behavior and responsibility is expected of the children of this Queen Mother that reflects her royal beauty and the loving power shared by the King. Ponder the fact of being a Queen whose King is God! Ponder the necessity of pleasing the Queen with a reflection of her kindness and service and obedience to the King. Ponder the joy that must permeate her children at the position of predilection given to her children who have been chosen; but also who accepted this honor offered by the Queen of Heaven herself by the Will of the King. Ponder and rejoice and be grateful, dear ones of My Mother's love and care, her concern for your future; her gifts of prayer and grace showered upon her little ones whom she desires to see growing in the purity and strength required for members of the family of God, members of His Kingdom.

It has been the desired duty and cooperation of this Queen to pray for her chosen ones who have responded to the grace she procured for you through her prayers and pleading for your response to her call to you, her little ones in danger of wandering into the web of Satan's subtle snares and losing the heavenly gifts she wishes to give you, her beloved ones. It is her prayers, her purity, her obedience that brings you along the path of the desires of the King for the perfection of His subjects whom He loves beyond the understanding allowed His vulnerable little ones, who need the help of His Queen to acquire the cleansing needed to enter one day into His Heavenly Kingdom forever.

The world in which you live and learn to become obedient and loving children has become a place of deadly opportunities to follow the enemy of this Queen, the woman who will crush the head of this serpent, Satan. Without her help, you cannot do whatever the King tells you! Stay closer than ever to her, My beloved ones. Listen closely to her whisperings of love, her call to purity. Come away from the world into the peace of her guidance, her holiness, her example and the words she has given these many years that will convince your heart of the dearness and protection to be found in the Heart of the Immaculate Queen. I, Who am the Son of the Queen, call out to you as brothers and sisters of the Son of God and son of Mary. She will bring you closer to Me. She will teach you how to love the King. My Mother sends words of love and gratitude to you, as your Queen and companion on the journey of those who serve the King by sharing words that will save the ones, who step out of the chaos and noise of the world, to pray for mercy on those still trapped by the lies of Satan and the dreaded Antichrist. Continue in silence and your present focus on My Father's Will for your time and energy and surrender."

8/22, "My dear ones, I am your Jesus of Mercy, here with you again. I speak again this day in honor of My Mother, My precious Mother and Queen, your precious Mother and Queen. In her great humility she has asked Me to speak, to ask you to come closer to Her. She has asked Me to tell you of the great love that exists between Us; how I listen to every plea and every request from My Mother.

This is the basis, My dear ones, for My request to you to come closer to her, to hold her hand, to listen for her voice. She has so much to share with you, so many things to tell your heart, so many words of love, so much encouragement that you need. Practice listening, becoming used to this new, perhaps, deeper relationship with Mary, the Immaculate One, our precious Mother; for in the days ahead, more and more you will need her strength, her comfort, her gentleness to soothe you, to reinvigorate, to bring you to a place of deeper commitment, of perseverance. She has told you in the past how difficult it will be to persevere. She knows this from her own experience, her own waiting for the Father's Will to be fulfilled in My life and in hers. She knows what it is like to see a loved one die before her eyes; but to be raised to defeat death and so to show all of you your own future: to defeat death and rise to new life, again and again in the coming months and years and then one day, forever!

We have this beautiful, loving Mother to celebrate together. What a great gift from God Our Father. You will see My Mother on occasions, My children, in the midst and in the heat of battle: the battle against the evil one that grows in the world, the battle against the darkness that descends, the battle against the evil that exists in the hearts of many now. Her presence will be something you know, something tangible that you will see, not for a long period of time, but now and then according to My Fathers' will for you as it is needed, because of His great mercy and His great love for you. Be encouraged by My words! There is so much ahead of you that is beautiful, that is sacred, that is holy and will be wholesome as you become whole and holy and wholesome; as you lead others through the Heart of My Mother back to their God and Creator, obtaining salvation through their repentance, their promises to remain faithful.

Oh, My dear, dear ones, how I love you. How grateful is every person in Heaven, is your God and all your loved ones who are smiling at this moment at each of you. It is a mighty group of warriors you have become. It is a mighty Communion of Saints you are becoming! Reread My words often, all of the words of Heaven. Only with this sort of reinforcement and strengthening can you remain faithful. Even at your level of commitment now, it will be that difficult and impossible without My Mother, without the strength of Our words. You have every promise for every gift, every strength, everything you need for the future. You are loved beyond words, My faithful ones, My beloved ones."

8/26, "Dear ones, I am your Jesus. I gather with you today bringing with me every person in the world; not only those who belong to My Body, the great Body of Christ, but more especially those who do not, those who do not know Me or My Father, know nothing of the Trinity, nothing of My Mother, who have rejected totally all of Us. I ask you to remember these rejections that occur constantly and realize, children, that when you are rejected, it is not truly you, but Myself, the Trinity, My Mother, all the words ever uttered by God and the Holy Mother, that are rejected. Yes, it feels and sounds as though you are personally being rejected, and there is some element of that in the criticism and rejection of many people;

but I mention this today, that you may see the greater seriousness of those who reject you verbally or even just in their hearts, to pray for them, for it is their God they are rejecting, and this is most serious! My children, this requires mercy: My mercy and yours. For, 'whose sins you shall forgive they are forgiven, but whose sins you shall retain and hold bound, are held bound! Think of this deeply, and allow forgiveness and compassion to well up into your entire being for these poor confused and misled people. They would have to be confused, or they would not lash out in such a mean and dehumanizing way, such a hurtful way, tending to almost destroy you. Those words, My dear ones, are certainly an example of how it feels when you are attacked by another, especially those close to you.

I tell you all these trials, all these hurts, all this purification is necessary, not just for you, but for the one who is rejecting, who is lashing out; for My children, when the truth becomes evident, how deep their remorse will be. Nothing could cause remorse like an incident of this kind. This will touch them most deeply and convert them most deeply, bring them to contrition and remorse most deeply. This is the desire of My Father, Who allows all these things in His plan out of mercy. You see once again, as I explain how mercy is always at the foremost of each action of My Father loving you, all of His children, bringing most quickly each one back to Him. There are such serious events in the very near future. I know you have heard this in the past. You have prepared to the utmost degree in the past; but now you see you are prepared for any event at anytime, and this is the desire of My Father for His faithful ones. It is not necessary that you know the time or the day; otherwise it would have been given many times in many ways. What is necessary, My children, is faith, the faith that will move mountains, the faith that will turn mustard seeds into giant trees, comforting many in their shade.

My children we have come a long way together, arm in arm. Truly, Heaven has watched you change into mighty warriors. You will see the depth of that word once the battle is heated, once you see casualties, once you see a removal of great numbers of people from the earth. You will know why the word (warriors) was used in the first place. A warrior is mighty, is fearless; uses the weapons at hand in every age, in every degree of development of weapons. It doesn't matter, and it does matter! The external, physical weapons are still a picking up of your Rosary, a picking up of your Scripture, a physical speaking prayers or reading My Word. The words of prophets in the past, the words of prophets now, the clinging; and it is physical as you **cling to a belief in My words in spite of delays and disappointments; and, yes, being made to look foolish and once again being rejected, humiliated, hurt.** My children, how I weep for you, how My Mother weeps for you and with you. Her tender Mother's heart breaks again and again, when you are hurt. When you are hurt, she is hurt so deeply. Rejoice that you have her to absorb much of the hurt, to comfort you, even though you may not feel her comforting words and prayers, her arms around you. How blessed and gifted and graced you are! I remind you once again, first and most of all because you have been given the gift of My Mother; that you have discovered how near and really she is your Mother, that you have come to love her as you have, and are comforted by her.

Outside of the gift of the Triune God, there is no greater gift in the world than My Mother. Praise My Father for her, My children. Praise and thank her as you prepare for the unfolding of the End Times: stories and events, one at a time, one following another, one linked to another. All will be well, My children. Remember the great Mantle of protection that surrounds you, individually and collectively now and forever. You are loved. Be especially prepared now. Although you might have received the Sacrament yesterday, I ask you to receive the Sacrament of Reconciliation again this week. The best you can do, My children, so you will be the best you can be! I love you, My warriors, My companions-at-arms! You are Mine. Feel My love. Cling to that. Never let go of My love!"

8/29, At Adoration, "Dear one, please pray to Our Spirit now, for the Father has important words. I am your Jesus, daughter, filled with love for you this day and come to help you receive the gifts you are about to be given. Child of My Creative Heart, be filled with peace. 'It is I, your Father and God Who comes with words of comfort and direction for My people. Believe in what you will hear now, for time is precious; and these words contain the seeds of salvation, watered by the faith in your own heart, nourished by the hope you carry to all who listen. Be strengthened by My power, little one. Be at peace please, daughter, about all that lies ahead of you. You have done all you are able to do each time your help is required by your dear little ones or by Myself. I will never abandon you to debilitating fatigue; and only allow a certain amount now, that you will remain calm and hidden and obedient. The human spirit is full of desires to accomplish much. As you succumb to the need for more rest, you are also trusting in My promises to sustain you on your journeys and fill you with words to stimulate the hearts and minds of everyone.

Please tell Our faithful ones their God and Creator calls out in near despair over the arrogant demands of His children: 'Now', they say to Me. 'Act now, if You mean what You say to us. Show us a sign to give us hope and renew our trust in You, if You really care for us. It is foolishness that You ask of us, when You ask for preparation for nothing! You have made a laughing stock of the very ones You profess to love and protect. How does a God of love allow His people to languish in ridicule and drought of spirit?' Oh, My people, how your try your God, Who desires only to heal your hearts and spirits by ridding them of the poison of Satan.... in a world filled with death and treason, especially through the lies and deception of facile words at every level of leadership. This time of waiting has been the result of My mercy pouring out and into the wounds you carry, inflicted by these poisonous fumes of hatred and not so subtle plans for your annihilation or slavery. The antidote to this sinful environment is a purging of your hearts of worldly desires, of impatience, of haughty attitudes and demands upon your God. The arrogance that has been solidified within pride-filled hearts has created a solid wall of resistance in too many, who were expecting instant rewards and importance for their prayers and initial response to the call of Mary, the Immaculate and obedient one, sent to you by My Will for you. You, as Church, have rejected her!

You have defied the leadership of your Pope, (John Paul II) who has given every ounce of energy and love to lead you to her, whom he honors and loves as example and vehicle of her Motherly tenderness. This holiest of Holy Fathers is shedding his earthly existence, as his last ounce of strength, to fulfill his promises to her and to you. Pray for him, My dearest people. It is the hour of immolation for the Church of My Son, its real crucifixion in spirit and in fact. **Do not ask for instant action from your God. Ask for mercy**! I have created each of you, and the entire world. Listen not to scientists and their plans to replace My Creative Power with their own. There will never be a good and acceptable reason to interfere with My Will, My Plan for the world of My children, made in My Image. **Confess your pride and impatience, My people. Your understanding of your own importance and opinions is beyond My tolerance.** I wish to give you love and healing and joy, My beloved little ones. My plans for you are perfect! You must allow Me to be your One and only, True and loving Triune God, All Powerful God, Who acts in the best and most perfect way for your present and your future. I love you, My people. It is why I wish to save you. YOU NEED ME, MY HELP, MY WAY!"

8/29, "My dear ones, I am your Mother. I am coming (to you) through a gift of my Spouse, the most Holy Spirit of God. My children, I am so happy to be with you. I have been in your presence this entire evening, praying for you, walking among you, praying with you, touching your hearts, transforming you into my children of grace and humility. **It has always been humility that is most needed, and the cause of the greatest struggle within Our people**. It is the way in America to be independent and aggressive, to be very confident, to be sure of yourself, and I say this night, my children, good for you! For you are aggressive in your love and your obedience to the Father. You are confident in His love and my love for you. When you are confident in all of the ways of your Triune God and your holy Mother; when you are strong in your ability to persevere, you are strong in working for your Lord, in being filled with His strength, in being independent in the right way: independent of the call of the world, the desires for the world now, independent of the lure of the world, its gratification, the call of Satan to give up, to give in, to turn away from the call of the Father. This call is given through me and the words allowed me by the Father, for they are words of love and encouragement, my children, words of delight for your faithfulness, your growth in holiness. As you come closer to me, your love for me grows; and I tell you I am so blessed by you. How precious you are to me. I say this again and again; but it has been a little while since we have visited like this; so I must tell you how precious you are, how much I love you, how dear you are to me. How I count on you, your prayers, your faithfulness, your desire to serve, to persevere in spite of delays and disappointments, in spite of the feeling... 'Will anything ever occur in my life as I pray for? Is the Lord listening? Does He hear me? Does He know of my love for Him?'

I tell you, children, I come here especially this night to tell you the Father does hear. He does answer. He does know everything about you. My Jesus lives in your heart. My Spouse, the Spirit of God, pours Himself out and His gifts again and again upon you, giving you the gift of openness to receive the Father's mercy, His plans for you. You are thinking it is difficult to persevere, and you are correct! But you are gaining strength, gaining the kind of perseverance that will overcome incredible obstacles in the future, **incredible events that will leave you stunned and wondering if the world can continue after such mighty blows! I tell you this by way of encouragement for your continued prayers and faithfulness.** In this dreadful heat, think of the time that will come of dreadful cold, my children! You will be taxed to the fullest of your own abilities, but **your abilities will far exceed those you know of yourself now; the self you are familiar with, the self who grows weary quickly; who does not pray as much as you would like; who is not the faithful one you know I call you to be. And yet, you ARE my faithful ones. Again I say, be encouraged about God, about me, about everything you question, everything you struggle over, most especially of course, the rejection and ridicule of others.** Oh my dear ones, how I weep with you, believe this, in your sorrows and your wounds. We are one, my children, you and I; for I bore every wound of my Son, and I **tell you I bear your wounds as well.** I love you, my dear ones. Think of that often. Be comforted. Be invigorated by the mere fact of my love, my presence with you and many Angels. **When you are discouraged and fatigued, stop! Become aware of my presence with your many Angels.** You will see how good you will feel shortly; ready to begin again, able to continue, to be joyful again, to smile, to keep on keeping on. I am with you, my children, every moment in love and encouragement and joy. And then, AGAIN, my dear ones..... Be aware of my presence with you!"

9/2, 2:45 a.m. At Desk: "My dearest one, please write quickly My words for you and Our people. The **days are hurrying into a time of change for the world, not only of seasons, but a time of upheaval and chaos.** There will be many of these, and each will become more violent in nature and degree of destruction. In the coming days, there will be a bizarre action of the Moon that will frighten the entire world, and totally puzzle scientists. (To my knowledge, this has still not happened in '06, but Jesus has said to my heart again and again…'Everything We have told you WILL OCCUR!' And then God's time comes into play again .. Cta.) These will be the strongest signs yet given by My Father, and many more will be moved to pray.

Events in Israel are becoming more violent. More lives are about to be taken by each side, and tourists will be in danger, as My Shrines are once again in peril. Daughter, I am your Jesus. You know Me by My words and the personality of the Lamb, the way I speak to you, and My Heart that resonates with love in your heart. Joy courses through your person, as you run to meet Me here in Our special place reserved for Me alone. Although I hold all of Our faithful in My Heart, **each**

of you is held in a special and unique and particular place within: reserved for you and taken by no other. Please encourage Our people to believe this, and to feel the special love and **unique character of their personal call from their Triune God and through the Holy Mother**. Imagine such personal invitations given for everyone, chosen before they were born, and lived out in a way that is unique to each beloved one!

When you see soldiers fighting in the streets, women and children being chopped down by bullets and violence, you are more able to imagine the state of siege soon to be lived out by Satan's plans. Each new attack, especially in this country, is a forerunner of larger fights, terrorist attacks and increased violence everywhere. This is designed and allowed by Our Father to draw you into the results of conflict at a reasonable pace, when possible. Then everything will seem to explode at once, and force decisions that will alter your own lives and form the choices of others. It will be dangerous in the streets, as police and soldiers appear to keep the order and peace of the city intact. This might seem like an exciting time, but it will be a time full of new dangers. Come back to Me now, little ones, in joy, in days given over to time spent with Me."

1 p.m. Same day, at Adoration. "Yes, daughter, let us continue. You are rested now and filled with My Presence in the Eucharist. You are filled with peace, little faithful one, and a desire to be here with Me in silence. People do not know, do not see or understand how or when they are becoming ensnared and trapped once again by Satan's subtle web. He knows the weakness of each person, and goes from one guise to another, each time with the same objective: that of tripping up those, especially who struggle to climb the mountain of perfection of My Father. **Hypocrisy, judgmentalism and haughty attitudes, critical, abusive natures are often family characteristics handed down through generations**. It is not until one person has the strength (accepted from Our Spirit) to stand out and say:

'STOP! No more will I live in such and such a way, choosing negative behavior, self-destructive and gratifying behavior, passing along abusive attitudes and words and actions to others, as they were passed along to me! No longer will I lash out in anger over events, even hurtful or harmful in my life, events I did not seek or choose or cause or deserve! From this moment, I choose to live in peace with all people; to become a person of mercy, of forgiveness, of love.' This is also what it means to know and do My Father's Will: to become a new creation, a purified soul and a healed spirit.

'No longer will I seek to place blame, to point fingers at another, to tear down another in order to build myself up! No longer will I perpetuate any words or behavior, especially attitudes that kill the spirits, break the hearts and minds and lives of others. This day I become a healer, a reconciler, a source of mercy and acceptance in a quiet and humble and prayerful way.'

This may require years to implement and mean the loss of the friendships, the association of many who still espouse worldly attitudes and values. This will definitely set up in your life the opportunity to share totally in My life on Earth and My Eucharistic Life now, hidden under the form of bread for the world, feeding the hungry with all you have and all you have become! Are you not excited by these possibilities, My beloved people? Do you look forward to a life of peace within, no matter what is occurring in your world? A life filled with quiet, grateful joy can replace a life of guilt and anger, resentment and bitterness when you allow Me, your Jesus, your Savior, to empty you of all harmful behavior and perceptions, all violence and chaos and noise.

Violence is the food of movies and entertainment in the world of Satan! Intensity and stimulation from rich food and drink, noise and violence feeds anger and illicit sexual expression. You know all these things, My people, but not the degree to which you are victim of them each time you watch and partake of these scenes presented on television, movies and story lines that pride themselves on offering real-life situations, that are not of MY life, children; but the death stories of Satan designed to appeal to and develop your baser instincts. You cannot imagine life without all the entertainment opportunities you crave and enjoy? Oh yes, it requires enormous grace and strength and discipline to leave the harmful lifestyle of the world. There is nothing impossible to God (Luke 18:27) I remind you, little precious children of My longing. It is why I call you to begin spending your free time with Me, united to the Father and the Spirit and the Immaculate One, Mary the Holy Mother. Joseph, too, and all the Saints are **praying for you and waiting for you to ask, to seek and so to receive help in your great need for purifying and healing, your emptying and transformation.** Pray more often, pleading **with all your might for the desire to desire this change: a total conversion into the humble child and peaceful servant you were created to be!** In the Name of My Father and Myself and Our Spirit, I call out to you in anguish, people of the earth. STOP. LOOK. LISTEN and be TRANSFORMED into the IMAGE OF THE LIVING GOD. Choose Life, My loved ones. Choose Peace. Choose Holiness. Oh my dear ones, **do not lose yourselves. Do not lose Me. Do not lose the last calls of this Age to accept mercy: your final bridge to My Father's mercy, to salvation for all Eternity!"**

**********September 11, 2001 Adoration, 2:35 p.m.**************

"Child, begin to write immediately. I am Jesus, Son of God, Second Person of the Trinity. Believe I am speaking, My precious one. Listen carefully.

'To all My faithful ones who read My words and believe, I send special greetings of love and peace. The events that have begun at the hands of terrorists are the most out of control attacks by Satan himself. They are a shout of defiance to all that is sane. They require the MOST CONTROLLED RESPONSE FROM FAITHFUL AND PRAYERFUL PEOPLE EVERYWHERE. FLOCK TO YOUR

CHURCHES, BELOVED ONES. SPEND YOUR HOURS BEGGING MERCY ON ALL THOSE WHO ARE ENTERING ETERNITY IN LARGE NUMBERS NOW. REREAD OUR WORDS OF WARNING TO SEVERAL FAITHFUL MESSENGERS THESE PAST THREE OR FOUR YEARS. YOU WILL FIND THEM FILLED WITH THE LOVE OF GOD AND PROMISES OF PROTECTION ACCORDING TO MY FATHER'S WILL FOR EACH ONE. RECEIVE THE SACRAMENT OF RECONCILIATION, ONCE AGAIN, MY DEAREST ONES. FOCUS ON MY PRESENCE IN MY EUCHARIST AND WITHIN YOUR HEART. I POUR OUT NEW STRENGTH, MY PEOPLE. I WILL BE WITH YOU EVEN MORE POWERFULLY IN THESE DAYS OF TERROR. BE OPEN TO THE TRUTH FROM THIS MOMENT ONWARDS.

DO NOT, I BEG OF YOU, GIVE IN TO PANIC. REMEMBER THAT SATAN IS ALLOWED VICTORIES TO FULFILL ALL OF SCRIPTURE UNTIL MY RETURN. BELIEVE, MY CHILDREN. PRAY, AS NEVER BEFORE. ALLOW ME TO COMFORT YOU. BELIEVE IN THE POWER OF YOUR PRAYERS FOR THOSE WHO WILL PRAY FOR YOU IN RETURN WHEN THEY ARE BROUGHT INTO PARADISE. THEY NEED YOUR PRAYERS FOR MERCY, MY PEOPLE. THEY ARE YOUR DEAREST FAMILY AND **MY LAMBS OF SACRIFICE.** I SEND YOU MY GIFT OF CALM PEACE WITH THESE WORDS, AND ASK YOU TO REMEMBER THAT WE ARE ONE IN PURPOSE, IN LOVE AND IN PRAYER BEFORE MY FATHER AND YOURS, IN SERVICE FOR AND TO THE WORLD. I AM WITH YOU. I LOVE YOU. I BLESS YOU AND THANK YOU FOR YOUR OBEDIENCE AND COMMITMENT. CONSECRATE THE WORLD AND ITS VICTIMS, MY BELOVED ONES. BE AT PEACE. I AM JESUS.' DAUGHTER, RELEASE THIS IMMEDIATELY AND STAY IN CONSTANT PRAYER NOW YOURSELF. BE ATTENTIVE, CHILD, FOR MORE DIRECTIONS. REMAIN IN PRAYER AS MUCH AS POSSIBLE. REREAD ALL OUR WORDS."

September 12, - 4 A.M. at home, "DEAREST CHILD, I AM YOUR MOTHER OF SORROWS. PRAY TO MY SPOUSE, THE HOLY SPIRIT NOW, LITTLE WARRIOR. LET US BEGIN:

'MY BELOVED CHILDREN, THANK YOU FOR TURNING TO ME IN GREAT NUMBERS AND FOR LONG HOURS OF PRAYER. CONTINUE TO UNITE YOURSELVES TO ALL OF HEAVEN WHO PRAYS FOR THIS WOUNDED COUNTRY AND ITS LEADERS. MY HEART CRIES OUT TO YOU WITH ALL ITS MOTHERLY COMPASSION. SEE THE SERIOUSNESS OF THESE EVENTS, DEAREST SOLDIERS OF MINE. DO NOT BE MISLED BY THOSE WHO CLAIM TO SPEAK WORDS OF HEAVEN THAT ARE CONTRARY TO ALL YOU HAVE HEARD THESE MANY YEARS. BE PREPARED NOW IN EVERY WAY, MY DARLING LITTLE ONES. MOST OF ALL, REALIZE THE EXTENT OF DANGER TO THE FUTURE OF THE WORLD AND THE WARLIKE AGGRESSION PRESENT IN THESE ACTS

OF TERRORISTS WHO CARE NOT FOR HUMAN LIFE; WHO CELEBRATE A VICTORY MEASURED BY LOSS OF LIVES AND DESTRUCTION OF PROPERTY. YES, MY PEOPLE, THESE ACTS OF WAR, THIS NEW SURPRISE ATTACK ON AMERICA IS THE GAUNTLET THROWN BY SATAN TO MOCK AND RIDICULE YOUR COUNTRY AND YOUR LEADERS.

YOU HAVE SEEN TREASONOUS ACTIVITY EXHIBITED, AS WELL!

CAN MY BROKEN, BLEEDING HEART BREAK THROUGH YOUR HARDENED HEARTS, AMERICA? WILL YOU REREAD WORDS I HAVE GIVEN BY THE MERCY OF GOD, OUR MIGHTY FATHER AND CREATOR? AS YOU READ THESE WORDS, PUT YOURSELVES IN THE SCENES VIEWED THESE PAST TWENTY FOUR HOURS. BE PRESENT IN THE HEARTS AND HOMES OF THOSE WHOSE LOVED ONES HAVE DIED HORRIBLY. BRING ALL OF THESE INTO YOUR HEARTS AND COMPASSION NOW. SEND THEM YOUR LOVE AND COMFORT, YOUR CONSTANT PRAYERS FOR MERCY AND CONVERSION FOR HEARTS BROKEN OPEN BY TRAGEDY. ALLOW YOURSELVES TO BE UNITED TO THESE SORROWFUL, SUFFERING ONES AND THOSE WHO ARE BATTLING HEROICALLY TO FIND AND TREAT STILL TRAPPED VICTIMS. DO NOT READ THESE WORDS TO SIMPLY RECEIVE NEW PROPHETIC WORDS, TO BE TITILLATED BY THE LATEST PREDICTIONS AND FRIGHTENING EVENTS. READ THEM TO BE GUIDED IN PRAYER, TO BE MOVED TO GREATER COMPASSION AND SERVICE TO THESE SUFFERING SERVANTS AND VICTIMS BY OFFERING YOURSELVES, THE HOURS OF THIS NEW DAY, AND ALL YOUR ENERGY PLEADING BEFORE MY SON IN HIS TABERNACLE FOR ALL WHO HAVE AND WHO WILL CONTINUE TO DIE IN CONTINUING RESULTS OF THIS FIRST AND IMMEDIATE DISASTER.

YOU, AS SOLDIERS IN MY ARMY, HAVE TRAINED FOR YEARS TO FIGHT THE EVIL IN HEARTS OF MEN WHO FOLLOW EVIL, WHO LISTEN TO EVIL SUGGESTIONS AND MAKE EVIL PLANS TO DESTROY. THIS IS THE BEGINNING OF A FAR GREATER EVIL THAN THE WORLD HAS EVER SEEN SINCE TIME BEGAN: A WAR BEGUN IN TREACHERY, ONCE AGAIN, THAT HAS THE FOCUS OF DIVIDING THE WORLD AND SETTING UP TOTAL WORLD CONFLICT. PRAY FOR YOUR COUNTRY, MY DEAR ONES. YOU CAN SEE THAT A GREAT MEASURE OF PROTECTION HAS BEEN REMOVED NOW BY THE WILL OF GOD. WHILE YOU SEE DEATH AND NEW DESTRUCTION EVERYWHERE, HOLD MY HAND AND DO NOT PANIC. ALLOW YOUR TEARS OF SORROW TO WASH AWAY EVERY LAST OUNCE OF RESISTANCE TO THE WORDS OF HEAVEN AND AGAINST GOD HIMSELF. HE WAITS

FOR YOUR PRAYERS OF MERCY FOR THE SOULS OF ALL WHO HAVE COME INTO ETERNITY. HE WILL ACT IN DIRECT RESPONSE TO YOUR PRAYERFUL AND TRUSTING REQUESTS.

THE DAWN BRINGS NEW HOPE AS LIGHT, ONCE AGAIN, FLOODS THE EARTH. **BE THAT HOPE, MY CHILDREN. BE THAT LIGHT TO THOSE AROUND YOU, ALREADY FILLING WITH DREAD AND DESPAIR. FIGHT BRAVELY, MY BELOVED CHILDREN, WITH WEAPONS OF LOVE AND PRAYER AND LIFE-CHANGING COMPASSION AND FORGIVENESS FOR EVERYONE IN YOUR LIFE AND IN THE WORLD. BE TRANSFORMED NOW INTO ALL YOU ARE CALLED TO BECOME.** BE STRENGTHENED IN SILENCE BY THE PRESENCE OF MY SON AND MYSELF AND MANY, MANY LEGIONS OF WARRIOR ANGELS. THE REAL BATTLE IS FOR SOULS, DEAREST ONES OF MY OWN SUFFERING HEART. WHILE MEN MUST BATTLE TO SAVE LIVES AND PROPERTY, YOUR TASK IS TO SAVE SOULS, (**UNITING OUR PRAYERS TO JESUS' REDEMPTIVE ACTS... cta.**), AS YOU PLEAD FOR MERCY AND FORGIVENESS IN REPARATION FOR THE SINS OF THE WHOLE COUNTRY AND THE WORLD.

YOUR REAL TRANSFORMATION BEGINS THIS VERY MOMENT. CONFESS YOUR SINS. ASK THE HOLY SPIRIT, MY BELOVED SPOUSE, TO ENLIGHTEN YOU EVEN MORE, THAT YOU MIGHT GIVE UP ENTIRELY ALL HURTFUL WORDS AND BEHAVIOR. **SEND ONLY LOVE INTO THE WORLD.** REACH OUT WITH PATIENCE AND UNDERSTANDING TO THOSE WHO ARE FEARFILLED AND WANT TO LASH OUT IN THE USUAL AGGRESSIVE WAY. RESPOND TO ALL WITH LOVE, MY DEAR, PRECIOUS ONES. **DO NOT SHOUT AND ARGUE EVER AGAIN.** I LOVE YOU, MY DEAREST, LITTLE ONES. I CALL OUT TO YOU: ANSWER WITH YOUR LIVES OF SURRENDER TO THE NEEDS OF YOUR COUNTRY. BELIEVE MY WORDS TO YOU AND <u>REMEMBER, EACH EVENT BRINGS YOU CLOSER TO THE RETURN OF MY JESUS AND THE TOTAL DEFEAT OF EVIL IN THE WORLD</u>. PRAY IN PEACE, LITTLE ONES, AND IN PROFOUND TRUST. BELIEVE THAT FINALLY SO MANY MORE WILL TURN TO ME AND THEIR GOD. THANK YOU FOR LOVING ME, AND LEADING THE WHOLE WORLD TO VICTORY IN HEAVEN ONE DAY. I AM MARY, YOUR MOTHER."

September 12, At Adoration, "My beloved faithful one, I am your God and Father, once again come with words of direction and warning, but also of comfort and peace. Thank you, daughter, for remaining available at all hours in order to fulfill My Will.

'My faithful people of the world, as you see events unfold (present and future) you know that My Will allows each attack by Satan and his followers. You have been warned that evil intent will seem so victorious that all must be lost (in your perception). I remind you again that the victory has already been accomplished by My Son's perfect obedience. I ALSO say to you: 'Make no mistake ... I will NOT be overcome, and this accelerating darkness WILL be overcome by the Light of Christ and the MIGHT of My Arm.'

Lucifer, the fallen angel who is Satan and his followers, have launched the most vicious and deadly attack on the lives of the whole world. I invite you to COME BACK TO ME in humble contrition to live My Commandments, to seek My forgiveness and to accept My mercy. NEVER LEAVE ME again, or stray for a moment, My beloved children. I pour out new mercy upon you who believe, to give you the strength to return and the perseverance to remain. Do not wait for My Warning! Seek the immediate help of Our Spirit for the enlightenment of your minds to all that needs reconciling and forgiveness in your life. Listen to no one who attempts to distract or divide or distance you from your Triune God and the Holy Mother. I created you, My dear ones. I enabled you to develop, to crawl, to walk, to run! Run to Me NOW, My own loved ones.

I know every thought of those who have totally embraced terrorism and evil. I tell you, there are many more such events that will occur, that WILL SUCCEED. I will continue to allow words of encouragement and reminders of the present kind (see above) to be given throughout these days of tragic consequence, that you might be filled with ongoing peace and focus; but you must ACCEPT THEM COMPLETELY, My little weak and fearful ones. USE MY WORDS AS A WEAPON AGAINST THE CONTAGION OF PANIC. REACH DEEP WITHIN YOURSELVES, ONCE AGAIN, AND FIND THE STRENGTH POURED OUT AND DEVELOPED THESE MANY YEARS. **You have all the gifts and virtues you require, My people. You have only to believe this and use them**! Now believe ALL My words!'

September 12, "Dear children, I am your Jesus, come with blessings this night, with gratitude for your prayers; for the love that pours out of each heart; for the devotion and the trust in My words, all of My promises, your belief in the special call you have been given to be these instruments of mercy and salvation. My children, we are more closely united now than even before, and we will become more closely united again and again; but remember, we are one! You have reached the level of preparation desired by My Father. You have reached a level of holiness that renders you able and ready to cooperate with every call of My Father. Remember, My dear ones, just because it may sound impossible or too much for you, or look impossible, it will NOT be impossible! Remember My Presence with you, My Mother's presence with her Angels. More and more and more, as days and events unfold, this will be the most important thing in your thoughts and your awareness: **Our absolute Presence with you**. I have said this so many times. Do not forget it, My dear ones, for this will mean you are allowing Heaven to strengthen you and gift you as much as possible. You have learned that We need your cooperation, that you would allow My Father's Will (at every moment) into your life, and you know now why this will be more and more important, as the days go by.

There is no need to speak of the events, My children, for you are all filled with them. The horror of these days is imprinted on your hearts and minds and spirits; and you weep as We weep and have been weeping in anticipation of these events. My children, I wish only to encourage you with My love, with My gratitude for all you have done, all you have become, and all you are ready and eager to become in the future. You have said, yes, again and again in union with My Mother. Thank you for being all you were created to be. How you are loved and held in the Heart of the Father. Dwell in joy and peace, a calm, quiet strength that could only come to you as a gift from My Father through My Heart and by the action of Our Spirit. Everything you have ever heard and learned and waited for has begun and, as happens in any tragedy, you are brought more closely together. I ask you to be as quiet, as silent as possible in these days, to stay recollected and focused on prayer and on the crying need of all. You are My beloved ones, My children. Never doubt that for a moment. My Mother wishes to speak briefly. I bless you, My children. I love you, My children."

Blessed Mother: "My dear ones, I am here with My Jesus always. Again I have been praying with you. Again I have poured out love and Motherly blessings. I wish to say also, how united we are in this effort. Become as aware as is humanly possible for you of my presence, with My Angels and with My Son. This will not only help you to remain calm and peace-filled and focused; it will help your level of sanctity and bring you to new holiness. My Son is the source of all holiness and all that is good in your lives; for He is the very face of the Father. He is the very mercy of the Father. He is the very love of God. Again **I invite you to hold my hand, to bind each other and your loved ones with the beads of my rosary, and the prayers you say for each other and the world now.** I have every confidence in you who have become strong warriors in my army of faithful ones: loving ones, dear ones who are ready for everything and anything. I thank you, my dear children, for becoming these strong allies in the battle against the evil one. Of course I say to you: PRAY MORE. Of course I will always ask this of you; and you will respond as I request, for your hearts are full of love for me, for your God and for the world. Rejoice that you have been brought to this peace, this new creation you have become: a creation more perfect, more in line with the Father's Will, more focused and patterned after the Father's Will. I say to you, my children, rejoice, as I rejoice! Be filled with my love, my dear ones. Be filled with me! WE GO FORWARD TOGETHER."

9/16, ADORATION, Blessed Sacrament Church, "My dear little weary one, rejoice, for I am your God and Father. Be filled with new strength and dedication now to this increased level of service. You are about to see more destruction this day, little one. Remain in prayer throughout the day and evening that many souls may be saved. Even now, new plans are in place to continue a level of terrorism designed to fill each heart with a level of terror not yet reached in the hearts of the citizens of this country, and then in the world. A state of hyper vigilance is desired by Satan and his followers to produce a state of irritability and ultimately chaos within all. Now is the time to pray once again for peace in the hearts and minds of Our faithful remnant. Pray again for each other that mercy may overcome the events designed to rob you of your peace and trust. Remember that My Will is perfect, and **will allow what is best for each soul to bring that one most quickly back to Me. Those coming into Eternity are given the opportunity to learn of My Kingdom, learn about Me, and to choose Me and My Kingdom**. In this terrible realization of the most destructive of Satan's plans to date, your hearts and desires are given greater impetus to pray for the dead and injured. Must it always take a jolt to your consciousness, to your spirits, to bring you to the place and degree of prayer I have begged for all these years? Must you pray out of a sense of horror, or will you now pray out of a sincere love for the entire world and the salvation of all? Do you now begin to understand, My people, how much the world will and does now need you? I tell you, Heaven is weeping. All of Us who have prayed for all of you unceasingly call out to say: YOU CAN DO MORE! When I allow you, My faithful children, to dictate to My actions, to share in the responsibility for the future of the earth, it is also a great gift (to you). Come together now and be united in prayer and pleading for the souls coming into Eternity who need only your love and prayers now."

Continued:

9-16 ADORATION, Blessed Sacrament Church (continued words about souls coming into Eternity, some of whom went to Purgatory) "Gone is the opportunity for the souls (in Purgatory) to improve their position in Purgatory! It is up to you now. Also, realize that many have come into My Kingdom as martyrs, as lambs and victim souls. Praise and thank Me for this, as they have been and are heroes in these events, and are praying in a heroic way now for all of you. They are coming to know about My Plans for these End Times that fulfill all of Scripture until the time of Jesus' return. They pray constantly for and with all of you, their loved ones, for the salvation of everyone on the earth; but especially you, their dearest loved ones. Invite all of them to pray with you, My people. Discover their nearness and ongoing love, ever purified now in My Kingdom. You are not only waiting for the next act of war, the next action of My Will. You are living out My Will for you, My beloved ones. Remember the presence and love of your Triune God and Holy Mother. YOU ARE CALLED TO UNITY WITH US AND WITH EACH OTHER AND ALL PEOPLE."

9/19, "Children, it is I, Jesus, Who comes this night. Be at peace, children. Be filled with My Spirit now, with new virtues, new strength, an increased desire to pray, an increased joy and gratitude for prayer. I come this night with words that may seem strong; but I speak of attitudes, children, that must leave your hearts and your minds and your lips. **All criticism must end, My people everywhere in the world, all judgmentalism, all haughty attitudes.** If you are seeing yourselves as different, or especially as better than or having more than anyone,

My people, you will not remain My faithful ones when times become so difficult. You cannot (only) *imagine* yourselves to be My faithful ones, My remnant people on whom I count so heavily, whom I need so dearly and love so much. When you are called to perfection as you are, My children, this means you must change totally. I ask you this night to practice being more aware of another, being more open, hospitable, friendly, warm, truly interested in each other. Not just with a greeting, but heartfelt sincerity. All good comes from the heart, My children; and hearts must now be emptied of the world so that only goodness and peace, mercy and tenderness dwell within each of you.

My dear ones, this is so important, and you must practice NOW! There can never be too much time put into practicing mercy, practicing gentleness, friendliness, **practicing the fact that you are each other's sisters and brothers in one huge family**. Recent events have shown the world the power of family, the power of reaching out to help. What you have seen, My dear children everywhere, is still a shadow of the reality to come, the need, the brokenness, the fear, the dependence My people will have on each of you. Prepare your hearts this night, My dear ones. I have given you so many gifts, all the gifts you need, all the gifts to render your hearts a place of refuge for all who come to you. You CAN DO THIS because you have these gifts and yet, so many of you are not using them. It is only in using the gifts you have received, that they will come to fruition. They will blossom and become a part of your very self, the very core of your being where I dwell, waiting to receive all those you bring to Me by bringing them into your heart and into your love and into your arms. This welcoming, this concern must be authentic. You know, My children, **how immediately you are aware when someone is not sincere.** You can see truth or pretense in each other's eyes. You can see in each other's eyes a sparkle of recognition as sister, as brother, as one who believes and loves as you do. You are never fooled by one who pretends and now, My children, YOU HAVE BEEN GIVEN THE GIFTS TO HELP YOU READ HEARTS. This too gives away the false one. DO NOT BE A FALSE ONE, My children. BE A HOLY ONE, A SINCERELY LOVING ONE: READY TO REACH OUT TO GIVE OF YOURSELVES AS MUCH AS NECESSARY, AS YOU ARE CALLED TO BECOME ANOTHER CHRIST, ANOTHER MARY, ANOTHER APOSTLE. How are you fulfilling this call? Is it heartfelt, is your love heart generated?

Are your prayers, PRAYERS FROM THE HEART, not just words still? Spend this time (in the light of destruction that escalates My Father's plan) reflecting on your own behavior. My people I beg of you, allow yourselves to be brought most quickly now to the place of perfection My Father needs you to be for the level of service you will perform. You will *become* service. You WILL BECOME refuge! You will *become* mercy and tenderness and compassion. You know the difficulties, My children. Practice every moment in your hearts and your minds, as well, for it is no good to harbor ill will. It is no good to harbor attitudes: critical and judgmental attitudes, lofty expectations of another, while you excuse yourselves and your own behavior. (How important can this be? How often does He mention it? Cta.) My dear ones, it is *NOW* YOU MUST CHANGE

COMPLETELY by giving Me your heart, by practicing this patience, the love I have for you, the gentleness of My Mother, her tenderness and concern for each of you. Oh My dear ones, I love you so. Do not be one who is left behind, who has given so many years to this call to become a soldier, a fine warrior in the Army of My Mother. ONLY GOOD CAN OVERCOME EVIL, MY CHILDREN. Open your hearts to Good. I love you. You ARE Mine, My children. Be and become My dear, dear, dear, precious ones of the Will of My Father NOW."

9/23, "My dear ones, I am your God, your Father and your Creator. I come this day with new power for you: empowerment, My dear ones. **Strive to overcome shyness: resistance to respond, to lead. Your *yes* includes a reaching out, a going beyond your own comfort.** Going beyond what you perceive as your abilities. Going beyond anything you have done in the past to minister, to see to the comfort of others, to see to their needs; be it in a group such as this, or one you see on the street or in a crowd: someone who needs help. These days, My dear ones, *are days of practice*. Practice ministering to others. Practice being the leader I am calling you to be, that I have gifted you to be. This is not a matter of feeling, My children. It is a matter of conviction in My promises. Conviction and faith in My words that you do have what it takes to answer whatever need you perceive in another: to help another, **to lend a hand or a shoulder or an arm or a word or a comfort, a look, a kindness, a helping suggestion, a patience, a comfort.** My dear ones, there will be so much of this. Think again of all the destruction you have seen. Think of the survivors of those destructive events: how it is for those versed in ministering to people in great shock: professional people, counselors, ones who are schooled in the right words, in the right actions, in the patience to deal with someone terribly shocked.

I tell you, My children, YOU ARE PROFESSIONALS, AND YOU MUST JUST ACCEPT THIS. Oh, not professionals in the *ISMS* and the OLOGIES, with letters after your names! You are *PRAYER* PROFESSIONALS, My children. You are *PEOPLE* PROFESSIONALS. YOU ARE *LOVING* PROFESSIONALS. YOU ARE *BROKEN AND WOUNDED* PROFESSIONALS, My children. YOU ARE *COMPASSIONATE AND UNDERSTANDING* PROFESSIONALS. YOU UNDERSTAND NOW WHAT I AM SAYING TO YOU, and I say this most lovingly.

HEAR ME, MY CHILDREN. HEAR YOUR LORD AND YOUR GOD. HEAR ME WITH ALL OF YOUR MIGHT AND YOUR STRENGTH, YOUR ABILITY TO RESPOND, TO SAY: *YES,* AGAIN, TO TRY MORE TO DO MORE, TO PRAY MORE, TO REACH OUT, EVEN IF ONLY WITH A FRIENDLY GLANCE, AN ACKNOWLEDGMENT.

My dear ones, you are now publicly in the eyes of the world as a country at war. We have been battling evil since the world was created, since mankind came to be and began to experience the struggle, the fierce battle against self, against the evil one. HE IS YOUR ENEMY! All you see today is propagated and promoted and propelled by Satan, the greatest enemy to good. My dear ones, think, ponder, reflect. Do not resist, My children. Do not refuse to serve, to practice, to become. I, your God, have given you the strength, the abilities you already need, the virtues, the conviction. Whatever it is you need, My children, you have NOW with My power, the might of My arm and My Spirit to enable you. Reach out and grasp all I seek to give you. I LOVE YOU. I LOVE ALL My children. ***You are a bridge to their salvation***. Accept this fact, this truth and this mighty gift. Accept the empowerment I give you now. Accept it in peace and joy and freedom with your *YES*. Oh My dear ones, you must be READY! You must PRACTICE. **Be healed**. Be healed in the Name of your Triune God. Accept love. Accept power and strength and joy. Be grateful!"

9/26, "My dear ones, I am your Immaculate Mother: the Holy one of God, the Mother of God, your Mother, my dear little ones. I am so happy once again to be with you here in your midst, as my Son does walk among you, does touch your hearts, your minds, your spirits. I come this night to ask a favor of you, to ask you to begin to pray for the healing of your spirits. So many of you, My dear ones, are so wounded, are so chided and ridiculed by others. Your wounds cause you to be impatient; cause you to be sensitive; cause you to take offense when no offense is meant; cause you, at times, to reflect on your own experiences with pity. Self pity is destructive. It is divisive. But I also ask each of you to be aware of the wounds in the hearts and spirits of others; to be more gentle, more patient yourself, knowing your own difficulties with patience.

Tolerance, My children, is the word! How difficult this is. If I had been intolerant, My children, I could never have followed my Jesus on that terrible walk to Calvary, nor could I have watched Him being beaten before He began that walk. My children**: woundedness, brokenness, sinfulness is always present when you see someone who is impatient, or quick to respond with defensive words. I mention this tonight because of the people who will come to you after the great Warning of the Father. They will be most impatient, My children, most wounded, most broken, most frightened, irritable, full of chaos and lack of understanding. It will take time, My dear ones, and patience to deal with them.** Oh My little ones, how far you have come in practicing virtue, in acquiring, accepting virtues, except this one virtue of patience. Irritability, or the lack of patience, is what clings the most, the longest, affecting most deeply each one of you everywhere. There is no one who stands out more than the others. There is not one who is less affected with these problems (this weakness) than another. So I ask you again to pray for each other, for you will become a fighting unit and unit you must be: united, thoughtful, kind, not making excuses, **no high expectations of each other**. Only the perfection My Son calls you to: His perfection, only accomplished with His gifts, His love, the results of all of His suffering for you, and the fact that He suffers still, as I do.

All of Heaven weeps again and again for events of the recent past; but especially for the events in your future. I know you wish to be all you are called to be for the people who will come to you, and you *will* (be) when you pray and ask for more help; when you pray for each other; when you think before you speak and act: asking mercy on your own shortcomings because, My dear ones, you are human!! These are very human traits, and you are all under more tension than ever. Heaven knows this; and I remind you to remember this about each other. Again, there is no one person under more tension than another. **In one way or another, each of you undergoes your own crucifixion and death to self, death to the world, death to your old ways of being and thinking and responding.** These are not new words, I know; but I remind you again, out of love and motherly concern for you, My children. For I wish to make everything easier for you, that your own lives will flow more smoothly and be more grace filled, that you might be more healed and more at peace, the peace of my Son. I love you, My dear ones. How I love you, my little children. Be like children. Be filled with joy, and joy with each other. Amen."

9-30, "My dear ones, I am the Holy Spirit of God, come once again, bringing you the joy and the gratitude of all the Angels most especially this day, as you have given honor to them, prayed to them, consecrated yourselves anew to them. Their delight is great, not only because of your prayers and your love; but because of the progress you make in goodness, children, the progress you make in holiness. In coming closer to them, you've become more like them, for you are thinking of their presence. You are aware of them. This indeed affects your behavior; affects your thoughts, your words, your inclination to patience and kindness and sweetness, as all of the Angels are sweet, My dear people. All of the people of God everywhere, who listen these days, have remained faithful and prayerful and are growing in holiness. I call out to all of you to tell you, also, you are being united more closely to the Trinity. That means (united) in love, in obedience, in oneness with each other, in oneness with the Will of God, Our Father, with Whom I Am One, and with Jesus, the Son. Reflect on this, and rejoice! Always reflect and rejoice in the words given to you by Heaven. Always give praise and thanks to the Creator of all: all people, all creatures, all of creation that groans more than ever with suffering, with trepidation, with anticipation.

Remember, children of God, **the Father's Will is perfect in all things, is present in all things and all events. It contains mercy first and foremost. It contains protection for you, His children. It contains what is best (for you).** You are growing. You are growing in My gifts. REJOICE! This in itself is another gift.. My dear people, be aware of God's Presence at every moment. Be aware of My power within you now: ready to help you, enable you, strengthen and empower you even more; building on the gifts of empowerment so recently given to you by the Father. Always there is escalation, My dear ones, either positively or negatively. Reflect on that, as well.

PRAY FOR YOUR COUNTRY, MY DEAR, DEAR ONES. DO NOT PRAY IN FEAR. DO NOT EXPECT FEARFUL THINGS. THINK ONLY OF THE FATHER'S WILL IN EACH EVENT. OFFER YOUR FEARS. GIVE UP YOUR FEARS. THEY ARE A KIND OF SUFFERING, A SUFFERING THAT YOU MUST OFFER IN REPARATION FOR THE SINS OF THOSE WHO PERPETRATE TERRIBLE EVENTS. CONTINUE TO BEG FOR MERCY.

As you become mercy, you send out the Father's mercy and healing to everyone around you and to the entire world. You have heard these words before. Do not forget them. Do not forget! You have been given great gifts that enable you to affect the entire world. Give up the world of pleasure, dear, dear ones. You must indeed worship in spirit and truth. (John 4:24) I pour Myself out upon you and all who listen, all who read, all who hope. I strengthen you again this day. I increase your ability to love for the sake of your God; to love for the sake of all (those) you meet, all whom you will love into healing, into wholeness, into unity with the Trinity. You are at peace, this day, My dear ones: the peace of Jesus that rests in you, the peace that allows you to sing *Hosannas* with the Angels and all the Saints and everyone in Heaven. Amen, people of God, amen. Be filled with MORE LOVE."

10/7, "My beloved ones, I am your Father, your God, your Creator, the One Who sustains you in My Will, in the might of My arm, in My power and majesty, in My great love for each of you here and all who come in fidelity and humility, in littleness and obedience. I bless you this day with the might of My arm. I increase your gifts this day, My dear faithful ones. Most of all, I increase your trust. My dear ones, you know that WITH THE NEXT EVENT, CHAOS AND FEAR WILL BE LOOSED IN THIS COUNTRY AND IN MANY, MANY PLACES IN THE WORLD WHERE EVENTS WILL ALSO OCCUR. I look to you, My faithful ones, to be strong. Not so much to be the one with the answers or explanations for others; but to be the one who begins to comfort, to listen to the fears of others, to allow them to voice these fears. **In your listening, in your comforting manner and attitude, your acceptance of their fear, your understanding, you will help to soothe and heal them.** It is peace that will heal My people. It is the acceptance of each of you by Heaven, by all of us here that has begun your own healing. Unconditional love, unconditional forgiveness, acceptance, understanding and patience have caused you to thrive, to blossom, to give forth an odor as a new blossom in My garden, as a new converted one, a new creation who blooms only in My Will and for My Will and because of My Will. My children, this is the Mission for which you are being prepared for so long now. Think of how many years you have heard My call and responded! This Mission begins again this day at a new level of involvement, of gift, of using these gifts most carefully, and especially in littleness and humility to serve. Oh, My dear ones, remember that he and she who would serve must lead by example, serving the needs of others. This, first and foremost, includes the fears of others, the lack of understanding. Humanly speaking, you will be moved to impatience first, and perhaps irritability and the inclination to explain. No, My children, I tell you,

FIRST YOU MUST LISTEN AND ALLOW THESE DEAR ONES TO POUR OUT THEIR NEEDINESS. FEAR IS OF THE EVIL ONE, YOU KNOW. SO OF COURSE THIS WOULD BE A FIRST REACTION. AND I DO NOT DENY FEARSOME EVENTS, OR FEARFUL RESPONSES IN HUMAN NATURE. I SIMPLY CAUTION YOU AND DIRECT YOU TO GO SLOWLY, CAREFULLY, GENTLY AND TENDERLY FROM NOW ON, WITH

EVERYONE. FOR YOU ARE ABOUT TO SEE (another immediate sounding phrase that is sent in the Father's time, that will ultimately happen… cta.) UNBELIEVABLE CHAOS, MY CHILDREN. DO NOT ALLOW THESE TO BE WORDS OF FEAR, AS YOU HAVE NOT IN THE PAST, AS YOU HAVE REACTED (EVEN SURPRISINGLY TO YOURSELVES) IN PEACE, KNOWING AND REMEMBERING ALL THE PROMISES OF PROTECTION THAT YOU BEEN GIVEN YOU. Count on these promises.

Then, for My dear lost ones, (and I mean this as those who are at a loss for understanding) then you may begin to share the promises of Heaven for all who are faithful. Then you may begin to explain My Perfect Will: that I am calling all to come back to Me as quickly as possible to be forgiven, to be healed completely (as only Heaven can heal,) as part of the gifts and the climate of Paradise. My children let your only response be gratitude and thanks for the mercy that has brought you to this place. Remember My need, and the need of all others in the world, for who you are and who you are ***becoming;*** for your industry in prayer, in mercy and in tenderness. Amen! Be filled with hope and joy."

10/10, "My dear ones, I am your Jesus. Thank you for your heartfelt prayers for your country. Indeed the times find this country for the first time in so many, many, many years in grave danger. I say this to you with the full knowledge that you understand My promises of protection. You understand the reason all of these things must occur now and that you are chosen to be an important part of My Father's plan. For He has chosen to share His power with you, His gifts, His mercy and His love, that you will be vehicles for every gift the Father has to give. Most of all, you will be amazed by the patience you WILL HAVE when the time comes; most especially, if you continue to pray for each other for patience and an emptying of the irritability that is such a result of fatigue, of hard work, of ridicule and rejection, of humiliation, of everything you are suffering now. Count on the promises of God. Count on the incredible love of My Mother and yours. How I wish words were not so inadequate to describe Her to you, and Her love and concern for each of you: your future, your perseverance, your humility, all of the virtues you need and will have at the right time. You see how blessed you are?

Do you praise My Father and thank Him for the amount of gift you have received, and will in the future? Do you praise and thank Him with delight, as He is delighted with you? Oh, My children, spend more time reflecting on the gracious goodness of My Father. This in itself will transform you more, will allow you to become the instruments of My Father's Will. All of these people (who come to the faithful after destructive events and then the Warning, C.A.) will need you, My dear ones, so very many of them. You have seen a great number brought into Eternity quickly in the recent destruction. That will be compounded; so you can imagine the condition of those relatives and loved ones who are left upon the earth grieving, frightened, angry, with all of the emotions you are seeing now in so many. These are human reactions and emotions. You know that, My children. And so you will be moved to great pity and compassion to offer whatever is needed, **to be available at every hour to soothe, to comfort, to share grief, to**

listen, to pour your love on the wounds of those who will be torn by all of the events.

Do not wonder why I continue to mention these same things to you. Realize, pay attention to all of these events (now) and the reaction of Our people who, for the first time, are realizing that **perhaps safety is not something that can be taken for granted**. The power and the might of the arm of God IS your shield, IS your defense against the evil one; and you have it! Again, I say, rejoice! Continue to pray more, as you have. Continue to thank My Father for moving you, inspiring you (through Our Spirit) to new places, new things, new tasks; to accept new trials and new sufferings that you might offer for the conversion of the world. My dear ones, how I love you. I pour My blood of protection over you now. Rejoice!"

10/12, "My people, dear ones of the Triune God, I am the Spirit of God, the Spirit of Joy, the Spirit of Advent. I bring you Advent joy. Your spirits grow and expand and heal, as you pray. Remember that prayer is as important and necessary for you as the food you eat each day. It is as necessary for those starving all over the world, and especially those starving for the Body of Christ. Unite yourselves, My dear ones, more totally now with those everywhere; not just because they are your brothers and sisters, not just because they are cold and hungry and homeless, but, my dear ones, because they are you, they are yours. Every person in the world shares the same weaknesses, the same human inclinations, lack of understanding, the same brokenness and the same neediness. As prayer is the focus for Advent, I ask you to call upon Me each time you pray. In a new way, ask Me to pour out Myself, My joy, My gift of gratitude for prayer, for this great vehicle: this vehicle that reaches every person in the world. No, you cannot completely or totally appreciate the power of prayer; but you are learning! You are understanding more, and this shows you how you can expand in your mind and your heart, in your spirit, in your whole being to embrace the world. Let this be your thought for Advent:

I EMBRACE THE WORLD WITH MY PRAYER. I EMBRACE THE WORL WITH MY LOVE, AND I SEND PEACE INTO THE WORLD TO PREPAR EVERYONE FOR THE GREAT FEAST OF THE BIRTH OF JESUS.

My dear ones, you are so beloved of the Father and the Son and of Me. Yo belong to Us. We are one. Let that realization steep your hearts with this joy and gratitud Let this not be mere words or a frame of mind that you manufacture or remember to sa Let it become now who you are. How much you are loved and needed by your God, you Holy Mother and everyone in Heaven; and as they come into Heaven, each new soul begir to pray for you in joy and gratitude. Remember that you are never alone. I pour out ne blessings this day, new graces, new strength. Again, My dear ones, be filled with joy an prayer and gratitude."

10-12, "My dear one, please take My words given, once again, for your comfo and understanding. I am Jesus, your Lord and King. See these next days as a buildup of th power of Satan who is celebrated and worshipped by so many at this time. Combat the power of evil with the power of your prayers, My faithful ones. Rid yourselves of hatred and critical words. Focus your attacks on the real enemy, the evil ones who gain power that is increased by the increased numbers of people who worship them, especially the young people hungry for excitement and bizarre experiences. They do not realize, in many instances, with whom they are dealing, or the lasting (everlasting) consequences of their foolish activity.

Oh, My people, your children need you! They need your patience and responsible behavior as an example of your sincere love and interest in them and their problems that would cease to be problems if only they could count on your support and genuine care for them. This does not mean more toys or treats or stimulating television movies that do so much harm. Yes, My people, they do! Look to My Mother for the patience and calm to read to your little ones. Do not be so busy that you cannot play wholesome games, help with homework, share a project, enjoy a walk or hike or other healthy activity. Plan to *dress in costumes as prayerful ones* who spend extra hours sending pleas for mercy on your country and the world!

DO NOT PUT ON FALSE FACES, MY PEOPLE! TAKE OFF YOUR MASKS: THE FALSE FACES OF A WORLDLY SELF, LOST IN SELF INDULGENCE. LET THE REAL YOU, MADE IN MY IMAGE, SHINE FORTH FOR ALL TO SEE THE GOODNESS AND JOY RESERVED FOR THOSE WHO LOVE, WHO ARE CLOTHED IN INNOCENCE, IN THE PURITY OF MARY, THE IMMACULATE ONE.

My requests are serious, and a failure to respond will result in serious consequences. I call out to you, My people. Discover ***peace*** in place of discord. Discover the soothing words of My Mother's Rosary, her teachings and guidance gathered in all the messages she has brought to the earth these many years. Are you weary of who you are, of how things are going in your lives? Then, My children, CHANGE! Become a new creation, a childlike follower of MINE. Leave the world and all its noise and distractions. *Do not wait for another to join you!* I AM CALLING YOU TODAY. Do not continue to make excuses for YOUR ABSENCE FROM MY PRESENCE.

It matters not what future events may bring, when you are secure within My Heart. It matters not where you live or (where you) move. I AM THERE! I am ALWAYS with you. Find Me by believing My call and requests. See the lives that ceased to be a part of so many families, who are now in Eternity. See that more will be taken, even as you are reading these words, and realize how necessary are your prayers for them. You own loved ones are longing for some of your time and more of your heart. SO AM I, MY DEAREST, LOVED ONES! Do not wait until warnings such as these are fulfilled before you pray and repent. Include your leaders in every prayer you utter. More than ever, they need your support in quiet, humble supplication for their openness to the Spirit of justice and reason. The world teeters on the edge of self-destruction, dear ones.

Counter the attack of Satan with your attack on Heaven! Bombard evil with good. Counterattack with love, begging the Father of Mercy to save the world from the plans of evil men to spread destruction and slavery. If you think I would not warn you in this way, My precious people, wait and see then; and repent in sorrow, once again.' My daughter, these are difficult words to take, I know. They need to be said to those who are running in circles with chaos and fear as a motive. If only a few more will respond wholeheartedly........"

10-14 , "My dearest ones, I am your God and Father. I come this day with special blessings: rosary blessings, My dear children. I tell you this day your prayers are answered in a special way for your country, for your families, for each other, and with healing for yourselves. It is healing that is most needed by all, everyone in the world, one kind of healing or another. You must be healed, that you might be a source of strength, a source of courage, solid, real, authentic courage and hope: not something you would learn to recite, or glib answers you might give. A strength within you that emanates to all, that permeates the atmosphere, that is a reflection of your belief in all the words of Heaven and the promises of your God. A reflection of the might of My arm, a reassurance to others that you have experienced this night; that you have experienced My mercy throughout your life at special times when you needed it most; My strength to BE for you, to be on your side, My children, to be in your corner, to be the One you know you can count on. There are so many, many people who do not know this kind of support, this kind of unconditional love of One who will come through every time. You, My children, in your ministry to the many, will be a sign of this reassurance; a sign that you know, that you have discovered, that you have found THE place of comfort, of protection.

No matter what happens in the lives of each one, My children, remember this: My promises are still in effect. It is Paradise that is your home. It is the Kingdom that is your goal, the Heavenly Kingdom. It is everlasting peace that is the climate in which you will spend eternity. Imagine: To be relaxed, to be peaceful, to be calm, to be at ease. And at this point I remind you that disease is an important word that describes the condition of those whose agitation, or stress or even genetic predisposition, brings them to a place where health is compromised, a place where total ease cannot be found. There is no place on earth where total ease can be found now, My children; except that time before My Son (I remind you again) in the Sacrament of the Altar where, if you will allow it, He will pour Himself out: His peace, His healing into the vessel of your person, of your being. The vessel you are becoming for all, the instruments of My Will. You will hear these words repeated again and again, for it is My desire that you remember them daily, that you live your life in this way, in this mindset, in gratitude for these gifts. You are Mine, little ones.

Remember that I am your loving Father. Praise Me, My children. Run to Me, as a child does to a father he or she adores and loves, depends upon, counts on, delights in. My children, the level of anxiety will only rise in the coming weeks and months, by design. These are the primary reasons for you to actively combat agitation, chaos, anxiety within others. I tell you, you are all strong enough and well enough, transformed enough to do this and, in whatever way you serve, it is not only ENOUGH, it is My Will and My desire for you (in your own way). I will send the people to you who will need you and your way, your experiences, your heart, your love. And it will be more than enough! I love you and I bless you in My Name, in the Name of My Son, and the Name of Our Spirit. The Holy Mother blesses you, as well. She showers kisses, hugs and gifts of joy today. Praise Me, My children. Thank Me. I am your Heavenly Father. I love you. Amen dear ones, Amen."

10/17, "Dearest children, I am your Mother. This night I wish to give praise and thanks with you to the Father for the many of you who are gathered, for visitors from other places, for children (present) who come to give me honor with my Rosary. I am honored, My dear people, by your presence. Praise and gratitude, My children, must be uppermost in your minds now. There are many gifts you cannot see that you have received. You must just accept this fact and indeed, be grateful for it. I remind you that there will be nothing you cannot do when the time comes: the time of great need by so many, many people, so many more people than you will believe you can even assist. You will be overwhelmed at first, so this night as I pray with you, I am asking the Father to increase your courage, to increase your trust that His words will be fulfilled. That you will have the perseverance to simply continue in spite of fatigue, in spite of overwhelming crowds of humanity that will wash across this country like a wave. I have used these words before. See them (people) in your mind. Pray for them daily. Pray for yourselves, that you will be open to every need, for I remind you, they will be great. These needy ones and their grief and fear might also overcome you, if you do not trust; and you will need to do this many times, My dear ones. Pray briefly *throughout* your dealing with each one; and before you pray and comfort, and pray with each one. At first, My children, they will be unable to pray. They will be sorrowful because of the sins of their lives; because they had passed up so many opportunities for grace and rejected my presence in the world. My Son's Presence in the Eucharist and in the Sacrament of the Altar; for refusing His Sacraments and all of the opportunities that you have and that you accept with such joy and gratitude.

You will not be teaching so much as answering questions and leading through patience, through humility, by listening to the words of the Spirit, also. For you have been promised that *every word you need* will be *given you* by My Beloved Spouse. Count on this, my children. You know your God would never let you down; and in times such as these will be, you will more than ever need to count on Him. You will have the might of His arm, the words you need, the perseverance of His great love and His desires for the salvation of all the people, of everyone in the world who will allow it. Oh my children, thank you for increasing your prayer when it is requested of you. Thank you for struggling to do everything requested by Heaven. You have no idea how close are you and I, yourselves and all of Heaven! I rejoice, and I give thanks for you and for all you do for the entire world. Remember, you are important in this great plan of the Father, not in a proud or boastful way, but in a deep and serious and loving and miraculous way! My children, I pour out my joy upon you again this night, and upon all of those who pray all over the world. I unite your prayers this night from everywhere, and take them to the Father. I pour them out before His Throne to obtain as much mercy and mitigation and peace as possible. I love you, my dear ones. You are so precious to me. Be filled with joy, my children. YOUR STRUGGLES WILL INCREASE. Combat these struggles with joy, and with my presence with many, many, many Angels, and with the Presence of my Son. Amen, my dear ones. I love you." (Again.. these words are meant for everyone, everywhere.... Cta.)

10-20, "My beloved people: I am your God, your Father and your Creator. I remind you especially that I WILL NEVER BE OVERCOME BY THE POWER OF SATAN; THAT HE ONLY HAS THE POWER I ALLOW THAT SCRIPTURE MIGHT BE FULFILLED. When you hear yourselves begin to fear, or when you feel doubts build or hope begin to vanish, grasp tightly these words, all of My promises to you. My beloved ones, there is nothing I would not do for you, only ask Me! You know that My Will is what determines each event in each person's life, as it unfolds in My Divine plan for them and for the world. YOU ARE BELOVED ONES OF MINE. I will not harm you. I wish not to harm anyone, but the life of My innocent ones has become an endangered situation.

You have been praying against these horrible sins of abortion and euthanasia and all of the sins of the flesh and the gratification present in the lives of so many people now. You see and you understand the condition of the world today, and why these conditions must end, why these atrocities must cease. There are those who have no regard for any life at any age or stage of development. This cannot be allowed to continue. Evil must be allowed to destroy evil and exhaust itself for that day when the evil one and all of his followers are chained in the deepest level of Hell. There is no other way now, My dear ones; but I continue to ask you to continue to pray for mitigation and for peace in the hearts of My faithful ones.

The condition of the world cannot continue and especially because of the secret plans of men, secrets which continue to cover the actions of so many in the world: the lies that are told, that condition in the world that is the unfolding of Satan's plans. All of these things you must remember and build as understanding to each event that is allowed, for you will see more now, as you have already been warned. You will know that I am acting according to justice and to mercy because you understand mercy, My children. You understand My great love for all of My children in the world. Remember all of these things. Ponder them again and again in your minds and in your prayers and in the quiet times when you sit before My Son. DO NOT BE AFRAID. DO NOT DESPAIR. **Whatever has developed in your life will come to good!** I love you. I trust you and your faithfulness. Trust Me and My faithfulness!! Be at peace. Remain in the peace of My Son. Receive increased virtues this day from the beloved Immaculate One, who IS the Mediatrix and Co-Redemptrix and Advocate for the world: My vessel and instrument of grace!"

10/24, "My dear ones, I am your Jesus, your Lord and your God. My children, how happy I am to see you gathered in this way. How happy I am to be here with you, lifting My Heart and My voice with you to the Throne of the Father, pleading for mercy on each one of you and your loved ones and on the whole world. Now there will be great sorrow in many areas of the world, as sons and daughters give their lives to protect this country, to protect the world from terrorism, from terrorists whose goal it is also to keep people terrified, to bring people to a place of chaos in their minds and hearts, as I have explained to you already. My dear ones, you must have great compassion for the people who are living in fear. Yes, these are fearful events and yes, there is great loss of life in the future, My children**, great loss of life**. Allow this to bring compassion and sorrow to your hearts, to bring you to pray for those who lose loved ones, to pray for the world that balance may remain in the hearts of those who have listened, who believe in all of the promises of Heaven. I tell you, **it will become more and more difficult to persevere**. There are not many new words to give to each one. See the gifts in each other to help you appreciate each other. Realize the change and transformation that is taking place, for it HAS OCCURRED to the level of My Father's Will now for all of you: each one here and each one who reads and hears and believes the words of Heaven. IT IS AND WILL ALWAYS BE, MY DEAR ONES, A TIME FOR REJOICING. Remember, no matter what is happening, it is the fulfilling of all of the prophecy, all of the words, the instructions and directives and teachings of My Mother all of these years. Give thanks for My Mother every moment, as I continue to do! I gave thanks for My Mother before I was ever born! Unite your thanksgiving and your joy for her with all of Mine throughout all time. My dear ones, I love you. Thank you for the time you spend with Me to ease the suffering Heart I possess. Amen, My dear ones. You ARE faithful warriors."

10/25, AT ADORATION, "My dearest one, please write these words for the world. I am Jesus, your Lord. Pray with Me and all of Heaven to Our Spirit for openness and a listening heart, once again: Please tell Our people not to miss a day of the prayer and adoration they have scheduled and begun now. Already they can see the numbers of people who are in need of this increased surrender to prayer I have requested of all of you. The dawn brings new tragedies, and Our people will be moved in a greater way to quit the world and its emptiness; to embrace peace and silence; to embrace Mary, the Immaculate Mother, and to embrace Me in the Trinity and ALL the requests of Heaven. Now is almost too late; but wait, My dear ones, there is ALWAYS the mercy of My Father!"

10/28, "My very dear ones, I am your Mother. I am here joyfully, praying with you, listening to your heart-felt prayers and these words of mine that I have given to my beloved and faithful priest-son (Fr. Gobbi messages having to do with the rosary, used as meditations for this last Sunday in October.. C) Thank you, children, for using these this day; for the industry that has gone into collecting the meditations for each week. (A woman in group has been doing this since we began to pray together. C) I ask you to continue to meditate upon these mysteries of my Rosary, the words that I have specifically given, that you have heard this day, (from 5-1-83 & 10-7-92) and others that might keep your focus on the power and the goal of MY ROSARY: THIS MOST IMPORTANT WEAPON AGAINST SATAN AND ALL OF HIS PLANS, HIS HATRED FROM WHICH ALL OF HEAVEN DESIRES TO PROTECT YOU; AND WILL PROTECT YOU, AS YOU USE THIS MIGHTY WEAPON ALLOWED ME AND ALL OF YOU BY OUR HEAVENLY FATHER.

My dear ones, again I must tell you how precious you are to me. How deeply I hold you in my heart. How united in prayer we are at all times now. I speak to my faithful all over the world this day with these requests and reminders. Oh, My children, the days become more filled with terror, with fear; and you must help me overcome this fear, refute the power of the evil one everywhere and his hold over the lives and hearts of so many people in the world. THIS IS A SACRED DUTY NOW THAT YOU HAVE ACCEPTED AS SOLDIERS IN MY ARMY, AS FOLLOWERS OF MY SON, AS FILLED WITH OUR HOLY SPIRIT, MY BELOVED SPOUSE, AS CHILDREN OF OUR FATHER. My dear ones, you are so important to this fight: a true battle that escalates every day. Do not be frightened by my words. Be made more serious and focused by them, while at the same time being made joyful! You will see more suffering now all over the world. The plans of Satan and the Antichrist are clever and this is the time in which he is allowed victory. Again, **DO NOT BE FRIGHTENED, but remember the protection promised by your God. See to it that you remind others close to you of these promises**. Help them to remain faithful to prayer and to offer inclinations to fear and panic as a suffering, as a penance; as you fight against them and as you choose trust and peace in your hearts. Each time it will be a conscious choice to decide how you will react or what you will do with your human reactions!

My dear ones, you are strong. You are prayerful. You are obedient. You are mighty! Do not be overcome by emotions. I AM WITH YOU. YOU ARE WITH ME, living in my presence every moment with my Son and many, many Angels. I will continue to repeat this, my children everywhere. Pray especially for those who are suffering war in so many places, who live moment to moment, not knowing what the next moment will bring! I love all of you. You are my dear, dear, dear children and companions in prayer, in love, in concern for the future of the world. Be brave, my children. The time will come when you will see the need for heroism in your own lives: a heroism of service, of bringing the needs of others into your minds and hearts as a FIRST STRIKE IN YOUR OWN LIVES; A FIRST STRIKE OF LOVE TO YOUR HEARTS AND MINDS AND ALL YOU POSSESS PHYSICALLY, MENTALLY, EMOTIONALLY AND SPIRITUALLY. GOD IS WITH YOU, MY CHILDREN. YOU ARE WITH GOD. Praise Him. Thank Him. Joyfully, we shall love Him together. Amen, my dear, dear ones. Rejoice. I love you!"

10/31, "I, Your God and Your Father, Your Creator and Your Lord, speak this night. I bring you into My arms, My children, that I might caress you, that I might hold you with the might of My arm by bringing you more deeply into My Will;

for **it is there, My children, that you become the perfect instruments of mercy, of My Will for you and for the entire world. I repeat that you will have every gift that you will need in the days ahead.** I ask you once again to pray as often and as much as possible. You still have no idea what lies ahead for the world, the great sorrow that will wash over many, many more of our people; but you do know how misfortune, how broken lives, how interrupted lives, changed lives, have a way of bringing people back to Me. It is unfortunate that after so many thousand's of years My people still do not listen until they are brought to their knees by an event, caught up in a sudden and abrupt sadness and misfortune or loss, but it was always thus with human nature. I did not create nature to be this way, My children. I created you to be more loving and grateful children: happy, living in My Will, surrendered to all I provide for you, all I desire for your lives. But the will of My people over the centuries has always been the same, only to grow stronger and more self giving (selfish), more self serving, more self gratifying.

My dear children, your will is a function of your soul, so it is your soul that is wounded by the choices that make you turn away from Me, that make you go towards the world and the plans of Satan. Be more aware in your lives (I beg of you everywhere in the world,) of the times you are cooperating with Satan! This happens many more times than you realize, and it happens for everyone. This is allowed to a greater degree now, as you know; but when you see your souls as I see them, you will instantly be filled with remorse. **You and all the people in the world whose hearts have not hardened beyond the place of repentance, you are My faithful ones. Pray for each other.** Pray for the world that they might listen and believe. My dear ones, as you come closer and closer to the Image in which you were created, you are able to live more deeply, more perfectly in My way, and more joyfully and more easily. Is this not a better way to be? Is it not truly easier to surrender to My desire, finally; once the struggle with your own will has finally ended, and you have accepted the graces I have given to you? Is it not more peaceful? Of course it is!

I wish only good for you, My dear little ones. Each week you gather, you hear many repetitions now. It is because you are so close to events that will cause more sorrow, more events, and I need you focused in prayer. This is your life now. Allow nothing to distract you, and no one to interfere with My call to you at this time. I stress this and will continue to repeat this call, to let go of the world and all activity within the world. This is more difficult for my young ones, and yet when you are busy with tasks, with the work your life calls you to, with your commitments and responsibility, if you are making enough time for prayer, you will not miss the world. I would not tell you this if it were otherwise. As you live more years in the world, you see the truth of My words and you begin to acquire wisdom, an advantage of the years. Praise Me and thank Me, My children, for the wise plan for your lives, for bringing you together. You need each other's prayers, you need each other. Such a bond is growing between all of you. That bond is held in the Heart of Jesus and the Heart of Mary. You are held in those Hearts as well. Be joyful! I am joyful with you. It is difficult to think of joy in the face of loss.

Yet I ask you to remember that **each event takes you that much closer to the return of My Jesus** and allows Me more and more to empty the world, and all the people in it of evil, in order to defeat the plans of the evil ones in this age. I love you, children of My Creative Heart. See yourselves, feel yourselves (emotions), enjoy yourselves. Thank Me for yourselves gathered into My arms. Amen this night. How I love you."

11/5, "My dearest children, I am your Jesus. Thank you for gathering. Know that many Angels and Saints have joined you here this day to swell your numbers, to multiply prayers, to unite all of you in the great Communion of Saints. I thank you again for your faithfulness. I come once again with love, with healing. I bring all of you, and all those who have ever attended this particular prayer group, new gifts from My Father this day. Always, My dear ones, there are new gifts. I have told you about many of them that you will not recognize until it is time to use them, until they are needed; but this day I bring you new strength. I bring to each of you new energy, improved health, a greater desire for holiness. It is holiness My Father desires for you, and for which all of Heaven prays most of all on your behalf. As the time goes by, and you tend to become impatient or distracted or even discouraged, My Father will bring the gifts you need, like these today. Much of the increased energy will be energy for prayer, an increased desire for the desire to pray, an increased ability to see into My Father's Will, an understanding in all of the things occurring in your own life and in the whole world; for you WILL see war escalate. You will see a breakdown, as well, in discipline; a breakdown in society and in order, for chaos is the environment of Satan. It is his fomenting of unrest that causes nations to attack each other. It is why I mention all of these things to you; for **I wish you to begin to take better notice of events, to discover the Father's unfolding plan that you might not be discouraged, that you might see each event (especially destructive ones) as necessary to fulfill Scripture or to allow evil to destroy itself.**

Everything is planned for your safety. Everything is planned for your long life in the service of Our people. Heaven has attempted to explain what this will be like. But there are no words that could truly define or outline for you how difficult this will be, how totally against everything you have ever known and all of the things you have become accustomed to without realizing the comforts, the little daily habits that you have**. All of these things will be interrupted and disrupted, and many things discarded that you have always used for your own comfort.** Of course, I say these things NOT to discourage you more; but to prepare you, to give you new food for thought, for your ability to perceive My Father's Will and enjoy it, the ability to surrender to whatever it is He calls you to become now. You are ascending to new levels of service all the time, My dear ones. You cannot see this, but all of Heaven watches and prays and supports you with great love and now with new strength, this new vitality that you will feel, and I know you will most appreciate. My children, you are LOVED! See these gifts and every change in the world as a sign of the Father's love. Even though your understanding only begins to expand, just believe that everything that occurs is a sign of the Father's love, His way of protecting you and ultimately cleansing the world and all people. I love you, My dear ones. Thank you again for loving Me, for all you do to witness to that love. You are precious. You ARE My dear ones! Rejoice."

11/7, "My dearest children, I am your God and Father, come once again to celebrate with you the gift of My love. Know that I am pouring out My Spirit of healing as you have requested this night. You will always need healing, My children, in some area or another. **Always beg for healing of your hearts, of your spirits, of your ability to make the proper choices;** for these will become so much more difficult as time goes by. **Pray for the healing of relationships past, but always in a way present within you.** My dear ones, **whenever I come as your Father and Creator and Healer, I bring many gifts. I see the entire world in an instant. I see every thought in every mind at the same time;** therefore, I WARN YOU, EVEN THOUGH THINGS DO NOT OCCUR AS RAPIDLY AS YOU EXPECT, AND I HAVE ASKED YOU TO OFFER THIS WAITING TO ME FOR THE SALVATION OF OTHERS. I TELL YOU AGAIN, THERE WILL BE MORE EVENTS SOON. There are events of a destructive nature every day, so it is not necessary that something earth shaking, as momentous as has happened in this country be visited often. I tell you, the events will escalate. Remember, I am acting in a merciful way all the time, and I am allowing you time to adjust, to change, to prepare more and always to pray more.

Remember leading your little ones by the hand: how they stop and become fixed on something for a long period of time without moving. You are like that, My dear ones! You stop and become distracted, and often it is a long time before you realize this. As a good Father, I am allowing you to adjust to an always new path; but **I need you to keep up with bigger steps, to move along more quickly now, to become so much more convinced of the important role you are playing in the salvation of the world.** THIS IS NOT SOME IDLE CONVERSATION OR SELLING POINT FOR PRAYER. THESE ARE ACTUAL FACTS ABOUT THE RELATIONSHIP BETWEEN YOURSELVES AND EVERYONE ELSE IN THE WORLD, ABOUT THE IMPACT YOU ARE HAVING ON LIVES WITH YOUR PRAYERS, ABOUT THE IMPACT YOU ARE ALLOWING ME, YOUR TRIUNE GOD, TO HAVE IN YOUR OWN LIVES. When this call came to you, you were nowhere near the obedient, faithful ones you have become. Praise and thank Me for enormous change in your hearts and in your understanding. You need understanding that you might explain to those who come to you the need for patience, the time it takes to change, to heal. **You all carry deep wounds. Some wounds are very fresh. Cherish each other, My people.** Realize your own weaknesses are no different than anyone else's. It might be in different areas of a life; but there are barriers that cause resistance, that cause distraction, that cause you to stop and stare or fixate on something as you walk along, still holding My hand, but distracted! YOUR FOCUS MUST BE TOTAL, CHILDREN. I have chosen to need you so very much, to allow you great power of prayer, of ability to change the world and its people. I do this because I love all of you everywhere; and yes, even terrorists are My children. My call includes them first of all. Remember, MERCY IS RESERVED FOR THE WORST SINNERS.

My dear ones, I do not speak in order to chastise you; but to speak deeply to your hearts and to your minds, that your will might activate a greater focus on prayer and the serious need of the whole world. There was always great responsibility when gifts are given. You cannot know how gifted you are. You cannot possibly see how many you are touching with your love and your prayers. Pray for those who pray, My dear ones. I count on you. I love you. You love Me and My Son; Our Spirit of Love; the great Mary, the Immaculate One. Thank you for listening with your hearts. I know you will respond more, for you have become such obedient ones. I can count on you to do whatever is necessary. Remember, this is a preparation for you, and that will always be included in your needs as things change; or there is more destruction as nature begins to erupt more in more violent ways. How blest you are. I am so pleased with you, so grateful, so happy to see your joy, to see your instant response always. You are dear little ones. You have gone from crawling to taking baby steps and some day, My children, beyond running, YOU WILL FLY! Be filled with gratitude."

11/17, "My dear ones, I am Jesus, come once again to bless you, to heal you, to strengthen you, to fill you with My love and mercy. Thank you for coming here, for all the places you go to pray, to join with others, to offer in many places a united heart and voice to My Father and yours. Once again you are brought to a more serious frame of mind by new tragedy, by events in which new lives are lost, new families are affected and visited with sorrow and many, many other emotions as well. This will continue, My people. There are many, many people to reach. You would not be able to take it if you were always in the state of realization about the number of people (who will enter Eternity) or the evil in the world or all the things Heaven continues to bring to your attention! It is humanly impossible to do this always, and so We remind you again and again that for this period of time and new awareness, you are united with everyone in the world who prays and with everyone who needs prayer so desperately. I thank you for your continuing faithfulness. I see your hearts flowering, growing and expanding to embrace more and more people: those who suffer everywhere. Lives are being lost all over the world, My children. Natural events are occurring, yet many of them you hear nothing about from your media. Smaller earthquakes occur in many places now, preparing for even larger destruction.

In His mercy My Father delays again and again, **waiting that more prayers might be said**, that He might respond to the goodness and generosity in the hearts of His faithful ones. In this process also, you are being united more with everyone in Heaven, who pray constantly and with such power from their purified state, and this is healing you. So there is one great dynamic of cooperation and reciprocal grace, cleansing, healing, strengthening, converting, transforming. My children, it is a time of great power in which God is acting in the world. The Spirit is being poured out upon the world in many different ways. See not only destruction, My dear ones, but recall all of the good that comes out of each event and be moved to continue to pray more and more; not only to pray more, but to remain in the frame of mind of prayer at all times. **Anything other than living in Our Presence is not what My Father calls you to be now. This requires even more change in behavior and attitudes and conversations, even in thoughts and reactions to people and things.** You are becoming such mighty warriors. If you were to see your souls now and your hearts, as opposed to their position and condition when you accepted this call, you would be astounded and quite possibly not even believe that you are the same person; and yet of course you are not the same person! That is how much each of you has changed. You have grown and learned. You have given up things and people you had hoped to have a relationship with or to be friendlier or closer to. Do not see this as punishment, but as focus on My face, on the needs of others and part of the trials that bring you to each new level of My Father's plan. Everything has a purpose. **Everything has been so well thought out by your God, as only your God could present this masterful plan for the salvation of the entire world! Remember that, and rejoice.** Rejoice in My love for you. You have no idea how close you are to everyone in Heaven. You have no idea how much you are being prayed for, and carried and comforted and protected even now. How important you are to the salvation of the world and to the Kingdom of Heaven on earth. Again I say, My dear children, rejoice."

11/18, "My children, I am your Mother. Thank you for coming here this day, for praying to me and for opening your hearts to my love and the love of Our God. I speak this day of Thanksgiving, my children everywhere, and of thanks giving. **I remind you again, you were created to give praise and thanks to Our Father.** That is who you are. You are children of thanksgiving. You are children of the creative act that formed you in your mother's womb and despite the difficulties, even possible rejection and hurt that has occurred since then, the Father created you in love: His love that does and has and will never cease. My children, because you are human and limited by your nature in your understanding, you do not realize the magnitude of the Father's love or the gifts He has given to you. If you did, you would be on your knees constantly praising and thanking Him. This is true, but also the Father has tasks and plans and His Will for you to fulfill. This means serving others, ministering to their needs, not just in the future when so many will show up at your door, (at the door to your heart most of all,) but now, at every moment.

Realize that you are offering thanksgiving for all you have been given by this ministry and your kindness and thoughtfulness to others, your awareness of their neediness. For, my children, you are all needy, yes some more than others; but you are my little ones and you have many weaknesses: still a predisposition to self-gratification, to self-pity, to self aggrandizement and these, my dear ones, are the result of Original Sin. These were the feelings, the motives which moved Adam and Eve to wish to be more than they were, to have more than God had given them; and so they gave in to pleasure, to the desires of wanting more, having more, being more. This, too, is a part of your human nature. These are elements within yourself that you will always fight against, even in the New Era when there is no temptation! These weaknesses yes, to a much lesser degree, will be present within you. And so your human nature, which is your heavier cross, will always remind you of your need to thank the Father and praise Him for offering to be the Source of your needs, the Source of your healing through Jesus and through their Spirit, my beloved Spouse.

I pray every moment that you are given more understanding into the great gifts you have received. I pray with all of my might, all of my gifts, all of who I am that you will have greater clarity in thinking, in knowledge, in wisdom; and that this will lead you to become mighty instruments and signs of praise and thanksgiving. Give thanks, too, my dear ones, for all those who have gone before you, fighting to obtain your freedom, toiling to reap the benefits of the Father's gifts to find a better way of life, to procure for you greater gifts and an easier way of living on the earth. There are many heroes who have gone before you and who now pray heroically and constantly in Heaven in joy. They see you (more and more) become warriors of thanksgiving and prayer of hope for the future, hope for your children, hope for the fulfillment of the Father's Perfect Will. Oh my dear ones, it is an exciting time. **Spend this week, my dear, dear, dear, children, united in your mind and heart with all the people in Heaven, as well as myself, with your God in prayers of thanksgiving for each other, for the gifts God has given to each other, for the friendship, the support, the joy you are for each other.** You are so dear. I pour out my thanksgiving for you now, upon you and before the throne of Our Father. I love you."

11/24, "My dear ones, I am your Jesus, come this day to welcome you with joy, with gratitude again for your presence here. I often say these words to you; for you have no idea of the joy in My Heart at this special time of being together that we have been given by My Father at this special time in your Church year: the preparation for My Birth. It is such a sacred time for you, for the entire world, and you are joined by all in Heaven. Think of this please, each time you pray. Billions of people (in Heaven) are praying with you individually, the great body of Christ, the great Communion of Saints, the great gift of unity I mention once again this day. You are not alone, My children. You are not isolated from others. You are more united than ever to each other, as you have remained faithful these many years to prayer, becoming more thoughtful, remembering each other, being instruments of grace for each other. Rejoice, if only because I ask you to rejoice because you are so blessed. This is truth, My children. I ask you again to ponder the fact that you are blessed mightily, that you are special in My Father's plan. All My children all over the world, I bring these words to you as well. You are special and precious in My eyes. You are a vehicle of delight to Heaven. Oh yes, there are some turning away and there will be some of the faithful who are caught up in the spirit of the Season, the spirit of the world, I mean. My dear ones, stay with the spirit of peace. Again I say, only in quiet and silence can you receive the gift of peace. Only by desiring this gift now at this level in My Father's plan NOW, can you receive this gift and many of the gifts. You know yourselves better now, as a result of the many gifts poured out these many years. You know more clearly your needs, your weaknesses, your compulsions, your irritability, your tendency to impulse, to become distracted. I must remind you again of these things, for it is so important that you reap the harvest of all the graces, the fruits of this Holy Season.

This year, I want you to be the Manger into which My Mother will lay My tiny Body. Open your hearts. Open your minds, your spirit and your lives to Me, to My Mother and to Joseph, who keep watch at your hearts now as you await My arrival in a deeper way, in a way more real than ever, ever in your lives. This I promise you, as you focus on the special prayers, the liturgy, and the needs of the world. It is winter now, with terrible cold in many parts of the world; and you know it will be a bitter winter in much of the world. I ask you to keep these things in yours hearts and your prayers, asking for comfort for My children everywhere. **My dear ones, you are important to every person in the world. Remember this every time you pray.** Keep this thought in mind as you shop, as you cook, as your write and read. Most especially, **bring the whole world with you as you sit before Me in My Blessed Sacrament. You will be bringing them in a way that is more real than you realize!** Rejoice! Again I say, your gifts are many, and My love for you and the love of all in Heaven is so very great. I bless you, My dear, dear children. I hold each of you. I cradle your hearts this day, as you become a cradle for Me!"

11/28, "I am your God and Father, and I come to say, I LOVE YOU! I come to say, please remember that you are My children. You are My creation, and you are being led into My perfection. I am allowing you, each of you, to suffer at this time in different ways, to different degrees, for different results; but for all of you, I am pouring out and desiring for you and from you: PATIENCE! This gift, this virtue, is not only important for those people who will be coming to you, but for **your own ability to remain in peace**. Without patience with Me, your Creator, your God Who moves everything that moves, Who holds you in the palm of My hand, tenderly, gently, lovingly, creatively: making of you something new at every opportunity.

Without patience, you will collapse in grief and fear, in irritability and unforgiveness. The need for patience is present in your dealing with each other, especially those who are difficult! Realize, My dear ones, **that difficult people are gifts to you directly from Me!** Rejoice in this, for it is My Providence. You ask for healing, My children. I tell you, **it is these dealings, it is this struggle, this striving that will heal you!** I could heal you in an instant; is it not so, My dear ones? But each of you understands why I allow you to try again and again to become who you were created to be, to become this mercy which is so very, very much more than it seems at first. I also wish to tell you again how well you are doing in your striving. Be encouraged, as I tell you these things. Again I remind you, you are persevering; and I give you these words tonight to help you to continue to persevere, for the struggles will increase.

Remember to pray for all of those who will come to you. THERE WILL BE NO PATIENCE IN THEM, MY CHILDREN! THERE WILL BE MUCH IRRITABILITY TO BE FOUND EVERYWHERE IN THOSE DAYS; THOSE DAYS THAT WILL SUDDENLY BE THESE DAYS! My children, I offer you every help you need, every strength and every opportunity to grow; and the quieter you remain, and the more you listen in the presence of My Son, the easier this growing, this learning and this struggle will be. I see joy in your hearts at My explanations that are not new; but perhaps new applications to help you understand again, and more deeply. I love you so much, My dear ones. Believe My words. Believe My love for you, My gratitude for you and for all My faithful ones in the world. My dear children, YOU WILL NOT WAIT FOREVER! Remember this also, and one day you will remember and long for the peace of these days of waiting. Amen, My children. See yourselves in the palm of My hand. I blow into you the breath of new life, new hope and new joy."

12/2, "Dear ones of the Triune God, I am your Holy Spirit: the Spirit of God, the Spirit of Joy, the Spirit of Advent. I bring you Advent joy. Your spirits grow and expand and heal, My dear people, as you pray. Remember that prayer is as important and necessary for you as the food you eat each day. It is as necessary for those starving all over the world, and especially those starving for the Body of Christ. Unite yourselves more totally now with those everywhere; not just because they are your brothers and sisters, not just because they are cold and hungry and homeless, but **because they are you, they are yours**. Every person in the world shares the same weaknesses, the same human inclinations, lack of understanding, the same brokenness and the same neediness. As prayer is the focus for Advent, I ask you to call upon Me each time you pray. In a new way, ask Me to pour out Myself, My joy, My gift of gratitude for prayer, this great vehicle that reaches every person in the world. No, you cannot completely or totally appreciate the power of prayer; but you are learning! You are understanding more, and this shows you, My dear ones, how you can expand in your mind and your heart, in your spirit, in your whole being to embrace the world. Let this be your thought for Advent:

"I EMBRACE THE WORLD WITH MY PRAYER. I EMBRACE THE WORLD WITH MY LOVE, AND I SEND PEACE INTO THE WORLD TO PREPARE EVERYONE FOR THE GREAT FEAST OF THE BIRTH OF JESUS."

My dear ones, you are so beloved of the Father and the Son and of Me. You belong to Us. We are One. How much you are loved and needed by your God, your Holy Mother and everyone in Heaven; and as they come into Heaven, each new soul begins to pray for you in joy and gratitude! Remember that you are never alone, My dear, dear ones. I pour out new blessings this day and new graces, new strength. Be filled with joy and prayer and gratitude. Amen to Our people everywhere in the world. Amen."

12/5, "I am your Jesus, once again here with you to praise My Father and thank Him for each one of you. My dear, dear children, thank you for the preparing you are doing in prayer, in spending more time with Me before My Blessed Sacrament, where I wait for you eagerly, and I pray joyously when you arrive! You have no idea of My joy and that of all in Heaven, nor can you imagine the graces poured out, and the unity with the Triune God you are attaining. You have seen new terror, new destruction. I tell you, Heaven weeps, for this too is another sign of an escalation, a deepening of hostilities, a bringing to a boiling point blood that courses through powerful men bent on controlling each other, the people of each other's country. **This part of the world (Israel and Palestine, cta) is so important in these End Times. It is a sign to you that Scripture is once again being fulfilled. This will continue, as you know. Pray for them, My dear ones.** Unite your hearts to all of those who suffer from this renewed hostility, and the many, many more who will know hardship. Yes, My Shrines, once again, are in danger; and I call upon you and your goodness and your prayers to save these testaments to My life, to outstanding events in My life. Imagine over 2000 years, how many people have come to visit these places and now, not only imagine but believe the very great possibility of their destruction! The danger is very real everywhere. Men seek to take all the power, all the land. You know there will be many more of these, for it is Satan's way. I can see in your hearts the seriousness with which you hear My serious words.

I know that your hearts are united with Mine in this great time of need. If these shrines and holy places are destroyed, it will be easier to wipe out the memory and the reality of My time on earth! You can see how true this would be, for you know the plans of evil men who wish only a One World Religion and must destroy others (religions) first. When you are attacked (by others or by evil directly), I am attacked. When I am threatened, you are threatened, for we are one; and we must combat the enemy together. Although it will look, for awhile, as though the enemy will overcome, you know he will never overcome the power of My Father. I speak to all Our children in the world, for these words are true for all of you. Remember**, the Father lets you know how much He loves you by what He asks of you and allows you to do.** You are needed, My people, by your God, by the Love that created you! There is nothing else important. Remember My love. Allow Me, children, to love you more. Amen, for now, My dear ones. I Am with you."

12/9, "My dear ones, I am your Mother. I am here this day with you in a more powerful way than ever. Thank you for the unity you and I and all my children everywhere in the world enjoy. Let us give thanks and praise together (for the gift of this day) to God, Our Father, for the unity He has given us, for the graces He has given to bring you more deeply into my Immaculate Heart and into my ways.

So very often now, your thoughts are my thoughts, your reflections are filled with my words for all of the times in my life: preparing for Jesus' arrival, His great birth, and all the events that followed. You have learned and become stronger and holier because of this. I bring you to Jesus, my children, because I brought Jesus to you! I thank you for allowing this in your lives, for all the love that has developed in your hearts. My children, we go forward together every moment preparing for each feast; for each day is a feast when you are able to receive my Son, the ultimate Banquet and Gift of the Father. My children, the rest of this day become aware of me standing next to you or kneeling next to you; for, my children, I am! And **when you sit and when you rest, I am still kneeling next to you.** Take this image, my children. Embrace it. Hold tightly to it. Hold tightly to me, my dear ones.

How excited I was in the months and weeks before the birth of our Savior. Not until I saw Him, although I felt His movement within as I carried Him lovingly and tenderly, yet not until I saw Him, did I begin to grasp the enormity of this gift in my life and to all the world for all time. Ponder this, my children. See the Infant in your mind's eye, in the eyes of your heart. Allow Him to grow within you these weeks; to grow in wisdom, in understanding and knowledge (within) yourselves, as He, Who is Wisdom, (Who is all things to us) grows within you. This too is a gift, for the Father will allow a flowering of your meditation, as you concentrate and as you embrace Jesus carried within me and now growing within you, as well. Yes, it is a mystery, all of these things. Yes, my dear ones, all of these things are true. Hosanna, my children. And this day we say: thank you, Father, again and again for the gift of your Son. I love you. It is a serious time in the world. Bring joy to the world, my children, as my Son grows! I bless you. I pour out graces this day upon the world by a gift of the Father: Advent graces, preparation graces, strengthening graces and all of my love!"

12/11, At Home, 12 a.m. "Dear one, be at peace now, child, that we might be united with these words for you and for the world. I am your God and Father, My daughter. I bring you Truth, not deception. I bring peace and clarity to your mind, not chaos and confusion. You know it is I, your Creator Who speaks for your healing and understanding. Daughter, I bring gifts of conversion and instruction for your heart and the heart of the world. Pray again to My Spirit for the openness and calm necessary now for your spirit. Please take words for My people now:

'My beloved ones in the world, I bring you news of great joy for unto you has been born a Savior Who is Christ, My Son! He is One with Me, My dearest children, and He is one of you. He is My greatest gift to you and sure proof of my love for you. I am your Father and Creator, and I rejoice with you and because of your love for Me and for Jesus, My Beloved One. You are a living example and sign to the world that Our Spirit dwells within you; for you return this gift of Love that I have given you through your prayers and ever developing gratitude, your love and adoration for Jesus, and your employment of the gifts of Our Spirit. My people, if there were anything or anyone more helpful and loving, more powerful or obedient to Me, more necessary to your salvation than Jesus, I would have sent him to you! But I am the Author of life, the Source of all good in union with Jesus and Our Spirit. Therefore, I have sent the greatest gift I could ever give, the most necessary to your passage through this difficult portion of your life, and the One Who has remained with you always to nurture and heal and forgive and teach and ultimately free you from the power of evil and the effects of Original Sin.

My love is everlasting, My people. The more you allow it, the more you are given peace and wisdom in order to receive the gifts I wish to continue to give you. You wish always to gather new facts about the future to fill you with powerful emotions and weapons with which to lord it over each other. **I desire to give you healing, that you might allow Me to remold you, reform you into a most perfect instrument of My Will** and a most perfect reflection of My Beloved Jesus, filled with Our Spirit and His power. I am listening to your requests for mercy, My dear ones. I have answered many of your prayers already and have every intention of continuing to mitigate destruction and confound the plans of Satan who is only the instrument of his own hatred and destructive revenge. You will discover new wisdom and understanding in your Christmas list of fulfilled desires to live in My Divine Will more perfectly!

Praise and thank Me, My precious ones, **even as you see new victories given to the followers of evil for many years to come. Do not become discouraged!** Enjoy the peace and joy of this blessed season when you are brought to a new vision of innocence and love in the Person of the tiny, miraculous Babe, born weak and helpless, dependant on Me and those around Him in spite of His power in His Divinity and humanity. These words are meant to lead you to adore at the manger, to beg for a time of peace for the world, celebrating the true reason for celebrating the birth of the tiny Infant Who lives forever as a sign of My love for you. My people, thank you for remaining faithful to your God, to His promises and call to you. Jesus is My Gift to you. Accept Him. Hold Him in your hearts, in your lives, in your will. Trust in My plan, My love, My desires for you."

12/12, "Dear ones, I am your Jesus, come with words for you and for the world. Be filled with My peace, My faithful ones: the peace of this season, the joy of anticipation, the hope that your prayers for the world, for everyone everywhere, especially those who suffer, may be fulfilled. I rejoice with you on this Feast of My Mother. (Lady of Guadalupe). Pray to her every moment. Again, I ask you to pray for the young ones everywhere: children who live in abusive situations, who live on the streets, who are cold and hungry. There are many of them. Ask My Mother to wrap them in her Mantle of warmth and comfort and love. I will touch their hearts, as you continue to pray for them. I will touch them with My love. Many children know very little love. It is one of the tragedies of these times. People are too busy to show love. They are angry or they are hurt and unable to find love to share, unable to accept love. MY DEAR ONES, YOU HAVE BECOME POWERFUL INSTRUMENTS FOR THE WORLD, FOR NEW GIFTS FOR THEM, FOR NEW HEALING. REJOICE!

I pour out My Spirit of rejoicing upon you, My children, for these reasons and for every reason, that you might thank and praise My Father, especially for the gift of My Birth, My remaining (with you) in the Eucharist, for all I have become in your lives. You are My faithful ones everywhere, My Eucharistic people. Now meditate upon this fact: Allow your behavior, your demeanor, your relationships with others to reflect the Eucharist you carry in your heart! As I pour out rejoicing, you will feel new joy and new delight in Me and all of the Gift I Am, and what it means to be one with your Triune God and your Holy Mother and Mine: this precious Mother whom I have given to you, who loves you so very much. Thank her again and again. It is never too often. It is never too much! Thank her for her 'YES', for bringing Me to you, for the great love in her Heart for each of you. You ARE her little ones, her precious little children. Bask in that image. Nurture your hearts, your minds and spirits with this fact, with these words. **Picture yourself on her lap,** the child in you who has always needed a loving and gentle and caring Mother. Allow this to heal you more. Thank you for persevering in all of the prayer you are called to say, to pray: **to praise, to adore, to thank and to petition according to My Father's Will**. You have grown in understanding of His Will, My children. What a great gift this is to you. What a great gift you are to My Mother and to Me, to your Triune God, to all in Heaven. They rejoice with you and for you and because of you. Hear them singing praises to My Father for each of you. Believe this, My dear ones. Believe that you are all so closely united within My Heart and, My children, rejoice!"

December 16, 2001 External locution @ Ameche Prayer group through Carol

"My dearest sons and daughters gathered here and everywhere in the world, I am your Jesus, come to speak briefly to your hearts, to your minds and to your will. My dear ones, I ask for a new consecration of your will this day, given more deeply, more sincerely, more lovingly and more lastingly now for the days ahead: days of grace and gift, new holiness, days in which I pour My light into your hearts. As you sit before Me and prepare; as you listen; as you give Me your heart that I might fill you with this light, fill you with Myself (this Holiness and Sweetness, My children), I bring you the love and delight of all in Heaven. Once again, your loved ones are cheering for you, singing praises to the Father for the gift given to their own loved ones. The world cries out from many corners in agony, My children. The very idea of war must be offered with your gift **of surrender to My Father's promises of protection, of a firm belief in His plans for you, in His loving Providence, in His Divine plan in which you have always lived and moved and had your being, although now more deeply in a more heartfelt way.** My children, you are loved. Rejoice! I speak not this day of destruction; but of life, of wholeness, of courage as one of My followers, as one who kneels before Me in the Manger, a Manger of Hope, My children, a cradle of love rocking to the hymns of Angels, the melodies of Heaven and the sweet stillness of that first night. Thank you for accompanying My Mother on this journey: a journey of hardship and closed doors, of no-room-for-you-either in the hearts of many. My dear ones, you are blessed beyond your understanding. Thank you for accepting these blessings, for using your virtues and for consecrating yourselves once again to your Triune God and your holy Mother. You are My little ones singing in your hearts: Hosanna in the Highest Heaven. I fill your hearts with peace this day. It will remain, whatever you encounter. My dear ones, I bless you. You bless all of us in Heaven."

FOR MERCY'S SAKE!

FOR MERCY'S SAKE

"If the sacrament of the Lord's Passion is to work its effect in us, we must imitate what we receive and proclaim to mankind what we revere. The cry of the Lord finds a hiding place in us if our lips fail to speak to this, though our hearts believe in it. So that his cry may not be concealed in us, it remains for us all, each in his own measure, to make known to those around us the mystery of our new life in Christ." (Friday, Office of Readings, 1976 pg. 257: third week of Lent: Reflections by Saint Gregory the Great, Pope)

IV

2002 Messages

1-02, At Adoration: "Dear one, please write. I am your Jesus of Mercy and Peace. It is a time of immense struggle for all the faithful in the world. Imagine and then remember the suffering in every part of this wretched world. Pray in gratitude for each other, My dearest people of My Heart. I pour out new perseverance at this time, and a new strength of purpose and fidelity to My Father's plan for you and for the world. These days of waiting are doing much to purify you, as the increase of the scorn and impatience of haughty ones causes increased humiliation and suffering. In return for harsh words, please continue to reply with words of peace and mercy and patience. You are changing daily, My dear lambs. Continue to trust in Me and all the promises of your God. Renew your own promises. So soon you will see renewed hostilities and a greater number of people brought into eternity. Increased prayer and response to Heaven's requests and directives will continue to fill your days. Do not look for justification, My dear suffering servants. Look for mercy! Be grateful that you are surviving each trial, each attack of Satan that attempts to discourage and distract you. You are loved by all of Heaven. Be stalwart and focused now. Be at peace, My beloved ones."

1/9, "I am your Jesus of Mercy, My little ones. I come to you this night, pouring mercy on your wounds, on your struggles, seeking to surrender your day to day journey into My Father's Will. I fill you with peace this night, My dear people everywhere in the world. There will come a time when you are together praying long hours, begging mercy, simply praying to maintain the peace within your hearts, the trust about which I speak so often; simply maintaining an atmosphere of love, of generosity towards each other and those in the whole world. When you pray, also bring these people into your hearts now. There are so many more than you hear about, than you realize, who are suffering in dreadful conditions. These must be part of your prayer. These must be alive in your hearts. These must be a greater part of your awareness every moment; that you might lift them up, begging the Father's mercy; that you might beg for relief and comfort and solace in their suffering. It is now, when winter brings harsh conditions, when so many are brought into eternity. You know they're being given My Father's mercy, where they will live in the warmth and the beauty of Heaven forever. Thank My Father for that gift, as well. It is true and truth when I say, 'What would Heaven do without you?' My Mother pours out her love this night for your faithfulness to her, for journeying with her throughout these last weeks and months before and after My birth. A new intimacy dwells within your hearts, which have come to know My Mother through her prayers, her Rosary, her presence with you. There is so much to be thankful for, is there not, My dear ones? I give thanks for you this night at the throne of My Father. I ask you to feel My Heart beating with love for you as I embrace each of you now, holding you, healing you and comforting you. (and each of us now, everywhere as we read... cta.) You are My precious ones. I will always tell you that! That could never change."

1/13, "My dear ones, I am your Mother, **To persevere through waiting is the cleansing and purifying act of God that you accept.** My children, how brave you are. What a sign for others: growing in patience and in obedience yourselves. These virtues strengthen you and change you like no others. I pour out my virtues upon you; that is, the purity and the innocence of the virtues I was given the instant of my conception. I place you deeply within My Immaculate Heart once again, my dear ones, for you are my beloved children. I wish only for you to succeed, to climb the mountain of the Father's Will, to joyfully accept each event and each turn of events which He, in His wisdom, allows for you, for your life and for those around you. My children, the Father knows each of you totally, completely, and knows what is best. It is His Providence that you experience every moment of your day, no matter how difficult, no matter how you struggle and sometimes resist. His love waits for you joyfully. **His mercy IS His patience, and His patience is mercy**. Rejoice that you are favored in this Mercy and this plan. Rejoice that you WILL OVERCOME yourselves! You have consecrated yourselves to God and to me. This is a most serious and solemn vow and consecration, which we in Heaven then help you to honor.

All mankind is weak, vulnerable and at times lazy. This is part of your resistance, and is so very human. Do not become discouraged with yourselves. My Son fell three times for you; again He arose and continued the journey so that you would see this human and Divine nature giving you a pattern: giving you hope, giving you endurance, and promising you the strength you would need. Oh my children, it is why nothing is impossible when you allow God to BE FOR YOU, to be your strength, to be your gifts, to be the answer to every dilemma. I love you, my children, with a love that is deeper than the ocean; that is higher than the sky and wider than the universe; that is brighter than the stars, more fragrant than the most fragrant and beautiful flower. Be comforted, my dear ones, by my love, my presence with you, my caring for you. We WILL be victorious! Together, we will go forward and overcome with Jesus at our side, because we have each other and we have Him and His love, the love of the Triune God. Be at peace, my beloved ones. You are so precious to me, and I thank you for all you have become, all you will do, all you will be for the world."

1/20, "My dear ones, I bring holiness. I bring happiness in prayer. I bring joy to your spirits. I bring perseverance for all the days ahead. It is your Mother once again: Mary, the Immaculate One who comes bringing solace to your hearts, to your spirits, healing to your minds, to your soul, deep healing this day. I, too count on you. I too need you. The days are coming, bringing events against which we have prayed for a long time. I wish to tell you that you have, by your prayers, mitigated much, so that you will appreciate how severe it would have been! Do not be alarmed by my words; but I come with serious warnings for you. **Gather your children into your hearts wherever they are, more than ever in your hearts that are so joined to mine and the protection in my heart. Gather your loved ones from everywhere, your country and the world. (Note: this is a spiritual gathering.)** Open your hearts more, my dear faithful ones everywhere in the world. Read the events everywhere, the struggles, the deep suffering of so many. Keep these dear ones in your mind as well as your hearts. They are yours, my children. They are you! These are not new words; but all of Heaven wishes you to know the seriousness of the times and pending events. You are wrapped in my Mantle. You ARE protected. Oh my children, you are loved. You will see that all of the struggles of the past, (those things that you thought so important,) you will see them fade beside the terror and the immediate fright of so many. Pray now for the strength for the world to withstand Satan and his cunning plans.

My dear ones, remember also the need of the world for you personally, your generous prayers. Sit and contemplate the state of the world with me, aware of my presence (with many Angels) as a loving, mothering, strong presence for you and for them. In the days to come, you will know my presence more than ever, as you practice this time of reflection and quiet. This awareness of my presence will only grow within you. Send this awareness out to others, to your dear ones, that they too might turn to me more, might reach out and take my hand; the hand that is held out to help them; the hand that brings comfort and tenderness and love; the presence that will keep everyone (who accepts it) from panic, from chaos, from disintegrating into a fear that is Satan's plan for you. You know there is nothing to fear in my arms, in my Mantle, in my heart. Send this conviction out with your prayers to the world. It will help, children. It will touch them. Believe this. How I love to be with you in this way. I love you way beyond what you imagine, far beyond your ability to imagine or even to desire. Be at peace. Be grateful for my presence. Praise the Father with me, My dear ones. Amen."

At Adoration after Prayer Gathering

Jesus said: "My daughter, please write for the benefit of all. Believe in the might of My arm to protect and maintain your place in My Father's plan. This time for the world is being controlled by the One World people who are using it to promote a false sense of security and well-being. Our people are so confused by this long wait, since they are unaware of the need for more change and conversion in their own lives. As long as people are praying, they are being healed and transformed into My Father's Will. Without a good deal of prayer each day, along with adoration and quiet reflection, Our people slide back into doubt and resistance. The waiting is beyond the comprehension of many of (even) Our faithful ones. NO ONE yet understands the degree of change still needed within all. Do not spend your time idly, My dear people, or in pastimes that divide your heart and attention to My requests. THE WAIT IS NEARLY OVER, My beloved faithful ones. Seek comfort in My Presence, My people. Seek answers before Me in My Sacrament. Seek peace, where there was no peace, in the comfort of My words and promises. Be assured of My love, the power of Our Spirit and the providence of My Father. It is only in My Father's Will that you will thrive and become the instrument of that Will. I shower you with new gifts and strength this day. HOLD ON TO MY LOVE, CHILDREN, AND FLOURISH!"

1/23, "My dear ones, I am your God and Father. Believe in My joy at being present tonight with this dear and prayerful and faithful group. I tell you, My children, all of Heaven cheers for you, and often the sound of Angel voices brings your name throughout all of Paradise. You gladden the hearts of everyone in Heaven. That is not just repetitious, My dear ones, it is something to ponder. **There are many human emotions in Heaven, and joy is a feeling, is a mode that we accept with delight at every opportunity because it is not always thus. Often there is sadness and in these days, even with joy, there is the sadness that clings with the awareness of events, of the terrible conditions in the world and of the cold which deepens now.** Your poor, dear, suffering family in Africa. Pray for them. Conditions are beyond your belief and, of course, you are not receiving the entire story from your media. It is very, very dreadful. They need you. Think of this often. Put them at the top of your list at this time.

I bring you graces as always. I bring My love and new strength. Your country, My children, is in grave danger from not just one, but many directions, grave events. I see in your hearts you do not jump to a fearful response, and I thank you for this. You could only do this because of trust in the promises of your Lord and your God, because of the gifts of Our Spirit that flow through you, bringing you balance and comfort in the real knowledge of My protection. Each time you pray in union with Jesus, with the Saints, with the Immaculate Mary and the Angels and all of Heaven, you come closer to all of us; you are more united in purpose and in deed, in heart, in mind and in spirit. This is much more powerful than you realize, MUCH more, My children. So I ask you to rejoice and to give thanks for this fact, this actuality. You are My own dear, little ones. I know you will look after each other and the needs of all. You are My champions, and all of My faithful all over the world. How you will shine! How well you will succeed. It has always been My plan for you. Be filled this night with peace and comfort and healing. Amen."

1/27, "I am your God and Father, come to be with you again this day in joy and thanksgiving for YOU. I welcome all of you to this time. My mercy is showered upon you and the whole world this very moment in response to your dear, heartfelt prayers, in response to the love in your heart, in response to the humility with which you beg for mercy, not only for yourselves, but most especially for the poor and suffering in the world. It is another day of giving praise and thanks to Me, to My Son and Our Spirit. I remind you to take rest in the words of your God and His promises to you. Do not become anxious for a moment and yet, do not become complacent because of your gifts. Always, **it is a balance to which you are called** to be on guard and yet, to surrender. I call for more surrender from each of you this day. I ask you to surrender all of your understanding; all of what you have come to know; all of your wisdom, your knowledge, new and old, that I might purify these gifts. Give them once again to Me, as I have given them to you, for I wish to fill you with new wisdom, new understanding according to My Will.

You have discovered along this journey that My Will is much different than yours; that My Will contains a waiting, much purifying, a much slower pace than you would desire, a perfection that is not of this world, a humility that contains boldness, a humility that contains a pouring out of yourself beyond your ability at this time. And so, you are growing into these new ways, new knowledge, new understanding and above all, new wisdom. You will begin to see things in a new way, in a greater depth, I tell you this day; for it is time, My children, to move forward once again, to take giant strides up the mountain of My Will, to take giant steps INTO My Will. You are growing and becoming all I desire for you. DO NOT RUN AHEAD. Seek only My Will. Seek only My pace. Seek only your God and your holy Mother, the virtues, the simplicity, the hiddenness and the silence of My call to you. Hear the songs and the cheers that resound in Heaven for you. Feel the delight and the joy over your progress, over you dearness, your fidelity, your consecration to Me. I bless you this day with a mighty blessing of strength and I cleanse you of little sins that cling, that stand in your way, that cause a barrier to these giant steps I wish you to take from now on. Always there is more, and today there is much to ponder in these words I have given to you. Pray to Our Spirit Whom I pour out now with the gift of openness to new gifts, to new wisdom. Stay close to Our Holy Mother who brings you ever closer to your God. Be at peace. Be about joy! Amen."

1/30, "My dear ones, I am Jesus, Son of God, Savior of the World, Second Person of the Trinity, your Lord and your God, and Spouse of your soul. It is time that more signs are given, that more people are touched, that more people realize the gift and graces being poured out from Heaven at this time. Praise My Father and thank Him, My children. It is also necessary that you become comfortable with this ability to obtain healing for others. By comfortable I do not mean complacent nor, of course, would I ever mean arrogance or the understanding that it is you who are healing. But there is always an element of surprise and delight and amazement when one is healed, and I wish for you to become comfortable with the fact that yes, you are being given a gift now to heal others. Perhaps you will not see this at first. Perhaps My Father will ask you to wait, as He has so many times throughout this journey; but it is given to you this night in a very special and powerful way. Soon this gift will extend to all Our faithful ones in the world. Pray for them, My children gathered here, that they will receive this gift of healing very soon; for all of Our faithful ones will be given this gift, and how you will rejoice! Praise the goodness of My Father. Praise His generosity, His overwhelming mercy. All of you in the world, of course, are His children and in this time those, who pray and listen to the words of Heaven and respond with all of who they are, are most certainly prized by the Father and are gifted in special ways for the days to come.

Do not fear to hope that many, many, many will be healed now by the mercy and goodness of My Father. Begin now to praise Him for healings, before you even see this. **Begin to praise Him for all of the gifts you will receive,** that you have received that will affect the lives and the eternity of so very many. Thank Him now for these facts, these events of the future. Balance your understanding of difficult events with joyous healing and conversion. I love you. It is so difficult to remain faithful to prayer. All of Heaven is aware of this; **and it is your fidelity and struggle to remain faithful that causes the greatest joy, causes new gifts to be given, causes hope to flower in your hearts and in the world.** Be filled with My peace in the midst of difficulties. Be filled with the sureness that all will be well in spite of everything and anything, that all will be well for all of you. My Mother sends her love. She smiles at you now with the greatest sweetness, nodding her head in agreement with My words. Go in peace this night, Amen."

2/3, "My dear ones, I am your Father, your Lord and your God, your Creator. I come to fill your heart with love and the awareness of the love of your God and your Holy Mother, My beloved daughter, the Immaculate Mary. I come to fill you with her virtues, her sweetness, her gentleness, her tenderness, her love of all the people in the world. Whether or not they are open to this is an individual situation. There are many who are not open to dear Mary herself. This then is a barrier, a wall, a block to this gift; for without Mary and her 'yes', there would not have been Jesus and His 'yes'! So, I ask you to **pray especially this week for all of those who do not accept Mary in their hearts, who do not acknowledge her, who do not give her honor and love and obedience as Mother of God and your own spiritual, heavenly Mother.** This then is a most important request, My children, for it is so, **so very important and necessary that all will accept this holiest of women, this most blessed and pure and Immaculate One.** Pray that the entire world opens up to the gift of her, the gift of her virtues, to all of the gifts she wishes to give you as mediatrix and co-redemptrix. Accept with new joy who you are becoming, all that you can be in My grace with My gifts, with My strength, for **the time approaches when you will see your sins as I see them.** You will be given an awareness of the reality and the truth of God. What a blessing this is, what a gift this will be, what a great help toward healing, what a great avenue to humility. All of these things are so necessary for you, for the future, and for every moment. My dear ones, in your obedience you have earned many, many opportunities, so I encourage you to grasp this opportunity of further help from your Mother, from the one who is giving birth again to Jesus in your heart as well, and to the world. This Mother, this beloved woman is the person all of you know personally. How precious she is as a friend, as a confidante, as one who walks with you on your journey, bringing you all of the aid, the comfort, the joy you will receive. You are the ones I count on, My children in the world who are faithful. You will never know until you reach Heaven, with a more perfect knowledge, how many you have assisted in accepting the gift of salvation. You ARE My beloved children!"

2/6, "My dear ones, I am your Mother. I cannot tell you how much joy fills my heart to be with you once again. How grateful I am to speak to you, to share my heart, to share my words of love and encouragement to you: to persevere, to reach out with my joy to everyone. It is a fact, my dear ones, that everyone's feelings, everyone's state of mind and heart and spirit are felt by others. So I remind you that **joy must be your state of mind and heart and spirit, that others be touched,** that others be lifted on this wave of joy that will wash across the earth, that will bring so many to realize that you have been touched in a special way, that this joy they feel about you is sincere, is healing, is peace, is something very much to be desired. This is what it means to be a sign to others, a source of mercy and a source of healing. It also involves **your taking command over sorrow or a feeling of depression or sadness or loneliness, and overcoming it with joy, allowing this to be who you are to others.** Oh, my children, you are a joy for me! I wish to be joy for you and the world, (not only) the world in which you live, but the entire world to which you send out these waves of joy. This will encourage others and lift them up. Pray to me about this, my dear ones. Pray that I might help you accomplish this sense of joy, not something that would be an affectation; but **to put on joy as a natural and comfortable clothing, as a colorful garment, as a sign that you are my child and this brings you joy, and this brings joy to others.**

My children, there are so many things you will do simply by being who you are becoming, who the Father created you to be. My dear ones, this increased relationship of ours that is a gift of the Father is a result of my prayer also, of my joy and my gratitude for the love in your hearts. How much we will serve the Father together! How much will be accomplished for the sorrowful and frightened ones who come. How much healing will be accomplished because of the joy with which you receive each one of these, the great welcome and hospitality that you will pour out upon each one. Be eager, my children, for this time. Be eager for the cleansing the Father wishes for your soul, your hearts, your spirits, that you might be a more perfect instrument as well. That is the **goal of all you do now: becoming the Father's Will, becoming the source of mercy** that will draw so many to you and ultimately to Him through my heart and through the Trinity. My children, we have much work to do. We have much prayer to say. We have much healing to accomplish. We have much joy to experience. Let us rejoice for each other! Feel my love embrace you now. Feel my love healing you, giving you comfort, giving you a greater belief and commitment to all the words of Heaven."

2/6, Jesus said:

"The world is about to explode with a particular event in this country that will grip the world in a new realization of the power of Satan and the state of terror allowed now", (another 'now' we await in patience. Cta.)

2/13, "My dear ones, it is I, your Jesus. I come with peace for your hearts; peace for your spirits, for your mind, for your soul; peace to permeate every act and thought and word and deed; peace to embrace you; peace for you to embrace. **Impatience is such an enemy of mankind**. You can believe this, My dear ones! Look how long you have been praying for this virtue, (patience!) Look how long you have been praying and struggling and hoping to change; and you have changed, My children, greatly! But I say with you: how impatience clings! It is a thorn in the side of all My faithful ones**. It is allowed to be an instrument of struggle, that you might gain strength, of course; but that you might gain the great love and gratitude of My Father,** for He knows so very well how patience goes against the very grain of human nature! And so I bring you the gift of peace this night with which you might deal just a little better each day that you might be aware of the virtue of patience, that you might stop for a single moment before you speak or act or react with impatience. Everyone struggles with this virtue. It is not the first time this has been mentioned to you. It is not the last time I will ask you to pray for each other throughout this time of Lent for the gift of patience.

There is no way you can imagine, My children, how many, many people will be coming to you and the enormous patience you will need. I can only remind you again and again, and ask you repeatedly to plead for this virtue, to practice with each other, children, to praise and thank the Father for this struggle; for this struggle is helping you to become mighty instruments for His people. I leave you with this thought tonight of My patience with those who jeered and scourged, who said the most terrible, terrible things to Me, those who ran from Me, those whom I had healed; the wait before My time of Passion and Death; how I was urged by My human nature to impatience for the very moment of My Father's Will to be enacted. So I do know how it feels to jump with impatience with each other. I bid you to be brave, and remind you also that HUMILITY IS A GREAT ANTIDOTE TO IMPATIENCE! I love you. I pour out peace. Carry this peace. Be aware of it. We go forward, My children."

2/17, "My children, it is I, your God and Father. I come this day to fill you with perseverance, with new resolve, new commitment and new strength; to shower My mercy upon you; to fill you, My dear ones, with Jesus, My Son. I speak to everyone in the world who listens and believes and acts upon Our words, who strives to live within My Will more fully. I welcome you here, My dear ones.

You bring a smile to Heaven, to each "face", each one. Gratitude resounds through Heaven once again, and as each one in the world reads and acts upon and accepts the gifts I am giving this day, this delight, these smiles, this gratitude continues. May I say to you there is a Holy Pride that rings throughout Heaven for all of the faithful ones in the world? Without you, My plan would not be fulfilled, would not be a success and would not be victorious. This is so because I have chosen it to be. I have chosen to include you. I have chosen to share My power with you and the needs of Our poor lost ones everywhere. I have devised a plan that includes their need of you, their dependence upon your response. Think of yourself in their place: counting on the prayers of others in the world you do not know; counting on these prayers to enable them to open to the gifts I wish to give them, open to the Spirit, to the virtues; to the gifts you and they need. Could there be any greater need than a dependence upon Me and the path I have chosen to share with you?

Feel that joy I wish to see growing in your hearts and lives, to help you to thank Me, to be truly happy about your place (in His plan) and the requests for so much prayer. I have created you in My Image. I wish for you to become more like that Image. I have given you My Son as an example. This great gift to you is meant to show you once again in the light of new graces and new gifts you have received, in the light of the new creation you have become, to see more and more what Jesus has always been teaching you and showing you with His words and His life and His acceptance of My Will**. There is nothing else as important as this mission you have been given, as this reflection and all the new understanding,** seeing and hearing and acting in a new way based on the life of My Jesus when He was with you and spoke and taught and healed, as He wishes to do for you now and every moment.

My dear, dear ones, remember the degree of gift you are offered. There is no parallel in history, for **the events of the future have no parallel.** Thus to be prepared, you must be able to accept everything I wish to give you now and in the future at every moment. These same thoughts are being repeated to you, and in this repetition you are meant to see their importance, to reflect again and again on all Heaven is sharing with you, giving to you, showering upon you. It is love I bring, My children. It is Myself, for I am Love in union with Jesus and Our Spirit. Reflect this week on all the loving things I have done for you, how much more you feel the love of your God, how much closer you are and feel to that Love. This too will heal you. As any loving, doting parent, I want you to receive the best and the most, the highest and the deepest, the greatest amount of all of My gifts that you can possibly receive. It is up to you, My dear ones. I am here with all of My gifts and My power and My love. I give them to you. Take them. Say to Me**: 'My Father and My God, I praise you. I thank you. I accept with joy and gratitude every gift you are giving Me now, in the past and in the future. I love You, My God. Help me to love You more.'** My children, I love you."

2/20, "My dear little ones, I welcome you this night. I am your Jesus. I gather you this night into My arms. I gather all who hear My words, who live the requests of Heaven. I come to thank you, especially this night, for your devotion to My Mother and yours, this precious Mother who is everything in our lives. What a blessing, what a precious Mother she is to Me. What a blessing to you. I ask you to join Me in praising the Father and thanking Him for dear Mary, Our dear Mother, this Immaculate One who holds each of you in her heart, who holds each of you in her prayers. Your well-being, My children, is her constant prayer and concern. Recall that you have a new and deeper relationship with her, that she is sent to help you reflect, to help you request, to help you repent and renew, My dear ones. Recall that I have told you this time, will be a peak of healing in your lives, and so it will be by the gracious gift of My Father: the healing of reconciliation, where healing begins; the peace that comes from reconciliation; the joy that grows and spreads throughout yourselves, your spirits, your hearts that causes you to be the source of mercy to others you are created to be. My dear ones, you can never reflect too often, that you might rejoice and repent and renew. Do not be alarmed at discovering new weaknesses, but praise My Father. Do not be afraid to see yourselves with new eyes; to hear yourselves with new ears; with new understanding, to embrace yourselves, as I embrace you, as I hold you this night. How grateful I am to see the joy that jumps within your hearts, as you hear My words of love. You KNOW it is I, and together we will see victory, and you will know peace and live the Father's Will as it was always meant to be. BE, My children, in My love. Amen."

2/ 24, "My dear children, I am your God and Father. I ask you to **recall that you are exactly where I desire you to be in My Will and in My plan** for you and for the world. It is always a human trait to desire to run ahead, to do more, to be more, to receive more in your own perception of events, of your prayer life, of your own conversion. I tell you, My children, to wait for My Will for you is another way to practice patience with yourself and obedience, obedience to the way things are, to the way I would allow things to develop and to unfold in your life. The more you think about it, My children, the more you will see the wisdom of My plan. It is necessary that you always see that IT IS MY PLAN; to realize My power; to praise and thank Me for it and to remember that My power will never be overcome by the evil one. This will lead you to more trust, as you know. This will take away every ounce of fear or anxiety or agitation or impatience with others.

I mention again, My children, that you have no idea how difficult it will be to be patient in the future with great numbers of people coming to your doorstep, taking residence in your homes, sharing your meals, your clothing and all of your time. Oh, My children, pray for each other. Pray for the world. Pray for peace. Although these words are familiar ones, if you will truly read My words often and meditate upon them you will find many new ideas for yourself; much food for thought; a new focus on My Will; a new focus on your own acceptance, your own graciousness. Impatience, My children, is NOT gracious, and you must be the heart of openness, hospitality and graciousness to each other now and to all who come. Remember the words of My Son. I am your teacher. Hear MY words. Follow My requests. Pattern yourselves after My designs and desires for you and you will know joy and peace and trust, surrender and patience. Nothing else can give you the sense of well-being, the sense of belonging to the Body of Christ, of dwelling in My Will that these virtues will produce. Oh My children, you are loved by all of Heaven. They pray for you. Unite your prayers to theirs. Invite them into your every task. Expand your understanding. Expand your horizons to include the Kingdom of Heaven with you in so many ways. Thank you for listening to My words. I urge you to reread them, to ponder them, to make them part of who you are becoming. You ARE faithful. Amen."

2/27, "My dear, dear people, I am your Holy Spirit: the Spirit of the living God. I come this night with many, many gifts to each one, according to your needs, by the gracious Will and desire of your Father God, your Creator and Lord. It is a time of strengthening, dear ones; a time of renewal; a time to put on the armor of God and thus, I clothe you this night anew in this armor. Read again the words of Sacred Scripture about this armor, (Ephesians 6: 11-17) and vow to personally accept what this means. I will give you a deeper understanding of what this will mean to you now and in the future. I bring you new understanding this night to many things that will be given as the days go by, and at that time you will better understand God's work in the world, in your hearts and the hearts of all His people everywhere. You will know what I mean when new mysteries unfold, when you will see the Father's action that may seem harsh, even unreasonable, something that before could not be explained; but now you will see through His eyes, Our eyes (your Trinity) the eyes of deeper understanding, the eyes of justice and mercy and fairness and above all, merciful goodness for each person in the world.

The world is on the brink of such destruction, of such change, of such hardship. Yes, you have heard these words many times in the past, and you may yet hear them again before the actuality of events; but it is the Father's desire that you might shore up your strength, your acceptance and the balance within yourselves that while you are preparing and expecting, you are also at peace and trusting. My people, I fill you also with the strength to seek reconciliation again at this time; to prepare beforehand with Me; to be open to every suggestion, every new look that I may give you at yourself, at your life, at the Father's mercy and at your place in His plan now and for the future. Many gifts are raining down from Heaven now because of your need for them, your need at this time that the Father's Will might unfold for the world at any time; that most of all, I wish for you to **remember protection and love and joy, conversion and healing, miracles and peace.** Your hearts, My dear, dear ones and the hearts of all those in the world who strive to be faithful, (as you do) your hearts are blossoming once again. Simply accept this fact. Believe My words and rejoice. Rain will come. Storms will develop and you will continue to blossom, to become more beautiful, radiant in the light of the Sun that will always be shining upon you. How you are loved. Amen."

3-3, "I am your God and Father. I come this day with strength for these closing days of this Lenten Season; strength to bear the events of the future; strength to bear the truth, strength to accept the truth about yourselves and about My plans for all the gifts I have given to you, for the wonderful gift of your person, of who you are. So often My Jesus and I will speak about being who you are, about giving to your Triune God all of who you are and all of who you are becoming in My plan and in My Will. These are the most important truths to accept, for it is the place where you begin your journey each day in surrender, in joy, in giving, in letting go, in offering all of your old ways of thinking and reacting, of the control you have always thought you had, of your needs, your expectations, your desires and as We have discussed, My dearest children, your own impatience; not just because of delays in expected events, but most of all impatience with each other. It is especially when you are weary or have struggled, or journeyed in new directions that impatience is the greatest enemy, for you are vulnerable, you are distracted, you face your own weaknesses and inadequacies. This sets up a perfect atmosphere for impatience, does it not, My children? I see that you agree with each of My words to you, that I know you so well, better than you know yourselves. It is because of all of these things that I love you so much, because you continue to struggle, to try with all of your might to accept whatever My Will allows in your lives at every moment to change you, to bring you to that place of new creation so necessary to serve in the days to come. And with all of these thoughts and words today, and food for thought and reflection, I tell you My dear ones, YOU ARE OVERCOMING!

You are becoming victorious over self, over selfishness, self-centeredness, self-absorption, anxieties and worries. How these have plagued the lives of Our people everywhere in the world. These are such distractions. These help you to play right into the hands of Satan. That alone is reason to change, to struggle against self. Believe that YOU HAVE every gift, every virtue, every power, every strength you need to combat the self that cries for notice, for gratification, to be the center of your own attention. Do not let irritations overcome you. Steel yourself against the way these are able to overtake you. Get the upper hand, as it were; for in the future, in the days of chaos and much destruction, these will still be your greatest enemies as you battle fatigue and new directions and situations totally unfamiliar to anyone. You will have your Lord and your God, your Holy Mother, more Angels than you can imagine and all of the Saints and every person in Heaven with you to see you through; bringing you comfort as well as strength, adding to your joy with the understanding of the final victory. Remember as you listen now, in spite of irritations, that I will always overcome. My power will never be defeated and you, My dear ones and My dear ones in the world who listen everywhere, are My shining ones, My holy ones, My precious ones, My victorious ones. My blessings, My mercy, My love are yours. Amen."

3/6, "Dear children, I come to you this night by a very special grace and gift of God Our Father, for I am Teresa from Avila. I have given you words in the past (printed in book, Do Whatever Love Requires) and I come again to encourage you to pray to us in Heaven for the strength and the help you need; to remind you that We are praying at every moment for you that you will not become discouraged, that you will not be overwhelmed by adversity in your life. This emptying of your will, this surrender of your will is the most difficult of all you attempt to do and to give to our Great God. I come to tell you that We are with you in all of your trials, in your struggles to become these mighty instruments of healing, of hope, of mercy, of compassion.

How I love you, my little friends in Jesus and Mary. We watch you, as you pray. I tell you, wonderful fragrances accompany your prayers, as you send them to Heaven. I tell you also to believe deeply in your hearts that you are never alone. We are in community with you, dear children of God! We are friends. We are soul mates; for we all have the same love for Jesus, our beloved Master, our King and the precious Mary, our Queen. Thank the Father for this gift, as I am thanking Him this night in union with all of Heaven. This gift is given, my children that you will understand gift more. What is gift? It is the unusual. It is the unexpected. It is very often the needed event or object in your lives; and so, my visit with you tonight is an example of the gift the Father can give. He alone allows these wonderful visits, and comes to you Himself with words of teaching, of wisdom, of the greatest love. When I was on the earth, I made so many mistakes, my children. I struggled so with myself; and so I remind you that I pray with the deepest compassion and understanding for your own weaknesses, and I encourage you to trust and to have patience with our Dear Lord! We all love you so very much. Be in joy, dear companions on this great journey to the Father. Praise God! Amen."

March 10, (For everyone in the world, whenever you read this!) "My very dear ones, I am your Jesus, children. I am your Suffering Lord. I come with a special request this day to My faithful ones everywhere in the world, as well as to all of you gathered here. I ASK FOR A DAY OF QUIET REFLECTION AND RECOLLECTION AMONGST ALL OF YOU WHO GATHER CONTINUALLY TO PRAY AND TO BEG FOR MERCY OF MY FATHER. I ASK YOU TO DO THIS ON A DAY BEFORE HOLY WEEK BEGINS, THAT YOU MIGHT PREPARE YOURSELF BETTER THAN EVER BEFORE TO SPEND HOLY WEEK IN A HOLY AND LOVING AND SACRIFICIAL WAY. When a special day of prayer is requested of you, remember that it is also a special day of enormous gifts, new graces, new strength, new outpouring of Our Spirit. This day I also ask that you would have a time of quiet reflection upon your own sinfulness; that you would do this in unity with Our Spirit; that you would do this and request His help with all your heart, with all your soul, with all your mind and all your strength; that you may truly benefit in a total way from all My Father desires to show you, to reveal to you at this time as a means of preparation, as a means of cleansing, as a means of rejoicing, My dear ones. For you will rejoice as you discover more that will prepare you, that will help you to become a more perfect instrument. These words you are hearing often, My children. Know that this is the basis of Our Father's Will for all of you, for all of

His children in the world, and I ask you to prepare for this day by praying for each other for a new unity with My Passion and Dying and Rising.

This will be a special day; however, remember to come without expectations, without asking gifts or particular needs. Come and surrender. Come in openness to whatever the Father wills, whatever He desires for you personally on this day. And I thank you in advance that you will be coming together, and bringing in spirit those who are unable; but that all of you will unite worldwide in spirit to offer yourselves to the Father as an open vessel into which He will pour these revelations of a deeper nature of self, of weaknesses yes, of vulnerabilities and what will lead to greater compassion, greater understanding, wisdom, empathy for the world and for each other; that you will, from that day forward, come together in greater warmth and appreciation of each other, My dear ones everywhere, in gratitude for each other, for who you are and who you are becoming. This day must be simple, with as much silence as possible. This day must simply be Heaven's gift to you, My children, as you have become greater gifts to each other and to all in Heaven. Rejoice, My children. Rejoice, as you prepare for My Passion and Death; but also in remembrance and preparation just a few days prior to the great Feast of My Mother and the Annunciation to her of My birth within her to grow and become your Savior and your King. There is much for which to give thanks, most of all for the love of your Triune God and all in Heaven. Thank you for listening. Thank you for your love. Heaven blesses you this day. Amen."

3/13, "My dear ones, I am your Jesus. I ask you this night to come to Me in your need. Pour out your frustrations, as well as anxieties. Pour out your feelings of confusion, any lack of understanding over what may be occurring in your lives. Give Me every need, everything with which you struggle, everything that wars against your human nature: the way things have always been, the status quo, familiar things that seem gone and replaced by those that are no longer familiar and leaving you feeling ill at ease, with a lack of the ability to relax or rest in your prayer, your Scripture reading, your meditation; an inability perhaps at this time, to concentrate or to pray. Remember as you are struggling, as you are attempting to fulfill My Father's desires through My Mother's requests to you, and the greatest needs of the world: As long as you are trying to do this, you are succeeding! **It is your motive, My children. It is the purity of heart. It is the sincerity with which you ask and pray. It is the love you bring to your prayers: asking help, comfort and healing for the world.**

Satan fights furiously these precious prayers of yours, My dear ones everywhere. He is given much strength now, and will interfere as often as possible; but you do remember, and you do believe that he will never overcome you, nor certainly will he ever overcome the plan of My Father which includes your own salvation, your own journey into perfection. Never become discouraged. Never give up. Never feel inadequate or ill prepared. It is openness to Our Spirit that is needed. Greater understanding fills your heart even when it is fatigued or divided or distracted: an understanding of the way people suffer, of how much each one is going through in their own way, especially those in foreign lands who have nothing; the desperate poor everywhere, who have nothing; the abused, the tormented who have nothing, not even a place of safety, who have had trust in anyone or anything torn from their hearts and their minds and their spirits. Just remember them when you pray. Hold them up to My Father for healing, for comfort, for new hope, strength and conversion.

IT IS NOT YOUR FEELINGS OR YOUR EXPERIENCE THAT IS THE POINT OF PRAYER. **It is the needs of others that you bring to prayer.** Persevere in love, as I persevered for you through My Passion, through the terrible suffering, the terrible wounding and the dying. Each day now, see yourself preparing for this Feast, for this reenactment of the gifts that gave you salvation and redemption. Oh, My children: WE ARE ONE!"

3/17, "My precious ones, I am your Jesus, come once again to fill your hearts with a greater desire to pray, to love, to serve, to surrender to My Father's Will for you. It is a special Feast in the world, and so I bring gifts from this special Saint: this dear Patrick whom the entire world loves and honors this day. All of Heaven joins you and the world in giving honor to him and to all the Saints who are praying for you constantly. They send you strength and hope; send joy to your hearts, that you might persevere, that you might face the truth of God with honor, with acceptance (again in surrender to the truth) that you might praise and thank the Father for the great gifts He is giving and about to give the world. In calling you to change, Heaven is giving you many, many tools, many teachings, many ways, new paths to tread, many paths to embrace. Some of them will be increased suffering. Some of them will be increased sorrow and loss; and in all of these, My children, I remind you with all the love of My Heart to realize that they are gift! Remember, the Father chastises those He loves (Hebrews 12:6) and He allows you to suffer in union with My sufferings as a means of bringing you ever closer to Me, to unite you more to My very Person. My dear children, more than anything remember how much you are loved, that there is love present in every breath you draw, in the sunlight and the rain. In everything you observe, there is God's love present, sustaining, maintaining, enriching and nurturing. Be filled with Our love this day. All of Heaven is pouring blessings out upon you now and upon everyone in the world, as they read and hear My words. YOU ARE PRECIOUS IN MY EYES. YOU ARE MINE, My beloved ones. Rejoice!"

3/22, Day of prayer (as requested by Jesus) through Carol. Our Lady spoke with such distress and sadness, heard and felt in my heart and spirit.

"Children of My Sorrowful and Immaculate Heart, I have been with you this day weeping tears of joy for the love in your hearts; weeping tears of sadness at the terrible conditions in the hearts of people everywhere in the world. I am your loving Mother, your Sorrowful and Sorrowing Mother. Today many souls have been brought to Heaven because of your prayer. Today many more will accept the mercy of the Father because of your prayer. Today you are given the gift of walking more nearly, more closely and in union with my Jesus on His dreadful walk to Calvary: the walk that allowed Him to walk directly into our hearts with redemption, with salvation; to be crucified for us; to take upon Himself, (that precious Child of mine) the dreadful burden of the sins of all time. Remember, My **Jesus has told you, as He hung on the Cross suffering unimaginable pain, He saw you, my children: your precious faces, your heads bowed in prayer for the world, begging mercy, begging protection, begging forgiveness and salvation for the world. He saw you ministering to thousands, healing them, bringing them to the Father, raising some miraculously from the dead!** My children, how blessed you are. In your worst sorrow, I am with you, sharing your sorrows. In the sorrows to come I will be with you, shouldering your sorrows with you. In your grief, I will be with you, united in your sorrows.

Oh my dear ones everywhere in the world, thank you for praying as Jesus invited you. Thank you for picking up your crosses daily to follow after Him. Thank you for the love in your hearts which prompts you to seek new unity with my Son's Passion and Dying. You are brave soldiers, my dear, dear ones everywhere. Remember (in the most trying times) that We will be victorious together, that together we will lead so many to salvation, to victory with my Son. You are my children of victory. I am your Lady, your Mother, your Queen of Victory. My dear ones, I ask you to attempt to touch even more people in the coming week with your recollection, your silence. Be soft and gentle. Be tender with each other, especially in the face of hostility and anger, sharp words, ridicule. You can know that you are truly united with my Son because you experience these things! You can know that you are walking the path to Calvary because you are united in this way. You can know that you and I walk behind Him, but **together we will meet Him face to face along the way; that we will stand at the foot of the Cross gazing into His Face covered with His precious blood, twisted by the agony of His suffering for you and for every person who has and who will ever live.** My dear ones, what love He has for all of you!

I come this day to share the grief in My Heart, and tell you of the support you give me, of the hope you give me, with the love and devotion you give me. Believe my words. You KNOW I am here and speaking. Believe that all that has been told to you will be accomplished**. As with the Passion of my Son about to begin, so too is the Passion and Crucifixion of His Church about to begin. Pray, my dear ones. Pray and pour yourselves out now. If you truly love me, pray. If you truly love my Jesus, pray. The world is about to be crucified, as well. Pray, my children. "**

4/3, "My dear people: I am your Holy Spirit, the Spirit of the living God; the Spirit of the Risen Christ; the Spirit of God, the Father and your Creator; the One Who fills you with the desire to be holy; the One Who brings you gifts and new strength and perseverance; the One Who inspires you to good deeds, to obedience, to desire to follow every action of Jesus during His life on earth, most especially in His dying: the way He handled His suffering and those who tortured Him, who questioned Him with foolish questions, who humiliated Him, trying to destroy Him in the eyes of His followers forever. I mention these things to you to remind you of the great power of the Resurrection; to tell you how the fire of My love is present within you and each resurrection you experience; to encourage you to seek Me and My power: the fire of love, the fire of desire to love and to serve, the fire of goodness and purity, the fire of longing to come closer to your God and My precious spouse, your Holy Mother.

It is a fire that will rain down from Heaven, as I pour Myself out on each of you this night and in the days to come. It is a fire that cleanses you: a fire that perfects, that burns impurity and gross matter within you, all of the things that are worldly, most especially inclinations to gratification. All of these are ingrained in human nature so deeply. Each one is convinced that it is impossible to be thoroughly cleansed; and I tell you that nothing is impossible for God! It will not be impossible to make of you more perfect instruments of God, the Father's Will; to make you instruments of joy and hope for all whom I will bring to you Myself according to a plan devised by the Father before the world began in His all-knowing; in His perfect wisdom, His perfect plan for every problem, every sin, every turning away, every weakness found in human nature. I mention these things to encourage you not to despair, for **I tell you there will be times when you will come so close to despair because of what you see and experience. You will not believe the events. You will not believe the fear. You will not believe the conditions that will develop. And as far as you can see, the eye will not understand how these conditions could be bettered or changed or improved!**

I ask you this night to begin a Novena to Me for the strength you know you will need; for strength beyond your knowledge of what you will need; for calm, ordered, peaceful acceptance of everything that now begins to unfold in the world. The Father's Will unfolds in many areas of the world, not only in your own lives. I ask also that you broaden your horizons of understanding, that you include the entire world in your world, in your vision; for it is necessary that **you continue now to pray to be aware on a global level, the whole family of God and your family: part of you and who you are, your loving responsibility, a gift to you.** This night I am giving you and all who pray in the world and listen and act upon the words of God and the Holy Mother that ability to broaden your horizons, to start thinking less about yourselves and your own needs, **to think only of the needs of others now. This will require much practice** and in reality, everyone is in need of great practice! Think, for example, WHAT YOU MIGHT SAY IF THESE PEOPLE WERE TO COME TO YOU IN THE MORNING. FOR EXAMPLE, WHAT WOULD YOU SAY? DO YOU KNOW? HAVE YOU PLANNED? HAVE YOU ANY IDEA HOW YOU WOULD PROCEED? Think about this dear, dear people. YOU are God's instruments of healing for them, of hospitality, of heroic service. **YOU, each of you everywhere will lead, will comfort, will heal, will nurture and will speak in answer to every question. Could you do that in the morning??**

I present these questions that you might begin to see the challenge ahead of you, the challenge that must be met by every faithful one in the whole world, that

you might become more serious about the requests of Heaven and all the words shared with you these many, many years. I am with you every time you call on Me. I come to help you, to inspire you, to give you the words you need.
You are blessed and beloved of God."

****

April 8, 1992

THE SORROWFUL MYSTERIES

Jesus: "Walk with Me. Carry My Cross with Me. Fall with Me and rise to continue to the Hill of Shame. Come now, and be lifted up with Me. Hang on My Cross and die with Me in perfect union with My Will for you. Stay close to Me. Lean on Me, for I am strong." Blessed Mother: "All of Heaven contemplates the beginning of my Son's Passion this night, and you will be more surely united to me if you walk this way in my company. Allow me to bring you to the foot of the Cross. Allow me to show you the depths of my love, as I followed my Jesus from a distance through the streets lined with shouting, jeering people, whose only thoughts were to kill my Jesus. Love for my Son allowed me to find the courage, the strength to follow Him to the foot of the Cross. It was a night that had begun earlier than I could remember. Perhaps for days we had not slept in preparation and prayer for this solemn event. There were no tears left in me, only a living out now of the things foretold for my beloved Child since the fall of Adam. Join me now, as we walk the streets behind Him and watch Him suffer and die. I love you and thank you for wishing to accompany me on this awful journey. It begins.....

1. THE AGONY IN THE GARDEN

"Allow the feelings to penetrate your heart, as you hear the sounds and terrible words. See what they are doing to Him Whom I love. See how they push and taunt Him. I long to run to Him and shield His bruised body with my own. A mother would always try to do this for her child, but I must stay away and allow all of Scripture to be fulfilled. The love of my Son for His Heavenly Father is more than anyone could ever comprehend. Please know that it was this love which gave life and breath to every single thing He did while on earth. It allowed Him to be single-minded in the face of a truly impossible human situation."

2. JESUS IS SCOURGED AT THE PILLAR

"I knew of the longing of my Son to fulfill every word that had been written about Him, and so I too bowed before the will of Our Almighty Father God, Who in His plan of salvation of His people emptied Himself of His precious Son in order to redeem mankind. Dwell on this thought and allow it to fill your heart with love and gratitude. My Son did not suffer alone. The Father and their Most Holy Spirit suffered each pain, each

humiliation with Him; although humanly He had been abandoned to the lust and greed of a crowd, a mob gone mad with the taste of blood."

3. JESUS IS CROWNED WITH THORNS

"My Son, the Lamb, must be slain for the very people who are screaming for His death. They are intent on destroying the One Who has loved and served them, taught them and healed them, eaten with them and visited in their homes; Who only wished to bring them knowledge of the Father and His great love for them. Can you bear to watch this scene? Can you bear to see His Sacred Blood poured out on the filthy streets to mingle with the dust and dirt of the crazed people yelling for my beloved Son's death?"

4. JESUS CARRIES HIS CROSS

"I was all alone when I met my Son in the street on His way. I approached Him slowly and with great trembling, for my own sorrow was so great; but I knew it would be the last time before His death, so I hurried to Him to touch and caress His face. He was nearly dead then. When we looked into each other's eyes, the greatest love passed between us, and a new strength, a new sense of purpose seemed to pervade His being. I know He would survive all the cruelties and impossible pain in order to fulfill the Father's Will for Him. As much as He loved and longed to comfort me, it was His Father's Will which gave Him the strength and courage to continue on His way."

5. THE CRUCIFIXION AND DEATH OF JESUS

"It was now time to behold His Crucifixion, and it was only through grace and the help of Angels that I was able to behold this horrifying scene. Imagine your own children nailed to the cross. The blood which was left in His body spurted afresh, as the nails pierced Him, and my heart broke completely with each sound of the hammer. I do not know what allowed me to stand in that place, yet I could not bear to leave Him alone with that hatred. You can never imagine such a scene, and I will never forget it. Until the day I left this earth, it was before my eyes at all times."

EPILOGUE

"Even though I knew He had risen and was now in Heaven with His Father and the Saints and Angels, standing at His right hand pleading for the world, it was with sorrow that I continued to contemplate the terrible scene of His agony. My heart was always filled with great longing to be reunited with my Son, and this was a longing which gave me an energy and love to serve His friends, who also missed Him so and spoke of nothing other than His words and recounted stories of His time on earth with them. Each day new marvels would be recorded, as awareness grew within them of all my Jesus had done for them. I was able to be comforted by the recounting of all these times in my Jesus' life with His beloved ones. It brought me comfort to hear the love and gratitude in their voices, and for a brief time He would live

for each of us again. We lived for the day that each of us would be called to Heaven to be with Him, all the while learning together from His words that were remembered. This was the way our days passed, in love and longing, never quite recovering from the horror of that dreadful time when my Son, the Lamb, was crucified."

4-10, "My dearest children, I am your Mother. I am Mary; Mother of Jesus Our Redeemer, Jesus the Savior, the Holy One, the Son of God. I bring this greeting tonight to the world to remind you of the great gift all who ever lived have received from My Precious Son. I ask you tonight to spend time during this week meditating upon the amount of gratitude I had and have and will always have for the tremendous, the glorious gift of My Son. It took (me) a lifetime to come to the place of realization (once He lived out the Father's Will for the salvation, the redemption of the world, of all mankind for this appreciation, for this overwhelming gratitude to develop day by day, step by step, event following event, for the fullness of my response to reach its' flower, its' full blossom; and then when I finally returned to Heaven, I would be filled with the Heavenly understanding and delight at all that Scripture had foretold, at all that Jesus had promised about Himself, about Heaven, about being in Heaven. I tell you, my children**, if you would meditate and ask me, I will shower you with a new understanding, a new wisdom in this area, and it will bring you to a new appreciation of the presence of My Jesus in your lives, in your heart, united to your spirit and your will.** This will be a gift, as all is gift, but it will be a great gift; for new appreciation always strengthens, always leads to new gratitude. New gratitude always moves one to love more, to desire to serve, to do more, to become more in the Father's Will and begins the circle, the cycle of appreciation again and again.

My children, your Lenten Season, your celebration of the glorious feast of My Son's Resurrection; your celebration and the great outpouring of love and requests for mercy on Divine Mercy Sunday have enabled this gift to be given now, of which I speak this night; has enabled many gifts to be given, my children everywhere: gifts you need, gifts the Father wishes to give out of His great mercy and love for you, out of HIS gratitude. Only in Heaven will you know how many people you have touched this very year of prayer and obedience to all the requests of Heaven. Your greatest gift and goal is unity with your God. The gift I bring this evening is a preparation and a further means of your more complete unity with your Triune God and His Will for you. Praise and thank Our God, my children. You know I love you, and I know you love me! How I wish there were words to explain my gratitude for you, for your love and your fidelity. Meditate with me, my dear ones, on the glorious gift of my Son, Jesus."

4/14, "I am your God and Father. Forbearance, My dear ones, is a gift, like all gifts needed by human nature because of the selfishness of human nature and the impatience that batters the peace trying to survive within each of you in spite of chaos, in spite of the fact that My Will reigns instead of your own. This alone can cause chaos at one time and another, as a realization sinks more deeply into your awareness **that My Will springs from My Divine Love for you**, My care, My desire that you would become all I have created you to be. Really understanding them (His desires) requires more acceptance, requires more surrender on your part, more docility and humility. Obedience to My Will means many things, and can only be discovered personally in deep reflection with that openness given you by Our Spirit, for which you also pray. Each step contains many steps on this journey into My Will. You can understand this statement now, being more familiar with these steps, with the **continued dying to self you must experience, that you might become a new creation.** Imagine taking a very varied group from all walks of life, from every level of education, different cultures, different ways of seeing and living; and turning them into a fighting unit, a group of warriors obedient to their commander**: the same commander for all these different people throughout the entire world.** And **you will begin to appreciate the time it is taking, My dear ones, from a new vantage, from a new look at humanity,** all the while Satan wars constantly within and around this varied group. My children, you are becoming these warriors; you are becoming this united fighting unit.

As you accept and as you give in to all I desire and request of you through the Holy Mother, through My Son, through My own words, through Our Spirit and through gift, **you only accept it in all of these ways with all of these steps; so each step is slow and must exist within a framework that is the same though adapted to each different person. I outline these steps today to give you a greater appreciation of My job, of My action within your lives; and when you hear the words "it's not just about you" My children, perhaps you can see that in a greater way: the larger picture from this new understanding. Understanding expands your hearts and your minds and your ability to accept and to grow and to become an even mightier warrior!** Appreciate that in this way I am also sharing My power with you, as I allow you to become a more pliant instrument, pliable in My hands, one to be used uniquely by Me because each of you is unique! There is much to this journey. Much of it you will never comprehend until you look back from Eternity and the vantage of Paradise. In the meantime, I desire to bring you as closely and intimately into My plans as possible, that you might be united with Me in purpose, in the desire of your own heart and will. This will make you desire to surrender more to whatever it takes to touch, to change, to save as many in the world as possible. **There is a universe to consider, My children. Think about that!** Do not become discouraged for one moment, for your struggles are My Will also. I bless you, My dear ones, My own, My warriors, My beloved. Amen."

4/17, Jesus said: "My dear ones, welcome! We gather in the midst of the beauty of My Father's creation, in the beauty of weather that is nearly perfect, in the midst of hearts that are being perfected! Your hearts, My dear ones, your precious hearts!! (His voice was so tender here.) I call upon the generosity of your hearts this night, and I bring word from My Father, a word of gratitude, a word of caution! Be on guard, because Satan is given more power now. His plans are escalating, and so you will see the results of these plans very shortly, and so I say, 'Be on guard personally and collectively, first and foremost of course, in your prayer. Pray for safety, not that you are personally in danger, but your country, My children, your dear country which you all love and whom you have all served throughout your lives, for which you are filled with gratitude.

YOUR COUNTRY WILL BE VICTIM ONCE AGAIN. I see your hearts, My dear ones, and I too wish that I could tell you exactly when! From all of the words from Heaven these many years, you are brought to a new understanding of the need to build your faith, to build your trust, to build your surrender, to build for the future, to build a mighty edifice within your hearts, a temple of trust, a tower of trust! You have seen already, My dear ones everywhere in the world, how **God alone could intervene and defeat the plans of Satan, and you know also My Father chooses to wait and to act in response to your prayers.** You are not the only ones waiting, My precious ones**. My Father waits for you,** for your deeper response, for ongoing, constant awareness on your part: awareness of Our Presence with you; awareness of the suffering everywhere in the world, of terrible need of so very many; awareness of the danger, all of these things, along with hope and joy and mercy in your dealings with everyone. Mercy as the environment in which you live, that all of these things will constantly be with you whatever you are doing at the moment. This new way of being is happening for you!

Great progress HAS been made; as the Father allows Me to tell you, to give you a glimmer of things to come. He knows that you are ready, that it is not necessary that you have the knowledge of the time or day because you are prepared. You are the soldiers ready for battle. It is difficult to think in these terms. It is difficult to carry the world with joy. It is even more difficult for each one of you to carry yourself, I know, with joy and yet, without joy, who could walk, who could respond to all the directives of Heaven? Always human nature needs new encouragement. I bring encouragement for you this night. So quickly, so easily the spirit lags, falls behind and becomes distracted. This level of prayer involvement, of the involvement in the story of every person in the world, brings with it a fatigue, a strain; and so I ask you again to immerse yourself in My Sacred and Eucharistic and Merciful Heart; **for I hold the world and every event there and thus you will more deeply be immersed in the world within My Heart!** My children, always I call you to Myself. Always I offer Myself, My Heart to you. PREPARE, MY CHILDREN, FOR A MIGHTY EVENT. DO THIS IN PEACE, WITH CALM, IN TOTAL SURRENDER TO WHATEVER THE FATHER WILLS THAT YOU MIGHT HAVE JOY! I LOVE YOU!"

4/24, "My dear ones, I am your Jesus, once again. I wish to thank you for your prayers, for the Novenas you are saying, for your increased awareness of Our Presence, as We have requested of you for your increased companionship: how you call upon My Mother in new ways and more often. All of these things point to obedience. What could be more important? Each of you thinks you have an awareness of the spiritual lives of others, of what makes a person holy or not holy, of what determines good prayer or dryness. And I tell you, My children**, it is OBEDIENCE that determines your readiness, your response to the call of Heaven, the state of your heart, your will, your mind, your spirit, your soul. It is obedience that forms and reforms each of Our children in the world**. It is obedience to the requests of Heaven, all of them. Those of you who reread Our words over the years know Our requests, know the words given for your encouragement and learning, begging you to beg for mercy and all of the words by which you are nurtured in Scripture as well. And so, of course, I encourage you again this night to continue your increase in response for all events occurring throughout the world of which you know nothing, as well as new signs of My Father's escalation of His plan, of His mercy, of His goodness, of His patience with His people. Only God could have this kind of patience. For in your reflections you look at yourselves and find yourselves wanting, with shortcomings, weaknesses and vulnerabilities. And, of course, this is true because you are human!

Focus on the Father's goodness for this week, My children, His patience with you and the world, in spite of enormous atrocities, in spite of continued plans of the One-World people, in spite of increased availability now of this chip, this instrument of Satan (microchip that will be the Mark of the Beast of Scripture). You see how the world moves forward in Satan's plan, but in your hearts is the understanding and the trust, the sure knowledge of My Father's power and of My victory. Remind them (the world) of the Father's power, of the gifts of the Holy Spirit so available, so powerful. You can feel the tension, as Heaven requests more prayers and prepares you with words of warning for events that are close. Yes, My children, this country is in grave danger, your beloved country. What sadness that your country must suffer and yet, you know in your hearts the terrible suffering of unborn babies who are torn from their mother's womb; of those who are abused: the elderly as well as the children. The world plummets into darkness like the comet you await, but I am Light. I am Hope. I am Joy and Strength. I am your Courage. I am your All in all, and you have Me and I have you, held so carefully and tenderly in My Heart. Reflect upon this. Be comforted by My love and My tenderness. Be comforted by all of My words, the love of My Mother. Continue to come closer to her. What joy you bring to her heart, My dear ones.

Do not tire of My words of love, for this is your food. This is a balm for your wounds, a soothing of your spirits; and the more you read them, the more you will be soothed and comforted and strengthened. My children, I am eager to begin this march into battle that will see the Second Pentecost (after the Warning when more people than ever before in the world receive and accept the gift of conversion, Cta.) and the outpouring of Our Spirit with the conversion and the healing and the return of so many of Our children. Heaven awaits this time as eagerly as I. Again I remind you to pray to the Father to hasten My return, for as My return is hastened, each event is hastened and will bring you that much sooner to the time of My return and the renewal of the earth. Let nothing else fill your desires, My children, but the needs of others and all the events for which you are prepared. Come to Me! I wait for you and thank you for all the time you do spend with Me. Feel My love this night and My gratitude. Feel this comfort and tenderness. Feel the healing you are being given. You will all have help in mind and body and spirit. Feel My love for you embrace you and wash over you and wash away your fatigue, your weariness. My children, be healed in My Name. Amen."

5/5, "My children, I am your Father, your Creator and Lord. Welcome to the deeper relationship with your Triune God and your Holy Mother that you have received and you are now living. Welcome to My love for you and all My children in the world. I thank you, My dear ones, for being faithful to the need I have for you. Thank you for bringing your devotion to My mercy**, the Divine Mercy shown through the face and the love and the heart of My Son.** My mercy, children, is a refuge as well as the Heart of God Who is Jesus and the Heart of Our Mother, Mary and the hearts of each one of you**. Mercy is that place of comfort, of sure knowledge of being forgiven, of being wiped clean, of being purified, of being united once again and more deeply into the great Communion of Saints.** In union with My Beloved Son, you too are the light of the world; you too are the light of mercy; you too are the experience of forgiveness, of patience, of all the virtues so beautifully presented through the Immaculate Mary; for **you too are all of the things I have given you through My Mercy.**

My dear ones, how you have matured in your hiddenness, in your surrender, in your becoming. How you are fulfilling My Will and filling My Will with new delight and gifts for you. It is that **on-going cycle of obedience to requests, followed by new graces and gifts, followed by new requests and more obedience on your part!** It is the cycle of your life, My dear ones**. It is the cycle of Life!** This day that speaks of summer here in this place, is also the beginning of more plans of Mine to bring the days of fulfillment of Scripture that much closer. When you say WHAT, you wonder HOW and WHO and WHERE? And this is part of your obedience, your patience, your surrender to **simply accept My words now without resistance, without the need for further explanation; but in trust, the trust that allows you to be purified more and strengthened more and filled with more patience.**

My dear ones, thank you for all you give to Me, your Father and Creator, joyfully, patiently. Thank you for being ALL I have created you to be. This next set of events of which there are portents throughout the entire world, and even now in this country, will bring great sadness, even greater sadness, an ongoing sadness to the people of this country. So I ASK THAT YOU PRAY NOW AND BEGIN TO TAKE INTO YOUR HEARTS THE PARTICULAR ONES, WHOM ONLY I KNOW, WHO WILL BE MOST AFFECTED BY THESE NEW EVENTS; THAT THEY WILL COME TO ME THROUGH THESE EVENTS AND BE CHANGED, BE OPENED; THAT THEY WILL BE MORE WITHOUT RESISTANCE AND BROUGHT INTO MY LOVING ARMS, MY ARMS OF MERCY. BEGIN TO PREPARE THEM, MY CHILDREN,

THOUGH YOU KNOW THEM NOT, FOR THEY ARE YOUR FAMILY: YOUR BROTHERS AND YOUR SISTERS.

Praise and thank Me for all of the ways you are needed and used in My plan, for the good that you do, for the graces and strength that you allow others through your prayers. I send you forth now in new strength, in new holiness, with a greater effect and strength for your prayers. I send you forth in mercy and a new desire to help, to prepare those who will grieve so terribly, who will be in such desperation. Thank you, My children, for listening, for believing, for acting upon My words, My requests; for accepting all I bring to you, most especially My love, My mercy. Amen, My dear ones, I bless you now by the power of My Name, in the Name of Jesus and in the Name of Our Spirit. I bless all those in the world as well, who hear My words and believe; and then again, I bless all My children everywhere and I call out to everyone, Come back to Me. Hear Me. Accept My Mercy and live."

5/15, "My dearest ones, I am your Holy Spirit, come once again, dear children of God, with many new graces and the strength for which you ask. When you ask for particular gifts, it is the result now of your further meditation and reflection on your life and behavior, on your own needs; but it is also the results of My inspiration. I ask you to praise and thank Me for these inspirations, for new understandings, for new wisdom and for prudence. The gift of prudence is what helps you walk away from harmful behavior and habits that keep you from repeating sinful behavior and activity harmful to your soul and so often to your body, to your mind, your spirit and your emotions. **Sin, My dear ones, is deadly**. It poisons the air around the sinner.

Occasions of sin are toxic and like poison, for they can poison your mind and your will, your vision of truth, your cooperation with the grace God the Father showers upon you constantly now! One who is wise avoids deadly situations, toxic places and people and occasions. Of course, I remind you of these things to encourage you, dear ones, to avoid all that is toxic and harmful to you and to ask Me for greater clarity of that which can be an occasion of sin for you; that you can quite easily avoid if you are more aware and attempting to do all to improve your standing in God's grace, your cooperation with His Will for you, your response to all the directives of Heaven and the increased prayer that is being requested constantly, everywhere and through so many messengers. There are many constants at which you can look, that you can find in messages being received all over the world. They are the basics, dear ones, the basics of prayer and adoration, fasting and penance, surrender and abandonment to the Will of God.

Peace, faith, daily Mass, reception of the Eucharist and reconciliation. All of these are your lifeline to God, to life as a child of God, to the ability to pray more, to an increase in love and a desire to pray, an increase in the love of God and the Holy Mother and for her rosary and all of the special prayers dedicated to her. All of these are the foundations built on the Christ on which you continue to build and allow Me to build within you and around you; to build around you a protection against the toxic places and people, the deadly behavior that threatens the life of every human being and (most especially) those who sincerely desire to follow

Jesus, to become more like Him every day. Take advantage, dear people, of the graces being given now. Take advantage of all the teachings delivered by Heaven... again, nothing new, perhaps a newer, deeper understanding of important things to your salvation, of important points for the salvation of the world and your role in that salvation, (united to Jesus and His sufferings, his death and resurrection).

Dear people, ponder these words in the coming days. Reflect upon the gifts of the Father and all that you DO have. Reflect upon how good you feel when you can truly praise the Father and thank Him for these gifts. Be encouraged by your place in the Father's plan, by your ability to persevere as you have; for you have accepted the gifts of perseverance We have given you. You ARE progressing in the great call to be more united to your Triune God. Ask now for the ability (as I give it to you) to see and understand and appreciate the magnificence of this gift. You will celebrate Pentecost and I will be there with all of My gifts, wherever you are, pouring them out, showering you, drenching you in gifts and grace. You are beloved of Heaven, dear, dear, ones. You are joy. You are hope. You are mercy. You are love. You are instruments of the Father's Will! Rejoice and praise. We shall celebrate this great Feast together in great unity, people of God everywhere in the world. Amen, dear ones, Amen. Be at peace about everything that develops."

5/19, "My dear ones, once again I am your Holy Spirit come with words of warning, words of comfort, words of encouragement and reminder. The warning in My words, dear children of God, has to do with the spread of fires, has to do with destruction from nature, has to do with events that will take many lives very soon. The encouragement I bring is, of course, much the same as the reminders I bring you of Our promises of protection. Pray much during these summer days for those who will suffer loss, displacement of homes: become refugees themselves. Pray for yourselves that you will have the desire, the eagerness to pray for all of them, as you would a family member. Again I say they ARE your family. You are one in the suffering all of you will do for the Father's plan, for the purchase of salvation in the lives of so many. I bring you the peace of Jesus this day. I bring you a new focus on prayer, new strength to pray long hours: more than one hour at a time, My faithful ones, as a preparation for the future when you will be together and praying many hours in great need yourselves; but also praying then for those for whom you pray now. I pour out My gifts upon you this day. I pour new healing into your minds, your memories, your hearts.

I mend your broken hearts this day, children of God. I mend the tear that sooner or later happens in the tapestry that you know as your own life. By this tear I mean a change, events that leave the picture as you know it changed, torn as your hearts are torn; and lives are torn apart again in preparation for the days ahead. Dear faithful ones, I bring each of you new wisdom this day, for wisdom is most important. Wisdom understands the Father's Will. Wisdom sees with the eyes of God, hears with the ears of God. Wisdom does not judge, for wisdom recognizes that all hearts are broken. Wisdom has compassion, for it reflects upon each life, each person in whom it dwells. Wisdom brings one closer to the virtues and to the heart of Mary, the Immaculate one. Wisdom chooses good, relies on prudence and understanding. Wisdom is the path to new knowledge, even and most importantly a greater knowledge of God.

Dear ones, know that even though you may not experience an emotion or a feeling of any kind, you are being gifted in new ways this day. You are being brought more closely into the Father's Will. You are being given greater protection against the attacks of the evil one, for he will attempt to attack even more because you are faithful, because you are affecting so many in the world because of your prayers. All things are brought to good for those who trust in the Lord, and so I tell you that I bring all of the events in your life this day to great good, and I allow them to bring that good to as many people around each of you as possible, that new understanding and conversion may be given to them also: this conversion you pray for with such heartfelt and strong conviction. Dear ones, your prayers touch the Heart of the Father, the hearts of all in Heaven. They are united with your prayers for your intentions. Dear ones, I bring you new freedom this day, a total gift of freedom to more totally pray and serve, and respond to all you are called for.

There is a new call, dear ones, a call of responsibility to the family of the world, as situations worsen everywhere now. You see this. You have experienced this. You believe this now. Act upon it. New joy is yours, little ones everywhere in the world. These gifts are given, and I pour out the fire of love, a fire of My love: the fire of eagerness and desire to serve, to touch others in the deepest areas of their hearts with compassion, with forgiveness, with tenderness, with gratitude to the Father for you and for the gifts the Father is giving to them through you, because of you. Reread these words, My dear ones, and rejoice. BE FILLED WITH FIRE! How I love you, My children. How grateful I am for your fidelity. Remember this too, your God exists in gratitude for your fidelity. Your God exists to bring you, His creation, to Heaven one day to be totally healed, to be united beyond your imagining with the Triune God, with happiness and holiness that will fill your longing with peace forever. These are mighty days of grace, My children. Take advantage of them, of every opportunity you are offered. Take advantage of your God, My children, and His mercy! Amen!"

5/1, Personal excerpt, "Dearest child, please be at peace. I am your Jesus and I love you. Remember the plan of My Father to renew you and all Our faithful ones when hoards of devastated people run to your doorsteps looking for every kind of assistance. Please tell My children of the world to RECHECK SUPPLIES OF BLANKETS AND PILLOWS THAT WILL BE NEEDED ITEMS OF COMFORT FOR MANY. It will be the only available sleep accommodations in many cases. Many will be sleeping on floors in every room, or porches and in makeshift tents in most cities. Rural areas will see fields given over to makeshift quarters where many will simply sleep outside, protected by whatever is available."

6/ 5, "My dear ones, I am the Spirit of God come again this night to bring each of you new wisdom, new understanding, new clarity of thought, of discernment. Always My dear, dear ones, these need purifying, strengthening, renewing in the hearts and lives of Our faithful ones who strive to do the Father's Will. I bring encouragement to each of you this night on your journey. Do not think that nothing is happening in your spirit and in your lives (for good) when nothing seems to be happening! Do not think you have been abandoned when everything seems to go wrong. It is a darkness yes; it is a kind of black night, a dark night as you understand it.

It is purifying. It is the time of waiting for Jesus to return to you in a new way, as the Apostles waited while He, their Lord, their Jesus was in the tomb seemingly dead to them, as though all had come to the end of the promises they had listened to and believed for those years of travel with Jesus; only to discover Jesus revealed to them in a new and more glorified way. Realize, My people everywhere in the world, that this happens again and again as you experience highs and lows, consolation and weakness, healing and woundedness, strength and weakness, all of the contrasts; and the signs of the escalation of the Father's Will for you, signs of new healing, of new discovery about yourself and about your Triune God and His plan for you and for the world. These things are so important now, My dear ones, to equip you at a deeper level in your hearts and spirits and minds and behavior for this most important time, when I will lead thousands to you everywhere in the world. Again, I bring a reminder from your God: there is no more important time now than to prepare for the Warning and the time immediately following, even though you may see and experience a holocaust of nuclear events before that. Remember, through all of these events (that you expect) you will be protected according to the Father's Will. He cannot go back on a promise, My children. He cannot forget His mercy and His love for you. He cannot be unfaithful, this God of yours. He cannot cease loving you according to My words this night, which have been offered for deeper understanding and deeper comfort, deeper encouragement, a deeper level of hope; for each of you will discover more weakness. Each of you will see yourselves in a new way either personally very soon or collectively with the world! Continue to ask Me for your experiences of discovery: behavior and attitudes, unforgiveness, all of the things that still cling to you, of which you are not aware. My dear, dear ones always the love of Heaven is showered upon you, as you listen and reread these words.

Always, all of Heaven is praying for you. Always, this great united effort of yourselves with all of Heaven to help effect the salvation of the world, (as many as possible) is occurring. Every second of every day, be aware someone is being touched deeply somewhere by conversion, by your prayers, by the prayers of the entire world who is faithful. **Always the Father's Will is being done. Always, Scripture is being fulfilled in a great way. Always, you are becoming who you are created to be: a holier, more honest, more grateful child filled with praise.** Rejoice, My children. Praise the Father. Praise the Son and praise the Spirit Who speaks to you. Be very grateful for these words, My people everywhere in the world, for I speak of YOU! Amen, dear ones, be filled with My Power. Be filled with healing and health and hope. You are loved, so deeply loved, Amen."

FOR MERCY'S SAKE!

6/9, "All of Heaven has rejoiced in the Sacred Heart of Jesus and the Immaculate Heart of Mary. I am your loving Father, and I come with joy for you this day: My own joy about you, My own joy because of you and with you. I increase your joy, your delight in My mercy and IN this new joy. My children, how necessary it is for you to be aware of My Will operating in your lives at every moment. Whatever occurs is what My Will allows for you, My dear ones. Often this is so hard for you to believe and to accept. Often the pain of emptying, the pain of loneliness, the pain caused unfortunately by selfishness causes you to wonder how and why I am allowing these things to occur; but when you stop and remember that My Will desires only good for you, you will be at greater peace, greater acceptance of this Will.

You believe that I am your God, your Creator, your Father. You believe that I love you, that I am speaking now and so, My children, the faith, the trust you feel this moment accompanies you. It has not changed. It does not change unless you turn away, unless you choose not to allow the strength of these gifts to work in you, to act in you, to cleanse and purify you. For this, My dear, dear ones, is always what I am about: to cleanse you; to empty you of sinfulness, of thoughtless habits, of giving in to your need for gratification, your need for the gifts of the world, these gifts that bring excitement and distraction and a false identity to mind and heart: and you know, My dear ones, this cannot be. You know you are My children, and you know what a gift and blessing is this fact, for you forget as soon as something distracts you; calls your name; takes your attention, your eagerness to flee in new directions, your eagerness to let go of the prayerful routine you have come to know, that you realize in the depths of your heart and spirit is the only way you will survive in the coming days!

You are seeing fires everywhere consuming acreage, homes and possessions. You are seeing and understanding this as a fulfillment of the prophesies given through so many of Our messengers. To you, Our faithful ones, this one occurrence alone is enough to give you new reason to be faithful, to pray for victims of fire; but there is so much more, so many more victims, My dear ones. Without My grace YOU would be victims of more, of worse. Instead you are victims of Love! You are victim for the world in union with My Beloved Son, and once again I say: 'How Blessed You Are!' You are asked to rejoice, and so I say again, rejoice! Seek a deeper knowledge, a deeper understanding of your blessings, your gifts, of all that would make you joyful, of all that would make you run into My Heart and into My Will. So many of you have consecrated yourselves now to My Heart. I thank you for these prayers, for all of the special prayers you have said these past days. Know again that your prayers have touched the hearts and lives of many throughout the world; and that they have touched YOUR hearts and your lives as well, bringing more good, more surrender, more joy, more sanctity, My dear ones, into every fiber of your being. How I love you, My children. How grateful I am for your fidelity. Remember this too, your God exists in gratitude for your fidelity. Your God exists to bring you, His creation, to Heaven one day to be totally healed, to be united beyond your imagining with the Triune God, with happiness and holiness that will fill your longing with peace forever. These are mighty days of grace, My children. Take advantage of them, of every opportunity you are offered. Take advantage of your God, My children, and His mercy! Amen."

6/12, "My dearest children, I am your Jesus, come this night and bringing you My strength; for IT IS STRENGTH THAT YOU WILL NEED, NOT JUST FOR THE COMING DAYS, BUT FOR THE INCREASED ATTACKS OF THE EVIL ONE THAT WILL ACCOMPANY THE PRAYER LIVES, THE SACRIFICES, THE PENANCES OUR FAITHFUL ONES EVERYWHERE IN THE WORLD ARE OFFERING. It may seem unjust to you that Satan is allowed to attack, to distract, to discourage, in many instances to bring dismay into your hearts because of the actions of others, when you are trying so hard to be the children We call you to be: all you are created to be and yet you do recall, you do believe, you do understand that **purification is the object of all suffering.**

In the end, all is well. In the end is the beginning; and each temptation, each challenge by the world merely strengthens you, merely points out to you your stand, your love, your commitment to My Father's plan, to all that is holy, to the Beatitudes and the Commandments. My dear ones, the Father will allow more purification now in your lives. You are prepared for this. Do not be surprised. Do not be saddened or disheartened, I beg you, for there is nothing that will overcome you by the word of My Father. I have given you warnings in the past (about possible events in the world) to strengthen you, to give you important reasons to pray for safety for the world; and now I ask you to pray for each other, especially for strength for each other, that you will put on the armor of God in a new way, couched in trust, shined with prayer till this armor gleams and blinds the eyes of the evil one and all who are not of Me. The world calls with greater strength, with greater aloneness, with tantalizing opportunities and events. Keep your focus on My face. Keep your awareness wrapped around My presence.

Not only am I within your hearts, but standing next to you as well. Embrace My Mother and her many Angels that accompany you everywhere. Be aware of them. They really ARE with you. Pray with them. Pray with them as you walk, as you ride, whatever you are doing. Do not be alone. Do not listen to the world. Listen to the sounds of the Angels who sing praises to My Father for your holiness, your sweetness, the gifts you have been given, your special place in My Father's plan. I say these words to everyone in the world who listens. It is true of all of you, I tell you, you fill heaven with delight. Call upon every person in Heaven to pray with you and for you. Thank them and continue to praise and thank My Father, for you are being purified beyond your understanding. When you BECOME the Will of My Father, your prayers and your gifts will know no bounds. You ARE becoming, My children! Remember your armor. Remember to polish your armor with prayer and to wear it with joy! I love you, My little ones. Be joyful. Amen."

6/26, "My dear ones I am your Jesus. Remind yourselves, dear ones, that you are precious to Me, that you are beloved of My Father, that My Mother delights and rejoices in you constantly, that the Angels chant your names before the throne of My Father constantly, that the Holy Spirit continues to pour out the fire of His love, all of the virtues and gifts that you need. In addition to your delight, your happiness, your gratitude for prayers answered, add a constant praise to My Father. I repeat this request again and again, because it is forming you; it is transforming you and turning you into the vessels of praise you need to be. You will bring this gift of praise to all that come to you after the great Warning of My Father. You will be an example, a source, a fountain of praise, and you will lead our people in praise to the Triune God and in gratitude for the holy Mother. The time draws so very near for the fulfillment of more events. You see terrible fires consuming huge acreage, homes and businesses, and you know this is a fulfillment of many prophesies. Pray for these people who are in danger. Pray with all your hearts; but remember at the same time, the Father's Will is being done. Remember the sobering effect of loss, the heroic deeds, the bonding between laborers and all who gather as a result of ongoing tragedies and loss. Remember the Father's Will is present in every event, and He draws the greatest good out of each event, although you cannot see it at the time.

You are being prepared vigorously now for the days for which you prepare! The vigor of the action of the Holy Spirit to show you new weaknesses, those of which you are unaware, is a mighty gift from My Father. Please praise and thank Him for all you discover about yourselves that needs reconciling, purifying, healing, forgiving. I bring the love of everyone in Heaven. You would be amazed at how close you are to all of them and they to you. Once again, your loved ones send support and cheers of happiness for your place in the Father's plan. You know I am speaking to everyone in the world as I bring these words. There is heaviness in My Heart this night, as I view present and upcoming events. There will be much more loss of life, My faithful ones. **Please begin to remember them in your prayers now**, that coming into eternity they will all choose for My Father's Kingdom. **Pray in reparation for their sins,** for they don't know it now, but they count on you totally to make reparation, to bring them the graces they will need. It is an increased responsibility, but what great gifts you are being given in all of these requests.

You can know that gifts are increasing when your responsibilities increase. Remember that, and **when requests increase, you know that the gifts which allow you to fulfill these requests have already been given.** You are learning so much about the Will and the desires and the action of My Father in your lives. How helpful is all of this to prepare you more to live most perfectly in His Divine Will. Do not despair or doubt, for you will see greater events, greater gifts, greater responsibility, but great miracles and healing and conversions, as well. Let My words be a cause for joy, My children, as you are a cause for joy for Me. I love you. There is nothing else you need. Thank you again for loving your God and your Holy Mother and each other. Are you not beautiful gifts to each other? Rejoice!"

FOR MERCY'S SAKE!

7-02 "My dear ones, I am your Mother. I come to you this day with blessings for your country for which you pray so ardently. I pray for the hearts of all those who are frightened, all of those who have despaired of receiving the kind of care and treatment and help they deserve as members of this great country, as children of God; for all of those who live in sorrow, who live at a level that is less than human in some instances. These are not necessarily people who live on the street. These are people who are abused, who are kept in horrific conditions, treated almost like animals, receiving food and love in a lesser degree than most animals that are pets, who are well cared for by their owners. My children in the world, this is a greater problem and occurs in greater numbers than you know; so I will ask you at this special time of celebration of your country that you would look and dig and reach deep within your hearts for love, for commitment to the needs of these dear ones, these sacrificial lambs, those who are helpless, who know nothing but a way of life that is cruel and heartless, that is mindless, that destroys the spirit of all those who are mistreated to a very great degree. Please bring them into your hearts now, into your prayers, into the love that has grown and developed as you have learned to reach out and make the needs and the sufferings of others your own.

I will celebrate with you the last vestiges of true freedom in this country, as great change occurs so quickly now. (Heaven's 'quickly', not ours!! Cta.) Believe my words. Believe in my choice of words. Believe in your need of each other in prayer, in hopes and dreams for the realization of the Father's plan for the whole world that innocence and purity may return soon to all of the Father's creation by the suffering, by the deprivation and in some cases by the enslavement of many throughout the world. My dear children, you have learned to receive words of warning with a level of balance and trust, and I thank you more than you will ever know for reaching this plateau in your minds and hearts and spirits and wills; for it enables you to pray in a better way, to pray in an unselfish way, to pray with the compassion and level of concern for all of those of whom I speak. Together we will make the difference. Together we will cause transformation within the world in spite of the evil and the ruin caused by evil fighting evil; and with the good of our prayers and actions, our desires for our brothers and sisters everywhere in the world to be victorious, to overcome, to heal, and to once again be whole and wholesome and happy and free children of the Father. Reread these words often. Make them your own as you explain, as you ponder, as you think of these needs and these terrible conditions which exist. I count on you to be my soldiers, my apostles of these dreaded new events that unfold in your future. Quickly they will unfold. Amen, my dear little ones. You are mine and I am yours! Rejoice children, **for we belong to each other and together we are the Lord's!**"

7/4, 10:40 P.M. At Home, Jesus said: "My dear child, please take words from My Heart to yours: My people, who wait and wonder over the next act of My Father's Will, I, your Jesus of Peace and Mercy, say to you: please be at peace, My strong and holy ones. These are days in which your armor and weapons are being polished by the prayers and acts of obedience of your brothers and sisters in prayer all over the world. You ARE impacting each other, precious little ones of My Father's Will. As the sun reaches high into the sky with its rays of heat and light, your own souls soar with the heat of the fire of your love and industry on behalf of those who live in darkness everywhere! Your faces glow with the love of My Mother and yours. They reflect the joy of Heaven which radiates to the earth and back again in mutual delight and appreciation. My people, clothed in the breastplate of salvation, you are a mighty and formidable army of My followers, trained by Mary, the Immaculate One, and brought to the place of readiness desired by My Father.

Allow My words to wash over you and caress you with the strength they are meant to bring. Clothe yourself with this strength and comfort and a polish that will attain for you the gleaming exterior by which you are known as soldiers ready for battle against the powers of Hell! You can see the level of fear and panic caused by a lone gunman in his attack on crowds (LAX) of holiday travelers. This alone will convince you of the need to begin again and continue to pray for all who will come to you after the great Warning of My Father. Imagine their panic and renew your visits to Me in My Blessed Sacrament, where I will fill you with a quiet strength with which to overcome the unimaginable panic and chaos that will exist after major devastation, followed by the gift of seeing the actual state of their souls at that moment. **Time will stop, My people!** Is this not a sign of My Father's love for His people and His supreme desire to save them for all Eternity? Do not waste valuable time wondering and discussing the views of many as to what events can be expected in the near future and when they might occur! **Think of the dreadful terror that will carry Our people in all directions like so many leaves blowing here and there in a gale force wind!** This image cannot begin to approximate the actual events and your need for greater strength with which to overcome the tragic, fearful reactions of so many.

You await news of specific events, and I tell you, **the element of surprise will continue**; for this speaks most directly to the dishonor and disgrace of those who follow Satan and perpetrate his lies and fear-producing tactics. There is one thing I wish to say to you, dearest people of the world: Do not let down your guard against the wiles and temptations the evil one holds in wait for you. He desires only your despair and disgust over the long wait willed by My Father, as He strengthens and allows persecutions and trials to challenge you at every turn. Your own purification is being accomplished by each struggle with self and each rejection of the lure and glamour of evil. DO NOT, I say, become discouraged or weakened in your resolve to do good and avoid evil. You ARE winning these preliminary battles. Pray again today and every day for each other and the necessary discipline needed to overcome Satan's plans to destroy you. DO NOT BE FRIGHTENED by My words of love and warning. You KNOW they are meant to protect you from weaknesses that are still present within you, and which continue to do the greatest harm when your defenses are down or less than required to defeat your willful self that continues to demand gratification. I am your sweet Jesus. My Mother and I are with you at every step. Be filled with peace and every gift and blessing you will need for the immediate future."

FOR MERCY'S SAKE!

7/11, Adoration, 3 p.m. First, Jesus was responding to the sadness in my own heart at discovering new levels of sinfulness within myself.... definitely a product of what I consider an "early Warning experience for me... (Carol.)

"My dear one, write words of love for your heart. You suffer torments of your own reality, little one; and I tell you this is but a shadow of the grief and pain that will be experienced by all who come to you soon (after The Warning). You can imagine the degree of despair that will exist within them at the sight and realization of the evil they have espoused for so long. I ask you to share these words with the world now, as they too face new realities about themselves and their own behavior." Then He continued with this direct message to the world:

"Dear people of the world, rejoice that I, your Jesus of Abounding Mercy, bring you words of comfort, as well as new reminders of your need for more reconciliation. Please, dear faithful children of God, do not add to the dangers to your souls by reading and promoting lies and scandalous charges against My chosen ones...words that are the products of Satan's plans to destroy those who suffer daily to do the Father's Will, and all of you who rush to believe and pass along hateful words with a hateful glee of your own! There will be many more such attacks because Satan fills with increased rage and vows to destroy the Father's plan and all His creation. Do not add to Satan's victories. Do not show the malice and lack of mercy in your own hearts by your promotion of malicious gossip and falsehoods. Remember, the Spirit of God is the Spirit of Truth. Without total honesty and integrity in your hearts and actions, you are without the Spirit of God Who is Truth! I hope you are able to hear and feel the strength of My words to you and the anguish I suffer because of your heartless and trumped up accusations against those who have served so faithfully these many years as the ones who share words of love and warning and direction from Heaven meant to be the means (for the instruments you are becoming) of the salvation of all who continue to live in darkness. Come now to My Sacrament of Love and Forgiveness, My people. When you attack the words of faithful messengers, you attack all of Heaven; and I tell you to beware, and Woe to you if you continue! I am your Jesus, Who wishes to save all of you. Do you not know Me yet? Are you not aware that you have a tender God of Mercy, Who longs to forgive all His children again and again and again: right into Eternity, My much loved people. You are My own if you will have Me!!"

7/19, (An excerpt from a personal message.) "I am Jesus, come with the gifts and strength you need now. The days go quickly to bring the world to the place of critical destruction and escalation of events in the plans of the One World Order. Those who will destroy so much of the world are full of confidence and the arrogance required to begin to implement the hateful desires of Satan for My Father's Creation. The people of the world will be alerted by you, and those who listen and believe will live to fight the presence of evil in their hearts and reach out to My Father and to each other. You must spend these days in an all out effort to organize and implement your supplies and foodstuffs. There is more you need to do by way of clearing out clothing and extraneous papers and books. More blankets are in order for your house, and a paring down of supplies you will take along for the times of hiding. A serious focus is required to accomplish all these chores and a succinct presentation filled with the most important facts and reminders for your talks." (Although these are directives for me personally, I am printing them in case your own situation might be further organized by these reminders! Carol.)

7/23, "My dearly beloved ones, I am your God and Father. I come with joy in My heart at the holiness that lives now in your hearts, at the firm commitment and consecration of your whole self that you make again and again to your Triune God and your Holy Mother. I give you *mitigation and mercy and peace, My children, (He was speaking to the prayer we say between decades, *'Father, we ask your peace, mitigation and mercy.') mitigation of events that will mean: not of delay any longer, but still a lessening of the effects of all the events of the future. I tell you, My dear ones, you have come to the place where THE FUTURE IS NOW, as We have foretold to you in the past. There is sorrow in Heaven because of destruction about to visit the earth, this country, many places where I am revered, as well as those places where Satan is a god. Pray for those who do not know Me. **Let them be your number one petition now. Beg for mercy and openness to grace for them. Beg that they will seek forgiveness when the time comes and the grace is offered. Beg for mercy on your country**. Each of you in the world, who hears or reads My words given to so many of you now, pray for your countries. Beg for mercy upon yourselves and your loved ones, and IT SHALL BE GIVEN! But you must pray humbly, knowing that each gift comes through mercy and the generosity of your God Who loves you beyond understanding.

When My people come to you, tell them of My mercy. Tell them that I am a God of love and instant forgiveness, when you seek forgiveness from Me. Tell them that eternity is forever and beyond your understanding. Pray that they will accept all of the grace and understanding I wish to give them. Your mission, (after the Warning .. c.) My children everywhere in the world, is close to becoming a reality in your lives and hearts, your lifestyle, your way of thinking and being. This will change you forever, My children, but as it is meant to do. Along with the sadness in Heaven, there is always joy, so I ask you to be very serious and very joyful. **Events are so close, and you will weep that you did not pray more.** I bless you with all the love of the Triune God and all in Heaven. I heal you. I strengthen you. I lift you up higher in My Plan and within the Kingdom that **is** beginning to blossom on the earth: little patches everywhere! And each of you is a tiny flower with your roots sent deep into the ground of the Heart of My Son. **All will be well, remember that**. Remember, you are never alone. Remember that you are precious children of Mine, and you are loved and loved and loved again and always and forever! Amen."

7/28, "My dearest children, I am your holy Mother, come by a special gift of Our dear God, the Father, Our Creator, Our Lord. I will prepare with you this week your Consecration to God, Our Father. Know that all of Heaven will be making this consecration prayer as well; that We continually and always consecrate you, have consecrated ourselves in a most perfect way to the Father, the One Who created us. Whose Will for us is perfect and Who pours out many new graces now, as the time for events to begin in the world comes closer, as the time for you to move into greater action arrives. My dear children, you are models of grace and fidelity. You are the hope of all in Heaven, united to the graces and the gifts of the Father, the love and the Eucharistic nourishment of Jesus, my dear, Beloved Son, and the fire and the gifts of my Beloved Spouse, the Holy Spirit. It is for these I ask you to lift your hearts in praise and thanksgiving. This week especially I remind you, children, for the rest of your lives you will be praising and thanking the Father in a more heartfelt way, as you see and use the gifts, the graces, the transformation you are being given for all of those who will come to you, for all of those who need your prayers more and more each day. Do not forget that Satan gathers strength each day also, and you must combat his plans and his power with the power given to you by the Triune God.

These are serious days, critical times in history, critical for the future of this country and the world. I do not speak to frighten you, but to remind you during these lazy days of summer when the heat distracts you, when vacations take you away from the routine that nurtures your spiritual growth. Not only will you see greater events soon, but you see ongoing events in the world that speak to the need for prayer, and speak to the unfolding of the Father's plan and the fulfillment of prophecy these many years to the world, as well as prophecies found in Holy Scripture. Remember how much you are needed. Remember how much you are loved and graced. Remember that you are still as needy as ever, that your weaknesses and vulnerability still lie in wait to catch you ùnawares, to pull you away from the Father's Will, to distract you from the focus on the face of My Son, to close your heart and your mind, once again, to the gifts of the Sprit. And so you must always be on guard. You must always be in a place of readiness to do battle, not only with the evil one, but your own weaknesses and sinfulness.

You will never be without the need to fight temptation while we are battling evil and evil's plans for destruction; but most of all, you will never be without the grace and presence of my Jesus, of my own presence with you with many Angels and the help you will need at every moment. Call on Us, my children. Practice this, that in times of danger you might not wonder what to do, or be frightened, or feel helpless or overwhelmed; but that you might **instantly defer to the strength and power of God, my own help and the help of the Angels, whom you will see so very often**! These are mighty promises, My dear children, that you must support with your trust and ongoing, repeated prayer and practice. You are in training! Remember this, my children, for greater battles; and you have made great progress and hold a mighty place, elevated now in the Father's plans for you and for the world. My children, I love you. Be joyful. Be trusting. Be aware every moment that you are my children, that together we can overcome everything and anything; and we will be victorious, for we are united with my Son in this great battle. My dear ones, be filled with the peace of my Son. Be filled with joy, and share the joy of all in Heaven for each other and for them. How blessed you are, my children. Remember this: ALL IS WELL! Everything, everything has been cared for already. **Everyone you love will be saved because of your own fidelity and the special promises and mercy of the Father.** Rejoice, My children. Remember that we walk together, my little ones. Amen."

7/30, "My dear ones, I am Jesus Who brings mercy this night, for which you thank and praise Our Father. Please remember that YOU ARE MERCY, My dear ones, to all you meet if you are living Our requests, if you are attempting to change and to be all you are able to be now because of all the gifts and mercy given to you. Think of the gratitude in your hearts each time you are forgiven, each time you are lifted up in My Father's plan, each time you say, 'Oh My God, I am heartily sorry for having offended you;' each time you promise to avoid the occasion of sin, to confess your sins, to do penance and to amend your life. To be able to say these words and mean them is in itself such a great gift. My dear ones, I ask you to focus this week (and I am speaking, of course, to all My children in the world) on praise and thanksgiving. It is so important for you to practice praising and thanking My Father, for soon you will be experiencing great difficulties, hardships, **ultimately even displacement from your homes, although that will be yet a while.** Even then you must praise and thank My Father, for again these things reflect His Perfect Will for you and for the world at that time. Such changes are ahead of you, My children. To think that you will make these changes and allow yourselves to be changed (**more by events and by the service you will provide to others**) is again, in itself, cause for rejoicing and praise and thanksgiving; for each of these also reflect a particular and special gift you have already been given. To meditate upon these things, My children, will increase your awareness of the degree and amount of gift you have been given. This too is very necessary for your growth and for your further ability to praise and thank My Father. Appreciation is a heart and mind expanding experience, My children. You know how good you feel when someone voices appreciation for something you have done. I do not call you simply to make My Father feel good, for that is not necessary; but **appreciation is necessary because it changes you** in a way you MUST be changed, to grow in a way you MUST grow, and expand your hearts, that you **will embrace with gratitude and joy everyone who comes to you from this moment on**. These numbers will increase gradually at first; but the time for which you have been prepared and of which I speak (after the Warning of My Father) will mean a **tremendous influx of huge numbers of people that will be overwhelming without the overwhelming grace and strength you will be given, that you have already!**

My dear ones, you know I speak of serious things because it is so important, not just for you, but most importantly for those who come to you. Thank you for responding as you do to all of Our requests now; so I say with confidence: you WILL comply with these requests made tonight, and for this I give you My gratitude and the gratitude of all in Heaven. How united we are, My children. How joyful this is. How precious you are! I am so close to you, My children.

Believe this. Meditate upon this fact. Let this awareness grow within your minds and hearts. Allow this fact to bring great joy to your spirit. There is no cause for sadness or fear or doubt or discouragement. On the contrary, there is every reason to rejoice, to celebrate. The victory is already won in which you will participate, My children. What joy! What gift! What grace! What favor each of you has received and lives in the Father's plan. How I love you!"

8/8, the Father spoke: "My children in their little, humble and tender ways will draw many to the Heart of My Son. All of you have no idea how many watch you and are changed, merely by your kindness, patience and very obvious love for your God and Mary, the Immaculate One. Become the holy ones I need you to be, as the enemy increases his attack. Do not be concerned as to when events occur. EVENTS ARE OCCURING EVERY MOMENT NOW. PLANS ARE MADE AND FINALIZED THIS VERY DAY. You are ready in minds, hearts and spirits. This is what counts. Do not fear little illnesses and set backs. They are nothing before My power. Be encouraged in the face of your own weaknesses. **These keep you where I desire you to be in humility and surrender**. It will be soon, I promise you, that events will take you and your families to a new place of conversion which you await in great hope. What joy will fill your hearts, as loved ones turn and embrace Me and all the words given by Heaven these many years. **Practice peace of spirit even in the face of excitement. Practice letting go of emotions connected to these events that, happy or sad, you might simply be at peace and acceptance of all I desire for you and for them. Believe I am speaking. A special place is allowed for patient ones, who will explain again and again and again the ways of My Will, the desires for all of My people.**

IT IS NO LONGER A MATTER OF PAST, PRESENT AND FUTURE. IT IS A MATTER OF NOW: A FULFILLMENT NOW OF ALL OUR WORDS AND PROMISES, A TIME OF PROTECTION FROM DANGERS YOU DO NOT SEE ... POSSIBILITIES ALLOWED BECAUSE OF THE PROTECTION OF MANY ANGELS WHO ARE WITH ALL OF OUR FAITHFUL. This fact, this presence of Angels is SO REAL, and will be so comforting for all who believe and accept this gift. To accept a gift is to enable it. Begin to remind each other of the constant presence of these precious ones who are filled with joy at this mission of protecting and praying for all of you, of being an atmosphere of holiness in which you live and move and have your being. Praise Me this day, for you are highly favored and blessed. You are needed by your God for His people. There is much to do, My children; but first, always there is praise, love and gratitude that your hearts might pour out constantly on Me and all of those who come to you. Praise and thank Me for them. Love them NOW. They belong to you as brothers and sisters in the great family of God. You are loved, My dear, dear ones, with all the tenderness and might and power and mercy in My Heart."

8/6, "Jesus said: "My daughters, thank you for your prayers and the love in your hearts. Thank you for your devotion to Me and for new levels of surrender to My Father's Will. You are becoming ones who will protect My weak and lost ones on many occasions. You cannot imagine the helplessness, the fear and fatigue in the minds and hearts of all of them. This will be the result of more than a sense of loss. **It will be a near death of each one: emptied so quickly by removal of everything they have known and everything they have loved.** Contemplate this situation, dear precious ones of My Father's Will, that you might **explain to others the near despair that will be present in all that come**. It is right that you focus on this period of time. It will help you pray and prepare for them now, for warlike destruction and annihilation of great numbers of people. **Imagine portions of this country and the world just disappear, destroyed, missing from the shape and outline that has been so familiar. Everyone, even Our faithful ones, will know great shock and an inability to move or speak, so great will be this annihilation! Pray for them: your brothers and sisters, who struggle just as you do to follow Our words. Hearts will be broken. Sorrow will be crushing. Disease will be rampant because of lowered defenses and a weakened will to live. I show you these things to prepare you, of course. You can see how necessary it will be to have the ability to remain calm, to have order in mind and will at this time. Share these words with those who listen, that more might be able to be a source of strength and understanding.** Your hearts are a deep well of compassion and patience and peace from which you will pour out these gifts upon the wounds of everyone. Again... you will have every gift and strength needed to tend to all, whoever they might be. Expect the mighty (perhaps priests or bishops or leaders.. c.a.) to come for strength from the lowly. Expect those who should be leaders to admit with sorrow their pride and many errors. Many of these will be soothed and comforted by your own words, forgiveness and compassion. You must offer every struggle from now on, and they WILL INCREASE, for healing and conversion for all these dear ones, led so far away from truth by the evil one. Remember how much you are loved. Believe it! Amen."

8/12, "Dearest child of My Immaculate Heart, how tender a heart grows as love grows, as sorrow for sin increases, as understanding of the wretchedness of the human condition renders humility a greater characteristic of the soul. Strength increases as you spend time meditating upon the goodness and mercy of Our God and of Me, your loving Mother.

It is a joy to contemplate the gracious generosity of the Father's gifts to us. This has been a core of My own prayer life since I was old enough to understand; and praise to the Father was My very breath from the moment of the Angel's first words to Me, and even throughout the terrible suffering of My Beloved Son and the joy mixed with sadness when He departed the earth to return to His Father in Heaven. Understanding gave a greater depth and richness to the praise (tinged with longing) that burst from My Heart and lips until the moment I was assumed into Heaven to be united forever with My Son, Jesus; with My Spouse, the Holy Spirit and with My Father and Creator God. Continue to offer this devotion to Me with a more perfect zeal from your loving heart and desire to embrace the Will of Our God. I will never leave you without my own gifts and strength and desire to serve My Son. I am your Mother and Companion in sorrow and in joy and in praise of God."

8/20, "My dearest children, I am Mary, the Immaculate One, your holy and loving Mother. I come to remind you of many things. My children, first of all, of My love. Remember that you are cherished in my Heart and held there, nourished and protected and hidden from the evil one. If you will accept this gift, this opportunity by living all of my requests; by living as a true child of Mary, as one devoted and committed to Me and My requests to all those who will come to you. It is so very important that you begin now, even more, to pray for them, that they will be open to one of the greatest outpourings of the Holy Spirit in the near future. My children, how far you have come on the path to the Father's plan for the world and His Will for you personally. Oh My dear ones, be encouraged, be joyful, be grateful, be filled with excitement, be filled with eagerness to fulfill the role given to you to fulfill the needs of Our people and the needs of God, Our Father! These needs are those He chooses to have, that He might acknowledge to you His need of your presence in His plan, your fidelity to His call, your honest and sincere response to all that is requested of you.

It will never be that these dynamics, these ways of life that you have chosen and accepted, could be mentioned too often or their importance belabored! My children, **let your hearts smile, let your spirits sing and jump with joy at your place in the Father's Plan!** It is, of course, His Will that you do not realize the enormity of the gifts you are given, but you also do not realize the enormity of the events on your horizon. It is difficult for me to speak of destruction to you and yet, I do all the Father commands me in obedience and gratitude, and so I mention this because of its imminence in the world. I mention the need for your focus not on destruction, but on the need of prayer and a constant focus on the people in the world, who will come to you and all of Our faithful everywhere; but just as important, My dear ones, are those who will be obstinate, and refuse and reject all the words of warning that will be given. There are many whose hearts have hardened because of the long period of time, the length of time the Father has taken to begin to fulfill His Plan at this new level by allowing Satan more power, by allowing destruction to occur everywhere in the world. You know, my children, how my Heart grieves for all of you, every one of my children everywhere. I need for you to be strong. You need for you to be strong, my dear ones, and certainly Our children who come will need you to be strong; but I tell you, you WILL do this! For in this outpouring of the Spirit will be enormous gifts for all the faithful: gifts of perseverance, of strength beyond human endurance, of endurance beyond your understanding.

The opportunities you are being given now and in the future are unmatched in history. Pray for each other, my dear ones, for your fidelity; that your strength, that your level of interest and the investment of your whole self might remain at a very high level. There is nothing more. You ARE as prepared as you are going to be now with supplies and water and bedding. For years now these have been requested, and now it is simply a matter of praying and focusing on the needs of the world. THE WORLD, MY CHILDREN, IS ABOUT TO EXPLODE. ONLY THE FATHER'S HAND HOLDS BACK THE DESTRUCTION AT THIS POINT. Praise Him and thank Him for all His goodness to you all of these years, for bringing you to this place, this point in this journey. You are loved. You fill all of Heaven with joy and gratitude, with delight that you live out and fulfill your promises to God, made on behalf of Our people. Be at peace with my words, my children, for there is nothing to do except trust in God's might and His Will, and to live out this trust in prayer and in joy and surrender. You are loved mightily by all of Heaven. I kiss each of your foreheads as I depart. Amen."

8/15: This is another excerpt from a personal message given by our God and Father as part of His words about nuclear destruction, and His desire to deliver His people from "annihilation and suffering that is beyond anyone's ability to imagine." He speaks of the safety of the world that will be enabled through warnings to everyone:

"Begin now to pray for them and their instant recognition of truth, their ability to accept it and move into action immediately in order to save their loved ones and themselves. They will be so blessed and gifted for this obedience. They will begin to lead others in making the proper choices, and saving them too. As you struggle with the difficulty of this mission, remind them what is at stake. Remind all to keep this in mind from now on, as they pray and prepare for all who will come to them according to My Will for each of My children. Begin to pray now also for those who will NOT comply. Remind them to choose life while they have this most important opportunity. Those who refuse will face a long time of suffering: first here on earth and then long years in a Purgatory of wretchedness and pain because of their pride and obstinacy. The time is upon the world. They are your first priority and reason to exist now! Your cooperation and obedience will be service to Me and the highest level of love and mercy on Me and the people of the entire earth. It is NOW!" (Refers to the Day of the Lord, a period of time… cta.)

8/27, Jesus said: "My very dear ones, I bring you greetings this night from all of Heaven to you gathered here and to everyone in the entire world who hears and believes and lives My Words and all the words of Heaven. The heat here (Arizona) is oppressive, while in other places a chill begins to fill the air; and so you know that seasons are changing. The oppressive heat reminds you of the progress (still in many places) of fires; reminds you of those who suffer in Purgatory, for this indeed is a deadly heat that goes on and on in your experience, that you and they (in Purgatory) know will end one day. And so you are filled with hope and joy and trust. It also reminds you of the suffering fires of Hell: these fires that never burn out; these fires that are chosen by those deadened by sin, by grievous sin: mortal, deadly, rejecting all good, all mercy, all beauty, all possibility. Remember this, My children, as you pray for all of these, for it is the cause of sadness in your own life for those in Purgatory. And the heat and the fire fills and feeds the hatred in the hearts of those who have chosen to be in Hell.

I speak these words this night, My dear ones, for you speak of patience and perseverance this night in your prayers gathered here. I tell you, you will have the patience and perseverance and trust you seek. For it is in living out the need for these gifts, the awareness of their lacking in your life that develops these gifts, that causes you to plead and beg for them, to call out to the Father for mercy once again upon yourselves, your loved ones and the world. And this is as it should be, My children. But remember it shall be yours, and it is in waiting that you are practicing. It is in practicing that you will be more prepared, I say again, for those who come to you; for **they will require more patience and perseverance than you ever could even imagine**! It is difficult now, yes, and you know it will be difficult in the future, and your whole being strains against the waiting for the time to arrive when My Father's promises are fulfilled. Remember My words this night FOR THEY WILL BE FULFILLED, A BEGINNING OF ALL YOU AWAIT. This fills you with joy and trepidation, as well it might!

It will be so necessary to have the most profound trust in the promises of protection, **for what you will see and experience in an ongoing manner will terrify, will defy the imagination, will overwhelm many; but not so for you, My strong and prepared ones,** not so for you, My warriors of prayer and obedience. This great Army of faithful ones throughout the world that prays for each other, that sustains and supports and nourishes each other in every corner of the world with the strength enabling always new gifts to be given! Oh My children, rejoice, rejoice that you are highly favored in My Father's plan. Though this is repeated often to you, there is no way you can imagine how blessed you are, how gifted: what **you will do and enable with your prayers, your openness to the words of the Holy Spirit, the miracles and conversions, the healing, the return of peace to shattered lives and frantic hearts. My children, let these images fill your hearts and minds as you pray, for it will be thus!** Increase your prayers, My dear ones, for they are needed. It IS possible, My dear ones, for YOU ARE NEEDED! Feel My love. Feel the tenderness in My voice and in My presence here with you. I LOVE YOU! Amen, My dear, little ones everywhere; thank you for the love in your hearts for Me."

9/3, "My dearest children, I am your God and Father. I come this night with special blessings and new strength once again for all of you and for all in the world who listen and live My requests. My dearest children, how close you are to understanding My Will for the world, to understanding My ways that are not your ways; and when there is a lesser understanding on your part, there is a greater act of trust and surrender in your hearts! I wish to thank you for this. I tell you, your gifts will be a hundred-fold: beyond your imagining for this new peace you have come to in your faith, in your obedience, in your cooperation with My Will. Truly you have learned to surrender. Truly this has been a monumental hurdle, a great distance that you have traveled, a mighty obstacle that you are overcoming.

Again I thank you for all of your efforts and struggles to learn My Will, to live it, to be obedient to every event that occurs in your lives, for this is how you know My Will for you. **It is simply that which occurs**.

You are also working at being joyful. Joy can only be part of your tapestry, of your story when there is trust and obedience and surrender. Joy is the fruit of these virtues, of this struggle; the gift that is given, the strength that will enable you to continue. Although each event may not seem like a gift, or something for which you would be joyful, yet I tell you, it is! JOY AND SORROW ARE TWO SIDES OF THE SAME COIN. IT IS A COIN OF GOLD, MY CHILDREN, WITH WHICH YOU AFFECT AND CO-REDEEM MILLIONS (uniting our actions with Jesus'… cta.) This very fact can increase your joy! It is a time before battle when gifts are finely honed, polished, brought to the best of their ability: the highest level of performance. So it is with you, who are weapons in the hands of the Almighty and your holy Mother, weapons against the evil that lives in the hearts of most of the people on the earth.

Continue as you are. Continue to praise Me, for this one act on your part does more for you than I could ever explain. It is one of those facts that you accept and act upon in faith. **Praise transforms you like nothing else can.** Believe this, My children. In the midst of a broken heart, in the midst of a broken life, of broken dreams and hopes, **praise will keep you from drowning in the many things that can overwhelm each one. Praise is a buoyant effort, keeping you on top of each situation, keeping you breathing, speaking, calling out your heart, and mind-expanding as you embrace each event. It is one of the great mysteries of life, this dynamic of praise** that (you must) simply be grateful exists, My children. It will save you from disaster, from depression, from dissolving into self-pity and worse. Always, My dear ones, I give you the opportunity to grow, to become stronger, to be more united with My Jesus and your Triune God. Praise and thank Me for all those I will send to you, for there will be many; and they, too, will transform you like nothing else on earth could do! This time of waiting is not a time wasted, is not a time that is unprofitable or lost, unless you use it foolishly. I have brought My gratitude this night, and so I pour out new gifts, the gifts each one needs particularly, as you request. Pray, My children. PRAY FOR THE HOLY FATHER, THE BELOVED VICAR, WHO'S TIME OF SUFFERING INCREASES. Thank you, thank you, thank you for acting in love. Be filled with the peace of My Son and know that you are cherished, yes, beyond words, beyond understanding, beyond your ability to grasp; but you will see the results in gift and miracle and conversion and harmony-out-of-chaos one day."

9/10, "My dear ones, I am your Jesus. I have come with gratitude again from all of Heaven. It is mercy My Father desires, and so We are most grateful when you request, when you pray for mercy for the whole world. It will be the answer for each one individually and collectively for the world as one family and especially for sinners. This night, children, the world realizes the possible dangers everywhere, realizes the irrational plans and behavior of terrorists, and so the world, once again, is on its knees tonight and will be so tomorrow. (First anniversary of 9-11-01 destruction of Twin Towers in New York City ..cta) This prayer is especially blessed by the Father, is given great power and fire by Our Holy Spirit and is joined by My Mother and Myself for every person in the world. Your beloved country falters in all that is holy, in all that is right and honest and true. If you only prayed for your country for as long as you live on this earth, you would be praying always. I have told you at length before of difficult, destructive and disastrous events about to occur in this country, and now we are closer than ever. And so I remind you and I request (from everyone in the world) prayer for this country, for it is indeed needed, and you are indeed My prayerful ones, My beloved ones whom I love and cherish and hold within My Sacred Heart. This night, My children everywhere in the world, be hopeful; for it is important to balance your understanding of difficult events to come with the joy of knowing that the Father's Will is being fulfilled, and in each event Scripture is fulfilled, and a little bit more of the evil in the world is removed.

You will see that it will be a LONG WAIT FOR MY RETURN, although **it will seem longer than it will truly be**. Continue to pray for patience for each other and for the world; but the dear ones in this country do not know suffering and deprivation of the kind that you will see and feel and taste. Think about joy again. **Think about being joy, making that choice for everyone around you and then for the world**; for you know now the possibility of sending joy to the farthest corners of the earth, if you would make time for this kind of prayer and do this. Joy is so healing and so comforting. It makes one feel alive and loved. You have become vessels of joy, and so I ask you to pour out this joy upon each other. You have become vessels of all the virtues and the gifts that We have given you. Remember that! And so you have this store, this treasure, this deep well in which to dip, in which to reach deeply for your own strength, your own comfort, your own peace of mind that will then pour out upon others also. I mention these things tonight, of course to prepare you for days ahead; for in frightened people during frightening times, it is those who are able to reach deep inside for strength and hope and courage and all the gifts you have, who will bring peace once again into the hearts of those who are so frightened and so lost, who lack understanding, who lack an anchor (which you will become) until you lead them to My Father and to Me and to Our Spirit and the Holy Mother. Dwell in the peace I bring this night, for you will not know peace much longer, peace as you desire it in sunshine and carefree days. Pray for each other that all might be friends, that all might be reconciled, that all might be and live as brothers and sisters, as you were created to be. Receive My gift of peace. Receive My love. Receive Me, My children. Amen."

9/17, "My dear ones, I am Jesus, Son of God and Son of Mary, the Immaculate One. Thank you for remembering and reflecting upon the Sorrows and the Sufferings of My Mother this night (feast of Our Lady of Sorrows on 15th.) Thank you again for your devotion to her, for coming close to her in these very critical times in your history. Thank you for all the love you share with her and in telling others about her, spreading devotion to her, whom I love beyond telling. This night I wish to bring you into My Sacred Heart in a special way for this night and the days ahead. In other words, I will keep you there! You will feel My Presence this night and the gift of peace I give you. It is a special gift from My Father to encourage you, to strengthen you, to bring you to a new level of holiness and commitment to His plan. You see and hear the danger in the world. Already there are aggressive attacks by the United States. Pray for your country, My children. Once war begins between two countries, nuclear intervention will most definitely be part of that conflict and spread to the world quickly. I ask you again to bring balance to all you are hearing from Heaven, to all of your preparations and your prayers. Thank you for all you are doing to answer the requests of Heaven. Thank you for loving Me. How united we are and again, how precious you are in My eyes. The world's prayers increase as events increase, and so you can see an answer to your own prayers in that area. I do not need to tell you more of coming events at this point, for there is so much for which to pray now and in general for the world. I call out to people everywhere with My love and My gratitude, and encourage you to continue.

Be the impetus behind your own decisions to pray each day! Do not wait for another conflict or event of destruction. As long as you are praying, your prayers are affecting the world. They are affecting events, mitigating and lessening destruction. That in itself is the first reason to pray, after the conversion of all hearts. My children, I simply wish to bring you into My Heart now, so there will be a long period of silence as you sit. Know that I am holding you, embracing you close to My Heart, and in a mystical way I bring you into My Heart and hold you there, bathing you in My love and in the protection of My Precious Blood. It is protection I have promised, and so a new level begins this night, as the world comes closer and closer to confrontation. My people everywhere, as you read these words, I ask you then to sit in quiet for a period of time. **Believe that I bring you, too, into My Heart, giving you many special gifts and new protection, new strength, raising you to new levels in My Father's Plan.** Focus on My love for you and be filled with a peace only I can give you: a healing and comforting peace, a cleansing and renewing peace, a loving and gentle peace."

9/18, Adoration, "Dearest little weary one, please take words of great importance for you and for the world. I am your God and Father. Please pray again to Our Spirit for the gift of openness and protection from the distractions of the world.

'My dearest people who listen to the words of Heaven shared by this and all Our messengers, please be attentive to what I tell you now. As your Creator and Lord, I call out to you for an alert and positive response throughout the next weeks and months. The world is on the brink of war. It is not a matter of if, but when. It is not a matter of how much destruction and loss of life, but the need for more prayers for conversion for all those who will be brought into Eternity. There will be another terrorist event in this country that will push your government and military past any hesitation to begin its own retaliation against the countries that support terrorism, supplying the weapons and opportunities for those who are instruments of the plans of the Antichrist and New World Order. Your military is poised and totally prepared to respond with might and aggression **toward leaders who have been chosen to launch the next surprise attack on your country.** Remember, My faithful ones, **each event has been agreed to by the superpowers of the world.** While your prayers will always be necessary for the salvation of the entire world, **the plans of Satan will be given many victories in order to fulfill Scripture**. As you view acts of terrorism, you can see plans and the need to retaliate brought to a peak. The necessary events to raise levels of pride and patriotism and defense will continue to set the stage for what will be obvious to the world as the need for a war and **all the excuses given for the aggression of your country**.

I ask you to begin now to pray for your own preparedness to act with heroic valor on behalf of the earth that is about to be scourged by the hateful lashes of Satan's army of terrorists, the instruments of destruction, through an incitement of world war. This will also give those proponents of a one world government reasons acceptable to the greater number (of people) for giving more power and control to the UN, thus losing more freedom at home, more privacy and the gifts obtained by those who died to obtain this freedom. Stay in close proximity in prayer groups and families and unity with your Triune God and Holy Mother, your special Saints and Angels. Pray that hardened hearts will begin to believe again to see a fulfillment of the words of Heaven, as the world moves towards certain war and fulfillment of Satan's plans. Do not dwell in fear, precious children, but in joy and gratitude that you begin at a new level today to affect the people of God throughout the world with deeper and more heartfelt and loving prayer for their eternal salvation and happiness, and your own continued journey into holiness. I shower you with new strength of commitment now. Be filled with joy and hope and gratitude, My loved ones."

9/24, "My darling sons and daughters, it is your Mother, come to you this night with a heart brimming with tears, with sadness, with heaviness of heart. Your country, your dear country; it is not my intention to frighten you or belabor the point of destruction, but you must pray more for your country. It cannot be something casually remembered. It cannot be that you would remember now and then, or not take this request most seriously. Your country, my children, is in grave danger. So many factions vie to be first. So many tensions develop on your national scene that will also impact the international scene. So many lives are at stake, and I call upon the world to pray for YOU this night, as you have prayed for the world and for many who have gone into eternity in large numbers in the past. It is not fear you should bring to prayer, but concern and sorrow, a serious commitment to supporting this dear country of yours, the freedoms you have now. **You have no idea what it will be like to live without freedom, to live with fears, to live with oppression, to live with many new laws, many restrictions, many opportunities you take for granted now that just disappear in developments that immediately are beyond your reach.**

My children, we have made a promise to each other long ago: a promise to pray together, to be companions in sorrow, in joy and in hard work. The amount of prayer that is needed, My dear, dear ones, will amount to what you think of as hard work! **I am asking you to forego all other activity now, to focus only on prayer, on time in silent adoration and praise and thanksgiving** before My Son, united to the Father and Their Spirit in the great Sacrament of the Altar. My dear ones, we begin at a new level, you and I, the great Communion of Saints to combat evil, to call out for mitigation and mercy as long as possible, for as many as possible. Do not think of this as drudgery, but as the kind of gifts given to the Saints of old; **for you are the Saints of new, of now and forever! My dear ones, we must be one: one in our pleading with the Father, begging for this mercy.**

I remind you that this does not mean that events will be cancelled or done away with; but **still possible is mitigation and a lessening of destruction, and mercy for all those who will go into eternity.** My children, the Father allows Me to speak to you this way, this night out of His great love for Me and for all of you and all of His children everywhere. Evil has **just begun** to manifest itself upon the earth. You do not yet know this level and degree of evil. You have not yet seen this kind of attack on the innocent, so I ask you to gather your courage and your strength to consecrate yourselves once again to My Immaculate Heart and to the Triune God, and pray with Me, that we will be victorious for as many as possible**; that as many as possible will accept the mercy of God, Our Father, for their everlasting salvation**. I count one you, My dear ones, to be with Me."

9/27, "My dearest children, I am your Jesus with you this night. You know My love for My Mother. Whenever you gather in obedience to her requests, you fill My Heart with a joy that cannot be named, that cannot be described, that defies words and joy that fills My Heart with such gratitude. New blessings and gifts, new healing pours out from My Heart this night as a cup would overflow, so filled with gratitude would it be! Continue to pray for people everywhere, that they will increase their prayers. Continue to pray as you are this night. Come together as often as you can. Throughout your day, consecrate whatever you are doing as a prayer of petition for mercy for your country, as a prayer for the conversion of all those taken into Eternity. Do not dwell on destruction; but **dwell on the Perfect Will of My Father, His perfect love for you, His desire to save and to bring into Paradise as many as possible. This will always be the intention and the reason for all of your intentions, for it is only goodness that is desired by your God.** It is only love that pours forth from Love, and it is a response of love that is requested by Love.

My children, it has been mentioned to you that these are golden opportunities for a greater unity with your God and your Holy Mother, all of the Angels and all the Saints and all of those, which is everyone in Heaven, who are praying now for your country. Your country, My children, has not responded in any way according to the hopes and desires of the Father, except for the few faithful, such as yourselves, and those who gather everywhere in every corner of the world to offer prayers of praise and to beg for mercy. Pray in thanksgiving for each other. Pray in thanksgiving for those who need your help and your prayers, for these keep you where My Father desires you to be in His plan for you personally to become more and more the holy ones of God, the holy ones of this most critical and important Era. **You will each be a rock for those around you, for you will not shudder or fall apart or embrace hysteria or chaos, and confusion will not flood you minds; and for this of course, you will continue to praise My Father.** And when all of these things, these emotions, a loss of self-control, attacks on so very many occur, it will only be your strength, your backbone of steel, your core of trust that will reach out and embrace each one around you, and they too will succumb to the might of My Father's arm (in trust.) All of Heaven is with you, so united are you becoming, so entered more deeply into the great Communion of Saints. Give praise and thanks, My dear ones. You are truly blessed beyond your knowledge, and most certainly it is pure gift of My Father's mercy and His love and His gratitude for each of you. I ask you to open to the love of your Triune God, that you might know that truly you are loved, appreciated, cherished. I love you. My Mother sends her love and her gratitude. Amen."

9/29, "My dear ones, I am your God and Father. I come to you this day of rest to tell you that you have earned a holy rest in the Presence of My Son and all of Heaven: a rest that is about to strengthen and renew you beyond your hopes and dreams; a rest and renewal that will be needed in the days to come. I speak to My children everywhere in the world who are praying; but especially those who are praying more for this country, who act in obedience, who obey with action of prayer, of adoration, of silence and surrender. Your response this time to prayers for your country is a more seasoned, more informed, more experienced response after the events of last September; after the ensuing months of heartbreak and greater realization of what it means to lose a loved one, especially in great numbers; for all of the people of this dear country that you love, of which you are proud to be citizens, whose freedoms you enjoy with gratitude, albeit taking for granted very much of your freedom and your gifts here. It has been mentioned to you that Satan has plans by which you would be deprived of your freedom. And so it is that events move this very day toward a loss of freedoms you have always known and have known for hundreds of years here in this great land of opportunity. I say this to encourage you to persevere, to continue in your prayer, to hold up this country and to uphold everything this country, **under God**, stands for and has stood for.

You will not believe the changes that will occur here, and it will be sudden and they will change your lives completely. I pour out the Spirit of

God this day upon this country and upon each one of you in the world who prays. There has been a response in this country to the call of the Holy Mother of God, but alas, never what it could be. Such possibility and opportunity is passed by, rejected, not listened to, is ridiculed as well as are those who uphold the call of Heaven. I, your Creator and your God, am proud of you who have become true warriors in a **battle that will go on longer than you would ever wish, longer than I would wish. Except that Scripture must be fulfilled, and Scripture is filled with events that will occur because they have been written!**

My children, love each other. Do not argue! Do not harbor bitterness or unforgiveness for one more second, no matter what occurs in your life. Do not be angry. Praise and thank Me for opportunities (suffering, struggles, disappointments, etc.) to offer for the conversion of this country. From now on, this focus of prayer will be yours. From now on, a threat hangs very seriously over your country (of devastating events.) Trust, My people; trust the mercy of your Father. Trust that you are protected in the plans for the salvation of everyone written in the Book of Life, of everyone who will accept the gift of salvation forever and ever because of you, and your love for everyone. Feel and taste the freedom you will always have: the freedom of a child of God, the freedom to give yourselves to your God and Creator, the freedom to rejoice in the Communion of Saints, in all I call you to be and to become. It is beyond your imagining. I love you. You ARE MINE! The Spirit pours out upon you now (this new freedom) and in the days to come. ENJOY IT, MY CHILDREN! Amen."

10/1, "Dear children of God, I am your Holy Spirit, come this night to bring graces and the strength of warriors, for that's what you are and who you have become. You are called in these critical days by your God to pray, to combat evil, to combat the plans of Satan, the great enemy of your God and Holy Mother and your great enemy. And so it is as warriors that you spend so much of your time praying, practicing obedience to the Commander, practicing being at the disposal of the Commander and all of His plans and all of His needs for your time and energy. I remind you again to say that prayer, to read that Scripture passage and put on the armor of God and all that it means. Do not be frightened, but be moved to action by these emotions, these feelings, these reactions you are having.

The world, My sweet little ones, is about to explode in different places, and then in many places and then all at once everywhere! You ARE prepared for this. Do not dwell on possibilities that 'might' happen. Do not, I tell you, dwell on headlines and sensationalism, for **it is the silent and peaceful warrior who does the most good in combating evil in this particular battle.** Pray for each other more, My people everywhere, in the spirit of unity, for it is this unity with which you must combat the strength and the wiles of Satan and his demons and all of his followers. It is in unity that you find your greatest strength; but also your healing, your comfort, your enrichment, your enjoyment, your encouragement, dear ones, for you will be encouraging and enabling each other all along the way.

You must begin now to lay the proper foundation for the time when you come into a community and stay in community until Jesus returns. These are momentous and great acts and events that will occur in your future even beyond your ability to grasp in importance. So they are mentioned again and again to make you more familiar, more comfortable with the ideas of so much change in the world and in your personal lives, in the very environment in which you will live, in the way you will live. All of these things take prayer and practice and surrender, but of course I tell you again, YOU WILL DO EVERYTHING REQUESTED. YOU WILL BE ALL YOU WERE CREATED TO BE AND YOU ARE CLOSE, SO CLOSE TO SEEING YOUR SOULS AS YOUR GOD SEES THEM. I know your hearts rejoice, as your Triune God rejoices and all of Heaven rejoices. Pray to Me for openness. **Pray to Me for an acceptance of all that you will discover; for I tell you, in many instances YOU WILL BE SURPRISED. It will take you a moment to accept the reality, the truth that you will see; and so prepare yourselves, children, in every way you can. But most of all, pray for each other's preparedness, for it is in reaching out to others that you are prepared the most and in the best way**. Remember these words. When you see them (all the people who come to us,) you will understand. There will be many, many, who come to you; and until then, you will be working and praying and reconciling your own sinfulness, your own thoughtlessness and carelessness and all of the things that make up being human. My children, rejoice! Each of you is so very blessed. I pour out new gifts again this night, new strength, new courage, new hope, everything you need. ENJOY, MY PEOPLE! Be merciful to yourselves, and accept joy, live joy, be joy for the world. You are loved so mightily!"

10/8, "My dear ones, I am your Lord and your God, your Father: the One Who has created you, Who sustains you in My plan and for My plan and through My plan. I greet you with special joy this night as you lift your hearts and minds and souls through this precious rosary of this precious, Holy and Immaculate One. Know that I am listening in a special way throughout this month (as you pray the rosary) to all the intentions for which you pray; and will give more mercy, more of whatever it is you desire, that you request, for which you pray, especially for your country. My dear ones, how happy I am to see you filled with new hope, filled with the trust that will enable more gifts to be given. Time is no longer an ally. Time is no longer something that you think of as endless or of which you have so much. For soon and very soon, **you will know what it means not to keep time the way you do now, not to have time as a guide, as a framework, as a structure as you always have. (This has been explained in the past, almost in the beginning at Medjugorje, as how we will live after the Warning and beyond.... Cta.)** This in itself will make life so very, very different. This will require a tremendous adjustment on the part of My people everywhere, an adjustment that includes a new way of being, of perceiving, of acting. Everything about your life will change. I can tell you this, but you have no real idea of what it means or of how it will feel or look! I can only tell you that **more and more, you will be drawn into My Plan when time is no more, for there will be less**

distraction also. You will be pulled more deeply into the Sacred Heart of My Son, into the gifts and the graces poured out by Our Spirit, requested by the Holy Mother for each of you. (As the time around the Warning is more completely described, it is more understandable why there has been such delay…. Even though we are going crazy for it to occur!! Cta.)

I ask you to begin to ponder time: what a gift it has been, although at times it seems like your enemy! It has been a great gift, and you have learned not to waste it. You have learned simply by surrendering, (learning) that **it will not matter about time! It will not matter about structure, for you will be responding to the needs of the moment of so many.** My children, as the days change now from Summer heat to Fall cool, different colors, different aromas in the air, a different feel to the air, you know that time has taken you into a new Season. Let this Season be a time of appreciation for all the time you have spent on the earth and, of course, I speak to My dear ones everywhere in the world. Appreciation and using your imagination just a bit, you can imagine life without time. Imagine how different your life would be now, had you not been brought to this peace in the time and the structure of My Plan because I am God and nothing is impossible! **I had no need of time, nor will you, My children**. This is a new adventure that we begin together, and I ask you to consider it that way. Ask Our Holy Spirit to give you an enrichment of your appreciation for all of the gifts you received, but **most especially thank your Triune God for the gift of time.** My children**, this might seem like a short and simple message, but I assure you it is not! For it will help to prepare you for a new way of being and living and thinking. All of your experiences have been framed in time. <u>Soon they will not be, and so you are facing one of the first and biggest changes that are part of My Plan, but are necessary for a transition to the next event and the next event and the new level of serving and a new way of being. You can only completely understand these words by living them!</u>** Until then, fulfill My requests of you. This will increase your appreciation of all the gifts because this will be such a great change, and I wish for you to be as comfortable as possible!"

10/13, "Dear little children, I am your Mother. Thank you for your dear words, your heartfelt prayers, your mention of my special Feast this day as I appeared so long ago at Fatima. Thank you for realizing the importance of every appearance of Mine throughout history, but most especially in these critical times. I ask you, in honor of this day, to find the messages I gave at Fatima and read them again, to realize their importance for your own time. Realize the unity in my messages everywhere and always the unity we share, My dear children everywhere in the world; and you have unity with each other now through prayer, through My Rosary and within My Heart. This very special day many gifts are given to you and especially those you long for the most, you pray for with all of your might, you desire with every ounce of strength, every breath within you.

Ask the Holy Spirit, My Beloved Spouse, to show you the state of your soul, to grant you the gift of openness to more gift, to further reconciliation, to increased healing. You will always need these things; but now more than ever and never more than at this time before the gift of the Father's Warning is given to you. Many of you think of or view this gift with trepidation. I tell you when you receive this awesome blessing and mercy, you will see there is nothing to fear. You will know what a great gift you are being given and how much more there is to the gift than you realize at this point. Please enable the gift and all the other gifts to be given by praising and thanking Our Father now for them, for His gracious mercy, for His concern, for His providence in your life. For always He thinks ahead of time and He is giving you mercy even before you need it, even before you ask for it or discover the need for it. Let this show you just a little bit more how much you are loved, how precious you are in the eyes of your Triune God and in My eyes. Rejoice with Me for YOU, for your place in the Father's Plan, for your place within My Heart and My Will, and all the graces I obtain for you. I give you My great love once again, My dear children everywhere. You are all My children, even those who do not know Me or who reject Me or who will never know of these times of gift, and how much I am loving and blessing and gracing you. Pray for the world. **Pray for your country. It is in danger you cannot imagine and it will be ongoing now, once there is another strike at the heart of this country and then at the world. Pray to combat the effects of terror in the hearts of each person in the world**. All of the little ones in Heaven have joined you in your prayer, and send you their great love and their prayers for you constantly, constantly. Be at peace, My dear ones. I ask you to sit now in quiet for a few more moments while I am blessing you and pouring out grace, pouring out My love, pouring out the peace of My Jesus. Amen."

10/15, "My dear children, I am the Holy Spirit of God, come again to bring you new strength and new blessings, new courage, new understanding of the amount of protection, the amount of strength, the amount of power and might of the arm of God that will be fighting and protecting and pouring out, and ultimately defeating evil in the hearts of so very many, **ultimately defeating Satan himself and his demons, all of his followers.** My people, it is only an understanding from contemplating, in reflecting (and most of all when I give you the gift of understanding and appreciation), that you will come to know and realize, and be comforted and strengthened by a new awareness of the PROTECTION you DO have, and of the NEW STRENGTH you will be given in an ON-GOING MANNER NOW. I ask you to open your hearts this night, your minds, your ability to grasp with all your hearts, with all your strength, new truths We wish to give you: a new depth of understanding, a **new awareness of the Presence of Jesus and dear Mary, My Spouse, with many, many Angels**. You must have this awareness in order to accomplish as the Father desires of you. This will enable everything in your lives and all the needs of those who come to you. The calm you must have to face the chaos; the maturity and the balance to be the anchor light; the steadiness to go forward in the face of danger, in the face of ongoing destruction, in the face of many things that will frighten you at first, and in the face of overwhelming need within **overwhelming numbers of Our dear, dear lost people. Your hearts will break at the sight of them, and compassion**

will carry you to their side and allow comfort and mercy to rise within you and embrace them!

Oh My dear ones, ponder these thoughts. Let these words build images within your minds and hearts to prepare you. It is the only way to prepare, as well of course, as Adoration and silence. You are already praying for these dear ones who will come. This has prepared your hearts more, as well as theirs, in the wonderful, mysterious way of the Father's Plan. Do not worry that you will not do something right or correctly or well, because **you will have all the strength you will need**. Always, when you prepare ahead of time, it is through this kind of reflection. There have been other instances that you might go back to in your lives that you prepared ahead for, even the arrival of family, of guests, of parties and dinners, of people staying in your homes. Think of the preparations those times required. Imagine and expect the same sort of preparation and organization in the face of **overwhelming waves of people**, but that too will be overcome, will be handled by yourselves calmly and sufficiently and sweetly. Those are the words that count, My dear ones: your sincere welcoming.

Think about the state of mind and soul these people will find themselves in, at first. Put yourselves in their place. Do not dwell in destruction, but **imagine what it might be like to be so totally and completely displaced**. My dear people, this time, THESE EVENTS ARE NOT THAT FAR AWAY because you have persevered and prayed and prayed and prayed, and will continue in this way. It is very apparent and should be to you also, that you WANT to do this work. You want to be prepared. **You want to help, to be obedient instruments of the Father's Will, His every desire to alleviate suffering, to ease fears, to help to overcome anguish, immense sorrow.** And these are some of the ways you can begin now to do more, to prepare yourselves and them. **When flower seeds are planted, the ground is made ready first. It is turned over, broken up into smaller, more receptive pieces.** These are some of the actual events you have been experiencing, dear ones: the action of the Father in your lives turning things upside down, fertilizing, sprinkling, showering with rain and rays of sunshine. The ground of your heart is ready. Continue to maintain the readiness with all of these suggestions brought to you with love, with every help and grace and strength you will need. Maintain your gardens, My dear ones! What precious and beautiful gardens you are becoming. How you are loved! Be filled with Jesus' peace. Serenity will follow you and never leave you again. You are beloved. I speak to everyone in the world with these suggestions and about these events and about each one of you everywhere, Our faithful ones."

10/22, "My dear ones, I am your Mother, the Immaculate one of God. I bring joy from Heaven at the sight and the sound of all of you gathered in this place, lifting your hearts and your pleading to the Father. The faithful ones are fewer in numbers everywhere ... everywhere, My children! This state of affairs brings sadness. It is also the impetus that keeps you praying, keeps you focused on My requests and on the face of My Son. There is so much heartbreak. There is so much abuse and terrible darkness in the hearts and souls of so many people. This terrorist act will incite your country to greater aggression, (doesn't mean it's here for sure… cta.) to greater-taking-sides by many countries, to a closer step toward world war, to the greater possibility of nuclear war! The beauty in your hearts sustains Me, fills Me with hope and with such gratitude. Believe that I am speaking to you, My children everywhere in the world. My sorrow is beyond words tonight, and so I just allow you to hear and to feel My sorrow.

You are called to be people of hope. You can see even now how difficult that will be. How necessary that will be in the face of destruction and tremendous change, tremendous upheaval and displacement. My children everywhere, we must be MORE UNITED. We must be MORE POWERFUL in that unity. We must be MORE JOYFUL in the promises of the Father and all of the words of Heaven. I tell you the good that is accomplished, the souls that will be saved are because of you, My dear ones who respond. Praise the Father for the promises He has given you **to allow each person coming into Eternity to find out about Him and His Kingdom, and choose then. The Father's love has the power to bring miraculous events out of every kind of chaos and loss; and so it will be**! My little ones, spend time with Me this week. Make it a point to invite Me to be with you. In a special way, I will do this. It is the Father's Will at this time that we are more united, for only in this way can anything be accomplished to mitigate and lessen all that is about to occur. My children, we WILL overcome; but it will be a long struggle, a long battle. As you know, Satan has much power at this point. **Do not ever despair. Do not ever give up. Do not ever, My dearest children, turn away from Me.** Thank you for your love. I shower you with love this night. As a heavy rain would fall, so My love falls on you now! It will renew and refresh you like nothing else. Thank you, My little ones, for listening."

10/29, "My dearest children I thank all of you for gathering in My Name this night and in the name of Our Beloved Mother, to whom you pray so ardently, hopefully and faithfully, so dearly and in such a heartfelt and sincere way. I assure you that I am your Jesus Who speaks. I assure you that your prayers have touched many more this night; that the effectiveness and the giftedness of your prayers increases every day, reaches out to more, brings gifts and a change of heart to so many. Do not continue in your deep concern for your loved ones, for **My Father has promised all of the gifts they need to receive the gift of salvation to spend eternity in Heaven.** Pray for your country, as you have been asked many times now recently. Most especially pray for your leaders, who wrestle with decisions to act in such aggressive ways so as to foment war throughout the world. My dear ones, this is not a new understanding for you; but you come closer, closer than you realize to the events that will trigger a massive response in the world, a massive retaliation, all planned by the followers of the Antichrist, the followers of Satan's plan to destroy the world. Praise My Father and thank him once again, My dear faithful ones, that you are to be protected and saved through event after event that you might continue to lead, to heal, to explain, to comfort. So many will continue to arrive at your doorstep, you will think to panic, to be overwhelmed by the numbers. But then there is the grace you have been given. Continue to praise Him for choosing each one of you in spite of your weaknesses; in spite of a continuation of self gratification and yes, My children, still a good deal of laziness! There is no other word to use, although I can see you do not care for this word. Remember once again that My words are words of love that condition you, that develop who you are by pointing out everything that needs reflection, that needs to be brought to the altar, to the Sacrament of Reconciliation. My dear children, you have come so far. Think of that often because it will be more and more difficult to persevere. **It will be long years of perseverance**. Look at this fact once again and realize a tremendous dependence upon your Triune God and holy Mother.

Your holy Mother and I are blessing you this night with new blessings, new hope and courage and new affirmation for your hearts. All you hold to be true in your hearts in all the words given by Heaven now is re-cemented, that your conviction is increased with energy and with a deep felt ownership; that you might give witness every time you are called upon, of this deep conviction of all of the events you expect because of the words of Heaven. Continue to ask My Father to hasten My return, for in so doing He will hasten the other events, especially the gifts of My Father's Warning which you await so acutely. It is so good to be with you, speaking words of love, of support, bringing you the love of all of Heaven. This blessing My Mother and I give to you is a renewal of all your gifts, is an increase of every area of weakness with its corresponding strength, that you might overcome more weaknesses now and at a deeper level in the heart of your very, very, dear self. Do not ever forget My Mother and I are with you. Many Angels surround you. The love of My Father sustains you. The gift of Our Spirit strengthens you."

11/5, "My children, I am your Jesus, come tonight with the gift of obedience. From the lives of the many holy ones who have worked and dedicated their lives to the Church, to My Mother, to their Triune God, you have knowledge of the importance of obedience. It will be more important than ever that you are learning to **obey every little request and directive. Your lives will depend on this some day; and only through a blessed habit of obedience, through practice, through offering this obedience as a penance for the world will you be able to build up that virtue, that quick response.** I repeat, each time you hear something new repeated and repeated so that it is then something old**, you also know that you are that much closer to the fact**, to the event that requires the request in the first place! Delays throughout the years have occurred to teach you the power of your prayers. Mitigation is given whenever possible, and it will continue to be given; but many times We have reminded you: nothing can be done away with in the plan of Satan as it is allowed by My Father. Each week that you gather, believe Me, you come very much closer to an event of terror within your own country once again, and then within the world. There is already terror living in the hearts of so many. This, of course, is the goal of terrorists. When you trust as I am calling you to trust, you will not worry. When you are prepared, as I have called you to prepare, you will not be concerned when an event occurs or is delayed; and always Heaven and earth rejoices together when there is mitigation. Continue to pray with all your strength, with all your concentration and the generosity in your hearts for mitigation, for what mercy is given in this gift! Prayer, My children, is the life blood of your soul, the life blood of your spiritual journey, of your unity with your God and Holy Mother.

I TELL YOU THERE IS SUCH JOY FOR YOU IN HEAVEN AS YOU CANNOT IMAGINE. LET THAT BE ENOUGH FOR YOU to encourage you to persevere! Let that be the impetus to remain faithful, to remain focused. I know how difficult it is for you to spend more and more and more time in prayer; but remember also to **consecrate each task and realize this is a prayer**. I have told you, 'Prayer is service and service is prayer'. In these many months ahead, you will be so happy that you have done all the things I have requested of you, that Our dear Mother has called you to do. Ask once again of Our Holy Spirit to show you hidden sins, roots of sin, your lack of charity, your lack of patience and tenderness with each other. As you look into the faces of all those who come to you for help, see My face. It will help you run to each one, to welcome and embrace them; for truly I will be visiting you in each person, in great numbers with many, many, many blessings, with much healing for you as well as for them. I say these things again to you that you might rejoice, not become tired or bored or disinterested or distracted; but more focused, more motivated to pray for these many reasons and especially for your country. These are not idle requests. **Your country will sustain immense damage, not everywhere, but in more than one area.** Your Angels fill the room this night. Listen closely and you will hear their prayers and feel their joy. I wait for you every day. Come and visit. Come and listen. **Just be with Me, My dear ones**! "

11/10, "My dearest ones, I am Jesus, here with you. Do you hear My words? I AM HERE WITH YOU, not in some far-off place listening, vaguely interested and at times distracted by the needs of others. I AM ALWAYS WITH YOU, and always I know everything in your lives: every struggle, every exchange of words, every difficulty, every situation, every temptation and decision. I come to encourage you again that you ARE choosing for good. Oh yes, **you are human and impatient and demanding, even of your God; but I look at you and into each heart and at each precious up-turned face, and I smile and tears of joy fill My eyes. It is the same everywhere My people gather.** I am with you. I am for you. I am upholding you and strengthening you. I LOVE YOU! Do not forget this, My children. Praise My Father for the love of your Triune God given to you through My Sacred Presence, through My Sacred Heart, holding each of you in My Heart, in My Wounds, in My love. YOU MUST REJOICE MORE! You must reflect upon the gifts you receive, and I speak to My children everywhere. You must praise and thank the Father for all you are given, for these great changes within you, for a peace in your hearts and minds that will never, never be disturbed, even by the occasional fear or even terror that fills your hearts and minds at the moment; but the great gift of peace that is given to you again and again will carry you through every tremor of the earth, through every sound of battle and explosions, the fear of so many around you reacting to the might of Satan's plan. In sunshine and temperate weather, you are able to enjoy and appreciate My Father's gifts; but what will you do when the air is rent with the sounds of attack and war, with the rumblings of Nature that split and destroy, with the terrified sounds of Our people tossed about in total confusion with no anchor such as you have, with no foundation, no understanding such as you have?

(Late development in '06, Jesus has told one of His messengers that a huge terrorist attack was to have occurred on Independence Day of this year, but did not because of the prayers of those saying Jesus' Novena of Peace given to her and shared with many.. cta.)

My dear ones, rejoice! Thank and praise My Father. It is a time just before battle, My children. You are soldiers and you are part of this battle: the most important part of this battle after My Angels led by My Holy Mother and yours, and the Saints and all in Heaven who pray for your safety; for you, for your country, your loved ones. Oh My children, you have no idea. I repeat, you have no idea!

Gather all of your energy, all of your plans and lay them aside. Go forward with that energy into prayer, into begging and pleading for mercy for your country and for the world. For it is only mercy that will mitigate, that will alleviate enough destruction to allow My Father to ultimately be victorious, to remove evil completely from the face of the Earth and to bring you triumphant into a beautified world and peace and purity and into My Eucharistic Reign. **My children, because these are familiar terms and expectations, do not think they are something about which you must or are allowed to become casual. Do not, I repeat, do not become distracted. Do not turn away.** Do not allow the allure of gratification to stop you in your relentless attack on Heaven, your relentless pursuit of mercy in the face of evil, in the face of many plans, well laid and ready to explode, to go forward to conquer. R**eread each word of this message to you given out of the concern of all of Heaven, Our great love for you**, Our need of you, the need of the world for you. Go forth in love. Go forth in new strength for this call, for this reminder of what lies ahead and your great role in My Father's Plan and the victory that awaits you when you remain faithful. My dear ones, **think of others first**."

11/12, "My dear children, I am your God and Father. It is with sadness that I see destructive events that are allowed now. You must keep at the forefront of your mind and your understanding that Scripture is being fulfilled by every event. Scripture must be fulfilled, and so there will be many, many, many events! You begin to see the long road ahead of you. Do not run ahead for that very reason. **You need to be in your lives where I am keeping each one of you: whatever that may be for your own good, for the process that must play out in your lives to bring you to the next step, the next level, the newest gift, the newest**

method of service. This is true of everyone who remains faithful, everyone who desires to serve. You can feel events closer than ever. When you see smaller ones, you know larger ones are on the way, are so much nearer. You can feel My Plan being enacted. You can feel My Will, children, now that you are living more completely within that Will; but you also feel the Presence of your Triune God and the Holy Mary, your dear Mother.

Spend time with Me this week, yes, in praise. Come once again before My Son in the Blessed Sacrament. I am united with Him there, and I too wait for you. There is more I would tell your hearts, My children everywhere in the world. There is more unity I would give to all of you in the world, your prayers, your concerns, your struggles, the continued vanity and selfishness and self-centeredness that plagues every human. Be grateful that My plan allows these visits between yourselves and many of Us in Heaven. Be grateful for opportunities to meet new prayers (people), to meet new groups, to meet new lost ones to whom you may minister; and see that as a practice, but also as a major gift to them through you from their God. So much more occurs than you realize ... every moment. It is a great miracle that the great numbers of people in the world, who are listening and are praying, are doing so at all! Besides not realizing how blessed you are, you **do not realize the great, great dynamic of My plan that unites you with the entire world who prays, that is turning you into a single weapon to fight the evil one.** One reason you will be astounded so many times, My children, is because you do not see now the gifts you have been given; how you have been honed and trained and are a more perfect result of My work in your life. Again I say to you, 'Praise Me. Thank Me. Have mercy on yourselves, for you are weak. Have mercy on yourselves, for you are helpless without your God and the might of His Arm! Have mercy on each other, and grasp that might and use it for each other's strength and healing as members of this great Army of the Virgin Mother, the Immaculate One.

One of your duties is to pray for each other, to care for each other in this way, to strengthen the ranks, to bring health and wholeness and soundness into this vast Army of weak and helpless ones; and then, My dear, dear ones, to rejoice at the great mercy that flows throughout all of these actions on your part, on their part and Mine! Be joyful, as I am joyful. Be delighted, as I am delighted. Be ready now for anything to occur of a new and more difficult nature in your lives personally, collectively and on the world scene. You see danger lurking, waiting to pounce. Yes, there is great evil in the world, but there are so many innocent little ones, weak ones, those who have no one to care for them. You are their help. **You are their lifeline of salvation in union with Jesus**. You know that! Rejoice; rejoice that you are loved, for you are SO loved. Thank you for your fidelity. Thank you for the love in your hearts. Be encouraged and strengthened and filled with joy by My love and My words to you this night."

11/12, "My dear children, I am your God and Father. My children, it is with sadness that I see destructive events that are allowed now. You must keep at the forefront of your mind and your understanding that Scripture is being fulfilled by every event. Scripture must be fulfilled, and so there will be many, many, many events, My dear ones! You begin to see the long road ahead of you. Do not run ahead for that very reason. **You need to be in your lives where I am keeping each one of you: whatever that may be for your own good, for the process that must play out in your lives to bring you to the next step, the next level, the newest gift, the newest method of service.** This is true of everyone who remains faithful, everyone who desires to serve. You can feel events closer than ever. When you see smaller ones, you know larger ones are on the way, are so much nearer. You can feel My Plan being enacted. You can feel My Will, children, now that you are living more completely within that Will; but you also feel the Presence of your Triune God and the Holy Mary, your dear Mother.

My children, spend time with Me this week, yes, in praise. Come once again before My Son in the Blessed Sacrament. I am united with Him there, and I too wait for you. There is more I would tell your hearts, My children everywhere in the world. There is more unity I would give to all of you in the world, your prayers, your concerns, your struggles, the continued vanity and selfishness and self-centeredness that plagues every human. Be grateful that My plan allows these visits between yourselves and many of Us in Heaven. Be grateful for opportunities to meet new prayers (people), to meet new groups, to meet new lost ones to whom you may minister; and see that as a practice, but also as a major gift to them through you from their God. So much more occurs than you realize … every moment. It is a great miracle that the great numbers of people in the world, who are listening and are praying, are doing so at all! Besides not realizing how blessed you are, you **do not realize the great, great dynamic of My plan that unites you with the entire world who prays, that is turning you into a single weapon to fight the evil one.** One reason you will be astounded so many times, My children, is because you do not see now the gifts you have been given; how you have been honed and trained and are a more perfect result of My work in your life. Again I say to you, 'Praise Me. Thank Me. Have mercy on yourselves, for you are weak. Have mercy on yourselves, for you are helpless without your God and the might of His Arm! Have mercy on each other, and grasp that might and use it for each other's strength and healing as members of this great Army of the Virgin Mother, the Immaculate One.

One of your duties is to pray for each other, to care for each other in this way, to strengthen the ranks, to bring health and wholeness and soundness into this vast Army of weak and helpless ones; and then, My dear, dear ones, to rejoice at the great mercy that flows throughout all of these actions on your part, on their part and Mine! Be joyful, as I am joyful. Be delighted, as I am delighted. Be ready now for anything to occur of a new and more difficult nature in your lives personally, collectively and on the world scene. You see danger lurking, waiting to pounce. Yes, there is great evil in the world, but there are so many innocent little ones, weak ones, those who have no one to care for them. You are their help. **You are their lifeline of salvation in union with Jesus**. You know that! Rejoice;

rejoice that you are loved, for you are SO loved. Thank you for your fidelity. Thank you for the love in your hearts. Be encouraged and strengthened and filled with joy by My love and My words to you this night."

11/17, "Beloved children of My Sacred Heart, I bring greetings to you from all in Heaven. I have united your prayers this day in a deeper way that they might reach and touch more deeply everyone in the world. I am your Jesus. I come to tell you that 'all is well, that all will be well' and I invite you and I plead with you that you **develop a prayer habit of telling yourselves** ALL IS WELL AND ALL WILL BE WELL; for you know there will be times of upheaval and destruction. You know there will be times when it will seem very much so that all is not well, that all will not be well, and so it will be necessary to remind yourselves and each other again and again as a means of maintaining balance and trust, a means of overcoming fear, a means of surrender to the action of My Father at that particular moment; to see that action, to see His Will as not only perfect, but necessary and a means by which all will be well eventually! This is a greater responsibility, and will be a greater help than of course you realize at this moment. This will be more difficult (then) than it would be now; and so I ask you now to develop this habit. It will be so helpful to you and others. Again, it will be that means to joy and peace that will allow you to rise to the top of each event that will carry you on, keep you going in strength, in that joy and trust, **as it will be the only means of your survival, especially emotionally and mentally**. Do you see what important tasks I am giving you, that great gifts and powers will be yours? It will be My power, the might of My Father's arm; but you will be using it and without using it, you would be overcome.

First, you must be accept the truth of My words and believe in them, and then practice using them, and then incorporate them in your every waking moment. And **there will be times, many times, when your sleep is disturbed, so I ask you (upon waking each day) to begin the day reminding yourselves** ALL IS WELL AND ALL WILL BE WELL! This is not some sort of mind control, some sort of fooling yourselves or escaping reality! The greater reality will be, My children, that all IS well and all WILL BE well! Do you see? Do you have a greater understanding? Can you hear the importance of this dynamic as incorporated into your lives now? I give you extra grace this day to accompany this new practice of yours, for I wish that you would receive success, that you would receive this gift the way it was meant to be received, that it would become part of you, that it would be and help you to become more of who you are created to be for yourselves, for those around you, for all of those who come to you. You will be passing this suggestion along that is greater than just a suggestion, when I tell you I am pleading with you to incorporate this new way of being into your lives! It is also a sign of escalation and a new level in the Father's plan that you are achieving by accepting grace, by accepting gift, by accepting ALL the Father wishes to give you. My dear ones, it is an exciting time. It is new armor you are asked to put on. IT IS THE ARMOR OF TRUST, THE ARMOR OF FAITH and

THE ARMOR OF OBEDIENCE to the practice of these words. You will do this, My children, and remind each other of the importance of this practice. I know I can count on you, for all of Heaven prays that you will be successful in this new endeavor. Remind each other, children, and be open to the reminders of others. Do not allow this to irritate you or build up a defense or a wall within you! Be gentle and tender with each other. Be sweet with your words, with your tone of voice. Simply say to each other: 'all will be well, all is well.' Amen for now, My dear ones, I bring you success. I bring you new wisdom to appreciate this gift and see how far-reaching it can become; and how it can transform you and everyone around you. I love you, my dear ones. Be grateful for this new gift and for My Father's plan for you. (These messages for 2002 are filled with suggestions for important behavioral changes, and so we are invited to read the words slowly and often, asking the Holy Spirit for the gift of openness to the gifts of the Father!! ... cta.)

11/19, "Dear children, I am your Mother. I come once again to encourage you and to warn you. Yes, it has been a long wait, and **at other times you will experience other waits of a long duration, waiting for the fulfillment of the Father's Will.** Do remember, My dear ones, that **the Father allows each event, each period of waiting in order to form and reform you, in order to make you more docile, more pliable in His hands, that you might be a perfect instrument for His people.** You ARE becoming pliable and more docile. You are agreeing more within yourselves with what you experience each day, each week, each month, each year that is all part of the Father's Will for you personally and for you collectively. Remember the rest of the community. Remember, **it is not just about you,** My dear ones; and others around you need as much or perhaps more time and prayer to bring them to that better place in the Father's Will. **It is the reason you are asked to prayer for each other. Simply pray for each other, my children!** It is such a special place that you occupy in the Father's plan. It is such a gift that we have been given to each other. You will only appreciate all of this in Heaven, when the greatest clarity will be given to your understanding, when you will see clearly in the light instead of darkly, as you do now. The veil will be lifted from your eyes, from your minds and understanding. What a great day that will be! Know also you become more perfected as you live into the New Era or are brought into Heaven, but especially know that **in the New Era your minds will have more clarity to see truth, to understand the mysteries of God, to understand His ways and thus give you that ability to surrender most completely, to live as completely as possible on the earth the Divine Will of Our Father**. I speak in this way tonight to encourage you, though it gets colder everywhere and there is less daylight and longer periods of darkness. It seems to be more difficult to do everything.

It seems there is still so much to do and it is up to you to decide how much to do: how distracted you wish to be, what you will allow in your lives that might distract you and turn you away from the focus you need to maintain as these instruments of the Father's Will; not just for that reason alone, but because that focus prepared you to praise and thank the Father more and to minister to His dear ones who will surely come to you in great numbers. Oh my children, it will not be overwhelming, although it will seem to be at first and at certain times throughout the rest of your life; but you and I are more united. You and Jesus in the Triune God are more united. You are more graced and gifted and blessed and you are stronger and yes, you are wiser, more prudent and more patient: all of the things you strive for. Be patient with yourselves, my little ones. How precious you are to me, my little chicks whom I gather under My Mantle to protect you from the darkness and the cold and the evil in the world. **You are my beloved ones, all who pray and remain faithful everywhere in the world!** You are all experiencing the same difficulties everywhere in the world, the same struggles and impatience, the same fatigue and strain from the many prayers and the modified lifestyle you now live. It will be better if you take care and slow down; if you resist the opportunity to do too much, to run in too many directions. You know by now how much damage this can cause, and you know I wish for you to be at peace and healthy and holy and humble, precious little children of mine. Give time for the Spirit. Give time to me and to yourselves. Make that your Christmas gift to yourself. Begin now building these gifts! Words cannot tell you how I love you. What you do for my Heart! Thank you for your love. It is a true and deep and pure and holy love, my children. Spend time with me, children."

11/24, 2002 External locution @ Ameche prayer gathering through Carol

"My dearest children, I am your God and Father. I come this day with the glory of God. I come this day with the glory being saved on your behalf as a result of your suffering. **Recall that suffering is a purchase of souls, the golden coin that is exchanged for conversion**. Your own conversion is involved in the same way, My dear ones. Imagine, one day your bodies will be glorified! One day you will know the happiness of Heaven, the bliss of Paradise, the peace beyond understanding. **It is difficult to save and to behave for a distant future!** It is even more difficult when you are anxious, when you think nothing is happening; and in that very thought and very anxiety, you are suffering. I tell you, My children, "ALL IS WELL AND ALL WILL BE WELL; and I ask you, once again, to allow this to be your theme, if you will: the attitude and composure and peace that you bring each day to each moment in joy, for if 'all will be well and all is well,' this is a joyous occasion!! These are part of the mysteries of God that I wish to share with you, a means of perseverance, a deep truth behind all of the events you will experience, but most especially all that it means to be human; to be human and to experience this can be a distraction from all that is Heavenly, of course, **for it is to be human that you are called to live most deeply.** Allow that longing for things of Heaven, things of God to be part of who-you-are to grow! It is a good thing to desire Heaven, to desire your God and your Holy Mother.

My dear ones, this very week you will spend time giving thanks in this country, to give thanks for her and for your freedoms. Give thanks for the protection afforded this country. Give thanks for faith and trust. Without faith and trust, there can be no Thanksgiving, no gratitude, no growth in holiness and wholeness and these are of utmost importance to you. This day **make yourselves a promise that your focus will be greater on the needs of all around you and the danger present in the world, especially to your country. Focus on the truth that Satan and his demons are ever lying in wait to trip you up that you might be on guard, that you might know that, in spite of all these things, many Angels surround you, and the might of My arm will protect you**. Praise the might of My arm, children. Praise My perfect Will and plan for you and the world. Offer thanksgiving from your hearts for mercy and forgiveness. You will be doing this at a new level of understanding, a new level of gratitude. It will be a new level because I give you this gift today. Do not take these words, or requests lightly. Always you must make progress, always avail yourselves to the action of Our Spirit lifting you to a new level. **You can cooperate with the grace I give you, but always it is first My grace acting within your hearts and your lives that causes you to grow and to move forward and to be elevated in My plan and in your ability to serve.** These things are so important, are all that is important along with your obedience and your surrender to Me; your praise and thanksgiving for My love, for loving you first, for calling you to love Me and the Holy Mother and each other more. Without My call, My dear ones, it would not have happened! Without My sustaining you, it would not continue. See yourselves in truth, and rejoice. Be prepared at all times and at every moment, so that all can be well and all will be well! I shower you with new strength.

I shower you with the ability to touch others with your sweetness, with an obvious love for Me, for your Triune God and the Holy Mother, with obvious love for each other, for obvious gratitude that will be lived out in the joy of your countenance, the joy of your spirit, the joy of your smile despite sorrow and sadness in your life. I tell you **each struggle, each problem will be resolved**! Believe this and rejoice. Follow My Son closely. Imitate Him. Love Him. Receive now the Spirit of Love, the love of My Son, My love, which is One. I bless you and shower you with all you need this day to continue to grow, to become, to blossom, to fly in the face of evil, fearless, victorious, joyful, Amen. My children, thank you for your love and your presence this day and everywhere in the world who listen and believe. This message is for all of you, as are these gifts and blessings."

12/3, "My dear children, I am Mary, your Mother, the Mother of Jesus, the Mother of God, the Mother of the world. Thank the Father with me this night for the opportunity to visit, to be, to share, to pour out my love, my gratitude for you, my delight with you. How much thanksgiving was given in Heaven this very week for each of you. Your prayers of thanksgiving ascended to the highest Heavens releasing new graces for the world and especially for this country. My dearest, dearest ones, I know that you suffer. I suffer too. Realize this, my dear ones, that although I enjoy the happiness, the bliss, the perfection of Heaven**, still I feel sorrow when I see you suffer, when I see so many in the world suffer. I see your struggles and, yes, the times you fall, the times you bring so much less**

than you might to your prayer, to your fasting and your penance, to your joy and your service of each other. My dear ones, you know how many there will be. **You have a very, very good idea of how difficult this great mission you have been given will be for you to accomplish: impossible, of course, without the help, completely the help of your Triune God and of my own help** that is given even now to hold you in this chosen place for you, this graced and blessed place that you occupy in the Father's plan and in the hearts of everyone in Heaven.

You are so loved by every person in Heaven, every Angel, every Saint and of course the Triune God and myself who loves you with a mother's tenderness, with a mother's watchful eye: praying for you, obtaining new blessings, little, special gifts that show you my love, my presence with you; trying (when I can) to make things easier, more palatable, more acceptable, for this is the Lord's Will: that you be more accepting, as we walk together, arm in arm, praying, just being together, learning to know each other, love each other more. We promise to be more faithful; we promise to do whatever it is God requires and requests. We consecrate. We recommit every ounce of our being, every fiber of our hearts, every ounce of energy, every wish, every desire, that it might be the wish and desire of our God and Father. There is more suffering in your lives, more difficulty, more struggle and a greater weight from waiting (!) and yet I tell you **this is the most blest and graced time you have known, and I ask you to be grateful. Realize, recognize that in each event, in each hardship, each sorrow and heartbreak, there is a greater unity with my Son and this, my children, is so much greater than you could ever imagine at this point.** It is true you will never understand or appreciate until you are face to face with the Divine Mercy in Heaven, My Jesus, My Beloved One. You, my children, are also my beloved ones! Be comforted this night in your weaknesses, in your heartbreak, in loss, in beginning to realize how much you depend on your God for everything. Rejoice. Rejoice that you have been chosen. Rejoice that you are allowed these sufferings, these challenges. My children, what will I say next? Of course I will say to you: All is well; and all will be well" for you and for your loved ones. It is in God's time, but it will be well! Be of good cheer, my dear ones of hope, my dear, dear ones of joy. Remember and know and feel and believe that I am with you, my children, every second I am with you, I am next to you. Hold my hand. I love you!"

12/6, in Massachusetts, "My dear ones, thank you for listening tonight with your hearts, for opening your minds to Possibility and to Truth. I am your God. I am your Father. I am your Creator. I come to tell you how grateful I am for you, to tell you that you fill Me with JOY, that you are precious and so necessary to My plan for the world; so necessary to be a life line to eternal life, a life of joy in Heaven, the bliss of Paradise. I come to bring a healing, My dear ones, and the peace of My Son Jesus. I come to tell you that I am removing you from the world MORE NOW. I am removing the world from your hearts MORE NOW, that you might become the instruments I call you to be. There are no words to explain or convince or show you how much you are loved. Spend time with your Triune God and find out. Experience the peace of My Son. Experience Our presence. You WILL, My dear ones, feel the graces and the gifts you are being given. You WILL fill with conviction, with trust. Trust that all you are hearing will be accomplished, that all you are hearing will begin so very soon, that your country is in great need of prayer; that your prayer is effective, more than words can tell you. I can only show you and convince you of these truths as each event plays out in your life. I am healing you this night of every infirmity, every disease, I am casting out every spirit that is not of God, every impediment, every resistance, every wall put up between yourself and Myself. Come to Me with trust that I will not harm you. Oh, My Dear ones, **do not be afraid**. Know that ALL IS WELL.

Whatever you see and whatever you experience, ALL IS WELL, AND ALL WILL BE WELL. For My Kingdom is developing, growing, blossoming on this earth and you are more important than you will ever realize. Thank you for loving your God, your Jesus. We are One, My Son and I and Our Spirit. So I too, invite you to come before Jesus in the Blessed Sacrament, where I am united with Him and with Our Spirit. There are so many gifts waiting for you--- if you only stop and receive them and believe. **Be hidden now. Simplify your lives more. Learn to appreciate quiet and silence and prayer. My children, do not be afraid.** DO NOT BE AFRAID. I fill you with joy. I fill you with peace and with hope. You are never, ever, ever alone. You are loved beyond your understanding. **Plan for the future, but pray now**. I LOVE you, I LOVE you. All of Heaven loves you, prays for you, and the Angels chant your names before My throne. I bless you in My Name, in the Name of My Son Jesus and in the Name of Our Holy Spirit. Amen children, thank you for loving Me."

12/10, "I am your Jesus, come to hear you once again and My children everywhere in the world. I come to empty you now of the world. As you ponder your weaknesses, your sinfulness, your selfishness, you realize why you still need all of My help, all the graces I obtained for you; that it was necessary for Me to be born into the world, that Love Itself would be born; that Heaven would touch earth in the Divine and human way; that I would lift humanity higher in dignity, in honesty and all the gifts you are given. And yes today, mankind has turned away more than ever, even rejects a public mention of My Birth, removes it from public as much as possible, denies the nature of this great feast, this great celebration that all of the world has joined in over the years, the millennia. More than ever at this time we see the results of coldness in the hearts of mankind; and for the greater part, man is no longer kind, no longer accepts a Savior, a God Who has created and redeemed and sanctified His people and sustains His people with life and grace and fidelity on His part. Of course, I now ask you to pray more for the hearts of everyone in the world. The suffering being endured in many parts of the world is beyond belief. It is beyond your imagination that you could help them. It is beyond anything you could stand yourselves! You can touch their lives in the midst of squalor, in the midst of degradation and abuse and the total destruction of dignity. You have the ability to help them, to affect their salvation, their ability to choose salvation. I died to obtain the redemption of mankind. I died to obtain the possibility for salvation for everyone in the world, and I ask you to live your lives now until the end of your life, dying to yourself and to the world and to everything that might distract you from the call of your God and your Mother, the Immaculate One, to keep, to save as many as possible from the clutches of Satan whose plans and power and victories increase now. Be still in a recollection of the great meaning of this feast, this great gift of this feast, the ongoing gift as I am born again and again in your hearts, in your spirits and your minds, your very lives. Praise the Father, children. Thank Him for the gift of My life, My birth and all that I had meant to the world now and for Eternity. Think Eternity, My children. **Do not disallow or waste the gift of salvation for all eternity**. Think and pray about this throughout the week and until My Birth is celebrated in the hearts of My faithful and loving people everywhere. Again, I ask that you unite this waiting, this period of time with the heart and the waiting of My Mother. She bore Me in joy**. I ask you to bear Me in joy, My children**! Amen."

12/15, "My dearest children, I am Mary, the Immaculate One, your Mother, your sweet and loving companion in this tiresome and fatiguing and difficult journey. Celebrate the great gift of My Jesus, born into the world and into your lives, but in a special way at this time. My children, what greater gift could you have received? He is being given birth in you always and by your behavior. By your own mercy and love you are birthing Him again and again in those around you and everywhere in the world, as you pray for the whole world. It is time, My children, it is a great part of your mission on the earth to bring Jesus to the world any way you possibly can, most especially through your prayers. Give thanks for Jesus. In so doing, you are rejoicing and giving thanks for me, and I thank you for the gift of surrender to all the words of Heaven gathered in Scripture, gathered now through faithful ones, given to help you to become these great instruments for the healing of the world and in union with Jesus for the salvation of the world. My dear ones, spend these next days in more silence with me whenever you can in the peace of waiting, the peace of allowing and accepting all the Father wills for you these next days, and until the Birth of Jesus is celebrated. Give thanks for the great gift the Father allows when I speak to you; when we come together like this in a greater experience of each other's company! Be of good cheer, my children. Be filled with joy now."

12/17, "My dearest little children, I am your Jesus speaking: **it is a difficult time in the world, to say the least.** Offer every action and every task for the world's protection: protection of their souls. It is a sadness when one of Our loved ones is taken away from you; but what a blessing for that soul, for that person who is closer then to the Kingdom of God in Heaven, who is given more direct opportunity to choose the Father and His Kingdom, given a more direct opportunity for total cleansing (if that is needed) in Purgatory which, as you have come to understand, contains much joy for those who are closer to Heaven. I ask you to rejoice for all of those who will be taken, who will be brought into eternity and given every opportunity, every grace, every encouragement by your prayers and a new gift of openness from Our Spirit. Allow these things to be the impetus this week for your prayers, and when you see a soul come closer to God and to Heaven and to peace everlasting, rejoice! Praise the Father once again and thank Him for His great mercy on that soul for an end to suffering, to confusion, to struggle, pain and loneliness.

Most certainly many of you will see My Coming on the clouds! These are amazing facts, and it is an amazing time. Although you are familiar with all of this information, still it is difficult to grasp, difficult to imagine and must just be accepted, given thanks for, prepared for, especially by prayer and adoration, reception of My Body and Blood as often as possible and more nearly now, a personal and intimate preparation of My Birth. You can do more to unite yourselves to My Mother's waiting, to ponder that time, to ponder your own waiting. I delight in preparing you this night for all that is to come, for being born again in your hearts.

I Am Truth, tiny, Baby Truth! Allow this feast, this pondering, visiting My Manger to be a time of healing, for you are all weary and you all suffer so much. It is a great sorrow to everyone in Heaven. You cannot see your hearts and your souls as I do, but I tell you that more and more they glisten, they shine with the brightness of the Star that shone upon My tiny Body. Use these images to comfort yourself and to help you to remember that 'All is well', whatever you experience, and 'All will be well'. **I encourage you to get rest, to slow down!** Spend more time in quiet, just to be with Me. Discover what this can do for you, how refreshed you will be and strengthened and renewed, and give thanks and praise to My Father. I bring you love this night as your gift from Me and from all in Heaven: precious, strong, caressing, comforting, enduring love. Be joyful, My children. Be joyful!"

12/25, Adoration, "My dear faithful ones everywhere in the world, I, your Lord and Savior, your infant King, bring blessings and healing to each heart that celebrates My Birth with renewed love and commitment to My Father's plan to give the gift of salvation to all who will accept it. Thank you, My faithful ones, for these days of preparation for the feast of My Birth and to prepare you for My Second Coming into the world. Believe that events go forward this very day to escalate plans for war and the need for martial law. You will see miracles of conversions and healing in your lives and the lives of those close to you, whom you love and pray for. I thank you also for your attempts to become the warm and loving instruments of the Will of Our Father for the good of others. My people, know that increased perseverance is also given this Day; that the year will be filled with what look like disappointments and loss, but will in reality fill you with new understanding and wisdom. So many learning experiences will bring you to a place of final readiness and surrender to whatever is required in your own life by the Father's Will to render you fit and battle ready. You know a further emptying is necessary to remove the distractions of your present way of living in the world, and to bring you to the knowledge of your own sinfulness and areas of vulnerability that will afford a total cleansing and healing of your hearts and souls.

This time will also be a sign that you are brought to a new level of service and holiness. And so with each new experience, I ask you to rejoice and give thanks and praise for a further preparation of your minds and hearts and bodies as a soldier of God's Will and desires for you: a total rendering of your lives, a distilling and purifying of every moment."

FOR MERCY'S SAKE

"How long will you people mock my honor, love what is worthless, chase after lies? Know that the Lord works wonders for the faithful; the Lord hears when I call out. Tremble and do not sin; upon your beds ponder in silence. Offer fitting sacrifice and trust in the Lord."

(Psalm 4: 3-6)

V.

2003 Messages

1/6, Adoration, "Dearest daughter, I am your Merciful Lord, Father and Creator. I give you special words now for the world on this special feast of Light and Beauty, as I call each of you who listens to and follows My words to become a source of the Light of My Son and radiant reflection of His Beauty and Presence within you. **Your own country is about to become aggressors in a war that will appear to be necessary to many, but in reality is an escalation of plans agreed to by leaders of major powers in the world who initiate steps to begin implementing (as members of the New World Order) the plans of Satan to annihilate much of the world's population and large portions of land in many areas of the earth in order to conquer the world.**

My people, you have waited years in fidelity and prayer in spite of hurtful ridicule, and spiteful behavior and words of many relatives and friends. Many have watched spouses walk away in disgust and contempt at your new life of prayer for the conversion of the world and preparation for the Second Coming of My Son. In a way that will vindicate all of you, but continue to break your hearts, you will see millions of lost ones come into My arms begging forgiveness and seeking reconciliation. The time of suffering begins for the entire world in wars and with destruction from **weapons never seen or used before in history. The only solace will be My promises (given these many years) of protection and eternal salvation for your beloved ones, as events begin to fulfill Scripture until the return of Jesus, My Beloved Son, to send Satan and all his demons and followers into Hell, to renew the Earth and begin a New Era of Peace and Purity. THIS WILL BE,** My faithful Remnant. Please see to a final collecting of supplies and water and especially Sacramentals. See to your own revitalized Consecration to this call through the Sacred and Immaculate Hearts.

Accept all that is revealed to you in humility and gratitude, and see this as a further outpouring of My mercy upon you that will bring you to the place of purity and readiness required for those who will be My instruments of salvation to millions throughout the entire world. DO NOT REJECT THESE WORDS BECAUSE YOU HAVE HEARD THEM OFTEN BEFORE! As your own soldiers wait in a state of ultimate preparation and readiness to begin a WAR that HAS NOT THE BLESSING OF HEAVEN, but serves as a mighty example for you, **so you are called to an ultimate preparation that will keep you at a state of readiness for whatever will unfold in this country and the world, maintained by My grace and gifts and My predilection of mercy beyond any you have yet experienced.** Do not attempt to figure out My plans for you! Remember it is a humble and obedient and silent servant who will win these wars and gain the Eternal Prize! Expect miracles of renewal and hope and strength, My loved ones. **I cannot, I will not go forward or succeed without you. You cannot know victory without union with Jesus' victory and the assistance of all in Heaven.** Do not worry. Do not fear. Do not be overcome by anyone or anything. Do not despair."

1/7, "My dearest ones, I am your Jesus. I come in delight to be with you again, to be speaking to My faithful ones all over the world YOU will bring gold and frankincense and myrrh to all of those who come to you, My children! You will be the gold: the shelter you provide, the clothing, the food; but most of all, the patient, listening heart you will provide that will be a sweet odor, an incense to their broken hearts, the confusion in their minds, the distress in their spirits, the remorse in their souls and the fear that will be eased by the myrrh poured out as you pour out your love, your compassion, the hard work and fatigue that will accompany all of your ministering: whatever task is needed for these dear ones. Remember these ones who will come, these dear, dear ones **will be nearly dead themselves from all their experiences.** And their needs will differ, in spite of the fact that the general condition will be much the same.

I say these things that you might ponder and ask the help of the Holy Spirit to prepare you mentally, spiritually, emotionally, as well as physically. Recall that **when you trust completely, you will not worry, you will not feel inadequate.** You will not look at yourself as you are now, but rejoice in the healing about to occur within you, the strengthening and the renewal! You have waited long for these gifts, My dear ones, I know. Your patience has been strained to almost breaking. Just a bit longer, My children, all the while realizing that when these gifts are needed and given, it will mean also that a tremendous change has occurred in your environment and in your world. Keep all of these things in mind that you might pray from the proper perspective, My dear ones, all the while surrendering to you know not what at this point, but that all will be the Father's Will and so, you are able to rejoice. You are able to wait in joy and hope and peace and surrender. Be filled with joy, My children, as the Father's plan moves ahead for good, for the destruction of all evil. Amen, My children. Thank you for your love and your prayers and your fidelity."

1/14, "Dearest children, I am your Mother of Sorrows. Never forget my love for a moment, or my presence with you. In the coming days it will be so necessary that you realize My Son and I are at your sides. I am, of course, speaking to every one of my faithful children in the world. I am blessing all of you with perseverance and new strength, with the ability to overcome fatigue quickly now; with the ability to persevere in spite of every danger, every fright, every loss, every instance in your life that brings such great change as will occur in the near future. They will cause you enormous struggle and pain. But if you will recall the outcome of each event that brings you closer to the return of My Son, you will be able to have joy and calm and a peace that will see you through each event. My children, there is nothing to fear. There is no concern that will not be resolved for the good. **There is no sorrow that will not be turned to joy, and there is no hardship that will not be replaced with a new and renewed and beautified world.** You are all struggling. Unite that with Mine. Ask the Spirit, My Spouse, our Spirit, to show you and to help you understand what it was like for Joseph and I and Jesus in all of the instances of our lives. How we depended upon the Father, and how this is an example for you to give each question, each puzzlement, each lack of understanding to the Father; knowing He is caring for you, knowing that you have the might of His arm always.

Seek and find the joy, My children, in My Son, with My help, in My company with many Angels and with all the prayers and support of all of Heaven. You must do this, My children. It is the way to follow My Son. It is the way to fulfill Our Father's Will for you personally and for the world; all the while knowing that you are cherished and loved and given every blessing, every strength, every healing, every renewal that will present itself at the proper time. My children, think of the people in the world who have nothing and no one, who are reviled and scorned and treated as objects, and then remember the embrace I give you this night. **Send it out to the world, to those who are alone**. My children, we have victory. We have success. We have eternal glory! For now, my dear ones, more and more you live more deeply in the Kingdom of the Father on earth as it is in Heaven. Convert every sadness, every struggle into joy. I am with you, and all is well and all will be well, My children."

1/19, "My dear ones, I am your God and Father, your Creator and your Lord. **Your God is your hope! The Holy Mother, My beloved daughter, the Immaculate One, is your hope. Remain in hope,** and rejoice and believe that you WILL do this because of the gifts I bring you this day. When I say mighty gifts, I speak of the might of My Arm, the power of My Arm to overcome, the power against which no other shall prevail. The power that no other power shall overcome**, the power that is only allowed by My power**, the power of your Triune God! My children, live in hope. Live in the sure environment of victory. You have no idea how necessary this will be for you; but I ask you today, (more than ever before in your life) to recommit yourselves to My plan, to remember all of the promises of Heaven; to renew them in your hearts and in your minds, in your spirits and in your will; to accept them as your future that is NOW. My children, it is with great excitement I give you these gifts today, according to My Plan, at the perfect time. It is in My hope for you and your victory in union with your God and Holy Mother, all the Angels and Saints, everyone in Heaven, that you will have this victory, already won by My Son. Rejoice and give praise and thanks to Me, for it is accomplished in your life and in My plan. There is no other way, My dear ones, that you could accomplish ONE thing, ONE overcoming, perseverance, any ability that you have and will have (in order) to go through each event that is before you. We are united this day, My dear ones, as never before for your safety, for your sure victory, for the ability to keep on keeping on. **Turn every event into an act of rejoicing;** into gratitude for the escalation of My plan to rid the world of evil; to cleanse you and to cleanse the world that it might be renewed. Continue to open your hearts to new possibility to become a new creation, to becoming the instruments of the might of My Arm! Amen, My dear ones, your are loved. You are blessed. You are cherished, and I shower you with gratitude. I bid you to persevere. Amen."

1/26, "Dearest people, I am your Holy Spirit Who speaks, the Spirit of God, the Spirit of Love. Even though you have been prepared; even though you are ready to face the future, (and most of all face each minute today,) there will never be a time when you are not in need of more, when you have arrived at a place of perfection, when you have all the gifts and all the power and ability that you will need. No one knows this better than you, if you are being honest with yourselves. I bring you the joy of all of Heaven and the gratitude of the souls in Purgatory, of your dear loved ones. They pray with you. They pray for you, as do these precious souls in Purgatory waiting for your prayers, waiting for the moment when they will be brought into Paradise and eternal bliss. I bring you unity, dear people of God, everywhere in the world: a greater oneness in the Trinity, a greater oneness with each other, with the hearts of Jesus and Mary. Believe that you are enabled today to go beyond fear; to go beyond (but feeling) these emotions of fear that will make you want to flee from your place in the Father's Plan, from your place as disciples, as instruments of all the Father wishes to give His people and increase in you now and every day. **Live in the unity that you are given today**, in an awareness of a new oneness with the world and all who pray.

IT IS THAT MIGHTY VOICE OF ALL GOD'S PEOPLE THAT MUST RISE TO HIM TO ENABLE MITIGATION, TO ENABLE THE OPENING OF HEARTS EVERYWHERE FOR WHICH YOU PRAY. Please, please, dear ones, feel the urgency, the need for action on your part. Go deep within yourselves, once again, reflecting on the Father's mercy. Come once again to the Sacrament of Reconciliation now. Pray for humility. Pray for a new look at yourselves and your OWN behavior. **You will struggle with your weaknesses until Jesus returns; until you are brought either into Eternity and to Heaven, or you are kept here by the Will and plan of the Father to enter the New Era of Peace and Purity.**

Dear children of God, **beg to be purified. Beg to be transformed. Beg to become a new creation once again and again and again**. You are in the place the Father desires you to be this moment. Believe that and accept it with joy. But now I say to you again: a new level of holiness, of commitment and conviction, of understanding and knowledge of God and all the words of Heaven (these past years) are so necessary to increase. Dear, dear, dear people of the Sacred and Immaculate Hearts, we are ONE to whatever degree you will accept unity with the

Triune God and the Holy Mother. **It is up to you.** Great heights can be acquired by yourselves and the choices you make. Ponder the Father's mercy and beg for mercy on your country, on yourselves and on the world. I come in love, as I am the Spirit of Love. Remember first the Father's Perfect Will. Remember that you are loved beyond your understanding and rejoice! Lift your hearts. Offer them to the Father. Offer your lives to the Father's Will. Whatever needs to occur because of the Father's Will, will be your will, and you will give praise and thanks from now on forever and ever and ever, as you ascend more closely to the Kingdom of God on earth as it is in Heaven. Accept these gifts. Live them. Live them. Live them!"

1/28, "My dearest children, welcome this night to such an important and critical time in the history of the world, to prayer for the world, for the universe! I am your God and Father, your Creator and Lord, the One Who sustains you in My love. My Heart overflows with love for you. My Heart overflows with gratitude for your fidelity. It is many, many years now that you have prayed, and only become stronger and only increased your prayers according to My Will for you and in obedience to the requests of the holy one, the Immaculate One: dear, dear Mary, your beloved Mother. My children, YOU ARE A NEW CREATION TONIGHT, ALL OF YOU EVERYWHERE! I ask you to dwell on that simple phrase and say to yourselves: **'this moment, I am a new creation, according to the Father's Will for me and His plan for me and for the world'**; for, My dear ones, it is so true. Much more is the importance of your place in My plan because of the many years and the many delays during which you have responded. You know that many have not, or have responded at first and then turned away and have bitterness in their hearts, more so than they realize. I WOULD ASK YOU THIS WEEK, MOST ESPECIALLY, TO PRAY FOR THE HEALING OF BITTERNESS IN YOUR OWN HEARTS AND IN THE HEARTS OF ALL WHO PRAY AND IN THE ENTIRE WORLD.

Bitterness immediately speaks of a strong and sharp and unpleasant taste in your mouth, and it brings unpleasant and unkind, bitter words to the mouth that are uttered in many different ways; but always in a negative way, in an angry way always blaming someone for the difficulty and hardships, the struggles, the disappointments in the lives of everyone who harbors this bitterness. I ask you to give any bitterness, any unforgiveness to My Son, to bring it to Him as you kneel before Him in the great Sacrament of the Altar. This bitterness, My children, corrodes your heart, your mind, your spirit, your will, your words; and I wish for you to be healed. I wish for you to speak and walk in tenderness. The two cannot exist together in the same heart, and **tenderness will not thrive where bitterness has eaten away**! Tenderness is very important for now, for always; but most especially (you KNOW this) for the dear, broken, terrified, sorrowing ones who will come to you.

Always, My children, Heaven speaks of preparation for the time when you will pour yourself out upon the wounds of so many, and **you will go deep into the bitterness you find within these people; for great will be their loss remember, and first of all reactions will be bitter, terribly sad words looking for someone to blame! Bitterness, My children, is a cross that is brought upon you, everywhere in the world, by those who cannot trust or forgive, or try to understand and then tolerate others.** These scars, this erosion is deep in the hearts of many, My people, and of course I turn to you, My faithful ones who speak loving words in your prayers for the world. I ask you this week to begin to pray more in this vein as a focus for your prayers, as a focus for your petitions for healing for this dread and dreadful condition. My dear ones, you are loved. You are healing. You are tenderness. You are joy!

I bring the delight and shouts of gratitude from all of Heaven, especially your dear loved ones. How very much they love you; you can imagine! Unite your prayers with theirs. Invite them to pray for the most important cause, for you will heal many because Heaven will be praying with you and increasing the power of your prayer. Praise and thank Me, My children, for the beginning on a new level now of healing for the world at this stage. With these prayers and this focus and this gift you offer to all those who will come to you; but NOW for those you do not know, have not seen, but love already because of your hearts that ARE love. My dear ones, I thank you for your gentle tenderness. Send this love I pour out upon you tonight out to the world, out to those around you. Allow it to be present in your own mind, that you might share it at every moment as instruments of My healing and My love. Amen, My children; thank you for loving your Triune God, your Holy Mother and all of Heaven. How blessed you are. Believe it! "

2/2, "My dear ones, I am your Jesus of mercy and love, the One Who forgives and brings all of the gifts of Heaven. My dear ones, you WILL persevere. You WILL be victorious through all the years of waiting for My return. Whatever you hear from Heaven, take into your hearts. Ponder the words. Praise and thank the Father for these words given to so many now in every part of the world. Thank you for your prayers this day, on this special feast. I do, at this moment present you to My Father again and anew, and of course I speak to every person in the world who listens and attempts to live the requests of Heaven, the Commandments, the Beatitudes, mercy. Know that you are mercy on your God! Your desire is the impetus for the desires in the hearts of everyone in the world; for your desires contain the Father's Will and His desires for you and for the world. Think of these things, My children, and rejoice. Rejoice that more and more you are prepared to be a mighty instrument of all the gifts the Father has waiting for the world. Remember children, **that evil will be removed from the world and from the hearts of every person who chooses to cooperate, to receive and to live the gifts of My Father. It is a glorious time, My children, in the history of the world**. My children, these are life-giving words. These are good for your soul and your mind, your spirit and your heart. Digest them as you accept them again and you become a new person, as I present you now before the

Throne of My Father to His Will, to His might, to His power, to His great creative love for you. Amen, My children. Sit now in quiet for a moment to receive My gift of peace for you this day on this Feast of Mine and yours! Amen, My children. How I love you." (We are invited to realize these are not just repetitive words, but times of new and greater help and ability given, and how we always need them, to all of us each time they are mentioned as newly given, and they are real! ....cta.)

2/4, " My dearest children, once again I am your Jesus of Mercy Who speaks this night, Who stands in your midst, Who showers you with grace, with strength, with mercy and with all the love in My Sacred Heart. It is a night when everyone is weary, and struggles to stay awake, but I tell you My words are truth and light. My children, I ask you to be attentive. I ask you to read and reread the words I give for you and for the whole world. I have begun to speak to you through this messenger of events in the future for this area and your entire country. Pray for mitigation, as you have begun to do this night. Pray for all those who will struggle with waters that rise and flood and destroy, that bring great hardship to those whose very property and lives are threatened. I bring these requests and this information, and I will continue to give more words because of your faithfulness. Again and again people all over the world will **struggle through natural events, through bizarre weather patterns, signs of My Father's work in each place with experiences and struggles, with loss and fatigue and sorrow. It also speaks of the escalation of His plan for you and for the world**. You say, My dear ones, that you wish things would hurry and begin, and yet you shrink from the life events that occur in your own lives and in different places in the world. Please, My dear children**, remember that all of Scripture must be fulfilled.**

I ask you all to take better care of yourselves. When you care for yourself, you enable yourself to continue in My Father's Will. You admit that you are human and frail and vulnerable, as are all My people, every human on the earth. Think of the areas in the world that have felt famine and starvation, deadly floods and storms, taking many lives. You would not (wish to) know of this, My children. Praise My Father for every hardship, for I tell you the **Kingdom of Heaven must be earned**. Love requires sacrifice and suffering always. My love and God-is-love are your goals, My children, the love of My Mother. While you must not think it is earned because We love you; still a necessary ingredient in your response to Love, to My love, to your own love will always be a curtailing of your own whims, your own fancies, a human waste of time and yet I tell you, you are strong and noble! Expect no more of yourselves than you are able to handle even with My help. If My help seems limited, My children, it is not; yet I tell you again, **you are all where My Father desires you to be in your spiritual journey, in your physical journey through your life's story.** Always it is necessary to reflect, to readjust, to ask that motives be purified, that agendas **be simplified**, that surrender accompany each response to the Father's Will. Oh, My dear ones, you are so precious to Me; and so I speak words of counsel, words to comfort, to give you food for thought, to invite you to new reflection upon each day you spend in this difficult journey; and I speak with love as a reminder, My children, that every moment of your life: ALL IS WELL AND ALL WILL BE WELL! You are held in the palm of My hand, and I love you. You are Mine. I will NEVER let you go. We are one, My children. Be at peace."

2/6, 11:55 p.m. At Home, "You know how floods devastate and erode and kill farm animals and pets and humans, and leave horrible destruction in their wake. The fury of the Father's wrath will be seen in many parts of this country through the reflections of swollen waters and swift-running current. **If all will begin to pray at the outset of these storms, most of the destruction will be delayed**. Daughter, do not be afraid, though the events will be so terribly fear producing. I tell you these things to encourage patience and trust. The dear ones who have gathered faithfully around you now (prayer group) are bonded together solidly with you and with each other and with Me. This will still be an important area of mercy and renewal. We will continue to record new events of the near future, little weary one. All is well and all will be well! Rest, child, and arise a new creation. I am Jesus Who protects and strengthens you."

2/9, "My dearest ones, I am your God and Father. I bring you the gift of openness to hear and believe every word you are being given in these critical days. I bring you new trust. I bring you peace, a new desire for renewed commitment and consecration; a renewed fire in your hearts, My dear ones. How difficult I know it is for each of you to continue as you are; but I tell you, nothing prepares you more than the ongoing perseverance you are living. Do not become weary, and if you do, My dear, dear children everywhere in the world, I tell you: rest more; for this waiting, this perseverance, this struggle, personal especially, drains you of strength, drains you of the ability to continue as you are, opens you to distractions, to the call and allure of our enemy, the lure of the world. My dear people, you continue to be My faithful ones. It is with great seriousness I come to you. There is so much fear, so much expectation and announcement of new attacks; and so a climate of fear and expectation of the worst is developing in your country and in the world. Remain in peace, in simplicity, My dear ones. It is a simple straight-forward routine, faithful adherence to what you have been asked to do in each day to the focus on My plan, on My call to prayer, on the Face of My Son, His Presence with you at every moment; on the dear, dear Holy and Immaculate One, Mary, the Beloved Mother, her presence with you and many Angels. My dear children, do you truly live in this Presence, this awareness, this focus, this quiet strength being given to you? If you are not living in this environment, which has been given to you in grace and gift and you cannot be at peace, you cannot avoid distraction, the strain becomes greater and you succumb to illness, to more stress, more fatigue, and it is ongoing." (continued)

2/9 cont'd. "As you consecrate yourself and your loved ones, your country and the world every day, My children, consecrate yourselves to joy, to trust and surrender. **These are weapons**. I tell you again and again. They are yours, you have them. You have every virtue, every strength and gift you need, My children, and they must be lived in simplicity. **Do not allow your days to become crowded** with activity that is not necessary to your ongoing prayer life, your ongoing spiritual stamina. My dear ones, how I love you! Feel My love. Remember that you are My chosen ones, My faithful ones who have responded; that Satan wars against you every moment. Oh My children, do not become discouraged and, even when you fall as you do and you will, do not allow that to be a discouragement. Do not allow yourselves to be disheartened. Do not allow yourselves to turn away for any reason. Remind yourselves at the start of each day that you are living in My Kingdom now, that you have grown and become the important and necessary instrument of the salvation of so many. Allow that to remain an important motive for your prayer, your focus, your desires and your choices!

As you see destruction again and again throughout the intervening years until My Son returns, you will need more and more strength. You will rely more and more upon each other for encouragement, mutual strength and comfort for the love to blossom and remain the atmosphere in which you live. I say these things to you, My children, as a reminder, as an encouragement; and as I say them, I am gifting you again and more and in new ways to equip you to continue to regain and retain joy and hope for the fulfillment of all of Our words for the swift return of My Son, for My mercy which is yours, for the ability to grasp and BE mercy for the world. I tell you, you bring great joy to your God, to your Holy Mother, to all of Heaven; and I thank you. I love you, My own, My dear ones."

2/11, "My dear ones of My Sacred Heart, I am your Jesus, children, your Jesus of Mercy, your Lord and your God. I am your Savior and your King, the King of your hearts. I see in your hearts such love for My Mother, and I thank you so much. She loves you, children and we all give praise and thanks for Her this night on this so very special feast. Many, many graces and healings are given this night in the Name of the Beloved Lady of Lourdes. She is queen of hearts, My children. Everywhere in the world She makes Her presence known and draws Her children into Her Immaculate and loving Heart; and I tell you truly, more and more hearts become like Hers. You are learning more and more to love Me with Her love and as She loves, and with a purity you have not known in the past. Let us give praise to Our Father for this great gift and for the blessings and the transformation that occur constantly within your hearts, your minds, your will, your lives and your spirits.

Let us think only of the call each of you has to be a child of Mary, to follow Her on the steps to Calvary, to follow Her every step to the foot of the Cross in love, in surrender, in gratitude for what each of you must offer daily, for what each of you offers freely and in love. Again I say, **true love requires**

sacrifice and suffering, and so it was for this dear Mother. All that has been written or privately revealed and recorded does not begin to touch the love My Mother showed to all the people we encountered while I was on this earth with Her; all She suffered for the sake of Love, all She sacrificed for Me. There were no needs of Mine She did not think about and provide before they were obvious or necessary. There was no opportunity that passed by for Her to tell Me of Her love, of Her gratitude for Me and of the great love which was the gift to all those who followed Me, to all those who looked after Her, took Her into their hearts, made Her a part of their lives.

Oh My children, this Holy Mother is the life of Our hearts, is She not? She is the inspiration, the motive. She is the strength I give you. She is the dedication of every fiber of her being that inspires you; and She prays for you every moment, as She did then when I walked the earth. **In her great wisdom and understanding She knew about you always, as She knew about My life, about her own, all that had been revealed to her through the mercy and gift of My Father**. Let these be the impetus also to bring you closer to her every moment; to pray with Her for each other every moment; to pray in thanksgiving to My Father for her, as I know you do as you come to a greater understanding of the gift she is, and all she does for you and Her great love for you: the many places that are Shrines to her appearances, to her words of love and warning to all of Her children at those particular times, as she is doing today, to bring you closer to Me and to the way of Love. My dear ones, you are blessed tonight by all of Heaven. A blessing is given in union with your Triune God and your Holy Mother to each of you now, a blessing that is filled with love, that you might **feel the love of God and all of Heaven** even more from now on, that you might feel the action and support of that love and all the prayers that pour out from Heaven at every moment. Be sustained and strengthened and encouraged by these gifts; by this love ever present with you, always growing in your hearts, always sustaining you and preparing you for the days ahead. Let love fill and guide and complete your life. I am Jesus Who loves you. I AM Love!"

2/18, My dearest children, I am your God and Father. I tell you this night to PRAY MORE FOR YOUR COUNTRY. DIRE EVENTS FOLLOW THE AGGRESSIVE BEHAVIOR OF YOUR GOVERNMENT. Pray more. Pray for a change of heart for these misguided ones, who know not the truth they think they know; who listen to false voices, false leaders, false values, follow the plans of Satan, their minds clouded with greed and a false sense of what is right. Do not be frightened, but be on guard! Satan and his demons roar like crazed animals seeking souls, seeking to devour My innocent ones. Pray, My children... more! Offer each moment of each day, each breath you take as a prayer. Offer obedience and surrender to My Will. You know not what lies ahead. I count on you to do My bidding, to answer My requests with all of your strength, all of your focus. Please, **attempt fewer distractions in your lives**.

Attempt a more contemplative and quiet lifestyle. You will see chaos soon; so much change in your lives; so many, many, many people who will need you. When you see them, you will understand My words and the need for total trust, or you would be overwhelmed immediately. you would turn and run! New openness is given this night to your hearts, to your minds, to your will that you will accept all that lies in front of you, that you will let go of the world more and all that lies behind you. MORE HUMILITY IS NEEDED, MORE PATIENCE, MORE TOLERANCE, MORE ACCEPTANCE OF EACH OTHER; for you know and love each other and you will not know or love yet those who come. Great and heroic change and deeds will be required of you, My dear ones; but you will do this, whatever it is, and you will come to a place of immense joy that is constantly present. Believe My words! Please I beg you, do not become discouraged by the struggles in your life**. Do not be saddened that a delay seems to continue**; but remember: IT IS MITIGATION THAT IS YOUR GIFT TO THE WORLD! It is support and comfort, a reaching out to bring into your hearts the entire world. My dear ones, think of it, what a momentous time and call to such a small number of people who are mighty, who are precious and able. This openness I give you this night. Believe this, for without My gifts, you know you would be nothing; but with Me and because of Me you are everything I desire and ask you to become**. It is time for new maturity, a new seriousness** and a reflection on all the words you have been given; **for there is so much you gloss over and forget**, and I need for you to know that you might be and become prayer warriors unequalled in all of history! Think of that, and rejoice. It is good to take care of yourselves! It is a waste of gifts when you do not. Take time to heal, My dear ones. You are loved and loved and loved every moment. Amen, My precious, mighty, little ones!"

2/23, "My dearest ones, I am your Jesus of Mercy, of hope, of joy, of surrender to the Will of Our Father: surrender for you, My dear ones, to each event that is about to unfold in your lives, in your country and in the world. Thank you for being so very faithful to this prayer time. All of you, all who have ever been here and your families are doubly blessed this day for your fidelity, for your accepting the gifts of wisdom and understanding, praying for the souls in Purgatory this day and resolving to do more for them. My Father has asked every person in the world to pray more for your country. It is not less necessary, but more necessary than ever, NOW, THIS DAY. Never, My dear ones, are you without the means of fulfilling the desires of My Father. Never are you without the grace to protect you from the evil one. If only you will accept these consciously, daily before you begin your day and your consecration for not only yourselves and your loved ones, but for your country and then for the world. Accepting gifts you recall, praising My Father and thanking Him for them, and then using them are what enables these gifts and moves the Father to give you new gifts, to raise you higher in His plan; which simply means that you will pray and act in surrender more fully, more totally, more deeply with all your might and all your heart and all your will. My children, the time comes closer for events, and you have seen destruction again now of a natural cause in several places in your world. You know that these are signs and an impetus to be serious about My serious words, but at the same time and above all, to be joyous and filled with hope. **Hope, My dear ones, is what will enable the gift of perseverance**; and as you persevere, you gain more hope, and so it goes in the wonderful plan of My Father. There is nothing to fear! There is no reason for discouragement or a lack of desire to serve your God, the Holy Mother and every person in the world. It is a great family you are, My children. It is a great and greater numbered family that you serve. Welcome them again into your hearts and prayers. From now on, the needy will be needier, the sad will be sadder; the broken will recognize their brokenness as they respond to the gifts of the Spirit. Again I say with all of the love in My Sacred and Eucharistic Heart, remember that 'All is well, that all will be well.' HOW I love you. Be filled with peace. Amen."

3/2, "Dear ones, I am your Mother, and I come by a very special request of God, Our Father this day to prepare you for this holiest of Seasons, the Season in which you renew all of your consecrations, all of your promises; and you come in trust, in fasting and in prayer and much reflection on your own weaknesses, your vulnerabilities, the peace, the people and the things that cause you to fall or even cause you to be distracted, to turn away for even a moment. Oh my children, you know what important and critical and serious days these are! Always the Season of Lent is given you to prepare yourselves to walk to the Hill of Calvary with me, with My Beloved Son, your precious Lord and Savior and King. But in these years you have been asked to pray more, to pour yourselves out as My Son poured Himself out for you, to walk every step in quiet, in obedience; contemplating the words, the sounds, the total environment of suffering of all of us in those times and more especially, of My Beloved Son; to unite yourselves to each suffering, each word, each renewal of self to the Father and His Will for yourselves and for the salvation of the world and to **rejoice, my children, that you DO co-redeem in union with My Son.**

What great gifts are yours, my dear children everywhere. Praise the Father and thank Him that you are given a listening heart, constantly given new wisdom and understanding, and that this Lent, new understanding of all Jesus suffered for you, of His great love for His people will be yours. There is nothing greater you can do for yourselves, for your God, for me and for the world than **unite yourselves to the suffering and death of Our dear, beloved, precious Jesus.** You will never know how many people you touch with this union. I tell you now because of God's love and His plans for you, because of the critical days in which you live; great gifts are given this day to every faithful one in the world, to the entire world. Beg that they will accept the gifts and the mercy the Father desires to give. You know not the day nor the hour when each step of the Father's plan unfolds; and so you are obedient and you WILL walk with me arm in arm to the Hill of Calvary these forty days in the most consecrated and focused and deep, deep giving of yourselves. (This opportunity is as new and available now as it was in 2003…cta.)

I am with you, my dear ones, and I hold you in my Heart; and because it is My Immaculate Heart, know that you are being purified more during these special days. You are wrapped in my Mantle and folded in my arms, held in my Heart and in my great love for you. All of Heaven blesses you and joins you on this most important journey for the world. As you walk, as you kneel, as you pray, bring the entire world with you to the foot of the Cross. We go forward in the most important time in history... together!"

3/4, "My dear ones, I am Jesus, come once again with new strength, with new energy and vigor; for it takes more of these gifts to maintain the level of prayer to which you are called, to walk this path with My Mother to the Hill of Calvary, to stand at the foot of My Cross, to weep with Her, to comfort Her and in this way to comfort Me. **This is a prayer of the finest kind, of the highest level: to comfort Me, My children**. Think of this. Place yourselves at the foot of My Cross when you are in silence and before Me; or wherever you are and there is time to be aware of the Cross holding My Body, as you see and hear Me uttering My last words, as you see Me suffering unbelievable pain. My children, you are being offered such great opportunities with these prayers, practicing YOUR presence at My crucifixion, at My suffering, every event that is immortalized in the Stations that you walk in your mind and in your heart and, as often as possible, in the Church before each Station: kneeling, bowing, recalling, uniting yourselves with each of these sufferings, present with Me. Believe Me, My children, this is a great gift; and believe Me that your attempts to unite yourselves to My sufferings and to be present to them will gain you a level of holiness you have not yet experienced or could even imagine. I encourage you tonight to pray more in this way, to walk the Stations often. Great, great graces are given with this prayer, with this effort on your part, sustained by Our Spirit and the Angels, as I was sustained on that terrible walk, carrying the heavy, heavy, heavy burden of the Cross of your sins and the sins of the world. Think of how many people, My dear ones everywhere, are involved in that act, that walk, that emptying of My entire Self for the redemption of mankind and now repeated again by yourselves often, giving great, great graces for the world beyond your imagining.

Always more is given than you expect, and you have learned to come to prayer to Me without expectations, without needs, without an agenda as you sit before Me in silence. This too is graced by Our Spirit. The Triune God blesses you this night. All is made ready each day, as you prepare for the final week of many prayers and preparations and the ultimate walk to Calvary. Pray especially for those who will be taken into eternity during these weeks of Lent. There will be many. Remember it is MERCY that they receive. Pray for their hearts to open, for their choices to be guided by the Spirit and the mercy of My Father. Pray, My children, for you will see many events of destruction, and in those events many brought into eternity and as many as possible given the gift of salvation that will save them ... most of all because of you and your prayers and your concerns and your hard work on their behalf. Oh My dear ones, words fail to convey the gratitude of My Father, of all of Us in Heaven, and most especially the souls that are saved as they realize what they had the courage to choose: for Truth! Keep these graced times in your consciousness that you might be moved to praise and give thanks, that you might rise above the struggles of each day as you fall on your way, as your weakness is presented to you in ways you do not enjoy, in revelations to yourself about yourself. You would rather not see and yet you know, My dear ones, to give thanks for these as well, and you know you are being led to the greatest perfection step by step, even as you fall! You are loved. HOW you are loved. How I will say that again and again and again until We are facing each other, and then I will say so again! Persevere in increased prayer and in joy. All IS well!"

3/11, "My dear people, I am the Holy Spirit of God: the Spirit of truth, the Spirit of love, the One Who brings you the gifts and the healing you have received, and Who will continue to bring these to you until the moment Jesus returns. It is not as though gifts will end at that time, but it will be the beginning of a new era, an era of peace and purity. You will still have need of gifts, but in different ways you will receive them, different levels of sanctity and unity with your God and holy Mother, My dear, dear Spouse. My dear people of the world, unite in prayer, unite in sacrifice, unite in penance and in almsgiving. Unite in humility. The dear people who serve the world now are praying for them by begging mercy for the world, by being available to the needs of all now and in the future. It is I, the Spirit of God Who enables your acceptance, your use, your sharing, your pouring out of each gift you have received, each measure of holiness, each height and depth you have achieved through the grace and the gifts I bring to you, and that are brought to you by the intercession and poured out by the Immaculate One, dear Mary, the holy Mother. My people, do not dwell on the fact that you are becoming holy ones, that you have achieved true grace, a higher level of sanctity that gives praise constantly for this fact, that every gift you will need, every ability you will need in the future has been given to you already. Praise the Father and thank Him that you are chosen to serve in any and every capacity millions of people who will be desperate and desolate.

Praise and thank the Son, Who suffered more terribly than you will ever know throughout His entire life; but especially the years of ministry that were public, the people He served with grace, with patience, with complete harmony, with their needs as the vehicle of your redemption. Praise the Father's Perfect Will which enfolds you with healing, with new formation. Always you are going forward and rising, being lifted up by the prayers that are said in Heaven and by the Will of the Father. Praise and thank Him. **To continue always requires praise. To enable always requires gratitude. To receive requires the openness that you pray to Me for:** to open your own hearts and the hearts of everyone in the world. Dear, dear people of God, rejoice! Familiar words, but do you? Will you and can you now because I am always here to help you, waiting for you to ask, waiting to pour out blessings and gifts and strengths far beyond that for which you ask; for you do not know entirely what you need, and always your God sees in a perfect way your needs and gifts them, nourishes you and lifts you up again, and again and again.

Each time you fall in even a small way, it is necessary to lift you up again, and many times you are not aware of the little, seemingly inconsequential, but hurtful words and glances and attitudes that you bring to others and the sorrow you cause. Just accept this fact, My dear ones, this truth for everyone, and come in sorrow begging mercy and forgiveness and openness to new understanding and new wisdom. There is a rhythm and (again) harmony to prayer, to becoming who you were invited by the Father to become, who you were created by the Father to be, who you were sustained and called forth by the Father to accept; and then in that unity to go forward to touch everyone, to pour yourself out as your God pours Himself out for you and for the world and upon the world. In your furthest stretch of imagination, My dear ones, you could never allow the reality of suffering in the world. As you dwell on the needs of others, you will begin to feel better, for **you will have left behind the burden of self!** Remember this. Ponder this fact. This is truth. We praise and thank the Father that this is possible for each one of you in the world. How blessed you are, how fortunate to be chosen. My dear ones, praise and thank the Father Who loves you, your Triune God Who loves you, and the holy Mother who holds you in her Heart, who loves you. Accept this love and rejoice. I pour Myself into your hearts now everywhere, as you hear and read these words. Amen. Praise and thank the Father!"

3/23, "My dearest children, I am your Mother. I greet you this day with all the love in my Heart. I welcome you. I embrace you. I am here with you. I walk among you and embrace you. I thank you for your fidelity. My dear ones, you and I walk together, walk with each other into battle; and I ask you and remind you that you are signs of hope, that you are a source of peace, a source of mercy to all. I ask you again to be patient and loving and tender and tolerant with each other and with your loved ones**. Each person responds to the call of Our Father at the right time in the Father's Will**, in the right way. You know it is the Holy Spirit, **my beloved Spouse, Who converts**. **Your call is to pray for openness in the hearts of your loved ones, in the hearts of all in this country and in the entire world.** My children, recall again how many your prayers are impacting, are turning towards the Father, opening to my Son, to Our Presence with you and with them, with so many Angels.

My children everywhere in the world, you are so precious to me. The Father counts on you, gifts you and graces you again this day, and all of your loved ones. Do not despair. **It is the Father's plan to convert your families, your loved ones. There is nothing to fear**. Be at peace always. Bring peace wherever you go, wherever you are. Bring My love and My Heart to all and do not succumb to impatience, to a lack of understanding. It is not always necessary that you understand; but only that you trust, that you believe in the words of Our Father, of my Son and my beloved Spouse, in the words I bring to you, the healing and the tenderness. You are my beloved little ones, and you must be beloved little ones to all of my children, for all ARE my children. Remember that always you are reaching out with love and kindness, or unkindness and the lack of love. How important you are in the Father's plan. How necessary are you with your prayers as instruments of the Father's plan. Be patient with each other and with the Father Whose Will is perfect, Whose love is beyond your understanding, beyond your imagination. My dear ones, I am with you. I am for you. I am helping you. I am interceding for you at every moment. Remember that your names are chanted every day, all day before the throne of Our Father by all of the Angels, that you are never alone and therefore, you need never be lonely. You belong to me. Thank you for loving me as you do, for your fidelity and your devotion. Open your hearts to my Son Who loves you, Who IS Love! Rejoice."

3/25, "My dearest children, I am your God and Father. Thank you for coming again this night, even in your fatigue. Thank you for overcoming whatever fills your lives with chores, your distractions. They are purified by the Holy Mother and they obtain graces for all of those who suffer the effects of war, all of those fighting to free people from oppression, to protect your country and others who are involved. YOU WILL NOT FAIL, MY CHILDREN. You will not turn away again, as you have in the past. You will not seek other gods or other pleasures, joy from any other direction than the joy I give you, the gifts I give you. They adorn your souls with beauty. **They strengthen your will to choose again and again and again for Me. Some day this choice may mean that you might lose your lives. You know that there will be martyrs for the sake of the Name of Jesus. You know to pray for those who will be martyrs. You know that they will come directly to Heaven for eternity in bliss, in unknown happiness (in this world).** You are a sign of hope for those who pray, but especially for those who do not pray. They know you are praying for them and secretly they are joyful and grateful, all the while you carry the burden of concern for them.

Continue to carry your brothers and sisters, for the burden is made light through love and the joy of sacrifice. When you love them, you are loving Me; and when you serve Me, you are always serving them! Remember you cannot lose in My service. You will always win, and ultimately it will be eternal life that you have won. Praise and thank Me, My dear ones, for My great mercy to you, as you have no idea how many gifts and what great gifts you have; **so too, you have no idea how often you are forgiven and given My mercy;** although this awareness increases, as it should, but increases more now. Praise and thank Me for forgiveness that you do not know about: forgiveness that you have forgotten about, or even that you may take for granted or count on. Do not become complacent, My children. I speak to you everywhere in the world with My great, great love, with My longing for your salvation to clothe your soul, to bring you into perfect unity with My Will. Oh My dear ones, WHEN YOU SEE HEAVEN, YOU WILL UNDERSTAND WHAT ALL THE FUSS WAS ABOUT!

I am your God, your Creator, your Father, the One Who made the entire Universe. I spoke and all was created! Ponder this in the coming week. Ponder the fact that all is gift and that you are here by the great gift of My sustenance, maintaining you in grace, in the proper place in My plan and in My Will. More and more you will see the need for this mighty prayer: the mighty power of My Son and His Name. My children, I thank you again and again and again. And your answer can always be: 'You are welcome, Father. You are always welcome to all the prayers, all the strength and energy that you have given to Me. I give it back to You now, my loving Father, in gratitude and in delight for this opportunity to pray for the world and its' salvation, and to come closer to You, to my Beloved Jesus, to Your Spirit and to Mary, the Immaculate One. I lift my soul, I lift my heart, I lift my mind and all of who I am and I give them to You, Father. I put myself at Your service and at Your disposal.' And, My children, I will say: 'Amen. Be at peace, dear children, dear little holy ones, dear, dear little precious ones of My plan, of My mercy, of My great love for you and for all.'"

4/6, "My beloved children, I am your Jesus, your Savior, your Lord. I am with you this day reflecting upon My Passion. **You are very special, important instruments of Mercy for the world. I wish for you to see yourselves in this way, for it will help you to remain focused on your mission, the call to so many who have remained faithful all over the world.** There is so much and so many for which to pray, and I come again with gratitude for the time and the degree of self you surrender. You cannot possibly understand the enormity of your gifts, or the gift you are giving to the world. Many are coming into eternity now. Many more will follow. The war will escalate. Your President reels in sorrow and remorse as he realizes more and more how he has been duped and fooled and led astray by the empty words, the false logic of evil men. Pray for him, My children. His heart is good, but he has been foolish. He has listened to flattery. He is my precious son. Pray that he has the strength to accept the decisions he has made, to remain faithful to Me. Pray for all those who suffer so terribly in war. War causes people to become something else, someone else, transformed by the ugliness of suffering, the ugliness of the sounds and the sights of people dying, being blown apart; lives being blown apart, families being shredded. My children: IT IS A TERRIBLY SERIOUS TIME IN THE WORLD. You know this. For the following weeks, bring everyone to the mercy of My Father, Who is involved in this terrible, terrible war; and remember you will only see an escalation.

Take the sorrow that My suffering allows in your hearts and your understanding, and apply it to the loved ones of those who lose their lives, who give their lives for the freedom of this beautiful country and their dear, dear families and all of you. IT IS A SERIOUS TIME, MY PEOPLE. You are at war! You are NOT engaged in watching something fascinating on your television sets. You are not only tuning in at the end of the day to see what is new. REMAIN TUNED IN, My people, to the horrors and the sadness of loss, to the travesty of justice. You know the power of your prayers so much better now. Trust the power of that prayer for individuals, that they might see and accept the mercy of My

Father. You are My Angels, even though you are weak, sinful, turn away so quickly, become absorbed by something else and allow distractions to steal your time, your focus. Get rest, My dear ones, that you might continue. Remember the world counts on you and your fidelity. My Father counts on you and in the meantime, gifts you with precious and enormous strength, graces, peace and joy. Can one be joyful in the midst of war? YOU can, because you have that grace; but it is the joy that results from gratitude for gift, from gratitude for the mercy of the Father waiting to pour out on helpless suffering little ones everywhere. There is no sense to war; but in suffering one touches another, one pours out self in union with Me, and you can rejoice for this unity. You can rejoice that you are allowed to affect the salvation of so many. These are beautiful days everywhere as Spring approaches. It was Spring when I marched to Calvary. **Your soldiers march to Calvary, My dear ones. March with them in prayer and in love and in generosity. You are soldiers in My Mother's Army,** remember that! You are My beloved ones. How I love you. How grateful I am for you. Be blessed and filled with new courage, new energy, and of course, new joy. We are one! My Mother and I bless you now, again in the Name of My Father and in My Name and in the Name of Our Spirit. Rejoice, My children. You are highly favored. You are the darlings of My Heart. Amen."

4/8, "My dear ones, I am your God and Father. I bless you tonight, for I see you proceeding according to the requests of My Beloved Son. I thank you for this obedience. How I thank you for the fire burning brightly in your hearts, in your spirits, in your words, in your souls. I give you tonight the ability to see yourselves better, to be aware of your behavior, to hear your own words, that perhaps could be softer, more patient, more tender, more loving. Hear not only My words, but the pleading in My voice. Come to Me, children, for the strength to carry Our wishes, and the desires of My perfect Will. Come to Me. Throw yourselves upon My mercy. Place the entire world in My mercy. Place all of your desires into My desires. This is easy to say and impossible to do without more mercy, more grace and strength. I see your desire to change, to improve, to be all you are called to be and, of course, I thank you again because you are reaching higher as well as reaching more deeply into your heart, into your behavior, into your own motives, asking that they be purified.

It is well that you do not realize how gifted and blessed you are! You know that I mean by this: it may interfere with your humility, and that is the most important of all. It is the foundation on which all other virtues are built and all behaviors are improved. Remember you heard tonight the words about the people healed by the hidden sufferings, the hidden surrender of My Son. This is what I ask of you. **Try not to take advantage of advantages, My children!** Try to be as small and hidden and humble and quiet as you can be. Pray for openness. Pray for an insight you have not had before. You are accomplishing so much by your obedience. War will only escalate, and so I simply repeat this tonight. Keep this in the forefront of your prayers as a motive, as a reason to stay quiet and reflective. Praise Me and thank Me again and again. Stay faithful, stay focused, stay prayerful and silent. Amen, you prepare for enormous events. "

4/13, "My very dear ones, I am your Mother, the Immaculate One who walks with you now, this week of Passion, inviting you once again to walk with me, to stand back, to listen to the crowd, to listen to each other, to listen to yourselves and all of the voices that clamor for attention; all of the distractions that clamor to divide you, your heart, your motives and your focus on the footsteps of My Son as He falls and rises, as He allows another to help Him, to share His suffering in carrying His Cross. Be that one, my children, to carry the Cross for My Jesus by carrying yourselves and your own weaknesses to Him again in the Sacrament of Reconciliation, and to remember My Son died for sinners. So I invite you to leave your righteousness and your judgmentalism, your criticism and your attitudes at the foot of the Cross of My Son. My Son's burden is light, but first you must unburden yourselves of these things that slow down your walk with Him Who loves you beyond words, Who suffered for you beyond imagination and understanding, Who loves you this day, this moment in overwhelming pouring out of Himself, in an overwhelming surrender of all He could have said and could have done and could have avoided for your sake, but did not, for love of you!

I invite you to avoid opportunities that might put you in a better light, a different light in the eyes of others, to surrender the opportunity to make yourselves important, or the one who is listened to, to be the one who would see themselves as savior of the rest. I do not accuse you, my children, but I remind you of the reality of the weaknesses of being human and, as you travel along in community, these temptations are always present; and in the cleansing and emptying of your souls, it is important to know yourself, to generously give of all of who you are. As you travel this journey, as you are emptied, allow yourselves to be filled with this reality, with this great, great, great heroic love, this great sacrificial love and then, do likewise! I thank you, my precious ones, for your generosity and your great hope to be all you are called to be, and to be little in doing so. Stay hidden with me. Stand back, my children, and listen. Amen, my dear ones, amen. I am with you and you are with me!"

4/16, Adoration, 5p.m., "Little messenger, rejoice! I am Jesus Who loves and protects you. It is the time of reflection now. Come away with Me for words to the waiting world. It is a time of gift and strengthening for the battle that rages for souls, especially those of My beloved ones who serve the needs of all and pray for the salvation of the world.

'My children of the world, each of you is suffering in a personal and special way of the Father's Will that brings you into greater harmony with each event of your lives and in the world. You are still unable to imagine or emotionally accept the horrors that await your future. Do NOT turn away because you do not wish to hear or believe. Do not reject words given to messengers that seem too frightening to be real, too impossible to accept as what would be said by a loving God. Know that you ARE stronger and more able to persevere through terrifying times that come to pass in your own land. The New World Order becomes bolder and more sure of itself each day, and will go forward with even more aggressive behavior. Use this important time of unity with Me to learn to say and mean: 'Not my will, Father; but Thy Will be done!'

4-17 At Home 11:30 p.m., "Let us continue, dear daughter of My Heart.

My people: **All your good intentions come to naught when you succumb to using harsh words and bitterness**. These wound Me most, for you are hurling these at My already bruised and battered Body that carries your sins on My heavy Cross, sick and trembling, weak from scourging and the lack of tenderness on your part. **Be patient with those who do not understand, who have not accepted the words of Heaven; or who have, perhaps been put off by your haughty behavior and sarcasm. The love in one's heart can only respond to the Love it hears and discovers in the heart of another. The weakness of sin can only be dispersed in an atmosphere of acceptance and patience and tolerance.** Prayer is your only recourse with which to battle the evil one and his hold on another or, perhaps, yourself! See yourselves in the light of My love for you, and My Father's mercy. You must follow up His forgiveness with whatever is necessary to change your lifestyle, or remove yourself from temptations and the occasions of sin. My dearest people, My beloved ones, I beg you, I call you from the Cross to come back to Me this instant and remain in My protection. Call upon My Mother, as she stands at the foot of My Cross. **Ask the one who has accepted the world in every Age as her child, whom I will deny nothing, to come to your assistance.** Run quickly to her standing here.

Leave your critical words and attitudes at the foot of this Cross on which I languish for love of you. Accept the healing and strength that pours from My wounds to push away the evil one and all of his temptations and subtle suggestions that continue to lead you astray, continue to fill your hearts and words with anger and unforgiveness. It is mercy I desire, My dear, dear ones! It is mercy you must desire for your loved ones and for yourselves. Give to Me this holy night all of your acceptance and cooperation with the graces and gifts My Father continues to pour out upon you. Do not throw them back at Him in disinterest. Do not, for love of Me, walk away from Me now, as the requests for your new level of surrender touch upon behavior and habits that cling. I have saved you from eternal death, dearest ones. Choose life! Choose peace and purity, patience and sincerity, tenderness and a merciful acceptance of each other. It is Me you will be loving, My pain you will be relieving, My woundedness you will be soothing. You have already received all the strength and the virtues you need with which to defend your weak humanity. I am your Buckler and Shield**. It is in the shadow of My Cross that you are defended!** I love you. I will never leave you or give up on you. Do not leave Me, little precious ones."

FOR MERCY'S SAKE!

4/24, at Adoration, "My dearest child, I am your God and Father. I bring healing to your heart. I bring the might of My Arm to your lagging and weary spirit. Continue to rejoice and praise Me, little one. Be encouraged, daughter, and now let us begin:

'I am the Father and Creator of all, Who calls out in gratitude and love for the perseverance of My faithful remnant. In spite of weakness and personal failures, you continue to make progress in My mercy. **Your very fidelity to rising each time you fall opens My mercy, causes it to fall upon the earth and enables a trust to carry each of you through loneliness and near despair.** You can see and feel the strong support of other's prayers, your mutual love and prayers and all of Heaven's love and prayers. Without this increased interaction and dependence within the Great Body of Christ, this Communion of Saints which you are living so acutely as My Church Militant, all would be lost! You would be lost and My Plan would fail. However, My beloved ones, I remind you again that the gates of Hell shall not prevail against My Church, My holy ones, the warriors you have become in the Army of your Heavenly Mother who continues to obtain mighty graces and mercy and perseverance in the battle that rages. You are about to see war erupt on a new front, requiring a transfer of troops to defend other countries and people. This will continue, as you have been told in the past through so many messengers. I speak these days mainly of transformation in My Son, the Christ, your Savior and King through this messenger who has served Me and all of you for many years, while remaining faithful to all I have desired for her life. Again I say, do not reject these words because they are not to your own liking or expectations. See that these words call to you **to continue to change, to struggle against your own sinfulness, not those of another!**

Each of you is dealing with personal sin and weakness and a revelation of new areas of sinful habits and behavior. This causes discomfort and depression and discouragement. **In a state of greater surrender to the reality of your own lifestyle, you will find the peace you need to continue this road to holiness.** I plead with you this day to accept My Will for you; to ask Our Spirit to show you new areas of unpleasantness, of a demanding spirit, a nature driven by selfishness and haughty attitudes. Look closely, My beloved children. These are present in most of you; but they are also coupled with broken hearts that you continue to defend with harsh words, lashing out instead of coming to Jesus, the Holy One. Accept the fact, dearly beloved ones, that a degree of all these ills is present in all of you as a part of your weak humanity. Accept My Jesus as the One Who heals you, Who will save you, Who will bring you to salvation: your Heavenly Home and just reward. You ARE heirs of My Kingdom, little loved ones. Accept your inheritance. I will do the rest! I will defeat evil and remove it from the hearts of evil men and from the earth. Trust Me, My children. Remain hidden and protected in the Sacred and Immaculate Hearts. Be gentle and patient with yourselves, My people. Be patient and gentle with Me, your God and Creator and Lord. All WILL be well. All IS well. BELIEVE IT!

4/26, 10p.m. At Home, "Dear child, thank you for sharing these words with the world that waits in humble and joyful hope for new wisdom and understanding. Remember that dawn brings the day of celebration of Divine Mercy and the opportunity to obtain indulgences and the removal of all the punishment due to your many sins. Make this a day of praise and thanksgiving for this great act of mercy to all who believe these promises to Our Beloved Faustina, Our little Saint and giant messenger of many words from Jesus of Mercy that explain My mercy; that promise these acts of mercy in response to all who have prayed the Novena of Divine Mercy given to her long ago to prepare all of you now in this Age of Divine Mercy for the great difficulties and change and struggle in these End Times.

I am the Father of all people. I offer My boundless mercy to all people, who need only accept this mercy by cooperating with My desires for each of you, and your surrender to My mercy and My Perfect Will. I salute you this day, beloved ones, for more obedience and surrender to these Heavenly promises and means of bringing you more deeply into My Divine Will by means of this astounding gift of my predilection and gracious goodness. Every day, My children, you are braver and stronger and **more prepared for the times of treachery and betrayal, martyrdom and daily suffering in hiding from the Antichrist and his followers.** When you live in obedience to My Will and desires, precious ones of the world, you are pouring out mercy upon Me, your Father God and Creator, your Jesus of Mercy, the Spirit of Mercy and Mary, the Mother of Divine Mercy. You are blest. You are victorious in Mercy and in Love. Amen."

4/29, "My dearest people, I am your Holy Spirit Who speaks. Believe this, My children. Believe that I am pouring Myself out upon you in a new way, as you desire for every faithful one in the world. The Father will never abandon you, nor let you down. He will never remove His protection, His mighty love, the strength of His arm. These images, My dear ones, are so important for you because they are so real, though you cannot see them, and you know that you experience these according to your trust in these promises; that new grace is given always, but you must be open to it and immediately begin to use it, to share it, to give it away. More than ever now, **you are the instruments of grace for the world**. Do not take this lightly, My dear people, for it is part of your mission. It is part of your identity as child of God and child of Mary: How very, very difficult, how totally against all you are, but in the line and the spirit with who you are becoming. Be joyful, be hope filled. It is not only necessary, it is time that you send hope and trust and acceptance out to the world. Think of the world. Think of what a big place it is, how many billions of people, (BILLIONS, My dear ones) and your prayers and your good works, your surrender, your obedience is touching them! Your success in your mission, as the instruments of the Father's Will, is having an effect upon them for the good, for healing, for salvation.

How faithful you are. Be encouraged! Be filled with a new fire. Be filled with new zeal for souls, for this day I fill you with new sanctity; this day I fill you with new understanding of your mission and of the graces and blessings you are receiving. My dear people in the world, when you think of each other, My faithful ones, think of each other as a brother or a sister and smile! Feel love for each other now. This CAN BE, this IS, My dear ones. What a calling you have to be instruments and a source of love: the love that heals, that binds wounds, that comforts spirits. Praise the Father! Allow Jesus to heal you now. Allow My gifts to strengthen you now as you sit and allow Me, allow your God to act in your life, to be for you who you need Us to be, not who you would like Us to be; but according to your real needs, the Father's Will for you. Ponder these things, My dear ones. They are everything to you. Amen. Amen. You are blessed."

(I urge you to read the following message many times. It is one of the most helpful guides given by Heaven for the future... cta.)

5/4, in Summerville, S.C., "My dearest people of My Merciful Heart, be lifted up now in the goodness and gracious mercy of your God. I am Jesus, Who loves you. I invite you into the tenderness that pours forth from My Wounds, placed there by the ingratitude of the world. No more harsh words and impatience! Listen to yourself first. Hear your sharp replies, your aggressive responses and haughty expectations of special treatment and places of honor. Understand that words wound and leave lasting impressions that can change lives and a belief in My love for those you harm. The state of mind of the poor lost ones, who will come to you after the Warning, will be total confusion and great fear. Imagine the chaos that would occur in your own mind, were you not prepared so well and filled with all the understanding needed to bring you through these enormous events. Imagine, My faithful people, the terror that will enfold these dear ones who know not the forgiveness and tenderness of the Father. Dwell often and long on their state of mind and anxiety, as they move across great distances in search of help and understanding. I say again, spend MUCH TIME putting yourselves in their place, their state of mind and heart; what that level of terror will be like, as they flee from ongoing destruction and the sight of your own countries as a battle zone covered with great numbers of casualties.

This will be an exercise in mercy as you attempt to alert your senses to the feelings and reactions, to identify with the reactions of the many who will struggle so to even reach your doorstep. Immediately you will discover the level of physical weakness and emotional fragility. Fragile, My beloved disciples, means easily broken, frayed nerves that will start or cower or run for hiding and shelter in response to every abrupt and loud noise, to every raised voice, especially those who shout! Hushed and tender voices will be the rule for each moment **as people continue to arrive day and night in a precarious emotional state.** I remind you of these facts, My dear ones, because you must imagine and reflect and prepare for these times. They will have specialized needs, and you must spend time with Our Spirit in quiet listening as He tells you more about these days. My Spirit speaks to many tonight to prepare Our faithful ones to focus on this need for emphasis on a new and heightened state of terror. It is time (in my Father's Will) to tell you about this now. Believe Me, My precious ones, **you will always be on call to come to the aid of these victims** who wander lost and lonely without trust, ready to fight to the death for those who remain behind in need and counting on the might of your arm, your cleverness to bring them into a place of safety from the perceived harm that will be everywhere. These are events that will be felt keenly by battered nerves, and **seen as a continuation of events that threaten life and sanity at every turn.** Ask Our Spirit for a clear understanding now of all they will experience and suffer. No other way will bring you into greater unity with their state of mind and fear and acute mental shock. It is My wish for you to begin to learn more in this new way about those whom you will find at your doorstep. To love someone is to prepare for their arrival. When you received Me for that first time in Holy Eucharist, you studied and learned about Me, and how loving and generous I would be at this special time in your lives. You learned how necessary it would be to greet Me with great joy, to treat Me as an honored Guest and tend to all My needs. It will be even more necessary for these frightened and heartbroken brothers and sisters you have not yet met. When you expect guests, you purchase special treats and tasty morsels of meats, and spend long hours preparing your hearts and souls and houses for this august occasion. Would you do less for ones who are broken and in the greatest need, whom you will consider it an honor to serve, as they are also your means of salvation? There they will stand, bearing many wounds, helpless and scared, completely at your mercy, so to speak!

Decide, write down what you would say, what you would like to hear and receive in a like situation. This use of imagination is a gift to them and to you in your attempt to be as prepared for them as possible, and an entirely-new-to-you experience. Do this for yourselves, My children. Do this for them. Make notes of your feelings and observations about yourselves and about them. This way of preparing is a legitimate and serious approach to a large group of people about whom you really know nothing, and can only conjecture as to the state of being they will inhabit. This WILL work. This WILL help, My faithful ones. I know how many of you hope to serve and comfort them as well as possible in the best possible way. You might do these mental exercises with others and compare notes: learning and teaching as you go. Continue in the guidance of Our Spirit and the dearest, most tender, most loving Mother of all, Our own Immaculate Mother who waits to be needed, to be helpful, to bring you a greater degree of success and victory in your joyful attempts to make each truly comfortable and able to rest and trust and begin to heal. Ponder My words, My loved ones. The more you practice and **observe these studies in the use of the gift of imagination**, the more you will learn, the more at ease you will be; and so, in turn, will they! Our Spirit WILL help you when you call. The Angels WILL help even now in simple practice rounds. It is your serious desire to do your best and help them heal most quickly that will move the Father to grant you more gifts, more opportunities to succeed. This will be such an exciting time, made more joyful for all by the love in your dear heart, the compassion you will immediately feel at the first sight of them. Ponder the possibilities, My beloved ones!"

6/2, At Adoration, "My dearest daughter, I am your God and Father. Be filled with peace now. Let us begin with words for My people. 'My beloved people who pray and hear My words, be at peace. You have seen, and many have experienced directly, terrible events of weather and attacks of Nature. These will continue, faithful children. Those who have come into eternity are being touched and encouraged by your special prayers for them. Believe that all have begun to pray for you. This fulfillment of My many warnings regarding fierce storms and damaging tornadoes is a mighty reminder of the truth of all My words to you. I beg of you to take seriously all the **invitations to increased prayer for your country,** and the need for your ultimate preparations for increased destruction and for the needs of so many who will come to you in the greatest need and most fragile conditions of mind and spirit. Please begin immediately the use of prayer of imagination with which you are now gifted as a further means of your own readiness to handle huge numbers of people who will be broken in spirit and terrified in mind and, in many cases, in body too. When you see devastation of this magnitude and hear these survivors who are now moved to a greater appreciation for the value of human life, you can more easily allow yourselves to spend time in this new kind of prayer and preparation. You see the power of Nature and what an overwhelming weapon it is in the hands of evil people. The warnings and descriptions of events to come that you have rejected as fear based ramblings begin to occur, as My Plan escalates.

Do you still disbelieve words of My simple and weak messengers? If you only realized how much they pray and suffer for you. I am a God of Mercy, My beloved ones, Who speaks and acts to bring a renewal to the earth and to the minds and lives of all people. To rid creation of evil will require an ongoing display of the power of evil in wars and natural events. Your prayers are weapons, My dearest holy ones. You ARE My holy ones when you accept the sacramental cleansing of Reconciliation; and then let go of your own haughty ways and become the humble and obedient instruments of healing and mercy for souls and the lives of those who are then graced and gifted to receive the salvation My Son died to obtain for all mankind. As you see many brought into eternity in subsequent events, those of you who are accepting the enlightenment of the Holy Spirit and repenting of personal sin, be assured that your prayers accompany them and enable salvation to be accepted, to be chosen by most of these souls. These fierce storms signal a time of increased union between Heaven and all Our faithful ones. Rejoice and praise Me, little darlings of My Will. Be even more grateful for whatever My Will allows in your lives. Unite your sufferings to the Passion of Jesus. Realize that the battle intensifies, and My need for your promises intensifies with it. You are My beloved holy ones as you live My Commandments more purely and your commitments to every person in the world more deeply. You are the Keepers of the Family of Man, My dear ones.'"

FOR MERCY'S SAKE!

6/17, At Home, "My beloved daughter, I am your God and Father, here to continue My call to you. You can tell from all the weather disasters that bigger changes are in your immediate future. I know you desire more exact information and a clearer understanding of 'when' and 'how'; but that you also know this cannot be, else how could you wait in joy and hope for all to occur, and be purified and given increased patience in My plan?? You DO know that escalation is occurring. Fight doubt and fear with the strength of My Beloved Daughter, Mary. You see Our faithful ones everywhere floundering as though they had no guidelines, nor had been given any wisdom or understanding. I bid you to continue in your work to aid Our faithful people who need more by way of examples and increased faith and trust before they can gather information on their own from Our Holy Spirit.

I am your God! The people of the world must spend some time to finish this new task I have given them: to use the gift of imagination as a new and large part of your preparation for the thousands who will come needing food and shelter and healing immediately after the Warning. **There will be other times first that you will accept those in need into your homes according to their helplessness and fragile state of mind.** Be in a constant state of expectation of God's Good Things to keep your anticipation and joy at a new level of increased joyful hope and eagerness to greet these dear ones, and bring them into your homes. IT WILL WORK, My precious little ones. You will see!"

****

I have been putting together a list of facts gathered from the message of 5/4/03, and my own understanding (with the help of the Holy Spirit ... cta) of what we will need to do and say and be when all these people show up at our doorstep. These people will be in total confusion and fear, possibly terror, from the events of Warning and destruction that has or is happening at that time also; many will never have known the tenderness and forgiveness of the Father. They will be anxious, exhausted from the long trip to reach our homes and from the emotional state of loss and fear brought on by the fact that many will have lost everyone in their families and all their possessions, thus they will be helpless and needy without an understanding of the times or events. They will have been in flight from ongoing destruction and the sight of our countries as a battle zone covered with casualties, and perhaps in shock. It will have been a terrible struggle to reach us as a place of safety and help, and a state of physical weakness and emotional tension could exist, which Jesus explained means easily broken and upset, further frightened, suspicious, no level of trust, frayed nerves, running for cover at each sharp sound or loud noise, which is often referred to as being hyper-vigilant. This would be a precarious emotional state, and they would have special needs: such as time to mourn and process the experiences and go through the five steps of process where there is great loss: denial, depression, anger, compromise and finally acceptance.

There may be nightmares at first as part of this processing. This all sounds very terrible and impossible for us to handle, but that is all the more reason it will be so important to remember the promises of Heaven: we will have all the help we need, and there will be nothing we are unable to do for them because it will be the power of God, the gifts and strength of Jesus and Mary, the help of Angels and the words and gifts of the Holy Spirit we will have. We will see Our Lady, not often, but when we need it the most for encouragement. Jesus also has said the sight of them and their neediness will bring enormous compassion to our hearts and the desire to welcome them. We must pray for pure motives, because our motives always need purifying; respect their fragile state and not begin by handing them bags of medals and rosaries and begin explaining the Father's plan immediately; that will come later when we are answering their questions and inviting them to pray with us... after they have spent time healing and resting and being restored with peace and our joy at their presence with us, and emphasis on their recovery. If they are startled by loud noises and especially by raised voices, then we will need to speak in hushed tones with no harsh or impatient words. Only loving welcome and comfort in the Name of Jesus and Mary, and the sight of our own willingness to nurture and help them, will convince them immediately of the truth of our later answers to their questions.

There will be people arriving around the clock, so some organization will be needed for simply responding to the need of the moment. We will not see, I think, eight hours of sleep and 16 hours of day time routine, and will have the ability to do this according to Jesus explanations in the past, that They will be standing right next to all of us (and these people!) to give us assistance and strength. This gives us some idea of how important repeated time before the Blessed Sacrament will be to renew us and refresh us. Remember, Jesus said we will know great fatigue and hard work and great struggle, but also will know the greatest joy possible on earth, and earn our own salvation by bringing these lost ones to the Father Who waits with open arms to forgive them and gift them as the heirs of His Kingdom all truly are. And they will surely be filled with joy and gratitude that shelter and peace has been found, although some will be too angry to accept healing, and then Jesus said, relinquish them to the Holy Spirit and do not think you have failed. I see this time as the greatest reason to go back over messages and become as encouraged and trusting and committed as possible. It looks as though our prayerful trust will be our greatest weapon against discouragement and fear. And it always helps to know what's ahead of us. Now if we only knew when!!! I am sure some of you will have many more results from your prayer of imagination (5/4 & 5/12) and putting yourselves in their places, Carol.

6/18, "Dearest ones, how happy I am to see you gathered once again; to see your beautiful faces upturned, giving Me honor and glory and all of the thanks in your hearts. I am your God and Father, My children. How I love you. All of Heaven resounds with your prayers, with a special time of honor to Mary whom you love so very much and hold in your hearts, whom you emulate as you practice patience and peacefulness and patience with each other. How grateful and delighted she is for each of you. Believe this, each one of you she holds so deeply in her heart, wrapped so tightly in her Mantle of protection and love; for whom she prays to the Holy Spirit, Her Beloved Spouse, to bring you the openness, the focus, the devotion called for in these times. YOU ARE A SIGN OF THE TIMES, MY CHILDREN. Think about that. Think about example.

Think about creating an atmosphere of joy and peace just by being who you are: made in My Image, the Image of the Triune God. My children, stay close to your Mother. Stay close to your God. Your focus these days must be listening to the voice of the Holy Spirit as He gives you new understanding, prepares you more for the time you will be My direct instruments of healing and hope and conversion for all of Our lost ones who will wander ... so lonely and terrified; but who will eagerly respond to the love in your hearts, the tenderness you provide for them, the patience as you listen to each one pour out his or her story, his or her sadness or fear. Do not become frightened yourselves while contemplating this time, My children; for that is not it's purpose; but you know now that I give you new tasks long before they are needed to come to fruition, long before you will be ministering to those you do not know, but whom you will come to know instantly in their need.

I commend you and I bless you and gift you this day, once again, for enduring, for surrendering to My Will; and it is an endurance, My children, I know, for you are being purified to such a great degree: a higher state, without being separated from each other or better than each other, just more prepared now, dealing with your own weakness, your own sinfulness, your own habits. Those who torment you must be offered in praise and thanksgiving, for they are instruments of your purification! **They are an instrument of your conversion.** How can this be, you say? And yet you know **that healing occurs in the shadow of the Cross.** My children, be like your God and be joy-filled because of each other, because of Me, as I am of you and for you and with you. We become more united, as you become more focused on the purpose of My plan to save as many souls as possible. Listen closely and you will hear the Holy Mother thanking you for your love, telling you of Her love for you. You are My warriors! I need you, My dear ones. Yes, I have chosen to need you, but the world needs you. Amen, My dear, dear, dear little ones everywhere. Many, many, many blessings and graces, much mercy, new strength, new energy and vigor, new joy, My children, always new joy. Be joy, My children. Always be joy. Amen."

6/20, "My dearest ones, I am your Jesus. I bring you welcome. I bring you greetings. I bring you gratitude from all of Heaven. All of Heaven is praying with you all the time and for you constantly, as well. Let this be a source of joy for, as it has been said, the increased need of prayer, the escalation of My Father's plan, the fulfilling of some of the prophecies and events foretold by Heaven signals a time of greater unity between Heaven and yourselves and all of Our faithful ones everywhere who read and listen and respond with surrender of their lives, their gifts, their energy. My dear children, you see an escalation of terrorist attacks. PREPARE AGAIN, AMERICA. PREPARE. As you prepare, offer surrender to the Father's Will as well, and remember that each event that occurs is allowed by the Father's Will to fulfill Scripture, to allow Satan's increased power in all of those who follow him to be realized. DO NOT PRAY IN FEAR. DO NOT BE IN FEAR. Give Me your fear, My dear ones. Respond with prayer for your dear country and for the world with tenderness and compassion and sincere hope for the future of each individual on the earth.

Realize that many people have lost all hope, all trust, all belief in God or in any goodness because all they have known are harsh words and a harsh reality. Think of these dear ones who suffer in so many different ways when you suffer yourselves. For I tell you, your sufferings are not as great as these, yet you pray with greater compassion and understanding because of your own suffering. Your news media allows some of the reality of the world to be told, but not even near to all of it; and so, pray for those you do not hear about. Pray for those whose sufferings are hidden by a special offering of their own, those dear victim souls who gladly suffer for the world. Pray for their continued endurance. You know many of them, My children. They are your neighbors. They are members of your prayer groups. In some cases they are members of your own family, about whose sufferings you know nothing. It takes heroic endeavor to suffer in silence without complaints, without questioning the wisdom of your God. Offer praise and thanksgiving for them, for they are bringing untold blessings and gifts to you, as well as the rest of the world. Ask that you might suffer in silence, for many of you need the cleansing that will lead you to this place. Remember that I suffered in silence, not answering those who attempted to scandalize My life, My words and My actions. My dear ones, how difficult it is to suffer; but in uniting those sufferings to Mine, you will receive the greater strength, the greater endurance, the greater joy in doing this.

When I say to you: 'Prepare America', you know I mean in prayer, asking for greater protection, for greater mercy, an openness to the Spirit for all of those who are being taken into eternity. Prepare for the feast of My Ascension, My children, for as you do, you too will be lifted up higher. Focus on ascension into more heavenly things and more heavenly focus, a purer love and surrender. Be filled now with My Spirit, the Spirit of love and all the gifts of Our Spirit. I speak to My children everywhere in the world. You are all, everyone, MY children! Remember, **this is something you will tell people again and again and again that they too, though separated, though unaware or unknowing are still, first of all, a child of God, a child of Mary, an heir to the Kingdom.**"

6/28, Adoration, Jesus said: "My beloved faithful throughout the world, begin this moment to fill with new trust and peace. Bring Me your doubts and fears of abandonment by My Father and all of Our promises to you. It is in this waiting that His Will IS accomplished in you for a renewed understanding of His plans. Time is a mighty gift to you, and these days are filled with a living out, an unfolding of all that has been described to you. As you ponder and reread Our words, you will see them being fulfilled in weather disasters all over the world. Realize that every day sees new events which are a result of the Father's merciful justice tempered by the mitigation your prayers have obtained. The ability to control weather events is something your government and military boasts about. The poison coming out of the sky from planes piloted by enemies of life and health are some of the most obvious signs of the daily attack on inhabitants of this country. Why are patterned contrails not mentioned by your media? Why does no one attempt to discover the source of this bio-terrorism? Why is the health and welfare of this once great country steadily deteriorating? Do you believe that your government fights for your freedom, My poor suffering people? The plans of Satan unfold before your eyes, and nothing is done to protect the land of the free and the home of the brave, who are freed only by your surrender to Me, your bravery in hours spent in the purity of prayer and service to each other and the suffering of the world. Life becomes more difficult for everyone everywhere. You can see your helplessness to change things with any weapons of defense save the mighty weapons of Rosary and Adoration to My Sacred Heart. How miserable does your life need to become before you **pick up these weapons and beg mercy for humanity**? Yes, your lives and hearts must be filled with Divine strength, but it is offered to you every moment through the Bread of Life and the Cup of Salvation. Already your commitment and promises of fidelity waiver, My beloved people. The ridicule and embarrassment become nearly unbearable. The loneliness of rejection is the food offered by the greater numbers who have turned away, who have filled their hearts with trash, and wonder why their God does not act the role of mighty avenger, Who would free you from struggle.

Do your attitudes not reflect the Pharisees of My day, who rejected all of Who I Am, waiting for a God Who would bring freedom from the ruling power who held them in submission and misery? Look again, My dear ones, at ways you spend your time: wasting precious hours watching violence and impurity. The lure of evil glitters with promises of gratification and a life filled with senseless corruption. I beg you to reflect upon these words, brought to you with all the love of My Sacred Heart. Come before Me and rest and be renewed, My beloved ones. Know that **suffering will only end in the purifying you still need**. **The fires of purification on this earth are nothing compared to the cleansing fires of Purgatory.** What will it take to convince you of the peace and mercy to be found in greater unity with Me in My Father's Will? There is nothing better anywhere, My people. It is your perception, sullied by the world of gratification that leads you away from Truth. I Am the Way and the Truth and the Life of your soul, your future, peace and true freedom, the fulfillment of your reason to be alive in joy and all the treasures of Our Father's Kingdom. I wait for you, My own, My all, My children!"

6/29, "You are a conduit of the Father's Mercy to everyone. You are the instrument that prays for openness to My Mercy, for I am your God and Father Who speaks, My children, My dear, precious, weak, weak children. Never has the world faced greater and more total destruction than it does at this moment. Never do the boasts of those with weaponry and destructive ability sound more hollow to the Triune God, Who is the God of all people. Look at yourselves! My children, are you faithful with the first love you felt when you were called, and discovered Jesus and discovered My Mercy and the great love your God has for you, in spite of your sinfulness and lack of interest? All of these events and conditions, states of mind and being have existed throughout history since the dawn of creation; but now I tell you, do not be more frightened. Be more aware of the need of yourselves as an active part of the great Army that will help Me to destroy evil, that will protect those who come to you, who will drive away the evil one according to My Will for you and for them. In spite of all your prayers, in spite of all the time and the fatigue, all of the changes you have made in your lifestyle, it is NOW the time of greater emphasis on all you are called to be and to become!

The fact that there is no active war, organized war or declared war in the world, in a new way at this moment, does not mean the plans of the evil one are not rumbling just below the surface of your consciousness and of the awareness of the world. I speak in this way because it is necessary to remind you that the plans for war and annihilation go forward, and they are always in someone's plans, and now in a more organized, a more hateful and more personally destructive way. HEAR MY WORDS WITH PEACE: another miracle that you would not be frightened and frantic; but that you would sigh deeply and understandingly and be led, once again, to the Rosary of the Holy One, the mightiest weapon against Satan and his evil plans. How weak you are, My dear ones! It is what brings My Mercy to a place of spilling over, almost in spite of Myself! My children, I cannot resist you and your neediness. Count on that and praise Me, My children, because you will be saved and the world will be saved, the greater number, not from any great and lofty and holy height that you have achieved, but in humble, holy gratitude. Remember **trust is belief in spite of the obvious evidence, in spite of what could happen.** Believe that you are protected in My Mercy, in My need for you; and in My love for you and in the glorious Mantle of Mary, the Immaculate One, I gather you into My Will. Find a comfortable spot there, My children, and remain!"

7/2, 3 a.m. Jesus said: "In order for My Father's Will to be accepted and accomplished by each of His children, a certain amount of UNLEARNING must occur in your hearts and minds first before the soul is emptied of misunderstanding and naïve thinking, and finally filled with Wisdom and Truth. This takes time and a certain degree of resistance to change on the part of each one. If a person is truly committed to following the Father's Divine Will**, it will quickly see the error of its ways and mode of perception, and in time humbly reconcile to the Triune God and within itself and with others.** This is where the soul can become an authentic instrument of mercy to itself first: accepting God's unconditional forgiveness and love and in turn, pouring out this same mercy on others, on her God and upon itself; forgiving itself, and in humble surrender to Truth, move quickly along the Path of the Father's Will and learn to soar with the

Spirit of honesty and true joy. It is only when one clings in stubbornness and haughty pride to originally held perceptions of its own importance and self esteem that it refuses to stop and listen to the voice of reason and caution in order to see the truth of its reckless ways, and plunges deeper into the pit of self destruction. **The Father allows this willful one to hurdle headlong into tragedy when the soul sees itself as God, as a final authority that must be obeyed.** These are the actions of our reckless ones! Only chaos can result in the heart and soul of such a one who is unguided and without discipline and proper restraint. This entire process of conversion can occur in a twinkling, an explosion of God's healing grace, or it can take a long and lonely and resistance-filled struggle as the soul grapples to retain a perceived control over its life, surrendering slowly and painfully to My Father's mercy and then merciful justice.

I ask Our children, who wonder why and how their lives have filled with so much conflict and suffering, (all of you, My dearest people,) to ponder these words and accept the truth of your own resistance to a clearer look at the reality of your own behavior that might continue to block out the Truth of the Heavenly Father's Perfect Will for the peace and salvation and holy joy He wishes to shower upon each of His beloved children. More than ever, My precious ones, it is time to begin making serious and proper decisions that result in freedom from the grip of Satan's plans for your demise, the freedom that allows you to become a mighty weapon in the hands of your God and Holy Mother in this escalating battle against the plans of the evil one to destroy the world and the souls of the many who race headlong toward the precipice of an eternity in the grip of hellish suffering without their God, without Love Itself. Reflect, My people. Slow down and listen to My words of warning to each of you. Shut out the voices of criticism and arrogance that clamor from within your own hearts.

Choose Life, My beloved children. Be filled with new strength and determination to help those less fortunate than yourselves to enter through the **doors marked Service and Patience and Welcome and Tolerance, Peace and Acceptance and Joy. You are the ones who must prepare now to run through the cleansing waters, that you might dress in garments of dazzling joy and humble obedience, that you might maintain the strength and trust to go forward, not looking back to the world that will continually call with what sounds like a better way, accompanied by familiar music and frantic speed and empty promises. Keep your eyes and hearts focused on Truth, My beloved ones. I Am Truth. Begin again, My precious people, to run into the waiting arms of your Abba, the Father and Creator of all."**

7/6, Jesus said: "My dear ones, the weather anomalies, fierceness and destruction must be an alert. Please, My children everywhere, when you hear of events that cause great damage, and you will in a continuing manner, be brought to your knees! Be stopped in your tracks. Be aware of the unity you have been given with the world and the power in that unity to protect people; and when they come into eternity, to give them the proper choice for My Father's Kingdom. You are each a source of wisdom and power for each other now. It is wisdom that allows you to accept the delays, that allows you to learn to live without time, without schedules, without agendas: totally, totally foreign to you. It is so totally necessary that you practice in this area as well. Prayer IS practice, My children. It is a far greater gift and a far greater task than ever you could realize without practice, without a long period of time during which you pray in this way. DO NOT EXPECT AN INSTANT RESULT OR AN INSTANT 'FIX' IN YOUR OWN NEEDS OR FROM YOUR OWN PRAYERS FOR YOUR LOVED ONES. IT IS TIME AND DELAY AND WAITING THAT IS NEEDED FOR CHANGE, FOR UNDERSTANDING TO TAKE ROOT AND TO BLOSSOM!

I bring you the gift of increased patience this day, My children everywhere in the world, and I thank you for your perseverance. The prayers you do offer and yes, the prayers that have increased in your lives every day, bring new sensitivity to the needs of others, new thoughtfulness and a new listening heart. You are becoming all My Father needs you to be, all Our people will need you to be. That is the answer to everything, as well as your own purification! Rejoice, though you struggle and even weep in frustration and humiliation and hurt from the actions of others. Rejoice, for **My Father chastises those He loves and teaches through hardship and struggle."**

7/3, "My very dear ones, I am Mary, your Mother. I come to you this day thanking you for honoring the Blood of My Son. You have heard that after the Crucifixion and Death of my Son, I followed the path He walked, saving, rescuing, keeping, adoring every drop of blood that my Son lost along the way, every bit that I could find: this Precious, Holy, Sacred Blood. Every time you honor and seek the protection and the great power in the Blood of my Son, you are giving honor and glory to the Triune God, to the Word of Our Father in Heaven: to my Son Who died to save you. Gather His Blood as I did, my children, and the power if offers. Seek His protection, His cleansing. Seek the graces and the power that are yours through the Blood of my Son. CONSECRATE THE WORLD IN THE BLOOD OF MY SON. Cover yourself every moment with the Blood of my Son. Drink the Blood of my Son and be renewed. Become a new creation, an extension: unite your own blood with the Blood of my Son as you drink, as you believe, as you reach out to share this power, this holiness, this sacred opportunity. The world needs the Blood of my Son. Bring It to them in your prayers, in your union with Him and with me and with the people who know not and who suffer because of it. I love you, my little ones. Be doubly encouraged, as you are bathed in the Blood of my Son. You are in my heart."

7/20, "My beloved children, I am the Holy Spirit of God. Most especially today, I bring you the gift of thoughtfulness of the needs of others and the needs of those everywhere in the world. **Thoughtfulness contains** many other gifts: patience for example, gentleness, tolerance, a listening heart and spirit and **a healing of the action of interrupting each other!** Interruption is a very human trait, but it is not a thoughtful action. It arises, yes from your enthusiasm, and that is so human. It arises perhaps from having the answer or having a word that another waits to remember. Practice, My dear ones everywhere in the world, waiting, for thoughtfulness certainly includes waiting on another.

When you think about all those who will come to your respective homes or wherever I, the Holy Spirit, will bring the poor lost ones who will be so needy and seeking much help and refuge, the spirits that are so jangled and frightened and confused within each person, remember this is still your primary goal for prayer. Remember that all of Heaven prays for all of your intentions. I ask you, as the Spirit of Love, that **you begin to pour the Blood of the Lamb upon all of those who will come to you after the Warning, to procure for them all the Blood of the Lamb will mean and does mean to prepare THEM for the great trauma in the lives of everyone in the world: mental, emotional, physical.** All these things will receive great jolts from the events of the future. Would this not mean that you would wish to prepare all of those you love, all of those who would come to you, in the best possible way with your best possible efforts? Thank you for listening to these words. Thank you for deciding already to respond to My requests this day. How blessed you are. How much you are loved. How much praise and gratitude is offered in Heaven constantly for each of you, no matter how you struggle, no matter that you fail. **What counts is that you rise again."**

7/31, 9:15 p.m. At Home: "My dearest one, be at peace. I am your God and Father Who speaks: The world staggers toward destruction on legs of wood and feet of clay. Ask all **to include the conversion of world leaders**, especially in your own country. It is a gift of many miracles that keeps those faithful, who are the weak and suffering remnant flock of My calling**. It is always a case of the greater numbers of humanity being saved by the few**. The battles that rage for souls and the defeat of My faithful remnant grow in intensity daily and will surpass any battles, spiritual or temporal, ever fought in the history of the world. Do not allow temptations (that rise out of delays according to My plans for your cleansing and purification) to keep you at a place of sneering disinterest. If you would remember just one fact: **My WIILL is perfect for your own life and for the life of the world.** It is superhuman trust I have begged from you, but it is superhuman trust and faith and strength to persevere that you have received from My Merciful Hand!

Rejoice, beloved followers, and do not fear. Think of pictures you have seen from past wars and times of destruction. Allow them to spur you on to a gathering of the supplies and food and blankets and bandages you will surely need for the refugees, the survivors of widespread destruction that arrives at any moment from now on. This is not a fearful warning, but more of My mercy showered upon the world to bring you to become the place of shelter these dear ones will need. Do not sacrifice your brothers and sisters out of an inflated sense of righteousness. Indignation and impatience with your God can destroy many needlessly. It is mercy I desire, not sacrifice! Once again, I am sending the Holy Spirit of God to shower the gift of openness upon your stubborn and obdurate hearts. I send the love and blessings of the Triune God as well, My beloved people. Hear Me and believe My words. I am your Creator Who keeps His promises."

8/3, "I am your God and Father. I invite you and beg you to come to Me AS My children, to count on ME as your loving and merciful Father, to expect miracles of healing of all your requests and needs. I have told you many, many, many miracles have been given to you already, and have occurred in your life: your very conversion and fidelity, first of all. Pray against hardness of hearts, My dear people everywhere. It is a formidable strength against which you will be praying, and I ask you to **unite your prayers to each other's**. Trust this, **for all those whom your hearts envelope in love will be healed, will be converted, will come to Me at last one day in Heaven, according to the time of My Will. Fear not, My children everywhere, for My greater desire is their salvation.** You know that nothing is impossible to God and nothing is impossible when you unite yourselves to Me, your God, and all of Our prayers are lovingly, sincerely offered for the conversion of the world. It is battle We do, battle in the name of souls and victory in the name of justice and mercy! Truly it can be said that you warm the heart of your Triune God and Me, as your Father. Rest when you are tired. Take care of yourselves. I mention again to pour out the Blood of My Jesus upon the world every moment you think of it. **Think of it every moment, My children!"**

8/10, "My loved ones, I am your Jesus of Mercy, bringing a new level of understanding for you, a new level of wisdom and knowledge. Some of this knowledge will come to you directly from the Holy Spirit of God. Others will be enlightenment during prayer; while you are reading Scripture, or a book about a holy one of God who has lived in the past. All are sources of grace and enlightenment, and all must be sought continuously. The gift of wisdom has such a high place that Scripture speaks of her in a full chapter and more, and promises that when you seek her, you will find the greatest prize.

Seek Wisdom and truth, for I am Truth. Seek honesty. Commit and consecrate yourself to honesty. Get away from the habit of saying what you know another wishes to hear, or what is convenient to say**. Dare to tell the truth, My children, about yourselves and about everything**! This does not mean that you would reveal a confidence of another or about another. This means charity and words of truth at every opportunity. My dear ones everywhere in the world, how much more prepared you are with these new gifts. You will see. You will feel them! Suddenly something will become clearer, or you will hear it in a new way, and understand better and more deeply. Praise and thank the Father for this. All throughout each event in the future you will be learning. For the rest of your lives you will be learning, and the rest of your lives forever and ever in Heaven; but these gifts, this particular wisdom is preparing you for right now, before the Warning, before events of destruction visit every shore. I ask you to take seriously My words and to seek Wisdom. Always openness to gift is needed. Is that not so,

My loved ones? Always you must seek what you know you need, and I am telling you these things to remind you of your need for wisdom and a depth of understanding you do not possess now. Rejoice, My children, these are special and sacred days as you prepare for the (feast of) Assumption of My Mother into Heaven. Thank you for loving My Mother. Continue to tell everyone about Her, for the source of comfort and peace and dearness She is for every heart that approaches Her; never turning away from you; always seeking your good, your graces, your gifts. Amen, My dear ones. Prepare."

8/17, "Beloved children, I am your Jesus of Mercy. I AM your hope. I AM your perseverance, for I am all things to you and for you and with you; for you are in Me and I am Hope. I am Truth. I am Love in union with My Father and Our Spirit. You cannot imagine the beauty of Our Mother and the beauty of Her Heart. You are beloved of My Heart. Imagine the Father on His throne, addressing your prayers, purifying them and purifying you this moment about My Father and Our Spirit, and about each other and your fidelity to prayer everywhere in the world. Prayer, like incense, rises to Heaven. It is the glorious Communion of Saints, and Mary is your Queen. Be lifted up in Her love this day and in My Peace."

8/23, "My dearest ones, I am Mary, the Mother of God and your Mother. I am the Immaculate One, the Holy One of God. I remind you this day that you are My beloved children everywhere in the world, that I intercede for you constantly when you are down or tired or discouraged, or even near despair, most especially. I invite you to remember that I am praying for you, interceding for you, asking strength, asking endurance, My children. You are overcoming yourselves! Believe this, for it takes a long, long time; and there will always be some weakness, some presence to remind you of Original sin. These tiny sins are an erosion of your supply of grace, of your treasures that result from your Corporal and Spiritual Works of Mercy, from all you try to do to fulfill the Father's Will. You do not wish to give away the results of such great effort and so many prayers. Think of it this way, also. In a human way, it is easy for you to guard something that you have worked hard to supply for your families, for yourselves, even something frivolous. How much more important it is to guard your spiritual treasures, and so I remind you in this way also that I am praying to protect your spiritual good and spiritual strength and the armor that protects you from the plans of the evil one that are always in progress, My children. You are reminded again that Satan never takes a holiday or vacation or rest, I am FOR you. I am in your corner. I am on your side. I am WITH you. I LOVE you. Remember Me, My dear ones, every minute. That is how I remember you!"

9/7, "Children of My own creation, My little ones, My beloved ones, I am your God, your Father and Creator. It is much I ask of you. It is a long time of waiting that you live. This waiting is securing for you, like nothing else could, your salvation, your place in My plan, your ability to be the instrument I need you to be, I have chosen you to be for the salvation of the world. To sustain you is something only your God can do, so I ask once again that you would praise and thank Me for something you are living now: your life at a level of holiness, a level of surrender and commitment not known by most of the people on the earth. Think of it and rejoice. **When you are frightened, when you are anxious, stop and praise Me.** When you are walking into the unknown, or letting go of a loved one, or a friend or a way of life or whatever it is that seems so familiar, I ask you to stop and rejoice, for it is only through these events that you are emptied **and prepared as the resting place for thousands of broken hearts,** a place where Jesus takes his rest with His Mother and yours to hear them there in your hearts united to His heart and Her Heart in a greater purity than you could ever imagine, **an environment of mercy and continuous patience and forgiveness without which no healing would occur, so dreadful will be their condition, as you recall.** Be filled with courage, My children, to continue on this bold march to victory and healing and conversion. We march together with all the others like you in the world, united in the Sacred and Immaculate Heart and in My plans. Rejoice!"

9/9, Adoration, 12:50 p.m. "Little one, rejoice that I, your Jesus and Lord, have come to speak. Remember, My beloved people, you come closer to events each time they are mentioned. I say this to encourage you to be prepared for natural disasters and plans of those who seek to conquer your country and destroy your freedom. Believe that I am seeking to PROTECT YOU WITH REPEATED REMINDERS TO STORE FOOD AND WATER FOR A DESOLATE WINTER WITHOUT THE COMFORTS YOU DEPEND UPON. I, your Jesus, will be with you throughout the coming months with the warmth of My love and the Light of My Presence. All who love Me, heed My words! All who love your brothers and sisters in the world, pray. All who seek to live Our Father's Will, rejoice that His plans to remove evil from the earth go forward. WE GO FORWARD, My beloved faithful ones.... TOGETHER!"

9/13, At Home, Excerpt from personal message, "My dear little one, please write My words. Dear one, I am your Beloved Jesus, come with graces and peace. It is no accident that each event is accepted or rejected, fulfilled or delayed, allowed or disallowed by My Church authorities. Most of the time, this frees the Father's hand to act in a way that will further His desires for His faithful messengers and the world. How could the Father ever be defeated, unless He allows this to seem to happen for a moment, so that His Will is fulfilled in an even greater way, AS NO ONE ELSE COULD ACCOMPLISH!! Do not fear or be disappointed, as you are asked to wait, yet again, for many events to occur and be accomplished for the best of all involved. Remember, do not fear: even though things and people take so much time to see truth and THEN change, IT WILL BE AT THE PROPER TIME."

9/14, "My dearest ones, I am the Holy Spirit of God: the Spirit of holiness, the Spirit of healing, the Spirit of forgiveness and mercy, the Spirit of Wisdom and Understanding and Knowledge. There is a saying among Our people:

'Well, it's not written in cement yet!' Let your commitment be written in cement so that it might harden like steel! That this commitment might be carried as a frame to hold you up, a framework within which to live and work and have your being, that outlines each decision that defines who you are. My dearest ones, as you come closer and closer to mighty events that define the End Times and the escalation of the Father's plan, it is more important than ever that you reaffirm your commitment; that you are aware of what you have promised to do for the Father, His honor and glory, and for the world: it's salvation. That you would remind yourself daily to renew this commitment through your consecration through simple words of loving promise, to affirm and to firm up your commitment to walk with a backbone of steel that reflects the steely commitment you have made to obedience to all the Father's requests and desires, to His Commandments and Beatitudes and to His mercy. You can work at being a reflection of your God's love in the way you treat each other and love each other and accept each other, especially accepting each other's weaknesses and the little things that irritate you about some people (!) Jesus' Blood courses through your commitment to keep you alive, to keep your commitments alive, to keep you safe and protected and strong and vigilant, to keep you holy.

There cannot be a commitment without a life of holiness, humility, peacefulness, tolerance: again, acceptance and openness to each other and each other's problems and needs. All of these works of mercy and charity are sanctified further by offering them each day as the day begins, as it always has been: your consecration of every act, every breath, every word and action: Do not think that nothing is happening, for YOU are changing daily, sometimes minute by minute, most especially when you are struggling with something or have pain or doubt, and you are praying so very hard for help and guidance to come through a dilemma. This is the 'stuff' of change. This is the 'goods' of a new creation. SEE EVERYTHING AS AN OPPORTUNITY OF PRAISE. You are strong, My dear ones, very strong. Very much you are soldiers and warriors. You ARE ready, for anything and everything. I shower you with the graces of My gifts today. Most of all, it is Fortitude I give you, fortitude in commitment. Be at peace, little beloved ones of God."

9/18, At Home 9:30 p.m. "My dearest child, please take My words of encouragement for the people of the world and for yourself. I am your God and Father Who speaks now for the further preparation of all who pray and prepare: 'My dear people of the world, I am your Father in Heaven, speaking words meant to heal your hearts of the fatigue and irritability caused by seemingly endless waiting, by the weariness that results from hearing repeated words from Heaven without the immediate fulfillment you have expected so many times. I tell you, **this kind of waiting builds up increased trust and provides the time needed for you to change in such a way that will be permanent and totally according to My Will for each one.** Before the Warning occurs, you must be the instrument needed by the people I will send to you. Before healing others, you must learn and be stronger and healed yourselves. I have showered you with all the gifts you need many times; but still you are in the process of absorbing them, allowing them to transform you and beginning to live out your promises to Me in a greater and more perfect way. You are each filled with more of My Jesus, Who Is the Way, and thus you become more like Him and an experience of Him to all you meet. This is exactly My desire for you and for them.

Each of you IS a miracle! Each of you is a fulfillment of My Plan and My Will for the world. I ask you to please believe My words this night as a sign to yourselves of the required level of surrender within your lives and hearts. Be encouraged about yourselves in spite of needing to struggle harder to pray and desire to pray and continue on this rocky road of becoming! Remember and pray to the added Angels, who now accompany you, especially when you feel your weakness most and are tempted to sin or to quit or to doubt My promises. Remember that each trial is designed to teach you and purify you and bless you with whatever you need to bring you quickly to Heaven or strengthen you to live in the New Era of Peace and Purity on Earth as it is in Heaven."

9/19, At Home, 9:30 p.m. "Daughter, let us continue. I am your God and Father, here to bring words of warning to you and all My faithful people. 'Do not continue in your sinful ways, My beloved ones. It is an eternity of suffering and horrible pain or of the Beauty and Glory and Perfect Joy of Heaven that awaits you, My weak and foolish children. There is no sincere request I will ignore when it concerns the salvation of souls and conversion of lives and hearts. You are helping every person in the world to a rebirth: a new beginning in the Kingdom of Peace and Purity and Joy. Ask Me for greater understanding and a mature patience while you wait through this time of purification for the perfect time to be reached for the realization of all We have told you about. Please, put your dreadful pride and critical analyses aside and bow in humble acceptance of the Truth I attempt to give you. The world will not survive without Truth! Accept Jesus, My precious ones. Unite yourselves, count on, become one with the Savior of the world. Do not present Me with a set of criteria to fulfill according to your own desires and decisions!"

9/21, "My beloved children, I am Mary, your Mother; yes, Queen of Angels and Saints. You are all My angels and you are all becoming Saints. To love you and protect you is My joy. Pray to be more aware of the people for whom you pray, more conscious of suffering people being touched, being comforted, being moved to pray themselves. The mercy and might of God, Our Father, is beyond words, beyond expectations, beyond anything you can even imagine, much less have ever known. It is no wonder We ask that you praise and thank the Father constantly, no matter what occurs; for it is all procuring good in your lives and the lives of others; for every mistake, every sin, every failure, every turning away, every hurt is a learning experience.

EXPECT MORE LEARNING EXPERIENCES NOW. YOU ARE READY FOR THEM. You are at a place of surrender that brings you strength to endure whatever is contained in the Father's Will. Thank you for allowing Me to be your Mother, to be your Queen, to be your Advocate, your Co-redemptrix. There is nothing to fear, nothing about which to worry, no matter what the suffering in your own life might be. You are protected. Your loved ones are protected. Believe this. Do not be guilty in your hearts. Do not look to place blame, especially on yourself, for this is not the way of God. Your God deals in and works through forgiveness. Remember, EVERYTHING FOR YOU WILL BE WELL. BELIEVE THAT, MY CHILDREN. It is important. It is life saving. It is heart healing that you believe. I embrace you again, and I leave you with a kiss!"

9/27, 2003, At Adoration, "My dearest child, begin now to take words for the world. Dear people of My own creation, listen to your God and Father. Dearest hearts, your plans for the immediate future are realistic and therefore, I promise you anew that protection will be the result of your obedience to My requests for preparedness. I am giving you strong words these days through several of Our chosen messengers and I tell you, you are beginning to listen! I do not wish to frighten you, but must break through your complacence in the face of danger to this country and ongoing destruction elsewhere. You, who have remained faithful in the world, are going to see the results of your fidelity and perseverance in protection you will recognize as miraculous. Begin now, my faithful ones everywhere in the world, to praise and thank Me now for the miracles of protection about to attend your lives and the lives of your loved ones. You see the disastrous results in the lives of children you know, whose parents appear to care nothing for them and who slough off their responsibility on someone else; or allow the child to dictate to them without any correction, all to the negative development of that child or children. You know deep within your hearts the positive effects of reinforcement of rules on behavior that reflects respect for the parent and his rules. That child knows deep within itself that he or she is loved and cared for by the rules, whether or not they are an interference in the desires of the child to follow every whim, and be one of the crowd of its peers! This is the kind of loving parent I desire to be, I MUST BE for all of you, My children. I know well the consequences of every thought and action of everyone, and wish to save you forever from your own willfulness and immature and spoiled behavior. To be selfish and self-centered, therefore sinful and given to self-gratification, is so human, My beloved ones. To give in to the call and lure of the world is to succumb to the plans of Satan and set yourself on a collision course with a life of suffering forever in Hell.

I love each of you, My dearest children throughout the world. I call to you again and again in mercy and patience, in anger and remorse for the lives of sin you continue to pursue. Your Triune God and Heavenly Mother, Mary, feel the lashes of your rejections; feel the hatred of all that is good that radiates from your sneering rejection of the words of warning I send to the world. I MUST act in a mighty way now to bring justice and balance and love back into your lives; to act in retribution for the terrible suffering inflicted upon the innocent unborn, the children who live in filth, the corruption that allows criminals to rule, the vicious attitudes of the powerful and terrorist alike, who see no value in human life except to enslave and corrupt and conquer, who have plans to annihilate the very people who follow them after their own perceived victories everywhere in the world. This is the future for those who choose evil now! Do not, I repeat, be led astray by empty promises of an easier life, a diabolical promise of power and money and exhilaration, all the while marching to the tune of Satan to certain and eternal death! It is prayer and fasting and self-discipline that will enable you to put pleasure-seeking-as-a-goal behind you once and for all. Choose Life, My beloved children. Pray unceasingly for those who refuse to listen to these words of your God, Who begs you to become a people of Hope and Joy and Peace and Love for each other and the world. YOU CAN DO THIS, BELOVED ONES. I HAVE SAID IT!!"

9/28, "My dear ones, I am your Jesus. I come with joy and hope for all of you. The messages that are given by Heaven these very days become more and more serious, and some of them are frightening. Please read them again this week and discern with our Spirit, the meaning, the truth held within. You come closer and closer to days of battle in your own country. It has been protected. It has been My Father's Will to pour out every kind of grace and good thing needed by the people of this country and the world. You will feel yourself abandoned when My Father holds back these special gifts. They will still be given; but much less often, much less will you be aware of them except that **you will succeed, you will be victorious in your march to victory. You will be victorious in your march to meet the Son of God when He returns to the earth.** For now, I wish for you to spend time this week above and beyond what you already do... in silence. I ask you to have patience with yourselves. You know that there is only a matter of time before your own dear country is hit by a major event of My Father's Will. I say this to prepare you. Look again at your supplies. Make sure you have what you need. There are many different types of visitation from My Father in world-wide and weather-wide events. And so, you must prepare for anything and everything. There will be so many! How many times have I said this to you, My dear ones? And yet, I feel the overwhelming response that you will have to all of them, wondering how you will survive this time, helping them to survive.

I remind you, it will be as you would wish it to be and it will be My Father's desires for them and for you. Make an effort to go through each day with peace, living within a 'shell' of peace, an atmosphere, an environment of peace and hope, for it is this that will be noticed by others; and when those people who are so sad and so lost come to you, **they will need strong signs to make them stay. It is not only before the time when they first come to you that there will be events of a destructive nature but afterwards and ongoing as well**. There is nothing you cannot do. I know some of you have particular requests and questions and wonderings this very day and I invite you to come to Me in quiet, and ask yourself and listen yourself and write and read and learn. I love you, My little ones. I count on you. Yes, there is a small bit of time left, but not much, not much! Pray. Pray for those who have encountered the might of My Father's arm, and who will again (as in storms and earthquakes, tornadoes and hurricanes). It is a difficult time now. Amen. My children, rejoice."

10/13, Shrine of Blessed Solanus Casey in Detroit. (Very important message for everyone!) "Dearest daughter, be at peace. Be emptied of all now except the sound of My voice. I am your Lord and your God, your Jesus of mercy, your Eucharistic Savior. I call out to the people of the world to repent of their sinful ways. Give time to the preparation before seeking reconciliation. Be rested and alert as you reflect through the power of Our Spirit all you will wish to bring for healing and forgiveness. **Your unconfessed sins and the possessions you cling to are your greatest burden.** Do not let worry be a distraction. Do not ever, ever again speak or act in anger. Do not ever speak or act in a haughty, selfish manner or with expectation of recognition or places of honor. Seek the hidden path to My Cross. Be a simple and humble servant who gives public thanks to all the gifts of My Father. When your response to any event is praise to the Father for His wisdom and perfect Will on your behalf, you are returning mercy to Him and will proceed in a deeper understanding of His Will and graciousness and perfect care for you. In this way, peace will be maintained within and without your entire being and demeanor. There is nothing and no one who will overcome you. You are fighting, seasoned and readied: mighty, humble, holy warriors. Rejoice!

The Agents of the Antichrist will seek to test their ability to control and cause weather extremes and storms of unprecedented ferocity. Earthquakes will escalate in number and degree of violence. People will literally be shaken from their complacency in every corner of the world. (This will be ongoing throughout the End Times…cta.) Pray for them from now on, that they will accept the gift of wisdom and understanding that all of these events **are signs of Scripture fulfilled and of time, as you know and live it now, running out**. You are entering a period of time marked by destructive events that will be above and outside any ever experienced in the world since history has been recorded. Floods and winds will devastate and destroy vast areas of land without the time or opportunity to recover and rebuild.

All I have told you for so many years through this messenger is about to be fulfilled. Pray for all My chosen ones, the poor and the little ones, who have for so many years left home and family for your sake. The attacks of violence increase, and danger to their persons lies in wait at every turn. **This time of the violence of Nature will continue to escalate, contain the Warning and continue beyond into the BRIEF PERIOD in which you will bring many, many lost ones into your homes and hearts; but will then be tempered by the outpouring of the Spirit that results in the greatest numbers of people accepting My mercy and conversion in the history of mankind. This brief period will see the triumph of My Mother's Immaculate Heart, followed closely by your departure with your Angels who lead you into safety of**

refuges, hidden from the eyes of the Antichrist and the New World Order, all followers of Satan.

An extremely dangerous time lies in your future, My people. I recount these events to move you, once again, in the direction of readiness of anything. DO NOT FEAR. DO NOT WORRY ABOUT YOUR POSSESSIONS OF FOOD AND WATER. GIVE AWAY ALL YOU HAVE GATHERED FREELY AND WITH JOY (i.e. when the lost ones DO appear at our doorsteps... cta.) GIVE YOURSELVES AWAY TO SERVICE TO MY HELPLESS, NEEDY ONES WHOSE LIVES AND SOULS WILL BE SAVED BY YOUR KINDNESS AND SHELTER. THINK NOT OF YOURSELVES, BUT ONLY OF OTHERS. Pray for them today, this moment, tomorrow and every day for the rest of your lives. THIS IS YOUR LIFE, your future **into an Eternity of prayer for the world in a Paradise of Union with your God.** I salute you, people of My creation, My delight. Hold on prayerfully to Me and to each other and to the Father, to the Immaculate Mary and her Beloved Spouse for the adventure of your lives! Whatever develops in each one's life is My gift to you for Eternity!"

11/2, "My dear children, I am your Holy Spirit, the Spirit of God, the Spirit of holiness, the Spirit of unity among you, the Spirit of wholeness and health. The souls in Purgatory are praying for all of you who are praying for them. Know that many of the souls will visit those who spend much of their lives and time praying for them, as they are released or as they need more prayers, by a special gift of the Father. There are more of these occurrences in the world than you realize, My dear people. I tell you this to encourage you to pray for the souls in Purgatory. There are billions, My people. Purgatory is the greatest gift a soul receives, for it means that soul has made the ultimate step and only waits now for entrance into Paradise. The Will of the Father is that ALL of you would by-pass Purgatory and go directly to Heaven. There are more going directly to Heaven now than ever. Rejoice as Heaven rejoices. Their prayers also are given great strength by the majesty and gracious goodness of the Father. BE encouraged, people. Be strengthened with hope and by hope. Know that your strength will NOT leave you, will only increase. Persevere, My dear, dear ones, in the Spirit. Worship in spirit and light. Praise the Father, united to the Heart of the Blessed Mother. Come to Me like a little child, knowing the petitions will be answered, your desires fulfilled, the wishes of your heart fulfilled. Feel the prayers of the souls in Purgatory this day. Be in joy, even as you are in sorrow. See the Father's Will in all things, My little holy ones."

11/9, "My very dear ones, I am your Immaculate Mother, Mary: Mother of God, Mother of every person who has ever lived, every person in the entire world. Oh, my dear children, thank you for remembering and honoring and praying for the souls in Purgatory. They are much closer to Heaven than you are, my children of the world, and so I ask you to appreciate their prayers and TO THANK THE FATHER FOR THEM. I THINK THIS IS SOMETHING THAT THE WORLD HAS FORGOTTEN TO THANK THE FATHER FOR: THE

PRAYERS OF THE SOULS IN PURGATORY. I know how you love each other. I know how you love them and each one who prays and who suffers in the world. Truly, my children who pray, you do love the world and all of the people in it. What a wonderful development within your souls and your spirits, within your petitions and intercessions to the Father of Mercies.

You WILL BE HEALERS, my children, in every sense of the word. Hosanna, Halleluia to the Father. Praise and thanksgiving to the Father for His gracious goodness to you. You want so much to please me and the Father and the Son and the Holy Spirit, my Spouse; and I tell you, so it is and so it will continue to be! NO ONE HAS TO WAIT FOREVER (!) and so it will be with you. Hope will turn you into a hope-filled person, a hopeful person, a source of hope for all who come to you. This is a much greater role than you realize because you do not know the state of a hopeless person, so you cannot yet appreciate what this will be like, what this will mean to hopeless souls, hearts dead with near despair. I am so grateful for the love you send to Me, the obedience. Faithful little children everywhere in the world, thank you. My children, the world grows darker, the sins grow greater and mankind sinks to a lower level with no thought of the future or no care in their hearts and minds and wills. It is a desperate world seeking gratification, seeking happiness through the eyes of the world, seeking some sort of escape from responsibility, especially to their God and reparation for their sins. You have been chosen, as you know, to be the lambs, the **victim souls offered for the reparation of the world's sin: a mighty task, a painful task often, a severe task, a serious task, one that you are fulfilling.** Hosanna! Praise the Father for each other, for each other's faithfulness and obedience and the joy with which you meet each day and with which you serve each other. I embrace you and hold you in My Immaculate Heart. You are such dear, little ones. Do not despair!"

11/16, "My very dear children, I am your God and Father. My dear, dear ones, I give thanks for you this day, as I ask you to combine these (souls in Purgatory) in your hearts and in your prayers with prayer for all of those who will die in events of the future. Begin praying for them today because it will be a time for greatest decision for all of them. For some the choice for My Kingdom, and to repent, will be easy. Others will only make the choice based on the strength and the power of your prayers for them; for though they will come to understand more about sin and My Commandments and My Kingdom, they will not have the background or the depth and it (their choice to convert after the Warning ...cta.) will be based on fear more than love at the first. Again here is a great opportunity to serve your brothers and sisters in the entire world by preparing them, though they will not know it, to enter Eternity and to choose (in the right way) happiness for all Eternity, **to be healed ultimately according to My Plan for them by waiting in Purgatory and experiencing your ongoing prayers for them.** Remember to give thanks for them and their prayers for you, for then they WILL know you are praying for them and be eager to return the favor. They will understand how important your prayers and yourselves are in their lives and that your prayers will purchase for them salvation, eternal glory with Me in union with the Triune God and with all people in Heaven, especially the Angels and Saints and the Holy Mother Mary, the Immaculate Queen.

You realize the eternal gifts that await them, and so your hearts will be moved this day to pray for all of those who from now on will be going into eternity in greater numbers. You see more of your soldiers dying on a silent battle front, a hidden battle front, a deceptive path, a treacherous road, and you get a picture of the terrorism waiting, hidden, yet suddenly exploding for all to see. You have experienced much of this in the world now, and even in this country, storms as well as explosions; but you are yet to experience war on your soil, so you must prepare each other for this as well. This greatest gift you can give each other is your prayer for your friend's preparation and the ongoing life of the soul in your friends! What greater gift can you give him than to lay down your life in service of the soul of your friend and loved one? My dear children, you are a magnificent sight as you gather to pray and listen and allow yourselves to be changed by all of these things and by My Will and by Our directives for you: Novenas, Rosaries, Chaplets, Masses, receiving the Body and Blood of My Son, reading the words of Scripture, spending time in silence; all of these, more than suggestions, but important requests that you have been given and respond to as well as you can. You see it took time. It took process. It took unlearning and then new learning, a new adaptation to the Kingdom of God on earth as it is in Heaven. Give praise and thanksgiving with all your might; for it is a glorious time in the world and for you, although destruction will rule the day for years to come. I am your God and Father, your Creator. Gather in preparation, whenever you can, for the great Feast of My Son as Christ the King. Amen, My dear ones. Live in My love. Live aware of My love. Be more changed, more strengthened, more consecrated and made stronger in your commitment to Me."

11/30, "My dear children, I am your Mother, the Immaculate One of God, the Mother who loves you as no other could, who has suffered for you as no other would and who stands by you as a loving Mother should. You are the Tabernacles who will carry the light of Christ, my Son, to a darkened world. The tragic events of the world are too numerous to name. It is enough to unite yourselves to the sufferings of people everywhere in the world and to those who will offer their lives for the Name of my Son in the future. It is a critical time. It is a critical Feast, one of great importance. Already there are continuous natural events occurring everywhere in the world. Many, many more will result from the sinfulness of this very season of holiness that we seek to celebrate in thanksgiving and praise to the Father for the gracious gift of His Son. Never leave My Son's side. Stay hidden in His Heart. Remain strong in your union with Him and in your belief in every word that has come from His lips at any time in history.

Purification is a most necessary and most painful gift from the Father; but it saves you from suffering far worse than you can imagine; and that, my children, is my goal for you, my hope that I might pray enough and protect you enough that you remain faithful and strong in your commitment to My Son; that you be saved from any more suffering, hardship or loss than absolutely necessary according to the Father's Plan. You are carrying a burden, yet you also know it is My Son's burden which is light and which We carry with you. That burden is the ENTIRE WORLD AND ALL OF THE SINS IN THE WORLD. You are able ministers, able instruments, able carriers and able servants. You are my beloved children in whom I am well pleased. WE SHALL REJOICE TOGETHER, MY BELOVED CHILDREN. ALWAYS. KEEP ME IN YOUR LIFE, IN YOUR HEART, IN YOUR MIND, IN YOUR SPIRIT AND IN YOUR WILL. YOU ARE EVERYTHING TO ME AND I AM EVERYTHING TO YOU IN YOUR QUEST FOR THE MIGHTY TRIUNE GOD. Pray. Pray. Pray and rejoice."

12/7, "My dearest children of My Sacred Heart, LET NOTHING SLOW YOU DOWN. LET NOTHING HAMPER THE TIME YOU TAKE FOR SILENCE AND FOR PRAYER AND PREPARATION OF YOUR DEAR HEARTS, THAT THEY MIGHT BE AS SPOTLESS AS POSSIBLE TO WELCOME ME INTO THEM AT THIS GREAT FEAST. MY BIRTH IS YOUR RE-BIRTH! SAY THIS TO YOURSELVES AGAIN AND AGAIN, MY CHILDREN: **'JESUS' BIRTH IS MY REBIRTH**." And so it will be every time you repeat this prayer, every time you lift your eyes and your heart to Me in joy and gladness for the great gift we have in each other. Pray in thanksgiving for your faithful priests, those who pray for their brother priests who struggle so. Pray to cast out the world of evil and sin from the hearts of your countrymen and the world. When you prepare for My Birth, you are prepared for any, any tribulation, and there WILL BE tribulation! You are My champions!"

12/14, "Children, My very dear and faithful ones, I am your God and Father, your Creator, He Who sustains you in grace and in perseverance. Give thanks for the increased trust that grows in your hearts, in your commitment, in the confirmation of Truth within your hearts. All of these things occur silently, miraculously, wondrously, My children. Be filled with joy, I tell you once again, as I am filled with joy; for there is little joy in the world and almost no gratitude. Unite all of the gifts in His life and in your lives, and offer them to Me as part of your thanksgiving for this great feast and for the gift of My Son. Holiness, My children, is a result of loving. Loving, My children, is the result of holiness!"

12/21, "My dearest children, it is I, your Mother. More than ever before, I tell you, your hearts have become that manger, that resting place, that holy site on that Holy Night. You know that you are also each Tabernacles which hold the Presence of my Son for the world, and that **soon there will be no light left in the world except that which shines from your hearts. Imagine not just the Baby in your hearts this day, the very same way He was that Night; but that shining from your hearts is that same light, that brilliance, the Light of the world; and that you are that light, as well, my children everywhere in the world.** You will be that brilliance of the Presence of Love, of holiness in spite of weaknesses. Each of you has traveled a longer distance this year, my children, than any other single year in your lives toward the Father's Will, and into the heart of my Son and the fire of Our Holy Spirit.

Rejoice, my little ones everywhere, my faithful ones, bearers of Christ with me. KNOW THAT AT MIDNIGHT ON CHRISTMAS EVE, WHEREVER YOU ARE, I WILL BE VERY, VERY POWERFULLY WITH YOU BECAUSE YOU WILL BE VERY, VERY POWERFULLY WITH ME IN THE STABLE AT BETHLEHEM. THIS IS A VERY SPECIAL GIFT OF THE FATHER TO ALL OF HIS FAITHFUL ONES IN THE WORLD. BELIEVE THIS PROMISE. BELIEVE THIS GIFT. BELIEVE THIS GREAT LOVE. BELIEVE IN ME, MY CHILDREN, AS YOUR COMPANION-AT-ARMS. I love you, my little ones. Anticipate this great night and this great gift about to be given. I do not promise you ecstatic experiences or extraordinary gifts of vision or transportation or anything that might come to your mind of that nature. I promise you my presence, and your presence with me and the Babe and Joseph. Once again I invite you, listen for the singing of the Angels!"

FOR MERCY'S SAKE!

FOR MERCY'S SAKE

"A shield before me is God Who saves the honest heart. God is a just judge, who rebukes in anger every day. If sinners do not repent, God sharpens his sword, strings and readies the bow, prepares his deadly shafts, makes arrows blazing thunderbolts". (Psalm 7: 11-13)

VI 2004

1/4, "My beloved ones, welcome this day. I am your God and your Father, I am your Creator, and you have just celebrated the Feast of My Son's Birth, the finest gift the world and each heart can receive. Thank you for gathering in groups everywhere, giving praise and thanks to Me and to Jesus for consenting to be born, helpless in a cold and dreadful, hidden place, only to be announced with great glory befitting His Kingship. My children, remember that you carry the Infant King with you every moment. Remember He has been given to you individually as well as collectively in the world and in the history of mankind. Always your reality is a result of My mercy and My plans for your life and for the future of the world. Allow yourselves to feel the love of the Triune God. It is a fatherly love, a creative love, a nurturing love, a comforting love, a saving love, a fiery love, a gentle love, a grateful love, grateful for each of you who love. Love each other, My dear ones. Serve each other. Help to save each other in the world. How you need each other. I bless you this day in My Name, in the Name of My Beloved Son and in the Name of Our Spirit."

1/18, "My dear, dear children, I am your Mother of Sorrows. I come this day sorrowing for the lives of the many millions of children that have been lost to greed and self-gratification, to selfishness and the lack of love in the hearts of their own mothers and those who support the terrible sin of abortion. It is true that many misguided mothers have repented, and thus are forgiven this murderous sin and have received the mercy of Our Father and Creator. For them and for His mercy let us all praise and thank the Father. It is goodness that is beyond our understanding as humans. Let us pray together as mothers and fathers, as those who reverence life in all walks of life: the elderly, many of them dear, helpless ones who should be honored and protected by their families, who should be nurtured and are not.

My children, you have reflected this day on the sanctity and the great gift of life. Give thanks to the Father for all life. Do not think of these words as redundant. Never for a moment stop supporting life, for you would not live without the constant, loving and mighty support of your God and Creator. And, my children, how you are loved by your Father in Heaven. How this love pours out constantly and graciously, patiently waiting for you and the world to come to Him more each day, praising Him, thanking Him for all of His gifts, for sustaining you in His might. My dear ones everywhere in the world, as children of Mine, as a child of God, I plead with you to remember the unborn: those who have gone before, who are praying for their parents even now and who have forgiven them, and who wait to greet them when they come to Heaven. Remember how you are loved by Me, your Heavenly Mother, and give thanks. Persistence in prayer is the obedience you practice to the call of the Father. Let us rejoice together for the gifts of your lives. We go forward, fighting against the evil one, fighting against the spirit of the world!"

1/25, "My dearly beloved children, I am your God and Father, your Creator and your Lord. I am the One Who sustains you in Divine Love and in My Divine Will and in My perfect and constant Providence for this moment, for everything past and every moment of your future. Live in the awareness of that Love and that Providence. My children everywhere in the world, I beg of you to be alert to the Presence of My Son, your Lord Jesus, your Savior and your King. He has saved you for a reason: to spend Eternity with your God in everlasting bliss with each other and your loved ones, to share in the Godhead in the power and the might and the glory offered to you in glorified bodies, and in praising and thanking Me in continuation of the praise and glory and gratitude that you offer to Me now as My children, children of the King!

PRAY FOR YOUR COUNTRY. PRAY FOR THE WORLD. PRAY ESPECIALLY FOR THE BORDERS OF THIS COUNTRY, ALL OF THEM! PRAY FOR COURAGE FOR THOSE WHO WILL SHORTLY UNDERGO GREAT DEVASTATION, MOST ESPECIALLY AT THE BORDERS OF YOUR COUNTRY. YOU KNOW I SAY THIS TO PREPARE YOU AND ALL PEOPLE, AND TO CALL YOU TO DEEPER PRAYER. By now you understand how powerful your prayers have become; how necessary they are for every person in the world, and so you respond with more understanding, to be My obedient servants, servant children and, as My Son has told you, 'I call you friends.' See yourselves in this new way: as warriors whose rosary is the sword focused on battle against all the evil in the world, gathering. You are very close to enormous events that most certainly will take the attention and the breath away from so many, that will catch the breath of all in the world.

I am serious this day, for I call you this day to be My serious warriors. Long ago Mary, the Immaculate One, explained to you that each event will cause more destruction and take more lives in an escalating manner. You will see that as well. It is with some fear that any soldier marches to war and kneels on the battleground in preparation for attack, and it is thus that I would wish for you to find yourselves a protected battleground, protected by Myself in union with the Son and Our Spirit, with the Holy Mother, all the Angels and Saints and all in Heaven, and the prayers of those in Purgatory; yes, entering a greater battle now, which will be played out in service as well to those who survive, your dearest brothers and sisters everywhere.

Rejoice, My children, that we come closer to the destruction of evil everywhere, the removal of evil everywhere and a glorious new beginning, either in Heaven or on a new and renewed earth. I count on you, My dear, faithful ones. Of course I say: 'Do not fear.' Do not fear beyond reason, for reason tells you of the presence of the Heavenly Court and the might of My Arm. You are My precious ones, My own children. To arms!"

2/1, "My very dear ones, I am your Immaculate Mother, My children. I enable you, through the gifts I have been given, to touch others in a deeper way, to allow them to recognize the Presence of my Son within your heart, and that it is only peace you desire and peace you bring. I bring the grace and gift of increased sanctity once again for all of you gathered here and in the entire world, who listen and follow all the words of Heaven these many years. Do not despair. Do not lose heart or hope. Continue to pray for your loved ones whose hearts seem never to soften, but only perhaps harden against the call to prayer and against the love and forgiveness of my Son, your Savior. I bring you **my promise that they will love me as you do**, they that will turn to their Mother, the Holy and Immaculate One, with all their hearts and great joy and relief that they have at last chosen truth, sanctity and peace. Again, you may not see this instantly, but gradually, the way a deep and lasting conversion must occur. Praise and thank the Father with me every moment for the rest of your lives here and in eternity."

2/15, "Dear children, I am your Mother, Mother of all hearts, but most especially the loving and protective, ever-present Heart of my dear Son. His love spreads wherever there is joy and acceptance and tolerance and encouragement and all of the virtues, most especially patience. I remind you again this day how great will be your need for patience when all of the lost ones come to you in agony. The Angels and Saints sing with joy this day for all of you who pray everywhere in the world and let love pour from your hearts into the wounds of others and, of course, into the Wounds of my Son Who has hidden each of you in His Wounds to guard you, protect, nourish and nurture you, to bathe you in His Blood, to cleanse you, to perfect you and simply and most gloriously to love you. You are my comrades-at-arms. The Father promised me a mighty army; and you are that army, you are that might, you are that strength, the perseverance that is required to win a battle, a battle of love for souls. Remember to have patience. You are my heart, my children!"

2/22, "My dearest holy ones, I am your Jesus of Mercy. I am YOUR Jesus, children; for I belong intimately and completely to each one of you and to My children all over the world who have turned to Me in a greater way through the Heart of My Mother, who knows Me! Some of you have responded more than others; and for this I thank you this day. Remember, My dear, dear ones, that you will see frightening things; that you will know moments of fear; that they will be overcome by the trust in My promises of protection, in the promises of the might of My Father's Arm and the place you hold in His plan for the salvation of the world to give this gift to each and every person in the world who will accept it. How you are loved! I must say this again and again to encourage you, for difficult times lie ahead: struggle and yes, confusion, as the meaning of My words begin to be lived out and understood more deeply by each of you. This is all preparation for each time and each event that becomes more difficult; each time more people come to you in more need, in more fear, in more sorrow and remorse, in more confusion. Think of these things and allow compassion to blossom in your hearts.

I thank you, little ones everywhere, for being you! Help Me to help you. I tell you of the Father's plans, but you know by now **that I do not know when He will act upon each word He has allowed Me and given Me to speak**; and so, **each year there is a greater possibility of greater destruction, of a greater unfolding of His plans to remove evil from the world, from the hearts of every person alive.** Dwell on the seriousness of these words and your place in My Father's plan. Allow these reflections to give you a greater understanding of the level of service that you will be to each one, the level and the amount of need in the hearts of those who know Me not, who reject Me, who ridicule Me still, and My Mother. I bid you to be filled with joy and hope. The more you pray, the more you reflect, the more you open to the gifts of Our Spirit. You are Mine and you belong to Me. Whatever your calling in life, We only become closer, more intimately united in My Father's Will. Thank you for your love. Amen."

2/26, At Adoration, 1:30 p.m. Jesus said: "Please take these words, given as an extra strength and guidance for all. 'My dear loving and patient people, I know and see your hearts straining to remain faithful to all the prayer you are called to offer for all of My Father's intentions on your behalf and for the world. Do not give in to fatigue, I beg of you. **A heart that is surrendered is at rest and at peace with each day of waiting and lack of understanding** of His Will and desire for you and for the entire world. You are hanging on with trust and hope to the truth of all My Father's promises, all the while wondering why He does not act in a more obvious way to change the hearts and minds of loved ones, who drift farther away from their God in ridicule and words of derision at all you endure for My sake. I hear the anguish in your voices and spirits, and see the fatigue and great price required for the energy to continue in trust to answer the call of Heaven. Oh My children, you are one with Me. Walk with Me. Hear My words of encouragement and reminder **that those of you who follow Me must suffer the loss of all expectations, any earthly rewards for your faithfulness in reflecting My life with your own!** Think of the areas of your country about to be destroyed by earthquakes and mighty storms. Ask Me daily to pour out My Blood upon those who will certainly be brought into eternity quickly. Love them with your own lives and the penance required to save countless souls who must accept Our mercy. To arms, once again, My beloved warriors. I call out to each of you personally, and beg your attendance with Me in the Most Blessed Sacrament in prayer and silence for your country.'"

2/29, "My dear beloved ones of My Sacred Heart, I am your crucified Lord. I am the One Who shed ever last drop of blood in My body for each of you, for everyone who has ever lived and will ever live. I poured Myself out for you until there was nothing left of Me, no drop of moisture within My Body, until My Body was like a shell that blew in the wind. I love you now with that same love that allowed Me to die, to suffer so dreadfully and to gather up all of the strength of the Godhead and rise for you. **Tell people sincerely, seriously, lovingly, how much they are loved**. Love each other with My love, with that sacrificial pouring out of yourselves. You will have this opportunity again and again. Come and see, My children, what I have done for you. Behold My crucified body within your heart. **Be My victim souls**. Do not be frightened by My words, for you know I am with you, sustaining you. You know the comfort of My Mother. Together we run to her for that comfort. Together we seek her glance, that loving and full of love and compassion glance that breaks your heart when you consider your unworthiness. Always My children everywhere in the world, remember that it is the love of your GOD that allows you to even approach My Mother. Come to Me in her company and be strengthened. Be one with the Immaculate One. It is mercy I desire. It is humility that is needed. I say again to you, I love you. Love Me. Come to the foot of the Cross and rejoice!"

3/7, "My beloved children, I am your God and Father, your Creator and your Lord, the One Who loves you. I come this day, with a new warning, a new hope and a new call and of course, this call is to prayer. This call is to **beg for the gift of salvation for the world**. Time grows very, very short before mighty gifts are given in the midst of chaos and upheaval and destruction. The mighty gifts, as you would suspect, are my great gift of ultimate mercy! **My gift of mercy will save millions.** Ponder, dwell on souls who have wandered through life without understanding, without wisdom, without love; and be motivated by the desperation and desolation in their hearts and their lives. Imagine yourselves wandering the streets with no home, no possessions at all, trusting that a meal can be found or will be available somewhere, at the hand of God through generous people in the world. Imagine yourselves in that condition. Anyone who wanders in the state of sin wanders in that sort of dependency on the gift of salvation from their God. You have an opportunity to intervene in the lives of these people, then as now, and you must seize the moment, seize the opportunity with all your might, with all the hope and understanding and wisdom in your own heart, your belief and trust in My words and promises.

Of course you will pray most powerfully for those you know, those close to you; but try, I tell you, to realize that everyone in the world is that close to you in My Plan; that you might pray for them as lovingly and filled with hope and trust as you do for your dear ones close to you. Unite your prayers to each other's and to those of the entire world. WEAVE A BLANKET OF COMFORT AND

GRACE THAT WILL COVER THE WORLD AND PROTECT MY POOR ONES, MY LOST ONES FROM INCREASED ATTACKS OF THE EVIL ONE. WRAP THE WORLD IN YOUR BLANKET OF PRAYERS OF LOVE, OF HOPE FOR THEM. I leave you with this image, My dear ones everywhere in the world who hear My words and follow them. It is a very serious time now, and you will soon see very serious events erupt, unfold and yes, even explode before your eyes. Do NOT be frightened. Be emboldened by My promises of protection and My great, great love for you. The might of My Arm enfolds you. Amen."

3/17, At Adoration, "Dearest little messenger, I, your Immaculate Mother, bring encouragement this great feast day (3-17 is always feast of St. Patrick in U.S.A.) from Patrick (!) and all in Heaven. Though many of Our Saints lived thousands of years ago, each one is united in prayer with you and in concern for the salvation of the world. Rejoice, child. Special gifts pour down from Heaven at this moment for ALL who pray and struggle to remain faithful. Proceed in joyful hope, little one. I am your Mother of Sorrows and Joy."

3/21, "My very dear children, I am your Jesus of Mercy. I come to prepare you this day for the mighty week of My Passion. I had prepared all of My life, and each year for forty days you, the Church, is asked to prepare in union with Me for that horrendous day and those ignoble deeds. My Mother gave Me so much strength and encouragement and bravery and lent Me Her courage. Lend Me your courage, My dear ones. In that way you will become more aware of it; for you will need courage in the future, and I wish for you not to be fearful, but courageous, to reach deep inside where I dwell, that together we might make this walk and meet whatever it is the Father Wills for you in your own journey as well as Mine.

Prepare to practice more trust than you ever have in your lives. Begin to say this to yourselves, My children: 'Trust in My Jesus will carry me through this event or that event, or these events of the present moment." For it is only in this way that each of you will survive according to My Father's plan for you. It is a mighty adventure we begin today; for as you walk into danger, I accompany you, as you accompany Me on My walk to Calvary. **You will know there is a deep correlation when these events begin.** Reread My words of the prior Lenten times of the past to prepare for the Lent and the Passion of the future. Each day you experience struggles that make you stronger, that prepare you to better walk with Me in joy with your head held high! The strength and the power of My words to move you, to strengthen you, to protect you is in direct proportion to your acceptance and your openness. Open your hearts now, My children. Open your minds and your will to accept. IT IS LOVE THAT SAVES. This day I lift you higher in My Father's Plan. I increase your sanctity and your humility, for they must go hand in hand. Dwell not upon gifts, but in gratitude to the Giver. Come to Me all of you who thirst. I wait to refresh you with My love. Amen."

3/28, "My very dear children, I am your God and Father. I come this day with mighty gifts for you who are mighty in My Plan, who are mighty in the

Name of My Son, in perseverance, in struggles; who are faithful, who are My precious ones and mighty warriors. My dear ones, very soon you will see dreadful events in this country. They may not touch every area, but they will touch every heart in this once great land of yours. They will bring you to tears and mighty sorrow. It will be as it was when My Son wept over Jerusalem, that you will weep over your country, and you will be given another point of union with Him and His journey. Praise Me and thank Me for all of the gifts I am giving you daily.

Years ago I told you I would not leave you bereft of the help you will need, and so it is or you would not still be a part of My Plan. This is not, My children, for any reason except My Own Mercy and the goodness in your hearts that you accept all of the help, all of the mighty graces that I pour out upon you all the time, not just when I announce them. My children everywhere in the world, I speak to you as well. Know that I count on you for mighty deeds, for the last ounce of your strength: the strength and courage and the act of will it will take to survive the coming days and months. You have heard words like this before, and yet there were what you consider delays. There will be no such delay now, My dear ones, (and yet in 2006, as I am editing this for publication, there is still what we see as delay….. Praise God!) The world has continued to ignore the call of Heaven, the call for prayer, the call for change, the call for listening hearts, the call for surrender, and there has been little or no response.

Many have turned away. It is NOW a time when you gather every ounce of strength, every gift you have ever received in your lifetime, and **make the decision to remain in My Plan for its entirety**. **This will be lived out moment by moment. All the strength you need will be given moment by moment, as well as all My love and protection, as well as the prayers of every person in Heaven and all of you praying for each other.** Above all, I call for joy!' It is bravery.

It is love which smiles while the heart is breaking.

It is a total giving of what it means to be human: to pour yourself out when your heart is breaking, or you may be in exhaustion or simply wish to run from overwhelming events. Feel the seriousness in My words. Hear it in My voice. I ask you to be serious as well, once again: a seriousness that will give you the focus you must have. Many, many, many Angels are released from Heaven now, and accompany all of you and help you to fight your personal battles against the evil one and his demons. Many years have gone by in preparation for this time. If you have accepted all of My gifts, all of My preparation, you are ready for everything; and yet, you know first and foremost that you must not, **you cannot walk in fear! Joy will raise your spirits, raise you out of a fearful place, and lift you to the level of sanctity and giftedness that I Myself, your Father, offer you.** Without this, you will not succeed, My dear children everywhere. Thank you for listening with all of your might and heart and soul and mind and will. You are My beloved beyond, beyond, beyond anything you know. You are Mine, My children. I have created you for this moment. Be brave. Be joyful. Be grateful. Amen."

4/12, Adoration, "Little one, please take My words, meant for your encouragement and new trust. I am your Jesus of Mercy, your King and Lord. The world will shake with a guilty trembling, as a fearful quaking seizes them and this country. Much of the borderland of this country will break off and disappear under mighty waves. There will be some areas not touched by the unfolding of the Father's plan to remove evil from the earth. Those of you who are not dealing with immediate, that is local damage, must wait for others to arrive at your door step. Neighbors will band together and pool resources to help unfortunate victims. Leaders will come to the fore in order to organize the rest in an orderly and serious manner. Those of you who listen and pray and believe will explain to others the need for rescue from the elements, for shelter and food and explain the Father's Wrath over sins of infant murder, genocide and the sinful lifestyle of all who reject the Commandments, the present day words from Heaven, and the call to prayer and mercy and reconciliation. (As we see this has not happened yet, but reading the effects described, we can only say, Praise God for Your mercy and hesitation to allow such damage in our country… Cta.) Child, we will continue after this Holy Sacrifice of the Mass which I ask you to offer for your country, your loved ones and in reparation for all your sins.

12:30 p.m. …. Same day: "Hello, My little one. You see that your life will be filled with times of delivering Our words directly to Our people: Now and until I return. It will also be a time of writing letters to people gathered in each place of protection that will carry news to them of others like themselves, who wait in joyful hope for My Return. 'Be at peace, people of the world. Wait in joy and serenity and preparedness for all you expect to begin by the Will of My Father. Remember, nothing will aid your own journey more than total trust in all Our promises. You ARE loved. You ARE protected. You are being DRENCHED IN NEW MERCY this very week in your Novena of Chaplets to the Divine Mercy for My intentions. Thank you, My beloved children everywhere. We are all one in purpose, one in grace, one in My Light, one in the Divine Will of My Father. Oh My darling ones, how you are loved by your Triune God and Mary, your holy Mother, the Immaculate One. I am your Jesus, King and Savior!'"

4/16, 12:40 p.m. At home, "My little soldier, how weary is the heart you bring to Me! All of these little ailments serve to keep you focused on Me, your loving Lord and God, your Savior and your King. It is good to continue to seek rest and quiet, daughter of My Will. You will see hard work and travel again soon enough. The messages you have received about your country are serving to alert Our people to preparedness for a journey to safety. If you accomplish nothing else by your obedience, think of the people who will be saved. Soon there will be storms and floods and high winds that bring trees crashing and mud sliding with many homes into the sea. (Then He followed with a long personal message which ended with....) .... You will begin a new life with all who survive this period of tribulation and chastisement. How wondrous will be the earth, filled with beauty and simplicity. Yes, this will take a while to accomplish, but YOU WILL ALL BE IN A DEEP SLEEP DURING THIS TRANSFORMATION! Ponder My words, daughter. Be filled with peace and joy and trust in My help and protection. I am your Jesus of Mercy and Love."

4/25, "My very dear children, I am your holy and most loving Mother, Mary. You have given much devotion and honor to Our little Saint Faustina, as you thank God for her and pray according to the many messages given to her. Reread them in her Diary, My children, to cement in your hearts the truths of the days to come and of the needs for your life, your sustenance and for those who will come to you looking for mercy, looking for shelter, allowing you in the greatest way possible to BE mercy, to be one with Jesus of Mercy in being that great tree that My Jesus spoke of years ago, that spreads out it's branches to give shelter to all who come, who take refuge in your goodness. These are important days, days of reflection still on the suffering of Our Jesus. Be grateful for him. Love Him. To honor each other is something that you can do quietly and in your hearts through your prayers. It will cement even more the great friendship that has grown among you, the unity in My Heart and in the Sacred Heart of Jesus where you all dwell, hidden from the world and blessed beyond your imagining.

Pray for perseverance once again, for the attacks of the evil one increase now. You see them and hear of them all over the world, so many coming into eternity now from acts of violence and hatred. Pray for these dear ones. Pray for your country. Pray for each other that nothing can separate you from each other and your love for your God. Recall that nothing can separate you from the love of Jesus as the Apostle so wisely has told you, (Romans 8: 35-39) except your own choice. Thank the Father again for the opportunities to affect the salvation of the world with your prayers and your love. My dear ones, what can I say? But thank you with all of who I am! ALL OF THE POWER I HAVE BEEN GRANTED BY THE FATHER GOES INTO SUPPORTING YOU AND PRAYING FOR YOU AND LOVING YOU. REMAIN FAITHFUL, MY DEAR ONES, AS I AM FAITHFUL TO YOU. Welcome each other constantly into your hearts in prayer and in greetings. I love you, little ones. YOU ARE MY HOPE, MY JOY and LITTLE WARRIORS."

4/29, Adoration, 9:30 a.m. "My dear people of the world, be at peace. Give all fear and anxiety to Me, your Creator and Lord. Allow Me to sustain you with the might of My Arm and Perfect Will for you and for the world. Do NOT turn away from words of warning by your God. Trust that all I have allowed in your lives has served to cleanse your heart or brought your weaknesses to light, and you find yourselves in a dilemma of your own choosing or have even reverted to your former sinful lives. My dearest people, you are battle-weary from awaiting the arrival of events that will convince loved ones of the truth of all My words and the dangerous condition of the world that precedes the time of the Return of My

Son into a world given over to pleasure and the lure of Satan. You long for specific dates of these events or have lost interest completely, lacking the faith necessary to continue in obedience to My promises. Even many who see themselves as living in My Will have no tolerance for those who remain hidden and obedient to My plans for them, which may differ from your perceptions of My laws of slow conversion. All of you who serve Me in any way - be it large and important according to the ways of the world or little and hidden from the eyes of the world - must remember the ways of the world are not My ways; and pray for the perseverance of all who serve in a sincere hope to accept My Will, guided by the Holy Spirit of God. There is much hard work and fatigue in any calling by your God to reach out, always humbly and joyfully, to serve your family of My people everywhere. Pray for a kind and loving heart for YOURSELVES, LEAVING CRITICISM AND INTOLERANCE AT THE FEET OF MY SON. Recall the words of My Beloved Jesus: All who are not against Me are with Me.'"

4/31, At Adoration, "Child, let us continue: 'My people, hear My voice. I desire for you to be BATTLE-READY as you prepare to flee to safety by following an Angel to a place of MY choosing. Your own fatigue and discomfort from being displaced from all that is familiar could leave you impatient and irritable at first. Knowing and directly experiencing this flight will prepare you more than anything for those who will come to you in greatest need! Your own homes may be a place of refuge for the weary who come from areas destroyed by natural events. All these possibilities will help to expand your understanding and compassion for others suffering from loss or need and fear. To feel helpless yourself will expand your heart and mind and spirit, allowing you to easily embrace great numbers wherever you are. My plans for the world are always for your good! I will be pouring out My mercy through My justice for the conversion and salvation of all.

Do not think yourselves perfected, My faithful ones! Satan will continue to tempt and attack your weaknesses until My Son returns!!! STAY CLOSE TO YOUR GOD. LIVE IN THE ENVIRONMENT OF PEACE. LIVE IN THE AWARENESS THAT ALL IS MY WILL TO REMOVE EVIL FROM THE WORLD AND FROM YOUR HEARTS. PRAISE AND THANK ME FOR ALLOWING YOU TO LIVE AT THIS CRITICAL TIME IN THE HISTORY OF THE SALVATION OF THE WORLD. It IS possible for each of you to travel through each new journey, in each new direction in perfect peace and joy! You CAN trust Me, beloved people. You can do this because I have said it. You are My children, My creation, and I love you and wait (for you) with unconditional love and forgiveness. You need only come to Me and surrender your will to My desires to heal you, to save you, to give you lasting joy and eternal life some day in complete unity and harmony with your Triune God. It is a new Heaven or a renewed Earth I offer you. Be at peace, children. BE Peace, children.' "

5/8, Mother's Day (We had a crown of flowers for Our Lady's statue and many fresh flowers on the altar at the house. The statue, Our Lady of Grace, has turned from very white plastic to a soft pink about three years ago at Christmas, along with several other sacred items in the house. She was very pink on Sunday.) "My very dear ones, I am your Holy Spirit, the Spirit of God, the Spirit of Truth, the Spirit of holiness, the energy that helps you to remain on this journey back to the Father through the Heart of Jesus and the Heart of Mary, My beloved spouse. Thank you for making this a special day of love and honor for her, whom I love. She is truly My spouse. She is truly the one whom I enable to bring you graces from the Father, won by the Heart and the life and obedience of Jesus and her own life, her own love, her own obedience. She prays for you so much more than you realize, dear children and people of the world. She enables graces to be given to you. She prays for special gifts for you without your knowledge: those you have asked for and those she desires for you that she constantly requests at the Throne of the Father. I honor her with you this day in union with your love and your prayers and your songs, the flowers you have brought.

The shrine within your own hearts is something I have helped you build. Rejoice! Thank your Triune God for the place you occupy in the Father's plan and on the path to a great victory and defeat of the evil one. Mary is a mighty leader of each of you, as well as your loving and gentle Mother. She also prays that you might have that backbone of steel mentioned to you periodically to remind you to remain strong or to return to the narrow path, and then she encourages you and 'gentles' you along the way. Let your hearts open to the love I pour into them this day so that, united in My honor of her in the shrines of your hearts every moment of every day, you may remember that she is your Queen also. You are little angels of God, little warrior angels and I tell you, together with all of Heaven and most especially on this day, you will help in union with Jesus to effect the salvation of the world. Rejoice. Give thanks and praise to the Father for His wonderful plan. Listen for My voice! Amen."

5/16, "Dearest children, I am your God and Father. I call out to you everywhere in the world, who listen and respond with all their hearts and souls and minds and strength. I pour out perseverance. Believe Me, you would not have survived in My service and in service to the world this long without these many gifts given again and again, and especially the gift of perseverance. Continue to pray for this. Ask for these gifts for each other and your loved ones, especially those who do not listen now. My dear ones, there will be rain and flooding in many places in this country and in those on the other continents. There will be severe thunder and lightening to alert you, to remind you of the JUST ANGER that rumbles over the earth at the sinful lives of My people: of those who scoff, who refuse to listen or having listened once, refused to change and turned away in coldness. There will be eruptions of mighty volcanoes that have been asleep for many, many, many years. These will be given as signs of a greater escalation of My Plan, of the fulfillment of so many prophetic words, graced and blessed words from Heaven to warn and prepare you. This will be an ongoing theme until these events begin; and then more will be given to protect you, to strengthen you, to allow you to remain courageous in your peace, reaching out to others, sharing all I have given you, and appreciating totally the enormity of these gifts. How you are blessed beyond any people in history.

I bless you by the tasks I give you, by the learning experiences, the wisdom and understanding gleaned through your everyday lives and struggle to maintain the level of sanctity to which you are called. This can only be procured and maintained through prayer, through the mercy you have and the patience you have with each other and for each other. I come to tell you that you are doing well because you are struggling to be obedient. You are struggling to surrender, to say 'yes' to each new event, each new learning experience, each struggle. I ask you again to pray for the borders of this country. There will be much destruction and such great sadness, wailing, weeping and gnashing of teeth as the light dawns in the hearts and minds of so many who have been closed to the possibility of the punishment of your God and His Just Mercy. There will be many events of Nature that are beyond what you have yet seen. These are not new words, not new warnings; but they come with a more IMMEDIATE AND SERIOUS SET OF CIRCUMSTANCES THAT ARE CLOSER, THAT WILL IMPACT ALL OF YOU IN A CERTAIN WAY, THAT WILL CHALLENGE YOU; AND WITH ALL OF THESE EVENTS, I ASK YOU TO HEAR THE WORDS OF MY JESUS WHO IS ASKING YOU PERSONALLY AND COLLECTIVELY, 'DO YOU LOVE ME, MY DEAR ONES. DO YOU LOVE ME, MY DEAR ONES?? FEED MY LAMBS. FEED MY SHEEP!'

Reach out with whatever you have to give, to share: every talent and ability, every understanding, all of the wisdom you have received and accepted over these many years. These words are repeated again because of their importance; because, in a state of excitement and fear at first, you will forget, your nerves will be on edge, you will be struggling just to maintain the peace that you are given in the midst of chaos. Remember, I am speaking to everyone in the world, in this great country of yours, of America. Many scandals, many shameful acts are rocking the complacence, the haughty attitudes, the righteousness of many; and more prayers are being said for your leaders. I have been asking you to pray for your leaders for many years. You can see now the greater need for greater prayer. Unite your prayers. Come together at times and on days you have not prayed together before, by twos and threes, smaller groups; and if you are praying alone, remember you are never alone, and you can invite everyone in Heaven and unite with everyone on earth who prays and with all the souls in Purgatory for this dear land of your own and for the entire world. More and more, as events become more harmful among peoples, a greater challenge to peace, more frequent attacks by terrorists, you can see the need for prayer. It is not that prayers are not being answered or not affecting the people of the entire world, even terrorists; but this is how great is the need for more prayers.

The sins of abortion continue. Marriages among like genders, all throw rejection against the Commandments I have given you. Throughout the ages people have rebelled; but this, believe Me, is the most rebellious, the most civilized, the most frivolous, the most selfish and yet, the most advanced ever known in history. As with so many gifts you have personally, collectively as a nation and the world, you throw these gifts away, for they will be removed as more destruction levels areas of the earth. Oh My dear ones, it is NOW that you are called upon as soldiers and warriors in the battle against evil to rush to the front lines with all of who you are, which is mighty; all of who you are becoming, which is beyond your understanding, which will mean gifts promised so long ago of healing, of transportation outside the normal range, protected by Mary, your dear, dear Mother, whom you honor still this day for this special month devoted to Her. I tell you: do not waste time on 'When or How or Who.' More and more you know Why! The world will change. Focus on My words. Know that your God is BEGGING YOU, all the while giving you the spiritual and natural tools you need to survive, to bring the earth to greater levels of salvation for everyone who lives. Pray for those going into eternity which are more now, that will occur in such great numbers. You might be overwhelmed at first. Offer every little discomfort, every ailment, every illness, every struggle for the salvation of souls, My children. Keep this in your minds.

Many events will occur that will change the face of the earth; but then look beyond to the Gates of Heaven or the New Era for the Earth. There have been many Ages in the history of the Earth. The New Era means another direction, another way of life: the Eucharistic Age, and all of you as **Our Eucharistic people in the greatest union possible with your Eucharistic Lord.** I speak at length this day because I wish to reach deeply into your consciousness, into your minds and hearts, that you would hear what I am saying, that you too would wake up from your daily routine which is necessary and important, but can be so distracting and numbing of your minds and hearts. So I CALL YOU IN A NEW WAY TO NEW AWARENESS, TO NEW COMMITMENT, TO NEW SURRENDER OF YOURSELVES AND TO REJOICE! YOU ARE ONE WITH YOUR GOD, WITH ALL THE ANGELS AND SAINTS, WITH EVERYONE IN HEAVEN AND THE SOULS IN PURGATORY PRAYING FOR MY MERCY; PRAYING THAT THE EARTH WILL NOT BE COMPLETELY DESTROYED, BUT WILL GO ON IN A NEW WAY, IN NEW SHAPES, IN NEW LOVE AND ONENESS WITH THE TRIUNE GOD. This is your goal, either in Heaven or on the earth in a new time, a new Age that will usher in after the glorious return of My Son. Keep focused on these things, My children everywhere. Do so with joy. JOY WILL BLOSSOM WHERE GRATITUDE IS SEWN. My children, I bless you all. I love you all. Believe that you are precious. Believe that you are victorious. Thank you for listening. Thank you for being here, so important in My plans."

5/23, "Dearest ones, I welcome you this day. I am your Jesus of Mercy, Your Crucified and Risen Lord Whose feast you celebrate this day, when I ascended into Heaven. What joy I felt. There is nothing like a homecoming! Recall when you travel and you are far from home, you are never quite at ease; and it was thus for Myself, waiting as you wait for the Father's Will. Then, when you return to your homes, you can relax, take you shoes off, know that all is well and feel the familiarity around you. This is what home means to each of us, and thus it was when I returned to Heaven. Pray in union with that joy this week, My dear ones. Pray in thanksgiving that the Father's Plan includes bringing as many people in the world as possible into Heaven, their Heavenly home and Mine; that all will accept the gracious mercy and gifts the Father waits to give; He also waits to shower upon each of His children everywhere.

My dear ones, thank you for your obedience in carrying out all of Heaven's requests through Our words these so-many-years. Thank you for struggling and when you fail, for getting up immediately. Thank you for your faithfulness to the Sacraments, to Adoration. Only when you come to Heaven yourself will you realize all of the gifts you have obtained for yourselves and for souls everywhere. Again, I stress the fact that it is salvation you helped to win with your prayers and your sacrifices and penances and your obedience. Obedience, by its very nature, contains doing things that take up time or that might be something you would rather not do, or you would rather do another thing at that time; but you are giving up your own will or another way of doing something, and you are giving up your selfishness! Nothing could be more healing than that, **because to be human is to be self-centered: another result of Original Sin**; but you ARE changing. My children everywhere in the world, I speak to you as well. How I love you all. More and more you are united through this obedience and this prayer.

More and more you become the children of God you were created to be, and instruments of His mercy, His forgiveness, His patience: all of the things you desire and need yourselves. You will be instruments of those for so many, many, many people who need comforting and healing more than anything at first; who will need shelter and food and clothing; who will need gentleness and patience and patience and patience, much like yourselves! Pray in this understanding, My dear ones, that you might be more sensitized to the needs of the people who arrive so desperate, so frightened. Pray that you will be more and more that instrument; for always, My children, on a spiritual journey or any journey there is a call for more. On vacations you eat more, you play more, you rest more, you enjoy life more; and so I call you to enjoy life more, knowing that you are serving the needs of people you have never met and may not meet until you are all in Heaven; but in a reciprocal way they will pray for you and impact YOUR salvation, the gifts and graces you receive. You may think and say to yourself: 'Well, we know all this, Lord. You have said this before.' And I tell you, NEVER can I repeat too often the words that will prepare you to be the proper instruments of salvation for the world. Could anything be more important, My children? I think not. Could any gift be greater to you? I think not. Could anything be more perfect than the Father's Perfect Will in every instance of your lives? We know it could not.

My dear ones, persevere. Hang on. Keep on keeping on. I love you. I love your dearness. I reach down and touch you as you implore the Triune God, the Holy Mother, all the Angels and Saints and everyone in Heaven to pray with you, to help you, to strengthen you, to send Heavenly joy to your hearts in spite of sadness and fatigue; and to remember that each day, each moment you are beginning again to have patience with yourselves and with your God. You are blessed beyond your knowing, and My Mother and I bless you this day in the Name of the Father and in My Name and in the Name of the most Holy Spirit of God. Continue and persevere in joy. Amen. Rejoice!"

5/31, Pentecost, "My little holy ones, I am the Spirit of God, your Holy Spirit, the Spirit of love, the Spirit of sacrifice, the Spirit that enables you to continue to follow in Jesus' footsteps, living the commandments of God, the Beatitudes and the mercy that is called forth from you in these final times before the return of Jesus. This special day I fill you with the fire of new commitment, new joy, new sanctity, new hope, My dear ones everywhere in the world. It is trust that enables hope and so I renew your trust this day, and fill you with a longing to be all you are called and created to be. It is a difficult and dangerous time in the world. Every day sees explosions and deaths, people being brought into eternity. You have been prepared for this and been praying for those who, by the Father's Will, are allowed to succumb to the acts of terrorists who are people filled with hatred, people focused on only destruction and death. Pray for them, beloved ones. Ask that My power might wash away, wipe away and, as the wind, drive away their evil intentions. Pray that they might be recreated in the Image of God, as they were meant to be, that they might be saved, that they may not have to spend eternity in the fires of Hell.

Think of yourselves. Think of your own eternity. Pray that you might surrender more. There is continued destruction ahead for the world. Greater numbers will be brought into eternity to face the Merciful and Just God. Pray for them. **Your prayers are their salvation**. Remember this. This day I pour out new strength with which to march forward into battle. Believe these words, children. Believe that you will receive more of My gifts now. You will see them and feel them and recognize them and use them in a greater way. Thank you for gathering and celebrating this feast of Mine and all I have come to mean to you in your life, in your journey. How you trust in Me and believe in Me and My power! I give you that power this day, people of the world. Use it for good! Use it for the eternal destiny of the world in Heaven, in holiness, in service to each other. This week celebrate the Octave of My Feast by continuing to repeat: **'Jesus, I love you. Holy Spirit, God My Father, I love you. I believe in Your love for me. I believe that I am Your child, Your soldier, Your chosen one, Your instrument of mercy and peace and victory over evil.'** Be filled with peace."

6/15, @ Sacred Heart Church, "Dearest daughter, I am your Jesus Who brings greetings from all of Heaven. We welcome you to this place of holiness, as you sit before My Presence. Each event My faithful ones here have experienced, no matter how painful or discouraging and confusing, has been a direct result of My Father's Will for the purification, new wisdom and understanding of everyone. This place of peace and refuge will be all they have hoped for; but it will now be a result of My Father's desires and mercy. There have been great changes and delays everywhere Our faithful ones have gathered that will result in all their desires being fulfilled also. Hearts have expanded here, as each one has surrendered to My Father's Will, and all will be very well for all! Their hearts will fill with new peace and joy, as they listen to your words of explanation in answer to their questions. Please, child, assure them again of Our Presence at every moment, Our protection and great love. I am your Jesus of Mercy Who loves each of you gathered here in faith and trust, and all those you love and pray for. Be filled with Truth, My beloved people. Be filled with Me."

6/27, "My dearly beloved ones, I am your Jesus of Mercy, come this day and pouring out love from My Sacred and Eucharistic Heart. I hold each of you close within My Heart, My children everywhere in the world. My dear ones in this country, think of other countries, the terrible conditions of war; the conditions of living in countries where Satan rules, where free love is allowed without commandments or discipline to guide the lives of Our children. Think, think of the terrible suffering experienced by so many in the world. Think of the heat in the great deserts of the world: the heat you have never felt as an everyday occurrence. Think of the pain and suffering of the dying. Unite yourself to all of these people, and send them your love and encouragement in union with My Sacred Heart. My Sacred Heart is a refuge for all the people in the world. Bring them to Me, My faithful ones. Bring them solace. Bring them the balm of My love to pour out on their wounds, their terrible sorrows, their terrible fears, their great discomfort. The world is a difficult place now, as all sorts of weather conditions prevail that are above and beyond the norm, that wreak havoc in many places; and this is just the beginning, for you know that all of these higher numbers of storms, greater destruction of storms and floods and earthquakes will only increase. This information has been given to many of those who take words from Heaven.

Do not allow yourselves (to be) or seek to be isolated, My faithful ones everywhere; but reach out to each other and those to whom others reach out. Open your hearts and allow people to minister to YOU, to HELP you. **Open your hearts to the prayer that is coming your way**, the love and the encouragement of the faithful everywhere. There is no greater weapon against the evil one than unity, and you too must seek and accept unity with others. How else could you have unity with Me? You know that **to suffer is a blessed state in life**. You also know that most of the people on the earth scoff at that idea, reject the Cross and thus, reject the Father's mercy. There is so much for you to do, My children! Do it by simply opening yourselves to unity with Me and then with everyone in the world; praying for those who suffer, who are alone and lonely and frightened, who see no end to their suffering, who do not understand the glory that awaits in the Kingdom of Heaven. I speak of surprises and new journeys to you. Each day is a surprise when you are listening and watching for signs of My Presence, for the little treasures I allow you along your day. Be united to My gifts, to the grace and mercy always available to you. Do not become discouraged. Never ever for a moment believe that you are alone. More and more you can see and understand how important this is now, and will be even more so in the future.

My children, I love you with all the love in My Heart. I hold you all in My Heart every moment of every day. What a beautiful vehicle in which to ride through life! Be at peace in this heat, in discomfort, in the irritability that rises in these summer conditions, whatever they are for you. Be at peace. Practice being at peace in the midst of chaos and the discomfort of **'dis-ease'**. The Angels accompany you, My beloved ones in the world. Open yourselves to that reality. Open yourselves to that beauty, and the wonderful songs and great love that pours forth from these Angels to the Triune God and Mary, the Immaculate One. I love, I love you, I love you, I love you! Remind yourselves often that you are Mine, and smile and rejoice! Be filled with My peace."

7/4, "My very dear people, My beloved ones, I am your God and Father. Thank you for coming together on this special day, My children here and everywhere in the world: praying for your world, praying for your countries, praying in thanksgiving for all of the gifts given, praying in sorrow for all of the gifts lost and given away by aggressive and greedy people everywhere in the world. There is no excuse for greed. There is no excuse for those who pursue power, who pursue the conquest of others, who pursue that which does not belong to them by law and by My Will. My dearest ones everywhere in the world, I plead with you this very week to PRAY MORE, for many will be coming into eternity much sooner than you would like to see; much sooner than you would hope for and certainly, much sooner than you pray would happen. My plan must escalate. My Will must go forward, for there are those who suffer and will suffer too much; and everywhere in the world there are those who continue with haughty attitudes, with an irresponsible attitude of disrespect for others, especially their brothers and sisters in the great family of God. This cannot continue. If it is necessary for you to experience loss, then thus it will be to bring you to an appreciation of the gift you are to each other; of the gift and sacredness of human life; of the gift of your own life and all the treasures you have been given throughout your lives. See how people throw them back in the face of their Creator.

I mean for these words to be most serious, My people everywhere. I mean for you to hear them in a serious manner, and commit yourselves once more to praying for the world, to praying for the conversion of hearts and souls everywhere; but especially those in your own families and for your OWN hearts. It is callous attitudes and indifference that hurts. It is thoughtlessness that cuts to the heart of My dear people everywhere. It is these that cause a rift, a division to occur within groups and within families because of a feeling of self-importance that still accompanies many of My faithful ones. I call you into an accounting this day, My people in the world. LOOK AT YOURSELVES. LOOK AT YOUR OWN BEHAVIOR. LISTEN TO YOUR WORDS. BE AWARE OF YOUR THOUGHTLESSNESS, I beg of you; for it cannot continue, if you are to continue as My faithful remnant on whom I count to help Me save the world and every soul in it! As it is, you have been told and your understanding is such that much of this country will change in shape because of destruction, because areas will be totally annihilated in the whole world.

Pray in sorrow for your own sins first, My children, and then for the sins of the world. I love you, else I would not have called upon you in this critical time to be a critical part of My plan. Ponder again the salvation of souls in the entire world. Ask the Holy Spirit to show you yourselves, My dear ones. There is NO ONE EXEMPT FROM THIS REQUEST. Think of your attitudes. Think, My children! Be filled with the peace of My Son. Be filled with joy this day for the freedom that you still enjoy and experience each day by the might of My power and My arm! We are walking into battle!"

6/27, (Personal msg.) "My dearest one, please be at peace. Look back on times past and realize how quickly things change. All at once, all is new. The past is over and much of it is forgotten. You lunge forward to new heights of service and gift; and so of course, to new depths of questioning and wondering; and tiny fears creep into your mind and worry your spirit. It is all part of this process of changing and waiting for your heart's desires to be fulfilled. And yet, little one, you ARE more patient and filled with new wisdom and understanding. The days are so formative, like another womb; but this time **you are your own womb**, out of which is and will be born a new you, completely transformed into a mighty warrior. I bless you this night in the Name of the Triune God. The world is about to explode literally with bombings and attacks, and many soldiers taken into eternity."

7/5, "My very dear ones, I am your God and Father. I thank you for all the love that has grown in your hearts, My children everywhere in the world, for Me: your appreciation, your new ability and desire to thank and praise Me for everything. I tell you, all of you in the world who give Me honor and praise are a source of great mercy for the entire world, are the recipients of special graces of Mine, of a predilection for each of you, a choice (again I remind you, before you were born) to serve Me and My people in mighty ways, sustaining you as I have said before, helping you to maintain your level of service and grace and gift in My plan.

New souls have come into eternity this day. Pray for them this coming week along with your Novena to Me. Pray that they will open to My mercy; that they will accept forgiveness and choose for My Kingdom; that they will gladly embrace a time in Purgatory that will cleanse them, for they will then pray for you and for the world, and most especially for their families and their dear ones. We see more destruction in the world now, and again I remind you, it will be ongoing way for those giving their lives in service of the world, defending the world; that their honor and honesty may be preserved; that those who have fallen to evil suggestions and actions will be renewed at this time by your prayers, your special remembrance in sending love and support to them. How the world needs you, My children everywhere. How I need you. How you need you, and of course, how you need your Triune God. Thank you for loving your Triune God and the Holy Mother at new levels of hope and joy, new eagerness to serve and to persevere in waiting; as My plan unfolds slowly and naturally in your own life and in the world. **Dwell in hope**. This is the environment I have given you to help save your own soul and the souls of the world. What a mighty task, and you are the mighty warriors who will complete this task in union with your God and all of Heaven. Do not dwell in anticipation of destruction. **Dwell in anticipation of a cleansing and a removal of evil from the entire world.** Be My source of mercy by praying in this way: by always reaching out, always being available to the poor and the needy. You know that together We are victorious. A new waiting and a new obedience and your surrender IS salvation. I not only hear your prayers. I gather them through the Heart of My Son and the Heart of the Holy Mother. How you are loved! We go forward again."

8/1, "On this day we welcomed the Pilgrim Virgin statue of Our Lady of Fatima into our home (for a week) with prayers and songs, as well as consecration to God Our Father on His new Feast Day. "My very dear children, I come to you this day, yes, as Mother, as Lady and Queen of Fatima, and I thank you for welcoming Me more deeply into your hearts and into this place where you gather regularly, begging mercy for the world, praying for souls, praying for healing, coming closer to me always and more deeply into My Immaculate Heart. I speak to the world this day, reminding you of my messages at Fatima, reminding you of the war: World War that was mentioned then and that **I mention again today; for your world hurtles towards war.** You see signs everywhere: terrible attacks, destruction of human life and now destruction very openly of all that is Christian (destruction of Catholic Churches in Baghdad last Sunday) and those who follow My Son.

My children, the world becomes darker, more evil, a more dangerous place in which to be. Stay very united and close to me. Think of me every moment of the day and pray to me and with me. I am your Mother who wishes to protect you even more now that the need is greater. Do not be frightened, but know that there is an escalation in the Father's Plan now this very day. As you beg for mercy on your country and your world, the Father also pours out more mercy as you desire. You are living His Will when you ask for mercy, when you praise and thank Him and you pray for others and their salvation. We belong to each other, my children everywhere, and we are one in our love for my Jesus, our love and service to the Father, our love and gratitude to the Holy Spirit, my Spouse, for all of His gifts, for enabling you to be filled with graces, as I am filled with grace. This grace grows in you daily, and sometimes by leaps and bounds!

You are my faithful soldiers, my beloved ones. Rejoice, that we have this great mission to fight the evil one and his plans for the world together. We shall praise and thank the Father now in a moment of silence together for giving us to each other, (We are given the promise that this is happening again for you, right now, as you read these words… cta.) for giving us this great mission and for sharing with us the power to accomplish the defeat of evil in the world and in the hearts of all men. Let us pray, my children...... (long pause) I invite you to pray to me this week as Virgin of Fatima, that the earth may survive the plans of Satan, the destruction about to begin that has already begun, that lives first in the hearts of evil men. Pray for your leaders, that they might hear the voice of God and open their hearts. I love you, my dear ones. Thank you for your love."

8/3, "My very dear ones gathered here and in the whole world listening for the words of Heaven, I am your Holy Spirit; the Spirit that leads you forward, **Who enables you to come back** again and again to the mercy and the forgiveness and the holiness of the Father, to His perfect Will and plan for you. Oh My dear ones, how brave you are! How patient in all of your waiting, even when you feel impatient, for you are still here! You are still praying and believing, listening and surrendering. These same words are what defines the character of your journey, the environment in which you live and move and have your being. (Acts 17:28)

Words of warning have been given more often recently regarding floods and earthquakes; and so I come also to remind you to be alert, to be on guard, to be praying, to be faithful to the needs of your family everywhere in the world, closer to you than you will ever know until we are all in Heaven together! I gift you this day as befits your needs, your own neediness, your own helplessness, your own weakness in the face of the evil one and his temptations and the lure of the world, the call of your own flesh, the call of distraction, the call to take an easier way, the call to self-gratification, the call to laziness and disinterest. Dear people, I mention these because they are so much a part of human nature, allowed by the Father so that you will experience your great need and dependence upon Him, so that you will experience His mercy and be led to gratitude.

I bring the sorrow of all in Heaven this day at the waiting, the sadness, the struggle each of you must endure now as you are emptied more, as you are faced more clearly with yourselves; but I also bring you joy and the rejoicing and feasting in Heaven, for Our daughter, Maria, has joined Us (Esperanza from Betania). Pray TO her, My dear ones everywhere. Pray to her for all of your needs, for great power and grace have been given to her by reason of her life and the abandonment she practiced with great suffering for your sake; but especially for the sake of sinners. You are all sinners, My dear children. Ask Me again to see yourselves as you are seen by your God. Ask again for the openness, the courage, the bravery, the acceptance of your own reality as the truth of yourselves; and with all of this truth is coupled the great, great love of your God and My beloved spouse, the Holy Mary. Cling to her, My people. Come to Me through her, asking for more gifts, more of those things you know you need or discover now in a new and deeper way.

Rejoice when you discover the need for forgiveness. Rejoice when you discover a new opportunity for grace and cleansing and emptying that you might be filled with the innocence and the beauty, the power, the humility of the Holy Mother, of the Triune God, of all you are meant to become. There will never be a time when you must forget about who you are becoming. Strive to move forward with your God and your Holy Mother and with each other, all the while praying for each other in the world. I pour out strength this day, for **one day you will see incredible destruction and you will be spending the rest of your lives dealing with the results of the plans of evil men and the Father's Will that allows them.** There are many broken hearts in the world, My dear people. Pray for them! Pray for your own broken hearts and offer them for healing, for mending, for unity with the Sacred Heart of Jesus and the great, loving and Immaculate Heart of Mary. Be blessed this day, children. You are the hope of the world everywhere."

8/5, recorded at home after prayer with friends: "My dearly beloved and precious children, I am your Mother. I am the Immaculate One of God and your companion in sorrow and in joy. I bring you great joy this night. Thank you for your prayers, for your special celebration of me on the day of my birth. (It has been said often this date was revealed to a Medjugorje visionary years ago as the actual date of the Virgin Mary's birth…. Cta.) How I long to wrap my Mantle around all of the children of the earth, to protect you from the evil one and his plans for domination of the world. You know, for it has been said many times: these are evil and wicked days. Satan, the adversary, has been given many powers and much victory in these end times. Do not be frightened. Do not be overwhelmed by all the destruction you are about to see.

Do not be overcome by the numbers of people who flock to your doors needing great assistance and shelter and food and clothing. YOU WILL SEE THESE THINGS! It is especially for them that so much preparation and prayer has been made throughout these many years. It is because of them there have been so many delays, and the Father's sorrow at allowing so much destruction upon the earth. There are not enough people ANYWHERE listening to my words and the words of Heaven from the Triune God about returning to the Father, about changing and living the Commandments, about the great love We have for EVERYONE in the world. My dear ones, how I love you: your wonderful smiles, the joy in your eyes, the concern you have for your loved ones. Believe that your every prayer and every wish is heard by the Father. You are one with the great Communion of Saints. Never forget that! Never forget the power of your prayer. Never forget the needy ones in the world and those who suffer TERRIBLY everywhere from war-like conditions, from hunger and INTENSE poverty. I thank you again for your faithfulness to me, to my Rosary. Be joyful, children. Rejoice. Praise and thank the Father."

8/6, "My dear children, I am your Jesus of Mercy. I tell you THIS DAY, NEW MERCY IS POURED OUT UPON YOUR COUNTRY IN ANSWER TO YOUR PRAYERS. Believe this. Believe in My love for you and My gratitude for your prayers. This is repeated again to you from all of Heaven. I ask you to be strong, to surrender to My Father's Will, to be brave in the face of hardship, in the face of pain, in the face of great fatigue.

(The power of world prayer)

THERE WILL BE EVENTS, AS HAS BEEN TOLD TO YOU; BUT THEY WILL BE OF A LESSER NATURE: FEWER TAKEN INTO ETERNITY, A LESSER AMOUNT OF DESTRUCTION AT THIS TIME. Thank the Father for all of your struggles, in thanksgiving to Him for singling out your prayers to answer; for they are according to His Will, as well. Children, your prayers are mighty."

8/21, "My dear ones, I am your Mother. I have been sent to you this day with words of love and words of caution, with words of warning and words of victory. Remember these words this very week, meditating upon them, reflecting upon their meaning in your lives. Though they might seem to oppose each other, they are the opposing sides, they are opposite sides of the same coin. My children, when I bring you words of caution, I call you back to a greater focus on prayer. I call you back to the reason you have been called to prayer, to change, to become warriors. There is no way you can imagine the evil plans of men which are indeed the evil plans of Satan, our greatest adversary and enemy: enemy of goodness, enemy of all that is right and holy, enemy of peace and purity, enemy of your hearts and the hearts of every faithful one in the world, as well as those who still do not know the Triune God and all He holds in reserve for them: their inheritance, rightfully theirs, won by the death and the resurrection of my Beloved Son, our precious Jesus.

Dwell in the love of my Jesus and myself. Live in that atmosphere, that you might be healed more, that you might be more patient, that this love might radiate out to all, not what YOU think love is, or your ideas of behavior, but to **become more this instrument through which the love of My Son flows out to all.** I have described His love to you on other occasions and, if you ask the Holy Spirit, He will refresh your mind, your memory and your hearts. How people are suffering, how they need relief; and it IS the love of my Son given through your hearts, through your generosity, through your time and energy and yes, surrender of all of who you are, of all you have been given that this relief will be given.

You will see shortly (Please remember, this 'shortly' is Heaven's Timetable!

Cta.) greater use of your talents and special gifts, as people begin to come to you actually, physically in greater need. As you view their plight and begin to realize and discover all you do have to offer and the solace you are able to give them, the healing in their hearts and their lives, you will indeed rejoice and praise the Father for His great wisdom, for His formation of your hearts and your bodies as a 'cup' that holds your suffering; but also that holds the graces you have and the talents, the abilities you have been given. Some of them you know nothing about as yet!

My children, persevere! Come back. Rest yourselves. Be mature in your suffering. Be joyful in your suffering, as you pour yourself out for the world. If you could see how they live; how they suffer, the terrible attacks on their person, the hunger, the dreadful heat and the filth, the dreadful unsanitary conditions that foster disease and greater suffering, terrible thirst. The pain in your hearts and in your lives is indeed a preparation of you, as instrument of the Father's mercy and healing for all those who will come, yes; but a greater effort is needed for those you cannot see and whose pain you cannot imagine. Together you can affect the state of mind, the state of heart, the state of being in which they barely exist. Pray for their souls, as the Father takes many, many more into eternity. Mitigation has been promised now for your country, for this time, for a certain amount of time; and I thank you for your prayers, for all of you who pray, who remain faithful even though distracted and grumbling: even more unhappy allowing discomfort to affect your prayers, to affect the state of love in your hearts. Unite your lives to mine as I lived very, very simply, barely surviving, barely existing. It was the love of my Son that sweetened our lives, the atmosphere. Our very existence, our thoughts, our hearts, our words allowed this to happen for you, my children. Allow yourselves to be reformed into finer instruments, purer instruments, joyful instruments which shine in the light of my Son. Thank you for persisting in the ministries and in all you do for those in great need. I am taking your prayers to the throne of the Father this day, as you request. He hears EVERY word you say. Always your prayers are answered. Allow your hopes to increase with trust, to blossom, to flourish, to fill the atmosphere of your life with the color of Love, with the peace of My Son."

8/29, "My dear children, I am your God and Father. Each time I mention that new destruction will begin, your hearts are gripped with an anxiety; but with a hope, with a new 'yes', with a new understanding and wisdom that this must be, and with a new joy and gladness that My Will is unfolding at all. It is a great sadness to Me as well, My children everywhere in the world, that the unfolding of My Will must contain destruction, bring so many people into Eternity; but remember the goodness and the perfection contained in My Will and rejoice. It is a beginning, and you all know how grateful you are for new beginnings, a new direction: the proper environment for you life, the proper heart, the proper hope, the proper mindset, the proper spirit to embrace My Will.

Practice a listening heart, a tender and merciful heart, that this will be second nature, that more and more it will be first nature for all of you, for all of them who come. In your own country this very day, people suffer from new storms, new hardships, a lack of electricity, a lack of the common basic needs now. This results in hardship and suffering. It also results in a return to Me, and so you can rejoice that these events are bringing people back to Me as I desire. Remember, there is nothing more important than souls returning to their God in love, asking for forgiveness; in sorrow and remorse for sin, for thoughtlessness, for haughty attitudes and critical judgments. These will always be your weaknesses for which you will pray, and which you will seek to drive away with My grace, for they are at the core of the ego and pride of Satan. Cherish each other. Make room in your heart for each other. My children, THINK! Think before you speak. Think before you act. Think in love. Think with the heart and mind of My Jesus. Yes, there will be continued events of destruction; but dwell in prayer. Dwell in hope."

9/5, "My very dearest children, I am your God and Father. I bring blessings to you and all of My children in the world, for you are the blessings of your countries with your prayers, your sacrifices, the time you give to praying and begging for mercy for your countries. My dear, dear ones, thank you for your prayers for the people suffering the ravages of nature in Florida. This will continue, as you can see, as another (hurricane) approaches, a great storm, My Will for all of you and for all of them; a further reason to pray hard, My children, to focus much on salvation and on eternity, to pray for them as your brothers and sisters. Pray that they will become truly inheritors of My Kingdom, for this is what I long to do for all My children. It was for this they were created!

My children, pray for places that are being terrorized. Believe that you ARE becoming stronger, although you fall. Believe that this is a way to victory and that is, coming to Me in the Sacrament (of reconciliation... cta.), begging My mercy and My forgiveness. You can see how totally dependent you are upon grace, and how you are nothing without My help. It is thus that you will realize your littleness, and practice the humbleness that is required and requested of you. You are dust, My children, and into dust you WILL return. I intend to use every gift you have been given, as you offer them and yourselves to Me daily. It is a great gift to you to be allowed to assist Me by praying for, and one day directly ministering to, all those who come to you, all those who are going into eternity. There will be many, many more, even in this country, this land of plenty.

My dear ones, today take time in quiet to consecrate yourself again to Me, to all that I request of you, to serving Me as I desire, to praising Me, to being humble, to being patient, to being gracious with each other. **Your own wounds make you impatient.** I love you so much! I remind you again of the beauty of Heaven, of the peace of My Jesus that is offered to each one who chooses to accept it, and of My mercy. There is nothing more. You are so precious to Me. Remember every day you are the flowers in My Garden. The fragrance of holiness, the innocence of children is offered this day. Accept all I offer you, My dear ones, and BECOME with My Son and the Holy Mother and all of Heaven THE prayer for the salvation of the world. Be mighty and little in My plan."

9/9, Adoration, "My dearest one, I am your God and Father. I bring great strength today, as you have requested. Daughter, the great storms are about to flatten much of the state of Florida. For years My Church there has taken a liberal and promiscuous turn. My priest sons, and those who think of themselves as holy, have hurled blasphemy and ridicule in My Face. They show their disbelief in My Commandments by their callous and unclean behavior. It is this continuous attraction to self-gratification that brings My wrath upon this state filled with the most beautiful of My Creation. Never is there thanksgiving save those who bring in from other places the grace and gratitude in their hearts, the fire of the Holy Spirit and the love of the Holy Mother of God. These poor and sinful examples must stop completely. Retired religious seek to escape My laws in the beauty of a Paradise of their own making and desires. I am not going to relent until many more repent and turn to Me in humility, begging My mercy and forgiveness. This is a prophecy that will surprise no one, who has ever visited or knows of the lax Christianity that exists in the hearts of so many, who should be leading My people in the later years of their lives into the peace and security of the Sacred and Immaculate Hearts. Be filled with sorrow for all the innocents who must suffer along with the guilty, who must suffer for the sins of their brothers and sisters who have not been faithful or believed in Me, in the Holy Trinity, and the call of the Holy Mother. Daughter, pray that some will see this new destruction as a result of the might of My Arm and the just anger of their God. You know how much it will take to shake these thoughtless ones from their slumber. Pray with all your time and might for the souls coming into eternity; for those who survive, but whose loss of personal property and loved ones will be great."

9/12, "My dear ones, I am your Mother, the Immaculate One of God. I come to say, 'I love you.' You give my heart such hope. You bring courage and patience to the world with your prayers. So many places in the world are bleak with suffering; bleak in their living conditions; horrendous in the treatment of innocent, helpless, vulnerable people by aggressive, warlike people. My children, in this week, when you will celebrate the feast of my Sorrows, join ME in MY Sorrows for the world, for you will see this behavior spread to other parts of the world, to other countries and always to innocent people, my poor, poor little ones. Offer their sufferings, take their sufferings to the Father for the salvation of the world. Take them (suffering people) with you to your Adoration time. Present them to my Son. Ask for His healing and blessing, for His peace in their hearts. Ask for a relief from the terrible suffering, the famine and drought. This is a great gift to you, my children everywhere in the world. It is living out the reasons for which you have said 'yes' to being a soldier in the war against evil. Someday this evil will be removed from the world and the hearts of evil men. So many plans are in existence to continue with further suffering. It is a reason to be sad. It is a reason to beg the Father for relief, for mercy for them. Pray with me, my dear ones, for the spirit of repentance and remorse in the hearts of all those who turn away from the Father, who reject me, who continue to batter my Son.

Remember your own humanity when you are judging others. Remember when you judge and criticize, you are sinning then! Remember how you feel when you are given mercy and forgiveness, and treated with tenderness, and receive the gentle, loving words of Heaven. How you hope always for gentle and tender words. Be a source of gentle and tender words. It is more necessary than ever. Their hearts are broken. Patience is nearly used up, and we must begin again asking for new patience for you and for the whole world who prays. Remain in my arms, resting against my Immaculate Heart. DO NOT, my children, give up! I count on you. The world counts on you. Amen. I AM WITH YOU, MY CHILDREN. BE WITH ME!"

10/3, "My very dear ones, I am your God and Father. Fear not, My children everywhere in the world. You WILL serve Me in mighty ways. You WILL serve My people in whatever way they need, to whatever degree it is needed. Although you have been prepared for so long and live in expectation for so long, think of **the hundreds of years** during which the people in the Old Testament awaited the first coming of My Son. Perhaps that will help you to wait! I know, I know, I know how wearing it is for you; how you struggle to maintain hope; how you fight to maintain a positive attitude and a firm conviction in all of Our promises and all of Our words. This is My role for you, My dear ones. This is molding you, changing you, turning you, transforming you into the mighty warriors you must be! You have no idea how difficult the coming days will be. You have no idea regarding the **terrible plans of Satan for world domination and for slavery, true slavery for all of you**. You have heard this before, but you see it more in the world now, and get a better understanding. My poor people who suffer the oppression of the henchmen of Satan, who must see their children die in their arms in great numbers, not just one, but many in families. These are heartbreaking and heartrending experiences, and I beg you to unite yourselves with them that you might lend your strength, send your love and offer their sufferings for their conversion, for their healings, for their salvation. This will be a long time, a long run of destruction, My children. It may even reach your doorstep. Be ready. Be in My Will as totally as possible for you.

Pray for those who deliver the words of Heaven, for great fatigue is washing over them now as this time and these words seem to go on and on and on with no resolution; and yes, I tell you, hearts ARE changing; souls ARE being touched; souls ARE being saved. This is our mission together. This is your time to serve the Triune God and My plan. There is NOTHING in your lives more important. These are awesome times, and you are mighty warriors. We have just begun! Stay with Me. Pray with Me, your Creator, your Father and your Lord. Believe in My great love for you."

FOR MERCY'S SAKE!

10/10, "My dearest ones, I am the Holy Spirit of God, your Holy Spirit; the One Who enables you to be sanctified, to be lifted higher in the Father's Plan and in His delight; Spouse of the Blessed Virgin Mary, your beloved Mother. Pray to her to pray to Me, for Our prayers are one to the Father. Appreciate more who she is for you; what she does for you; how she loves you; how I love you, for I AM Love: the love of the Father for the Son and the love of the Son for the Father. This love lives in your heart now, for I am in your heart. You are children of the Triune God. Pray to Me for strength, for openness to the gifts the Father continues to desire to give you and the entire world, especially those who war against the children of God; who war against the Church of God; who war against the creation and creatures of God.

My dear, dear, dear people, I bring you enormous strength today. Always you need more strength everywhere in the world. Unite yourselves to those who are coming into eternity. Loan them your faith, your understanding, your wisdom, all the while asking Me for these gifts for them. What a great plan of the Heavenly Father to give the gift of salvation to the entire world! Think of that often and be moved to pray more for the salvation of the world. Imagine the number of prayers that are needed for the greater numbers of people always going into eternity; for it is a special time, this time of mercy, this time of free gifts won for them by your prayers, by your fidelity and your devotion, your faithfulness to the Mother of God, your precious Mother. Thank her for all She asks of you. Thank her for her guidance. Thank her most especially for interceding for you before the throne of the Father. Without her prayers, you know you would be nothing! Allow yourselves to be inspired to great love and new surrender to her as her servant, her child, the ones who love her and fight for her, the ones who give gratitude and praise to the Father for her.

How she loves you, and My children remember, she does so much more for you than your realize; so praise and thank the Father for the unknown gifts, for helping you to persevere. She knows the difficulty of perseverance, for that was Her mainstay; that was what she prayed for most after Jesus returned to Heaven and to His Father. My children, praise the Father for the new holiness that you find within yourselves and your prayers. Praise the Father each time He asks you to do more, for this means that you have been raised in holiness and strength and CAN do more. Come to Me, My dear people everywhere in the world, for My gifts. Without Wisdom you would be fodder - food for the great Beast that stalks the earth, for the error that becomes more apparent in the Church now. YOU ARE THE CHURCH, My people. Remember this, so it will be within the people of God, the people of the Church that error will come, will be apparent, will show itself and manifest its strength. Come to Me for protection against error, against lies, against falsehood and the subtlety that is Satan. Remember his strength, his gifts (far greater than your own), and yet you are protected with grace obtained for you by the Holy Mother, My beloved and precious spouse. Believe that it is waiting that has purified you to this point and enables more, always more to be given. Again you are reminded, you will not wait forever! Pray for each other, for the faithful all over the world. Not all groups such as yours have the comfort and the peace you enjoy. Pray for those who have not, who go hungry, who struggle mightily to keep faith, who struggle to believe and to trust. There are many, and they too need your prayers.

I pour all of My gifts upon you again this day. I will be with you in a special way, as you honor the Lady of the Rosary, the Queen of Heaven and earth, My Queen, My Spouse. Be filled with peace now and rejoice that all is well in spite of struggles. Praise and thank the Father for how very, very blessed you are. Appreciate this, My dear ones. Acknowledge it. Give thanks. Amen, dear, dear children of God and remnant people of the Father. Amen."

10/17, "My dearest and well loved children, I am your Mother, Queen of the Rosary, which feast you celebrate today. (This was Rosary Sunday in the Diocese of Phoenix...cta) Thank you for your prayers. Thank you for the love in your heart for me and for the whole world, when you pray. I LOVE YOU (said with great intensity.. cta.) I am your Mother and helpmate. I am your Queen. I am the one who purifies your prayers and your hearts with MY prayers for your needs, for your intentions, for your increasing holiness, for a new commitment in your hearts to prayer. Children, the call to prayer is always greater and is always mentioned because your prayers do SO MUCH GOOD! You have become mighty prayer warriors which has been my hope in my interceding for you. In prayer, you become holier; you become stronger to fight the evil one in your own lives, as well as the entire world.

Again I ask you, my children everywhere in the world, pray for each other who pray. Be alert and aware that Satan has designs upon your soul. When someone attacks you, or seeks to distract or undermine a life of prayer, visit my Son in His Blessed Sacrament. Yes, this is the beginning of the Year of the Eucharist: your greatest gift, your greatest ability to continue in holiness, in surrender of your lives; to prepare you for all of those who will come to you in the future, more needy than you have ever witnessed or could ever imagine; a time that will be chaotic at first and difficult; and you must be OPEN COMPLETELY to the Spirit of God, to my Son Jesus and to myself who will be standing next to you offering so much strength, so much power; and open to the words of the Holy Spirit, my dearly beloved Spouse. I mention these again so that you will not become cold or feel hopeless yourselves when you see great numbers of people arriving. NOTHING IS IMPOSSIBLE TO GOD, my CHILDREN, AND SO IT WILL BE ON YOUR BEHALF AND ON THEIRS.

I am so grateful that you gather week after week and pray daily my Rosary. Pray in thanksgiving this day, my dear ones, for the great gift of the Rosary, the great power that is given to these special prayers. ALWAYS, ALWAYS I am with you, praying for you, praying with you. Pay no attention to the noise and the chaos of the world. (Recently the Father said in a personal message as I sat before the Blessed Sacrament, 'Hug the silence as a refuge from the noise and chaos of the world. Store up treasures of silence.' cta.) Remember, as you pray and prepare, you become more united to your God and to me. My children, go in peace now, loving and serving your Lord. I am with you. Be aware of my presence, please."

10/27, "Dearest one, I am your Jesus Who speaks with great joy and continued gratitude. Dearest faithful ones, I am your Eucharistic Lord Who calls out once again, pleading for your presence before Me in My Sacrament of the Altar. If you are wondering why there is still unrest, a lack of the gift of My peace, confusion and lack of clarity in your direction and understanding, please just increase the time you spend with Me DAILY in My Tabernacle in silent adoration. You CAN do this in order to store up treasures of strength and patience and perseverance. These are qualities you MUST possess if you are to care for the great numbers of frightened, weary and broken people you will soon be welcoming into your homes and hearts. So many of you began Adoration before Me, and now have allowed busyness and empty chores to crowd into the time you once gave to Me. Come back, My beloved ones. Slow down, My warriors of the Holy Army of God and Mary, the Immaculate One. Allow that understanding you possessed so recently, and now have cast aside, to flood your entire being once again, that you might be emptied of chaos and exhausting, worthless activity; and filled with the peace that will heal you, comfort you, renew your energy to continue the battle against the evil in the world and in the hearts of so many of Our people. They will come to your doorstep seeking shelter and protection from the **elements and many events of destruction sent by My Father in an attempt to awaken the world from its slumber, its complacency and disinterest in anything sacred.**

As the earth rocks and splits, so will the hardened hearts and defenses of My people who have been too busy to listen to the Call of My Mother and theirs. INVITE YOUR FRIENDS WHO PRAY TO JOIN YOU FOR PRAYER: A ROSARY AND CHAPLET AT LEAST, before you share family news and inquire into needs for the wellbeing of each one. This need not be a long time of gathering or large crowds, but an opportunity to build community around prayer and concern for the world, mercy for your country and mitigation of the Father's justice against sins of abortion, of the flesh, of greed and dishonesty among government leaders.

Try to imagine a person without faith, without a relationship with God or even just goodness and honesty. Be moved to greater compassion for the victims of abortion, for such is everyone (a victim) connected to this tragic killing of helpless infants. Their own hearts are already dead and filled with hatred toward any responsibility required from those who carelessly regard life as products of conception and give no thought to the great gift of a life or **a soul: that spark of the Divine infused into each new person from the moment of conception.** How blind. How heartless. How selfish are the actions of all who throw away human life as so much inanimate material, instead of the life producing heart that develops so quickly in each microscopic human infused with this God-given soul that develops according to the Father's miraculous plan for creation. Yes, this practice will continue as long as Satan is allowed victory for his plans to destroy the Father's creation: both young and helpless and old and helpless; but your prayers can and will obtain reparation for these sins and the punishment due to them.

To allow salvation and repentance to be received by so many who act in oblivion, and commit the murder of others coming into the world or spending their last days depending upon the charity of those who should be protecting them, takes hard work, a solid commitment to the time needed for the amount of prayer needed for these ones who would answer only the call of their own desires and callous attitudes. You HAVE BEEN GIVEN THE STRENGTH to do this, My beloved and mighty warriors. Turn off your noisy and sin-filled television sets that have once again occupied the center of your lives with stories of anything-goes-lifestyles in order to lower your resistance to shameful behavior. You KNOW I speak the truth. You know the call for increased prayer is based upon the increase of sin in the world and a perceived license for any behavior that is not found out, that is carried out in darkness and secret. No, My dear ones, not much time remains before enormous destruction descends upon the inhabitants of the earth. My Father has given you more than enough time to change, to travel deeply into His Perfect and Divine Will for His people. Will you not listen and respond with compassion for a world that revels in a death culture that listens to the call of Satan for souls for all eternity? Believe and remember, beloved people, 'You Can Make a Difference!'

I am Jesus Who pours out new gifts from My Father for the success of your personal and collective response to this call. I bless you all in the world who listen and act to change, once again, into the selfless instruments of Mercy you were created to be for these times of perilous events that will eventually remove evil entirely from the world and self-centered hearts of too many of Our people. I love you, little precious ones. I desire your own journey into the Father's Will to be blessed with the success you beg for. Daily prayer is NOT too much to ask. Open your hearts. Let the world in. Embrace your brothers and sisters everywhere!"

10/31, "My very dearest children, I am your Lord and your God, your Jesus of Mercy. I come with the joy of Heaven and greetings to all of you from everyone there. The Saints send their thanksgiving for the special prayers you are praying today and the plans you have tomorrow to honor them. How they pray for you! My dear ones, when you are feeling blue or tired or discouraged, remember the greatest Saints that the world has ever seen, the greatest examples of loving their God and the Holy Mother are praying for you constantly. Be renewed by this word, by these prayers, by the love they pour out with every word of prayer for you. How you need them! How fortunate you are. Let us spend a moment now in praise of My Father, in quiet, in thanksgiving for all He has given to you, in thanksgiving for all He has given to you, for how much concern He has for the souls of every person in the world. Of course He does, children!

You are all His own creatures and creation, fashioned and made in His Image, in My Image and that of the Holy Spirit. Are you living that image, My children? It is a question to ask yourselves and to ponder, allowing the Holy Spirit to flood your minds and your understanding with the answers. Come now, we shall kneel together at the throne of My Father. Believe these words, My dear ones everywhere in the world, when you hear them, that <u>at that moment</u> We will kneel and pray before the Father, thanking Him and begging mercy on each of your countries; for destruction, My children, is not far away. Your Father and Creator is touched by the dearness and sincerity of your prayers and the love in your hearts. Believe these words. Believe that we are all one in the Father, truly, truly one: more united than you have ever been in your lives. You are being brought to new levels of holiness that will enable your great levels of service to Our people. They WILL come to you, My dear ones; and you will see miracles and you will see conversions in the hardened hearts of so many; and you yourselves will be brought to tears of thanksgiving and joy.

Tomorrow in this country, pray, pray for mercy, pray for guidance for your government, for your leaders, for the direction your country will now take. You know it is serious. You know the power of your prayers. Be all you were created to be in My Father's plan. Support those on the streets, those who suffer needlessly, and pray for the sufferings that are ahead of you. Pray especially for those who have no one. YOU are their family. YOU are the ones who will enable their salvation. YOU are the ones they will pray for in gratitude. As you see destruction, you will be tempted to doubt the goodness of the Father. Remember that you are living in His Kingdom on earth, sustained in His love. Remember that all will be well at the right moment, in the right way, at the right time. My Mother and I bless you this day. Be healed in all of the important, deep down ways you need!"

11/3, the Father said: "I salute you, My people who have responded to the call to choose life! (Voting Pres. Bush into office again.) Know, however, that Satan is poised to attack on many fronts and will not cease his restless prowling for souls to ensnare in his culture of death and destruction. Many lives have been saved this day by your choice for life. Yet lives will continue to be vulnerable to the secret plans now in place for world domination. **I charge you with acts of patience and listening to the needs of My people!** It is not just the faithful who are in need of My Son's Presence in their hearts, but especially those whose hearts are closed to the words of Heaven and the call to sanctity; those who refuse My gifts of grace and mercy; those who have vowed to fight decency and fidelity to My commandments. The battle escalates today. Still the earth will rock and split and rebel against the beauty of My Will."

11/6, Adoration in Shreveport, LA for people who attended talk at St. Joseph Church, "My dearest little one, welcome to this place of My Abode. Welcome into the heart of the South where love for Me beats in the hearts of many who will one day be a refuge to so many lost and confused and hurting, frightened people who will be in the greatest need. This area will see many refugees from great inroads of water devastation. A sense of panic and hasty flight will accompany all those who arrive after difficult flight from flooding waters and destructive storms. (These words have already been fulfilled once from the destruction of the Hurricane that devastated New Orleans. Cta.) I speak to all who listen this night. Welcome, My beloved ones of My Sacred Heart. I come with the gratitude of all in Heaven, My Holy Mother, the Immaculate One, and the Triune God. Blessed are you, My people, for responding to this call to gather in faith and trust, opening your hearts to Our words of warning and promises of protection. As is the case with Our remnant people, you are a small, but mighty group, who will be allowed by My Father to impact the lives and salvation of many of Our people who come to you, led by Our Spirit, seeking refuge and shelter, food and clothing, healing and hope. (This will happen again in many places in this country and the world. C.) This will be a time of chaos and confusion at first, but quickly grace and the power of Your God, the gentle hand of My Mother, and the help and prayers of countless Angels will bring peace and order to your focus. Do not be alarmed by the overwhelming numbers. My Father gifts you by what He asks of you, by all you will need to be in the lives of these very needy ones. It is the greatest gift you could receive on this earth, and will be a time of nearly total immersion in the Father's Will for all of you who serve them. This will be the greatest mission of your lives and, though you will know struggle and fatigue and hard work, you will know the greatest joy possible in this life. Be attentive now, My beloved ones, and listen well to all the words about to be shared in order to prepare you and guide you on the next step of your powerful and grace-filled journey into the Perfect Will of the Father and Creator. I am your Jesus of Mercy Who has called you here to heal you and strengthen you. You are the light of MY Heart, and I love you."

11/11, At Adoration, "There is nothing in the least amusing about the Antichrist and his plans for the world. Remember he IS the ENEMY OF FREEDOM AND THE SUCCESS OF THE JOURNEY OF ALL MY CHILDREN INTO MY KINGDOM. It is time for all to become more serious about the critical stage of developments in the world. There is not one of My people who can imagine or appreciate the danger ahead for the world and the depth of evil planned by Satan to interrupt these lives of My faithful in this most important journey into My Will for your ETERNAL LIFE!

I am your God and Father, little warriors of hope. I bring words of further encouragement to persevere in your commitment to prayer, no matter what occurs in the future. Lives are always vulnerable to the plans of the evil one. Lives and hearts will be challenged by terrible deeds of evil men, but NO ONE CAN SEPARATE YOU FROM THE LOVE OF YOUR GOD AND YOUR LOVE FOR US. Times are becoming more filled with the acts and deception of devious leaders. Nothing is as it seems and CAN ONLY BE SURVIVED IN TOTAL TRUST AND SURRENDER TO MY WORDS OF LOVE AND CARE FOR YOU. Whatever you see occurring in the lives around you, be not discouraged or defeated in your promises to Me to remain faithful to My Commandments and My call to you. You are MOST VICTORIOUS when you enter the Kingdom of Heaven! You are most completely healed by life in the perfection of My Will in Paradise. There is NOTHING TO FEAR. Surrender your fear to Me again this day, My beloved ones."

11/14, "My dear ones: I, your Holy Mother, have been with you; am here now speaking; come with joy; come in gratitude, the gratitude of all in Heaven. I speak this day to my children everywhere in the world. I speak with sorrow, knowing the future of the world. I ask you to pray with renewed hope, to concentrate on BEING hope, on being positive in your outlook whatever occurs in your lives and around you. I pour out the gift of compassion this day upon the world, as the world grows cold, as Satan is given victory. I come as Queen of your hearts as well as Mother; and as Queen, because I call you forth to enter into the majesty of being so united to the Triune God, to realize that not only is the world your family, but **so is the Triune God and so am I**! How this will expand your hearts and minds and your ability to encompass the entire world with your heart. This is so important to your role in obtaining salvation for the whole world as co-mediators for the world!"

11/21, "My very dear children, I am your God and Father. I repeat what I have said in the past: that never before has so much been asked of a group of people and so many gifts and graces, talents, abilities and promises been given, ever in history. My children, the world grows colder. The world grows darker and although you are promised a reprieve in this country because you have chosen it, because you pray for mitigation, because you choose life, because you choose holiness, do not think that many of My plans will not go forward; for they will, they are, they must!

Although My timetable is different from yours, I have one! It has always been as it is now; and it must go forward because the evil one and his plans go forward; and never will I be overcome by those plans. Families will heal, as I have said in the past, and become mighty, fighting units against the evil one, against greater power than you have ever seen or could imagine, that will be displayed in the world in your future; but for now give thanks, for now be grateful that you have been chosen to walk this incredible journey, going places and someday meeting people that you would never otherwise meet: your family, the great family of the human race. Ponder these things, My dear ones. Ponder the amazing grace that is given. Ponder the opportunities to save souls. You ARE My hope. You ARE My instruments of peace and healing, mercy and salvation. Give thanks, My children, as I give thanks for you!"

12/8, Personal message, Adoration. "Dearest one, take My words now for the world and for your own heart. To the world on this special Feast Day (Immaculate Conception) I say: 'Rejoice, for the Virgin Mother, the Immaculate One is your own Mother forever. She is your mighty companion and intercessor and mediatrix before Me. Rejoice, My people, for she is the one who stands by you for better, for worse, in sickness and in health until death unites you to Me in union with the Trinity and to her own Immaculate Heart. Rejoice, My beloved, faithful ones; for the Virgin Mother begs mercy for you and for the world. I am your Father and Creator. You are My precious, chosen, remnant people whom I favor with My requests to you. You are the gift I have given to My Jesus, HIS inheritance! I love you, My faithful ones. I call you My own."

12/12, "My very, very dear children, I am your Lord and your God, your Father and Creator. Prepare for the feast of the Birth of My Son. Your prayer must be that He would be born in the hearts of many, many more; that many more would open to accept Him, embrace Him, to accept Him for the rest of their lives and eternity: never to turn away, to walk always with Him. My dear ones, it is you I count upon: all who listen, all who pray, all who come before My Son in His Blessed Sacrament (daily, if possible); but more now than before, always more! Is that not true, My dear ones? Always more giving to those you love; so of course, always more giving of yourselves and your prayers to My Jesus and to the world. Think of the world in dreadful agony because that is what it is. Sinners are suffering. They may see it as pleasure. They may see their lives as a wonderful way to live. They may see light as darkness and darkness as light. Take pity upon the world and with Me, have mercy.

Pour out your mercy as you pour out yourselves with more hours spent reflecting, begging, praying for souls, begging for mercy, begging for acceptance in the hearts I have just mentioned. That is NEARLY THE ENTIRE WORLD, My people. Pray for each other at this special time, that you will allow Jesus to birth Himself more completely within YOU. It is the focus of My words once again: **the needs of others, the terrible condition of the world and its suffering people.** There are many kinds of sufferings, My dear ones. Pray for all of them. You ARE your brother's keeper. Be your Father's instrument of healing. Thank you for being Mine. Someday you will understand how blessed you are, and how dear and precious and holy you are becoming. Yes, you struggle, but struggle produces strength and strength produces fine soldiers. Be with Me in the Trinity. (talking about our union here, to the degree we are able as remnant people..C.) Be with your Triune God and prepare! Amen, Amen, My sweet and humble people. You are loved so mightily. "

12/26, in Iowa for Christmas.

"Dearest one, please take My words for the world and your own heart-peace. I am your Jesus, New-Born King, lying in a manger and surrounded by the glory of Heavenly Hosts ...... and bits of straw! In My condition of newly arrived upon the earth, I stare in wonder and joy upon the beauty of dear Mary and precious Joseph, several large beasts of burden (recognized by My state of perfection,) but also surrounded by many, many Angels, who have accompanied My journey, singing Hosannas. My world is a small environment filled with light and new feelings of cold and discomfort, a gnawing in My center that is quickly assuaged, as My dear and beautiful Mother lifts Me to her breast and begins to feed and fill Me with a warm, soothing liquid." (An interruption that lasted until we returned home and I am at Adoration...

12/28 "The light, little one, is so bright, yet soft and soothing. Dear Joseph is ever attentive to Me and My Mother, his sweet spouse. They had journeyed from place to place seeking refuge to the point of exhaustion; yet are completely renewed by all the miraculous transformation of this more than humble cave. The manger is as a throne for Me, and its humble origin is a sign of My own life on the earth. Humble is the word that describes Who I will be every moment of My life, as I journey toward a terrible and humiliating death. Spend these days after My Birth-celebration reflecting on the hardships that immediately accompanied this little, holy family. Reflect on the way **My Presence in the center of your life will always transform events and environment, no matter how harsh or disruptive the conditions.** Joseph and dearest Mary and I were always able to gaze lovingly at each other and thus, we overcame hardships, cold and hunger, always fed and comforted by our love for each other**. Keep Me in your midst**, My dearest, faithful ones. Carry Me, newborn and helpless, in the manger of your heart. Be comforted and strengthened, as we gaze at each other each moment. Distractions and chores are a part of your daily routines; but, please I beg of you, practice more now focusing on Me, your tiny, Baby King, radiating light and peace and all the sweetness you have ever known filling your hearts, comforting your spirits, purifying your beings. Watch Me grow each day, and grow with Me into the holy one of God, with Mary and Joseph, as you were created to be. My dear, dear people, you see in recent events how many have entered eternity. How many remain behind to struggle and die in terrible conditions. I invite you to live with My holy family, not apart from this overwhelming suffering and sorrow; but united to them in a compassion that allows you to lift up each of them to My Father, begging His mercy. We go forward from the stable together on a new and perilous journey."

FOR MERCY'S SAKE!

For Mercy Sake VII 2005
Messages

"HOWL, for the day of the Lord is near; as destruction from the Almighty it comes. Therefore all hands fall helpless, the bows of the young men fall from their hands. Every man's heart melts in terror; pangs and sorrows take hold of them,

Like a woman in labor they writhe; they look aghast at each other, their faces aflame. Lo, the day of the Lord comes cruel, with wrath and burning anger; To lay waste the land and destroy the sinners within it!" (Isaiah13: 6-9)

1-2, "My very dear children, I am your Mother Mary, the Immaculate One. You are loved and gifted by the Father, as He wishes to change you; for it is His love which allows you to change, to become more powerful, to become more a part of the Father's Plan: more necessary, more gifted, more humble; and it is through His gifts that hopefully you are humbled, that you realize you are not worthy of the great gifts being poured out upon you. That goes for everyone in the world, only because you carry the effects of Original Sin which lead to weaknesses; which lead to distractions; which lead to a continuous division in your hearts, always between the world and the Kingdom of God in Heaven, the Will of the Father, His Will for you, children. Never before have so many followed the Will of the Father more faithfully or in greater numbers with any greater gift and blessing. Else you would not be able to sustain this level of prayer.

You notice each time you hear, the call for prayer is greater and the call to more prayer, there is that little hesitation within your heart, that little question: 'Can I do this? How could He possibly mean me, when I pray so much? How could He possible mean more when there is no more time already in my life,' and yet, because of grace and gift, you DO TRY. You DO CHANGE. You DO BECOME MORE. These dynamics within your heart and soul and spirit are mentioned often, that you might appreciate, that you might give thanks and praise for a heretofore unseen level of gifts. For all of you in the world who listen and it is also understanding, and understood first by Heaven, that the nature of conversion is off and on, forward and backward; always some backward movement, always some sliding, always a cooling of ardor, a lessening of the ability to sustain the level of prayer to which you are called.

I mention these things today again, for we start a New Year together in which even more devastation will be seen, in which more innocent will be taken into eternity. **Most often it is not their own sins for which they suffer. It is not the reason they are taken into eternity; but it is the sins of the evil ones, those who follow the evil one, who live in that country or in that area.** You are seeing so many victim souls, my children. Pray to them as well as for them, for they have been blessed that they are in eternity and have an even greater opportunity to choose for the Father, to understand the mysteries of God, to be showered with graces .... again, beyond anyone's understanding. Praise the Father for His mercy on their behalf. It is humility to which you are called, my children. **There is no gift to any one person that is greater than a gift to another.** Remember this and do not feel a comparison forming within your heart. Do not allow that to develop, for that is not of God.

Fight for humility. Fight to become greater warriors. Fight against the evil one and the inclinations all find within themselves to sin, to sliding back, to turning away to the call of the world: all of the things you guard more closely against now. Understand that attacks of the evil one will increase in everyone's life, for Satan becomes more furious, as you become more the warrior you were created to be. It is 'serious times'. Our call to you is serious, as you can see in the recent devastation. Pray for them as you would a dearest loved one, for they are your family. They are your loved ones and they too are a means of your obtaining salvation. I desire your success as the children of God and my own dear children. Be filled with peace and joy: joy that you still respond, that you pray more, that you are gifted so mightily. Oh my dear ones, I love you. I rejoice for you. The battle increases."

1-9, "My very dear ones, I am your God and your Father, your Creator and Lord. My dear children, you are the light of the world. You are immersed this day in the waters of hope, the waters of Baptism with Jesus, My Son. Today is your feast, as well. Each day is a feast for you, as you are faithful and go more deeply into the waters of grace. Submerge yourselves with My Son, in union with Him, into My Will. The **waters of Baptism flow throughout your entire lives**, and I speak to My people everywhere in the world who are faithful; who struggle to do My Will, to hear the words of Heaven and to live them. You are cheered this day by all of Heaven, as **you swim through daily events, casting aside those which would help or hinder you. My children swim in the waters of My Will. You swim immersed in the Blood of My Jesus, for this is an immersion into the healing power of His Blood, and the healing power of My grace given through the hands and the requests of the Most Immaculate Mary.**

My dear ones, the remnant people of God are the hope of the world! That is YOU, MY DEAR ONES EVERYWHERE. PRAY IN A NEW WAY FOR EACH OTHER NOW, for Satan sets many traps, many diversions, many subtle and hidden worldly agendas. Be on guard! So many years ago I asked you to be on guard. I ask you that again now. The waters become murky, as Satan's plans go forward. Always he seeks to deceive you. Always he and his cohorts are busy, busy: attempting to distract you with busyness. Remember, My children**, nothing is important now except saving souls, begging for My mercy for the world**. Remember that you are a sign to others of the Presence of My Jesus, of His light. People notice your love. People notice that you are more recollected, that you have changed. Most people do not know why, they just know there's something about you. It is because you are about Heaven, and all of the heavenly gifts I have showered upon you. I rejoice with you this day, for you are persevering. Be on guard with incidents around you, as well as new destructive events in the world. To be on guard is to be prudent, to hear yourselves, to stop and think before you speak or act, to welcome being a source of hope and, yes, even of grace for all those you meet, without being obvious, without putting on airs or a false piety. It is most important that you would be real, authentic and sincere; and so I give you these words today to ponder, that you might prepare more than ever for events of a destructive nature that will bring many, many onto your horizon, to your doorstep and into your homes and hearts. Always, always you are preparing for them and for those times (still) before you welcome My Jesus in His return to the earth to fight that immense battle against the evil one. You will know many small battles, many events for which you prepare and wait eagerly. My dear ones, I am most grateful for you and I need you. Think of how much you need; and multiply that by all the people in the world. This might give you a glimmer of how much I am counting upon you and your fidelity. BE mercy, children. BE hope. BE joy! I AM your Father. I AM your Creator. I AM your Lord. Amen, My children, Amen."

1-16, "My dear children, I am the Holy Spirit of God. My dear ones, today, as every day, you are asked to pray for the world. There are serious events on the horizon once again; but there are serious events occurring every day in many places in the world. You will see war escalate and will realize the contrived reasons. You will see the collusion involved in Satan's ongoing plans for the destruction of the world. This, My children, IS serious! These events, as you know, will take many people, more each time there is an event. YOU, My children, are their hope! You are the vehicle of their salvation. You are their champion. Remember that! Pray to dear Reyes (Ruiz, Estella's husband, who died last year.... cta.) who was everyone's champion! (Whenever anyone of us said, 'Hi Reyes, how are you? He would always answer with great gusto? 'Like a Champion'!! cta.) He waits to pray with you and help to obtain your petitions and requests. All of Heaven awaits your invitation to pray with you, as they pray for you and for the world.

Oh My dear people, please realize how totally blessed and gifted you are to be allowed to be such an important minister and vehicle for the poor lost souls who are bereft of even a small knowledge of their Creator; and so many who have no one, no one but you. YOU ARE THEIR FAMILY. You have accepted them. Accept them more deeply into your hearts and your lives, your prayer life..... NOW, My people. If you could see face to face the destruction, the many who die and those so terribly saddened, heartbroken, beside themselves with grief; you would understand MORE the serious tones of these requests.

The world teeters on the edge of total destruction. It is only your prayers and the mercy of God that keeps it intact. Believe this! The human family is being decimated by very definite plans of the One World Order, the followers of Satan. Remember this total plan, and then remember the great power of God, Our Father: your Father. Remember how much He needs you. Remember what an important part you are in His plan. Believe this. Let it bring you peace and a tender joy and a tender gratitude that you are allowed to help so many. **One day destruction will visit your area.** Then how happy you will be that you have prayed and remained faithful. Do NOT fear. PRAY. Remember how much you are loved, that every person alive is loved, and that you all belong to each other. Great blessings I pour out this day upon all of you gathered here, and listen throughout the world. Amen. To arms, My children!"

1-23, "My beloved ones, I am your Jesus, children. I thank you once again for gathering today, this special day when the terrible legalization of abortion is mentioned most especially in prayer; not to be celebrated, but to beg mercy upon all of those involved with this heinous act, for the healing of those women who have aborted their babies everywhere in the world ..... and you know the Father has mercy on each one who repents! Only the Father knows the fear in the hearts of women, in the hearts of all of His children; therefore, He is ready to pour out mercy and forgiveness the moment it is requested. Most especially this day, pray for mercy on the acts of abortion, on those who give out information and speak as though they counsel wisely young pregnant women, and then lead them to the terrible act of murder. It is these sins for which you also are asked to make atonement by your prayers, by your sacrifices and penances.

A victim soul offers him/herself wherever it is needed, to whatever degree is required. These words can be frightening, and cause you to hesitate and yet, I tell you, you DO have the grace and the strength to offer yourself in complete surrender as this victim soul for the world: the special and precious and most blessed soul the world needs so terribly. The world, My children, is reflecting the chaos in the hearts of evil men; is reflecting the chaos of the lives that people lead as they turn away from God and His Commandments; reflects the chaos about to erupt in many parts of the world again. It is not that you wait eagerly for chaos and destruction. It is that you are alerted in your prayers, in your spirit, in your mind and thoughts and will to pray for the people of the world, especially the sinful people; not that you are not sinful, but those who have plans to destroy My Church, My faithful people. Yes, My dear ones, there are people who have plans to destroy you; but you continue bravely, courageously, looking forward always in trust to the promises of protection you are given by your God.

To begin to get a glimmer of the power of God, look at the universe. Look at the power of nature. Look at a tiny baby, and celebrate God's might and power and the great gift of creation. Be a fountain of thanksgiving, a fountain of joy that will praise the Father and give Him honor; and bring great blessings upon yourselves and all of those for whom you pray, all of those you love, especially your dear, dear children and families. Be positive in your outlook, in your praying. Prayer is not a negative thing. You are always asking for mitigation, for healing, for new hope, new gifts: positive life-giving gifts. My children, I love you. Thank you, thank you for loving Me. Be filled this day with My peace, My children everywhere. My peace is the warrior's shield, the protection you need for your body and mind, your spirit, your soul, your will, your choices; and over all of this I pour courage; and like Our Holy Spirit, I say to you: 'To arms.' (See msg. of 1-

16-05 from Holy Spirit.) Remember that we are marching together arm in arm: your Triune God, your Holy Mother, all the Angels and Saints and everyone in Heaven. How blessed you are, My dear ones, and how precious. Amen, Amen."

1/30, "My very dearest children, I am your God and Father. It is important to Me as well, that you are built up in all the areas of your life, your spiritual life most especially, for you know I need you to be most perfectly My instruments! I am your God, My children. I am your Creator, and I speak to you everywhere in the world who listen. I am calling you into greater perfection this day. If it seems to you that you are less than, that you are weaker, that you are discovering more vulnerability and sinfulness ... rejoice, My children, because by this you will know and become more humble; by this you are made aware of the areas to work on, to beg My grace and mercy upon; to see yourselves as you are ... totally dependent upon Me, to be grateful. My children, there are more earthquakes in the world now than ever before in history, since the dawn of creation. There is great destruction that no one hears about; but believe the words you have heard this day.

Know that evil powers are preparing the earth day by day to be more vulnerable, to cause greater damage, yes, in areas already hit. With the vulnerability of the earth in those areas that are prepared, you must join your prayers to these people. You must beg for mercy upon them because you have said, 'yes' to Me. You have remained faithful because they count upon you without even realizing it; because **salvation is the price of your fidelity**; because you nurture them in union with the Triune God and the Holy Mother; because you prepare them to say, 'yes', to enter more completely into the family of God, to impact their entire existence for eternity. There is no greater gift than the love of My Son. The love of My Son pours out upon you now. Do not look for things that would excite you insofar as they are news, they are a cause of things to talk about. They can be a distraction, if they are not a source of your prayer, the ground from which you blossom and cause the fertilizing of the ground of the people everywhere in the world. Nurture them as you would sick family members. Pour your concerns over them as a balm to heal their wounds in union with My Son. You are being given greater power in your prayer this day, My people everywhere. Believe this. Act upon this. Become, My children, more powerful instruments this very day, this very moment. Be healed yourselves, My children everywhere, more deeply, more profoundly, and become all I have created you to be. You as yet have no idea, yet you pray, 'Jesus, I trust in you.' Act upon that trust. Act upon those words, My children. The world has such need of you. The world cries out to you. Hear them and respond to their call! Amen, My dear, dear ones, My sweet children, My instruments of hope for the world. I love you. You are loved SO MIGHTILY and blessed this day. Amen."

2-09, At Adoration: "Dearest child of My Will, please take these words and good wishes and gifts of strength and vigor for the coming days. There is only joy to share with Our people because of the graces and mercy poured out now. Love blossoms where hearts reach out to the world. Love conquers when hearts open to forgiveness and new healing. Love is victorious when offered in union with Love for the salvation of the world. Please tell My people that their God and Father waits no longer for the response of cold and disinterested hearts; but gathers His faithful ones into His arms in order to cast down from the heights of arrogance the proud and disdainful through many events of destruction: many kingdoms destroyed, many a castle crumbled by the shaking of the earth. Pray for the ones who turn a deaf ear to My call to them. They are to be pitied for their foolishness. It is a wicked generation that runs headlong into the pit... racing each other for first place! All of Heaven is grieving the destruction of the earth ... when it could have been otherwise. But now, My faithful one, we focus on new life after death; the resurrection that follows crucifixion; the Light that rises out of darkness; the hope that arrives with the dawn. 'My dearest faithful people, I salute you and your perseverance in prayer. Come to the aid of your country, Americans. A mighty enemy is loose within, ready to catch you unaware and sleeping. The battle breaks on your shores, once again. Prepare your defenses with fasting and much penance. I, your God, am with My holy ones: To arms!'"

2-20, "My very dearest ones, I am Mary, your Immaculate Mother, who loves you beyond, beyond, beyond your understanding, beyond your hopes and desires. I pray for you, my children, every moment. Do not give up. Do not despair. Do not become too tired. It is up to you, my dear ones, to balance your days, to get enough rest; and you know the call of the Father is first. You are not meant to exhaust yourselves, my children, at this point; and the gifts of the special powers and strength the Father will give you have not yet been released but are saved for the time when you will need them so desperately for all those who come to you. They must be uppermost in your prayers and petitions, my children. The Father has described to you in a beautiful and clear way the state of being they will inhabit when they reach your doorstep; and you will hear this again and again and pray about it. Pray for strength for all of those who pray, for we go into a time of greater strength given to Satan and his demons; and you know that will escalate as events unfold. Most certainly you hear about and see greater evil in the world today. It is so easy to get caught up in the world, in what you think is important in your projects. My children, be brave. Say NO when it is necessary. SPEAK OUT and defend the plan of the Father. Defend my words., my love for you, my presence in the world now and for so many, many years. My children, we are so closely united in these efforts. I praise the Father and I thank him every moment for the gift of YOU, and I know you do the same. We would be bereft of any comfort without each other. How all of Heaven and all the lost ones count on you.

My dear ones, I am always with you. Do not feel the loneliness, **the emptiness with which Satan visits you**. He knows you are vulnerable in these areas; and the need for trust is so very, very great, and only increases. You hear of events to come and you do pray more, but this makes you more weary, more tense perhaps, more impatient certainly; and yet together we believe the Father knows what he is doing for the good of the entire world. Trust this, my children. Trust the fact that you are loved and carried through every struggle in your life. Remember the love of your God and your Mother. Remember the prayers and love of all of Heaven. Call on the Angels and Saints. Ask them to give you new strength, to take away fatigue and distractions. Oh my children, I am your companion in waiting. **Waiting is part of being a handmaid, a hand-servant of the Lord, You are doing it, my children!**"

2-27, "My very dear ones, I am your Jesus of Mercy. My dear children, I thank you for your prayers again this day. They have brought great protection for your country. Know that whenever you see destruction in this country, it would have been much, much worse except for your prayers. This is the same for everyone in your country who listens and who attempts to live the requests of Heaven for this critical time in history. My children, have patience with each other! Each of you has, to one degree or another, a demanding spirit. Each of you has expectations of others: how you should be treated; how you should be listened to; how you should be understood. In other words, My dear ones, you have an understanding of yourself that makes you think you have a right to preferential treatment, and I do speak to everyone who listens because it is human to have this condition, a of Original Sin. But children, be aware if this. Listen to yourselves. Feel your feelings in response to the treatment or the behavior, (of others) even if it is unjust and impatient. Pay attention to your response, your reaction to the behavior of others. **It is not others you can change, My children! It is only yourself**, and so I speak to you individually in that way.

Do not be saddened that I would speak in this way, for I attempt only to help you to see yourselves as I see you; to hear yourselves and thus to modify your behavior. **It is sweetness that changes hearts**. It is a slow and understanding and patient nature that draws people to itself, and thus I would caution you to listen to the demanding pattern of your speech. My children, I desire your perfection. I desire your sweetness, your holiness, your success as instruments of My Father's Will; and I speak to everyone in the world these words because human nature does not change, is not different from one region to another. It is so important, as you know, that you are the instruments you were created to be. Words have been given as to the state of mind and emotion that people who come to you will inhabit. There are no words to add to those, so I ask you to reread, to remember, to reflect upon the condition of the poor ones who struggle to make it to your doorstep. They will be, My children! You have waited so long that now you forget; now you are less alert, less inclined to practice, to reflect, to prepare. The thing **about preparedness is that there is never a call for less; but always more** because We begin by asking in small ways for small numbers of prayers and then they increase and then they increase, and the need increases. The need will never be greater, My children, than when you are face to face with hundreds and hundreds of people. Imagine even that, My dear ones!

I ask you: Be serious, My children. It is hard work to prepare for battle and yet, this is what you are called to do .... BATTLE READY IS THE CALL!. My children, I pour out new strength upon you this day, new patience, a new inclination, a deeper desire to be all you can be. Without the gifts of My Father, no one would progress on this journey. I call you to greatness, My people, not in a proud or self-interested way; but greatness in serving the Father and each other. Oh My children, I want so much for you to be with Me in these times, most especially. I love you, My dear, dear ones. I thank you for the love in your hearts. Be holy, My little ones. Be serious. Be joyful. Be one with Me!

cont'd 2-27, "Listen to the words of the Scripture readings these special, special days: all of My words taken to heart again. Ask Our Spirit for the ability to receive them in new ways, more deeply into your hearts, into the very ground of your spirit. Oh My darling ones, My precious and beloved people, how I love you. Be aware of My Presence. Be aware of My love. Be changed, My children, by My love! Amen, little ones. We go forward together!"

3-12, At Home, "Dear child, please write My words for the world. Be at peace, daughter. All is well. Please pray to Our Spirit now, and then receive these important words. 'My dearest people, I am your God and Father. I speak this night of the need for ultimate preparedness. MORE WATER MUST BE STORED BY YOU WHO HAVE TOTAL TRUST IN ALL THE WORDS OF HEAVEN THESE MANY YEARS. Remember, dear ones, all the dried food you have stored, and how much extra water will be required for its preparation. The days speed quickly by when you are living in My Perfect Will and desires for you. The time of deliverance from sin and evil is upon the world. And I need you to be ready in heart and soul, mind and spirit and will to be a haven of healing and of peace; an experience of mercy and patience to the poor frightened and sorrowing ones who come to you shortly. I repeat: you cannot imagine how difficult and different will be these experiences. You all know what it is like when you are terribly stressed, or as the aging process slows your memory. You forget words. You repeat the same stories or needs often. Imagine how this might occur in the lives of these dear ones who are in a critical state of fear and sorrow, and ask Me again for the gift of patience! Oh My dear people, on whom I depend so much to give these lost ones a listening heart, patient attention, sincere hospitality: voicing your gratitude for the opportunity to shelter them, share your food, hear their woes. Please remember to include them in your prayers each day. They are so important to your own salvation!

Again I say: Expect miracles, My beloved people. My plans will continue to unfold slowly in the life of the Remnant Faithful. Some events will follow quickly upon each other, but will be followed by periods of waiting for the next level to arrive and be experienced in your lives. Again, ponder all that must occur to fulfill Scripture to the time when Jesus returns, that you might bear the enormous changes ahead of you, coupled with long periods of routine and sameness, as I purify you to an even greater degree. Remember My Perfect Will and great love for you; that I desire only what is best for you and that, My beloved ones, is unity with your Triune God through My Will!! Come to the water, My dearest ones, and be cleansed and healed and renewed by grace and gift and Love. You are loved beyond your ability to grasp with your human understanding. You are so precious to Me. I am your Father God Whose love you return more perfectly every day."

"Dearest little one, please take the words of your Lord and your God, your Creator and Father, your Abba. Welcome to the heart of the Triduum, (the three days before Easter Sunday… C.) Bury yourself these next hours with My Jesus, the Lamb; and discover the mystery of ultimate sacrifice. Stay hidden from yourself, My dear messenger. Do whatever chores are required to prepare for your family; but in silence, and recollected with all the events of these days. Read and reflect, dear little one. Learn all you can at the foot of the Cross.

Plunge yourself into the Blood of My Jesus and immerse yourself in all HIS sufferings. You have been gifted by Me with the saintly Maria (Esperanza ... just returned from a beautiful trip to Betania on Monday of Holy Week .. cta.) with whom you have visited and who obtains new graces and gifts for the near future. There is no change in all I have told you... only an escalation of events. Worry not about messages to share. You have the advantage of years of material to share that is so very timely right now. Do you not know that I have prepared you in every way necessary for each event and eventuality? Pray as I have asked you to practice, little one. Be quiet and focused on this special time. You are still recovering from your long journey." (We were very blessed to be invited to visit Maria Esperanza's grave site and kneel on the grass right next to her grass-covered grave. I placed all of your names: everyone everywhere who prays and listens to the requests of Heaven, right on her gravestone, and it was amazingly peaceful, and Maria seemed very present.... cta.)

4/3, Mercy Sunday, "My very dear and beloved and faithful ones. I am your Jesus of Mercy, the Lover and Bridegroom of your souls. I am the One you seek, when you seek truth and goodness, kindness: all the virtues, all that is good. I am the One Who loves you beyond words, and I bring My gratitude and the gratitude of all of Heaven this very day for your Novenas, your precious uplifted faces earnestly praying for all of My requests given to Faustina so many years ago. You see the dear, dear Holy Father, all that is presented to you through the media, and you pray for him and to him constantly now. He is in good hands, My children. (I guess so. He is in Heaven!!... cta.) I ask you this week to reflect upon all the wonderful and sometimes astounding things that you have heard these very days about the Holy Father: what a leader, what an example, what a Shepherd! How he will be missed and yet, his spirit lives on in all the good he has accomplished and in the many ways he has influenced your own lives, your prayer lives, your heart life! What more is there to ask than more prayer; except that it would be said in a more meaningful way, directly from your hearts, meaning every word, concentrating on the words, concentrating on those you pray for all over the world; and there are so many, and We have named so many of them. I will be brief this day, My children, for your prayer and devotion are continuing. (The group left our house after this message, and convened at Church for Divine Mercy Devotions... cta.) Let Me assure you, your prayers are answered, especially those prayers personal to you, those requests deep in your heart, for you do not ask for yourselves, as befits a warrior in My Mother's Army. Your focus is on others now, as it should be; and for this, all of Heaven thanks you and raises cheers of gratitude before the throne of the Father. Be at peace this day, My dear ones. It is a time now for rest, as you have all accompanied the Holy Father on this journey. Be at peace. Be at peace. Be at peace. Remember My merciful love that accompanies you always and everywhere."

4-10, "My very, very dear ones, I am Mary, your Immaculate Mother. I come today with great joy, with Faustina who is with me, our dear, dear Saint, with all of the Saints who are new to Heaven whom you have prayed for and prayed to over the years: all of your special Saints as well. All of your own loved ones, who are in Heaven, are gathered today, my dear children. Yes indeed, this is a special gift for all of you and for Our children everywhere in the world, a gift from the Father for your fidelity: many, many, many prayers said for dear, beloved John Paul, for the Mercy Novenas and the continuing prayers for the world; for all We have requested, the prayers you pray (now) TO Our beloved Pope son. He will indeed impact your lives in many ways, in ongoing ways from now on. Praise and thank the Father for this gift. Know that He has been given to each one of you this day, who listen and pray, as your own Saint, as your precious benevolent one.

Rededicate and consecrate yourselves to that perfect love and Will of Our God. You are found faithful in God's sight, in His Will, even though you may fall; and I caution you today not to continue in the easy path or in easy ways or in repeated sins. Be firm with yourselves, my children. You can do this because my Son, Jesus, has said it is so; because all of Us pray for you unceasingly. How very specially called is each one of you, and united to the Trinity in the great Communion of Saints. My dear ones, you WILL persevere in all of the promises Our God has made to you these many, many years. Praise and thank the Father for all the gifts you have received this day."

4-17, "My very dear children, I am your God and Father. Oh My dear ones, time is so short before major events sweep away portions of your own country; and I say this about every country in the world. You are more than warriors, My dear faithful ones. You are the HEROES of this Age; and history will record your faithful prayers and service, **for which I will be given praise and honor throughout all of the Ages to come.** Perhaps you feel a sense today of the seriousness in My voice: the spirit of dread that permeates even your God, that My hand is forced to fall again on the world by escalating sin and a lack of response to all that is good. A mighty call goes out from Heaven this day directly to your hearts, filled with hope as well as sorrow. Remember that Jesus is your answer to every problem, every struggle, every sorrow, every need and weakness that assails you. Remember My mercy; My great, great love for everyone in the world, all of you. My precious, My beloved ones who are faithful, occupy a great place in My plan as instruments of My Will, as hope for the future, as the presence and experience of Jesus to all who come to you. My dear ones, be brave now. Proceed in total trust, counting on your God, your holy Mother. Do not be afraid, My children. When you trust, you will not know fear. It is the might of My arm that sustains you, that allows the peace of My son, My Jesus, to fill you."

4/24, "My very dear children, once again it is your God and Father Who comes to bless you with My Presence, to raise you higher in My plans for you, in My plans for the world. Be encouraged by the grace that has been give you anew by Our Spirit. It is the Holy Spirit of God that enables you to pray more; that inspires you to good works, to thoughtfulness of others, to compassion, to all of the virtues that you have been given that you might use them, share them, pour them out on all those you meet, not just in the future but NOW, My children everywhere, every moment; for you can be praying, as you know, every moment by consecrating all of your works and actions, your kindnesses towards others. **It is kindness that most emulates My Son**. It is kindness that touches the hearts of others most and opens their hearts to you and to Me. Ask Our Spirit for these gifts, My dear ones everywhere in the world, for I know you desire to serve at the best of your ability to answer the tremendous needs that will confront you in the days to come.

Pray more for each other because you know each other and are close. You are each other's FIRST NEIGHBORS because you are family, your NEAREST RESPONSIBILITY AND GREATEST GIFT because you are family. NURTURE each other with kindness, with prayer. You see and will see all sorts of new things in the world: change, escalation of My plan, escalation of My allowing the plans of the evil ones to go forward and most certainly, you will see the results of those plans. Be open to My plans for you, My children, My Will and desires for you. Again, I thank you for remaining faithful, remaining faithful to this group, for it is greater might when greater numbers of prayers in union reach My Throne. I HEAR YOU, MY CHILDREN, AND I ANSWER YOU IN THE BEST POSSIBLE WAY for each person for whom you pray, for each person in the world. Remember that, My children, because you will see much destruction and devastation. Be at peace with My words. Be at peace with the unfolding of My Will. When you feel a sense of joy that you cannot account for, or that sweeps over you suddenly... that is MY joy, My children, and another gift to you! It is a gift of encouragement, of gratitude. It is another call to remain My faithful children. Be aware of the peace, for it is given when you stop, ask for it, open up to it! Rejoice in gratitude for it!

5-1, "My very dear ones, I am your Jesus. I speak this day about My Ascension that you might be better prepared to experience the lifting, the turning, the surrender of all of who you are to My Father in Heaven, that you may arrive more closely united to His Will, that you might spend time in prayer and recollection and reflection before His Throne. This is a gift I also offer to you this day, if you will but spend the time and the quiet and yes, more surrender, to all My Father calls you to become. On that day when I was lifted up into Heaven to return so happily, so gladly to My Father, it was a culmination of so much emptying; (yes, of course, so much suffering;) but a greater appreciation (in your own understanding and in your own words) of all the Father meant to Me. Although We were One, I had felt His absence dearly, although I was always united to Him and always standing at His right hand in the Kingdom of My Father. Reflect on all of these things, My children everywhere. Reflect on how you are sustained in the might of My Father's Arm, how you can be more united or less united to Him through your obedience; and especially reflect on His great mercy and constant forgiveness. Yes, My children, as faithful as you are, you are constantly in need of My Father's patience and new forgiveness.

Never for a moment think that you do not have more ascending in your spirit, in offering yourself! Never think for a moment that you are without all the graces that you need. Never think that you can rest from prayer. I remind you that Satan takes no vacations, that he is more powerful than ever, that his own plans unfold to interfere as much as possible and in every way with your own ascending, in union with Myself, more deeply into the Father's Will. As you reflect upon all of these things, My dear ones, rereading these words often, be filled with astonishment at the gifts and the level of holiness you have been given, even though you struggle with your humanity, your weaknesses. As you sit before Me in My Blessed Sacrament, imagine the moment when I was lifted before the eyes of My Apostles into the heavens, then disappearing from their eyes. Feel their desolation. Feel their joy. Feel their new dependence on Me: seeming to be leaving them: so many, many, many things that you, each one of you, experiences in your daily lives that only points to Our greater unity, your unity with them, My followers, My Apostles and disciples. Oh My children, we will go through so much together now, for without Me, you could not bear it. You walk in the Company of Heaven, My children. Come now and ascend with Me to new levels of service and rejoicing. Rest, My children: rest in My Heart. Ascend with Me. Feel My love. Bask in My sweetness."

5/8, "My very, very dear children, I am your God and your Father, your Creator: grateful for your new commitment, for the new conversion you accept from My hands.... often in ways you would never choose, often in ways nearly overwhelming, often in ways that nearly crush you, exhaust you, stop you in your tracks, as conversion is meant to do. It forces you to think, forces you to realize new truth and come to Me and My Son and Our Spirit in true sorrow. Nothing will change you, My children, like sorrow: a realization of all you have NOT become in My plan; a face to face look at your weaknesses, your pride and egotistical desires.

This special month, dedicated to My beloved daughter, the Immaculate Mary, is a perfect time to reflect upon your own behavior once again in Her presence, with Her help, with Her special and precious and loving company, in Her tenderness, holding you in Her Heart every moment; but welcoming you in times of trouble, grateful that you have turned to Her always waiting for your call, your need, your love, your trust; the knowing that grows daily that you can count on Her and your great need for Her companionship. The world becomes darker, more difficult, more evil, a more threatening place in which to live, and so you look in the direction of Our Spirit for the comfort and the beauty, the peace, the gentleness that is found in this Holy and Immaculate One, to surround yourself with Her holiness, to borrow the strength you will need to look honestly at yourselves, My people everywhere, and you realize I do not chastise you, but I lead you to truth. My Son has told you that He IS Truth, and so the Holy Mother takes you to Her Son where you encounter ALL TRUTH. You are loved this day, as you are every moment in your lives. No matter what you have done or what you have failed to do, you are cherished by all in Heaven. Be healed of all that assails you. Be strengthened. Be made whole and new. Amen, My dear ones. Go forth now to defeat evil!"

5-15, "My very dear children, I am your beloved Pio, who comes this day by a special gift of the Spirit of God, Whose Feast we proclaim and celebrate. I bring my admiration and gratitude to each of you who prays and perseveres with fidelity. Do not be discouraged if you struggle to reach some former place you have experienced in your prayer life. Remember all of us have struggled to maintain the gifts of prayer, the gifts of loving God and being a servant. I always thank the Father that I was kept and spent most of my life in one place, so I admire you more than ever, seeing you balance so many different calls for your time, your energy, your talents, all the while maintaining these lives and these chores in the presence of the Triune God and the Holy Mother. My very dear ones to whom I speak also in the entire world, praise the Father and thank Him for blessing you in mighty ways. Do not wait to discover your gifts. Believe that they are given, that you have them because it has been said to you and promised to you.

I go where suffering flourishes and is welcomed. The wounds of Our Jesus bear a sign to us. They are our spiritual markings that no one can see but the Father. The wounds of Jesus are your protection, your badge of honor and courage, your identification as one who not only follows Jesus, but strives to become more like Him every moment of every day. We are joined these days in newer and deeper ways because of the escalation of the Father's Plan for you and for the world, and as a means of fighting evil that only escalates from now on until Our Beloved Jesus defeats him (Satan) and chains him in hell for so many, many, many lifetimes, as you know them. Be aware of this, my children everywhere.

How well you have learned to use new weapons of patience and peace and tenderness, friendliness, interest in each other's welfare. How much more you will learn; how many miracles you will see. How much closer we shall all become as the heat of battle rises, takes many, many more into eternity where they too will join this Army and continue or, maybe for the first time, understand and accept Truth and the Father's Kingdom and His Commandments, and seek forgiveness. Think of it, my children, for you are my children and my brothers and sisters: this great spiritual family that seems to diminish, and yet grows in spiritual ways and according to the Father's Will. I bring you greetings from all of Heaven today, and a celebration that includes all of you with all of us for all those still in enormous need. Be good to each other! Be tender. Be loving. Be attentive to each other's needs. Today is a mighty feast indeed, and I bring you the gifts of the Holy Spirit, as your spiritual father and the one who keeps your needs in my prayers. May God bless each of you everywhere, and He does, My children. He does! Amen."

Note: St. Pio spoke these wonderful words to my heart on May 13th that I thought you would like to hear, and realize that they are for all of us, so think daughter or son!

"Be happy to suffer, daughter, for the sake of His Sorrowful Passion. Have mercy on the whole world!"

5-18, (another Pio collection) at Adoration today, "My dear one, please write quickly. I am Pio, who speaks now to your heart. You give out of your own need and must add this healing more often to your words and suggestions to others for their preparation as God's instruments of mercy to the world. When I was receiving people for reconciliation and direction, it was joy and an open smile that reached through their sorrow and fears most quickly. You can heal and open hearts with these approaches to openness of face and acceptance in your eyes; focusing on a positive approach to people; treating them with great respect and honest devotion as new sisters and brothers in your heart and soul. Maria is waiting to greet all of you who travel to Betania at this time to invite all more deeply into her heart and plans. Remember, daughter, 'love will conquer all.' Be filled with peace."

A few excerpts from personal messages:

6-3, "I am Mary, your Heavenly mother, who speaks words of comfort. Continue to pray much for all these intentions and the world, but especially for this country. Time is gone for leisure, except the quiet preparation for battle when soldiers reflect on battle results and possibilities of many casualties. Events, My dear one, are very close to erupting and taking great numbers into Eternity again. Simply pray and spend all your time in preparation."

6-14, "I am your God and Father, your Creator and Lord. My plan for the world's cleansing is escalating quickly. The people who have remained faithful will receive new gifts and charisms from Our Spirit this very day. These will become more apparent to you and to them. The New World Order forces of evil work furiously behind the scenes to attain new footholds of power in major countries of the earth. You see struggles already among financial leaders and those who realize they are losing power and control in their countries. The United States works in secret with many world leaders to weaken the centers for control in various parts of the world. Know that amazing changes will begin in this country, once continued natural events drain the resources of this once great land. Be ready to see more infighting and wrestling for power among your leaders. Do not be afraid when martial law is finally and suddenly put into place for flimsy excuses and with dire consequences. You know there are many places of detention and annihilation prepared and in waiting for those who refuse the power of the Antichrist, who will so soon appear upon the International scene. Only trust can maintain a peaceful and calm demeanor within our entire faithful remnant. Remember the calm understanding that pervaded the hearts of all, who pray and listen to the words of Heaven, after the terrible destruction of the Towers of power and finance on the Eastern borders of this country? Count on the same heavenly assistance as the next attack on this land will bring to their knees the same ones and more, who reacted in sorrow and loss that first time. I call all My beloved people in the world to prayer, once again, **with a mighty emphasis on the souls going into eternity**, that they will choose for My Kingdom, repent of their sins and receive the gift of salvation I long to give everyone who will accept My mercy."

6/12, (with excerpts from 6/3 & 14) "My very dearest ones, I am your Jesus, My children. I place all of you more deeply in My Sacred and Suffering and Eucharistic Heart. This is a month dedicated to Me, and so I tell you as a gift to all of you and because you will need this gift: I give each of you in the world who listens, who prays, who struggles to change to become who you were created to be, I give you this day a closer relationship with Me. Praise and thank the Father, My children, Who allows this gift. You will each experience it perhaps in different ways; but most definitely you will notice My Presence more completely in a more realistic way, a more tangible way, a more heartfelt and joyful way. Oh My dear ones, this pleases Me too. I praise and thank the Father with you. We will accomplish mighty deeds, My children. We will accomplish all that the Father has planned for each of you. You have been patient, you have been obedient to a great degree, you have learned, My dear ones. The sweetness in your hearts is a sign of My Presence and the presence of the Holy Mother, the fact that you are surrounded by Angels who pray for this very gift: My sweetness. Love will conquer on every occasion, My dear ones, and so I bring you joy this day, joy and encouragement and new hope, for with My greater presence, with My joy, with My power, in My Name, you will accomplish more in the plan of My Father and by way of conversion for the entire world.

Continue to beg for mercy ….. yes, especially for your own country. Pray for the souls of all of those who will enter eternity quickly and in great numbers once again. Pray for an end to any fear of any kind in the hearts of all who will listen and of course, for an increase in trust, without which people cannot receive the mercy of My Father, except also through your prayers for them. The way you beg mercy for the world, My children, your prayers are a symphony that rises in a beautiful crescendo, filling Heaven with a melody: the melody of hope, the melody of obedience, the melody of the fulfillment of My Father's Perfect Will. How I love you. How all of Heaven loves you, My children, and sends their gratitude and great joy to each of you this day. Know that there is an escalation in My Father's plans. You will see this reflected in news around the world, especially where War takes a greater toll than you can imagine. Be strong, as warriors are strong, as prepared warriors and soldiers who anticipate battle. Please be filled with trust. Be joyful, for your great, great gifts and blessedness are the cause of Heavenly joy. All is well, My dear ones."

6/19, "I am your Jesus of Mercy, your Eucharistic Lord. YOU are special, My dear ones! Believe it through the eyes of your God; special to the plan of My Father; special in your endurance, in your trust, in your keeping on keeping on, in your love for My Mother and for Me, in your struggle to say, 'yes' each day; in the enormous strength you draw upon, not even realizing that you are acting in an heroic way as true warriors in My Mother's Army, as the true Eucharistic people that you are becoming, the **Eucharistic people who are present in the New Era, building understanding and knowledge and all of the virtues in the hearts of those who gather at the table of My Father.**

My dear ones, it is a momentous time. It is also Father's Day, and so I give special blessings to all fathers in the world, and as a sign to each father and each holy family who struggles to follow My Way. My children, I only come to encourage you this day; to give you new hope, to give you strength to imitate hope each day in your own lives; to begin each day with new hope. Hope springs eternal! Remember that all virtues spring eternal, that your soul springs eternal, and that My Father feeds you with Me through the wellspring of His Mercy. This is the month you honor Me in a special way as all of Who I Am to you, but most especially in My Eucharist where I wait for you, where I welcome you and invite you to accept so many opportunities to become the giants you are meant to be in My Father's plan. I love you, My dear ones. Feel My love. Hear the love in My voice, My delight with you, My happiness over your success each day of simply being who you are created to be. You ARE becoming, My children, absolutely and entirely all My Father calls you to be: an answer to all of His desires for you. Amen to you, My children. I love you. I rejoice with you."

7-10, "My very dear, dear children, I am Mary, the Immaculate One, and your very loving and grateful Mother. Horrific destruction is in your immediate future in this country. Pray especially now. I will pray with you, as we sit momentarily in silence that all those going into eternity will choose for the Father, His commandments; will choose to repent and accept that every suffering might be due in reparation for their sins; but that will save them, that will give them eternal life. Let us pray together, children. I kneel before you, My dear ones. (LONG PAUSE, AS WE PRAYED SILENTLY)

Your hearts, My children, are fertile ground for compassion that grows and reaches out to all of those in need. Together we approach the Throne of the Father now, asking for mercy. Together we surrender whatever area of your lives, my children everywhere, that you cling to as your own, your special private place that has not yet been surrendered, relinquished, offered up to the Father. Let us do that together now. I pray with you, my children everywhere, to give you strength. You CAN OVERCOME weaknesses. You CAN OVERCOME chronic, sinful habits. You CAN OVERCOME the 'self' which still rules your heart. These storms are the beginning of new levels of the Father's wrath, of a manifestation of His justice. More of the story with which you are so much more familiar will play out in your own lives and your own country and yes, in new places in the world. The numbers are small on whom We count to help in the great plan of the salvation of the entire world. Remember that We are together; that I walk with you, with my Jesus; that Angels surround you. This is Truth. This is the Father's gift to you. Let us begin again at this new level, hand in hand; our Rosaries swinging with our steps, glowing with the gold of your love, strengthening you for just a little longer, just a little more, just a little farther along the path of waiting. Be at peace this day. Feel my love. Feel the peace of my Jesus. Remember, little ones, we go forward TOGETHER into Love. Amen."

7-17, "My very dear children, I am your God and Father. I speak to My faithful ones everywhere in the world. You see a continuation of the might of My arm, and My wrath and My justice. Again, pray for those who are impacted by the tremendous winds, the water and the destruction that occurs with this mighty hurricane. Pray especially that all of those who are going into eternity will choose for My Commandments, will choose Me, will choose to repent and be given My mercy. Pray in reparation for their sins. As always I ask you to do this as the little victims I have chosen throughout the world. Truly, you carry the weight of the world on your shoulders; but it is not a weight you cannot carry, for these burdens are made light by the love of the Triune God, by the light of Christ, by the fire of Our Holy Spirit that burns in your hearts for the poor lost ones who are desperate for help, though they know it not. These storms will continue, My children everywhere. It is another means of rallying the entire world for a single cause, which is so important to the unity My remnant people must share, that you will recognize yourselves as members of this one great family with Myself as your Creator God; with My Son, your Redeemer and King and your Lord; with the Sanctifier and Enabler of good deeds. Think often, My children, of this great Communion of Saints. It is your fondest identity right now and the one that is needed most by the world; for there is safety yes, but there is great strength in numbers, and you are the chosen numbers who have responded to My call. Carry the world in your hearts, My dear, dear children everywhere."

7/31, "My very dear ones, I am your Immaculate Mother. I come again with the glory given to me by the Father, with all of the power that is mine because of Him. I ask you this day, this last day of the month dedicated to the

Precious Blood of my Son to spend the rest of this day praising the Father for the suffering, the dying, the Blood of Jesus that cleanses you, the Blood of Jesus that remains to nurture you and to cleanse you; the Blood of Jesus that I have asked you in the past to pour over all the people for whom you pray, *your* enemies, children. Sometimes you know who they are; most often it is subtle and hidden. But you know that the enemy works against all of you as the great Body of Christ. In the Blood of Jesus is your first defense, and the battle increases now, and very, very soon, you will see signs of the escalation of Satan's plan. **There has been time given for more conversions and yet events will be ongoing**. I ask you to avail yourselves of the healing given in the Blood of Christ. Ask Jesus to pour his Blood over you and to unburden you of yourself. How this holds you back. How this weighs you down. How this causes you to be distracted, disappointed, always having expectations or desires, or needs that can be put to rest at the feet of my Beloved Son. Remember it is He who first carried the Cross, Who invites you to carry your crosses, but not (to be) *immersed* in them. Carry your cross lightly, realizing it is not the great burden you make it, joyfully realizing it is not the great sorrow and weight it seems, when you dwell in it. Again the outcome of every event depends on your choices. Choose to be joyful. Choose to think of the needs of others, to pray for others generously. Oh my dear ones, get rid of resentments, get rid of anger, let go of unforgiveness. It is killing you! I speak to you everywhere in the world, for people do not change easily or quickly even over generations, and there is so much hatred in the world, that you are afflicted by it without knowing, without realizing that you may have picked it up in the air from others, from spirits that are not of God, that are not of joy, that are not of peace. They are running rampant now, and I offer you these reflections today so that you may be better prepared, you might choose your Lord and your God as your buckler and shield against all of these negative and harmful, life threatening feelings that you carry, that you are allowing to destroy, to pull you down. Allow my Jesus to pick you up.

I love you. I am with you. I am praying for you every moment. How much I long for you to be healed, to be freed of the burdens you create for yourselves. Let go! Let go of everything and everyone, especially those who annoy you the most and there are those people for everyone. Be free, that you might be joyful. Be filled with my Jesus. Bring Him to everyone. Prepare for an event of great magnitude in the world that will still impact the entire world. Be full of peace now, children: healing, deep, abiding peace. When you begin to become agitated over events in your life or people, let go of them immediately! Ask my Jesus to pour His Blood over those people or that situation and over you to heal you, to free you, to bless you, to transform you. Let us be joyful and praise the Father together, my dear ones, forever! Thank you for loving me. Thank you for loving my Jesus. Remember His great power, that He is your All in all."

8-7, "My very dear children, I am your God and Father Who speaks. I thank you with all of Who I Am for your precious and heartfelt prayers. When you pray, children, I know that you mean your words of love and all the words that reach out to others, for them. I thank you especially this day. (Feast of Consecration to God the Father)

I repeat this day, you are My gift to Myself! You are My hope for the fulfillment of all My desires for the world. You are a large part of the strength and might of My Arm, as the Army of the Blessed Virgin Mary, your dear Mother. We have come a long way together in this particular endeavor. Of course, since the beginning of your own lives, but think back to the day when you were touched deeply by My call, by My grace. Your heart took fire, and you knew that you wanted to be part of My plan of salvation for the world. It was a marriage of wills: yours and Mine! Today, as you celebrate a feast dedicated to Me, you are also living out more fully My Will for you and for this time, this very critical time when you need all of the Godhead: all of Our strength, given to you as you were born into this world by your God. The wisdom of My plans, the way they are coming to fruition is too slow for you, of course, but as you see people suffer as a result of destruction that has already visited your land, your earth, you are perhaps more able and more ready to accept the pace of My Will, My timetable, My perfect plans for you and for the world. They are always given in the greatest love for you.

You ARE responding to this call to know Me better, to love Me more, to honor Me constantly in all you do, to praise Me and thank Me, to realize that all IS gift; and thus you are fulfilling My Will for this Age! It is in these prayerful and subtle ways that My Will unfolds in your lives; not in great events that you can see or talk about, but in the following and in the responding that occurs within your hearts and your own will and in your spirits. LET THIS NOT ONLY BE ENOUGH FOR YOU, BUT WHAT YOU WOULD DESIRE, AS WELL! I bless you now, My dear ones, by the power of My Own Name, by all the might of the Godhead, in the Name of My Son, Jesus, and in the Name of Our Spirit. Thank you for being faithful to prayer, faithful to community. This is most important in My plan for the world. Think of all those who are orphaned, who have nothing and no one; and rejoice in community, and give thanks for this opportunity and the great strength that is present in community. Be filled with the peace of My Son now, My children. Let it carry you through the coming week and each event that unfolds in your lives as part of My plan. Do NOT be lonely, I beg of you. Turn to the Angels who accompany you. Turn to the Holy Mother, to the peace of My Jesus, to the power and the gifts of Our Holy Spirit and to the great, great creative Love that exists in your life, as My gift to you. Amen, little ones. We go forward!"

8-14, "My very dear children, I am your Immaculate Mother. Thank you for your prayers, especially this day honoring another feast of my life. Recall, my dear ones, how Jesus has told you in the past of the joy, the glory, the excitement, the light that shone through Heaven, even brighter as it were, welcoming me for whom they had waited, fulfilling the moment for which I had waited so totally. I relive that moment now with you, and I gather all of you everywhere in the world who love me, who listens and prays, who tries to be the child I am calling you to be: the warrior-child, the docile and obedient child, the loving child who will welcome so many of Our dear ones into your arms, into your homes and hearts. It is in every opportunity that you practice this welcoming, this purity of heart with which you approach each other. Imagine with me the feasting in Heaven: how I was greeted with such joy. It will be the same for you, children, at the appointed time. Even though you still wait in joy and hope, START LIVING IN THE VICTORY OF THE ACCOMPLISHMENT! Prepare your hearts, your souls, your lives, your minds and wills for the return of my Son and for the victory of all whom you will help choose salvation. There is much for which to rejoice, my children. LET US REJOICE IN EACH OTHER THIS DAY, THAT WE HAVE EACH OTHER! More and more and more, we are FOR each other. Thank you for honoring me this day. How honored I am, my dear, dear ones."

8-29, "My very dear children, I am your God and Father, your Creator and your Lord. I come today, once again with My mighty power, giving more power to your prayers, as you plead for mercy and beg protection for those in the path of the storm. Imagine how much good your prayers will do in their eternal lives. Imagine how much help many of them need. Feel joyful and grateful, My children, that you are needed so much by them and by Me, that we count upon you to be the faithful ones you have chosen to be. Think of the Old Testament stories, when those (who stayed behind) prayed for those going into battle. Is it not a matter of staying behind now, but staying hidden and praying for those who experience the battle and the battering of storms: those of you who stay hidden, yet are the mightiest warriors?

Take care to remain humble in your lofty position as warrior, as one who shares My plans, who shares My power to save the world, for I have put you in union with all of the redemptive suffering of My Son; and we are one, all of us, My children, all of us, through the Power of Our Spirit. Rejoice, for these are great gifts, though nothing you can see or feel. You know in your intellect as well as your heart that these are great gifts and this has put you in a special place, a place of co-redeeming with My Jesus and the Holy Mother, a vehicle for the salvation of the entire world. Keep yourself fueled, as you would a road vehicle, for you need to have the energy to continue on the road to salvation for yourselves and for the entire world. You travel along that road of My Will into salvation; more deeply into My Will, My plans for you: the many gifts waiting along the way that you will receive even more so in the future. How you have grown in your gifts is still as nothing compared to the future: what you will do for Me and for My people. Remember and believe this, My dear ones, for you will and you do impact the choices made by those coming into eternity, the most important choices of their lives and of 'forever' for them.

Gather the love that wells up in your heart when you think of those who struggle, those who suffer in storms, in floods, in terrible conditions, many of them giving their lives to the rage of the storm. Let all the love and compassion in your hearts come to the fore, come to the top, that you might pour out this love through your prayer, through your time and your energy on the wounds of these poor lost ones, perhaps on their very souls in eternity. My dear ones, (this, of course, is said to the whole world who listens and prays...cta.) more and more you are united in My plan. You are raised higher this day in My need for you, in My plans for you, in your place in My plans. Just quietly praise and thank Me for choosing you, for bringing you to a new place and yes again, I am always asking for more from you: more love, My children. You see I know how much more love you have to give, better then you know! Just believe, My children, that you can (and you will) do all that is possible for you. Thank you for listening. Thank you for taking these words seriously, as you recognize the serious condition of the path of this storm, and all the people on it. Pray for them. They are your family! They belong to you, and you all belong to Me! I pour out My great love upon you now and again My gratitude for all you do. You are part of the victory, My children. The victory that is already won by My Son contains YOU and your little victories, your patience, your perseverance, your commitment. Rejoice! We go forward once again together in victory!"

9/11, "My very dear ones, I am your God and your Father, once again: come to speak to you, to visit with you, My children everywhere in the world who hear My words; who answer My requests with your life, with your prayers, with your commitment and your consecrations. My dear ones, I come to encourage you to continue in the increased prayers that you are offering for this country, for the hurricane victims, for the victims of terror attacks in your country, for the victims of new storms that will surely visit this land and soon. It will come to be, as I have prophesied to you years ago, that eventually your country will be exhausted of funds and the ability to care for all the victims of storms and attacks, and will have to reach out to other powers; that this will be the beginning of a greater infiltration and presence of the New World Order people, of Martial Law, of an end to your freedom and privacy. Harsh words, My children, but a necessary reminder of what is ahead of you, and the reason for all of your prayer and the request of Heaven that you change. Yes, you have changed, My dear ones, as I have told you; but it must be more now. Discipline is at the forefront of your needs and this, of course, is obtained by FASTING!

New strength, a backbone of steel and the sweetness and tenderness and gentleness of My Mother is obtained through fasting and the practice of greater discipline in your life of all the good things you allow yourselves. PRACTICE EATING LESS, MY CHILDREN! IT IS AS SIMPLE AS THAT!! At each meal, be conscious and aware of the amount of food you eat and simply EAT LESS! I come to you with this request as an encouragement, but as a greater help for you to attain this discipline, to attain the toughness of spirit that a soldier is known for: that characterizes those who are committed to a cause, to a goal, to overcoming a great enemy. This is how you are to be described and understood, My children. Do not worry. It IS possible for you to do this. I speak especially to those in this country who have a surplus of everything, who have a great plenty and every kind of food imaginable. It is a matter of habit with you, My dear ones, I realize that. And so it is a matter of breaking old habits and forming new ones with the greatest goal possible: the defeat of the enemy and all of his plans for world domination; the conversion of souls that as many as possible will accept the gift of salvation I wait to give them. What could be a greater gift to give the world? And you are part of the great, great plan of Mine, without whom I choose to be helpless in this area; (that has just been described...cta.) so that you might feel and realize you are called to a very important mission and rise to the occasion of serving at your best, at your most involved, your deepest commitment, your greatest strength and focus on all you are called to become and to do and to be! I come this day to tell you that more than anything, I love you! I am so grateful for you. You will never know until Eternity. I welcome you now into a new day, a new level of service of loving Me and your brothers and sisters in the entire world. Be healed by the might of My Arm this day."

9-18, "Dear ones of My Sacred Heart, I am your Jesus of Mercy. How I have longed to be with you again in this special way. I watch over you, as I am with you every moment. Let us rejoice this day, that we belong to each other because of My Mother who has given birth to Me in your hearts again and again and again; who calls you again and again to come closer to Me, to listen more closely to the words of Heaven, to listen to all the Father says and invites you to be, who He needs you to be! Can you not see the condition of the world? And yet, **you know there is so much that is kept from you**, so much terrible treatment of little ones, so much terror in the lives of so many. Trust these words: that you must **pray more for those who are terrorized by terrorists, yes, but by people in their own families: those who live in fear of physical abuse, those who live in fear of the world, of Satan's plans.** How could you not give every spare moment of your time and energy to prayer for the salvation of the world, of these dear ones who suffer, who live the rejection in the hearts of the haughty. Bring My Mother to all you meet. Be an experience of her. Believe and practice being a source of My Mother and her gifts, as you are a source of Mercy and all the gifts My Father has given you. It is a time in the world now that you are to be more (for people) an experience of holiness, to be an experience of joy and hope; but also gentleness. **The world begins to weep as one giant wound in the Universe**! Pray for your world, My beloved people who listen to Me and to all the words of Heaven."

9/25, "My very dear children, I am your Mother of Mercy. Be filled with my strength this day everywhere in the world. My sorrows for the world increase, as devastation and destruction visits once again in many areas. The Father's wrath must be expressed in an ongoing way that hardened hearts and deaf ears may finally hear and respond to the need to change, to the need to come to the Commandments, to come and beg forgiveness, to repent and be transformed. Among you there is great suffering that is hidden because of your love of the suffering of my Jesus and your unity with Him. We enter more serious times now in many ways, more serious suffering; but more serious attacks by the evil one through particular, powerful people who are becoming more visible and more powerful in the world and in their ability to sway and gather evil men for evil intentions, for One World purposes for Satan's plans. We enter shortly the month of my Rosary: It is our greatest weapon, my dear ones. Do not forget this! Pray an extra Rosary for those for whom you grieve and worry. Remember that we pray together, that your petitions are my petitions and intentions; that your loved ones and your children are my loved ones and my children. Ponder our unity, my dear ones. I am your Mother, and I love you with the deepest and greatest and most powerful and tender love, beyond anything you will ever imagine. You heal my suffering heart as I attempt to heal yours, and you allow me more deeply into your heart and into your lives and your lifestyle. Oh my dear ones, how blessed we are in each other! You ARE MY little ones!"

10/10, "Oh my dear ones, I am your Mother of Sorrows, filled with sorrow today at the tremendous destruction in Asia. I know that you know how many prayers these dear ones need; how dreadful are their living conditions now, the lack of sanitary conditions. My dear ones, it is dreadful when people must experience such terror in their lives, such upheaval, such displacement, such confusion and a total rearrangement of everything they have ever known. Think of this, that you might appreciate more what they are going through, that you might pray with heartfelt love, grieving with them over their losses; and with all of this, my children, you will have no idea of the plight of these dear ones, and of course, it is so many innocents who also suffer. Look at your sunshine and clear blue sky, the flowering that occurs everywhere, the beauty of your surroundings, and praise the Father. Take this goodness, these gifts that He gives you, and send them to My poor, poor suffering ones in the world. IT IS UP TO YOU, MY DEAR ONES, TO COMFORT THEM. Yes, you CAN DO THIS!

You know the power of your prayers has increased. Love them with your prayers and your thoughts. Nurture them with your concern for them and for their eternal future. My children, we are seeing destruction everywhere, and so we are convinced now that the Father's Plan escalates and goes forward; but the purification of the world continues in the hearts of everyone alive. What a tremendous work. What a tremendous gift this really is from the Father: bringing people into eternity, giving them the opportunity to see for themselves, to choose instantly for salvation. You are fulfilling the role for which you were called; for which you were converted again and again and again; for which you were formed in the Image and Likeness of Our God! I say all of these words again to remind you of the prestigious place you hold in the lives of the entire world. Appreciate this, my dear ones. Feel the graces falling upon you this moment that bring you into a new place; yes, another new level of service for Our people and for Our God. It was for this you were created, my children. Rejoice!

Pray more and with joy, with peace; praising and thanking the Father for the peace of Jesus with which He showers you, that you might share that peace with everyone, that you might hold your temper, hold your words, hold your impatience. Hold your anger! Let go of your anger. Let go of all contentiousness within yourselves and FOLLOW ME. BE LIKE ME IN ALL YOU DO. BE LIKE YOUR GOD WHO LOVES AND HAS MERCY, WHO HAS PATIENCE AND FORGIVENESS ALWAYS. Let us rejoice because you can do this! If you could see yourselves as Heaven sees you, you would not believe it; for a great shining of light and grace comes forth from this room and your hearts and your faces, and reflects all the way to Heaven! Believe this, my dear ones, and be comforted. Be filled with joy. All is proceeding for the whole world. Rejoice! Let us give thanks together. My dear ones everywhere, hear these words. Know that your prayers, your hearts, your faces reflect the light of my Son and the goodness growing within you. Believe this. HOLD ON TO THE GOODNESS, MY CHILDREN. HOLD ON. HOLD ON TO ME!"

10-23, "Dearly Beloved Ones, I am your Mother, once again come to be with you to strengthen you. My children we go forward in this month of my Rosary as this call of the Father shakes the complacency of mindless, thoughtless, heartless people everywhere. Pray with St. Dominic, as this day you have honored him by reflecting upon his life and the immense fire that burned in his heart and soul, his mind and his will for the poor lost ones in this world. Ask him for the gift of understanding that he had of the suffering, who do not realize why they suffer or how they suffer or that they cause themselves to suffer away from the Almighty God and from myself; and the help that I could give them. Share this goodness. Share the peace, all that you have learned, have received, have become. Share your gratitude and hope for each other. I welcome the visitors here (from Canada and Australia...C.) that you might take a special portion of my love, my blessings back to your countries. Thank you for joining this group, for bringing your blessings, your prayers, your holiness to bear and offer to God, Our Father in thanksgiving. You are all one, and as you gather in greater numbers each week, each month, (and this will happen, most especially as storms continue, and desolation and destruction spreads) you will gather in greater numbers and offer greater numbers of prayers to the Father begging mitigation.

My children, remember that we are one, that we are a vast army, that we battle evil, that we battle inclination to sin, in even the most faithful, the most blessed of my remnant people, my precious children that you are. How difficult it is to carry your humanity. But this day each of you carries new graces, new gifts, new strength, as well as new hope to all you meet this week. You have not left each other behind when you leave (every prayer group, Cta.) for your homes this day; but carry each other in your hearts, your prayers, your good wishes and your mercy for each other and for the world. Ponder these words, dear ones. They are a sign of your power over each other and for each other and for the world. This is our theme: the power you have to be the mercy, to be the hope, to be the instrument of healing, of graces, of conversion for the world. My dear ones, rejoice!"

FOR MERCY'S SAKE!

10-30, "My dearest children, I am your God and Father. I welcome you this day. I count you as My faithful soldiers, as favored in My plans and in the Army of the dear Mother of God. I count upon you to treat each other with mercy, with a holy gratitude for all each of you does for Me and for each other. I would like to speak to the people of the world about appreciation and gratitude for your brothers and sisters, not being demanding or impatient or critical or unkind, even in the name of humor. It is time now to develop the greatest gentleness possible within yourselves. I say this most seriously, My children everywhere in the world, because the time approaches for destruction even closer to your own homes, to your own area; and the time when you will see refugees, people fleeing from that destruction with nothing of their own. It will be the beginning of the time when you will serve these poor victims of the wrath of Nature and of My Will that **might act in a more noble and giving and gracious way.**

Know that each of you is a fine soldier, is a prayer warrior; and I am asking you to identify with those names, to think of yourselves in that way for those who will come to you. There is no other way to prepare for this time, for these people than to keep reminding you, keep giving you suggestions, keep requesting more of your behavior, change within your attitudes and your words and yes, your appreciation of each other. You can appreciate those who will come to you because they will obtain so much grace in your ministering to them: the grace that YOU will need to obtain salvation, of course. You know that I call you to perfection. This is mostly a matter of attitude and behavior, and the most vulnerable place for all of you, and the place of greatest need for change and renewal, patterning yourself after your Mother, the Saints and Myself. We have spoken in the past about patience, and how it is the most difficult virtue to practice; so I remind you of this again today. I call upon you for humility, not some lofty attitude, but a sweet and generous SERVANT'S ATTITUDE. I call upon you to be My children, the children you were created to be in My Image, the Image of Jesus and Our Spirit. YOU CAN DO THIS!

As I ask these things of you, I ask you also to remember that you are beloved to Me; that I ask more of you because I count on you to be the vehicle of miracles, that this will begin soon; to cherish each other as We come into a Season that is about cherishing the tiny Baby, My Son, in your hearts, and present in the hearts of all you know and love. My dear ones, I am pinning a medal, a ribbon upon each of your chests today as a sign of new holiness, of new advancement in the Army of the great Virgin. Be aware of this, for it is real. It is a new sign for you. You have greater status in My plans, thus you have more responsibility and My greatest love and appreciation Myself for you. I speak at length today because this is unity that I present to you, the possibility of becoming more, as well as doing more. Please practice becoming more like your God. A great embrace for each of you! Amen, My children. Satan will be stronger at this time of preparation. Be on guard! Walk in My love and My protection."

FOR MERCY'S SAKE!

11-14, "My dear children, I am your Jesus of Mercy. I am your Lord and your God, your Savior and your King. I come to you this day with arms filled with graces for you, each of you, with gifts of strength. It is always necessary in battle to stop and be renewed; to rest and recover; to recuperate from excessive fatigue; to eat well and rest well and often. I ask this of you this coming week, My people everywhere, to unite this preparedness with each other's. It will not be the only preparedness I give you or ask of you. There will be more when We speak again. My children, I love you. You are the ones Heaven counts on. You are the ones the world needs. This becomes more important as each week goes by, as each event occurs and more are brought into eternity. Rejoice for them, for they have a great opportunity to learn about the Kingdom of My Father and choose eternal salvation. Great and ultimate are these gifts, My children; and you are the vehicles for them to choose correctly and rightly and in a holy way. I love you. Love Me. BE Me. Prepare for My Coming!"

11-20, "My dear children, once again... I am your Jesus of Mercy, come with greetings from all in Heaven, especially your own loved ones there. Realize that you ARE struggling. Realize that We are with you and that you have the strength you need to overcome that situation, that temptation, whatever it is. By now you know truly and deeply that all of Heaven wishes to help you do the very best you possibly can; and that is the reason, the object of all of the graces and gifts given by the Father at every moment, and always at your disposal. Years and years ago, it was explained to you that when gifts are given, which is always, your job is to be open to them, to accept them and then, to use them to remind yourself: I have this gift that I need. I can do this! I am equipped to handle this situation, and then just grasp the gift anew and move forward to victory! It works, My children! It is the path to victory!! It is the reminder I give you now, and will give you again, that you can give yourselves to make that victorious leap across the chasm of ruin; across an experience of defeat, of moving backwards and away from your God, instead of more deeply into the Divine Will of Our Father. Always that is your goal, but always you will struggle to do that because always remember, you have your humanity with which to deal and struggle.

Remember athletes who practice long hours, sweating from the exertion. Remember dancers, as I have mentioned in the past, who study, study, study; or anyone who has a particular job they have to learn, who studies and focuses and gives energy and desire to the goal. I ask you to remember your heart as a fledgling Manger, as bits of wood that you are meshing, that you are weaving with your prayers and your good works into that Manger in which I will be laid on Christmas Day. These are small images I give you again because I love you. Feel the love in My words and in My voice. 'I love you. This is Truth. I Am Truth. You are Mine. This is your greatest truth: I am yours.' Be healed again today, and strengthened and uplifted by My love. Be filled with joy because you DO go toward victory now; and all of Heaven accompanies you as you accompany each other in a new adventure, a new journey, a new victory. Amen, My dear ones. Let us go forward together."

FOR MERCY'S SAKE!

11/27, "My very dear children, I am your Jesus of Mercy, here to continue My words of encouragement and support: ideas from Heaven to help you prepare for My Birth. Children, nothing will help you more than openness to all the words of Heaven; but you must be so familiar with them that they remind you of what is going on in your life; or you are reminded of how to react in a certain situation, or what I have said about a certain situation you may find yourself in at that moment! Always the words of Heaven are meant to fortify you in the battle, not only against the evil one, but against your own self and self-absorption; your lack of awareness of what is being said around you: not listening with all of who you are to what is being said, or the particular action or prayer at the time. That is being alert; and if you recall, one of the first things you were called to do here in this place, in this city, in your original prayer group, (at St. Maria Goretti Church) your original coming together in response to the requests of My Mother for increased prayer for the salvation of the world. The messenges from Heaven and the words talked about being alert to what was going on, to the gifts being poured out, to being aware of the needs of everyone, to being respectful to a person who is speaking; who is trying to lead, to teach you the words of Heaven, most especially that are given through the mercy of God, Our Father to form you, to help you become the warriors you are called to be. I have said before, there is nothing more important in your life now than to prepare for all of those who will come one day, and that day is so much closer!

Through the years, you have heard the words about 'one day', 'some day', or 'soon'; and now you know that 'soon' has begun, that 'now' is here. To be alert is a state of preparedness for battle. It is also a state of preparedness for prayer, most especially for group prayer. I have explained to you that prayer must not be approached as a means of your own gratification, your own experience of the mystical! The very fact that you are hearing Me speak is a great gift given by the love of your Triune God in gratitude for you and your devotion, your perseverance and endurance these many, many years for so many in the world now who are so needy, whose needs are not being met as they should be by government officials here and in so many places in the world. My children, you know the importance and the power of your prayers now, and I speak to everyone.

Oh My children, the world, the conditions grow more critical. You hear of storms and events to come soon, and you know they will. Bring all of who you are to the table: the prayer table, the table of the Lord, the table of the children of God, the refugee people. WHEN YOU SEE THEM, MY CHILDREN, YOU WILL WISH TO RUN! Remember that! Grab the chair you sit in now to remind yourselves that one day you will wish to run; and I ask you to grab your chair then and to STAY and to BE all you are becoming and created to be! Know that I am your Jesus, that I AM here, that I DO pour out Mercy and healing and many, many, many blessings. Whatever you need this day, I say once again, 'IT IS YOURS'! Let us go forward: awake, watchful, alert! Amen, I love you!"

FOR MERCY'S SAKE!

12-4, "My dear children, I am your Holy Spirit, the Spirit of God. I thank you for the efforts put forth to be more open to Me and My gifts; and I promise you that I am always there for you with the words you need at the moment, with the gifts you need to overcome whatever you struggle with each moment, each day: each doubt, each lack of understanding of the Father's Will in your own lives, each hardship and struggle to answer the call of life's chores, the changes, all that is required of you in your present roll. I tell you that all is well for each of you in spite of weakness that persists, or attacks by the evil one that confuse you. Doubt is such a human condition! It is what plagues humanity most when dealing with something, with gifts as great as words from Heaven and teachings, and perhaps new understandings. Doubt is a weapon of the evil one, never forget that; and when you begin to doubt, cast out that doubt in Jesus' Name! Recognize it for what it is: an attack on your commitment, on all of your promises, all of the hard work you bring to each prayer, each day, making time for Adoration, making time for kindness in word and deed. Truly you are becoming the warriors that have been chosen, that have been requested, that have been decided by God Our Father; and by the grace and great love, the sweetness, the tenderness of Mary, the Mother of the world, My beloved spouse, your great, great gift and Queen who accompanies you each and every second. It is a very special time in the world, especially in the world of those who pray. Pray for those who defend countries, who are defending your own country in their hearts and in all of their actions and commitment to truth.

Dear ones, I am the love of the Father for the Son; and when the Father pours out love, it is Myself Who is the Vehicle. Remember My Presence. Ask for My help. Ask always for an increase in My gifts. Remember that one mighty voice for mercy is being lifted, calls out to the Father: 'Mercy, Father, Mercy.' We praise and thank the Father together, and in unity with Me, we continue in the Father's Plan for you and all the help that you are to the whole world. Remember to pray for all of those coming into eternity that they will choose for the Father, choose for salvation and choose life wherever they are! We are warriors and soldiers together; and we are at battle and We ARE victorious! Amen, My dear, dear ones. Blessings and peace and My gifts shower upon you now, everywhere in the world."

12-11, "My dear ones, I am your Jesus of Mercy: the Jesus Who is Bridegroom of your soul, your only Jesus; Second Person of the Blessed Trinity, your Triune God, your only God. I have come to ask you to be more focused on prayer in spite of a very busy time. All of you are tired. Everyone is tired, especially those who pray; yet when you come together, I ask you to speak out your prayers with your heart, because it is a mighty voice that the Father hears for mercy. Your country needs mercy. Your world needs mercy. You, My dear ones everywhere in the world, need mercy. I love you. I wish to give you every help; and I remind you to ask for it. Ask Our Holy Spirit for His gifts, His strength. Ask for the gifts you need that will support your weaknesses, your vulnerability, your quickness to judge, and especially a healing of your great ability to criticize! Do not look for the weak in each other, look for the good. See the good. Be thoughtful, My children, of the many chores of each of you. Be thoughtful of the humanity of each other, which at times is impatient and irritable. Unfortunately, this time of year sees increased irritability because of your increased tasks, of course; your shopping, of course; your greater amount of cooking and preparation for the holidays. Remember the primary purpose of these preparations, of these holidays: My Birth, that I might birth myself again and anew in your hearts.

Oh My dear ones, hear Me: I love you. I need you. The world needs you. Do not be distracted, My children. Do not become careless. Do not give up your devotions for another task. Try with all your might to be patient with each other, to be thoughtful of each other's ministry, of each other's ministering, of each others needs. lt is always more than you realize (the needs... cta) in the lives of each one of you, for much of your life is hidden with Me as it should be; and so I ask you once again to pray for each other more in the midst of busyness. Hold each other. Carry each other in your hearts, that you might share the warmth and the comfort each of you has to offer! Be aware of the cold, My dear ones here, in so many places and the people who suffer terribly because of it. Be aware of the hungry. Be aware of the unloved, the forgotten, the lonely. Be aware that each person in the world is a child of God and loved by God. My dear ones, My Mother and I bless you now in the Name of My Father and in My Name and the Name of Our Holy Spirit: a Christmas blessing for all of those who pray in special ways as a response to the requests of Heaven. Remember those who are sick, those who have no one, the souls in Purgatory, especially those who have no one. THE WORLD IS YOURS TO CARRY IN PRAYER! I know you can do this because I have said it, because you are Mine, because you are blessed. You are loved so much. Amen."

12-19, At Home, "I AM your Father God Who speaks words to you now for the world. These will be a confirmation of other words Heaven has spoken this day and a repeating of My concern for all who refuse to listen and prepare. The very theme of this time is preparation; the very essence of all We have spoken by way of teachings and warnings has been a preparation first of your soul and heart, your physical needs for the times of destruction and personal and collective chastisement. These times are here, and only the wise ones whose souls have been purified, their hearts emptied of the world, their wills reformed in the fire of My Love have lighted their lamps from this holy fire and maintained the blaze in obedience to My Will! Daughter, the world is a place of coldness that is reflected in the fierce wintry weather experienced in so many areas of this land. Yes, little weary one, we will continue tomorrow. Rest well."

12-20, "Let us continue for the world, child: The words that now come forth to many from Heaven for the world are some of the most serious and perhaps too frightening for some. As always, I remind you that these words are meant to strengthen you, to increase your prayers, and fill you with trust and hope in Our promises of protection. Remember that I, your Heavenly Father, have chosen to need your prayerful presence upon the earth, interceding for the lost souls everywhere in the world. My plan is proceeding for the world, accelerating for those who pray and listen and adore. As the snow falls in heavy flakes in so many areas now, so will My graces be falling upon each of My faithful ones throughout the world; but also upon those for whom you pray, interceding for them and especially for sinners. The many, who are brought into eternity at this sacred time of the Church year are, for the most part brought quickly into Heaven by the power of My mercy. Remember this, My beloved, faithful people, and allow this promise, this gift to assuage your sorrow and loneliness. I call you to accept the peace of this holy Season, to take time before the *Creche in your churches and homes to ponder the great gift of My Son, born into the world and into your hearts, *His present day manger. I have described three years of war to one who is faithful: fire raining out of the sky. These are plans made and agreed to long ago by world powers. When you see these horrors, be moved to pray for these leaders, to beg mercy on the earth, to fill with peace and trust the hearts of the faithful remnant people everywhere. DO NOT DWELL IN FEAR. It is the Season to rejoice that Love is born, and remember 'Peace on Earth to men of good will.' When you feel overwhelmed by fear, reread Our words of comfort and promise, explanations and teachings about the might of My Arm and the protection available wrapped in the Mantle of the Holy Mother, the Immaculate One. Be strong in your faith. Be the rock of strength and hope needed by all those less prepared than you. PRAY FOR THE GIFT OF WISDOM AND UNDERSTANDING FOR ALL THE PEOPLE IN THE WORLD. I have won the victory, dear ones. You too are victorious wherever you are! I love you! I have chosen you to be My faithful **prayer warriors throughout a long period of waiting** for the return of Jesus, My Beloved Son. This WILL be, My people. Whatever happens, it is best for you in My Perfect Will! DO NOT FEAR. YOUR GOD IS WITH YOU... FOREVER!"

For Mercy's Sake

"FOR THIS REASON I KNEEL BEFORE THE FATHER, FROM WHOM EVERY FAMILY IN HEAVEN AND ON EARTH IS NAMED, THAT HE MAY GRANT YOU IN ACCORD WITH THE RICHES OF HIS GLORY TO BE STRENGTHENED WITH POWER THROUGH HIS SPIRIT IN THE INNER SELF, AND THAT CHRIST MAY DWELL IN YOUR HEARTS THROUGH FAITH; THAT YOU, ROOTED AND GROUNDED IN LOVE, MAY HAVE STRENGTH TO COMPREHEND WITH ALL THE HOLY ONES WHAT IS THE BREADTH AND LENGTH AND HEIGHT AND DEPTH, AND TO KNOW THE LOVE OF CHRIST THAT SURPASSES KNOWLEDGE, SO THAT YOU MAY BE FILLED WITH ALL THE FULLNESS OF GOD." (EPHESIANS 3: 14-19)

VIII

2006 Messages.

FOR MERCY'S SAKE!

1-16, "My dearest child, please write words to live by, to sing with, to praise and thank Me for, to be healed by! I am your Father God, come again to heal your heart and understanding, increase your trust and waiting power. You are right to begin to focus on the fact that Jesus is returning, and soon (oh not in immediate fulfillment of My Plan, but quickly in the great scheme that now plays out on the world's stage.) This WILL WORK, little one, because it MUST WORK in order to fulfill all of Scripture **and perpetuate the human race**. You are also correct that you know some of the remnant people who, in spite of needed continued conversion (as do you also!) will come into the Renewed Earth as renewed people themselves. Then ALL you await will begin and be accomplished. You get a glimmer, daughter, of how this will unfold and who some of these people will be. All has become most serious. Gone will be all contentiousness, criticism or competition from any of them. All is poised to burst open upon their immediate environment, allowing My plan to continue. The waiting now occurs to allow a series of events to become aligned in My Wisdom and Will.

When you see an event that seems straightforward and without a hitch, this looks simple. Most often, the mighty storms of every kind are not simple; but need perfect timing to occur in just the right conditions. The evil one interferes with My plan so as not to gain the greater good for each person involved. It is not good he desires, but destruction and division and displacement of people. The more confusion he causes, the more vulnerable My people become. That is why We tell you to trust in Our promises and the protection of Jesus and the Angels, and just GO FORWARD ONE STEP AT A TIME, EITHER INTO SHELTERS, PLACES OF SAFETY OR HOMES ON HIGHER GROUND, WHATEVER THE SITUATION CALLS FOR AT THE TIME. It is good that many of you prepare to need to leave your homes for a period of time in different areas. It is a BLESSED SITUATION WHEN MY FAITHFUL ONES CAN PREPARE WITHOUT PANIC, AND REMAIN READY TO LEAVE AT ANY TIME, WHILE AT THE SAME TIME GOING FORWARD WITH DAILY TASKS AND LIFE AS USUAL. THIS, MY DEAR ONES, IS OBEDIENCE AND SURRENDER TO MY WILL AND PLANS, AT MY TIME AND IN MY WAY! Only I can see all elements of a statewide or nation wide or world wide condition, and know when the time is absolutely right. Believe this, children, and please stop trying to figure out every detail of a portion of My Plan you think you see coming together! Perhaps you are meant to recognize many signs, but My dear ones, allow Me, your God, to care for you now and in the so-near future especially.

THERE WILL BE LIFE-CHANGING EVENTS THAT WILL CAUSE GREAT UPHEAVAL AND MOVEMENT OF PEOPLE SEVERAL TIMES NOW ... FOLLOWED BY PERIODS OF MORE PRAYER, ADJUSTMENTS, GREAT CHANGES WITH NEW COMMUNITIES AND NEW EXTENDED FAMILIES GROWING OUT OF THE CHAOS AND INTO A SEMBLANCE OF ORDER AND PEACE. FEAR WILL LESSEN AND FAITH GROWS STRONGER, AS YOU SEE PORTIONS OF MY PLAN 'WORKING!!!' THE WORLD WILL BE AT WAR DURING MOST OF THE PERIOD OF WAITING

FOR MY JESUS TO RETURN. BUT MY FAITHFUL REMNANT WILL WORK AND PRAY AND STRUGGLE WITH ALL THE NEWLY BAPTIZED AND CONVERTED ONES WHO WILL ALSO LIVE IN JOYFUL HOPE AMIDST CHAOS AND ENORMOUS CHANGE, WHILE THE ANTICHRIST (WITH SATAN) SEEMS TO ENJOY CONTINUED VICTORIES. YOU HAVE BEEN TOLD YEARS AGO THAT THIS IS HOW IT WILL BE .... AND SO IT ARRIVES BEFORE YOUR VERY EYES, BROUGHT ABOUT BY THE ATTEMPT TO CAPTURE AND SUBDUE THE WORLD BY THE PROPONENTS OF ONE WORLD ORDER AND GOVERNMENT, RELIGION AND CULTURAL DEVELOPMENT; WHICH WILL ALL REALLY BE OPPRESSION UNDER SATAN'S PLAN WITH EVIL MEN. PRAY, CHILDREN, FOR EACH OTHER. Oh pray for your children and all children of Christian families, that they will accept My mercy and the cleansing action of Reconciliation after the Warning"

1-29, "My dearest ones, I am the Holy Spirit of God, the Spirit of all the graces and gifts you receive. Again I bring you new ability to speak out; new ability to be comfortable while leading the people who will come to you; new ability to have compassion on them, to put yourselves in their place, to nurture them with your interest in them, with your care for them, with all you do to make it possible for them to pray better, to be more comfortable while praying, to be more comfortable in their neediness. A gracious host and hostess see to the needs of their guests or those under their charge. You will be in charge! It will be your home they will be visiting. It will be your compassion and generosity they will be accepting, that will be healing them, through which they will be experiencing the compassion, the thoughtfulness, the generosity, the gentleness of God! I mention these things to alert you once again to the fact **that you are not just coming together to pray in these days; but to learn, to practice to become leaders, to become the strength these people will need; and so I bring new strength once again.** I bring you the awareness, the attention that you will bring to what is going on at every moment in these gatherings, so that you will always know what to do and what to say at the right time, so that you will be aware of the needs, again I say, of terribly needy people! You show your love for them by how you care for them, just as your Triune God does for you. There is never a moment that goes by that you are not in the consciousness of God, and so you can bring this level of service to all the people who gather. It will be a most trying experience at first. Everyone will be stumbling. Everyone will be learning. Everyone will be counting on you, depending upon you, thus the need for practice, for being open to Me, your Holy Spirit Who brings you strength and all the gifts you need at these times.

Alertness and awareness are a state of being by which you are able to minister to people at your very best; but practice is what allows you to do this, to come to that place. Because you have prayed together in a certain way for so long, you no longer pay attention or think about what you are doing. It is automatic, and then **suddenly you will be in a whole new environment, in a whole new place with new people. This sounds frightening**. This sounds perhaps like something you couldn't do; but I tell you, you can and you will do whatever is needed, most especially, My dear ones, when you practice!! **Remember the team that wins is the one who practiced the most! You are a team, a mighty fighting team.** Try not to resist change in your heart because it is **change most of all that you are facing in the future.** Jesus has reminded you that the human body resists change as it would an invading virus. How strong is that, My children? And **so you must learn to be flexible for GOD'S sake, for the sake of hundreds of people who will need you, who are so grateful for you.** Remember, My children, gratitude enables more gifts to be given, so praise and thank the Father whatever is happening, however good or however difficult something might be; and you know that you can learn because you always do and you always have and you always will; and you are loved so mightily by all of Heaven, and you will be loved so mightily by all of these poor people who will be so dependent upon you! I bring you the love of the Triune God. I bring you every strength and grace you need. I bring you victory once again. I bring you hope that you might be people of hope, signs of hope, a sign of light, a sign of the promise of the Father. Protect each other now with your prayers. I speak to you everywhere in the world once again with all of My words today. Be filled with the peace of Jesus, My dear ones. Continue with your growth, with your practice, with your victory. You are beloved of the Father. Amen."

2/5, "My dear ones, I am your Holy Mother Mary, filled with delight and gratitude to be with you in this way. My children, the struggle is becoming greater! I not only know this from Our God, but I see it in your hearts and in your minds and spirits, your very souls. The Father has allowed greater trials in your life, a taunting by the evil one to creep in after all these years. I come to tell you that I am praying for you individually and as a group here; individually and for groups in the entire world that you might persevere. I had mentioned to you years ago that perseverance would be the most difficult virtue to practice and, indeed you see it is. It is now when you must get tough with yourselves, My children; when you stand up and let the Lord know that you will make every effort to be faithful, every effort to be the true warriors you are becoming and are created to be; that you will give all your efforts when you pray; that you will speak out, realizing **that prayer is not about yourself**. It is not only for you, but it is for those who need it the most.

This IS a battle; so of course, you will battle with yourself: the self that seeks more for self; the self that is still spoiled, that is still eager for gifts, for signs, for special feelings, for special gifts of special prayer. Remember the backbone of steel that I wish to build within you. Think not about yourselves, I beg of you. As you persevere, you must think more of others. Lay down your lives for them. Lay down your perceived needs, the little candy kisses you hope for, you look for, that are not a part of true valor, of true giving and sharing, the events of true battle. As you war against 'self', you will see greater changes within yourselves, changes for the good; but you must NOT JUST SIT AND EXPECT THEM TO BE GIVEN, BUT ASK THE HOLY SPIRIT FOR AN INCREASE

OF STRENGTH; AN INCREASE OF THE ABILITY TO PERSEVERE, OF THE ABILITY TO SPEND EACH TIME YOU GATHER, EACH TIME YOU PRAY ALONE, EACH TIME YOU READ SCRIPTURE TO BRING A GREATER ATTENTION, A GREATER EFFORT TO THESE TIMES, FOR THESE ARE THE TIMES WHEN YOU ARE USING THE WEAPONS YOU HAVE BEEN GIVEN!

You know that the evil one accelerates his plans when you are being distracted more, when you are praying with less fervor, less attention. It is so throughout the world. Please remember you are always loved. Please remember that those who pray are fewer in number, and yes, We do request more of you! It is so among officers in an army. You are all mighty warriors, and when you are raised in the level of the Father's Plan, you are as officers whose rank is increased! Who must learn more about leading. Who must take to heart this new call upon you, this new level of leadership, of practice, of commitment joyfully, eagerly; preparing to lead those who come knowing nothing. Who have known no God, no grace, no Holy Mother, no sweetness! I pour my sweetness into you now, my warriors throughout the world. Know that I am always praying for you with all the Angels and Saints and all of Heaven every moment. DO NOT GIVE UP! PERSEVERE! BE MIGHTY WARRIORS, THE ONES I CALL YOU TO BE! WE SHALL SURVIVE IN LOVE, MY CHILDREN. We shall survive BECAUSE OF LOVE! Rejoice!"

2/12, "My beloved children, I am your God and Father here with you, pouring out graces, pouring out the healing you desire, the healing I desire for you. My dear ones, I come in love, I come in peace, to call you to the peace of My Jesus this day; peace at every moment in your lives that you might not argue with each other, especially with those closest to you. There is another way, there is not only compromise, but there is gentleness that needs to come into a conversation of differences. I have told you and explained the condition of the people who will come to you. They will need the utmost of diplomacy, if you will, the utmost of patience, of choosing just the right words to handle a tense situation: a delicate situation that may be fueled with fear on the part of one who has just arrived, on one who is frightened and feeling ill at ease, feeling strange and uncomfortable, feeling out of place. Remember you will be with these people as their leader, as the one who is thoughtful of everyone present, seeing to them as the mother hen does her little chicks. There is so much for you to think about. There is much awareness of others to develop in each of you. There is much awareness of the needs of others, of taking turns, of waiting for the needs of others to surface, of checking on the comfort level of all present, on a **discomfort that might develop in the midst of prayer which would then take precedence over your needs, over your attention.**

You must learn to be alert at all times in order to deal with the many people who will come. It is about a comfort level as well, to overcome your own niche in a prayer group which is so comfortable, which is so automatic that you are hardly paying attention. This must be overcome by the mother hen in each one who will be a leader. Do not think it is something you cannot do but **something you were born to do,** not only for people who have never come to your home before, but who have come in misery, terribly needy, still frightened, still totally out of place in their hearts and minds. Please reflect upon these words, My dear ones everywhere in the world. A listening heart is needed by a leader, perhaps more than anything. It will be your home to which they come. It will be your home in which you will make them comfortable, tend to their needs, make them comfortable with clothing, with something on which to sleep, not a bed surely after a while; but on the floor, every available space, sometimes somewhere outside in a yard, in a garage, in a shed, an attic, and in basements. This preparation should certainly aid your spring cleaning! Always when you keep large numbers of supplies, those supplies must be checked now and then, when you are able. **More water is always in order, drinking water or utility water, a means to purify this water.** There are lists of things to have on hand as you become more serious once again about gathering supplies.

Look around your own home for what it is that you use every day, that you would know they would need everyday. This call can be answered by each of you, not elaborately or in huge numbers of supplies, but some, My children; and most of all with every bit of your heart, every inch, every corner, every bit of your energy; and again I say all of who you are, and most of all, all who you are becoming. It must be serious for you, My children, although it has been requested for years. As I have said before, **there will come a time when the need will be now: instantaneous**. You will not want to go into this situation unprepared or unpracticed. Know that My words come from My concerns for you as My children, as My leaders, as My warriors; but also as a concern for those who come to you, for they will be the needy ones, they will be the ones who need your help. Pray for them My children everywhere. Pray for them now. Do not forget them! Do not allow distractions to get in your way of focusing on the needs of the world and remembering that every event we have mentioned through messengers all over the world will be fulfilled. My children are you asking, pleading, begging for mercy, for salvation on the world? Think of it. Together we have mercy on the world, always in union with My Jesus together. Take care of each other. Think about each other kindly, patiently with understanding, with peace. I love you. Please believe and feel and experience this more than ever this very day: the love of your God. It is what maintains your life!"

2-19, "My dearest children, I am your Jesus of Mercy. I am your Jesus of Healing and Hope. I am your ALL, My children. You need nothing else and no one else, although you need each other! You need the people the Father will send into your lives and has sent already. You need the love from them and for them that softens your own heart; that teaches you to love selflessly as I love you; that puts their needs before your own. My dear children everywhere in the world, I appeal to you once again to love each other and first to love yourselves. You cannot heal others until you yourselves are as healed as the Father desires for each of you. More than anything, that healing contains and your love contains a warmth, a compassion, a reaching out in understanding and support for each other. You have grown so mightily, as We have told you, and there is always more growth needed and expected and requested by the Father because, as you love more, you grow into Love more, so as you know, God is Love! You are growing into God, into being God-like, into being like Me, the Beloved Son, the Lamb Who was sacrificed, the Bread and Wine: the Eucharist on whom all will feed and depend, as My Apostles, My Disciples and all who followed Me learned first hand.

YOU HAVE ME FIRST HAND, MY CHILDREN! You have Me with you at every moment, standing next to you at every moment, desiring your success, your progress, your victory; desiring you to become more like Me and less like the person you are of the world. THIS is the Father's Will for you. THIS is what you are called to do and to be and to become: like Me, My children, a humble child of the Father, Who does the Father's Will before My own. Most especially, you heard that, when I was on the earth the first time: 'Not My Will, Father; but Thy Will be done': is always the cry of one who follows Me, and there must be a cry, a banner, a slogan under which you live, something that defines you to yourself first and then to others; not in words of course, but in deed; not in a showy, flashy way, but leading. You know and recall this is very important to remember when all the people who are refugees, (as orphans) such needy ones will gather and learn to pray with you. They will never have prayed before, so they will need your voices at every moment to be strong in leadership of prayer and song: to not only minister to their bodily needs, but their spiritual needs, which are more important, and a relationship and a friendship and an understanding with your God, your Triune God, which happens through prayer.

When you teach and lead, My children, you do so with a voice that can be heard. You know that My voice rang out clearly and strongly over the five thousand gathered; that a teacher speaks up, speaks out, makes sure everyone present can hear; speaks and prays with enthusiasm, meaning every word; speaking and praying from your heart, the first condition of authentic prayer. It must involve your heart, My children, not just repetition, not using prayer time as a good time to rest, although rest is sorely needed by all those who follow Me; and you know and I know that I am right with you at every moment. No, you cannot touch Me tangibly and yet I tell you, I AM a tangible God! You can touch Me most of all in the Eucharist; in each other, but also in each other's needs, in each other's sorrows, in each other's weaknesses, as you have patience and forgiveness and understanding for them. It is a wonderful dynamic to love! It causes such beauty and change in the heart and souls and actions, and mind and spirit and even facial expression of those who love. So I remind you again, as We begin to prepare for the great Season of Lent, that you are called at this time, as always, but more than ever to focus on what it takes to love: all of who you are, children, all of your energy for each other and with each other for the Father.

Come, My children. Come to Me and learn. Come and be transformed by My love for you, that you might respond by loving as I do all the people in the world; but most especially those nearest you, those around you, the people who come into your lives. Remember, how much practice is necessary and then of course, remember that you are being loved into this time, into every moment! Remember that you are kept alive by the supporting love of the Father for each of you. KEEP EACH OTHER ALIVE WITH YOUR LOVE, WITH YOUR CONCERN AND YOUR CARE FOR THEM! Love each person in the world into new life, perhaps to even learn to live for the first time! HOW EXCITING FOR YOU. HOW LIFE CHANGING AND LIFE-GIVING FOR THEM! I love you, My dear ones. Words are so inadequate that I tell you, and you hear this and you feel this in your hearts and in your lives through Reconciliation, through forgiveness, through patience and compassion and all the gifts your Triune God pours out upon you, making your life livable, worth living, worth loving! Let us love each other!"

2-26, "My dear ones, I am your Mother of Sorrows. I come with a heart filled with sorrow today. I come pleading with you to pray for your country, most especially to pray for those who used to pray, who used to listen and who do not at this time. I ask you to pray for re-conversion, a new response in the hearts of everyone who prays, a return to your FIRST LOVE of my Son and of me**, to the fire of your first response to my call!** Remember those days: the excitement, the focus of your prayer, the firm commitment within your hearts! I speak to my children everywhere in the world. Prayer always calls for re-commitment. Those who follow my Jesus must faithfully and continually renew their hearts, their minds and spirits, their promises to follow and believe in the promises of the Father. Always a renewal is needed by everyone in every Age… often, and for this, ATTENTION must be paid to your prayer, to what is going on in your life, to the new struggles, to the sinfulness which continues to make itself known and recognized by each of you. It is so very important that you know yourselves; and this first and foremost contains the knowledge of your weaknesses, of your sinfulness, of your chronic sins, the little ways in which you do not pay attention, in which you let your mind wander during prayer, in which you forget the call of the Father to you personally as His warrior: needing you and all of your gifts, needing your recommitment often that you might return to the fire that always accompanies a new conversion and remember, conversion occurs all through your lives, always at new levels you are raised higher in the Father's plan, but in His call to you and your response to Him. IT IS A LIFE WORK, a life gift, a gift that renews life always and often! I thank you again and again for loving me. Thank you for loving my Jesus. Thank you for listening each week, for re-reading the words you are given, for they are making you, turning you into who you are created to be, to become! They are guiding you.

I am the Morning Star! Allow me to light your way each day more closely into the Sacred Heart of my Son. I am the Morning Star! Allow me to light your way into the Light, into Life, into holiness, into joy. I am the Morning Star. I have been given to you as your strength, your protectress, your companion, your

Mother: lighting your way into the Light of Christ, my Son. We have said for many years to each of you who prays, this Lent is the most important and powerful you will ever live! Each year there is a truer and more powerful call for your response. Become excited about the opportunities to impact the world. Become more grateful, more filled with praise. Always praising the Father helps you to think of Him constantly, realizing that He sustains you constantly in His love and His power, in Our presence with you, with all the gifts the Father has given to you to this point. Faithful is your name!

I am the Morning Star, my children. I come to light your way. Live in the glow of my love for you. We go forward together into a time of Penance, into a time of giving up little things that please you, into a time of more thoughtful reflection upon the world and its terrible condition. The events occurring everywhere, the threats, the dangers DO increase! Remember this when you pray. As you pray for mercy on every individual in the entire world, you are helping them. You are bringing me to them with your love, with your prayers. Be healed in the Name of my Son, Jesus, this day in a new way, to a new degree. Be lifted higher in the Father's plan this day. Let us love each other!"

3-5, "My dear ones, I am your Mother of Sorrows. I am here once again pleading with you to pray for the world. You see events unfolding from within your country, instigated by your government: by your President, by people of authority who are, as I had told you, being goaded by people in the background who are fomenting war; who are fomenting the schedule of the One World order, the plans of Satan to conquer the world, to render your country more vulnerable, to render you someday **helpless and under the power of foreign governments**. Do not be surprised at these words, for they are not new; but you must remember them because you watch events develop on the international scene, on your own horizon, you see mighty change in the offing, and you know that prayer is more important than ever. (It is more important) that you pray with your hearts, not when you feel like it, or remember to do it, or happen to be feeling serious or focused on a particular day; but overcoming yourself, your selfishness, and realizing that prayer is for others, and **your greatest attention will bring the greatest power from your prayers and take the focus off yourself.**

My children, we are at war NOW! Most of you are too young to remember what this country was like during what is called the Great War, the Second World War. People's thoughts and every action was geared toward safety and peace on the home front, supporting the soldiers and war effort wherever it was, realizing that a certain amount of secrecy must be kept so as not to give away plans or secrets to the enemy, who had agents everywhere. TODAY THERE ARE AGENTS OF THE ANTICHRIST EVERYWHERE, AND YOU MUST BE ON GUARD; BUT MOSTLY ON GUARD AGAINST FRIVOLITY, A FRIVOLOUS ATTITUDE, REALIZING THAT AS SOLDIERS, AS WARRIORS YOU, OF ALL PEOPLE IN THE WORLD, ARE ON THE FRONT LINES NOW WITH THE SOLDIERS WHO FIGHT WITH ACTUAL

WEAPONS OF DESTRUCTION. YOUR ROSARY, YOUR ADORATION, READING OF SCRIPTURE ARE ACTUAL WEAPONS OF DESTRUCTION AGAINST EVIL; AND THEY ARE AS EFFECTIVE IN YOUR HANDS AS THE ATTENTION YOU GIVE THEM!

A good soldier keeps his weapons clean, working properly, paying attention to orders from the Commander, realizing that a group effort is the one that will win the day! Joy is the umbrella under which you pray and live and move and have your being with everyone in the world who prays. Be aware that it is a world-wide effort with these others with whom you join your prayers. Be aware that we are reminded again and again that Satan will be given many victories, and it will be more difficult to persevere in your positive attitude for victory, for victory will seem elusive and later on, LOOK IMPOSSIBLE!

You practice now, so you can be people of immense hope for those who have none, for those who know nothing of perseverance in the Father's Will, who know nothing of the Father's Will; but who will as helplessly depend upon you (then) as you should realize you are called to do now upon Our God! You are hope for the world, My dear ones everywhere who listen and respond. Be encouragement in prayer, speaking out your prayer, singing out your songs as songs of hope, as signs of trust and faith in the promises of the Father: to take your prayers, more powerful all the time, and one day defeat Satan and all evil completely. Thank the FATHER FOR THAT! ASK THE HOLY SPIRIT FOR THIS NEED. PRAISE THE FATHER FOR THAT ANSWER, FOR THAT BLESSING, FOR THAT NEW INSIGHT, THAT NEW UNDERSTANDING OR WISDOM YOU HAVE JUST RECEIVED. It is ongoing, for your change is ongoing, your transformation. It must be! You have lived long enough, each of you, to realize that you are totally formed by the world as you begin the first time to pray, to respond to My call; so it takes a long time to allow yourselves to be changed from that person of the world. I know how much you want to be what the Father calls you to be, but it must be according to His Will, His plans for you. **Do not decide what you will be, what you will do!** Have openness to the Holy Spirit through Whom gift and grace are given. My dear ones, polish your weapons this week! Clean your garments. Press them between your prayers that you will be new and shining and an example of hope and joy and love-of-God (to all who see you) with no effort: not intending to be seen or noticed, but humbly just to be a sign of love and commitment to the call of Our God and to me, your Holy Mother, who loves you so much. We go forward now into a new time, new times, new directions, new levels of service, new hope. You are my precious children."

3-12, "My beloved ones, I am your Jesus of Mercy. I am your Crucified Lord. I sustain you in My Sacred Heart, My children everywhere in the world. Send your love and your comfort and healing prayers to the world. Pay attention to the weather patterns, My children. They are a sign and a fulfillment of My words to you this year. Pray for your country. Pray for your government. Pray about all of the things done in secret that they may continue to come into the light to bring people an understanding of all that is being done without your knowledge in the first place: **that any conditions without representation no longer exist in this once great democracy, in the freedom this country was given by the Father.** It is more serious than you know, My children: the condition of your country, the events about to break upon the shores of this once great land. Pray in unity, I ask you again, with those who suffer. I can only encourage you to continue to spend less and less time in a frivolous manner. Give up those favorite television programs for now, My children. What frivolous distractions they are!

Remember My suffering, that you might suffer with a greater ease, with greater meaning, with greater effect upon the suffering ones in the world. OUR UNITY IS EVERYTHING, My children: My Sacred Heart, the Immaculate Heart of My Mother and yours is everything. Think of others first. Practice this. Give up self-pity. Give up a lack of respect for each other. There are many ways you practice respect or disrespect that is immediately felt by others. With your hearts opened by grace and prayer, you have become more sensitive to the actions, to the thoughts and feelings of others, and so you suffer more because of this. Be thoughtful, My dear ones. Be careful of each other. Be careful FOR each other. Be caring for each other. How much love and healing you obtain for each other by these thoughtful actions. How much love and healing you obtain for yourselves by thoughtful actions and words and attitudes! Always, My children, attitudes need so much to be purified. Bring them to Me. I love you. Remember the victory is won, and it will be ours in unity! Be like Me, My children. BE ME. Thank you. I love you!"

3/19, "My very dear ones, I am the Holy Spirit of God, the spirit of your sanctification, the spirit of the new you, an enhanced Spirit, the spirit of all you do for God, the Spirit of your conversion, the One Who implores you silently in your heart to pray as often as you can, to be as consecrated to the Father's Will and plan of salvation for the world as you are able.; Who gives you new energy when your spirits are flagging. Who gives you new desire when prayer is requested, when you see someone in need, or helpless or feeling hopeless. Who inspires you with just the right words to lift them up. Who fills you with hope that you might be hope for others., that you might send the spirit of hope, your own spirits to the world, that you might think of others first, that you might pray for their needs before your own, that you might trust the Triune God and all of His promises, that you might let go of anxiety, of worries, of concerns about which you can really do nothing by yourself. Who encourages you to bring your worries, your needs, your weaknesses and your sinfulness to the Foot of the Cross. Who gives you the means of conversion in your own hearts. Who enables the graces given by the hand of the Holy Mother, My beloved Spouse that you might accept them and immediately employ them in your actions, in your service to others? Who prepares you to be the warrior you are becoming? All of these things, I do for you, My children, because I am Love. I am the love of God, but I am the love in your lives as well, that you might be the vehicle chosen by the Father to spread mercy throughout the world, to spread word of the Father's mercy, Jesus Christ, the

Divine Mercy of the Father. You belong to the greatest training ground in history, and you are winning this battle against self and against the evil one. All of Heaven rejoices for you this day. The great St Joseph showers you with new graces, new gifts, new ability to respond to Mary, the Immaculate One, who loves you beyond words. My dear, dear people, time is short. Time is running out, for this very year will see great change. Time is a gift. Use it well, My dear ones everywhere. People in this country of plenty, use your time well and wisely for the world, for the needy, suffering world. Amen to all of you and from all of Heaven, most especially dear Joseph (His feast day.. cta.). Remember his innocence, his humility, his great service to Jesus and Mary, and do also."

3/26, "I am Jesus, your Crucified Lord. I come to you this day with new strength and the gift of perseverance. Always during Lent or any time of difficulty, extraordinary prayer, fasting, penance, My people need renewal! I needed renewal along the way of Calvary! I received renewal from My Father many times when I went away by Myself in the desert to converse with Him, to pray. The Angels ministered to Me with new strength and perseverance and encouragement**. I give you each, My children everywhere in the world, an Angel of encouragement this day, a special Angel to be with you at every moment, to be a source of strength for you, to be a support above and beyond anything you have known before**. This, of course, is a time of preparation (for the time) when you will know greater want, greater suffering, a need for greater faith and trust. Remember that you have this Angel. Listen for the name of this Angel that you might converse directly and intimately with this precious one, a gift to you for these times, these very difficult times! Our Spirit is allowing you to see yourselves in a new and perhaps more difficult way, more clearly hear yourselves, more honestly experience your own weaknesses, but also your own failings, **your sharp responses where gentle words would do better, would do more for both you and the one you address.**

My children, it is difficult to continue. All of Heaven prays for you. It is one thing to hear about the love of Heaven, the love of your God and your holy Mother; but at the same time to be alone, to be suffering through some particular situation or condition. All of Heaven is aware of this with you. **All of Heaven IS with you.** Please accept the gift of openness to the realization and awareness of Our presence and Our prayers for you and Our love for you, Our loving support for you. **Slow down. Fatigue is your greatest enemy. Slow down!** Noise and chaos is next on the list of enemies that would rob you of your peace, of your ability to hear My voice to strengthen your awareness of Our presence when you are rushing here and there as, yes, you sometimes must do, I know. Think of the chaos that will exist when you are no longer living the lifestyle that you have always lived. A time for peace and silence: it will be beyond difficult! Please, slow down. Take walks in this beautiful weather, even if it's snowing. I have said that before. It will always be a good idea! Breathe deeply of Our really, truly, loving, nurturing and strengthening presence**. Most of you will see My return!**

Remember why you are doing all of these things, why you are praying so much. Remember the changes in your future, in the world, great changes. Think about them as the reason you are living and doing and praying and being and suffering. My return will be glorious. Our victory will be glorious. My children, I only can encourage you to continue as you are, to get more rest. Do not be the cause of your lack of strength and perseverance, for then you are cooperating with the evil one and his plans. I am always with you; and you are healing when you allow me to heal you, and you are becoming stronger warriors. Be brave! Warriors are brave. You are becoming brave warriors! We shall overcome; and peace and purity will flourish in the world, a world of beauty and holiness and joy and peace. It WILL be, My children, because we will do this together. My Mother and I bless you. We are with you."

4-2, "My very dear children, I am your Mother, the Immaculate One of God and your holy, holy companion. Another reason We ask you to concentrate on Our presence with you is that you become more aware of the fact that you are surrounded with holiness. Not only an increase of your own; but the fact that my Son and I and many Angels surround you means that Our holiness accompanies you at every moment. This is a beautiful and sobering and important thought for you, another meditation and another reason to be grateful. Holiness is something that you wear, as well as practice. You know what I mean by that immediately. It is not a pious, affected way of being or dressing or looking or sounding. It is to be perfectly natural, to be approachable, to make people comfortable, to let them know that you are happy to see them, to be joyful in their presence, to be gracious, to watch what you say. Unkind or unpleasant or hurtful words must never cross your lips now or forever again. Think of Our Presence. This will be a great assistance to your climbing the mountain of holiness of the Father. As you become more accustomed to walking and being in Our presence, gratitude and humility, a quieter way of being will naturally develop within you. Again I say this must **not be an affected way of being or what you would think you should sound like or look like; but a thoughtful way of being, a new awareness of the environment in which you live.** This is contagious, My children; and it is a good contagion. It is a good attitude and environment to share, to allow to spread throughout the world, throughout your day, to everyone you meet. Be more interested in them and in Us than you are in yourself; and you know what I mean by that immediately also! Your sincerity is obvious to people as well as your insincerity to anyone. Do you have a name for your Angel yet, to help you persevere, to allow you to accept new strengths? All of these things can be part of your meditations, your thoughts, your reflections in the coming week. Perhaps others will notice a change within you.

If you are treating each other very kindly and thoughtfully, it will bring out the goodness and the grace within each of you. Think about that, My dear ones. It is the way of the Father's plan of transformation of each one of His children in the whole world. As you allow grace to come through you and to flow from your lips and your actions and your attitudes, you will be more healed, more comfortable, as well as comforting, more aware of the needs of others, their own sufferings, **and so your focus can be more easily on them instead of yourself.** This is certainly a sign of growth and a means of growth in your spiritual life as well as your social life. You will be much more pleasant to be around, much more delightful company, much more healing in your own presence.

My children, although I was born without sin and I was always sinless, I was always aware of attitudes within people and of difficulties in relationships. It led me to pray for the people involved in a particular exchange. I always had the ability to hear the sorrow, the suffering, and to feel the pain within each person I met. It is greater than ever for me now, this awareness, in my close and intimate relationship with each one of you. I see your pain. I see the reason for your sufferings. This will happen more and more for you, and you will be more at peace, I tell you. You will know more joy and true happiness: what it is truly like to live in the Kingdom of God on earth as it is in Heaven. Some of you live in very difficult surroundings, environments filled with at least one or maybe many very difficult people. Again, I speak to everyone in the world. Pray for them, my dear ones who do not know this sorrow, this struggle. Pray for each other and progress in this journey toward the Father's perfection for you. Do not try so hard to have all the answers or to even find the answers to your many questions! Concentrate now on just being in Our Presence always, every moment. Spend this week with joy and happiness at the new thoughts and meditations and awareness you are being given today. Amen."

4/09, "My dearest children, it is I once again, your Holy Mother, your sorrowful Mother, your very loving Mother who walks with you, inviting you now to walk with me. This is a serious invitation. It is a serious and huge gift for each one of you who accepts this, to spend this entire week in meditation and as much quiet as possible. You say you will do this, and then once again so easily you become caught up with the world, and the demands, and the routine, the way you have always done things; and I ask you to do my will, my requests in a new way, to be with me, to listen for my voice most especially this week; to write down each thing I tell your heart, to walk in my presence and my love. You will know sorrow, as you have not felt it before. You will know a longing to end the suffering of Jesus as you have never known it before. You will know love for my Jesus and for me as never before. You will know love for each other and appreciation of each other's gifts and prayers, for those who provide for you, for those who have gone out of their way to serve you, to be patient with you, to be thoughtful and gracious and generous with their time and prayers and with themselves; for all of those in the world who pray for you, for those who have gone beyond, ahead of you to smooth the way for you with their prayers, with their dying, with their suffering, with their love. There are many like this, many you know nothing about; so pray for everyone with an open mind and heart, those who have gone before you not knowing the contribution they have made to your life personally, to your sanctity, your strength, your perseverance and the consecration you make daily.

All of Heaven is consecrating you daily, especially this holiest week of your Church year. Realize how the very life of Jesus, the very person of Jesus is the reason for your life, the center of your existence, the guiding light, the motivation, the power behind every good you do. Appreciate my beloved Spouse, Who sanctifies your actions and your prayers, all you are becoming; Who strengthens you to do more, always more, becoming that soldier for the greatest battle in history which each one of you will fight together arm in arm, heart in heart, united to my Jesus and to me, to the Godhead and to all the people in the world, especially those who do not pray. Carry them this week. They are your Cross! Bring yourselves each day, each moment to the possibility of that moment desired by the Father: known only to the Father, blest by the Father, chosen especially for you each moment by the Father.

Your commitment is serious and should become more so by the end of this week, spent in such a special way answering the requests of Heaven, my requests, too, my dear ones. Know that I am spending every moment not only at the foot of the Cross, but before the Throne of the Father, uniting you in my heart and to the Perfect Will of Our God and Father. You are blest beyond your comprehension, beyond anything you might earn or deserve! Even in answer to your requests and your desires, nothing could touch (i.e. compare to…cta.) the desire of the Father for your good, your holiness, your spiritual growth, your success and victory in His Will. It becomes more difficult now to focus on my Jesus' face. His face becomes bloodied and beyond recognition. His flesh is torn. His blood is lost, ultimately, totally for you; and only the shell of His body remains. Embrace Him, as you unite to this Passion. He is embracing you. He is thanking you for all you do to ease His present pain, His present suffering as well, at the dreadful conditions in the world. My dear ones, I give you my strength. I hold out my hands to you, to embrace you. I love you. You are my own. I am with you. You are with me!"

4-23, "My very dear children, I am your Jesus of Mercy, come here with delight in My Heart, with as much gratitude as you can carry for the special week you have spent in this Novena of Divine Mercy, praying for My requests as given to dear Faustina. I pour out unimagined mercy and gifts upon you this day and to My children everywhere in the world. Thank you for the serious approach you bring to prayer for sinners and for the world. You are increased in the gift of mercy, increased in the gifts you need to be the instrument of mercy to Our people. Think of yourselves in that way every day. I am an instrument of the mercy of God, My Father. I am the Instrument of Mercy for the world; and, of course, most especially for those around Me and closest to Me. O My children, this week was the kind of prayer Heaven hopes for, a united prayer, a begging the Father for mercy upon the entire world. Dear Faustina, who is here with Me, blesses you this day in the Name of My Father and in My Name and the Name of Our Holy Spirit. You have her love and gratitude. Know this for certain, My children."

4/30, "My dearest ones, I am your Immaculate Mother, here with you to give praise to God, Our Father; in thanksgiving for the Divine Mercy of the Father, My precious Son, Jesus; in honor of the Holy Spirit, my beloved Spouse, and in thanksgiving and joy for all of you in the entire world who will be honoring me this special month of May; who will be gaining new gifts and graces through my hands and my intercession for you; who will be rising higher in the Father's plan; who will be offering your hearts in new ways to me and through my heart to the Triune God.

Again, I bring you news of great destruction in the world and in your country, and ask you to pray for your country and for all countries, many of whom are being betrayed by their very leaders. It is a dreadful time for the weak, the poor, the disenfranchised, the forgotten people of the world. Entire groups of people will be taken into eternity in some of these events. Pray for their souls that as always, we would ask for the grace that they embrace the mercy of the Father and choose for His Kingdom while repenting of their sins, and then to praise and thank the Father for the mercy freely given to these poor lost ones. Remember that you pray in reparation for their sins, my children: so many things, so many people to pray for. I bring you new strength for prayer today. Please be aware of my presence with you always, giving you strength, support, holding you up when you think you cannot walk another step from fatigue. This is a mere shadow of the fatigue of the future. Pray for yourselves for that time, that you will not succumb to the fatigue, to the chaos, to the lack of understanding in everyone that will worry you at first. **'How', you will say, 'am I to explain to all of these people', and then it will be, 'how can I explain these things one more time to all of these people?'** I bring you special graces now for all of those times of struggle and wonder and questioning, feeling faint at the prospect of more people, of more events, of more struggle and sadness and need among them. My children, recall that we are so very united now through your faithful prayers, through the love for me that has grown in your hearts with the help of my beloved Spouse, the Most Holy Spirit of God.

Remember that Our God is Love. He will never want for love for all of these people, **some of whom will come to you before major events because of smaller events**; and, so I urge you to be on guard once again against the turning away, against any division within your hearts, a lack of support for each other. My children, as always, all will be well, and very, very truly, my dear ones, all is well. Let us praise and thank the Father together this very week for all of the gifts and special graces given to all of you faithful to your Novena, the prayers of Holy Week, the devotions, the special focus you placed on the sufferings of my Divine Son that bring you so many more graces, as you dwell in His sufferings with

Him. Allow this to continue in your prayer, in your reflections, in your life, dear ones everywhere in the world. It is the means of so much power, power that you will need: conversion that all of you still need and yet, all is well! Stay close to me, little ones, as I stay close to you. Be grateful to the Father. Give great thanks, my dear children, for you are greatly blessed. Rejoice!"

5/07, "My very, very dear children, I am your Mother of Sorrows and Joy, a Mother who never leaves you for an instant, a Mother who loves you beyond your ability to comprehend. I come this day with new sadness at the terrible crimes against nature everywhere, at the attacks upon innocent people, at the increase of abuse against children and infants, against the terrible murder of infants in their mother's wombs. O my dear ones, we must pray more strongly, more fervently against these terrible crimes against humanity; against the original plan of Our Father, the Creator of all life; against the sanctity of life. If you would work this week at having more respect for each other, especially those who irritate you most; especially those who challenge you, who are impatient with you, who are obviously at odds with you. It has always been so that all of Our people are aware when others are at odds with them; and so, you can pray most truly and most seriously for those whom you know you have offended; those whom you make uncomfortable; those with whom you have been offensive; those with whom you have been impatient.

Your behavior is everything to another: to present the true Christ, to present a loving Mother, to present a merciful instrument of God, Our Father. It will make all the difference when the poor people who come to you in such agony cross your doorstep and take residence in your home, in your hearts, in your lives, and lifestyle. **This will not be for a long period of time; but still you will need to gather every bit of strength, every bit of goodness you have ever been shown,** you have ever received from Heaven: sweetness from my precious Jesus, sitting before Him in the Blessed Sacrament, absorbing His Spirit, absorbing more the Will of God Our Father, absorbing Mercy Itself in my Jesus! I beg of you to renew your hearts, renew your commitment, renew your consecration this week as you focus on respecting each other.

Each of you struggles with waiting; and so, impatience is natural. Each of you struggles with being different from the rest of the people in the world, which is God's Will for you, most certainly. Each of you struggles against temptation because Satan is allowed so much power now. Believe that each person in the world is made more irritable by Satan's desire, his deceptions and his plans for the world. I count on you so totally; and I speak to my faithful children everywhere in the world who will listen. Smaller numbers of those who pray are a greater call to you! Bring your fatigue, the lack of desire to pray that plagues you, and place it at the foot of the Cross, at the feet of my Jesus. We will overcome evil together. If we are not together, you are in greater danger than ever! Pray for those who have stopped praying. Hold them in your hearts as you adore my Son. They have loving hearts; just too much hurt in their own lives to remain patient, to surrender, to remain docile and pliable in the Father's hands. These are not repetitious words, my children. You are hearing them for the first time at this new level of sanctity that you enjoy, that you are given this day. Together, my children, we ARE together! Let us remain together. Believe all my words. When you see destruction, when you see terror, you will believe. I love you, my dear ones, as I always tell you. You are my precious little ones. Believe these words!"

5/14, "My beloved children, I am your Jesus of Mercy, Son of God the Father, Son of Mary Immaculate, Virgin and Queen. My children, I speak this day to you to give praise and honor to My Mother, to give thanksgiving, appreciation for Her presence in My life as I know you are giving all honor to Her and gratitude for Her presence in yours. Even if you cannot feel a great appreciation, know that it is the greatest honor you have received and the greatest help outside of My own Eucharist and My Presence in your heart. She is the greatest gift you have received on the earth, especially in this present journey more deeply into the Will of the Father. My children, is she not wonderful? Is she not so precious to your hearts, as she is to Mine? Are we not grateful for her and all she obtains for you? Believe Me, My dear ones, her prayers and intercession in union with the might of the Father's arm and His Will are what sustains you in this call by the Father to be mercy for the world. My children, you are very, very close to very, very serious events. I know that many of you can feel this in your hearts; that you are beyond being frightened by words like this; that you will take it as a reminder to pray every second you have (that is free), that you are able to offer to God, the Father, for the safety of the whole world.

When you see these events, you will know why We have talked to you, requested of you for so long more and more and more prayer; and spoken of the difficult conditions of living in so many areas of the world. It is always the poor who suffer the most, as We have mentioned. You are aware of this; and so you have prayed for them, especially those who have no one, those who think they are alone, although they are not. I cannot tell you of the gratitude of My Mother for you. She has mentioned this every time she speaks to you. I see it from a perspective of the Triune God; and all of her gifts that have enabled her to be so much, and so dear, and so necessary for your own salvation: her companionship, her strength. How she pleads for you, My children, before the throne of My Father and yours. This is such a great gift you are given, that you have this intercessor, this co-redeemer, co-mediatrix, co-advocate before the Father.

Thank you for your faithfulness to her. Believe it when I say it warms her heart. It fills her with gratitude. You give her hope; although she knows the outcome as well as you do, and the end of evil and Satan and his followers. As she has reminded you, a human heart beats within her; and so, you give that heart hope! You could not be loved more tenderly than she loves you. You could not have anyone 'rooting' for you more, in your corner, on your side, at your beck and call with every gift she has been given. Praise the Father in thanksgiving for her, My dear ones. Give all of your spare time to her, listening for her voice. Give your prayers to her that she might distribute them according to her desire. Give her all your love, all of your energy, all of the compassion she has given to you. Spread this compassion among all her children, whomever you meet, and be joyful. Again, joy is that wonderful state of mind and spirit that reflects her so well, so totally; and by which you touch hearts in the best possible way. Remember her backbone of steel! Practice that, My children. Again, I say praise and thank the Father for her on this wonderful day when you all honor your earthly mothers. Wherever they are, unite them to her heart in a new way as your gift to your mothers.

Rejoice, My children, all over the world. Thank you for listening, for still following her requests and ours. All of Heaven prays with you this day in thanksgiving for the Virgin Mother. All of Heaven is feasting on her behalf, singing hosannas, singing songs of praise. Join them in your minds and hearts. You are very, very close at this moment to the Kingdom of God in Heaven. Believe these words. You have prayed and remained faithful through struggle and sorrow, fatigue and hard work. This is a special gift to you now. Remember, you have a Mother that will never ever leave you or betray you. Let us continue this entire week giving thanks for her, coming closer to her, availing yourself of the gifts she wishes to give you. Thank you for taking this time out of your own busy day to be here to pray for the world in such great danger. Amen, children, I love you so much. Amen."

5/21, "My dear ones, I am your God and your Father, your Creator and your Lord. I bring the joy of Heaven this day for the beauty of your hearts, the sincerity of the prayers this day, of the reverence and devotional and beautiful sacrifice of the Mass that was offered at which all of Heaven attended. I give you each other in a new and different way, so I am asking you to rejoice in each other as given to you in a more heartfelt way. You are responsible for your family, and so for each other. Pray for each other's ongoing conversion that you might be ready to do whatever is required of you by Myself and each one who comes to you. Never will we stop preparing for this time, because always you will need renewal and strength, new hope and new trust. You will need patience and all the virtues every day and sometimes every moment because remember, these poor lost ones will not know Me! In many instances they will be in the deepest sorrow from loss of loves ones and property and the way of life they always knew. Remember how impatient they will be. Remember how difficult patience is for you and how most important is this virtue for each one of you. Beg our Spirit for the gift of patience.

I am proud of you as My children, as My warriors in the Army of the Blessed Virgin Mary whom we honor this month and this day. How close she is to each one of you, yes holding you in her heart, holding you by the hand and leading you through each event, each new trial, each new formation that leaves you more able to serve, to be obedient, to surrender, to fill with joy no matter what occurs within your lives. These are not easy things to do without focusing on the suffering of My Son, you could never continue without opening your hearts to the suffering of My Son. You could never allow them to be reflective within your own lives without the presence of My Son, within your hearts and at your side. You would fall away never more to return.

Think of the tragedies that are avoided because of My Son and your precious Jesus. He is your All in all, My children. He is everything to you and to Me. I love you so much more than words could ever express. I am so grateful for you, remember this, believe it. Your Triune God rejoices for your presence in My plan. All of Heaven rejoices for you and for the gifts that are given to you along the way. You are prepared; and when the next major event occurs in this country, do not seek to run! **Do not be worried that you will be held by the grief and the fright that grabs you at first, for very soon all these gifts and graces will take over, will return you to the calm collected composed warrior that you are at this moment.** We have many battles to fight together! Some will not seem to be victorious, **but it is the last battle that is already won which you must claim,** to which you must look forward in hope and in trust. I bless you. I strengthen you. I heal you this day in the way down deep and hidden things, My children. I heal you and I give you the gifts I know you need. I love you, My dear ones. I call you forth to be ready at any moment to serve and I thank you for loving Me, for all of your special prayers that honor Me. I share the might of My arm with you this day and all who pray in the world. Pray for each other. How you need each other! I have enjoyed being with you like this. I have enjoyed listening to your prayers, seeing your beauty reflected in your upturned faces and in your words of petition of faith and gratitude. Amen, little ones, we are so united this day."

6/4, "My dear and faithful ones, I am the Holy Spirit of God. I thank you for praying to Me this day in a special way, on this special occasion of My feast. The entire Communion of Saints, the entire Church of God is joined this day in special graces and new strength poured out by My hand. Rejoice and give thanks and praise, dear people of God, for it is a special day for you, too. It is a day in which you are empowered by My gifts and graces, by special gifts for each of you. Different from each other, but according to the Father's Will for your particular gifts, your particular personality and Image of God that you were created to be. My dear ones, pray for each other.

The enemy of God and all the Holy Ones, the enemy of the Church of Jesus in the line of the Apostles mounts tremendous attack. You are feeling the attack in particular weaknesses and particular vulnerabilities in these days. All of Heaven brings you thanksgiving and gratitude. All of Heaven brings you new joy, new strength and fire through My hands today for they have been praying for this for each of you; a new respect in each other's lives and behavior that you have practiced, that you have thought about and prayed about. This is so important for your preparation for those who will come to you through My hands and through My power and guidance. Patience, too, My dear ones, is poured out this day because still you struggle with irritability and impatience. It is a sign of pride, My dear ones. It is a sign of the special need of new healing in this area. Only love will conquer, patient love, patient listening, patient tending to wounded hearts and spirits, patience of a kind that is God-like. Think of how Our Father has been patient with each of you and continues to do so. This battle with self, dear children of God, will not end until you are entering Heaven.

When you live in your own world consumed by your own needs or the events in your life, you have no time or room for others. Believe Me, My people, you need to make time in your hearts, in your minds and spirits, in your will, in your decisions for the needs of others, not running around looking for people who are needy or have trouble or problems. There is no need to look for trouble, is there My dear ones everywhere in the world? For it is everywhere, and it is never as great as you think it is because you are still centered so strongly upon yourselves and your own situations. Beg for healing in this area, My dear faithful ones. It is possible for Our people to be very prayerful, to adore often and for long periods of time, to have changed greatly, to have come to new understanding and **still be very wounded.** Heaven desires to heal your woundedness as the ultimate preparation for all of those who will come.

You are a mighty edifice of My presence, that temple always spoken about where I dwell. **You will be a temple for others, or you will be disastrous for others!** Think of that, My people. For I know in your hearts, you wish to be a healing, soothing, miraculous experience for others; and this is offered to you as an opportunity to prepare more, to be more serious about being healed yourselves. This opportunity is offered to each of you in a new way today, a deeper, more cleansing, more thorough way. Rejoice, because it is addressing a great need within yourselves everywhere in the world. Accept My words as truth, as a new look and acceptance of yourselves becoming that mighty warrior desired by the Father, becoming that place and experience of mercy shown to you and shared with you by the Son. Becoming new gifts, greater gifts to all you meet, with everything you say and do, and with your patience and your awareness of others and their needs. This is so important to you, My people, but more important to them. For how can you be a healing instrument for them if you cannot be aware of them and their needs? All of Heaven begs you to take seriously these words given in great love, through Love, because of love. Amen to you, My people everywhere. You are loved."

6-11, "My very dearest children, today you celebrate the Trinity. My dear ones, I am your God and Father, come to visit with you, to help you reflect upon the Trinity, upon Three Persons in One God. We are all you need, My children, in every event of your life, in every happening in your soul, in every call to more. We are your greatest gift. We are your God. Honor the Trinity specifically in your prayers, that you might remember that you have three Persons to call upon, that you might remember you are never alone but always accompanied by this mighty Power of your God. Events will unfold in this country, again I say very shortly to you; but I have also told you that the more often something is mentioned, the closer you come to that event. I call you especially this day in the Name of the Trinity to be prepared, to prepare yourself more, to remember the promises of Myself, the mercy of My Son, the sanctity of Our Spirit and the great love that is the umbrella that covers all, that overcomes all evil, ultimately. My very dear ones, Heaven counts on you so very much, and I speak to everyone in the world who listens and prays. All of Heaven prays for you because of the "waiting"! It is such a hardship; and yet it is destruction that you await, My children. Remember that your prayers must continue, begging Me for mercy on all of those who suffer terrible hardships in the destruction to come, Remember they are your family.

Remember that your prayers are so powerful now and can bring comfort to those who suffer; and remember, there are so many suffering that you know nothing about, who are not mentioned by your media, who are forgotten immediately. Once something is in your media these days, that is nearly the last (of it.) If something is not a big, newsworthy all-day-long-on-television absorption of you and your time, then it is not deemed important enough to even mention again. This, too, is by the plans of the New World Order, a group of heartless people who are guided by Satan himself. My children, fatigue, in itself, is distracting; so I ask you once again to get rest, to take better care of yourselves. You are honoring My requests and being obedient when you are caring for yourself as a temple of the Holy Spirit, as the Presence of Jesus within your hearts; because I maintain you in My love every second of your life. Thus, you know what a great gift you are, most especially these days, to the great Army of Our Mother, the Immaculate One, who prays for you always, who is with you in such a powerful way. Thank her, My dear ones, for her presence, for her prayers especially for your perseverance. Perseverance is becoming a major factor in your lives as these soldiers, as these weapons-against-evil that you are. Beg for this gift, for even if you are not aware you are in need of perseverance. You notice this in your (lack of) attention to prayers, how your mind wanders and gets caught up with everyday affairs. It is necessary for you to pray with your hearts more deeply, more focused in a begging posture before Me.

My children, I call you to attention, as soldiers would be called to attention! I bring you increased perseverance this day. It is also difficult because these are repetitive words; but can you not feel the urgency in My voice and hear through these words how you must come to attention? Remember your family of the world, how they need you, how they suffer. My dear, dear ones, on this Trinity Sunday, pray to your Holy Trinity. Give praise and thanks for Us. You are so closely united with the Trinity. Believe this. Remember this. Act out of this unity, My children, that you might have all the power possible for the rest of your lives. Danger hovers, My dear ones. Be brave and prepared. I love you. Do not fear.

Count on the power of the Trinity and your holy Mother. Thank you for listening. Thank you for trying with all of your might to be all that I call you to be. Persevere!"

7/9, "My very dear faithful ones, here and everywhere in the world, I am your Jesus of Mercy Who speaks, Who has walked among you, Who calls to you for attention, for peace in your hearts. I call you to attention, as a Commander would call his soldiers, for it is most important that you learn to listen first to Heaven, to your duties, all that you have been called to become, to the needs of others and to your own needs. More than anything, the world and that includes everyone, needs healing: healing of your hearts, of your minds, of your spirits. Many of you need physical healing. I grant this today to a new degree, in a new way for everyone who listens. You will be listening to so many, many people; and it is your full attention that they will need: your patience, as we have spoken about so many, many times. You know that this a time of training, of practice, of formation to be all My poor lost people will need you to be. Because of the 4th of July celebration, there is emphasis this entire month on your country, on all your countries everywhere. How you must pray for your countries. Who else will do this? Who else will give them, your countries the best and finest protection possible; calling down the might of My Father's arm for that protection.

It is a time of unrest everywhere. Offer your own quiet, your own silence, your own peacefulness to combat the unrest in the hearts of so many, especially the enemies of Our church. It is thoughtless when people are suffering so terribly, as little children are everywhere, as helpless infants are everywhere; it is thoughtless, and yes even self-centered, when you do not include them first in your prayers. Little ones are so helpless, so dependent. Remember that. Remember your own childhoods. Perhaps they were unhappy. You can ask for healing again and again and again for yourselves and receive it; but, at the same time, ask for healing for the children of the world. How innocent and helpless they are. Appreciate the gifts you are being given, My children, as a good soldier appreciates his training, the call of his Commander, the rules by which he is called to live, the growth, the change that is expected in the life of a soldier; putting the protection of others as a goal, training for the protection of others as a goal, remembering all that is required of a soldier as a goal, and doing that.

My dear ones, I reflect with you this day, on all you are called to become by Our Father, more than any other people in history in such great numbers. It has been a long, long wait for you. Impatience nags at the corners of your minds, at the heels of your feet! Think about this, dear ones, this week. I give you new patience today, more perseverance because the wait is not over. Remember that there will be events, followed by another period of waiting as more change occurs, as recovery occurs from devastation. I speak in a serious manner this day because of the serious state of the whole world, so many you know nothing about; and still men make plans to destroy. It is a great cry from Heaven that you hear in your own hearts. It is a great cry for mercy that you are offering to Our Father. Remember all of the people in Heaven who are listening with you, praying with you and for you. Imagine the numbers of people of Heaven, My children, since the beginning of creation! They are all praying for you, and with you, and for the world. It is a mighty effort; because it will be a mighty battle, ultimately. First you will see skirmishes, surprise attacks again; people ambushed, yourselves ambushed if you allow it, if you are not listening, paying attention, being on guard as I have called you to do. I love you. You are My precious, blessed, dear, dear ones. I call out to remind you of the obedience and the surrender that you have promised, that you practice. You are loved. Always I will say that, for always it is true. And you know what you say about your children: 'it is the squeaky wheel that gets the most attention!' I am giving you My attention today, My children, and asking for yours. We are one. We are so united in the Trinity, in your prayers, in your obedience. Be there for the world, My dear ones, as I have always been here for you. Amen."

7-2-06 Excerpt from Personal Locution: God, the Father said:

"Our book of words will lead and teach, guide and protect, bless and gift all those who read with an open heart. The words and teachings are beautiful, and will transform hearts that desire new hearts, new eyes to see and new ears to hear. It is exciting to be on the brink of great change in the world, but especially in the hearts of many. The future is Mine to save, to renew, to give salvation as a gift of My Mercy, and yours to assist My plans for the world. Be joyful, My people."

Carol Ameche
Scottsdale, Arizona